A BETTER FUTUF

Policymakers, advocates and scholars have long concentrated on the importance of equal access to primary and secondary education as a foundation for a democratic and just society. Despite the growing importance of higher and specialist education in an increasingly technological and skill-focused global market, tertiary education has attracted much less attention. And yet universities and colleges are epicentres of egregious disparities in access, which impinge on traditionally marginalised communities, such as racial minorities, migrants, indigenous populations and people with disabilities. By drawing attention to this issue and assembling first-rate material from scholars and policymakers across the globe, this book performs an invaluable service for those interested in understanding and fighting a highly significant violation of educational opportunity and social justice.

JACQUELINE BHABHA is Professor of the Practice of Health and Human Rights at the Harvard T. H. Chan School of Public Health, USA. She is also Director of Research at the FXB Center for Health and Human Rights at Harvard University, the Jeremiah Smith Jr Lecturer in Law at Harvard Law School and an adjunct lecturer in public policy at the Harvard Kennedy School.

WENONA GILES is Professor Emerita and Senior Scholar in the Anthropology Department and Resident Research Associate at the Centre for Refugee Studies, York University, Canada. She is also a Fellow of the Royal Society of Canada.

FARAAZ MAHOMED is a clinical psychologist and a Visiting Research Fellow at the Center for Applied Legal Studies at the University of the Witwatersrand, South Africa. He also holds the position of research associate at the FXB Center for Health and Human Rights at Harvard University and Harvard Law School Project on Disability. In addition, he works with the Public Health Program of the Open Society Foundations on mental health and rights. He writes in his personal capacity.

A BETTER FUTURE

*The Role of Higher Education for Displaced
and Marginalised People*

EDITED BY

JACQUELINE BHABHA

Harvard University

WENONA GILES

York University

FARAAZ MAHOMED

University of the Witwatersrand

CAMBRIDGE
UNIVERSITY PRESS

CAMBRIDGE
UNIVERSITY PRESS

University Printing House, Cambridge CB2 8BS, United Kingdom

One Liberty Plaza, 20th Floor, New York, NY 10006, USA

477 Williamstown Road, Port Melbourne, VIC 3207, Australia

314–321, 3rd Floor, Plot 3, Splendor Forum, Jasola District Centre,
New Delhi – 110025, India

79 Anson Road, #06–04/06, Singapore 079906

Cambridge University Press is part of the University of Cambridge.

It furthers the University's mission by disseminating knowledge in the pursuit of
education, learning, and research at the highest international levels of excellence.

www.cambridge.org
Information on this title: www.cambridge.org/9781108496889
DOI: 10.1017/9781108655101

First published 2020

A catalogue record for this publication is available from the British Library.

Library of Congress Cataloging-in-Publication Data
NAMES: Bhabha, Jacqueline, editor. | Giles, Wenona Mary, 1949– editor. | Mahomed, Faraaz,
1985– editor.
TITLE: A better future : the role of higher education for displaced and marginalized people /
Edited by Jacqueline Bhabha, Harvard University, Wenona Giles, York University, Faraaz
Mahomed, FXB Center for Health and Human Rights.
DESCRIPTION: New York, NY : Cambridge University Press, 2020. | Includes bibliographical
references and index.
IDENTIFIERS: LCCN 2019057475 (print) | LCCN 2019057476 (ebook) | ISBN 9781108496889
(hardback) | ISBN 9781108655101 (ebook)
SUBJECTS: LCSH: Education, Higher – Aims and objectives. | Educational equalization. |
Refugees – Education, Higher. | Students with social disabilities – Education, Higher.
CLASSIFICATION: LCC LB2322.2 .B49 2020 (print) | LCC LB2322.2 (ebook) | DDC 378.086/94–dc23
LC record available at https://lccn.loc.gov/2019057475
LC ebook record available at https://lccn.loc.gov/2019057476

ISBN 978-1-108-49688-9 Hardback
ISBN 978-1-108-73899-6 Paperback

Contents

Figures

viii

Tables

Notes on Contributors

TANYA ABERMAN recently completed her PhD in the Gender, Feminist and Women's Studies Program at York University, Toronto. She is Coordinator for the access programme for students with precarious immigration status at York University. Aberman is also a co-founder of a non-profit organisation that supports sanctuary students and advocates for increased access to education.

CARLOS AGUILAR is a doctoral student at the Harvard Graduate School of Education (HGSE). His research centres on issues related to undocumented youth in particularly harsh contexts. As an undocumented immigrant and DACA (Deferred Action for Childhood Arrivals) recipient, Carlos' underlying emphasis is to complicate current narratives and theoretical frameworks surrounding undocumented immigrants by highlighting the complex experiences of individuals, their families and communities.

A. KAYUM AHMED is Division Director at the Open Society Foundations in New York where he leads the Public Health Program's global work on access to medicines and innovation. He also teaches a class on socio-economic rights as an adjunct faculty member at Columbia Law School. Before joining Open Society, Kayum served as Chief Executive Officer of the South African Human Rights Commission from 2010 to 2015 where he led a team of 178 colleagues to monitor, protect and promote human rights in South Africa, and he oversaw the management of nearly 45,000 cases. He holds a PhD in international and comparative education from Columbia University, various degrees in law from the University of Oxford (MSt), Leiden University (LLM) and the University of Cape Town (LLB), as well as degrees in anthropology (MA) and religious studies (BA Hons.).

OLIVIER ARVISAIS is a Professor at the Faculty of Education of the Université du Québec à Montréal. He is the scientific director of the Canadian Research Institute on Humanitarian Crises and Aid. Professor Arvisais is also co-president of the scientific committee of the UNESCO Chair in Curriculum Development. His research focuses on social studies teaching, educational initiatives in refugee camps and education under armed groups or totalitarian proto-states.

NELLY ASKOUNI is Associate Professor of Sociology of Education at the School of Educational Sciences at the National and Kapodistrian University of Athens. She has a long-standing interest in the social class relations in education and the processes that (re)produce inequalities at school. Her research focuses on education of immigrant and minority children, class inequalities in education, teachers' practices and professional identities. Since 1997, she has been a member of the scientific board of a large-scale educational project aimed at the social inclusion of Muslim minority students in Western Thrace (the north-east region of Greece).

SIMONA BARBU is a human rights activist and researcher who has specialised in working with Roma communities in Romania, as well as across Europe. Simona has experience with academic ethnographic research, holding an MA in anthropology of education and globalisation and from working as a research assistant at the University of Copenhagen, Denmark. In Romania, Simona worked with Romani CRISS, a leading Roma rights organisation that defends and promotes the rights of Roma. During her placement there, Simona worked to enhance access of Roma communities to education and public health services. She has contributed to writing reports on education for organisations such as the Organization for Security and Co-operation in Europe (OSCE) and the RomArchive platform. Since 2014, Simona has been working in Denmark, assisting homeless migrants from Central and Eastern Europe. This work experience allowed her to gain knowledge on the Free Movement Directive within Europe, as well as on national immigration frameworks.

JACQUELINE BHABHA, JD, MSC, is Professor of the Practice of Health and Human Rights at the Harvard T. H. Chan School of Public Health. She is Director of Research at the FXB Center for Health and Human

Rights at Harvard University, the Jeremiah Smith Jr Lecturer in Law at Harvard Law School and an adjunct lecturer in public policy at the Harvard Kennedy School. She received a first-class honours degree and an MSc from Oxford University and a JD from the College of Law in London. From 2001 to 2010, Bhabha directed the Harvard University Committee on Human Rights Studies. From 1997 to 2001 Bhabha directed the Human Rights Program at the University of Chicago. Prior to 1997 she was a practising human rights lawyer in London and at the European Court of Human Rights in Strasbourg. She has published extensively on issues of transnational child migration, refugee protection, children's rights and citizenship. She also conducts research on social and economic rights for vulnerable populations. She is the author of *Can We Solve the Migration Crisis?* (Polity Press, 2018), *Child Migration and Human Rights in a Global Age* (Princeton University Press, 2014); the editor of *Coming of Age: Reframing the Approach to Adolescent Rights* (University of Pennsylvania Press, 2014) and *Children without a State* (MIT Press, 2011); and the co-editor of *Research Handbook on Child Migration* (Edward Elgar Press, 2018) and *Reframing Roma Rights* (University of Pennsylvania Press, 2017). She was founding chair of the board of the Scholars at Risk Network, and she serves on the board of the World Peace Foundation and the *Journal of Refugee Studies*.

FRANCESCA BORGONOVI holds a British Academy Global Professorship at University College London and is a senior policy analyst at the Organisation for Economic Cooperation and Development (OECD), where she has been responsible for analytical and developmental work in the OECD-led international assessments (PISA and PIAAC) and the Education for Inclusive Societies project. Her research interests include gender and socio-economic disparities in academic achievement; student engagement and motivation; the outcomes of migrant and language minority students; and the role of education in shaping trust and attitudes towards migration. Francesca held research positions in the Department of Social Policy and the Centre for the Analysis of Social Exclusion at the London School of Economics and Political Science and has been an adjunct professor at the Paris School of International Affairs at Sciences Po since 2013. She also held visiting positions at the Goldman School of Public Policy at the University of California, Berkeley.

VIDUR CHOPRA is a post-doctoral fellow in the International and Comparative Education Program, Teachers College, Columbia.

Situated at the cross-disciplines of education, forced migration and citizenship studies, his work focuses on examining the experiences of inclusion within national education systems for refugee youth and the ways education enables or complicates global, local and transnational understandings of membership and belonging for conflict-affected youth. He has a wide range of research, policy and practice-based experiences within humanitarian and development contexts with the United Nations (UNHCR and UNICEF) and NGOs in East Africa, the Middle East and South Asia.

MAURICE CRUL is a Distinguished Professor of Sociology at the Vrije Universiteit in Amsterdam. He is a specialist on school and labour market careers of children of immigrants and refugees in Europe and the United States. He has coordinated the TIES project, which was the first European comparative study on the second generation in Europe. He has further coordinated two European Research Council (ERC) grant projects. The first looked at the upcoming elite among the second generation (ELITESproject.eu) and the second, an ERC-advanced grant project Becoming a Minority (BAM), looks at the new minority in super-diverse cities: the people of native descent (BAMproject.eu). He has written extensively about issues of diversity and inclusion. Some of his books include: *The New Face of World Cities* (Russell Sage Foundation Publishers, 2012), *Coming to Terms with Superdiversity: The Case of Rotterdam* (Springer, 2019) and *Superdiversity: A New Vision on Integration* (Free University Press, 2013).

NEGIN DAHYA is an Assistant Professor in the Institute of Communication, Culture, Information and Technology, and the Faculty of Information at the University of Toronto. Dahya's research is focused on understanding the social and cultural conditions in which technology is created and used, particularly on digital and social media in educational settings. Her research in refugee education and technology has centred on applying socio-technical theory to understand the role of mobile phones and social media to support teaching and learning among refugees pursuing and enrolled in post-secondary training and higher education.

CHARLOTTE E. DAVIDSON is Diné and an enrolled member of the Three Affiliated Tribes (Mandan, Hidatsa and Arikara). She earned a BA in American Indian studies from Haskell Indian Nations University and an MEd and PhD in educational policy studies from the University of

Illinois at Urbana-Champaign. She is an independent scholar living in Madison, Wisconsin, following over ten years as a student affairs professional, diversity higher education administrator and lecturer of undergraduate and graduate level courses in the fields of education and American Indian studies. Her practice and scholarship focus on the reinvention, embodiment and application of Diné and Indigenous epistemologies and pedagogies in the context of higher education. She has presented nationally on Indigenous higher education and co-authored a chapter in *Beyond the Asterisk: Understanding Native Students in Higher Education, Indigenous Leadership in Higher Education* and *Reclaiming Indigenous Research in Higher Education* (2013).

ELIZABETH DONGER is a researcher and current JD candidate at the NYU School of Law focusing on issues of migration, child protection and access to justice. She previously worked at the FXB Center for Health and Human Rights at Harvard University as a research associate, where she ran several advocacy-focused studies on the health and well-being of adolescent refugees living in urban areas of Ecuador and Zambia, and on community-level preventative approaches to child protection in India. Previously, she worked for non-profits in Colombia, Jordan and the United Kingdom on issues of land restitution, refugee resettlement and forced displacement. She holds a master's in public policy from the Harvard Kennedy School, where she was a John F. Kennedy Fellow.

DACIA DOUHAIBI is a doctoral candidate at York University in Toronto, Canada. Douhaibi spent five years working with the Borderless Higher Education for Refugees (BHER) project and travelled to Dadaab over three years as a teaching assistant and a course director for the project. She also travelled to Dadaab to conduct interviews and surveys for research on the role of technology to support education. With over ten years of research experience, five years most recently in the East African context, she currently acts as the Research Coordinator for Justica Africa, an advocacy and research-based organisation in South Sudan, and Research Advisor for aidx, a technology company working to develop peer-to-peer mobile applications to support systems of mutual aid among refugees. Douhaibi also serves as Advisor to the Emerging Scholars and Practitioners on Forced Migration Issues (ESPMI) network and Editor-in-Chief of the *Refugee Review*, an online, open-access, peer-reviewed journal on migration issues.

THALIA DRAGONAS is Professor of Social Psychology at the School of Educational Sciences at the National and Kapodistrian University of Athens. She has co-directed the 'Project for the Inclusion and the Education of Minority Muslim Children' in Western Thrace (1997–2019). Her specific areas of research include psychosocial identities and intergroup relations, intercultural education and ethnocentrism in the educational system, prevention and promotion of early psychosocial health, transition to parenthood and construction of fatherhood. She served as MP with PASOK (2007–2009) and has participated in Parliamentary Committees on Education, Culture, Equality and Human Rights. She was a Special Secretary on Intercultural Education at the Greek Ministry of Education (2009–2010) in charge of vulnerable communities such as displaced people, the Roma and the territorial Muslim minority.

SARAH DRYDEN-PETERSON is an Associate Professor at the Harvard Graduate School of Education. She leads a research programme that focuses on the connections between education and community development, specifically the role that education plays in building peaceful and participatory societies. Her work is situated in conflict and post-conflict settings and is concerned with the interplay between local experiences of children, families and teachers and the development and implementation of national and international policies. Her research reflects connections between practice, policy and scholarship and is strengthened through sustained collaborations with UN agencies, NGOs and communities. Dryden-Peterson's long-term research on refugee education has played a critical role in shaping global policy on the importance of quality, conflict-informed and future-creating education in all phases of conflict. She is the recipient of the Palmer O. Johnson Award for an outstanding article and a National Academy of Education Postdoctoral Fellowship.

JOHN L. GARLAND is an enrolled member of the Choctaw Nation of Oklahoma and an advocate for Indigenous inclusion in higher education. He received his bachelor's and master's degrees from Northeastern State University in Tahlequah, Oklahoma, and his doctorate in College student personnel administration from the University of Maryland–College Park. John also earned a graduate certificate in vocational rehabilitation counselling from the University of Arkansas–Little Rock and is a certified rehabilitation counsellor. Serving as the Director of Research and Student Success with Indigenous Education, Inc. – Home of the Cobell Scholarship – John's higher education career has spanned more than two decades. From administrative roles in student affairs to tenured graduate faculty, John's deep understanding of College student development and institutional processes provides him with unique perspectives for supporting Native students and their success. John actively publishes and presents nationally on Native students in higher education and has received recognition for his teaching, research, mentorship and advocacy.

WENONA GILES, PHD, FRSC, is Professor Emerita and Senior Scholar in the Anthropology Department and Resident Research Associate of the Centre for Refugee Studies, York University, where she has taught and published in the areas of gender, forced migration, globalisation, migration, education, nationalism and war. In addition to many articles, she is the author of *Immigration and Nationalism: Two Generations of Portuguese Women in Toronto* (University of Toronto Press, 2002) and the co-editor of *Development and Diaspora: Gender and the Refugee Experience* (Artemis, 1996), a two-volume issue of the journal *Refuge on Gender Relations and Refugee Issues* (1995), a volume of *Refuge on Higher Education for Refugees* (2010–2011), *Feminists under Fire: Exchanges across War Zones* (Between the Lines Press, Toronto 2003), *Sites of Violence: Gender and Conflict Zones* (with Jennifer Hyndman, University of California Press, 2004), *When Care Work Goes Global: Locating the Social Relations of Domestic Work* (with Mary Romero and Valerie Preston, Ashgate 2014). Most recently, she co-authored *Refugees in Extended Exile: Living on the Edge* (with Jennifer Hyndman, Routledge, 2017). She co-founded and co-coordinated the International Women in Conflict Zones Research Network (1993–2004). She initiated and then co-led a multi-year project (2013–2019) funded by the Canadian government and Open Society Foundations that continues to bring degree programmes from Kenyan and Canadian universities to refugees in the Dadaab refugee camps of Kenya (www.bher.org).

ROBERTO G. GONZALES is Professor of Education at Harvard University and Director of the UnDACAmented Research Project. His research examines the effects of legal contexts on the coming-of-age experiences of vulnerable and hard-to-reach populations. Since 2002, he has been carrying out one of the most comprehensive studies of undocumented immigrants in the United States.

TANJA JOVANOVIC is a Roma Feminist Scholar specialising in the sociology of education, currently as a postdoctoral fellowship at CEU-Harvard University. She holds a PhD in education from the University of Sussex, UK, and MA in international education and development. She worked at the University of Sussex, UK, as a graduate teaching research associate as part of the Centre for Higher Education and Equity Research (CHEER). Before that, since 2003, she worked intensively as a Roma activist in local and international organisations focusing on Central Eastern Europe. Her work focuses on overcoming barriers of Roma in education in regard to institutional racism, social exclusion and equity in accessing the mainstream school without segregation, bullying/discrimination and low quality of education. Tanja's area of interest is how inclusive education, equity and social inclusion play a key role in reducing poverty and in overcoming the socio-cultural-economic obstacles in developing settings such as Roma community or any other community faced with profound poverty.

RICHARD KAZIS is a non-resident senior fellow at the Brookings Institution Metropolitan Policy Program and a senior consultant to MDRC, an organisation that partners with US organisations and foundations on education and workforce development reform. He was previously Senior Vice President of Jobs for the Future, where he led the organisation's research and advocacy agenda. He has written widely on community College student success, low-wage worker advancement, and College and career readiness. A graduate of Harvard College and MIT, Kazis has also taught at an alternative high school, helped organise fast-food workers and built labour-environmental jobs' coalitions. Kazis currently serves as Board Chair of The Institute for College Access and Success.

ORLA KELLY is a doctoral candidate and teaching fellow in the Department of Sociology, Boston College. She is also a research fellow at the FXB Center for Health and Human Rights at Harvard University. Between 2010 and 2015, Kelly worked as a research associate at the FXB Center. In this role, she was involved in a number of projects relating to the determinants of educational attainment among disadvantaged groups in North India. Based on these projects, she co-authored several publications on gender and educational exclusion. Kelly's research interests include comparative education, gender and development, and sustainability. Her current research project is a macro-level investigation into the relationship between national educational attainment rates, well-being and environmental stress. She holds an LLM in international human rights law from NUI Galway and an MSc in international business from University College Dublin.

WANGUI KIMARI recently received a PhD in anthropology from York University in Toronto and is a Postdoctoral Research Fellow at the African Centre for Cities (ACC) at the University of Cape Town. She is currently working on an ethnography that elucidates the layered socio-ecological strategies, survivals and memories of residents in Mathare, a 'slum' in Nairobi. Her work draws attention to how an increasingly militarised urban governance (re)produces what she calls 'ecologies of exclusion'. She was also a teaching assistant and instructor for the Borderless Higher Education for Refugees (BHER) project in the Dadaab camps in Kenya between 2014 and 2018.

ADITI KRISHNA is a social epidemiologist with experience in global health and international development, working in the areas of education, maternal and child health, nutrition, child development, family planning, reproductive and sexual health, and water, sanitation and hygiene (WASH). She is the Director of Research at Iris Group, a woman-owned consulting firm specialising in social inclusion in international development. Aditi has conducted research on the impacts of gender-transformative interventions on adolescent health and maternal and child health, as well as on the effects of menstrual hygiene management on women's economic empowerment. She supports the WASH portfolio through her work on two USAID-funded projects. Prior to working at the Iris Group, Aditi conducted primary research on women's education and adolescent reproductive and sexual health services and used complex statistical methods to analyse data from large, secondary datasets. Her work has been published in leading peer-reviewed journals (*International Journal of Epidemiology* and *American Journal of Clinical Nutrition*, among others) and presented at academic conferences (Stockholm World Water Week 2019, UNC Water and Health Conference 2017 and 2019). Aditi earned a Doctor of Science (ScD) in Social and Behavioural Sciences from the Harvard T. H. Chan School of Public Health, a Master of Science in Public Health (MSPH) in Health Policy and Management from the University of North Carolina at Chapel Hill and a BA from Carleton College.

FRANS LELIE is a Fellow at the Department of Sociology at the Vrije Universiteit in Amsterdam. A social worker by training, she worked with women and their families with a migration background. In the last fifteen years she has worked on the topic of education of the children of immigrants in two major international projects: TIES (The Integration of the European Second generation) and ELITES, Pathways to Success. She produced five short movies looking at role models belonging to the second generation, telling about their pathways to success in Belgium, France, Germany and the Netherlands: www.elitesproject.eu /educational-kit. Currently, she is the project manager for the ERC-advanced grant project BAM on people of native descent in majority-minority cities in Europe. She is also a matchmaker for Takecarebnb, pairing people who obtained refugee status but are still waiting in the asylum seeker centres for a house with local families.

FARAAZ MAHOMED, MA, DRPH, is Clinical Psychologist and a visiting research fellow at the Center for Applied Legal Studies at the University of the Witwatersrand, Johannesburg. He received a Doctor of Public Health Degree from the Harvard T. H. Chan School of Public Health focusing on mental health and human rights. In addition, he received an MA in clinical psychology from the University of the Witwatersrand, Johannesburg, South Africa, and an MA in international policy from the Middlebury Institute of International Studies in Monterey, California, as a Fulbright Scholar. In addition to his position at the University of the Witwatersrand, he is a research associate at the FXB Center for Health and Human Rights at Harvard University and the Harvard Law School Project on Disability. Currently, he works with the Public Health Program of the Open Society Foundations on mental health and rights. He has been a research consultant to the UN Special Rapporteur on the Right of Everyone to the Highest Attainable Standard of Physical and Mental Health, assisting with the drafting of the report on the right to mental health of people on the move. He previously held the positions of Senior Researcher for Equality at the South African Human Rights Commission and Clinical Psychologist in community health settings in Johannesburg and Cape Town, South Africa.

GABRIELE MARCONI works in the OECD Directorate for Education and Skills, where he has been involved in drafting and developing the statistical framework for several projects and reports, including the OECD Benchmarking Higher Education Systems Performance report. He has a PhD in education economics from Maastricht University and has worked for the Center for European Policy Studies and Empower

European Universities before joining the OECD. His main research topics are education policies and statistics, unemployment and economic growth.

MARGARETA MATACHE is a Roma rights activist from Romania, Director of the Roma Program at FXB Center for Health and Human Rights at Harvard University and also a Harvard instructor. In 2012, she was awarded a Hauser fellowship at Harvard FXB and founded the Roma Program. She co-edited *Realizing Roma Rights* (University of Pennsylvania Press, 2017) with Jacqueline Bhabha and Andrzej Mirga. The volume investigates anti-Roma racism and documents a growing Roma-led political movement engaged in building a more inclusive and just Europe. From 2005 to 2012, Matache was the executive director of Romani CRISS, a leading NGO that defends and promotes the rights of Roma.

MELVIN E. MONETTE-BARAJAS was raised on the Spirit Lake Reservation in North Dakota and is an enrolled member of the Turtle Mountain Band of Chippewa Indians. He attended the University of North Dakota (UND), where he earned a BS in (elementary) education. While pursuing his master's in educational leadership, he served as a student affairs officer for UND's American Indian Student Services. Melvin completed his master's while working for the Minnesota Department of Education, Office of Indian Education. He then returned to campus-based work at the University of Minnesota School of Public Health. Melvin later took a job at the American Indian Graduate Center in Albuquerque, NM. In 2016, he founded Indigenous Education, Inc. – Home of the Cobell Scholarship – where he is President and Chief Executive Officer.

PREM KUMAR RAJARAM is Professor of Sociology and Social Anthropology at Central European University. He is also Head of the university's Open Learning Initiative (OLIve), which ran education programmes for refugees and asylum seekers in Hungary until the government's anti-migrant laws in the summer of 2018 forced the university to stop these programmes. Prem is also Project Leader of the Refugee Education Initiatives (REIs), an Erasmus+ Social Inclusion programme that runs refugee education projects in Austria, Greece, Germany, the United Kingdom and Hungary. REIs also advocates for change in European policies to foster access to higher education for refugees and for inclusive university environments and pedagogic practices. Prem's research interests are in capitalism, colonialism, migration and their intersections.

MATTHEW S. SMITH, ESQ., has supported cutting-edge disability rights advocacy in the United States, Bangladesh and Latin America for over a decade. He coordinates the Supported Decision-Making New York project for the City University of New York's Hunter College on alternatives to guardianship for New Yorkers with intellectual disabilities. As Research Associate with the Harvard Law School Project on Disability, Smith studies the transfer of rights for special education students, advises self-advocacy organisations on guardianship reform and researches Mexico's mental health system. He also manages a USAID-funded disability rights advocacy project in Bangladesh for Blue Law International, LLP. He has authored amicus briefs in domestic and international cases and has published in journals (*ABA Journal of Labor & Employment Law, Nordic Journal of Human Rights*) and books (*Derechos Humanos: Retos y Perspectivas*, Oxford University Press, 2012). He received his Juris Doctor from American University and his bachelor of arts from Harvard University.

CRAIN SOUDIEN is the Chief Executive Officer of the Human Sciences Research Council and formerly Deputy Vice Chancellor at the University of Cape Town, where he remains an Emeritus Professor of Education and African Studies. His publications include three books, four edited collections and over 200 articles, reviews, reports and book chapters, including a 2017 publication entitled *Nelson Mandela: Comparative Perspectives of his Significance for Education.* He was educated at the University of Cape Town and UNISA, South Africa, and holds a PhD from the State University of New York at Buffalo. He is the Chairperson of the Independent Examinations Board, the former Chairperson of the District Six Museum Foundation and a former President of the World Council of Comparative Education Societies. He had been the chair of the Ministerial Committee on Transformation in Higher Education and of the Ministerial Committee to evaluate textbooks for discrimination.

CORINNE SQUIRE is Professor of Social Sciences and Co-Director, Centre for Narrative Research, University of East London. Her research interests are in refugee and asylum-seeker education, HIV and citizenship, subjectivities and popular culture, and narrative theory and methods. Publications include *Voices from the 'Jungle'* (Africa et al.; ed., with

Godin, Hensen, Lounasma and Zaman, Pluto, 2017), *Living with HIV and ART: Three-letter lives* (Palgrave, 2013), *What is narrative research?* (with Davis, Esin, Andrews, Harrison, Hyden and Hyden, Bloomsbury, 2014) and *Stories changing lives* (ed., Oxford University Press, forthcoming).

MICHAEL ASHLEY STEIN is the co-founder and Executive Director of the Harvard Law School Project on Disability and Visiting Professor at Harvard Law School. Considered one of the world's leading experts on disability law and policy, Dr Stein participated in the drafting of the UN Convention on the Rights of Persons with Disabilities; works with disabled peoples' organisations and non-governmental organisations around the world; actively consults with governments on their disability laws and policies; advises a number of UN bodies and national human rights institutions; and has brought landmark disability rights litigation globally. Professor Stein holds an Extraordinary Professorship at the University of Pretoria's Centre for Human Rights, is a visiting professor at the Free University of Amsterdam and teaches at the Harvard Kennedy School of Government. He earned a JD from Harvard Law School and a PhD from Cambridge University.

LISA UNANGST is a doctoral candidate at Boston College's Center for International Higher Education (CIHE). Her research interests include access to higher education for migrant and refugee populations in Germany and the United States, international alumni affairs and quantitative textual analysis. Lisa worked previously in higher education at Harvard University, Cal State East Bay and the California Institute of Technology. She earned a master's degree in international education policy from the Harvard Graduate School of Education and a bachelor's degree from Smith College in American studies. Lisa was also the recipient of a DAAD (German Academic Exchange Service) postgraduate fellowship from 2003 to 2004. Her work has been included in the *Journal of Higher Education Policy and Management* and *European Higher Education Area: The Impact of Past and Future Policies* (Springer, 2018).

PALOMA E. VILLEGAS is Assistant Professor in the Department of Sociology at California State University, San Bernardino. She works at the intersection of migrant illegalisation, race, class and gender, focusing on schooling, employment, policing, surveillance, artistic expressions and affect. Her work is situated in relation to Mexico, the United States and Canada.

TAHIR ZAMAN is currently Deputy Director of the Sussex Centre for Migration Research (SCMR) at the School of Global Studies, University of Sussex. He was awarded a PhD in Refugee Studies from the University of East London in 2013. His work explored the social and cultural life-worlds of Iraqi refugees in Damascus, where he undertook fieldwork in 2010 and 2011, and was published by Palgrave Macmillan in 2016 under the title of *Islamic traditions of refuge in the crises of Iraq and Syria*. Tahir has since worked extensively with a leading peace-building and conflict transformation NGO on considering the role of Syrian Diaspora actors in responding to mass displacement and contributing towards peace-building. His current research interest focuses on the intersections of displacement, humanitarianism and social economy.

Introduction

Jacqueline Bhabha, Wenona Giles and Faraaz Mahomed

Inequity in Higher Education and Its determinants

The importance of primary and secondary education as fundamental drivers of empowerment, achievement and inclusion is widely acknowledged. So is the increasing need for higher education (HE) – education that extends beyond secondary school graduation and that delivers academic, technical or professional instruction – as an essential prerequisite for advancement in contemporary, global society. A single data point from the United States provides compelling proof: the gap between the earnings of high school and College graduates doubled between 1980 and 2000 (Kazis, in this volume). Yet access to the benefits of higher education remains particularly skewed in favour of dominant majorities. Little attention has been paid to the impact of this form of educational exclusion on marginalised or otherwise disadvantaged populations, whether they are in the global North or South.

This book makes the case that the systematic lack of access to HE and its benefits for some populations has a serious impact on life prospects and social justice. We are not just concerned with the question of physical access and initial enrolment, critical though those two factors are. We are also concerned with differential completion rates, with the quality of the credentials secured and the skills developed, with the networks built and the employment possibilities secured, and with the disproportionate financial burdens that follow HE for some student populations.

We assemble in this volume a broad range of critical perspectives to examine these manifold challenges. The populations that are the subjects of the ensuing chapters include citizens and non-citizens, residents of the global North and the global South, people who have migrated and people who have never left their homes. They share the experience of stigmatisation and or marginalisation, and with it the experience of exclusion from the full benefits of HE.

Though exclusions are the products of different historical, contingent and other proximal *determinants*, the *vectors* or consequences of exclusion for the very diverse populations we analyse encompass overarching similarities. Education-related commonalities such as inadequate academic preparation, insufficient financial support, geographical inaccessibility, linguistic difference, low-quality teaching and mentorship emerge across constituencies that are as different as Indigenous peoples, refugees, disabled persons, racial or ethnic minorities, and undocumented or irregular migrants. Meticulous analysis of these exclusionary forces and their multifaceted drivers and consequences can, we believe, stimulate greater awareness and promotion of strategies to redress the highly impactful injustices to which they contribute. In the following pages, we identify a number of these determinants of exclusion from HE and their vectors, thereby contributing to an understanding of the many and diverse forms of marginality. The chapters of this book consider sources of discriminatory exclusion based on gender, racialisation, disability, class, ethnic identity, location and citizenship. While not an exhaustive list, these factors are central to many situations of endemic discrimination, including in the context of HE. Often, exclusion from HE is based in an interrelated way on more than one of these phenomena, so-called intersectional discrimination.

A useful framework for understanding intersectional discrimination and its *determinants* is expressed in Fraser's research on three intertwined dimensions – redistribution, recognition and representation – that can result in exclusion from justice (Fraser, 2005; Giles, 2010). In this book we recognise claims for access to HE as claims for justice. Fraser argues that all three dimensions must be addressed in order to achieve justice. Applying this framework to our concerns, we take her dimension of redistribution to pertain to economic or class issues that stall or prevent people from accessing university and thus hinder their ability to participate fully in the development of the profession or livelihood of their choice. Recognition, in our analysis, refers to the ways that the forms of discrimination we have mentioned (and others) are used as reasons for exclusion from HE. Finally, we consider the representation dimension as the space available to any group to voice 'their claims and adjudicate their disputes' (Fraser [2005] in Giles, 2010, 28). In many of the cases described in this book, groups or individuals who have attempted to access HE have experienced all three dimensions of exclusion. They have, for example, encountered exclusion due to economic inequality, the dimension of redistribution. Aspiring students have also experienced the impact of a failure of recognition – stigmatisation by those who hold the power to exclude them from HE. The representation dimension, too, has obvious relevance to our material. Its results include silencing and various forms of sequestration of the students we are concerned with. Some of the consequences of these intertwined deficits are immediate, as where exclusion denies students the opportunity to advocate in favour of their right to university access; other results are long term, as is the case where the absence of university accreditation vitiates the ability to fully engage in the public sphere, with predictable consequences for further marginalisation.

The contributors to this volume write about the locations of marginalisation and what they mean for the groups they focus upon. While the global South is all too often the site of enduring educational exclusion, many of the exclusionary factors that characterise the global South are evident in wealthier and more educationally endowed settings in the North. The dichotomy is thus useful but of limited applicability. It is useful because demographic trends reveal an asymmetry between educational need and opportunity in ever starker terms. More and more demand for education, including HE, arises in the global South, most especially in sub-Saharan Africa, where birth rates are accelerating as state-funded educational opportunity is shrinking (UNESCO, 2014), compounded or at least partially caused by the low share of education in total humanitarian aid at just 2.1 per cent (UNESCO, 2018a).[1] At the same time, traditional sites of plenty in educational provision and tertiary education excellence, largely in the global North, are home to rapidly ageing populations with shrinking domestic demand for educational services (UNESCO, 2014). And yet educational access continues to be highly skewed, as evidenced by the enduring discrimination against African American and Roma populations. The global North–South dichotomy is also of limited applicability because of the impact of significant refugee and other distress migrant populations on the landscape of educational equality. As Squire and Zaman (in this volume) report, for example, newly arrived and mobile populations in France experience overwhelming challenges to access HE; the same is true for many migrant communities in Germany (Crul & Lelie, in this volume).

---

[1] This statistic is based on the Global Humanitarian Assistance Report (Development Initiatives, 2018). It is noteworthy that more humanitarian aid for post-secondary education is directed to middle-income countries than to low-income countries: 'low income countries received 13% of the total aid to postsecondary education in 2016, and their share has been declining since 2010' (UNESCO, 2018b, 6).

Our book explores the kind of education that is 'delivered', who is doing the delivering and how this is accomplished. It considers higher educational provision in a range of settings – from mainstream state institutions to dedicated facilities in refugee or migrant camps, from free state universities to expensive profit-making Colleges and universities, from provincial contexts to transnational collaborations. Where evidence is available, the contributors also consider the impact of the educational intervention described, on both output and outcome – in other words, the numbers of students enrolled, the courses delivered, the life impacts achieved or not achieved.

Marginalisation and Its Many Forms

The primary constituency of concern in this volume are marginalised populations excluded from the benefits of HE. As already noted, this constituency encompasses populations affected by many vectors of exclusion – economic, social, political, legal. The terms 'marginality' and 'marginalised' may, themselves, be contested. Margins are socially constructed interpretations of the boundaries of a society (or country or region) and the effects of being inside or outside those boundaries. Solorzano and Villalpando (1998) refer to marginality as a complex and contentious location or process whereby people are subordinated because of their race, gender or class. A recent volume by Danaher, Cook and Coombes (2013) examines the naming and sociological framing of 'marginalised communities', particularly in relation to education, and concludes that, at its core, the experience of being marginalised is associated with being located, physically or otherwise, far from centres of cultural and economic power. Many stigmatised populations have this experience despite living in some of the most vibrant contemporary centres of global cultural, intellectual and economic production.

The conception of marginalisation just offered is necessarily broad because sources of marginalisation are ubiquitous in contemporary society. Yet those who are somehow 'removed' from the 'inside' of the privileged constituency are likely to share characteristics that are cross-cutting, the most common being, perhaps, economic disenfranchisement and female gender. Within such commonalities, however, there are gradations, which generate distinct, even unique individual experiences of stigma and social isolation. Female and/or disabled refugees often face more acute challenges than do their male or non-disabled counterparts (Morrice, 2013), and undocumented migrants face restrictions which their citizen or documented peers (even if equally economically disadvantaged) may not experience (Ruge & Iza, 2005). Roma populations in Europe and Dalit populations in India face unique forms of denigration, including in societies that pride themselves on their inclusionary human rights records (Matache et al. & Kelly et al., in this volume). By attending to intersectional marginalisation, which generates distinctive forms of discrimination, we hope to illuminate the complexity of the rights challenges ahead.

While not minimising the pervasive disenfranchisement of many residents in the global North, we have sought to direct substantial attention towards the experience of students and scholars in or from the global South, cognisant of the conspicuous absence of HE research in this domain. In so doing, we align ourselves with those scholars and activists, many of them quoted in the following chapters, who challenge the centrality of the global North as the repository of pedagogic excellence, curricular primacy or institutional innovation. Concepts such as the 'pluriversity' are usefully provocative in this regard (Mbembe, 2016). Debates about decolonisation of university curricula, restructuring of HE funding structures and levelling of infrastructural inequalities – all featured in this volume – are critical for the broad and cross-cutting analysis of educational marginalisation that we seek to promote.

No population illustrates the pervasive, global impact of intersectional discrimination more vividly than refugees. Geographic displacement, economic deprivation, racial stigmatisation, religious and ethnic marginalisation and enduring institutional and colonial bias generate educational environments that vigorously militate against the inclusion of this growing and highly diverse population into the HE constituency. The population affected is substantial: 25.9 million people globally, the highest number ever recorded, according to recent data from Amnesty International (2019). In addition to refugees, other populations, including the internally displaced, the recipients of humanitarian status, the undocumented, the stateless and those who fall in between these arbitrary categorical divides but have also moved because they lack fundamental security at home, compound the size of those now termed 'distress migrants' (Bhabha, 2018). Together they constitute close to 70 million people (UNHCR, 2018), more than the population of large countries such as the United Kingdom, Canada, Australia or Kenya.

Eighty per cent of the current refugee population are hosted in poor countries, a percentage that has not changed for decades. Germany is the only global North country among the world's top ten refugee-hosting countries (Amnesty International, 2019). Meanwhile, countries long riven by conflict and economic distress – such as Lebanon, Jordan, Kenya, Pakistan, Bangladesh and Uganda – continue to provide humanitarian reception on a massive scale. This assistance is often offered in exchange for desperately needed development aid from wealthier countries that engage in this quid pro quo as a convenient way of externalising their humanitarian responsibilities. In 2018, less than 7 per cent of those who wished to be officially resettled (amounting to a paltry 92,400 persons out of over 20 million recognised refugees) were accepted from their location in zones neighbouring their home to countries of the global North (Amnesty International, 2019). Meanwhile, the majority remain trapped, sometimes for decades, in long-term refugee camps and other situations, such as detention centres and temporary border camps, zones of de facto social exclusion that generate a debilitating sense of temporary permanence.

Until recently, states and international agencies have evidenced little interest in offering HE programmes to refugees and other distress migrants. Their apparent impermanence on the host territory has provided a rationale for limiting educational investment to primary and some secondary schooling, often with little attention to the quality of the education offered. Almost a decade ago, with a focus on the global South context, Dryden-Peterson pointed to an imbalance between the humanitarian rhetoric in United Nations High Commissioner for Refugees (UNHCR) policy, which highlighted the importance of education at all levels for refugees, and the financial commitment underpinning that rhetoric: 'Education receives only 2% of humanitarian aid, the lowest of all [UNHCR] sectors' (2011, 9).[2] She called for a serious reconceptualisation of the education policies and programmes directed towards refugees, away from a 'humanitarian approach' predicated on short-term, emergency provision to one focused on a 'human-rights' and a 'developmental approach' that would be enduring and rooted in local government structures (UNHCR, 2011).

This book asks why only 1 per cent of those who define themselves or are defined as refugees are able to access accredited HE programmes (UNHCR, 2001, 2019b).[3] It also questions the gross gender inequities

---

[2] Dryden-Peterson attributes this lack of financial commitment to the fact that the UNHCR, at least in 2011, was not recognised by other international agencies as an 'actor in education' (see UNHCR, 2011, 9–10).

[3] According to the UNHCR, 'The 1% estimate was compiled in consideration of the following: 1) estimated tertiary enrolment rates of Syrian refugees in the five main hosting countries in the Middle East and North Africa region (Lebanon, Iraq, Turkey, Egypt and Jordan); 2) global DAFI

evidenced by refugee enrolment in HE. As the chapter in this volume by Kimari and Giles on the Dadaab refugee camps in Kenya notes, only a fraction of refugee girls who would benefit get access to HE of any sort, a dramatic form of gender discrimination that compounds the other gendered obstacles to female empowerment, such as early marriage, premature child-bearing responsibilities and many other sexual and reproductive health norms. As scholars have noted, in humanitarian crises, gender is routinely put on the back burner while the 'emergency' is addressed (Hyndman & de Alwis, 2003).

Gendered exclusions are not confined to refugee populations or humanitarian crises. As the chapter by Kelly, Bhabha and Krishna on 'low' caste, first-generation Indian girls attending College highlights, the obstacles to gender equity in this peacetime context are also persistent. They are the result of a complex intersection of deficient state policies and oppressive social norms common to disenfranchised populations across the globe. Askouni and Dragonas, in their investigation of HE engagement by the Turkish minority in Greece, also address what they call 'the intricate interplay of economic and gender constraints' that affect young minority women who take advantage of new affirmative action measures that facilitate College attendance. The excitement of a more open and expansive social and intellectual setting abuts against the economic and emotional stressors generated by the distance from home and family expectations of young women.

Methodologies

The methodological approach adopted in this book is syncretic. Acknowledging the complexity of exclusion and its multifactorial nature, and committed as we are to a holistic perspective that stimulates cross-cutting dialogue and intersectoral collaboration, we have gathered together experts drawn from several scholarly disciplines to illuminate our topic of interest. One approach to HE for forcibly displaced persons, a large subset of our population, draws on the framework of 'critical humanitarianism'. For some time now, anthropologists, geographers and others have used this framework to interrogate the priorities and preconceptions of those intervening in emergency situations. While some point to the importance of those aspects of humanitarianism that relate to 'safeguarding human life'

enrollment; 3) global Connected Learning enrollment; and 4) a grouping of other known enrollment' (UNHCR, 2001–2019a).

(Hyndman, 2000; Malkki, 1996), many of these same scholars and others point to humanitarianism as a 'political concept' (Nyers, 2006), which is also gendered and racialised, 'contraposing the needs of displaced peoples against the more powerful interests of states' (Hyndman [2000] in Giles, 2012, 210). Refugee camps have been described as 'the hidden flagships' of humanitarianism, an oxymoron, but one that helps to expose the invisible and unmonitored, yet hugely costly, nature of this type of protection. By making the connection between humanitarianism and so-called emergencies, that is 'humanitarian emergencies', Duffield draws our attention to the power relations inherent in current neoliberal forms of intervention, where strategies deployed are, in his view dangerously, defined as 'above politics' by Western states (Duffield, 2007, 71). This characterisation limits collective opportunities to engage with and challenge the forms of intervention or aid introduced by international actors, including the forms of educational provision offered. Outdated and contextually inappropriate syllabi, authoritarian teaching methods and gender-insensitive physical arrangements exemplify the results of this approach.

Sites are defined as humanitarian emergencies (sometimes for decades), and people in these sites are defined as refugees, whether in the global South or North, in effect (whether or not by intention) to facilitate their control and management by the states that host them. Their situation is thus quite different from the millions of asylum seekers who make their protection claims individually and, where successful, achieve a status that can facilitate social membership in the medium to long term. In these sites of humanitarian emergency, states responsible for ensuring the protection of fundamental rights of the resident populations pay scant attention to promoting access to higher forms of knowledge. A troubling recent example of how some neo-liberal humanitarians are sidestepping access to the right to education, including HE, for refugees is the promotion of the right to work for displaced people in 'special economic zones (SEZs)' or 'industrial incubator zones' (Betts & Collier, 2015, 2–3), where large corporations stand to profit from the vulnerable status (and exploitability) of refugee workers.[4]

The laudable goal of supporting refugee self-sufficiency is, in these contexts, subordinated to the profit-driven incentives given to private

---

[4] Scholars (e.g. Mitter, 1986; Nash & Patrica Fernández-Kelly, 1983; Wright, 2006; Cohen, 2011, among others) have documented, from the 1970s onwards, the deleterious impact of export processing zones (EPZs), similar to the special economic zones (SEZs) advocated by Betts and Collier, on the health, well-being, livelihoods and futures of refugee, displaced and marginalised workers, many of them women.

investors eager to take advantage of a captive (often highly skilled) population through highly regulated and restrictive labour conditions. A better approach is to provide access to quality HE, since it is indisputable that refugees and migrants who are educated, like their counterparts in the majority population as a whole, have substantial relative advantages compared to their uneducated peers. They are more likely than those who do not have educational opportunities to be resilient throughout the trials and tribulations of refugeehood (Nicolai & Triplehorn, 2003; Tapscott, 1994). What is more, from a broader, geo-political, perspective, there is evidence of 'a direct link between a refugee programme focused on higher education and national reconstruction' of a homeland, with significant contributions by university-educated former refugees filling key positions in building a new government (Morlang & Stolte, 2008, 63, in Dryden-Peterson, 2011, 52). In addition, refugees and migrants who have access to HE are more likely than those without such access to regain protection through their own agency and efforts, seeking out productive employment and living opportunities. Regrettably, despite persuasive claims that education, and specifically HE, is a crucial 'tool to . . . reverse this narrative [of the passive refugee]' by making people into their own 'agents', empowered from within, rather than by emergency aid imposed from without (Zeus, 2011), most education in long- and shorter-term encampments and border zones is of very sub-standard quality, inferior to that offered to the majority, host population.

While these entrenched governance failures persist, there is also growing acknowledgement of the urgency of redressing refugees' de facto higher educational apartheid. Thanks to the pioneering work of some scholar/advocate groups, a few represented in this volume, innovative work is underway to rectify the legacy of past and enduring educational exclusion. In part, this overdue correction has been stimulated by the insistent demand of the affected constituencies themselves for a better deal. Triggers include mass movements such as the 'Rhodes must fall' and 'Fees much fall' campaigns (Ahmed, in this volume) and the mobilisation of DACA youth (see Gonzalez et al., in this volume), the careful advocacy promoting universities geared to native or minority constituencies (for native peoples in the United States, see Garland, and for Turkish-speaking minorities in Greece, see Askouni & Dragonas in this volume), creative programmatic innovations – in Europe, Africa and elsewhere – enabling access through fee forgiveness or scholarship support, by improving access, credential equivalence schemes and intensive preparatory tutoring (see chapters in this volume by Smith and Stein, Unangst, Rajaram and

Kimari and Giles). But the legacy of past exclusion and stigma is enduring, and much work remains to be done. As chapters on the persistent educational disadvantage of historically marginalised populations such as African Americans, Indigenous communities, people with disabilities and Roma demonstrate, legislative reforms alone do not achieve parity, nor do they erase the multiple drivers of long-standing discrimination.

Summary of Chapters

This volume is divided into three parts. The first part, entitled 'Encountering Marginalisation: Disparities in Higher Education and the Broader Society', articulates the numerous challenges faced by marginalised groups in various contexts, pointing to significant sources of disadvantage and the material and intellectual deprivations that arise out of marginality. A common observation that emerges from this part is that HE marginalisation is a product of multiple intersecting factors of exclusion and inequity, what Askouni and Dragonas call 'overlapping disadvantages'. Borgonovi and Marconi demonstrate this pointedly by shedding light on the way in which migrant origin affects access to, and completion of, HE across the countries within the Organization for Economic Cooperation and Development (OECD). They show that, contrary to widely held stereotypes, immigrant background students are not less but more motivated to achieve educational success and to hold ambitious expectations, and that their lack of commensurate educational achievement is a product of states' failures to capitalise on this motivation and to ensure access to the necessary foundational skills. As a result of these institutional shortcomings, immigrants are under-represented in the more academic HE programmes and, because of prior linguistic and educational disadvantages, are more likely to drop out than their non-immigrant background peers. Crul and Lelie make a similar point in the context of HE in the Netherlands through their 'integration context theory'. They show how institutional arrangements, starting before primary school, block pathways to HE by compromising dominant language acquisition, exposure to quality academic education in school and opportunities to select competitive academic higher educational pathways as opposed to more technical, less prestigious ones. The broad relevance of these arguments is clearly highlighted by their relevance to other contexts discussed in the book. Matache, Jovanovic, Barbu and Bhabha point to the compromised early pathways that militate against higher educational success for Roma communities across Europe. With a careful case study of Serbia, they illustrate the intersecting mechanisms of segregation and stigmatisation across multiple domains, from housing to employment, to health and education, which generate dramatic obstacles to Roma higher educational success. All three of these chapters address circumstances in prosperous countries of the global North, countries where resource scarcity is not a compelling justification for inadequate provision. They illustrate the considerable need for students with migrant or minority backgrounds to secure improved institutional support across a very broad range of social domains that impact their educational outcomes. For example, parental income, a critical variable in the HE equation, depends on employment opportunity, which in turn depends on childcare support, often lacking in immigrant communities. School academic performance depends on teacher engagement and early exposure to the majority language, again factors that are far easier for majority than minority communities to access.

In a similar vein, Chopra and Dryden-Peterson focus on what they term 'Higher education in exile', focusing on the experience of newly arrived students in the United States and the experience of integration (or lack thereof) into the educative experience. They conclude that an ahistoric and acontextual approach to HE continues to predominate in that context and illustrate, in very human terms, the meaning and impact of experiences of marginalisation inside and outside of educational settings. Crain Soudien, meanwhile, explores the changing landscape of HE in South Africa and the evolving nature of disadvantage there, noting that efforts to 'transform' HE have been only partially successful because mere 'massification' of access has not adequately addressed prior contributory disparities, most centrally those derived from economic determinants driving HE success. Ultimately, these class disparities (and the social movements that they have spawned, as described in the chapter by Ahmed elaborated upon below) reconstruct processes of marginalisation that had previously been predicated on race, clear evidence that more holistic and systemic efforts to truly 'transform' HE in South Africa are urgent.

Racial discrimination and socio-economic disadvantage are also the subject of Richard Kazis' contribution, though the setting in his chapter is the United States. Similar to Soudien, Kazis makes the argument that equality is more than the absence of overt discrimination. Rather, effective promotion of equality is a concerted and active process by which barriers to inclusion generated by social marginalisation can be overcome, thus rendering equitable outcomes possible. Sadly, as Kazis demonstrates, this goal remains an unachieved aspiration. African American and Latino students, who are much more likely to enrol in higher educational institutions than they would have been two decades ago, still face disproportionate obstacles to educational success: they are far less likely to enrol in selective, academic Colleges than in lower-level technical institutions, they are more likely to drop out and they leave HE with far greater debt and less deployable credentials than majority and other minority students. Likewise, and also with reference to the United States, Garland et al. highlight how marginality in society, so starkly demonstrated by displacement and geographical peripheralisation, has impacted HE for Indigenous populations. The significance of 'place', and its relationship with educational opportunity, is explored in this chapter, in which the authors demonstrate that marginalisation from society and marginalisation from opportunity are a cruel cycle. Nonetheless, they argue, this cycle need not be a foregone conclusion, as their discussion of efforts to introduce education programmes for Native peoples and to reclaim Indigenous knowledge as part of the process of reclaiming the 'place' of Indigenous peoples in the United States demonstrate.

Part II of the book, entitled 'Deconstructing Marginalisation: Political and Legal Solutions to Marginalisation and Their Limitations', highlights the various ways in which scholars, policymakers, activists and educators have sought to, or are seeking to, address marginalisation in HE, by working within the structures of established institutions and political processes. Rajaram's contribution explores the ability of refugees to access HE and the role of the university in Europe. In doing so, he notes the need for new ways to engage institutions, to legislate and develop HE policy and to conceptualise the pursuit of education as a global good rather than a national one. He details efforts by the Central European University's Open Learning Initiative (OLIve) to advance this goal, in the process shedding light on some successes and numerous challenges in law, pedagogy and institutional culture. On this point of challenges that arise despite concerted efforts aimed at reducing marginalisation, Unangst looks at the ways in which institutions in Germany have (and have not) developed and adapted their efforts to accommodate the specific needs of female refugees. Using a quantitative textual analysis, she illustrates, in compelling fashion, that many initiatives may have been developed to address the needs of large influxes into the country, but that these continue to fall short in facilitating learning for particular individuals and groups. What these chapters demonstrate is that much has indeed been done to support higher education for refugees in Europe, but these efforts remain nascent and are not unproblematic.

Donger's chapter is equally circumspect about the many progressive shifts in Ecuador's regulation of forced migrants, recognising the considerable potential of that country's commitment to non-discrimination in HE, while also noting the substantial challenges that arise when questions of implementation become apparent. She demonstrates that stigma, lack of resources, lack of technical capacity and sheer ignorance of the legal framework can be impediments to the realisation of well-meaning legal guarantees. The chapter by Askouni and Dragonas, meanwhile, considers the impact of affirmative action measures, both at the school and university level, for Muslim minority students in Greece, striking a more hopeful tone in its recognition of the success, albeit partial, of such measures in 'transcending socio-cultural barriers', dramatically reducing student dropout rates and increasing higher educational enrolment, including of girls.

Two chapters in Part II focus on disability as a marginalising factor in HE. Smith and Stein illustrate how legislation and jurisprudence have markedly altered the aspirations of the US HE system insofar as students with disabilities are concerned. Even so, they also demonstrate how complex the day-to-day pursuit of education can be for these students, highlighting the patent gaps that still need to be overcome if equality is to be felt in lived experience. Mahomed's chapter emphasises the 'invisible' disabilities, namely psychosocial and intellectual disabilities, which require specific accommodations. Regrettably, HE institutions in South Africa are difficult spaces to navigate for students with such conditions, and this chapter documents the myriad ways in which laws and policies at national and institutional levels have further marginalised them. Even so, there is hope for improvements, in the form of present and future policy developments, and the chapter highlights some key ways in which these developments can be harnessed to bring students with psychosocial and intellectual disabilities out of the periphery in HE settings.

Part III of the volume is entitled 'Confronting marginalisation: Narratives of Affected Students and Educators and Innovations in Higher Education Settings'. It elaborates upon current efforts to address the challenges of marginalised populations, reflecting on what can be learnt from good practices and what complexities still require navigating. Villegas and Aberman use the terms 'counterspaces' and 'counterstories' as signifiers of the way in which undocumented students in Toronto confront their marginalisation and build an identity that incorporates both their past and their present. This is not without its challenges, but it is demonstrative of the value of narrative framings of marginalisation. Ahmed's chapter is similar, in that it documents and analyses a burgeoning movement to shift the way in which access to, and success in, HE is manifested. The 'Fallist' movement, with adherents from Cape Town, South Africa, to Oxford, UK, has captured the imagination of students who, because of race and class, have been excluded from the pursuit of an education. The chapter delves into the movement's formation, its impact and, ultimately, its implications for those at the periphery of society whose adherence to 'Fallism' is, at once, a source of pride, consternation, hope and disappointment.

Kelly, Bhabha and Krishna also consider the way in which marginalised students engage with HE, in their case in Rajasthan in India. Their narrative and ethnographic exploration of the role of familial relationships and systemic barriers to women's education adopts a 'positive deviance' approach, focusing on the strategies employed by young women from illiterate families to access HE and the success triggers – most importantly mentorship and family support – that enabled young women who made it to university to succeed where their similarly placed peers failed. Aguilar and Gonzales also focus on the narrative of marginalisation, in the context of so-called Dreamer students in the United States, a population of young people without regular immigration status who have spent all but the early months or years of their life in the United States. The authors show how these students, admitted to universities, but with no prospects of regularising their immigration status, are affected by the uncertainties facing them, the continuous threats of deportation and other challenges they must endure in order to achieve and take advantage of a HE. Here, too, there is reason for optimism despite the clear precariousness of their situation, with the authors illustrating that individual resilience can be a key factor in withstanding considerable pressures and obstacles.

The chapter by Kimari and Giles is a compelling portrait of efforts to innovate in HE. Documenting the work of the Borderless Higher Education for Refugees (BHER) Project in Canada and Dadaab, Kenya, one of the first degree-granting transnational educational programmes to be established in a refugee camp, the authors provide an honest assessment of the many ways in which the inspirational project's aspirations to generate access to Canadian university teaching and credentials in a refugee camp are subverted by inherent inequities and ethical challenges. The chapter provides a highly instructive narrative from the perspective of instructors, whose dedication, vision and experience in the provision of HE for marginalised people remain exemplary. Squire and Zamman also focus on innovations in the provision of HE, documenting an education programme at the Calais refugee camp in France, where students and instructors challenge stigmatisation and find not only an institutional home for the purposes of learning but also a community where identities are developed, relationships are formed and new pedagogical materials and strategies are generated. This, they suggest, is of equal if not greater value than curricular training.

Douhaibi, Dahya, Arvisais and Dryden-Peterson also explore innovative methodologies that promote access to quality HE among refugees. The authors describe the use of technology to support communication between female students in the Dadaab and Kakuma refugee settlements in Kenya and their instructors in Nairobi and Canada. They demonstrate an important point, namely that these innovations do more than simply facilitate learning; they offer a means to deconstruct often oppressive systems of patriarchy and colonialism and serve as a tool for empowerment.

In sum, this book sets out to map the social and political landscape of HE as it impacts marginalised populations today across a broad but overlapping set of drivers of disadvantage. Its goal is to probe how legacies of exclusion and oppression can be subverted within the HE context and to examine how normative and practical intervention can propel social change and stimulate greater social justice. Throughout the volume, we argue that HE is a critical redistributive part of the human rights toolkit and that those who dismiss preoccupation with it as elitist or premature are misguided.

The chapters collected here demonstrate clearly, we suggest, the ongoing effects of educational discrimination, stigmatisation and inherited disadvantage that continue to plague minority groups across the globe. These effects deprive people of critical tools for intellectual, social and economic self-fulfilment, and deny their families and communities opportunities for redistributive justice despite legal and political claims to the contrary. We show that all too often, minority communities continue to be blamed for their own educational failures, failures which are laid at the door of their 'culture' or 'temperament'. The volume also provides cogent evidence, we hope, that whereas one-dimensional innovations, such as scholarship schemes, or mobility programmes, or non-discrimination edicts, have limited impact, more holistic and integrated efforts to address intersectional discrimination and the institutional structures underpinning it can be hugely impactful. Examples where minority populations are integrated into quality educational settings before kindergarten along with their majority peers, where curricular innovations address historical myopia and distorted accounts of the past, where power hierarchies between and within communities are carefully challenged inside and outside the classroom, all attest to the feasibility of progress. Illustrations of original and courageous experiments in educational innovation – from Calais to Dadaab, from Cape Town to Berlin, from Jaipur to Thrace – are spread throughout this volume. They fuel the hope that rates of HE disparity, illustrated by the fact that only 1 per cent of refugees and 1 per cent of Roma access this form of education, can be drastically reduced and that, within our lifetimes, the educational opportunities that have so benefited us can be enjoyed, as they rightfully should, by populations unjustly excluded from them for generations.

REFERENCES

Amnesty International (2019). *The World's Refugees in Numbers: The Global Solidarity Crisis*. 4 July 2019, Amnesty International: www.amnesty.org/en/what-we-do/refugees-asylum-seekers-and-migrants/global-refugee-crisis-statistics-and-facts/

Beckett, G. (2013). The Politics of Emergency. *Reviews in Anthropology, 42*(2), 85–101.

Betts, A., & Collier, P. (2015, November/December). Help Refugees Help Themselves: Let Displaced Syrians Join the Labor Market. *Foreign Affairs, 94* (6), 84–92.

Bhabha, J. (2018). *Can We Solve the Migration Crisis?*. Oxford: Polity Press.

Canadian Council for Refugees (2019). *Statelessness*. 4 July 2019, Canadian Council for Refugees, https://ccrweb.ca/en/statelessness#whatisstatelessness

Cohen, D. (2011). *Braceros: Migrant Citizens and Transnational Subjects in the Postwar United States and Mexico*. University of North Carolina Press.

Danaher, M., Cook, M., & Coombes, P. (2013). *Researching Education with Marginalized Communities*. London: Palgrave Macmillan.

Development Initiatives (2018). *Global Humanitarian Assistance Report*. London. 20 July 2019, http://devinit.org/wp-content/uploads/2018/06/GHA-Report-2018.pdf

Dryden-Peterson, S. (2011). *Refugee Education: A Global Review*. Policy Development and Evaluation Services. Geneva: UNHCR. 19 August 2015, www.unhcr.org/4fe317589.html

Duffield, M. (2007). *Development, Security and Unending War: Governing the World of Peoples*. Cambridge: Polity Press.

Fraser, N. (2005, November/December). Reframing Justice in a Globalizing World. *New Left Review, 36*, 69–88.

Giles, W. (2010). Livelihood and Afghan Refugee Workers in Iran. In W. Lem, & P. Gardiner Barber (eds.), *Class, Contention and a World in Motion* (pp. 23–40). New York and Oxford: Berghahn Books.

Giles, W. (2012). Humanitarian and Livelihood Approaches: A View from the Dadaab Refugee Camps in Kenya. In P. Gardiner Barber, B. Leach, & W. Lem (eds.), *Confronting Capital: Critique and Engagement in Anthropology* (pp. 208–221). New York and London: Routledge.

Hyndman, J., & de Alwis, M. (2003). Beyond Gender: Towards A Feminist Analysis of Humanitarianism and Development in Sri Lanka. *Women's Studies Quarterly*, *31*(3–4), 212–226.

Hyndman, J. (2000). *Managing Displacement: Refugees and the Politics of Humanitarianism.* Minneapolis: University of Minnesota Press.

Hyndman, J., & Giles, W. (under review). *Living on the Edge: Refugees in Extended Exile.*

Kagawa, F. (2005). Emergency Education: A Critical Review of the Field. *Comparative Education*, *41*(4), 487–503.

Malkki, L. (1996, August). Speechless Emissaries: Refugee, Humanitarianism, and Dehistoricization. *Cultural Anthropology*, *11*(3), 377–404.

Mbembe, A. J. (2016). Decolonizing the University: New Directions. *Arts and Humanities in Higher Education*, *15*(1), 29–45.

Mitter, S. (1986). *Common Fate, Common Bond: Women in the Global Economy.* London: Pluto.

Morlang C., & Stolte, C. (2008). University Degrees for the Benefit of Reconstruction. *Development and Cooperation International Journal*, *35*(3), 103–105.

Morrice, L. (2013). Refugees in Higher Education: Boundaries of Belonging and Recognition, Stigma and Exclusion. *International Journal of Lifelong Education*, *32*(5), 652–668.

Nash, J., & Patrica Fernández-Kelly, M. (eds.). (1983). *Women, Men and the International Division of Labour.* Albany: SUNY.

Nicolai, S., & Triplehorn, C. (2003). *The Role of Education in Protecting Children in Conflict.* Overseas Development Institute. Humanitarian Practice Network. https://odihpn.org/resources/the-role-of-education-in-protecting-children-in-conflict/

Nicolai, S., Hine, S., & Wales, J. (2015). *Education in Emergencies and Protracted Crises: Toward a Strengthened Response: Background Paper for the Oslo Summit on Education Development.* The Overseas Development Institute. 21 August 2015, www.ineesite.org/uploads/files/resources/EiE-_Toward_a_strengthened_respo nse__Oslo_Summit_paper_-_DRAFT_2015-05-11.pdf

Nyers, P. (2006). *Rethinking Refugees: Beyond States of Emergency.* New York and London: Routledge.

Ruge, T., & Iza, A. (2005). Higher Education for Undocumented Students. *Indiana International and Comparative Law Review*, *15*(2), 1–22.

Solorzano, D., & Villalpando, O. (1998). Critical Race Theory, Marginality and the Experience of Students of Color in Higher Education. In C. Torres, &

T. Mitchell (eds.), *Sociology of Education: Emerging Perspectives* (pp. 211–241). Stony Brook: SUNY Press.

Tapscott, C. (1994). A Tale of Two Homecomings. In T. Allen, & H. Morsink (eds.), *When Refugees Go Home* (pp. 251–259). Trenton, NJ: African World Press, Inc.

UNESCO (2014). *Teaching and Learning: Achieving Quality for All; EFA Global Monitoring Report, 2013–2014.* Geneva: UNESCO.

UNESCO (2018a). *If Education Cannot Wait, Then Humanitarian Aid Needs to Increase.* 3 July 2019, World Education Blog: Global Education Monitoring Report. https://gemreportunesco.wordpress.com/2018/06/29/if-education-cannot-wait-then-humanitarian-aid-needs-to-increase/

UNESCO (2018b). *Global Education Monitoring Report: Policy Report 36.* Geneva: UNESCO.

UNHCR (2001–2019a). *Tertiary Education.* 4 July 2019, UNHCR, www.unhcr.org/tertiary-education.html

UNHCR (2001–2019b). *What We Do.* 4 July 2019, Connected Learning in Crisis Consortium, www.connectedlearning4refugees.org/what-we-do/

UNHCR (2014). *A Special Report: Ending Statelessness Within 10 Years.* 4 July 2019, www.unhcr.org/protection/statelessness/546217229/special-report-ending-statelessness-10-years.html

UNHCR. (2018). *Global Trends: Forced Displacement in 2018.* 20 July 2019, https://www.unhcr.org/5d08d7ee7.pdf

Wright, M. W. (2006). *Disposable Women and Other Myths of Global Capitalism.* New York: Routledge.

Zeus, B. (2011). Exploring Barriers to Higher Education in Protracted Refugee Situations: The Case of Burmese Refugees in Thailand. *Journal of Refugee Studies, 24*(2), 272.

PART I

Encountering Marginalisation
Disparities in Higher Education and the Broader Society

CHAPTER I

Disparities in Participation in Higher Education among Migrants

A Comparative Perspective in OECD Countries

Francesca Borgonovi and Gabriele Marconi

Introduction

Issues of equity and inequality are receiving increasing attention in both academic research and public discourse. The academic literature has revealed that within-country income inequality is on the increase and that wealth is even more unevenly distributed (OECD, 2015b; Saez & Zucman, 2016). This increase has been affecting both high-income and middle-, lower-middle and low-income countries. Increases in inequality harm social cohesion (Alesina & La Ferrara, 2002; Kawachi, Kennedy, Lochner, & Prothrow-Stith, 1997) as well as economic growth (Barro, 2000). In particular, increasing cross-country evidence based on data from Organisation for Economic Co-operation and Development (OECD) countries reveals that in the presence of high levels of income and wealth inequalities, social mobility is lower (Krueger, 2012).

Disparities in educational attainment and achievement are generally considered both a cause (Oreopoulos & Salvanes, 2011; Card, 2001) and a consequence of broader social and economic disparities (Holmlund, Lindahl, & Plug, 2011; Björklund & Salvanes, Education and Family Background, 2011). Given the expansion of higher education (HE) (Marginson, 2016; OECD, 2017a), the returns associated with participation in it and the high costs associated with participation, the study of disparities in participation in HE has become crucial to understanding inequalities in incomes, wealth and social outcomes more generally.

Because of the policy relevance of this topic and the relative paucity of cross-country comparable data, this chapter describes a set of indicators that can be used to map disparities in HE access, participation and graduation across the countries that are members of the OECD. In order to paint a comprehensive picture of disparities in HE cross-nationally, a variety of data sources are used: data from large-scale international assessments such as the Programme for International Student Assessment (PISA), the OECD Survey of Adult Skills (PIAAC), as well as ex-post harmonised national administrative, survey and census data. The use of different data sources enables the examination of a wide spectrum of disparities in HE.

The chapter begins by examining differences in the expectations of enrolling in and completing HE held by secondary school students with and without an immigrant background in OECD countries. It then assesses disparities in access and graduation and how an immigrant background influences not only the probability to access or attain HE but also the probability to drop out, to graduate from an advanced research degree (PhD or equivalent) and to have a research and teaching career in HE settings. Finally, the chapter presents cross-cohort evidence suggesting that the expansion of HE that occurred in the past decades in OECD countries was associated with a reduction of inequality in HE participation but not in skill dispersion.

For all outcomes considered, the chapter compares differences observed among individuals with and without an immigrant background with differences observed between other key socio-economic and demographic groups, most notably differences related to socio-economic status (SES). This enables a consideration of whether the specific outcomes observed among immigrant populations in specific countries mirror broader disparities in access and progression across the HE sector or whether these disparities are specific to migrant groups.

Broad factors that shape access to HE institutions and progression in HE programmes include (i) the ease of access to HE given where individuals live and the location of HE institutions; (ii) the availability of financial and logistical support to attend HE; (iii) exposure to individuals with HE credentials; and (iv) opportunities to use skills acquired in HE settings in the labour market. Although these factors do not affect migrants specifically, the socio-economic circumstances of many individuals with an immigrant background in many OECD countries make immigrant-heritage individuals especially vulnerable. Furthermore, many migrants experience migration-specific barriers to participation, including language barriers, lack of recognition of prior qualifications, prior non-standard educational careers and legal issues related to their status (e.g. eligibility for financial aid and scholarships) (Camilleri et al., 2012). These can vary widely across countries (Camilleri et al., 2013), leading to significant variability across countries in the representation of immigrants among entrants and graduates in the HE sector.

The process of comparison (across units and across conditions) is the basis of scientific evidence. Being able to make comparisons across countries enables the testing of alternative explanations, highlighting differences and similarities, and demonstrating the usefulness of a theory or concept in relation to a specific policy challenge (Imbeau et al., 2000). For this reason, in this chapter we build a knowledge base on the accessibility of HE to people from different socio-economic backgrounds across countries. Across the world, countries have devised a variety of approaches and solutions to address similar educational challenges, including how to reduce disparities by immigrant background in access to as well as progression and participation in HE. Evidence of the relative standing of countries in relation to common challenges, objectives and implemented solutions can be an important input for policy makers who need to design, plan and roll out inclusive education policies (Psacharopoulos, 1990).

Emerging Disparities: The Educational Aspirations of Secondary School Students

Students who hold ambitious expectations for their educational prospects are more likely to put effort into their learning and make better use of the education opportunities available to them to achieve their goals (Beal & Crockett, 2010; Borgonovi & Pál, 2016; Feliciano & Rumbaut, 2005; Portes, Aparicio, Haller, & Vickstrom, 2018; Perna, 2000; OECD, 2012, 2017b). Therefore, expectations of attending HE are, in part, self-fulfilling prophecies. When comparing students with similar levels of skills and similar attitudes towards school, those who expect to graduate from HE are more likely than those who do not hold such expectations to eventually earn a HE degree (OECD, 2012). Therefore, in order to provide a complete picture of HE-related disparities between individuals with and without an immigrant background, it is crucial to evaluate the expectations to obtain HE degrees and the readiness of students to attend HE courses as they approach post-secondary educational choices.

OECD countries vary widely in the overall number of students who expect to obtain HE, a reflection of historical differences in levels of participation in HE, the availability and quality of vocational education and training, the relative wage returns associated with attending HE, the structure of the local labour markets, as well as the incentives available to students to pursue HE (such as financial incentives, deferral of military service and social status associated with holding a HE degree). Interestingly, while in many educationally relevant domains immigrant-heritage individuals perform less well than native-born individuals (OECD, 2018a), the literature indicates that they are more likely to expect to attend and graduate from HE institutions than other students (Brinbaum & Cebolla-Boado, 2007; Jackson, Jonsson, & Rudolphi, 2011). This is remarkable because immigrant-heritage individuals tend to have a more disadvantaged socio-economic condition and to have lower levels of educational achievement overall (OECD, 2018a).

We use data from the 2015 Programme for International Student Assessment Study (PISA)[1] to examine differences between immigrant-heritage students and students without an immigrant background in expectations to earn a HE degree. Examples of HE degrees considered in the PISA educational expectations are: Bachelor's and Master's degrees in English-speaking countries (e.g. Australia, Canada, Ireland, New Zealand, the United Kingdom and the United States), as well as the Graduate and Postgraduate Certificate or Diploma; the Fachhochschulen and Universitäten Diplom, Bachelor's and Master's in Germany; the Corso di Laurea Triennale, Specialistica and Magistrale in Italy; the Bachillerato, Licenciatura, Carrera Profesional (conducente a grado academico), Postítulo and Magíster in Chile.

PISA data reveal that in many OECD countries immigrant-heritage students hold high educational expectations. In Australia, Hungary, New Zealand and the United Kingdom, for example, immigrant-heritage students are over 15 percentage points more likely to expect to complete tertiary education compared to native students. By contrast, in Greece, Mexico and Estonia they are over 15 percentage points less likely to do so. The result that in many countries immigrant-heritage students are more likely to expect to obtain HE degrees is particularly remarkable because immigrant-heritage students are often socio-economically disadvantaged

---

[1] PISA is a triennial large-scale low-stakes standardised assessment conducted since 2000. The number of participating countries has increased from 32 in 2000 to over 70 in 2015. Each PISA cycle assesses three core domains (reading, mathematics and science), one of which constitutes the major domain in a given cycle (reading in 2000 and 2009; mathematics in 2003 and 2012; and science in 2006 and 2015). The assessment is complemented by a background questionnaire designed to gather information on students' background, attitudes towards learning and behaviours. In 2015 and 2003, the editions used in this chapter, participating students were asked to report the higher level of education they expected to complete. Students who indicated that they expected to complete a degree at the 5A, 5B or 6 levels according to the 1997 International Standard Classification of Education were considered as expecting to complete a higher education degree. Since the target sample of the study is 15-year-olds who were in school at the time of the assessment, individuals that had already left formal education by that age are not represented in the study. Since school dropout is associated with socio-economic and demographic status, results represent a lower bound of potential disparities in educational expectations.

and exhibit lower academic performance – two of the factors that influence the probability of expecting to complete tertiary education. When comparing students of similar SES and, even more so, when comparing students of similar SES and academic performance, immigrant-heritage students are more likely than students without an immigrant background to hold ambitious expectations for their education in most, but by no means all, countries. Moreover, the educational expectations of students with an immigrant background vary markedly across countries. This difference reflects the political and regulatory environment encountered by such students and the resulting barriers or opportunities they encounter in different systems.

On average across OECD countries, the percentage of immigrant-heritage students who expected to earn a HE degree was 8 percentage points greater than the percentage of students without an immigrant background and similar SES and performance who expected to do so. The difference between students with and without an immigrant background of similar SES and academic performance was greater than 15 percentage points in Australia, Belgium, Canada, New Zealand, Norway, the Slovak Republic, Sweden and the United Kingdom.

However, while the fact that many immigrant-heritage students harbour ambitious educational expectations reflects their high level of motivation and commitment to education, many education systems in OECD countries fail to capitalise on such motivation and ensure that motivation is matched by readiness to participate in and obtain HE qualifications. When students who expect to complete tertiary education also have foundation skills, they are more likely to be able to achieve their goals. Figure 1.1 reveals that many immigrant-heritage students who hold high educational expectations often lack the academic skills to fulfil them. Students who do not reach baseline levels of proficiency in the core PISA subjects – science, reading and mathematics – are unlikely to be able to realise ambitious academic goals and unlock their full potential.

On average across OECD countries, only 74 per cent of immigrant students who held ambitious expectations for their education reached baseline levels of academic performance in reading, mathematics and science. By contrast, 87 per cent of students without an immigrant background who held ambitious educational expectations attained baseline academic proficiency, about 15 percentage points more than the percentage of immigrant students who fit this profile.

Immigrant students whose academic skills match their educational ambitions are more likely to be successful beyond their secondary

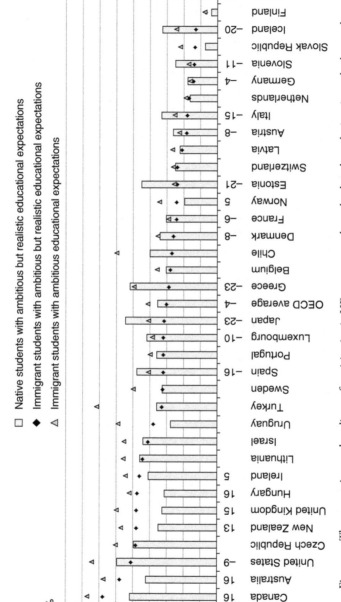

Figure 1.1 The expectations and readiness of participating in HE among secondary school students, by immigrant background

Source: PISA 2015 Databases

Students with ambitious educational expectations and who are ready to participate in HE are those who expect to complete tertiary education (International Standard Classification of Education (ISCED) levels 5a and 6) and also attain at least PISA proficiency level 2 in all three core PISA subjects – science, reading and mathematics. Statistically significant differences between immigrant and native students who expect to complete HE and have solid foundation skills are shown next to country/economy names.

Students are considered to expect to complete HE if they reported that they expect to obtain a degree at level 5A, 5B or 6 according to the ISCED.

□ Native students with ambitious but realistic educational expectations

◆ Immigrant students with ambitious but realistic educational expectations

△ Immigrant students with ambitious educational expectations

education. Too many immigrant-heritage students who harbour the ambition to obtain HE degrees lack the level of skills that are needed to succeed in HE. Unless the lack of alignment between ambition and readiness to attend and graduate from HE is tackled, the long-term integration of migrant communities can be undermined. Unrealized ambitions can lead to psychological distress among adults in general. Among immigrants, unrealized ambitions can be detrimental to labor market integration and overall social cohesion.

Cross-Country Evidence on Disparities in HE Access and Completion

Individuals with a HE degree are more likely to be employed and earn more (OECD, 2018b; Woessmann, 2016) but also seem to be more healthy and socially engaged than other individuals (OECD, 2015b; Lochner, 2011). Higher education brings agency to otherwise excluded individuals, enhancing their confidence and ability to improve their condition and helping them break down some of the barriers raised by social inequality (Marginson, 2011).

The previous section illustrated that while many immigrant-heritage individuals are motivated to enter HE institutions, lack of academic skills may hamper the opportunities they have to access HE. This section studies disparities in access to HE by comparing the share of immigrant-heritage individuals among new entrants in HE programmes[2] and among the general population. Similarly, differences in completion are assessed by considering the share of immigrant-heritage individuals among first-time graduates and in the overall population.[3]

Data come from the OECD's Indicators of Education Systems Network (INES) Pilot Survey on Equity in Tertiary Education (OECD, 2017c). Officials from ministries responsible for HE or national statistical offices of OECD member countries provided the underlying data using national sources (see Marconi, 2017b, for a description of the sources, year of reference and country-specific methodologies). Despite some differences in the year of reference, the dataset discussed in this section provides the most updated comparative picture of disparities in access to and

---

[2] New entrants are individuals who enter a higher education programme for the first time in their life.

[3] In this section, immigration-heritage individuals are those who are either foreign-born or have two foreign-born parents (first- and second-generation immigrants). First-time graduates are individuals who graduate from a programme at a certain level of education for the first time in their life.

completion of HE in OECD countries. Other existing data sources tend to rely on surveys of adults, who sometimes undertook HE several decades earlier.

The INES Survey covered demographic groups according to four equity dimensions: parental education, immigrant background, having children and provenance from rural areas. These four dimensions were chosen based on their high policy relevance and wide data availability across countries (OECD, 2016a; Marconi, 2017a). While focusing on immigrant background, this section will use data on the other equity dimensions for the purpose of comparison.

The INES Survey covers two entry-level educational programmes in HE: (i) short-cycle tertiary programmes and (ii) bachelor's and long first degrees or equivalent programmes. Short-cycle programmes are relatively short (up to two years) and are typically more occupationally specific and practice-based than other HE programmes (e.g. tertiary vocational education, or *fagskoleutdanning*, in Norway). However, they can also have a more general character and prepare students for access to HE programmes at other levels (e.g. some associate degree programmes in the United States). Usually, short-cycle programmes are offered not by universities but by other HE institutions. The bachelor's level is, in the large majority of countries, the most common level through which individuals access HE. Bachelor's programmes tend to last three or four years. They can be practically based programmes oriented towards the labour market as well as theoretically oriented, research-based programmes preparing for more advanced qualifications. Long first degrees are classified at the master's or equivalent level. However, they are generally accessible with an upper-secondary or post-secondary, non-tertiary qualification. In this respect, they are more similar to bachelor's and short-cycle programmes than to other master's programmes. A typical example of long first degrees is medical programmes (UNESCO, 2015).

Figure 1.2 shows country-specific percentages of 18- to 24-year-olds with an immigrant background who are in different HE programmes, as well as their share in the general population. In an equal society, the markers indicating the share of individuals with immigrant heritage among new entrants and first-time graduates at different levels of education would approximately coincide with the bar, indicating their share in the population. Differences across the series highlight inequality of participation in or graduation from HE in a country.

Individuals with an immigrant background are under-represented among new entrants and first-time graduates, relative to their share in

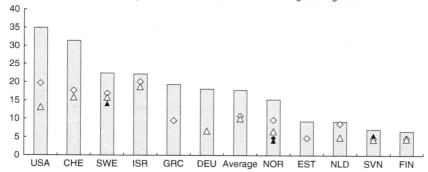

Figure 1.2 Percentage of 18- to 24-year-olds with immigrant background in HE and
in the overall population (2015)
Note: Individuals with an immigrant background are either foreign-born or have
two foreign-born parents. All markers and bars refer to the percentage of people with
immigrant background within a broader group of individuals.
Short-cycle tertiary education corresponds to ISCED 5, while bachelor's or long first-degree
corresponds to ISCED 6 and some ISCED 7 programmes with direct access from upper-
secondary education.
Source: OECD Pilot Survey on Equity in Tertiary Education.

the 18- to 24-year-old population. This is the case for all countries with
available data, and both for the short cycle and the bachelor's/long first
degree level.

However, there is a large variation across countries. For example, the
difference between the share of 18- to 24-year-olds with an immigration
background among new entrants in bachelor's/long first-degree programmes and among the overall population is negligible in the
Netherlands, and it is also small in Israel. By contrast, it exceeds 10 percentage points in Switzerland and the United States.

On average across countries with available data for entrants at the
bachelor's and long first-degree level, the proportion of 18- to 24-year-
olds with immigrant background is 11 per cent, as compared to
18 per cent in the overall population. This implies an estimated
39 per cent gap in the probability of accessing bachelor's or long first-
degree programmes between individuals with an immigrant background
and other individuals.

In all nine countries with available data on both new entrants and first-
time graduates, the share of immigrant-heritage individuals among first-time

graduates is lower than among new entrants, even though the difference is small (less than 1 percentage point) in Slovenia and Finland. This finding indicates that immigrant-heritage individuals are less likely to complete a HE programme at this level than to enter before the age of 25. This could relate to a variety of factors, including lower completion, delayed graduation or entering HE at a later age.

The finding that young individuals from under-represented demographic groups are less likely to complete (as compared to entering in) a HE programme does not hold generally across equity dimensions. For example, the share of 18- to 24-year-olds whose parents do not have a HE degree among new entrants and among first-time graduates at the bachelor's/long first-degree level tends to be quite similar (the difference is less than 2 percentage points, on average across 11 OECD countries with available data).

Immigrant-heritage individuals are also under-represented in short-cycle tertiary programmes in the three countries with available data (Norway, Slovenia and Sweden). This stands in contrast to other dimensions of socio-economic background. Short-cycle tertiary programmes often provide a point of access to HE to demographic groups that are otherwise under-represented. For example, in all countries with available data (including Norway, Slovenia and Sweden), the share of 18- to 24-year-olds whose parents do not have a HE degree is at least as large among new entrants and first-time graduates of short-cycle HE programmes as in the overall population. In Norway and Sweden, individuals coming from rural or intermediate regions (OECD, 2011) are also over-represented among new entrants in short-cycle HE programmes, as compared to the overall population (data on Slovenia and on first-time graduates are not available).

In each country, there could be a range of reasons why short-cycle HE could stimulate participation among certain under-represented groups, for example their short duration relatively to other HE programmes, their occupationally specific nature or their geographic location. Whatever these reasons, the available evidence suggests that short-cycle programmes in Norway, Slovenia and Sweden do not play the same role of widening HE access for immigration-heritage individuals as for individuals from other under-represented demographic groups.

Beyond Participation

The previous section mapped disparities in HE first-time entry and completion rates at the short cycle, bachelor's and long first-degree levels using ex-post harmonised national administrative and census data. In this section we use cross-country comparable data from the OECD Survey of Adult Skills[4] to identify disparities in HE participation and graduation as well as graduation from advanced research programmes such as PhDs, HE drop-out rates and employment in HE as academic staff. Finally, we examine how the skills individuals acquire in HE can differ across socio-economic groups and consider the implications of unequal returns for the long-term outcomes of immigrant-heritage individuals.

All analyses in this section were carried out on the pooled sample of OECD countries participating in the Survey of Adult Skills. This approach prevents us from exploring differences across countries which, as shown in the previous sections, can be substantial and also qualitatively important. However, pooling the data was necessary because of the limited sample size within most countries for some of the groups (e.g. academic staff in HE institutions or dropouts) included in the analysis. With the exception of academic staff in HE, we restrict the sample to 20- to 40-year-olds. We identify and compare the following groups of individuals: those who were foreign-born (versus native-born individuals) and those who are not foreign-born but have two foreign-born parents (versus those with at least one native-born parent).

Table 1.1 presents the association between having an immigrant-heritage background and various forms of participation in HE. Across OECD countries, between 10 per cent and 12 per cent of individuals were foreign-born. This figure was similar among HE students and dropouts, while foreign-born individuals were under-represented among graduates but over-represented among doctoral graduates and HE academic professionals, presumably due to the internationalised labour market for individuals with a doctoral degree (Auriol, 2010) and the traditional role of international mobility in the career of academics around the world (Welch, 2008).

Individuals with foreign-born parents represent a relatively small fraction of the 20- to 40-year-old population across OECD countries, and they account for a similar share of individuals among HE graduates. However,

---

[4] The OECD Survey of Adult Skills (PIAAC) is a large-scale international assessment of 15- to 65-year-olds in 33 (mostly OECD) countries and economies which was carried out between 2012 and 2015. Individuals participating in the assessment were administered a standardised test in literacy, numeracy and problem-solving in technology-rich environments. They were also asked to respond to a background questionnaire designed to identify the professional and educational background of the respondents, the level of education of their parents and their immigration background (see OECD (Skills Matter, 2016) for a brief overview of the survey and the main results). Results presented in this section focus on participants who were residents of participating OECD countries.

Table 1.1 *Share of individuals by immigration background in selected categories relevant to HE (2012 or 2015)*

		HE teaching academics	Doctoral graduates	HE graduates	HE dropouts	HE students	Overall population
First-generation immigrant	Percentage	19.1	29.2	9.5	12	11.2	11.7
	Standard error	3.9	5.6	0.6	1.5	1.1	0.3
	Sample size	745	421	26069	2715	10168	75837
Second-generation immigrant	Percentage	1.4	9.8	4.1	5.1	7.4	4.2
	Standard error	0.6	4.3	0.3	1.5	1.2	0.2
	Sample size	745	421	26069	2715	10168	75837

Source: OECD Survey of Adult Skills 2012 and 2015 Databases (PIAAC).

they are over-represented among dropouts, and while their proportion is about twice as large among doctoral graduates, they are significantly under-represented among HE teaching academics.

Conclusion

The evidence presented in this chapter indicates that in OECD countries large disparities exist in readiness to, access to, participation in and completion in HE. This is problematic because participation in HE is generally associated with better labour market and well-being outcomes and because individuals who participate in HE typically sustain only a fraction of the costs associated with their instruction, with significant public investments being directed towards HE. For example, in 2015 tertiary-educated workers aged 25–64 earned about 55 per cent more on average across OECD countries than their upper-secondary educated peers. However, the earning advantage varies greatly across countries: this advantage ranged from less than 20 per cent in Sweden to over 100 per cent in Brazil, Chile, Colombia, Costa Rica and Mexico (OECD, 2018a).

Although the earnings advantage associated with participation in HE is typically lower in countries where the share of individuals who completed HE is higher and among older cohorts (given the expansion in HE participation in recent decades), the returns to participation in HE remain substantial. Moreover, technological progress and globalisation are likely to lead to even more polarised employment patterns featuring high-skill/high-paying jobs on the one hand and low-skill/low-paying jobs on the other. When jobs are classified into different skill categories, OECD countries have seen an average increase of about 5 percentage points in jobs with high skill requirements and an increase of about 2 percentage points in jobs with low skill requirements. Employment in medium-skilled jobs decreased by 7 percentage points between 1995 and 2015 (OECD, 2017d).

We find that, in many OECD countries, students with an immigrant background are more likely than other students with a similar SES and academic performance to expect to enrol and graduate from HE institutions. Nonetheless, in the vast majority of countries students with an immigrant background leave secondary school with a level of skills that is not sufficient to enable them to be admitted into competitive HE degrees or to successfully complete such degrees if they are admitted. Some of the reasons that hinder the opportunities and progress of many immigrant-heritage students in HE are rooted in disparities during the school years.

These include lack of opportunities to participate in high-quality early childhood education and care; lack of adequate language support; lack of teachers qualified to teach multilingual and multicultural classrooms; lack of flexibility in the education system to account for non-standard education journeys; lack of knowledge of a country's education system and low-quality orientation programmes; lack of parents' voice or lack of ability on the part of teachers to listen to the parents of immigrant-heritage children; and concentration in socio-economically disadvantaged schools with few human and educational resources (OECD, 2018a). Working to ensure the readiness of immigrant-heritage students by promoting high-quality education during their schooling trajectory is crucial to ensure that they will be able to capitalise on their motivation and ambition and will be able to not only access but succeed in HE.

Our analyses suggest that short-cycle HE programmes can play a role in reducing inequalities in HE access and attainment among some socio-economic groups that are traditionally excluded from HE participation. However, our analyses reveal that short-cycle programmes do not appeal to immigrant-heritage individuals who, in sharp contrast to other socio-economically disadvantaged groups, hold ambitious educational expectations. For many immigrant-heritage individuals the only form of acceptable participation in HE is a long, academically intensive programme rather than shorter, more occupationally specific and practically based HE programmes. Lack of knowledge on the part of immigrant communities about the content of such programmes and lack of effective orientation and counselling targeted at ambitious immigrant youngsters may mean that some individuals who could greatly benefit from these programmes as a way to continue their studies and develop their skills beyond secondary schooling will be prevented from doing so.

Inequalities in HE pertain not only to access and attainment but also to what programmes people enrol in and what value added these programmes bring to them. There is some evidence that HE graduates from socio-economically advantaged households typically display higher skills than HE graduates from more disadvantaged households, an indication of potentially increased polarisation in the quality of institutions attended. Widening participation by encouraging attendance in short-cycle HE programmes may run the risk of further contributing to disparities in outcomes among HE graduates. Therefore, more evidence on the outcomes of graduates from short-cycle programmes is needed to understand whether they can play a role in effectively reducing the inequalities in the distribution of the benefits that different individuals reap from HE.

Overall, this chapter illustrates that, in most countries, immigrant-heritage individuals have a strong motivation to invest in education, see HE as an effective way to build a pathway into professional occupations and consider HE as a springboard for social mobility. However, many education systems in OECD countries fail to equip immigrant-heritage students with strong academic skills and, as a result, prevent them from being able to participate in HE programmes, from being able to complete them or from being able to enter the most demanding and prestigious institutions. The fact that we identify large differences across countries, even countries with similar immigrant populations (OECD, 2018), suggests that the organisation of schooling and transition pathways can play an important role in shaping how ready immigrant-heritage students are to make the most from HE opportunities.

REFERENCES

Alesina, A., & La Ferrara, E. (2002). Who Trusts Others? *Journal of Public Economics*, *85*(2), 207–234. DOI:10.1016/s0047-2727(01)00084-6

Altbach, P., Reisberg, L., & Rumbley, L. (2009). *Trends in Global Higher Education: Tracking an Academic Revolution*. Paris: UNESCO. https://unesdoc.unesco.org/ark:/48223/pf0000183135

Auriol, L. (2010). *Careers of Doctorate Holders: Employment and Mobility Patterns*. OECD Science, Technology and Industry Working Papers. Paris: OECD Publishing. DOI:10.1787/5kmh8phxvvf5-en

Barro, R. (2000). Inequality and Growth in a Panel of Countries. *Journal of Economic Growth*, *5*(1), 5–32. DOI:10.1023/a:1009850119329

Beal, S., & Crockett, L. (2010). Adolescents' Occupational and Educational Aspirations and Expectations: Links to High School Activities and Adult Educational Attainment. *Developmental Psychology*, *46*(1), 258–265. DOI:10.1037/a0017416

Björklund, Anders, & Salvanes, Kjell G. (2011). Education and Family Background: Mechanisms and Policies. In Anders Bjorklund and Kjell G. Salvanes (eds.), *Handbook of the Economics of Education*, vol 3, Amsterdam: Elsevier.

Borgonovi, F., & Pál, J. (2016). *A Framework for the Analysis of Student Well-Being in the PISA 2015 Study: Being 15 in 2015*. OECD Education Working Papers. Paris: OECD Publishing. DOI:https://dx.doi.org/10.1787/5jlpszwghvvb-en

Brennan, J., & Naidoo, R. (2008). Higher Education and the Achievement (and/or Prevention) of Equity and Social Justice. *Higher Education*, *56*, 287–302. DOI:10.1007/s10734-008-9127-3

Brinbaum, Y., & Cebolla-Boado, H. (2007). The School Careers of Ethnic Minority Youth in France: Success or Disillusion? *Ethnicities*, *7*(3), 445–474. https://doi.org/10.1177/1468796807080237

Brooks, R. (2012). Student-Parents and Higher Education: A Cross-National Comparison. *Journal of Education Policy*, *27*(3), 423–439. DOI:10.1080/02680939.2011.613598

Camilleri, A., Griga, D., Mühleck, K., Miklavič, K., Proli, D., & Schneller, C. (2013). Evolving Diversity II. *Participation of Students with an Immigrant Background in European Higher Education*. EURASHE, Brussels. www.eurashe.eu/library/equnet_report_2_evolving-diversity_migration-pdf/

Card, D. (September, 2001). Estimating the Return to Schooling: Progress on Some Persistent Econometric Problems. *Econometrica*, *69*(5), 1127–1160.

Clancy, P., & Goastellec, G. (2007). Exploring Access and Equity in Higher Education: Policy and Performance in a Comparative Perspective. *Higher Education Quarterly*, *61*(2), 136–154. DOI:10.1111/j.1468-2273.2007.00343.x

Crawford, C., Gregg, P., Macmillan, L., Vignoles, A., & Wyness, G. (2016). Higher Education, Career Opportunities, and Intergenerational Inequality. *Oxford Review of Economic Policy*, *32*(4), 553–575. DOI:10.1093/oxrep/grw030

Cullinan, J., Flannery, D., Walsh, S., & McCoy, S. (2013). Distance Effects, Social Class and the Decision to Participate in Higher Education in Ireland. *Economic and Social Review*, *44*(1), 19–51. www.esr.ie/article/view/62

Feliciano, C., & Rumbaut, R. G. (2005). Gendered Paths: Educational and Occupational Expectations and Outcomes among Adult Children of Immigrants. *Ethnic and Racial Studies*, *28*(6), 1087–1118. DOI:10.1080/01419870500224406

Frenette, M. (2006). Too Far to Go On? Distance to School and University Participation. *Education Economics*, *14*(1), 31–58. DOI:10.1080/09645290500481865

Hauschildt, K., Vögtle, E., & Gwosć, C. (2018). *Social and Economic Conditions of Student Life in Europe: EUROSTUDENT VI 2016–2018 – Synopsis of Indicators*. Bielefeld: Bertelsmann Verlag.

Hillman, N., & Weichman, T. (2016). *Education Deserts: The Continued Significance of 'Place' in the Twenty-First Century*. Washington, DC: American Council on Education. www.acenet.edu/news-room/Pages/CPRS-Viewpoints-Education-Deserts.aspx

Holmlund, H., Lindahl, M., & Plug, E. (2011). The Causal Effect of Parents' Schooling on Children's Schooling: A Comparison of Estimation Methods. *Journal of Economic Literature*, *49*(3), 615–651.

Imbeau, L., Landry, R., Milner, H., Pétry, F., Crête, J., Forest, P., & Lemieux, V. (2000). Comparative Provincial Policy Analysis: A Research Agenda. *Canadian Journal of Political Science/Revue canadienne de science politique*, *33*(4), 779–804.

Jackson, M., Jonsson, J. O., & Rudolphi, F. (2011). Ethnic Inequality in Choice-Driven Education Systems: A Longitudinal Study of Performance and Choice in England and Sweden. *Sociology of Education, 85*(2), 158–178. https://doi.org/10.1177/0038040711427311

Kawachi, I., Kennedy, B., Lochner, K., & Prothrow-Stith, D. (1997). Social Capital, Income Inequality, and Mortality. *American Journal of Public Health, 87*(9), 1491–1498. DOI:10.2105/ajph.87.9.1491

Krueger, A. (2012). *The Rise and Consequences of Inequality.* Presentation made at the Center for American Progress, Washington, DC. www.whitehouse.gov/sites/default/files/krueger_cap_ speech_final_remarks.pdf

Lochner, L. (2011). Non-Production Benefits of Education: Crime, Health, and Good Citizenship. In S. Machin, E. Hanushek, & L. Woessmann (eds.), *Handbook of the Economics of Education, Vol. 4* (pp. 183–282). North Holland, Amsterdam: Elsevier.

Marandet, E., & Wainwright, E. (2010). Invisible Experiences: Understanding the Choices and Needs of University Students with Dependent Children. *British Educational Research Journal, 36*(5), 787–805. DOI:10.1080/01411920903165595

Marconi, G. (2017a). Equity in Tertiary Education: Relevance and Data Availability across OECD Countries. In *GAPS Think Piece.* GAPS. www.gaps-education.org/news-events/closing-gaps-thinkpieces/

Marconi, G. (2017b). Pilot Survey on Equity in Tertiary Education: Results and Discussion. Declassified OECD Document Nr. EDU/EDPC/INES/WP (2017) 7. https://ssrn.com/abstract=3386937

Marginson, S. (2011). Equity, Status and Freedom: A Note on Higher Education. *Cambridge Journal of Education, 41*(1), 23–36. DOI:10.1080/0305764X.2010.549456

Marginson, S. (2016). The Worldwide Trend to High Participation Higher Education: Dynamics of Social Stratification in Inclusive Systems. *Higher Education, 72*(4), 413–434. DOI:10.1007/s10734-016-0016-x

OECD (2008). *Tertiary Education for the Knowledge Society.* Paris: OECD Publishing. DOI:10.1787/9789264063518-hu

OECD (2011). *OECD Regional Typology.* Paris: OECD Publishing.

OECD (2012). *Grade Expectations: How Marks and Education Policies Shape Students' Ambitions.* PISA report. Paris: OECD Publishing. DOI:https://dx.doi.org/10.1787/9789264187528-en

OECD (2015a). *Education at a Glance 2015: OECD Indicators.* Paris: OECD Publishing. DOI:http://dx.doi.org/10.1787/eag-2015-en

OECD (2015b). *In It Together: Why Less Inequality Benefits All.* Paris: OECD Publishing. DOI:https://dx.doi.org/10.1787/9789264235120-en

OECD (2015c). *Progress Report with the Development of Indicators on Tertiary Education and Outcomes of the Third INES Rating Exercise.* Declassified OECD document. Paris: OECD Publishing.

OECD (2016a). *Ad-hoc Survey on National Preferences and Data Availability on Equity in Tertiary Education: Results.* OECD internal document. Paris: OECD Publishing.

OECD (2016b). *Education at a Glance 2016: OECD Indicators.* Paris: OECD Publishing. DOI:https://dx.doi.org/10.1787/eag-2016-en

OECD (2016c). *Skills Matter.* Paris: OECD Publishing. DOI:10.1787/9789264258051-en

OECD (2017a). *Benchmarking Higher Education System Performance: Conceptual Framework and Data.* Paris: OECD Publishing.

OECD (2017b). *PISA 2015 Results (Volume III): Students' Well-Being.* PISA report. Paris:OECD Publishing. DOI:https://dx.doi.org/10.1787/9789264273856-en

OECD (2017c). *Pilot Survey on Equity in Tertiary Education: Results and Discussion.* Declassified OECD document. Paris: OECD Publishing.

OECD (2017d). *OECD Employment Outlook 2017.* Paris: OECD Publishing. DOI:https://dx.doi.org/10.1787/empl_outlook-2017-en

OECD (2018a). *The Resilience of Students with an Immigrant Background: Factors that Shape Well-Being.* OECD Reviews of Migrant Education. Paris: OECD Publishing. DOI:https://dx.doi.org/10.1787/9789264292093-en

OECD (2018b). *Education at a Glance 2018: OECD Indicators.* Paris: OECD Publishing.

OECD (n.d.). *Benchmarking Higher Education Systems 2017/2018: Estonia, Flemish Community, Norway and the Netherlands.* Paris: OECD Publishing.

OECD/Eurostat/UNESCO Institute for Statistics (2015). *ISCED 2011 Operational Manual: Guidelines for Classifying National Education Programmes and Related Qualifications.* Paris: OECD Publishing. DOI:https://dx.doi.org/10.1787/9789264228368-en

Oreopoulos, P., & Salvanes, K. G. (2011). Priceless: The Nonpecuniary Benefits of Schooling. *Journal of Economic Perspectives, 25*(1), 159–184.

Perna, L. (2000). Differences in the Decision to Attend College among African Americans, Hispanics, and Whites. *Journal of Higher Education, 71*(2), 117–141. DOI:10.2307/2649245

Portes, A., Aparicio, R., Haller, W., & Vickstrom, E. (2018). Moving Ahead in Madrid: Aspirations and Expectations in the Spanish Second Generation. *International Migration Review, 44*(4), 767–801. https://doi.org/10.1111/j.1747-7379.2010.00825.x

Psacharopoulos, G. (1990). Comparative Education: From Theory to Practice, or Are You A: \neo.* or B:*. ist? *Comparative Education Review, 34*(3), 369–380.

Ritzen, J. (2010). *A Chance for European Universities.* Amsterdam: Amsterdam University Press.

Saez, E., & Zucman, G. (2016). Wealth Inequality in the United States since 1913: Evidence from Capitalized Income Tax Data. *Quarterly Journal of Economics*, *131*(2), 519–578. DOI:10.1093/qje/qjw004

Shavit, Y., Arum, R., & Gamoran, A. (eds.). (2007). *Stratification in Higher Education: A Comparative Study*. Stanford: Stanford University Press.

Smalley, K., & Warren, J. (2013). Rurality as a Diversity Issue. In K. Smalley, J. Warren, & J. Rainer (eds.), *Rural Mental Health: Issues, Policies, and Best Practices* (pp. 37–47). New York: Springer.

Sørensen, E., & Høst, A. (2015). Does Distance Determine Who Is in Higher Education? In *MPRA Paper*. MPRA, Munich. https://mpra.ub.uni-muenchen.de/74517/1/MPRA_paper_74517.pdf

UNESCO (2006). *International Standard Classification of Education ISCED 1997*. Montreal: UNESCO-UIS. www.uis.unesco.org

UNESCO Institute for Statistics (2012). *International Standard Classification of Education ISCED 2011*. Montreal: UNESCO Institute for Statistics.

UNESCO Institute for Statistics (2015). *ISCED 2011 Operational Manual: Guidelines for Classifying National Education Programmes and Related Qualifications*. Montreal.

UOE (2018). UNESCO-UIS/OECD/EUROSTAT Data Collection on Formal Education – Manual on Concepts, Definitions and Classifications. UOE, Montreal, Paris, Luxembourg. 7 March 2018, http://uis.unesco.org/sites/default/files/documents/uoe2016manual_11072016_0.pdf

Usher, A. (2004). A New Measuring Stick: Is Access to Higher Education in Canada Equitable? Educational Policy Institute, Toronto. www.yorku.ca/pathways/literature/Access/usher%2004.pdf

Welch, A. (2008). Myths and Modes of Mobility: The Changing Face of Academic Mobility in the Global Era. In M. Byram, & F. Dervin (eds.), *Students, Staff, and Academic Mobility in Higher Education* (pp. 292–311). Newcastle: Cambridge Scholars Publishing.

Woessmann, L. (2016). The Economic Case for Education. *Education Economics*, *24*(1), 3–32. DOI:10.1080/09645292.2015.1059801

Access to Higher Education and Retention of Students with a Migrant Background in the Netherlands
A Comparative Analysis

Maurice Crul and Frans Lelie

Introduction

For over forty years the school careers of children of migrants with low levels of education have been a prominent topic in research in Western Europe. School failure, year repetition, early school leaving and streaming into vocational tracks have been widely studied (for an overview, see Crul 2013). By contrast, this group's school success and enrolment into higher education has hardly been on the research agenda. Only in the last decade has this become a focus of study (Alba and Holdaway 2013; Crul 2000, 2013, 2015; Gandera and Contreras 2008; Heath and Brinbaum 2007; Jong 2012; Louie 2012; Nanhoe 2012; Rezai et al. 2015; Santelli 2013; Suárez-Orozco et al. 2009). Some of the children of Turkish or Moroccan descent, the two largest immigrant communities in Western Europe, have made remarkable gains in education (Alba and Holdaway 2013; Crul et al. 2013; Wolf 2013). While the parents had very low levels of education, including many who were illiterate, a considerable share of their children have made it into higher education (Crul 2015, 2018; Schnell et al. 2013; Wolff and Crul 2002, 2003). At the same time, their access to and retention in higher education still show considerable gaps when compared to those of children of native descent (Inspectie Rapport Onderwijs 2016; Sociaal Cultureel Planbureau 2013). Throughout this chapter we will try to find out what is causing the difference in educational outcomes. We will look at children of Turkish descent in the Dutch school system to analyse whether these gaps are the result of socio-cultural background characteristics related to their ethnic group (being of Turkish descent) or of the migration (their own or that of their parents) or whether the gap in educational outcomes compared to the group of native descent can be explained by how educational institutions provide opportunities or, on the contrary, block the path to higher education for children of immigrants.

This chapter begins by comparing access to higher education across a number of Western European countries making use of the Integration of the European Second Generation (TIES) survey. This international study lets us analyse and compare school careers of the children of Turkish migrants in seven European countries: Austria, Belgium, France, Germany, Sweden, Switzerland and the Netherlands. The comparative perspective will show the impact of national institutional arrangements in pre-primary and elementary education and the permeability of the school system in relation to access to higher education (e.g. if the school system allows you to stream up from a vocational to an academic stream). Based on these findings in earlier research we developed the *integration context theory* (Crul and Schneider 2010, Crul et al. 2013; Crul 2017). This theory explains how institutional arrangements in education play a crucial role in explaining access to higher education.

From the comparison of the seven European countries we will further focus specifically on the Netherlands. Of all the countries in continental Europe, research in the Netherlands is most advanced on the topic of access to and retention in higher education, providing detailed information on students' performances in it. Based on the information available in the Netherlands we will show more in detail how differences in the preparation for higher education that students get can lead to important differences in their study success later on.

Access to Higher Education for Children of Migrants from Turkey in North-Western Europe: An Institutional Perspective

The more than 4 million migrants and their descendants from Turkey form the largest immigrant group in Europe. From the 1950s and 1960s onwards, the first generation came to Europe in large numbers. Germany, with more than 3 million people of Turkish descent, now hosts the largest group of Turkish labour migrants and their descendants. Sweden, Austria, Switzerland, France, the Netherlands and Belgium also have all received considerable numbers of Turkish labour migrants (Akgunduz 2008). Most of the parents belonging to the first generation were low educated, being specifically recruited by factories to work low-skilled jobs. On average, the men went to primary school. Many of the women, who joined their husbands after a few years, had not attended school at all. The vast majority of the labour migrants came from rural areas in Turkey, like the Konya area, where in the 1950s schooling beyond primary level was not common. A lot of the research done in continental Europe on the school careers of students of Turkish descent attributes low levels of participation in higher education to socio-cultural, ethnic and religious characteristics (for an overview, see Crul et al. 2003). The international TIES study enabled us to also take into account the institutional context, like the school system in place, the age of entrance in formal education, the streaming system and the length of compulsory schooling. In the TIES survey, the first large-scale survey among the second generation in Europe, we took a representative sample of people born in Europe to migrants born in Turkey in thirteen cities in seven countries. In each country 500 respondents between 18 and 35 years old were interviewed face to face about their entire educational careers and their labour market careers. This offered the unique possibility of comparing school careers from pre-school up to higher education for the same ethnic group with the same starting position (being born in Europe) in different educational institutional settings. To make the comparison even stricter, we reduced differences further by selecting only children from labour migrants with low levels of education (parents with lower secondary education at the most) in the data set. For instance, children of highly educated refugees who fled Turkey after the military coup in the 1980s or children of Turkish professionals who came to work for multinational companies were not included in this comparison.

International Comparison

In Table 2.1, looking only at children from parents with low levels of education, we found that the school outcomes and school careers of the second generation showed major differences across the seven countries. In Sweden and France, six to seven times as many respondents entered

Table 2.1 *Second-generation Turks (18–35 years old) in HE who have parents with low levels of education in seven European countries*

	Austria	Belgium	France	Germany	Netherlands	Sweden	Switzerland
Higher education	15%	17%	39%	5%	27%	32%	15%

Source: TIES Survey 2008.

Table 2.2 *Second-generation Turks (18–35 years old) in academic tracks in secondary schools who have parents with low levels of education in seven European countries*

	Austria	Belgium	France	Germany	Netherlands	Sweden	Switzerland
Academic tracks	18%	50%	47%	11%	23%	53%	NA

Source: TIES Survey 2008.

higher education than in Germany. Given that we could control for the education of the parents and that all these children were born in Europe, the differences between the countries were truly huge.

The differences alert us to the importance of the educational institutional context in different countries. Since we reconstructed the school careers retrospectively, we saw that big gaps between countries already appeared at the first selection point after primary school. The retrospective data on school careers in Germany in Table 2.2 show us that, in secondary school, only 11 per cent of the respondents were in the pre-academic Gymnasium track that gives access to university, while this is true for 53 per cent of the respondents in Sweden.

Institutional Factors That Hinder or Help

These outcomes inspire a look at the influence of specific institutional arrangements at work during the first part of the school trajectory that either hinder or help respondents to become successful in school. A number of institutional factors play an important role: the starting age of schooling, the number of contact hours in elementary school and the selection age for the different tracks in secondary school. In Sweden, more than a third of the Turkish second generation is already attending pre-school before the age of 3. In contrast, in Germany none of the children of the Turkish second generation was attending pre-school at that age. Furthermore, in Germany, elementary school is only a half-day school system in which children are at home in the afternoon. Both factors influence second language learning. In Sweden, the Turkish second generation learns Swedish at a younger age and transfers into an educational environment with much longer school hours. In Germany, many Turkish second-generation children really start to learn German only at age 5 when they enter compulsory school. By that time, they speak Turkish fluently but do not have a good command of

German. On top of this, in most German *Bundesländer* (provinces; educational policies in Germany are partly decided at the province level), children are already streamed at age 10 into three different types of secondary education that are consequential for post-secondary education or university. This gives them only four years to bridge the language gap, and that in a half-day school system, which means they have even fewer contact hours. By contrast, selection in Sweden only takes place at age 15, giving these children much longer to close any gaps with children of Swedish descent. The result is that in Sweden many more children access academic tracks that directly give them access to higher education.

These general school system factors interact with parental background characteristics. Because of the half-day school, the German school system transfers a large burden of language acquisition and homework support to the parents. By contrast, because of the full-day school in Sweden, most children do all their homework under the guidance of teachers at school. Our data analyses show clearly that in Germany only those children whose parents were able to help with homework could make it into Gymnasium, the track leading to higher education. In Sweden, on the other hand, many children who never or rarely got homework support from their parents also made it into the pre-academic tracks in Gymnasium (Crul et al. 2013, 137; Schnell 2015).

The Long Route

In all countries mentioned, streaming into the pre-academic tracks in secondary school is no guarantee of access to higher education. Many do not continue in higher education or, if they do, drop out. In general, the percentage of immigrant children in higher education is lower than it was in pre-academic tracks in secondary schools. The exception, however, is the Netherlands. Here we find more second-generation Turkish students in higher education (27 per cent) than in pre-academic tracks (23 per cent). The explanation lies in a rather unique characteristic of the Dutch educational system, called 'the long route' (EP and Nuffic 2015). In the Netherlands it is possible to use lower and senior vocational education (somewhat comparable to community Colleges in the United States) as stepping stones to higher education (higher vocational education). Completion of the first year of higher vocational education grants access to a four-year university. Though it takes three years longer than the direct academic route, it gets you into higher education in the end. No less than half of the students of Turkish descent in higher education have indeed taken this longer route, which entails more time out of work, larger study loans, higher debt and more pressure to combine studying with work.

Though it requires considerable determination and persistence, the long route compensates in many ways for the negative effects of the children's late start in the Dutch school system (somewhat comparable to Germany) and the early selection they face at age 12 (two years later than in Germany, but three years earlier than in Sweden). Twice as many children of immigrants take this long route compared to children of Dutch descent (Crul 2018). It is also typical for migrant children in other countries. In the United States, for instance, community Colleges are a common stepping stone to transfer to a four-year College (Crul et al. 2013b), and in Austria too, vocational tracks are used as a stepping stone to an academic track (Schnell 2014).

The Waterfall System

Belgium is almost the opposite, when compared to the Dutch case. In Belgium, like in Sweden, children start full-day school at two and a half and are selected for high school at either 12 or 14. Half enter academic tracks that lead directly to higher education. While the Dutch case is characterised by upstreaming through the vocational column, the Belgian case is typified by down streaming or what the Belgians call the 'waterfall system' (Crul et al. 2013). The most prominent characteristic of the waterfall system is that children in academic tracks who cannot keep up with academic standards (typically because their parents are unable to provide the practical help needed) are streamed down to vocational tracks, despite their initial academic abilities.

The Integration Context Theory

The outcomes we found across countries point to the importance of the local educational context. The *integration context theory* was developed to explain differences in outcomes in education but is also relevant to other domains like the labour market, housing or income. For instance, local institutional arrangements regarding childcare facilities, both the availability and the costs of childcare, explain why in Sweden twice as many female second-generation Turkish respondents in the TIES survey work (including women working in the informal economy) compared to Germany (Crul 2015). The resulting additional income in second-generation households in Sweden is one of the most important explanatory factors for this generation's social mobility.

The integration context theory (Crul and Schneider 2010) corrects the overemphasis on ethnic and cultural characteristics advanced by other explanatory frameworks. Traditional gender norms are often cited as the reason for low participation rates by second-generation women of Turkish descent in higher education in Germany, Austria or the Netherlands (De Vries 1987; Lindo 1996). However, in Sweden women with the same socio-cultural family background access higher education in far larger numbers, clearly a reflection of institutional factors at play (as the integration context theory would suggest). To be sure, individual characteristics may also play a role in academic success, as the point about the importance of parental help with homework makes clear. Where, however, students can work on their homework at school under the guidance of their teachers, these characteristics have less impact on school success. Integration context theory thus stresses the interaction between institutional arrangements and individual and group characteristics.

Access to Higher Education in the Netherlands

Unlike any other country in Europe, the Dutch national funding scheme for students combined with municipal register data on the birthplace of both students and their parents makes it possible to identify children of immigrants in higher education and to study retention rates for students with and without various migrant backgrounds.

The Expertise Centre for Higher Education (ECHO) was the first organisation in the Netherlands to integrate data and report on students with an immigrant background across all major Dutch cities (Zijlstra et al. 2013). The so-called Randstad Area is home to about 5 million people and houses five universities of applied sciences and five research universities.

Table 2.3 shows that a third of the students in universities of applied sciences (where students study to get a BA) are either migrants themselves or have parents who came as migrants. A quarter of the students with a migrant background have parents who have come from non-European countries, and 10 per cent come from other European countries or the United States. The prestigious research universities, which require a higher-level high school diploma for entry than do the applied science universities, are clearly less accessible for students with a migrant background.

Table 2.3 *Students with a migrant background in HE*
in the Netherlands

	European countries or the United States (%)	Non-European countries (%)
Universities of applied sciences	10	26
Research universities	12	17

Source: ECHO report 2013.

The students with a non-Euro-American migrant background (hereafter migrant background) are not equally distributed across study sectors. In universities of applied sciences, about half of the students with this background are enrolled in departments of Economics and Business, an 11 per cent difference with students of Dutch descent. There is also a slight overrepresentation (5 per cent) in the Social Work degree programmes. In research universities we find the same overrepresentation not only in economics (6 per cent) but also in Law (11 per cent). Almost a quarter of the migrant background students study law. Students with a migrant background tend to choose subjects leading to professions with high status.

Generational and gender differences have evolved over time. Whereas in 1997 half the migrant background students reaching higher education were first-generation immigrants (with women only 45 per cent of the students), by 2011 second-generation students formed the overwhelming majority for both communities, and women constituted 53 per cent of this student population (consistent with the general predominance of female over male students (Zijlstra et al. 2013, 66)).

In the 1980s and 1990s, young girls of Turkish or Moroccan descent were often forced by their parents to stop their studies prematurely and were married off early according to traditional gender norms. However, this trend has been reversed through the emancipation of young women in the two communities. In our study from 2000 this change became apparent (Crul 2000). Young women who stopped their studies and married early often broke up their marriages, bringing shame on themselves and their families. Those who continued to study in higher education, often against the will of their parents, proved that it was possible to postpone marriage and build a financially stable and respectable life with a partner later on.

Retention Rates in Higher Education in the Netherlands

Dropout (defined as departure from the institution rather than course switching) is most common in the first year of higher education (see, for instance, Cuseo 2012; Smedley et al. 1993; Wolff and Crul 2002, 2003). Table 2.4 shows that students with a migrant background drop out at a considerably higher rate than their non-migrant peers, evidence that a migrant background generates a more complicated start to higher education. The explanation for this difference is to be found in the institutional preparation that the two different cohorts of students receive; it has little if anything to do with their socio-cultural background.

The Institutional Preparation Students Receive

Slightly over a quarter (27 per cent) of the students with a migrant background have come directly from an academic track in high school while a third (33 per cent) have taken the so-called long route through lower and senior vocational education. The institutional preparation the students receive in the two routes explains the sizeable gap in dropout rates between students with and without a migrant background. Table 2.5 shows that of the students with a migrant background who have gone through an academic track in high school, 26 per cent dropped out in the first year. However, if they came via senior vocational education, the dropout rate increases dramatically to 39 per cent. Students with a migrant background who come through the direct academic route only show a 2 per cent gap difference with their non-migrant peers following the same route, evidence of the importance of the preparatory track taken. The gaps between the two groups mainly come about because students with a migrant background twice as often take the vocational route than students without.

Table 2.4 *Students with a migrant background compared to students without a migrant background in universities of applied sciences: dropout in the first year (cohort 2010)*

	Dropout from the institution within one year (%)
Students with a migrant background	35
Students without a migrant background	28

Source: ECHO report 2013.

Table 2.5 *Students with a migrant background from
non-European countries compared to students without
a migrant background in research universities: dropout in the
first year (cohort 2010)*

	Dropout from the institution within one year (%)
Students without a migrant background	20
Students with a migrant background	26

Source: ECHO report 2013.

The majority of non-migrant background students receive much more favourable preparation for higher education than their migrant background peers. Vocational education, the path taken by most migrant background students, is aimed at a transition to the labour market, which means that academic skills are not high on the agenda in the teaching programmes. Writing essays or doing individual work on projects is not a skill acquired in these tracks. Also, working on projects in groups with fellow students is not done to the same extent as in academic tracks in high schools. It is precisely this skill set, however, that is crucial to survive the first year in universities of applied sciences. (For more detail on curricular difference between academic and vocational preparatory routes, see Crul 2018.)

The ECHO report also gives dropout figures for students in research universities. Here too, students with a migrant background drop out more often than their non-migrant peers, but the gap is much less pronounced than in the universities of applied sciences.

This is because fewer students with a migrant background have taken an alternative pathway through vocational education into a research university (24 per cent) than is true for universities of applied sciences (33 per cent). But we do see the same strong effect from taking an alternative route. Of the students with a migrant background that directly came from an academic track only 22 per cent drop out within the first year, while those who came through the vocational route show a much wider gap with a 41 per cent dropout rate.

The findings for both the universities of applied sciences and the research universities show that institutional deficits – the different accessibility of academic versus vocational tracks for migrant background and non-migrant background students – seem to be the primary cause of the variation in first-year dropout rates. This should warn us against looking through the 'ethnic lens or migrant lens' (Glick-Schiller, Çaglär, and Guldbrandsen 2006).

Study Success in Higher Education in the Netherlands

We can see in Table 2.6 that the gaps in speed of graduation between students with and without a migrant background are substantial and do not seem to be shrinking over time. Though students with a migrant background who make it through the first year do not show significant dropout rates thereafter (suggesting that the first year is the most challenging part of academic adaptation), they do take longer to complete their studies than their non-migrant background peers. Interestingly, it is students coming from a vocational route who do slightly better in terms of the speed with which they complete their studies than their peers coming from an academic track in high school (see Table 2.7). This suggests that the adaptation in the first year is the most difficult part for the students coming from the vocational route, given the different skills taught in their education leading up to higher education. Those able to adapt seem equally, or even better, equipped to succeed in higher education.

The most important other trend we see is the huge gap in graduation rates that remains between students with and those without a migrant background (see Table 2.7 & 2.8), even when they have had the same preparation (either vocational or academic). Gaps of 14 per cent and 17 per cent after 6 years show that migrant background plays an important role (see Table 2.7).

Table 2.6 *Students with a migrant background from non-European countries compared to students without a migrant background in universities of applied sciences: diploma after four or six years*

	Diploma after four years (%)	Diploma after six years (%)
Students without a migrant background	51	75
Students with a migrant background	33	59

Source: ECHO report 2013.

Table 2.7 *Students with a migrant background from non-European countries compared to students without a migrant background in universities of applied sciences: diploma after four or six years compared to the type of preparation*

	Type of preparation	Diploma after four years (%)	Diploma after six years (%)
Students without a migrant background	Academic	44	73
	Vocational	62	79
Students with a migrant background	Academic	30	59
	Vocational	37	62

Source: ECHO report 2013.

Table 2.8 *Students with a migrant background from non-European countries compared to students without a migrant background in research universities: diploma after six years compared to the type of preparation*

	Type of preparation	Bachelor diploma after six years (%)
Students without migrant background	Academic	74
	Vocational	65
Students with a migrant background	Academic	61
	Vocational	54

Source: ECHO report 2013.

Here, for the first time, migrant background comes up as an important factor independent of the type of preparation for higher education.

To distinguish between migrant background in general or specific ethnic or cultural differences, we also looked at differences between the four largest migrant background groups. The differences between different migrant background groups are, however, relatively small. The gaps therefore are more likely the result of a general effect of being of migrant background. One can think of different treatment by the teachers or guidance staff, or, since we address study delay here, it could also be that more students with a migrant background needed to work while studying to maintain themselves because of the socio-economic position of their family. Our data cannot explore these factors further. Other studies have shown, however, that students with a migrant background more often have to work while studying (Lens et al. 2105; Wolff and Crul 2003) and that they have more family related responsibilities to fulfil, both factors which can interfere with their study.

For the students in research universities we see the same trends as for the students in universities of applied sciences. Students without a migrant background graduate much more often, even when they followed the same preparation. Graduation gaps with students with a migrant background, after 6 years of studies, of 11 per cent and 7 per cent remain. These are smaller gaps than we saw for students in universities of applied sciences, but they are still considerable.

However, big gaps remain even when students followed the same preparation to higher education. Again, a further analysis for the four groups separately does not point to specific ethnic or cultural group characteristics.

Discussion: A Transformation Model for Higher Education

Our analysis challenges the frequent assumption of a link between high dropout rates and insufficient study success on the one hand and student migrant background on the other. We demonstrate that the preparation of students guiding them towards higher education is most significant in determining these outcomes. For migrant background students who entered higher education directly from academic tracks, the gaps with students without a migrant background are very small. On the other hand, students who came through the long route do show considerably higher dropout rates. It is important to make these nuanced distinctions to avoid stigmatising students who actually perform well. Academic and administrative staff in universities of applied sciences and research universities have been known to target migrant background students, as a group that is performing less well or at greater risk of dropping out. We show that it is not the ethnic background or the migrant background that puts students at risk but the institutional preparation they receive. This has huge consequences for future policy interventions. Remedial programmes need to only target those students who have come through the long route, whatever their background, emphasising the acquisition of additional study skills and Dutch and English academic writing skills.

The Three-Phase Diversity Transformation Model

Based on the analysis of diversity policy programmes in the Netherlands and elsewhere we have developed a *three-phase diversity transformation model* (see also Crul in press). We distinguish the *awareness phase*, the *deficit phase* and the *institutional phase*. In general, higher education institutions go through these three phases sequentially. The *awareness phase* largely covers the period during which institutions start to acknowledge the new demographic reality they face. Data gathering on migrant and ethnic background often plays an important role in this phase. Are the numbers of students with a migrant background growing? Are groups accessing higher education represented in numbers equal to their share in society? Do the students with a migrant background drop out prematurely during their freshmen years? Answers to these questions frequently generate pressure to develop specific policies aimed at modelling the new immigrant student after the 'traditional student' of native descent.

With still limited research on the topic to rely on, we suggest that the analysis made in the first phase usually results in what we call a *deficit approach*. The students with a migrant or ethnic minority background are described in terms of deficits: lacking certain study attitudes, lacking language or lacking study skills. As a result, programmes are developed to repair migrant background students' language skills (Cuvelier et al. 2014) or to teach them how to study in higher education. Some of these efforts, however well-intended, are laden with stereotypical images of students with a migrant background and their families. Another common approach within this phase focuses on enhancing a sense of belonging. Universities embark on supporting ethnic minority student organisations or set up programmes where students with a migrant background can meet and support each other, for instance through mentorship programmes and summer courses. The idea is that this will increase their feeling of belonging to the university. In this phase diversity officers are often appointed and a structure is developed for consultation of migrant and minority students and staff (Foo & Ariss Fong 2009).

Often these deficit-inspired policies aimed at students with a migrant background fail to deliver, or only close a small part of the gap in outcomes (Inspectie van het Onderwijs 2016; Lens et al. 2015; Zijlstra et al. 2013). As we have shown in the data analysis, socio-economic background characteristics or the migrant background is only partly responsible for the retention gaps between students with and without a migrant background. Institutional deficits that result from a different kind of preparation offered by the vocational route influence the likelihood of first-year dropout much more than cultural factors. These institutional deficits are quite specific. It is a lack of academic language competency, rather than a general deficit in the national language, and academic competencies such as the ability to do research or develop an essay that hinders migrant background students coming to higher education via the vocational track. The vocational track (not a general lack of motivation or learning ability) is responsible because it never afforded the students training in these skills. Because of limited institutional resources and because remedial programming is often stigmatising (because it targets migrant background students as a whole rather than vocationally trained students in particular), students often reject what is offered and as a result supplementary programmes achieve meagre results.

Instead of these approaches, higher education institutions need to enter what we call the *institutional phase*, where attention is shifted to proper institutional practices and policies that encourage study success, either in the preparation for higher education or within higher education institutions (see Hurtado 2013; Tinto 1987, 2012; Wolff 2013). Institutional deficits in routes leading up to higher education should be addressed well before students enter higher education. Alternatively, in this phase, higher education institutions could target specific students at risk of failing in higher education because they have followed a vocational programme. This approach not only avoids stigmatisation of students with a migrant background, it also targets students without a migrant background that experience the same lack of academic skills. So-called bridge programmes for vocational students or international students have proved to be effective (Zijlstra et al. 2013). Higher education institutions might also explore why some faculties and institutions are able to close study success gaps better than others, perhaps by investigating teaching methods (Hurtado 2013; Meeuwisse & Severiens 2012; Wolff 2013), curriculum design, the College campus climate (Milem et al. 2005) and how guidance and counselling and mentorship are practised (Hurd et al. 2016; Wolff 2013).

Who Is the Norm?

Another important outcome of our analysis is the insight regarding university entrants. The norm used to be the student without a migrant background coming directly from high school after graduating from an academic track. However, if we look at all the students that diverge from this norm in big city universities nowadays, together they comprise more than half of the student population. The awareness of this fact should ideally result in a completely different approach to the student population. It no longer makes sense to treat so many students as exceptions to the norm, while they actually constitute the majority and thus shape the norm. While a university might accept the dropout of a few non-mainstream students as an inevitable consequence of resource limitations, it cannot afford to adopt this approach towards a majority of students. Apart from impugning the university's academic credentials, such high dropout rates are also likely to affect its financial base and the funding it secures.

We suggest that the current situation calls for a new approach by universities to their changed student populations. It calls for a holistic approach in which the starting position is that students crossing the threshold to enter university should be considered talented students, who in principle should be able to finish their studies successfully. Students of migrant origin coming from families with low levels of education who make it into university against the odds should find their talent and persistence valued and should be assisted as they navigate the university system. This, of course, requires a huge institutional effort, probably one of the biggest challenges our universities are facing today.

REFERENCES

Alba, R., & Holdaway, J. (2013). *The Children of Immigrants at School*. New York: New York University Press.

Akgunduz, A. (2008). *Labour Migration from Turkey to Western Europe, 1960–1974: A Multidisciplinary Analysis*. Aldershot & Burlington, VT: Ashgate (2016) London & New York: Routledge (Second Edition).

Crul, M. (2000). *De sleutel tot success. Over hulp, keuzes en kansen in de school-loopbanen van leerlingen van Turkse en Marokkaanse jongeren van de tweede generatie*. Amsterdam: Het Spinhuis.

Crul, M. (2013). Snakes and Ladders in Educational Systems: Access to Higher Education for Second Generation Turks in Europe. *Journal of Ethnic and Migration Studies, 39*(9), 1383–1401.

Crul, M. (2015). Is Education the Pathway to Success? A Comparison of Second-Generation Turkish Professionals in Sweden, France, Germany and the Netherlands. *European Journal of Education, 50*(3), 325–339.

Crul, M. (2018). How Key Transitions Influence School and Labour Market Careers of Descendants of Moroccan and Turkish Migrants in the Netherlands. *European Journal of Education, 53*, 481–594.

Crul, M., Ghorashi, H., & Valenzuala, A. (in press). Introduction. In M. Crul, H. Ghorashi, & A. Valenzuala (eds.), *Different Faces and Practices of Decolonization. The Challenges of Critically Informed Academia in Polarizing Times*. Stellenbosch: SUNMedia.

Crul, M., & Schneider, J. (2010). Comparative Context Integration Theory: Participation and Belong in Europe's Large Cities. *Ethnic and Racial Studies, 34*, 1249–1268.

Crul, M., Schneider, J., & Lelie, F. (2012). *The European Second Generation: Does the Integration Context Matter?* Amsterdam: Amsterdam University Press.

Crul, M., Keskiner, E., Schneider, J., & Lelie, F. (2017). The Multiplier Effect: How the Accumulation of Cultural and Social Capital Explains Steep Upward Mobility of Children of Low Educated Immigrants. *Ethnic and Racial Studies*, *40*, 321–338.

Crul, M., Holdaway, J., De Valk, H., Fuentes, N., & Zaal, M. (2013). Educating the Children of Immigrants in New and Old Amsterdam. In R. Alba, & J. Holdaway (eds.), *The Children of Immigrants at School*. (pp. 39–83) New York: New York University Press.

Cuseo, J. (2012). *Academic-Support Strategies for Promoting Student Retention and Achievement during the First Year of College*. Ulster: University of Ulster.

Cuvelier, P., Berckmoes, D., Rombouts, H., De Beuckelaer, W., & Vandenbussche, P. (2014). *Monitoraat op maat. Taalondersteuning academisch Nederlands Universiteit Antwerpen*. Antwerp: Universiteit Antwerpen.

De Jong, M. (2012). *Ik ben die Marokkaan niet! Onderzoek naar identiteitsvorming van Marokkaans-Nederlandse HBO studenten*. Amsterdam: VU University Press.

De Vries, M. (1987). *Ogen in je rug. Turkse jonge meisjes en jonge vrouwen in Nederland*. Alphen aan de Rijn: Samson.

EP and Nuffic (2015). *Education System, The Netherlands: The Dutch Education System Described*. The Hague: EP and Nuffic.

Foo, K., & Ariss Fong, N. (2009). *Best Practices in Equity and Diversity: A Survey of Selected Universities*. Project Report for the Equity Office of the University of British Columbia.

Gandera, P., & Contreras, F. (2008). *Understanding the Latino Educational Gap: Why Latinos Don't Go to College*. Cambridge, MA: Harvard University Press.

Glick Schiller, N., Çaglär, A., & Guldbrandsen, T. (2006). Beyond the Ethnic Lens: Locality, Globality, and Born-Again Incorporation. *American Ethnologist*, *33*(4), 612–633.

Heath, A., & Brinbaum, Y. (2007). Explaining Ethnic Inequalities in Educational Attainment. *Ethnicities*, *7*, 291–304.

Hurd, N., Tan, J., & Loeb, E. (2016). Natural Mentoring Relationships and the Adjustment to College among Underrepresented Students. *American Journal of Community Psychology*, *57*(3), 330–341.

Hurtado, S. (2013). *Diverse Learning Environments: Assessing and Creating Conditions for Student Success: Final Report to the Ford Foundation*. Los Angeles: Higher Education Research Institute, University of California.

Inspectie van het Onderwijs (2016). *De staat van het onderwijs. Onderwijsverslag 2014/2015*. Utrecht: Inspectie van het Onderwijs.

Lens, D., Levrau, F., Piqueray, E., De Coninck, D., Clycq, N., & Timmerman, C. (2015). *De universiteit in een tijd van toegenomen diversiteit: Een studie over de in-, door- en uitstroom van 'maatschappelijk kwetsbare studenten' aan de UAntwerpen.* Antwerp: Centrum voor Migratie en Interculturele Studies, Universiteit Antwerpen.

Lindo, F. (1996). *Maakt cultuur verschil? De invloed van groep specifieke gedragspatronen op de schoolloopbanen van Turkse en Iberische migrantenjongeren.* Amsterdam: Het Spinhuis.

Louie, V. (2012). *Keeping the Immigrant Bargain: The Costs and Rewards of Success in America.* New York: Russell Sage Foundation Press.

Meeuwisse, M., & Severiens, S. (2012). Studiesucces en leeromgeving. Een studie naar thuisvoelen, inzet en tijdsbesteding. *HO management, 4*(1), 18–20.

Milem, J., Chang, M., & Antonio, A. (2005). *Making Diversity Work on Campus: A Research-Based Perspective.* Washington, DC: Association of American Colleges and Universities.

Nanhoe, A. (2012). *Mijn ouders migreerden om erop vooruit te gaan. Onderwijs en de dynamische habitus. Succesbevorderende factoren in de onderwijscarriere van Marokkaanse, Hindostaanse en autochtoon Nederlandse academici uit lagere sociaaleconomische milieus in Nederland.* Antwerp–Apeldoorn: Garant Publishers.

Rezai, S., Crul, M., Severiens, S., & Keskiner, E. (2015). Passing the Torch to a New Generation: A Qualitative Study of Highly Educated Second Generation's Receiving Parental Support and Giving Support to the Younger Generation. *Journal of Comparative Migration Studies, 3*(12), 1–17.

Santelli, E. (2013). Upward Social Mobility among Franco-Algerians, the Role of Family Transmission. *Swiss Journal of Sociology, 39*(3), 551–573.

Schnell, P. (2014). *Educational Mobility of Second-Generation Turks.* Amsterdam: Amsterdam University Press.

Schnell, P. (2015). Behind the Scenes: Family Involvement and Educational Achievement of Second-Generation Turks in Austria, France and Sweden. *Journal of Comparative Migration Studies, 3*(2), 10. DOI:10.1186/s40878-015-0013-8

Schnell, P., Crul, M., & Keskiner, E. (2013). Success against All Odds: Educational Pathways of Disadvantaged Second Generation Turks in France and the Netherlands. *Educational Inquiry, 1*(4), 125–147.

Sociaal Cultureel Planbureau (2013). *Jaarrapport integratie.* The Hague: SCP.

Slootman, M. (2017). *Diversity Monitor VU 2017.* Amsterdam: VU.

Slootman, M., & Wolff, R. (2017). *Diversity Monitor 2017: Enrolment, Dropout and Graduation at Three Universities (EUR, VU and UL) A Synthesis.* Amsterdam and Rotterdam: VU/EUR.

Smedley, B., Myers, H. F., & Harrell, S. P. (1993). Minority-Status Stresses and the College Adjustment of Ethnic Minority Freshmen. *Journal of Higher Education, 64*(4), 434–452.

Suárez-Orozco, C., Pimentel, A., & Martin, M. (2009). The Significance of Relationships: Academic Engagement and Achievement among Newcomer Immigrant Youth. *Teachers College Record, 111,* 712–749.

Tinto, V. (1987). *Leaving College: Rethinking the Causes and Cures of Student Attrition.* Chicago: University of Chicago Press.

Tinto, V. (2012). *Completing College: Rethinking Institutional Action.* Chicago: University of Chicago Press.

Wolff, R. (2013). *Presteren op eigen bodem. Een onderzoek naar sociale hulpbronnen en de leeromgeving als studiesuccesfactoren voor niet westerse allochtone studenten in het Nederlandse Hoger Onderwijs.* Amsterdam: UvA.

Wolff, R., & Crul, M. (2002). *Talent gewonnen. Talent verspild?* Utrecht: ECHO.

Wolff, R., & Crul, M. (2003). *Blijvers en uitvallers in hoger onderwijs.* Utrecht: ECHO.

Wolff, R., & Severiens, S. (2011). De weg naar een keuze, een afslag naar success. *Thema,* 2, 16–21.

Zijlstra, W., Asper, H., Amrani, A., & Tupan-Wenno, M. (2013). *Generiek is divers. Sturen op studiesucces in een grootstedelijke context.* Utrecht: ECHO.

CHAPTER 3

Roma in Higher Education
Access Denied

*Margareta Matache, Tanja Jovanovic, Simona Barbu
and Jacqueline Bhabha*

Introduction

'God created school for the *gadje* [non-Roma]', a Romani student from
Serbia recalls being told by her grandmother.[1] And indeed, the extremely
low numbers of Romani graduates in Europe raise serious prima facie
questions about the exclusion of Roma from higher education and, beyond
that, about the quality and equity of Roma education at all levels. Across
Central and Eastern Europe, less than 1 per cent of the Romani population
have completed higher education (UNDP, 2011). For example, in the
Western Balkans, less than 1 per cent of Romani youth are enrolled in
tertiary education in Montenegro and Bosnia and Herzegovina, while
3 per cent of Roma in the Former Yugoslav Republic of Macedonia
(FYROM) and Kosovo attend higher educational institutions. In
Albania, only 1 per cent of Roma have a higher education degree (Nelaj,
Kaçiu, Dundo, & Dervishi, 2012: 54) in comparison to 27 per cent of non-
Roma (UNDP Regional Roma Survey, 2017). In Serbia, only 0.7 per cent
of Roma have a university degree (Serbian National Strategy for Roma
Inclusion, 2016), compared to a 23 per cent rate of tertiary education
completion by Serbians as a whole (UNDP Regional Roma Survey, 2017).

It is this low number of Romani graduates that drives us to probe the
factors that generate the underprivilege of this section of the population
and the broader circumstances that influence Roma's access to higher
education. In so doing, we reject the damaging but pervasive racecraft[2]

---

[1] Interview Romani student in Belgrade, September 2016. Harvard FXB's 'Romani Champions'
Project. Additional information about the research project can be found here: https://fxb
.harvard.edu/research/adolescent-empowerment/roma-program/rights- and-participation
/#champions

[2] Term borrowed from Karen Fields and Barbara Fields, *Racecraft: The Soul of Inequality in American
Life*, Verso, 2012.

that holds Romani culture responsible for devaluing education and insist, instead, on exploring the roots and false 'justifications' for the enduring and systematic exclusion of Roma from education, including at the level of higher education. (For an analogous argument about indigenous populations, see Garland et al. in this volume.)

The fact that only one in every hundred Romani youth compared to one in every 2.5 non-Roma European youth in the European Union (EUROSTAT, 2019) enters higher education is a troubling marker of structural racism across the continent. Romani students at all levels of education fall behind their non-Roma peers in rates of educational enrolment, attendance and attainment. These discrepancies are the product of both overt and covert forms of exclusion, cumulatively generated by structural and historical inequity, and pervasive economic and political inequalities. And a century-old policy and/or practice of school segregation of Romani children stands as a clear example of overt exclusion.

The legacy of discrimination and inequity generates enduring and pervasive disadvantages – material, social, psychological and symbolic – with daily impacts on Romani children, youth and their families (Matache, 2017). But, as we argue in this chapter, these processes also generate and perpetuate racist ideologies and a belief in Roma 'inferiority', which continue to influence policymaking as well as the behaviours and attitudes of both non-Roma and Roma populations.

Throughout the history of public education, policymakers, scholars and social practitioners have reproduced the same racecraft about Roma: they form part of an inferior culture, and they do not value education. Because of this overriding preconception that has fed a false moral justification for the disparities, the dramatic underrepresentation of Roma in higher education has not generated the appropriate sense of concern and urgency among policymakers charged with realising non-discriminatory educational rights and attainment.

Instead, since the advent of universal public education, there have been continuing accounts of Romani children and youth being rejected, ignored or neglected in schools. For instance, in the early days of public education, in 1881 in London, 'Trinity Cooper, a daughter of this Gypsy family, who was about thirteen years of age, applied to be instructed at the school; but, in consequence of the obloquy affixed to that description of persons, she was repeatedly refused ... ' (Hoyland, 1816). In 1927, the government of Czechoslovakia adopted a law that 'condemned the Roma as asocial citizens, limited their personal liberty, introduced Gypsy identity cards, and decreed that Romani children under 18 be placed in special institutions' (Barany cited in M Stewart, M Rovid, MRR VID – 2011). In 1941, the Serbian government ordered 'that schools must stop enrolling children of Jewish and "Gypsy" background'. School segregation, a more institutional form of discrimination, has been a reality for Romani children across Europe for almost a century.[3]

In this chapter, we argue that public education has historically been an institution designed for *gadje* (although less so for *gadjo* girls and the poor), while Romani children and youth, seen as 'inferior and nomadic others', have had no functional option for education and even less for higher education. We explore patterns of exclusion, fear, racism and racialised poverty. We look at historical and present-day instances of state-sponsored injustices, and the so-called moral justifications and reinforcements that have been advanced to support them, in the context of their contemporary consequences for Romani youths' opportunities for higher education.

We argue that schools and universities today, as in the past, remain highly unwelcoming for Romani children and youth, failing in large measure to address pervasive structural racism or to advance inclusion and equity (FRA, 2018). Over the past decades, state efforts, including affirmative action, have been made to correct these failures, efforts that have led to higher education opportunities for some, though not the most marginalised Roma. Thus, in the ensuing pages, we discuss triggers and factors that have been considered particularly beneficial by Romani youth.

We use Serbia as a case study to discuss anti-Romani policies that endure up to the present day. We have chosen to focus on Serbia for several reasons. Serbia is a small country (around 7 million people) with a reasonably large Romani population. Also, the authors have conducted extensive research in Serbia, and one of us is a Serbian Roma.[4]

We rely on data from surveys by the European Union Fundamental Rights Agency and other groups. We also draw on quantitative and qualitative data collected in the course of our own research projects in Serbia. These projects include the Harvard FXB Centre's project,

---

[3] In 1927, Czechoslovakia started to assign Romani children to special schools, allegedly because they exhibited mental disabilities, as shown by Yaron Matras (2015) *I Met Lucky People: The Story of the Romani Gypsies* (Penguin 715 Random House UK).

[4] According to the Statistical Office of the Republic of Serbia, the Roma population numbered 147, 604 in 2011 (the latest census, Statistical Office of the Republic of Serbia, 2011). Other estimates put the figure of Roma in Serbia at about 500,000 (UNICEF (b) (2007, p. 9). The discrepancy in population size is, in part, a reflection of the fact that many Roma lack personal documents, but also that they frequently have to live in unregistered houses, and feel compelled to conceal their ethnicity from official entities whom they consider oppressive or untrustworthy (Joksic, 2015; Milankovic et al., 2015; Jovanovic, 2018).

Reclaiming Adolescence: Roma Transitions to Adulthood, a participatory action study that explored opportunities and obstacles facing Romani youth trying to access higher education, training and jobs; the FXB Centre's Romani Champions project and One in One Hundred study, which aimed to understand the triggers of success and resilience among the 1 per cent of Roma youth who make it to College (Harvard FXB, 2018); and Tanja Jovanovic's University of Sussex PhD thesis (2018) that examines the influence of socio-political and socio-cultural practices and barriers on Romani youths' access to higher education.

The State of Education for Roma Today

Across the world, the quality of education and skills young people acquire continue to depend on the advantages and opportunities they inherit at birth.[5] The 'Education at a Glance 2018: OECD Indicators' report under-lines several critical factors that determine inequity in education, including social and economic status. These include *the level of parental education, immigrant background* and *gender* (OECD, 2018). Thus, although overall all children and youth are legally guaranteed the right to education, reality does not mirror this theoretical entitlement: high-quality education remains a privilege enjoyed mainly by members of families that are rela-tively wealthy, native-born, educated and non-minority. This is particu-larly true in the case of higher education.

The quality of education and access to skill training continue to vary both across and within states. Over the past ten years, in most OECD countries, levels of enrolment in educational institutions have risen. In 2016, across OECD countries, an average of 90 per cent of children and youth aged 4–17 were enrolled in education. However, equity in attain-ment has not improved, with enduring impacts among disadvantaged children and youth and in poorer countries. Parents' education level continues to have a large impact on the educational progress made by their children, too (OECD, 2012).

The school achievement of Romani children and youth across Europe in the past decade underscores these observations and the more general claim that states have yet to ensure equity, inclusion and non-discrimination in education. Evaluations of the implementation of the OSCE Action Plan

---

[5] Margareta Matache and Simona Barbu wrote the second and fourth sections of this chapter for an unpublished background paper entitled 'Guaranteeing Access to Quality Education for Roma and Sinti Children in the OSCE Area: Obstacles, Practices, and Solutions' in 2018. The text has been improved and updated.

(OSCE/ODIHR, 2013; European Union, 2016), the EU framework (European Commission, 2012) and the Decade of Roma Inclusion (Rorke, Matache and Friedman, 2015), along with recent studies concerning Romani education, show that Roma enrolment in compulsory schooling is improving too but not yet equivalent to that of the majority population overall (FRA, 2018; OSCE/ODIHR, 2013; European Union, 2016). According to the Fundamental Rights Agency, enrolment rates of Romani children increased in several EU countries between 2011 and 2016: '9 out of 10 Roma of compulsory schooling age are enrolled in education, converging towards the general population's enrollment rate' (FRA, 2018). However, in Greece and Romania, enrolment still lags behind: only 7 and 8 out of 10 Roma, respectively, are enrolled in education (FRA, 2018). In Serbia, while 99 per cent of children attend primary school nationwide, this is only the case for 85 per cent of Romani children (Statistical Office of the Republic of Serbia and UNICEF, 2014).

Moreover, despite this notable progress in primary school enrolment, alarming numbers of young Roma continue to be pushed out of school early. In 7 EU countries – Bulgaria, the Czech Republic, Spain, Hungary, Portugal, Romania and Slovakia – though the average rate of early dropout fell from 87 per cent to 68 per cent between 2011 and 2016 (FRA Statements in European Commission, 2018), 7 out of 10 Roma aged 18–24 still left school early (FRA, 2018). The dropout and completion rates are even more problematic in the Western Balkans; in Serbia, 36 per cent of Romani children do not finish primary school, compared to only 7 per cent of non-Romani children (Statistical Office of the Republic of Serbia and UNICEF, 2014). As a European Commission (2014) report underlines, 'beyond compulsory schooling, enrollment differences between Roma and non-Roma become even larger'.

The effects of exclusion are highly visible if one compares the data on Roma and non-Roma populations. In the case of Serbia, the Regional Roma survey conducted by the United Nations Development Programme (UNDP), the World Bank and the European Commission in 2011 found that Roma attend school for five years less on average than non-Roma. The preschool enrolment rate of children in the age group 3–6 years differs by as much as 30 per cent between Roma (18 per cent) and non-Roma (48 per cent). For compulsory education, only 80 per cent of Roma compared to 95 per cent of non-Roma children aged 7–15 in Serbia attend school. These differences increase through children's educational careers: only 22 per cent of Romani children compared to 89 per cent of non-Romani children enrol in secondary education (Statistical Office of the

Republic of Serbia and UNICEF, 2014). Also, for the 16–24 age group, only 25 per cent of Roma are enrolled in education, compared to 71 per cent of their non-Romani peers (Jovanovic, 2018). The participation of Roma in higher education is thus 16 times smaller than their Serbian peers (EQUI-ED, 2012). In sum, Romani enrolment in high school and College in Serbia remains extremely low and disproportionately so when compared to the majority population (Danvers, Smith, Jovanovic, 2017; FRA, 2012).

These alarming numbers and trends regarding Roma participation in secondary and tertiary education reflect realities and policy design at the European level. The disparities noted for Serbia apply across Europe: only 12 per cent complete secondary education and only 1 per cent are enrolled in higher education[6] (FRA, 2014).

The Serbian government has attempted to address these disparities by introducing measures designed to increase the numbers of Roma enrolled in higher education (Jovanovic, 2018). The 2003 affirmative action policy included reserved seats for Romani youth in universities and tuition-free places; the Secretariat for Roma National Strategy was charged with forwarding a list of Romani candidates who had passed relevant qualifying exams to the Ministry of Education, which in turn had the power to authorise free access to higher education institutions. This affirmative policy concentrated on one outcome of cumulative discrimination, the question of physical access to higher education. While a critical issue, changing physical access alone is not sufficient to address the multifaceted effects of racism, including the persistent and fundamental issue of discrimination and stigmatisation in compulsory Serbian education, and alongside that racism the culture of racist impunity that persists throughout Serbian higher education institutions. These accumulated legacies of oppressive behaviour have not been addressed and thus continue to negatively impact Romani students' journeys throughout their studies (Jovanovic, 2018). This approach to affirmative action is what Ahmed (2012) has called the 'tick box' approach to inclusion policy implementation, where insufficient attention is paid to the actual implementation of inclusion (Jovanovic, 2018).

What is more, even the well-intentioned affirmative action policy has been retrenched over the past year, with the number of available reserved

---

[6] Survey conducted in eleven EU countries (Bulgaria, the Czech Republic, Greece, Spain, France, Hungary, Italy, Poland, Portugal, Romania, Slovakia) with Roma respondents between 18 and 24 years.

seats in universities decreased and entry conditions increased, making access increasingly difficult for Romani students.

The challenge of improving Roma higher education enrolment numbers and attainment remains, while many policymakers and academics continue to draw on the racist imagery of an 'inferior' Roma culture to inform the measures they design for Roma education (Matache, 2017). The EU Roma Framework merely aimed to 'encourage' the Roma to 'also' participate in secondary and tertiary education, instead of setting clear benchmarks for governments, with the predictable result that only minimal enrolment changes occurred (Matache, 2017).

These numbers, challenges and factors unveil a complex web of root causes, starting with the long history of racialised marginalisation and exclusion and racialised rights intersecting with economic exploitation and consequently with deep poverty, ideological hatred and institutional racism. We discuss some of these factors in the following sections.

The Racecraft of a Culture that 'Does Not Value Education': A Case Study of the History of Public Education in Serbia

Across the centuries, anti-Romani racist ideologies, policies and practices have, in various ways, justified the rejection of Roma from school systems. Along with the institutions themselves, European scholars have shaped or contributed to the racialisation of the Roma that underpins and justifies this exclusion (Matache, 2017). For instance, in 1927, the creation of special schools for Romani children in Czechoslovakia (Matras, 2014) was justified through the lens of scientific racism. By using 'science' to label Roma as 'inferior', specialists offered 'moral reinforcement' for school segregation, perpetuating the deeply held collective belief that 'Roma culture does not value education'. This racecraft presented 'itself to the mind and imagination as a vivid truth' (Fields and Fields, 2012). Romani children were considered inferior and undesirable, and the same arguments have been used to justify the continuation of school segregation to the present day in the Czech Republic, Slovakia, Serbia and elsewhere in Eastern Europe. Thus, the racecraft of an 'uneducated people' continues to have the power to reinforce and 'morally' justify the exclusion and rejection of Roma from schools and universities up to the present day. And indeed, race and racism 'arise historically', and as Karen Fields and Barbara Fields argue, racecraft is 'imagined, acted upon, and re-imagined, the action and imagining inextricably intertwined' (Fields and Fields, 2012).

At the same time, education is a product of the cultural practices and the history in which it is rooted. As Altbach et al. have noted, the content and structure of educational institutions are socially constructed realities, which are influenced by external socio-cultural factors and traditions (Altbach et al., 1996). Educational institutions are thus deeply rooted in the historical experience of a particular country and community and are the result of accumulated historical changes.

In the case of the Roma in Serbia, we argue that the racecraft of the Roma as an 'inferior, uneducated people', combined with racialised poverty and rights and a history of state-sponsored injustice, has contributed to the situation that exists today: an educational caste system, with Romani children segregated, bullied or mistreated in schools, and, consequently and predictably, dramatically low higher education outcomes for Romani youth.

For centuries, Serbian Roma have been met with violence and rejection, from the cruelty of enslavement[7] and the violence of deportations and killings during the Holocaust to the assimilationist policies and educational caste system still in force today.

Public education in Serbia proved to be hard to establish. Monasteries were the earliest sites of education and literacy, starting with the Middle Ages when the clergy acted as teachers for the children of noblemen. The critical role of religion and of the church in spreading education is evident in Serbia, where 'conditions for literacy development among the Serbs were created by accepting Christianity' (Spasenovic, Petrovic and Maksic, 2015) from the nineteenth century onwards. In 1844, the first law on public education was adopted ('Law of school establishment') (Karanovich, 1979). And although laws, policies and efforts to increase the educational network throughout the country continued, towards the end of the nineteenth century only one-fifth of Serbian children were in school.

Serbia's public school system only grew substantially in the first half of the twentieth century (Spasenovic, Petrovic and Maksic, 2015), more or less at the same time as the belief in Roma's 'racial inferiority' was being reinforced 'scientifically'. This period coincided with an increase in Roma murders, anti-Romani sentiments and Roma rejection from schools.

During the Holocaust, Roma experienced systematic genocide. Once the German occupation was established, Serbia submitted to the order to

---

[7] The literature documents instances of the enslavement of Roma in Serbia as early as 1348, when a document noted that Serbian emperor Stefan Dušan donated a number of *gypsy slaves* to a monastery in Prizren (now in Kosovo) (Djordjević, 1924).

work towards the *final solution* and applied this to both the Roma and the Jews, considered equally inferior (Pisarri, 2014). In the former Yugoslavia, legislators made it legal to discriminate against Roma. A series of measures towards Roma and Jews called the 'twenty-two articles' were adopted between 1941 and 1942. One article required both Roma and Jews to wear yellow armbands, to distinguish themselves in public: for Jews, the armband read 'Jevrejin', and for 'gypsies' it read 'Ciganin'. Both groups were also forbidden from working as public servants or as lawyers, doctors, dentists, veterinarians or pharmacists and were not allowed in public places such as theatres and cinemas. Another article stated that Serbian authorities were obliged to keep Jews and Roma separated from the majority of the population.

In September 1941, a notorious act of institutional racism, built on the racecraft of Roma and Jew racial inferiority, took place: the Ministry of Education ordered schools not to enrol Romani and Jewish children, 'if they belong to the territory of the Military Commander in Serbia'. On 21 October 1941, another order read, 'quisling authorities issued the Main directive about the University, within which article 27 stipulated that "Jews and Gypsies cannot attend University [Colleges]"' (Pisarri, 2014).

While the situation of Roma in communist Yugoslavia was regarded as more acceptable than in the other communist countries, after the dissolution of Yugoslavia, although the Roma were a recognised national, ethnic minority, their conditions of life in Serbia have still been extremely harsh. Some live 'displaced, subsisting in camps, shacks and metal containers, facing the constant threat of forced evictions; harried and harassed, enduring ethnic profiling, police violence and racist intimidation' (Rorke, 2016), with little practical recognition or effort from the state to improve their lives.

One policy measure in particular disproportionately hurt Roma access to education: the government reduced the numbers of rural schools. The so-called rationalisation of the school network meant the closing of small schools and the merging of classes; this increased the number of students per school, mostly in the rural marginal areas where many Roma live. With little or no transportation, many children had no way to reach school or higher educational institutions. As a 2003 study found, 23 per cent of children had no access to transportation and children in some communities had to walk between 4 and 15 km to reach a school (Bogojević et al., 2003). Even in 2010, 'less than 40% of Roma settlements' had a preschool institution within a 1 km radius, and 'for 20% of the settlements, even elementary school is inaccessible' (Government of Serbia, 2010).

Segregation has also constituted an alarming practice of public schools, schoolmasters and teachers in Serbia. A 2010 study underlined 'widespread discrimination in the educational system' and confirmed that 'approximately 30 percent of children within special education in the Republic of Serbia are Roma', although Roma represented only between 2 per cent (official data) and 8 per cent (estimated) of the total Serbian population. World Bank data from 2004 estimated that 50 to 80 per cent of the children enrolled in special schools in Serbia were Roma. (Open Society Foundations, 2010).

Among other factors, these examples of institutional racism, executed across these key political regimes, have had dramatic and enduring impacts on Roma as targets and Serbians as perpetrators or bystanders of discrimination. A 2018 study by the Harvard FXB Centre and the Belgrade Centre for Interactive Pedagogy found that in Serbia, Romani youths, whether or not enrolled in College, face ongoing hardships and discrimination. Most adolescents belong to low-income families and have experienced poverty. Discrimination and stigmatisation in schools and biased teachers and peers continue to prevent Romani children and youth from fulfilling their actual educational potential. Some of the Romani youth participating in the study had internalised mainstream anti-Romani racism (Bhabha et al., 2018) – racism does convey itself not only through ideologies, institutions and dominant societies but also through the internalisation of stigma and racism.

Thus, when Roma believe that school is made for *gadje*, they are not pointing to the values of their own culture. They are reactive to a structural system of oppression and an education system that has cast out Roma from the start.

Present-Day Factors Affecting Roma Access to Higher Education

A multiplicity of intersecting societal and institutional present-day factors also prevent Romani children and youth from acquiring higher education. The following are some of the key elements.

Racialised Poverty and Politics that Punish Poverty

The social and economic environments in which children grow are strong determinants of inequalities and opportunity gaps in education and the labour market. The intergenerational transmission of poverty compounds the impact of those factors (Walker, Sinfield & Walker, 2011). The UNDP

Regional Roma survey found that in Serbia, 10 per cent of Romani people live in households with a per capita income under US$2.15 per day (Dotcho, 2012); 30 per cent of Roma in Serbia live on an income of US$4.30 per day or less. The generalised and racialised poverty of Romani people means that parents cannot provide the basic preconditions for their children to continue school or even to live decently. Given this situation, many Romani parents cannot afford the preschool education critical for child development and eventual enrolment in higher education.

Kindergarten Experience

Early childhood services lay the foundation not only for attainment in education but also more broadly for future learning, achievement and professional and social life. In some Romani communities, especially in rural areas, kindergarten facilities either do not exist or are seriously under-developed, 'often located under bridges, squeezed between factories, in the dump areas, or other degraded sites' (Milovanovic, 2013).

As the OECD data show, the kindergarten experience shapes the level of education for children across the OECD countries. Preschool education experiences provide children with the skills and abilities they need to perform well in school and advance successfully through the education system. This is as true of Romani children as of any other group. A recent study found that a significantly larger share of Roma College students in Serbia (63 per cent) had attended kindergarten compared to a comparable group of Romani non-student respondents (44 per cent) (Bhabha et al., 2018).

The Levels of Parents' Education

As the OECD data show, the level of parental education also provides a strong predictor of children's level of education. Among Romani children and youth, the likelihood of having a family member who has completed higher education is very low: in the past decade, across countries, the enrolment of Roma in higher education has remained at around 1 per cent in College and 12 per cent in high school. A 2018 Harvard and Center for Interactive Pedagogy study found that in Serbia, the lower level of education among their parents and close relatives wounded Roma youths' educational attainment and trajectory. Primary education consti-tuted the highest level of education for 35 per cent of the parents of Romani youth non-students. The parents of Romani College students, by contrast, had higher levels of education, with only 17 per cent of them reporting primary education as their final educational attainment (Bhabha et al., 2018). The report also found that 'the College students had more close relatives attending or who had graduated from College: 64% in the Romani student group, compared with only 43% in the comparison Romani non-student group' (Bhabha et al., 2018).

Unwelcoming Mixed Schools

The combination of deep-rooted anti-Roma racism and discrimination in the school environment persists as a reality for Romani children and youth in Serbia. Of the Romani students who are enrolled in regular schools as part of the compulsory education system and attend classes in mixed (Roma and non-Roma Serbian) classrooms, between 10 per cent and 30 per cent report exposure to peer harassment experiences that seriously disadvantage them and leave them, and their families, questioning whether to continue attending school (Jovanovic, 2018). Peer harassment can be viewed as an 'uncompromising clash', including physical and verbal violence, mistreatment, oppression and social manipulation – involving social exclusion, itself a form of what Johan Galtung has called 'structural violence'.[8]

Negative peer relations can lead to negative outcomes such as psychological difficulties and dropping out of school (Rubin, Both and Wilkinson, 1990; Jovanovic, 2018). Bullying is a constant in many classrooms. In Serbia, 75 per cent of the Romani pupils interviewed by the European Roma Rights Centre in 2014 answered that they are bullied in mainstream schools because of their ethnicity (ERRC, 2016b), confirming the more general finding that in ethnically diverse classrooms, students who are in a statistical minority are more likely to be exposed to harassment and vulnerability than their majority peers (Phillips, 2011). What is more, children who are victims of peer harassment or rejection frequently experience problems later in life, including a lack of confidence, feelings of isolation, social anxiety and depression (Jovanovic, 2018; Juvonen and Graham, 2001; Olweus, 2003, 2007). Such phenomena affect Romani children's participation and performance in education and can disturb their social and emotional development. In 2014, the Fundamental Rights Agency found that a 'hostile school environment' and 'safety

---

[8] Johan Galtung was referring to a form of violence wherein some social structure or social institution may harm people by deliberately preventing them from meeting their most basic needs.

concerns' were issues that Roma expected to encounter in school. School attainment, along with enrolment and attendance, is heavily influenced by the experience of discrimination and anti-Roma racism at school.

In a 2017 article, the Harvard FXB team demonstrated a correlation between Roma youths' experience with discrimination and career aspirations: as discrimination grows, Romani youth become less confident and more pragmatic about their aspirations and desired careers (Bhabha et al., 2018). Even those Romani students who make it to College report earlier experiences with discrimination: 58 per cent of Romani College students interviewed for a study in Serbia said they had experienced discrimination in either primary or secondary school (Bhabha et al., 2018). Students shared experiences when they were met with dehumanising and racialised verbal messages by peers in school:

> 'Little Gypsy girl' was the only way they described me in class. I just felt humiliated, I was fifteen, and I just felt miserable and humiliated.

> They called me a Roma, said I lived in a garbage container and these are some of the reasons why I withdrew into myself . . . (Bhabha et al., 2018)

But by contrast with Romani non-students, the College attendees had had the fortune of mentorship by teachers who had not based their expectations or support on skin colour and class. These students also reported close contacts with friendly non-Roma peers who had supported their Romani peers against discrimination (Bhabha et al., 2018).

Moreover, in nearly all schools, the vast majority of teachers are non-Roma. Along with the bias against or neglect of Romani people in the syllabus, this sets up the attitude that it is normative to be white European.

A Caste System in Schools

Although public policies related to Romani children include ideas of justice and equity in education, these ideals are often not applied or achieved in practice. The segregated educational institutions where Romani children are placed feature classrooms which, though described as 'inclusive', routinely relegate Romani children to the back rows, whereteachers ignore them (ERRC, 2017). At best, these spaces and practices focus on preventing illiteracy; they do not encourage Roma children to succeed.

In the Serbian context, because of isolation, some Romani children start school with poor comprehension of Serbian, an obstacle that is used to create barriers to enrolment and learning in mainstream schools. School representatives have highlighted the language difficulties of Romani children in Serbia whose families originate from Kosovo, but frequently Serbian-born Romani children are also forced to learn separately from their Serbian peers (ERRC, 2003). Some Romani children do not perform well in entry testing, because of inadequate prior exposure to preschool and, related to this, poor Serbian language competence (Bhabha et al., 2018). Yet, as the European Court of Human Rights jurisprudence shows, 'language deficiency cannot serve as a pretext for racial segregation' (James A. Goldston in ERRC, 2010).

Overrepresentation of Roma in special schools in Serbia is high (Open Society Institute, 2010). In 2009, UNICEF estimated that 50–80 per cent of the children placed in the 80 special schools across Serbia were Roma (UNICEF, 2009), while the Strategy of the Serbian Government showed that '30% of all children in 'special schools' are of Romani ethnicity' (Government of the Republic of Serbia, 2016). This discriminatory practice of consigning Romani children to so-called special schools provides a substandard education that inhibits educational progression or future gainful employment.

Increased segregation of Romani children in separate classes within the 'mainstream education facilities' is striking, too (Civil Rights Defenders, 2017). Some school representatives justify the segregation of Romani children by citing a lack of space (ERRC, 2016a). In 2007, reports mentioned 'satellite facilities close to Roma settlements'; in other words, schools had built separate buildings for Romani children (OSI, 2017). These practices perpetuate the sense that Romani children are inferior and undermine the rights, dignity, motivation and self-esteem essential for educational success.

Poor Quality of Education

Researchers have found that teachers tend to encourage and work more with higher-performing students (Henricsson and Rydell, 2004) and to favour children from families with higher socio-economic status (Brophy, 1998). Children who achieve less often do not benefit from positive interactions with teachers. As a result, the school can become a space where they are uncomfortable, which often leads them to drop out. Teacher expectations might also differ based on the children's gender.

Such discouraging behaviour among teachers has a particular effect on children belonging to marginalised and minority groups (McKown & Weinstein, 2002). In particular, it has had a boomerang effect on the attainment of Romani children. All too often, teachers approach their interactions with Romani children, parents and community members with minimal expectations and with prejudice based on their perception that Romani families and the culture reject education. Children absorb their teachers' expectations when they should be developing their sense of self-esteem and their motivation to continue in education.

Moreover, schools with a higher portion of Romani children often lack qualified personnel; skilled teachers are more likely to move to more urban, non-Roma and wealthy schools. Also, as in Romania, absenteeism among teachers is higher in educational establishments where Romani children study (Romani CRISS, CURS, REF, 2012). But in Serbia, a practical problem with teaching competences is that the teachers often ignore the absences of Romani children; they hold lower expectations and lesser educational objectives for them, and schools rarely include Romani students in extracurricular activities (Jovanovic, 2013). Similarly, Baucal observed that teachers tend to place more Romani than non-Romani students into classes with the lowest quality of teaching; in these settings, students are not encouraged adequately and typically receive 'shortened' or 'simplified' curricula (Jovanovic, 2013).

The training of Serbian teachers may also be problematic. It is mainly focused on subject knowledge and neglects components that are essential for an inclusive education practice, including trans-cultural educational and communication skills (Zgaga, 2006). Inclusive education and anti-racist skills should be factored into initial teacher education as an integral and organic part of the core curriculum, rather than included merely as an optional add-on component (Jovanovic, 2013).

A White Curriculum

In the schools that Romani and other minority and marginalised children attend, the curricula continue to neglect or misrepresent the history, realities or culture of these people. Teachers in Serbia regularly fail to adopt curriculum topics that relate to the life experiences of all children in their classrooms (Jovanovic, 2013). A variety of 'innocent' teaching strategies used by teachers have the effect (whether intended or not) of completely excluding some children from classroom discussion (Macura-Milovanović, 2008b). For example, it is common for teachers to give children homework essay topics such as 'A view from my room' or 'My holiday . . .'. For children who live in tin or wooden shacks, and who rarely go outside their neighbourhood, let alone on holiday, these topics are likely to provoke feelings of pain and lack of belonging. Not only would these students be unable to relate to these assignments meaningfully, but more insidiously, they might well experience humiliation and embarrassment as their poverty and exclusion from the rest of the class are highlighted (Macura-Milovanović, 2008b).

Ethnocentric, chauvinistic and parochial attitudes to education on the part of the Serbian authorities reproduce discriminatory, nationalistic social norms and institutionalise racism and prejudice (Jovanovic, 2013). They deny Romani and other minority and marginalised children positive role models and instead project onto them feelings of 'othering' and exclusion. In turn, these factors and other aspects of exclusivist, white curricula reduce the chances that Romani and other minority and marginalised children will proceed with their education and accumulate the pedagogical experiences required to attend higher education.

All the factors mentioned above that are informed and fed by the racecraft of 'inferior people' have contributed and continue to this day to contribute to Romani children's negative school experience and to the indifference of societies and policymakers towards the urgent imperative of generating substantive educational change.

It is this toxic mixture of historical and present-day factors that also leads Roma to internalise the self-image of a group who 'do not want to integrate' or 'do not value education'. Recent studies have shown that an extremely low number of Roma manage to enrol in and graduate from higher education, across Europe. In this context, one of the most relevant questions is: *what makes the difference for the 1 per cent who succeed and achieve a higher level in education?*

Few researchers have focused on the elements of success and resilience to understand how to overcome challenges. One such study is the Harvard FXB and Center for Interactive Pedagogy study 'One in One Hundred' (Bhabha et al., 2018), which analysed the success triggers influencing the educational outcomes of the outliers among the Romani youth[9] who, despite all the odds, succeeded in securing a university education. Among the factors identified by the study, one of the most salient was the influence of an inclusive environment that provides students with confidence in themselves.

Other factors highlighted by the study reflect the points made above. They include access to early childhood education services, financial aid,

---

[9] Two groups of children have been involved in the research, one of 89 Romani adolescents attending College and a comparison group of 100 adolescents who were not students.

moral support from families and teachers, prior role models within the family, mentorship and friendship of non-Romani allies, including both teachers and peers. More than 60 per cent of Romani youth who received a higher education had attended kindergarten, compared to only 44 per cent of Romani youth who only had reached secondary education. Almost half of the College group compared to 18 per cent in the other group also received some form of financial support during secondary school. Also, 64 per cent of the College group, compared with only 43 per cent of the comparison group, had close relatives who attended or graduated from higher education (Bhabha et al., 2018).

The Harvard FXB and Center for Interactive Pedagogy study found that an additional contributory factor to Roma higher education enrolment was the involvement of teachers with a belief in Romani students' intellectual potential and an active commitment to countering discrimination: 'They believed in my potential and always wanted to find out whether there was any problem underneath what was happening' (Bhabha et al., 2018).

As the study concluded, '[w]hat Romani children most need for educational success is what all children need: good schools, characterized by equity and inclusion, with unbiased, supportive, and well-prepared teachers' (Bhabha et al., 2018).

Reflections and Conclusions

For too long, a collective belief in Romani laziness, criminality, illiteracy and inferiority has been used as 'moral reinforcement' for justifying racialised poverty, racialised neighbourhoods, racialised education and, more generally, racialised access to rights in Europe.

For generations, Romani families have struggled to overcome obstacles to ensure their children have access to a good education. They have been told that school was not for Roma, and many believed it. Rejection by schools from the early stages of education but also a toxic, unwelcoming or culturally insensitive school environment made Roma believe that schools were only for the *gadje*. The racecraft of 'inferiority' has enforced, reinforced, justified, imagined and reimagined ideas, policies and measures that have kept Romani children away from high schools and universities. Structural racism, social and economic obstacles, and other intersectional factors (discussed above) have been the means to achieve these ends.

Identifying tools to dismantle the racecraft of a 'backward culture that does not value education' is essential to success in achieving better educational outcomes for Romani children. There will still be families that will not enrol their children in school or value school because of previous negative experiences and internalised apprehension about the educational environment. But regardless, inclusive and anti-racist education and the belief in Romani children's potential are a must for all teachers, as such steps make an essential difference in enabling Romani children to attend and thrive within an educational system. Those Romani students who succeeded in getting a higher education in Serbia pointed to the support from non-racist and anti-racist teachers who did not look at them as inferior and who believed in their capacity to learn. They also emphasised the importance of a welcoming school environment and non-racist peers (Bhabha et al., 2018). Thus, teacher training and support are critical. To facilitate inclusive education, teachers need to have practical experience of promoting it, and they need support in introducing higher educational standards and expectations across the school population.

The fact that many more Romani children now have access to primary school than they did is a most welcome development but one that cannot stand on its own. As enrolment ratios grow, so does the number of Romani children learning in segregated and low-quality school environments. Segregation persists in mainstream schools. Romani children across Europe continue to be placed in separate classes or not allowed into common areas. In such classes, the quality of education is much lower, and teachers expect less from the students. These enduring inequities vitiate the potentially beneficial impact of expanded educational access. Negative results will only perpetuate the racist belief of Roma failure and educational incompetence.

Despite policies and practices aimed at removing historical barriers to rights, racism – in all its forms from ideological to structural, and from interpersonal to internalised – persists on multiple levels. Racism also intersects with a range of factors that include gender and class, constantly thwarting the progressive intent of inclusivist educational policy and practice (Mirza, 2006). This combination of factors continues to push Romani children and youth out of school and deny them their right to higher education, even as educational institutions and governmental agencies attempt to promote more inclusivist agendas.

Gadjoness,[10] like whiteness, has been privileged and institutionalised and can only be effectively countered and deconstructed if educators,

---

[10] As defined by Matache here: https://fxb.harvard.edu/2016/10/05/word-image-and-thought-creating-the-romani-other/

activists and broader state institutions recognise the reality and the effects of anti-Roma racism, stigmatisation and discrimination. Education reform needs to start by dismantling the racecraft of 'inferiority' from ideology, policies and practice and by promoting anti-racism and inclusion in education.

REFERENCES

Ahmed, S. (2012). *On Being Included: Racism and Diversity in Institutional Life.* Raleigh: Duke University Press.

Altbach, P. G., Davis, C. H., Eisemon, T. O. et al. (1989). *Scientific Development and Higher Education: The Case of Newly Industrializing Nations.* New York: Praeger.

Bhabha, J., Matache, M., Chernoff, M. et al. (2018). One in One Hundred. Available online at https://cdn2.sph.harvard.edu/wp-content/uploads/sites/114/2018/12/OneinOneHundred.pdf

Bogojević et al. (2003) quoted in Pesikan, A., & Ivic, I. (2016). The Sources of Inequity in the Education System of Serbia and How to Combat Them. *CEPS Journal, 6*(2), 101–124.

Brophy, J. (1998). *Motivating Students to Learn.* Boston: McGraw Hill.

Civil Rights Defenders (2017). The Wall of Anti-Gypsyism. Roma in the Republic of Serbia, Stockholm. Available online at https://crd.org/wp-content/uploads/2018/03/The-Wall-of-Anti-Gypsyism-Roma-in-Serbia.pdf

Council of Europe (2017). Fighting School Segregation in Europe through Inclusive Education: A Position Paper. Available online at https://rm.coe.int/fighting-school-segregationin-europe-throughinclusive-education-a-posi/168073fb65

Deem, R., & Morley, L. (2006). Diversity in the Academy? Staff Perceptions of Equality Policies in Six Contemporary Higher Education Institutions. *Policy Futures in Education, 4*(2), 185–202. https://doi.org/10.2304/pfie.2006.4.2.185

Djordjević, T. R. (1924). *Iz Srbije Kneza Milosa. Stanovnistvo – naselja.* Beograd: Geca Kon.

Dotcho, M. (2012). The Health Situation of Roma Communities: Analysis of the Data from the UNDP/World Bank/EC Regional Roma Survey 2011. Roma Inclusion Working Papers. Bratislava: United Nations Development Programme. Available online at www.undp.org/content/dam/rbec/docs/The-health-situation-of-Roma-communities.pdf

European Commission (2012). Communication from the Commission to the European Parliament and the Council, Koninklijke Brill NV. Available online at https://doi.org/10.1163/2210-7975_HRD-4679-0058

European Commission (2014). Communication from the Commission to the European Parliament, the Council, the European Economic and Social Committee and the Committee of the Regions. Report on the Implementation of the EU Framework for National Roma Integration Strategies, Brussels. Available online at https://eur-lex.europa.eu/legal-content/EN/TXT/PDF/?uri=CELEX:52014DC0209&from=EN

European Commission, DG Education and Culture (2014). *Proposal for Key Practices of a Quality Framework for Early Childhood Education and Care.* Brussels: European Commission.

European Roma Rights Centre (2003). Segregated Education for Romani Children in Serbia and Montenegro. Available online at www.errc.org/roma-rights-journal/segregated-education-for-romani-children-in-serbia-and-montenegro

European Roma Rights Centre (2010). Europe's Highest Court Rules Roma School Segregation by Language Illegal. Available online at www.errc.org/press-releases/europes-highest-court-rules-roma-school-segregation-by-language-illegal

European Roma Rights Centre (2016a). Romani Children Segregated in Serbian Kindergarten. Available online at www.errc.org/press-releases/romani-children-segregated-in-serbian-kindergarten

European Roma Rights Centre (2016b). Written Comments by the European Roma Rights Centre for Consideration by the European Commission Concerning Roma Inclusion in the Western Balkans Progress Reports 2016. Available online at www.errc.org/uploads/upload_en/file/ec-submission-on-roma-inclusion-in-the-western-balkans-july-2016.pdf

European Roma Rights Centre (2017). ERRC submission to the European Commission on the Enlargement Component of the EU Roma Framework. Available online at www.errc.org/uploads/upload_en/file/submission-on-roma-inclusion-in-enlargement-countries-may-2017.pdf

European Union, European Court of Auditors (2016). EU policy Initiatives and Financial Support for Roma Integration: Significant Progress Made over the Last Decade, but Additional Efforts Needed on the Ground. Available online at www.eca.europa.eu/Lists/ECADocuments/SR16_14/SR_ROMA_EN.pdf

EUROSTA (2019). Educational Attainment Statistics. Available online at https://ec.europa.eu/eurostat/statistics-explained/index.php/Educational_attainment_statistics

Fields, K., & Fields, B. (2012). *Racecraft: The Soul of Inequality in American Life.* London, New York: Verso.

Fundamental Rights Agency Statements in European Commission (2018). Commission Staff Working Document Evaluation of the EU Framework for

National Roma Integration Strategies up to 2020, Brussels: 2018, 4.12.2018 SWD (2018) 480 final.

Fundamental Rights Agency (2012). The Situation of Roma in 11 EU Member States. Available online at https://fra.europa.eu/en/publication/2012/situation-roma-11-eu-member-states-survey-results-glance

Fundamental Rights Agency (2018). Fundamental Rights Report 2018. Available online at http://fra.europa.eu/en/publication/2018/fundamental-rights-report–2018

Galtung, J. (1969). Violence, Peace, and Peace Research. *Journal of Peace Research*, 6(3), 167–191.

Gillborn, D. (2006). Rethinking White Supremacy: Who Counts in 'WhiteWorld'. *Ethnicities*, 6(3), 318–340. https://doi.org/10.1177/1468796806068323

Government of Serbia (2010). Strategy tor Improvement of the Status of Roma in the Republic of Serbia, Belgrade. Available online at www.undp.org/content/dam/serbia/Publications%20and%20reports/English/UNDP_SRB_Strategy_for_the_Improvement_of_the_Status_of_Roma_in_the_Republic_of_Serbia.pdf

Government of Serbia (2016). Serbian National Strategy for Roma Inclusion. Available online at www.minrzs.gov.rs/files/doc/2016_godina/Strategija_uljucivanje_roma/Nation al_Strategy_for_Roma_Inclusion_2016–2025.docx

Government of Serbia (2017). Strategy of the Social Inclusion of Roma in Serbia for the Period from 2016 to 2025, Quoted in Civil Rights Defenders, *The Wall of Anti-Gypsyism. Roma in the Republic of Serbia*. Available online at https://crd.org/wp-content/uploads/2018/03/The-Wall-of-Anti-Gypsyism-Roma-in-Serbia.pdf

Gray, P. (2008). A Brief History of Education. To Understand Schools, We Must View Them in Historical Perspective. Available online at www.psychologytoday.com/us/blog/freedom-learn/200808/brief-history-education

Guy, W. (2001). The Czech Lands and Slovakia: Another False Dawn? In E. Marushiakova & V. Popov (eds.), *State Policies under Communism, Roma History* (pp. 293–310). Strasbourg: Council of Europe.

Henricsson, L., & Rydell, A. M. (2004). Elementary School Children with Behaviour Problems: Teacher-Child Relations and Self-Perception. A Prospective Study. *Merrill-Palmer Quarterly*, 50(2), 111–138.

Hinton-Smith, T., Danvers, E., & Jovanovic, T. (2018). Roma Women's Higher Education Participation: Whose Responsibility? *Gender and Education*, 30(7), 811–828.

Hoyland, J. (1816). *A Historical Survey of the Gipsies; Designed to Develop the Origin of This Singular People, and to Promote the Amelioration of Their Condition*. York: William Alexander.

Joksic, T. (2015). Discrimination of Roma in Serbia. [online] Available online at: www.aktionbleiberecht.de/blog/wpcontent/uploads/2014/10/Tijana_Joksic_Roma_Discrimantion-1.pdf

Jovanovic, T. (2013). *Teaching Competencies as a Means of Overcoming Roma Educational Exclusion in Serbia: A Critical Appraisal of Current Policy*. MA. University of Sussex

Jovanovic, T. (2018). Roma Student Access to Higher Education in Serbia: Challenges and Promises. PhD. University of Sussex.

Juvonen, J., & Graham, S. (2001). *Peer Harassment in School: The Plight of the Vulnerable and Victimized*. New York: The Guilford Press.

Karanovich, M. (1979). The Beginning of Girls' Education in Modern Serbia, 1838–1858. *Balkan Studies*, 20(2), 429–441.

Kovács-Cerović, T. (2006) National Report Serbia. In P. Zgaga (ed.), *The Prospects of Teacher Education in South-East Europe* (pp. 487–527). Ljubljana: Pedagoška Fakulteta.

Macura-Milovanović, S. (2008b). Barriers to the Inclusion of Roma Children. 30 April 2012, www.childrenwebmag.com/articles/child-care-social-issues/barriers-to-the-inclusion-of-roma-children

Macura-Milovanovic, S. (2013). Pre-primary Education of Roma Children in Serbia: Barriers and Possibilities, CEPS Journal 3. Available online at www.pedocs.de/volltexte/2013/7953/pdf/cepsj_2013_2_MacuraMilovanovic_Pre_primary_education_of_Roma.pdf

Matache, M., & Barbu, S. (2019). The History of School Desegregation for Roma. Available online at www.romarchive.eu/rom/roma-civil-rights-movement/history-school-desegregation-roma/

Matache, M. (2017a). Biased Elites, Unfit Policies: Reflections on the Lacunae of Roma Integration Strategies. *European Review*, 25(4), 588–607. Available online at https://doi.org/10.1017/S1062798717000254

Matache, M. (2017b). *Dear Gadjo (non-Romani) Scholars . . . .* Boston: FXB Center for Health and Human Rights at Harvard University.

Matras, Y. (2014). *I Met Lucky People: The Story of the Romani Gypsies*. Harmondsworth: Allen Lane, Penguin.

McGarry, A. (2017). *Romaphobia: The Last Acceptable Form of Racism*. London: Zed Books Ltd.

McKown, C., & Weinstein, R. S. (2002). Modeling the Role of Child Ethnicity and Gender in Children's Differential Response to Teacher Expectations. *Journal of Applied Social Psychology*, 32(1), 159–184. Available online at http://dx.doi.org/10.1111/j.1559–1816.2002.tb01425.x

Milanković, J., Ivkov-Džigurski, A., Đukičin, S., Ivanović, B. L., Lukić, T., & Kalkan, K. (2015). Attitudes of School Teachers about Roma Inclusion in

Education, a Case Study of Vojvodina, Serbia. *Geographica Pannonica*, *19*(3), 122–129.

Mintz, S. (2012). Education in the American Colonies. Available online at www .digitalhistory.uh.edu/database/article_display.cfm?HHID=36

Mirza, H. S. (2006). 'Race', Gender and Educational Desire. *Race Ethnicity and Education*, *9*(2), 137–158.

Nelaj, D., Kaçiu, E., Dundo, J., & Dervishi, Z. (2012). Factors Affecting Roma Integration in Albania: A comparative study. Open Society Institute for Albania, Institute for Development and Research Alternatives. [online report]. Available at: www.romadecade.org/cms/upload/file/9662_file1_comparative-study-factors- affecting-roma-inclusion- in-albania-final-docx.pdf

OECD (2012). Equity and Quality in Education: Supporting Disadvantaged Students and Schools. Available online at https://doi.org/10.1787/9789264130852-en

OECD (2018). Education at a Glance 2018: OECD Indicators. Available online at https://doi.org/10.1787/eag-2018-en

Olweus, D. (2003). A Profile of Bullying in Schools. *Educational Leadership*, *60*(6), 12–17.

Olweus, D. (2007). *What Is Bullying?* Center City: Hazelden Foundation.

Open Society Institute (2007). Monitoring Report: Equal Access to Quality Education for Roma. Available online at https://fra.europa.eu/sites/default/fil es/fra-2014_roma-survey_education_tk0113748enc.pdf

Open Society Institute (2010). Research on Schools and Classes for Children with Developmental Difficulties: Roma Children in 'Special Education' in Serbia: Overrepresentation, Underachievement, and Impact on Life. Available online at www.opensocietyfoundations.org/uploads/b61d6fa6-a304 -4a65-917c-2110aa53e24e/roma-children-serbia-20101019.pdf

OSCE/ODIHR (2013). Implementation of the Action Plan on Improving the Situation of Roma and Sinti within the OSCE Area Renewed Commitments, Continued Challenges Status Report. Available online at www.osce.org/odihr/ 107406?download=true

Pesikan, A., & Ivic, I. (2016). The Sources of Inequity in the Education System of Serbia and How to Combat Them. *CEPS Journal*, *6*(2), 101–124.

Phillips, C. (2011). Institutional Racism and Ethnic Inequalities: An Expanded Multilevel Framework. *Journal of Social Policy*, *40*(1), 173–192.

Pisarri, M. (2014). The Suffering of the Roma in Serbia during the Holocaust. Available online at www.starosajmiste.info/userfiles/files/download/Pisari_The_ Suffering_of_the_Roma_in_Serbia_during_the_Holocaust.pdf

Roma Education Fund (2007). *Advancing Education of Roma in Serbia. Country Assessment and the Roma Education Fund's Strategic Directions.* Budapest: REF.

Romani CRISS, CURS, Roma Education Fund (2012). *Absenteismul cadrelor didactice şi situaţia elevilor romi din şcolile primare din.* Bucharest: O analiză exploratorie.

Rorke, B. (2016). 25 Years after Yugoslavia: Roma Exclusion (Part 1). Available online at www.errc.org/news/25-years-after-yugoslavia-roma-exclusion-part–1

Rorke, B., Matache, M., & Friedman, E. (2015). A Lost Decade? Reflections on Roma Inclusion 2005–2015. Available online at www.rcc.int/romaintegra tion2020/romadecadefold//decade%20implementation/5.%20Decade%20Sec retariat%20Reports/A%20Lost%20Decade.pdf

Rubin, K., Both, L., & Wilkinson, M. (1990). *The Waterloo Longitudinal Project: Correlates and Consequences of Social Withdrawal in Childhood.* Waterloo: University of Waterloo.

Sameroff, A. (2010). A Unified Theory of Development: A Dialectic Integration of Nature and Nurture. *Child Development, 81*(1), 6–22.

Shonkoff, J. P., & Phillips, D. A. (2000). *From Neurons to Neighborhoods: The Science of Early Childhood Development.* Washington, DC: National Academy Press.

Spasenovic, V., Petrovic, A., & Maksic, S. (2015). Serbia. In W. Horner, H. Dobert, L. R. Reuter, & B. von Kopp (eds.), *The Education Systems of Europe*, 2nd edn (pp. 710–724). Geneva: Springer International.

Statistical Office of the Republic of Serbia and UNICEF (2014). Serbia Multiple Indicator Cluster Survey and 2014 Serbia Roma Settlements Multiple Indicator Cluster Survey, Key Findings. Available online at www.unicef.org/serbia/sites/un icef.org.serbia/files/2018–08/MICS5_2014_SERBIA_Key_Findings_and_Roma_ Settlements.pdf

Statistical Office of the Republic of Serbia (2011). Census, 2011. Available online at http://popis2011.stat.rs/?page_id=2988&lang=en

Stewart, M., Rovid, M., & Vid, M. R. R. (2011). *Multi-disciplinary Approaches to Romany Studies.* Budapest: Central European University Press.

Pankhurst, S. (1918). *Education of the Masses, Dreadnought Pamphlet No. 1.* London: The Dreadnought Publishers.

Telles, E., & Paschel, T. (2014). Who is Black, White, or Mixed Race? How Skin Color, Status, and Nation Shape Racial Classification in Latin America. *American Journal of Sociology, 120*(3), 864–907.

UNDP/World Bank/EC regional Roma survey (2011). Roma Inclusion Working Papers. Available online at http://ec.europa.eu/transparency/regdoc/rep/1/20 15/EN/1-2015-299-EN-F1-1.PDF

UNDP (2017). Regional Roma Survey 2017: Country Fact Sheets. Available online at www.eurasia.undp.org/content/rbec/en/home/library/roma/regional-roma-survey-2017-country-fact-sheets.html

UNICEF (2009). *When Special Means Excluded, Roma Segregation in Special Schools in the CEE/CIS Region*. Geneva: UNICEF Regional Office for Central and Eastern Europe and the Commonwealth of Independent States.

Walker, A., Sinfield, A., & Walker, C. (eds.). (2011). *Fighting Poverty, Inequality and Injustice: A Manifesto Inspired by Peter Townsend*. Bristol, UK: Policy Press.

CHAPTER 4

Higher Education in Exile
Developing a Sense of Self, Belonging and Purpose for Newcomer Youth

Vidur Chopra and Sarah Dryden-Peterson

Introduction

Zaid[1] was barely 15 years old when he moved to Boston from Syria in the fall of 2010. While his family desperately sought freedom from a politically oppressive regime, his mother led him to believe that they were in fact moving 'to obtain knowledge, to gain degrees, *just* to learn'. Six months later, in 2011, conflict broke out in Syria. As an adolescent, Zaid recalled feeling like he 'didn't have any power over the situation'. In those early moments, he wanted to focus on his schooling, but his experiences within and beyond high school were confusing. In Syria, he'd been told that America was a 'country of freedom', but as he experienced discrimination at school and realised 'nobody smiles in public . . . there's loneliness', he asked himself, 'What caused this to occur?' Lowering his voice to express sadness, Zaid shares, 'Even though Syria was a dictatorship, people could still get together, get along.'

In the five years since his move to the United States, Zaid experienced multiple transitions, including graduating from high school and moving to community College; combating discrimination and xenophobia targeting him and his family; watching the blaze of conflict grip his homeland in Syria from thousands of miles away; and acknowledging the way he was now perceived in contemporary America as he transitioned from being a 15-year-old to a young Arab male. Reflecting on his first five years in the United States as he watched an unyielding and bloody conflict in Syria unfold, Zaid felt like 'I got sucked into a movie. Like I'm, I'm somehow inside a TV and it's just a movie goin' on.'

---

[1] All names have been changed to protect the identities of research participants.

In this chapter, we present a portrait of Zaid, to explore the inequalities and opportunities encountered as he fled conflict and pursued higher education in the United States. We investigate how his experiences shape and reflect his sense of self, sense of belonging and sense of purpose. Our findings illuminate the ways newcomers fleeing conflict use education as a space to grapple with, and contest, questions of identity, belonging and xenophobia in host societies. We highlight in particular how higher education not just serves the function of enabling social mobility but also becomes a strategic tool for newcomers to navigate their personal aspirations and home community expectations while simultaneously navigating unfamiliar host communities.

Zaid represents one of the nearly 1.2 million recently arrived newcomers in the United States in 2010 (Camarota & Zeigler, 2017). Newcomers like Zaid blur and complicate the boundaries between traditional categories of refugees and migrants. Though conflict had not yet broken out in Syria when Zaid and his family left, one of their main reasons for leaving was the lack of social and political freedoms. Since 2011, nearly 12 million Syrians have been displaced within and beyond the country's borders as a consequence of widespread conflict (UNHCR, 2018). However, even before 2011, Syria was known to have among the most constrained civil and political liberties globally (Freedom House, 2011). Emergency rule, which was first imposed in 1963, continued to stay in effect, severely repressing individuals' rights to freedom of speech, expression and association, and fair trials, along with cases of arbitrary detentions and torture (Human Rights Watch, 2011). Unlike refugees who must be officially accepted for resettlement to the United States, Zaid and his family were able to move to the United States owing to his mother's ties to her extended family already settled there. Through an examination of Zaid's pre-higher education trajectory and his pursuit of higher education, we focus on a broader category of 'forced migrants', individuals who may not be traditionally classified as refugees but find themselves in 'refugee-like' situations (Crawley & Skleparis, 2018).

We also focus on community Colleges as particularly important social institutions for recently arrived newcomer youth to the United States; more newcomer youth attend community Colleges than any other type of post-secondary institution (Szelényi & Chang, 2002; Teranishi, Suárez-Orozco, & Suárez-Orozco, 2011). Through their lower tuition costs and programmes geared towards language acquisition and workforce development, community Colleges provide newcomer youth with pathways to access formal higher education and, subsequently, the job market (Erisman & Looney, 2007). As youth come of age and experience 'emerging adulthood', a unique developmental stage (Arnett, 2000), low-income, newcomer youth within community College contexts, in particular, experience complex tensions as they navigate competing individual and social responsibilities (Katsiaficas, Suárez-Orozco, & Dias, 2015). Through Zaid's case, we find that though these tensions are accentuated and shaped by conflict, higher education institutions, such as community Colleges, can play particularly important roles as immigrant youth navigate their sense of self, belonging and purpose.

The particularities of Zaid's case reveal and illuminate several universal themes that can further inform higher education research, policy and practice as tailored to meet the needs of refugee and recently arrived immigrant youth. Zaid is one of a growing number of forced migrants who are members of a conflict-affected diaspora, who seek to use higher education in ways that will positively impact peace and development in their countries of origin (Brinkerhoff, 2011; Dryden-Peterson & Reddick, 2019; Van Hear, 2006). Zaid's pathway through education embodies a common strategy of many newcomers and their children, including enrolment in community College. Unlike many in similar situations, community College was not a dead end for Zaid, and he is currently pursuing his undergraduate degree in engineering, with financial aid, at a renowned US university. Though Zaid was also able to secure permanent residency and citizenship in the United States far more quickly than most refugees, given his mother's American citizenship, his education and life trajectories reveal many challenges that accompany refugee and newly arrived newcomers' pursuits of education. These trajectories simultaneously illuminate relationships and spaces that Zaid shaped and engaged in, actions taken intentionally to bolster and accelerate his education. At the end of the chapter, we discuss implications, including ways that institutions of higher education can adapt existing structures to foster deep and productive, respectful relationships towards the development of welcoming spaces of learning for all.

Conceptual Framework: Sense of Self, Sense of Belonging, Sense of Purpose

Schools have a long history as primary institutions with which newcomers to the United States have contact and thus serve as central spaces for learning about and building relationships within the host society. While couched in the rhetoric of humanitarian concerns for the well-being of newcomer children, deficit models of thinking around newcomer students' learning abilities have hindered relationship development between schools and newcomer students. The school, throughout history, 'was an apparatus designed to subject immigrants to control, and to safeguard society's existing social and economic hierarchies' (Olneck, 2008, 104). In Gramscian terms, schools are mechanisms of control, not through violence or political force, but through 'the ideological, where the values of the elite become normalized as values that everyone can accept, even if they do so passively' (as described in Durrani, 2016).

Recent studies have identified ways in which schools can and do meet the needs of newcomer students, not through normalising the values of established elites, but instead through radical re-envisioning of individual identity and collective belonging. We focus here on relevant research, specifically with students who arrive as refugees or who have fled conflict. Through our analysis of this literature, we identified three critical spheres that shape the educational experiences of newcomer youth who have fled conflict: sense of self, sense of belonging and sense of purpose. In this chapter, we use this analytic as a way to think about both individual experiences and institutional structures, and how the two interact.

Until recently, literature on education of refugees in the United States has erased, by omission, the experiences of young people prior to their arrival in the United States (see, e.g., Bigelow, 2010; Gahungu, Gahungu, & Luseno, 2011; Isik-Ercan, 2012; McBrien, 2005, 2011; Nykiel-Herbert, 2010; Prior & Niesz, 2013; Szente, Hoot, & Taylor, 2006; Walker-Dalhouse & Dalhouse, 2009). Beyond vague descriptions of refugees forced from their homes often in violent ways before they arrive in the United States, there has been no nuanced understanding of the experiences of young people that may span periods of peace, conflict and/or transition. New research demonstrates the importance of school-based relationships of care and support for newcomer youth that recognise and honour previous schooling experiences in home and host countries and connections to place, family and ideas that may be transnational. Education that demonstrates these characteristics can spur connection to and investment in school as well as academic performance (Bajaj & Bartlett, 2017; Bartlett, Mendenhall, & Ghaffar-Kucher, 2017; Dryden-Peterson, 2017; Dryden-Peterson & Reddick, 2017; Mendenhall, Bartlett, & Ghaffar-Kucher, 2017), true for refugee education in countries of first asylum as well (Dryden-Peterson, Dahya, & Adelman, 2017). Across this literature, the idea of attention to 'sense of self' emerges, with connections to past experiences and meaning-making about home, conflict and personal identity. These processes of understanding and coming to a sense of self occur both through ways young people negotiate who they are in new spaces and how the people around them – parents, teachers, peers – choose to see and understand them.

Sense of self is inextricably linked to sense of belonging, particularly for newcomers who are racialised and othered. Refugee young people often have experiences in schools and communities that send explicit and implicit messages that they do not belong. Abu El-Haj documents the ways in which being Arab in a post-9/11 America, for example, is rife with everyday discrimination (2007, 2015). A 2017 survey by the Center on American-Islamic Relations found that among 1,000 Muslim-American students in California, 53 per cent had experienced mean comments and rumours about them because of their religion, a bullying rate more than twice the national average, and 36 per cent of female students had their hijab tugged, pulled or touched offensively (Council on American-Islamic Relations, 2017). Schools, including community Colleges and institutions of higher education, can be spaces to interrupt islamophobia and xenophobia, and to foster a sense of belonging. In particular, these spaces can enable active discussion of stereotypes and allow individuals to recognise and confront their own biases. Moreover, they can be spaces to develop both 'radical empathy' and 'radical hospitality', which seek to actively, not passively, create conditions for welcome and negotiation of belonging premised on each person's sense of self (Ghiso & Campano, 2013; Bajaj, Ghaffar-Kucher, & Desai, 2016; Shafer, 2016).

Refugee students' senses of self and belonging are not singularly located. Bajaj and Bartlett, for example, identify newcomers' 'multidirectional aspirations' (2017) that are situated in the United States, in the home country, and transnationally. These multi-sited identities are often connected to a sense of purpose, especially for individuals who have experienced or fled from conflict. Individuals stay connected to those who remain and to other geographically dispersed forced migrants by sharing resources as well as through 'social remittances', such as the sharing of information and ideas (see, e.g., Levitt & Jaworsky, 2007). Conflict-affected young people are motivated in these actions by strong commitments to, emotional engagement with, and shared identity among those who remained (Brinkerhoff, 2011; Iskander, 2010; Lyons, 2007; Nielsen & Riddle, 2009) as well as by aspirations for more peaceful trajectories for their countries of origin (Chopra, 2018; Dryden-Peterson & Reddick, 2019).

In examining educational inequalities and opportunities for youth flee-ing conflict, we focus on the interplay of student experiences, institutional structures and what happens in these processes of coming together. The three concepts of sense of self, sense of belonging and sense of purpose shape our investigation of how one Syrian student, Zaid, balances his sense of self, nurtured in Syria, with transformative experiences of belonging and purpose, fostered through his experiences living in the United States while war ravaged his home.

Methodology

To understand the ways recent newcomer youth in the United States experience and navigate higher education opportunities, we draw from portraiture, a social science methodology rooted in the phenomenological paradigm. Portraiture seeks to capture the fluidity and complexity of individuals' experiences in the context of their lives (Lawrence-Lightfoot, 2005). For some time, research on recently arrived newcomer children and youth in the United States has disproportionately focused on the many barriers they confront in their educational pursuits (see, e.g., Addams, 2008 [1908]; McBrien, 2005; Portes, 1998). Instead, we were keen to understand the ways that recently arrived newcomer youth navigate their higher education, in spite of these barriers. In staying true and committed to this goal, portraiture naturally lent itself as a methodology, as it concerns itself with a search for 'goodness', recognising that goodness is simulta-neously 'laced with imperfections' (Lawrence-Lightfoot & Davis, 1997, 9) and that social science interventions must not only acknowledge barriers and vulnerability but also locate and examine individuals' sources of strength. In so doing, portraiture seeks to convey the 'authority, wisdom, and perspective' of participants (Lawrence-Lightfoot, 2005, 6).

In the context of a graduate methods course on portraiture, Zaid was first introduced to one of the co-authors through a common friend. This co-author then observed and interviewed Zaid through the course of an academic semester in 2014 and, since that time, both have remained in touch. Central to this research paradigm and to our study is the develop-ment of respectful and reciprocal relationships with participants to better understand their ongoing decisions and meaning-making around critical junctures and transitions in their lives. Developing deep and meaningful relationships entails effort and time. Given our focus on the multiple educational transitions recently arrived newcomer youth experience, it was important to not only engage with our participant at one point in time but to continue following his trajectory and transitions across different settings and time points.

Our study draws on multiple sources of data, including several in-depth, semi-structured interviews with Zaid; an interview with his mother, Halima; informal conversations with student members of the Arab Student Council where Zaid was the president; participant observations at the Arab Student Council's meetings and its annual celebrations. This dataset consists of ten hours of interviews; a full day of participant observations in different settings, including Zaid's home and the community College he attended; and ongoing texts and social media messages that have continued since the development of the research relationship between the co-author and Zaid. Zaid reviewed versions of this work and participated in an education conference with the co-author where they shared the work together.

Each formal interview was audio-recorded and transcribed. Following each interview and observation, the same co-author wrote impressionistic records that informed our early analysis and emerging themes. The other co-author coded the interview and fieldnote data in Atlas.ti. Together, we took a grounded approach in our analysis, arriving at a set of codes that emerged from the data. For example, codes included 'creating community', 'unlearning and relearning', 'sense of self', 'sense of belonging' and 'sense of purpose'. At various stages of the work, we checked and refined our analysis through conversations with Zaid.

Findings

In this section, we present and interpret our study's findings through a portrait of Zaid's experiences in Syria and then in high school and community College in the United States. We divide our analysis into five themes: seeing the sun, unlearning and relearning, higher education and transnational roots, damaging the love spring and creating community. Through these themes, we examine the experiences and relationships that shaped Zaid's senses of self, of belonging and of purpose.

Seeing the Sun

In our first conversation, Zaid paints a vivid picture of his hometown in the suburbs of Damascus, Syria. He uses his hands animatedly to draw imaginary, majestic mountains with his school perched on the top and a scenic, verdant valley with fertile orchards and vineyards irrigated by the gurgles of the river Barada. Most of all, Zaid reminisces about the people of his hometown whom he refers to as 'simple' and for whom 'what's in their heart is on their tongues'. To ensure that we make no facile assumptions regarding migration and class, Zaid declares, 'I come from abundance'. Zaid's mother's siblings had migrated to the United States in the 1970s, although she remained in Syria. His father's family owned vast fruit orchards that exported 'peaches, apples, pears, and grapes'.

But not all has remained lush and abundant in the country. In stark contrast to the abundance of nature's gifts for Syrians like Zaid and his family, stands the dearth of personal freedom, civil rights and liberties that all Syrian people confront on an ongoing basis. Since 1963, Syria has remained in emergency rule, with people detained indiscriminately and in the absence of arrest warrants. From a very young age, Zaid's elders cautioned him against the vociferous expression of his political views for 'even walls got ears'. Zaid paid little heed to this until he personally experienced the reverberations of tyranny and injustice in his own school.

In grade 7, as is common in several language classes across the world, 15-year-old Zaid's Arabic teacher asked him to write about his future goals. Naïve and innocent in character, but ambitious in his approach, Zaid proudly read his essay in front of his class. 'I wanna become the President', he declared. Even before he could finish reading his essay, his teacher snatched it and dragged him to the school principal. Gentle, yet firm, in his approach, the principal told Zaid: 'If someone reports this incident, you could be gone . . . they will put you in prison. They'd probably torture you. They'd probably torture your family. You can't be saying stuff like this in public.'

Luckily for Zaid, his mother, Halima, worked as a grade 3 teacher in the same school. The school principal called Halima to the office where Zaid's Arabic teacher retold the incident in horror and reminded Halima and Zaid to 'never speak' of what had transpired in the classroom. By contrast, Zaid recounts the message to his mother as direct and severe. 'They told her, "You need to take this kid away from here . . . We all love him here. That's why we're not going to report it. But we don't know who he's going to have for teachers in the future."' Indirectly, Zaid's Arabic teacher was alluding to the Syrian government's security and intelligence apparatus, *Mukhabarat*, or 'secret police', notorious for surveilling and arbitrarily detaining its citizens (Human Rights Watch, 2011).

Halima knew that the time to move was coming close. Already an American citizen, Halima frequently visited her family in the United States each summer. She had even birthed her youngest daughter in

America. Halima was 'afraid for Zaid' and called her brother to 'prepare the papers' for her children to take up their American citizenship. Meanwhile, Zaid's father, a mechanical engineer and a civil servant, also lost his job. He refused to succumb to a bribe and was subsequently *made* to resign because there was 'no choice'. Like an orchestra conductor, Zaid moves his hands rapidly to outline the cancerous nature of corruption that has riddled the Syrian public sector. Describing the consequences of not paying periodic bribes to policemen and the unfettered and indiscriminate use of 'emergency law', Zaid's deep brown eyes widen and creases appear in the folds of his cheek as he scrunches his nose. 'We call it "beyond the sun." You get locked under the ground and you never see the sun again. You literally don't see the sun again.'

Halima was determined that her children continue seeing the sun. A year later, in September of 2009, Zaid and his sisters and parents made their way to Damascus airport. Unable to make sense of his relatives' tears, Zaid knew in his heart that he would return to Syria, well educated and soon. As the bus whizzed past the majestic green mountains and the gurgling teal river, reality struck Zaid. The reflections of his first and perhaps most impressionable fifteen years of his life whirled past. 'I realised I wouldn't see Damascus anymore. I wouldn't be able to see my family, the people who truly care about me for who I am . . . The supportive network that I'm going to leave and come to the unknown.' Reflecting on these moments now, he knows those were his last glimpses of the Syria he loved. 'My family from my Dad's side have bad history with the government . . . we have what we call a "red dot" next to our name, our last name, in the government's record', his left hand moves in a circle to emphasise the finality of this red dot. 'If I go to Lebanon and I try to get into Syria, and I get to an army checkpoint, and they see my ID, they'd read my name . . . they would just kill me right there.' Zaid understood his mother's desire for him to see the sun. But that didn't change the fact that, as Zaid said, 'it broke my heart leaving Syria'.

'You're Reborn': Unlearning and Relearning

Newly arrived in the United States, Zaid quickly learned that 'people of colour' are 'looked at differently' and that 'discrimination is a part of my life'. Zaid is struck by the 'labels' people attach when they see him, a young Arab male with a visible stubble. Despite these labels, Zaid remained steady and composed trying to remember that 'not all fingers [in the hand] are the same'. From the bus driver who made eye contact with Zaid but did not stop the bus for him to the rejections on his high school's playground and football team, Zaid knew that these instances of exclusion and discrimination were those of 'judgment', of being rendered invisible as a young Arab male and yet simultaneously being viewed with the gaze of hyper-visibility, as a 'fanatic' or 'extremist'. 'Injustice's what makes your heart break ... a little by a little', he said. In those early years, Zaid did not know how to make meaning of these instances and he recalls asking himself, 'what did I do to deserve all of this?'

On his arrival to the United States, Zaid was able to resume his sophomore year (grade 10), in a high school where 26 per cent of the student body consisted of minorities. With limited English language skills – Zaid described himself as 'a newborn' – his first friend was a Lebanese student he met in gym class, with whom he spoke in Arabic. Unable to communicate in English, Zaid was often mocked at school, re-affirming his belief that he needed to 'speak well ... to understand every word'. Determined and gritty in spirit, and optimistic in outlook, Zaid's mother often reminded him to take the 'negative pressure, turn it into positive energy and dedicate it to hard work'. During this time, American songs and rap music were Zaid's first English teachers. He read widely to be 'effective' in writing and to be able to 'deliver the idea'. It is perhaps his self-taught English that has resulted in him amalgamating words like 'right-eous' and 'virtuous' to in turn create 'rightuous', among others. As he rolls the 'r' in his words, it is hard to imagine that the young man seated opposite, speaking effortlessly in a fluid American accent, could barely speak a word of English just four years ago.

Though his teachers in the English as a Second Language department emphasised the value of diversity and equality of treatment, Zaid found this rhetoric irreconcilable with his experiences in and beyond school. 'I don't want people to treat me equally. I want you to be just.' Moving his hands like a see-saw demonstrating the delicate balance between equality and justice, Zaid finds the notion of equality too passive. In his eyes, justice is an active endeavour. 'Treat me like I treat you ... When I see you like stepping forward one step, I'll step ten ... If you're just, you can't discriminate.'

Zaid is unable to offer more detail about specific instances of discrimination at school, but the wounds of exclusion that 15-year-old Zaid once experienced are still raw. 'Would it really matter if I had heard it or if it was said it to me? The point is that I got the feeling they're trying to deliver. Whether I got it emotionally or whether I got it verbally, they're trying to get a certain point across and *I got it*.' Acknowledging the lack of resources within schools for newcomers to understand and navigate the structural barriers that are often a confluence of race, class and ethnicity, among others, Zaid sought the counsel of a White, Jewish teacher in his school, Miss Greenberg. Through her, he learned that intent drives action and that perpetrators have 'limited understandings of the world'. As he shares his wisdom, four creased lines dart across his forehead, 'Discrimination doesn't affect me. I know who I am ... [If] you grew up to hate, to dislike certain types of people, I can't blame you ... you were brought up like that. If someone is discriminating, you can only feel bad for them.'

Higher Education and Transnational Roots

In the darkness of a cold, black February night in 2011, a group of 15-year-old Syrian high schoolers gathered, scrawling graffiti on their school wall in the southern Syrian city of Daraa. Inspired by the onset of the Arab Spring in the region, a youngster scribbled, 'No teaching, no school, till the end of Bashar's rule.' The children were soon tortured and killed for inciting and sparking a revolution in the country. A month later, on 15 March 2011, the protestors' rage knew no bounds. The dam walls had burst open and Zaid marks the moment as an epiphany, a realisation that 'people in Syria have voice'. Angrily, they took their booming demands of freedom to the streets. In response, they were met with the army's tanks and bullets – symbols of brute and garish might.

Thousands of miles away in his home in the United States, Zaid followed the protests with interest, through social media. Concerned with the growing rumbles of a revolution that later turned into a bloody conflict he could not then imagine, Zaid phoned his paternal grandfather, 'If you want me to come to Syria, I will come tomorrow.' With reassurance and comfort, his grandfather said, 'Syria doesn't need men. Syria needs educated people. Get your degrees and when Syria's okay, you come back.'

As the death toll rose each day and accounts of protestors being jailed and tortured streamed in on Zaid's social media, he grew increasingly disillusioned. When Zaid lost two of his friends, he thought, 'this life's worth nothing'. Zaid had barely settled into life in the United States and was mentally 'prepared to excel' but 'then this struck me'. Raising his hands to size greatness, he elaborates, 'I've lost more than 40 cousins of mine', while his forehead breaks into creases. 'People I grew up with, you know, like beloved ones? ... When you lose the great things, little things don't matter no more.' Zaid's interest at school dwindled and his grade point average (GPA) GPA dropped, but he eventually passed his three advanced placement (AP) courses and graduated from high school. With an admit to a renowned public university, the family decided that community College was a better option since it was 'cheaper' and would enable opportunities for financial aid when Zaid transferred to a four-year university in the future.

Zaid enrolled at a local community College, an institution that prides itself on its diversity. The College is home to 1,000 international students, from 105 countries, who speak more than 75 languages. In fact, it is hard to miss the 67 international flags that hang from the ceiling just as one walks through its main entrance. In his two years there, Zaid's goal was to take as many classes to ultimately transition to a four-year university where he could major in biomedical engineering. His eventual goal was to 'develop artificial limbs . . . new interventions that will help the healing process of patients', those who had been directly and violently disabled by the Syrian conflict.

Zaid knew that the path to supporting Syria by eventually becoming a trained biomedical engineer at a four-year US university was a long haul. A longitudinal study examining all students enrolled at community College in the United States in 2010 found that only a third transitioned to a four-year university (Shapiro et al., 2017). Though formally enrolled in College, all Zaid wanted to do was to find meaningful and productive ways to 'make a difference' for the Syrian people caught amidst conflict.

In this time, Zaid's transnational involvement took multiple forms. Zaid initially protested at his city's public square with other members of the Syrian diaspora. However, 'when it [the revolution] became armed [in Syria]', Zaid 'backed up, a little bit'. Instead, Zaid tried his hand volunteering for a local NGO packing medical equipment as humanitarian aid for Syrians. Zaid plays with the drawstrings of his grey army camouflaged patterned hoodie as he describes wiring money to his displaced Syrian friends living in Lebanon. Though Zaid was thousands of miles away from the epicentre of the Syrian conflict, he was aware that sometimes even an effusive WhatsApp message to his displaced friends that reinforces, 'I'm here for you', is critical. In the summer of 2015, Zaid wanted to spend time teaching children in a camp hosting Syrian refugees in Jordan, Turkey or Lebanon. He wanted to act on his belief that the Syrian children have suffered the most from conflict. Displacement, with the unprecedented and bitter loss of home, family and education, has 'killed childhood', he said. He painted a dark and bleak future for Syria's next generation. 'They'll grow up to become criminals, thieves . . . this is the atmosphere they grew up in . . . They'll rise to become something we don't want them to be.'

While Zaid continued his education in a community College with the goal of becoming a biomedical engineer in the United States, his time at home was imbued with many of the same rituals from Syria that his mother Halima insisted the family maintain. Her melodious hum of a special Syrian song, the affectionate morning greetings to the children in Arabic, the use of well-roasted, dark, Syrian coffee or the family's coming together over Sunday breakfast – these rituals are anchors in reminding the family that despite life being turned 'upside down', some constancy has remained.

When we first met Halima, Zaid's mother, she explained that in nature the 'small pieces of rock hold the big rocks'. Leaning forward while smiling gently, she twirls her hands, unencumbered and free flowing like a graceful dancer, and shares, 'All families are trees. They *have to have* roots. With no roots, no strong in life.' With these strong roots, and aware of his capabilities and the experiences that have shaped him, Zaid knows that he must use his education well. 'Having an experience and not sharing that experience is betraying that experience. I have to share the knowledge I have acquired.'

Damaging the Love Spring

Zaid recalls enthusiastically encouraging Halima, his mother, a teacher with twelve years of experience in Syria, to enrol part-time in evening classes at his community College. Despite her long-time American citizenship, staying in the United States was new and 'hard'. Halima knows 'it's not easy . . . to change your skin'. Each Wednesday and Thursday, after a full day of work in a middle-eastern grocery store, Halima would begin her English and psychology classes at six and end at nine. Some nights she would stay awake past midnight to complete her homework. One day in her psychology 101 class, her Asian professor told her and another Haitian student to withdraw from class because of their limited English-language skills. Another time, the professor asked her in front of the rest of the class, with this pronunciation, 'Are you Mizlim?' Halima remained silent, while the rest of the class laughed out loud. Her silence was met by the professor's insensitivity. 'Why don't you answer? You have no religion?' he said. He went on to harangue her and inquired about the handful of radicalised youth from the United States joining the fundamentalist Islamic State (ISIS) group . His line of questioning revealed his own limited understanding of diversity. 'Is it true? Every woman in your country, they cover their hair, and nobody sees them? And they don't talk? And they don't do nothing?' As if these slurs weren't enough, he called Halima one evening on her phone to let her know that she had a C in her midterms. Halima recalled the professor's exact words that so clearly communicated to her that she didn't belong in class: 'If anybody gets a grade C, you cannot pass.'

Enraged at the misplaced labels and crestfallen at being pushed away from being able to learn, Halima acquiesced to the ludicrous demands of a bigot. She remembers silently withdrawing from the course without telling anyone at home. 'I will never take Psychology in my life', she shared, forcing a chuckle in between. 'I hate it. I don't want to take it. That's it. No more. Yeah!' Her chuckle did little to disguise the emotional charge the incident has held over her, and over Zaid.

Zaid only learnt of the incident a few days later. Unable to fully understand the gravity of the situation or what he could do, he took to social media. As he watched the Syrian conflict unravel, he had observed transformative effects of this kind of action. As the Arab Spring took hold, he said,

> Syrians remembered that they have voice. That they can actually, if they're feeling the pain, they can scream. So, this was the turning point in every Syrian's life. The turning point when you realize that you don't have to suck it up and just pretend that it does not exist. People had walls of fear, and when those walls broke, they can, they felt like they have a voice, they can, and since they were together, like, gathering, they felt like they can, they have a, they have a voice to say what's inside of them, to describe the pain, to describe the injustice.

These experiences fresh, Zaid took his understanding of pain and injustice to social media and wrote: 'Someone has initiated an enormous fire in my heart, and all the water on this earth cannot tone it down an inch . . . I forgive people when they do me wrong, but when it comes to my family, it is a survival matter.' The next morning, red in his face with anger and impatient in his stride, he sought an appointment with the dean. The dean assured him that either she would personally observe the professor's class or send a colleague on her behalf. However, to tame expectations, she quickly prefaced it by informing him that they might not be able to act swiftly or do enough because the professor 'was a part of the union'. Zaid expressed his frustration at the predicament. 'Sometimes you just have to suck it up. Not sometimes. *All the times* you have to.' A long silence punctuated our conversation.

Zaid has continued to feel personally responsible for all that his mother had to confront in her psychology class. While explaining the guilt he bears, simply for encouraging her to learn, he thrust his palms and arms forward with a sudden jolt, comparing the situation to being 'thrown under the bus'. He paused and, almost as if with remorse, his tone softened, 'When I see God, I'm gonna ask just one question: "Why? Why did all of this have to happen? Why life showed us everything beautiful and then all got taken away? Why?"' For the first time in the series of our conversations, Zaid showed vulnerability. Twenty-year-old Zaid, who otherwise had always seemed brimming with optimism and agency, seemed in this moment helpless and unable to navigate the immense institutional barriers in his way. 'If he [the Asian professor] discriminated against me, I don't care. But I can't see the person providing for me going through that. You can't damage my love spring.'

Creating Community

In light of news coverage around ISIS and Halima's personal experiences of discrimination at College, Zaid 'felt the need for people [here] to *see* us. And what I mean by us is Arabs . . . not just [as] Muslims'. To build bridges between the Arab students and the larger community at the community College, Zaid volunteered to re-initiate a then defunct club and become president of the student-run Arab Student Council. Though several Arab students were already a part of the Islamic Club at the community College that focused specifically on the study of the religion and its applicability in daily life, Zaid's goals were different. He wanted students and staff to know and learn about the diversity of the Arab world that is inhabited by Christians, Muslims and Jews. Zaid knew that 'somebody needed to step up to show the goodness . . . What you see on TV is marking every Muslim as a terrorist. And this is not the case.'

Over the two months that one of the co-authors observed the Arab Student Council's meetings, the club's membership remained nearly the same. Each time roughly the same group of eight to thirteen students attended the club's meeting for ninety minutes, strolling in and out at different points. Every now and then, a member would bring along a friend and the group would formally welcome the new attendee by briefly introducing themselves. Even though the club's meeting had a predictable format, students from different backgrounds, including those from Algeria, Brazil, Morocco, Iraq, Syria and the United States, were regular attendees. The first half hour of the meeting was usually spent introducing Arabic letters and key words; the next half hour focused on any aspect related to the region's culture such as variations in the *dabkeh*, a folk dance, performed across different countries in the Arab Levant; and the final half hour was left open for discussion. Most of these discussions pertained to the students' preoccupations with their club's upcoming event, 'Insights into Arabic culture'. Would there be a henna station? Should the group perform the *dabkeh*? How would everyone learn without much time for practice? These among others were all questions that entailed much of the club members' discussions. Though the majority of students in the club were native Arabic speakers, they still showed up to help the small handful of non-Arabic-speaking students curious about Arabic and the Arab world. Despite the banality in the club's meetings, it was clear that the club, through its desire to build and bridge relationships and foster belonging, was a powerful antidote to what Zaid believed to be an 'atmosphere where everywhere there is tension'.

Almost as a way to quell this 'tension', the club's leadership team with Zaid at its helm had clearly written into the club's constitution that no political or religious discussions were acceptable during the club's meetings. Zaid shared his early motivations for reopening the club and for volunteering to spend time organising the students, 'My belief is to promote the language and the culture *despite* religious or political views.' In so many ways, this dictated the design of the upcoming student event that was to focus on the 'good part, the fun part'. Zaid was determined to show that his people were not 'backwards' and 'uncivilised'. Instead, he wanted to make a point: 'There are nice Arabs, there are people who are willing to dance, some people who are willing to sing, there are people who are actually, capable of having fun. Arabs are not all about religion and promoting Islam.'

Despite the club's rules to not discuss these issues, politics permeated relationships. Rida, the secretary of the Club, also Syrian, had recently gone to Damascus for three weeks. Zaid knew that she and her family were 'definitely with Assad [regime]'. Reflecting on his own inability to return, he shared, 'If I go to Syria now, they'll kill me right there ... But if someone can go to Damascus, they're definitely with the government.' Zaid recalled being 'speechless' because he now 'knew where she stands'. He took his fingers to his head like a gun and clicked his tongue to mark a gunshot, 'I used to like her ... Liking someone and then seeing what they *actually* think and believe ... you kinda, just, like, kill 'em in your head.' But Zaid knew that he couldn't entirely sever relationships with Rida, for they have to 'work together to promote this club'. Beyond the club, though, 'is where the restraints come'. Zaid and Rida used to hang out earlier, but now Zaid described their conversations as 'limited', for there is no scope for the 'relationship to grow any further'. As Zaid reflected on his life's experiences, he is aware of the fundamental contradictions between the 'personal' and 'political' across time and place: back in middle school in Syria, and now in community College in the United States. 'The world is not ideal, it's not Utopia', he knows. 'But that doesn't mean it has to be hell. My role is to show people that there's still good people out there, willing to help.'

Discussion

Several circumstances and individuals supported Zaid's development as he learned and unlearned about inequalities and opportunities. Foremost, we acknowledge that Zaid's legal status as a US citizen upon arrival played an important role in his swift yet tumultuous transition to American society. Halima, his mother, served as the central 'root' in his life who lent nourishment, strength and stability in times of turmoil. Through her, Zaid was able to develop a sense of self that eventually propelled him to build a sense of purpose and connection with his many communities – local and transnational. The first social institution that Zaid closely inter-acted with on his arrival to the United States was high school. Though some students and teachers contributed to his sense of being hyper-visible, as an Arab, as a 'fanatic', and excluded him in the playground, one of his teachers helped him to decode American scripts of stereotyping and dis-crimination. It was through her that Zaid learned and internalised that 'not all fingers are the same' and that perpetrators of exclusion and bullying were 'limited' by their narrow views of the world. Her sage counsel validated his sense of self and enabled Zaid to begin to create a sense of belonging at high school, in ways that felt productive and authentic to him.

However, as the literature notes (Yuval-Davis, 2006), Zaid's belonging was contradictory and fragmented. As conflict unfolded in Syria, and given Zaid's family history, he realised that he could no longer entirely belong to Syria. His grades at high school fell, he lost motivation and studying advanced calculus, even with the pathways it created for university study, began to feet pointless. The American Dream of becoming educated that had been so profusely promised during his move as a 15-year-old from Syria and that had provided him a sense of purpose was ephemeral. Unable to afford a four-year university, Zaid enrolled at community College. Here too, his sense of self, belonging and purpose were inextricably intertwined. He sought to use his education to transfer to a four-year university to major in biomedical engineering for a specific purpose: so he could learn to develop artificial limbs for individuals physically disabled by the Syrian conflict. Yet as Zaid actively sought ways to make meaning of the Syrian conflict, and to even support those directly impacted by it, he found no opportunities within his community College to engage with these broader goals and purposes. Moreover, his senses of self and belonging were deeply wounded when his mother was discriminated against by her professor at the same community College. Unable to stand up against an academic institution or to protect her in the moment, Zaid continued to blame himself. In that moment, his sense of belonging to his institution rapidly evaporated. It was then that his sense of purpose shifted. From wanting to solely focus on the Syrian conflict, Zaid knew that there was work to be done right here in his community College, and for students, faculty and staff to unlearn their stereotypes about being Arab and to think differently about what it means to belong.

In the years ahead, the student population within community Colleges and universities will continue to become increasingly diverse (Szelényi & Chang, 2002; Teranishi et al., 2011). As higher education institutions seek to create conditions in which recently arrived new-comer youth can thrive, they will be usefully informed by considering ways and strategies to foster youths' sense of self, belonging and purpose. First, educational institutions need to better understand youths' pre-arrival experiences and educational trajectories, and to offer targeted academic and socio-emotional support that respond to the needs they encounter in their new classrooms. Furthermore, educational institutions and broader communities need to foster avenues for long-time residents – including students, teachers, administrators and community members – to take responsibility for their roles in building welcoming communities that are inclusive and caring. These opportunities should enable more authentic understandings of each other's culture and move beyond temporary, one-off events that celebrate diversity merely through food and music, tending to offer few opportunities to develop deep and productive relationships with one another. Though formal or informal language training is often provided to newcomer youth, these programmes tend to omit explicit instruction in the society's socio-cultural scripts, including the 'rules of the game' required for social mobility and inclusion.

Institutions also need to understand, acknowledge and honour the ways in which newcomer youths' simultaneous, transnational embedd-edness within multiple sites and communities connect to their senses of purpose and how these purposes can be enacted in both academic and non-academic pursuits. Filling these gaps in institutional understandings is critical to the creation of programmes that support productive relationships among students, faculty and staff and that can enable students in the development of their senses of self, belonging and purpose in connection with, rather than in opposition to, their academic institutions.

REFERENCES

Abu El-Haj, T. R. (2007). 'I Was Born Here, but My Home, It's Not Here': Educating for Democratic Citizenship in an Era of Transnational Migration and Global Conflict. *Harvard Educational Review, 77*(3), 285–316.

Abu El-Haj, T. R. (2015). *Unsettled Belonging: Educating Palestinian American Youth after 9/11*. Chicago; London: University of Chicago Press.

Addams, J. (2008 [1908]). The Public School and the Immigrant Child. In D. J. Flinders & S. J. Thornton (eds.), *The Curriculum Studies Reader* (pp. 25–27). New York: Routledge.

Arnett, J. J. (2000). Emerging Adulthood: A Theory of Development from the Late Teens through the Twenties. *American Psychologist, 55*(5), 469–480. DOI:10.1037/0003-066X.55.5.469

Bajaj, M., & Bartlett, L. (2017). Critical Transnational Curriculum for Immigrant and Refugee Students. *Curriculum Inquiry, 47*(1), 25–35. DOI:10.1080/03626784.2016.1254499

Bajaj, M., Ghaffar-Kucher, A., & Desai, K. (2016). Brown Bodies and Xenophobic Bullying in US Schools: Critical Analysis and Strategies for Action. *Harvard Educational Review, 86*(4), 481–505.

Bartlett, L., Mendenhall, M., & Ghaffar-Kucher, A. (2017). Culture in Acculturation: Refugee Youth's Schooling Experiences in International Schools in New York City. *International Journal of Intercultural Relations. 60*, 109–119. DOI:http://dx.doi.org/10.1016/j.ijintrel.2017.04.005

Bigelow, M. (2010). *Mogadishu on the Mississippi: Language, Racialized Identity, and Education in a New Land*. Chichester, West Sussex, UK; Malden, MA: Wiley-Blackwell.

Brinkerhoff, J. M. (2011). Diasporas and Conflict Societies: Conflict Entrepreneurs, Competing Interests or Contributors to Stability and Development? *Conflict, Security & Development, 11*(2), 115–143.

Camarota, S. A., & Zeigler, K. (2017). *1.8 Million Immigrants Likely Arrived in 2016, Matching Highest Level in U.S. History*. Washington, DC: https://cis.org/sites/default/files/2018–01/numbers-dec-17_0.pdf

Chopra, V. (2018). Learning to Belong, Belonging to Learn: Syrian Refugee Youths' Pursuits of Education, Membership and Stability in Lebanon. Unpublished Dissertation (EdD), Harvard University, Cambridge, MA.

Council on American-Islamic Relations (2017). *Unshakable: The Bullying of Muslim Students and the Unwavering Movement to Eradicate It.* California Chapter of the Council on American-Islamic Relations and is an online report https://ca.cair.com/sacval/news/2017-bullying-report/

Crawley, H., & Skleparis, D. (2018). Refugees, Migrants, Neither, Both: Categorical Fetishism and the Politics of Bounding in Europe's 'Migration Crisis'. *Journal of Ethnic and Migration Studies, 44*(1), 48–64. DOI:10.1080/1369183X.2017.1348224

Dryden-Peterson, S. (2017). Family–school relationships in Immigrant Children's Well-Being: The Intersection of Demographics and School Culture in the Experiences of Black African Immigrants in the United States. *Race Ethnicity and Education, 21*(4), 1–17. DOI:10.1080/13613324.2017.1294562

Dryden-Peterson, S., Dahya, N., & Adelman, E. (2017). Pathways to Educational Success among Refugees: Connecting Local and Global Resources. *American Educational Research Journal, 54*(6), 1011–1047.

Dryden-Peterson, S., & Reddick, C. (2017). 'When I am a President of Guinea': Resettled Refugees Traversing Education in Search of a Future. *European Education, 49*(4), 253–275.

Dryden-Peterson, S., & Reddick, C. (2019). 'What I Believe Can Rescue that Nation': Diaspora Working Transnationally to Transform Education in Fragility and Conflict. *Comparative Education Review, 63*(2), 213–235.

Durrani, M. (2016). Normalization is Control: Telling Stories to Survive. http://religiondispatches.org/normalization-is-control-telling-stories-to-survive/

Erisman, W., & Looney, S. (2007). *Opening the Door to the American Dream: Increasing Higher Education Access and Success for Immigrants.* Washington, DC: www.ihep.org/sites/default/files/uploads/docs/pubs/openingthedoor.pdf

Freedom House (2011). *Freedom in the World: Syria.* https://freedomhouse.org/report/freedom-world/2011/syria

Gahungu, A., Gahungu, O., & Luseno, F. (2011). Educating Culturally Displaced Students with Truncated Formal Education (CDS-TFE): The Case of Refugee Students and Challenges for Administration, Teachers, and Counselors. *International Journal of Educational Leadership Preparation, 6*(2), 1–19.

Ghiso, M. P., & Campano, G. (2013). Coloniality and Education: Negotiating Discourses of Immigration in Schools and Communities through Border Thinking. *Equity & Excellence in Education, 46*(2), 252–269. DOI:10.1080/10665684.2013.779160

Human Rights Watch (2011). *World Report 2011.* New York: Human Rights Watch. www.hrw.org/world-report/2011/country-chapters/syria

Isik-Ercan, Z. (2012). In Pursuit of a New Perspective in the Education of Children of the Refugees: Advocacy for the 'Family'. *Educational Sciences: Theory and Practice, 12*(4), 3025–3038.

Iskander, N. N. (2010). *Creative State: Forty Years of Migration and Development Policy in Morocco and Mexico.* Ithaca: ILR Press.

Katsiaficas, D., Suárez-Orozco, C., & Dias, S. I. (2015). 'When Do I Feel Like an Adult?': Latino and Afro-Caribbean Immigrant-Origin Community College Students' Conceptualizations and Experiences of (Emerging) Adulthood. *Emerging Adulthood, 3*(2), 98–112. DOI:10.1177/2167696814548059

Lawrence-Lightfoot, S. (2005). Reflections on Portraiture: A Dialogue between Art and Science. *Qualitative Inquiry, 11*(1), 3–15.

Lawrence-Lightfoot, S., & Davis, J. H. (1997). *The Art and Science of Portraiture.* San Francisco: Jossey-Bass.

Levitt, P., & Jaworsky, B. N. (2007). Transnational Migration Studies: Past Developments and Future Trends. *Annual Review of Sociology, 33*, 129–156.

Lyons, T. (2007). Conflict-Generated Diasporas and Transnational Politics in Ethiopia. *Conflict, Security & Development, 7*(4), 529–549.

McBrien, J. L. (2005). Educational Needs and Barriers for Refugee Students in the United States: A Review of the Literature. *Review of Educational Research, 75*(3), 329–364.

McBrien, J. L. (2011). The Importance of Context: Vietnamese, Somali, and Iranian Refugee Mothers Discuss Their Resettled Lives and Involvement in Their Children's Schools. *Compare: A Journal of Comparative and International Education, 41*(1), 75–90.

Mendenhall, M., Bartlett, L., & Ghaffar-Kucher, A. (2017). 'If You Need Help, They are Always There for Us': Education for Refugees in an International High School in NYC. *The Urban Review, 49*(1), 1–25. DOI:10.1007/s11256-016-0379-4

Nielsen, T. M., & Riddle, L. (2009). Investing in Peace: The Motivational Dynamics of Diaspora Investment in Post-Conflict Economies. *Journal of Business Ethics, 89*(4), 435–448. DOI:10.1007/s10551-010-0399-z

Nykiel-Herbert, B. (2010). Iraqi Refugee Students: From a Collection of Aliens to a Community of Learners. *Multicultural Education, 17*(3), 2–14.

Olneck, M. R. (2008). American Public Schooling and European Immigrants in the Early Twentieth Century: A Post-Revisionist Synthesis. In W. J. Reese & J. L. Rury (eds.), *Rethinking the History of American Education*, 1st edn (pp. 103–141). New York: Palgrave Macmillan.

Portes, A. (1998). Children of Immigrants: Segmented Assimilation and Its Determinants. In A. Portes (ed.), *The Economic Sociology of Immigration* (pp. 248–279). New York: Russell Sage Foundation.

Prior, M. A., & Niesz, T. (2013). Refugee Children's Adaptation to American Early Childhood Classrooms: A Narrative Inquiry. *The Qualitative Report, 18* (39), 1–17.

Shafer, L. (2016). Dismantling Islamophobia. www.gse.harvard.edu/news/uk/16/11/dismantling-islamophobia

Shapiro, D., Dundar, A., Huie, F., Wakhungu, P. K., Yuan, X., Nathan, A., & Hwang, Y. (2017). *Tracking Transfer: Measures of Effectiveness in Helping Community College Students to Complete Bachelor's Degrees.* Herndon, VA: National Student Clearinghouse Research Center https://nscresearchcenter.org/wp-content/uploads/SignatureReport13_corrected.pdf

Szelényi, K., & Chang, J. C. (2002). ERIC Review: Educating Immigrants: The Community College Role. *Community College Review, 30*(2), 55–73. DOI:10.1177/009155210203000204

Szente, J., Hoot, J., & Taylor, D. (2006). Responding to the Special Needs of Refugee Children: Practical Ideas for Teachers. *Early Childhood Education Journal, 34*(1), 15–20.

Teranishi, R. T., Suárez-Orozco, C., & Suárez-Orozco, M. (2011). Immigrants in Community Colleges. *The Future of Children, 21*(1), 153–169.

UNHCR (2018). *Global Trends: Forced Displacement in 2017.* Geneva: UNHCR.

Van Hear, N. (2006). Refugees in Diaspora: From Durable Solutions to Transnational Relations. *Refuge, 23*(1), 9–14.

Walker-Dalhouse, D., & Dalhouse, A. D. (2009). When Two Elephants Fight the Grass Suffers: Parents and Teachers Working Together to Support the Literacy Development of Sudanese Youth. *Teaching and Teacher Education: An International Journal of Research and Studies, 25*(2), 328–335.

Yuval-Davis, N. (2006). Belonging and the Politics of Belonging. *Patterns of Prejudice, 40*(3), 197–214. DOI:10.1080/0031322060076933I

CHAPTER 5

Continuing Inequalities in South African Higher Education

The Changing Complexities of Race and Class

Crain Soudien

Introduction

Using higher education sociologist Martin Trow's (2007, 243) analytic framework, South Africa's higher education system 'tipped over' in the second decade of the twenty-first century. It had become a 'mass' system. Trow, in this framework, described three kinds of systems: elite systems where participation by the eligible age group of young people was between 0 per cent and 15 per cent; mass systems where participation rates were greater than 15 per cent but below 50 per cent; and universal systems where more than 50 per cent of the eligible population were enrolled at a university or College. The South African system, in terms of this, became a mass system in 2013 when 16.3 per cent of the eligible cohort among people classified African enrolled in higher education.[1]

The purpose of this contribution is to critically engage with the important achievement of massification in South African higher education. Its focus is on the nature of the shifts that have taken place in student enrolments and the significance of those shifts for understanding the nature of inequality. It does not address the larger question of what in South Africa is described as the 'transformation' of the higher education

[1] Race and ethnicity, and the accompanying ways in which people and groups are described and classified, are subject to intense political contestations. In the current period, the dominant practice is to use the classifications which were developed in the apartheid era. In the closing years of that period, South Africa's population was formally classified into four groups: African, white, coloured and Indian. 'African' referred to people who were black and indigenous. The term 'black' was developed during the apartheid struggle by the liberation movement, under the influence of Black Consciousness, firstly as a rejection of the term 'non-white' and, secondly, to foster unity among oppressed and disenfranchised African, coloured and Indian people. There is, in this current period, a shift underway where the term 'black' is being used, even in official documents, to denote people who would before have been described as African. This usage, contrary to the Black Consciousness usage, excludes people described as coloured and Indian.

system (see Soudien, 2010). That discussion focuses on the governance, the curriculum and the academic profile of the universities.

The question being considered here is not whether young people in South Africa are being afforded the opportunity to be able to explore, on an equitable, fair and just basis, their talents and abilities. They clearly are not. The system, even as it has tipped over into becoming a mass system, still excludes more than 80 per cent of those who are age-eligible. The question is whether inequality is still primarily racial, or, is it, as the sociologist David Cooper (n.d., 1) suggests, taking a different form? His argument is that with massification has come what he calls 'restratification' of the social character of the South African university. Race remains pertinent as a social determinant in his analysis, but class, which was always a factor in the South African social dynamic, has become significantly more important in the post-apartheid period. The gender dynamics of inequality also require analysis. A feature of the changing nature of access and participation in South Africa is, as McGregor (2010, 1) observes, the fact that there are now more women (55.5 per cent) than men (44.5 per cent) in the system, but they congregate in the lower levels and in particular fields of study. This analysis, for reasons of space, does not work with these developments.

The argument that is made in this chapter, using several sources of data, is that a shift is taking place in the nature of inequality in higher education. Central in this process is the increasing salience of socio-economic class. Important in making this argument, however, is the need to acknowledge the provisionality of the data. Cooper is pointing to important nuances in the nature of inequality as it bears on higher education enrolment patterns in South Africa. The evidence, however, has not yet been integrated to show how the changes that have taken place in the broader society play themselves out at the level of the university. The discussion has been advanced somewhat by the debate that took place at the University of Cape Town around its admissions policy after 2009 and the demand for 'free higher education' that was made during the 2015–2017 student protests in the country (See chapter by Ahmed elsewhere in this volume). These developments support Cooper's argument but do not categorically settle it. It is evident, as data adduced here from the National Income Dynamics Survey (NIDS) of the University of Cape Town show (see Hino et al., 2018), that the class structure of South Africa has changed. Most significantly, the black middle class has grown in size and complexity. What the precise implications of this for the higher education system are, it will be argued, have yet to be fully demonstrated. Cooper's restratification thesis is useful but awaits stronger empirical grounding. What is required, it will be argued, is a much clearer analysis of the relationship between the growth of the African middle class in South Africa and the shifts that have taken place in the student population. The implications of the changing class structure have not been adequately tracked and studied in analyses of the changing form of the higher education system and how policy should be developed to deal with access.[2]

The chapter begins with a description of the racial nature of the colonial and apartheid higher education systems and, building on this, proceeds to develop a high-level analysis of the shifting form of this system from 1993 to 2016. This shift is juxtaposed with determinative shifts that take place in the socio-economic structure of South Africa during this same period. The chapter concludes with the argument that higher education has moved, as a result of these socio-economic changes, from a heavily race differentiated system to one which has distinct class features. At the beginning of the making of higher education in South Africa, conditions of entry into the system were decidedly racial in their nature. In the present period, class is beginning to play as significant a role.

The Institutionalisation of Race in South African Higher Education

It is important to see the development of the education system in South Africa, including that of higher education, as a socio-political process rather than, as some analyses suggest (see, e.g., Kasibe, 2015), the fulfilment of a clearly thought-through racial project. There is, as Hendricks and Vale (2005) show in their history of Rhodes University, contestation about their purpose at the beginning of the history of many institutions. This involved the questions of both access and content. They become racial projects. This socio-political process solidifies, after almost three-quarters of a century at about the turn of the nineteenth century, around a set of institutions which are, extraordinarily in some senses, like and equal to their sister institutions emerging elsewhere in the world at this time. But, they are distinctly South African. They become, quite unselfconsciously, vehicles of racial exclusion. They are all unambiguously white.

---

[2] The reasons for this are in themselves an issue of sociological contention. The Higher Education Management System (HEMIS) for the country does not collect demographic data on socio-economic class. It concentrates on race and gender. Lost, it is argued here, is the opportunity to understand important developments that are, maybe, or maybe not, in the country's social formation. An example of this is the factor of social geography. This includes, obviously, the distinction between urban and rural but takes in also the big changes in class, cultural and economic factors that arise as mega-cities such as Johannesburg develop.

Higher education in South Africa begins with the establishment of the South African College School (SACS) in 1829. Critical about this beginning, as it is argued below, is that it takes place in an official policy environment of liberalism in the Cape. The South African College School was primarily a high school, but it had classes which prepared students for the examinations of the University of London in the United Kingdom (see Maharajh, Motala & Scerri, 2011, 197; Lulat, 2005). This College model, essentially the first phase of higher education in South Africa, contained the upper end of the schooling system and the undergraduate degree. It was replicated in several institutions in the Cape Colony: Stellenbosch Gymnasium in 1866, Gill College in 1869 in Somerset East, Grey College in Port Elizabeth and the Graaff-Reinet College around about 1871 (Boucher, 1975), Diocesan College in Cape Town in 1874 and St Andrew's College in Grahamstown in 1878 (Buckland & Neville, 2004, 2). At the turn of the nineteenth century only two of these institutions were permitted to continue university-level teaching, SACS and Victoria College, the successor to the Stellenbosch Gymnasium. SACS's university-level division became the University of Cape Town (UCT) and Victoria College became Stellenbosch University (SU), both of them through the granting of their formal charters in Acts of Parliament in 1918. Earlier, in 1896, a School of Mines was established in Kimberley. This institution was moved to Johannesburg in 1903 where it became, first, the Transvaal University College, then, in 1910, the South African School of Mines and Technology and, finally, in 1921, the University of the Witwatersrand (Wits). The name Transvaal University College was handed over to a new institution established in Pretoria in 1910 which became the University of Pretoria (UP) in 1930 (Maharajh et al., 2011, 197). Rhodes University College and Grey University College, later to become the University of the Orange Free State, were founded in 1904 (Buckland & Neville, 2004, 1). The South African Native College, later to become the University of Fort Hare, was created in 1916 under the administrative aegis of Rhodes University College. The Natal University College was established in 1909 (Maharajh et al., 2011, 197).

Supporting these Colleges was the University of the Cape of Good Hope (UCGH), which was established in 1873. Modelled on the example of the University of London, it was an examining and accrediting authority for the Colleges which had come into being in the country. It did not provide tuition. That took place in the institutions. It conferred, as the country's official accreditation body, the degrees for which students in the Colleges were registered. It was reconstituted in 1918 with a tuition function as the

University of South Africa (UNISA), one of the world's first distance-education institutions. It provided, not by design, the main opportunity for higher education for students of colour. Because students studied on a distance basis the University did not implement racial restrictions for access.

The autonomous institutions such as UCT and SU were reconstituted around the same time as the making of modern South Africa. The country was established as a Union in 1910 after the subjugation of the indigenous people in what are called 'The Frontier Wars' of the nineteenth century, the discovery of gold and diamonds in the Kimberley and Johannesburg areas between 1860 and 1890, and then the South African or Anglo-Boer War of 1899–1902. The universities were critical sites for the struggles between Afrikaner and English-speaking white South Africans, between black and white people, and between the emergent elites and working-class people. As Dubow (2006) notes, the higher education institutions were mobilised behind a complex 'race'-class project. This project was not explicitly articulated at the birth of the higher education system, rather it emerged. The liberal lobby for a non-racial franchise, after the abolition of slavery in 1838, was insistent that the education system had to be 'open'. It had to be led by a Superintendent-General for Education who would be 'able to estimate at their practical value, or rather at their *real nothingness*, with respect to his office, the microscopic differences of colour, Nation, Language, Rank and the Sectional distinctions of Religion' (Kies, 1939, 22, and see also Cape of Good Hope Report, 1854, 32–33). In the rapid shifts which took place on both the local and global fronts, this liberal sensibility was deliberately undone, over about half a century. Two dynamics contributed to this: on the one hand, the fervour of racial eugenics and, on the other, the demands of the burgeoning capitalist economy emerging out of the country's 'mineral revolution' – its discovery of gold and diamonds – which required large numbers of low-skilled and, as a consequence, cheap labour.

The eugenics movement has deep footprints in South Africa (see Breckinridge, 2014). They are visible in the person of Francis Galton tramping over the South African landscape with his toolkit of calipers and statistical charts, and solidified in the 'science' of white superiority and black inferiority as a principle of national unity in the nascent country's political imagination.[3] This principle was championed by Sir Langham

---

[3] South African racial terminology shifts and changes from the very beginning of the period of Dutch settlement in South Africa. In the period under discussion, 1820s to the present, the terms European,

Dale who became the second Superintendent-General of the Cape in 1859 and the first chancellor of the UCGH in 1873.[4] Education was central in Dale's politics. People of colour could not be allowed the opportunities for self-improvement through the educational system that were being made available to the emergent white elite. They had to be forced onto the labour market on terms of structural inferiority. The Colleges were central to this project.

While some of the early Colleges were relatively liberal-minded in terms of gender – institutions such as SACS begin to admit women as early as the 1870s – they quickly adopted Rhodes and Dale's racial approach. The first institution where this approach became evident was SACS, which came under pressure in 1910 from Dr Abdullah Abdurahman, a prominent 'coloured' politician from Cape Town, to accept a young 'coloured' man, Harold Cressy.[5] Having been turned away from Rhodes, after having initially been accepted, Cressy applied to SACS. As Adhikari (2012, 19) says, 'after much deliberation, and in the face of strong opposition within its ranks, the Council of the South African College finally decided to admit Cressy'.[6] The challenge would be repeated in 1923 when the Council again demurred: 'it would not be in the interests of the university to admit native or coloured students in any numbers, if at all' (Phillips, 1993, 114–115). It would yield for a small number of students.[7]

Native, Boer, Brit, Bantu, white, non-white, black, the highly pejorative term 'Kaffer', coloured, Indian and African are all used both officially and unofficially. Other pejorative terms are also in circulation.

[4] Not only was Dale concerned about 'the mixture of the sexes in so many of the established schools . . .', but he was '*alarmed*' (author's emphasis) at 'the greater or lesser intimacy into which European children, especially in the country, are thrown with the unrefined nature and habits of the native calls us to be watchful in regulating and maintaining a proper standard of morality' (Cape of Good Hope, 1860, 5, and see Beinart, 1994, 68–69).

[5] Cressy had made successful application to Rhodes University College in 1909 (Adhikari, 2012, 18). Believing that he had been accepted, 'Cressy set out for Grahamstown. There he intended to fulfil a burning ambition . . . . One can readily imagine Cressy's anguish and frustration, when university officials, upon seeing the colour of his skin, summarily rejected his application' (ibid).

[6] The Council met twice over a period of a month to come to this decision. Despite its constitution which made it clear that 'the departments of the College are open without restriction as to creed or colour to all applicants', important members of the College's Council, such as F.J. Centlivres and WT Buissine, argued that it 'would be detrimental to the interests of the South African College to admit coloured scholars' (Adhikari, 2012, 16). The decision held, however.

[7] Phillips describes this attitude in the following ways:

> This (to keep students of colour out) it was felt was especially true with regard to its medical course, which was closed to blacks lest it lead to mixed classes and white patients being examined by black medical students . . . . A similar bar was put on Fine Arts courses in which white models posed for black undergraduates . . . . The handful of 'coloureds' who were admitted to UCT in these years . . . were mainly teachers registered for Arts or Education degrees. Up to 1929 five had graduated. (Phillips, 1993, 114–115)

Similar issues played themselves out elsewhere in the country. At the University College of Natal, for example, a Mr Wahed, 'an Indian resident at Pinetown ... [made enquiries] regarding admission to University classes' (Brookes, 1966, 43).[8] Only after an order of the court in 1926, indicating the presence in the political system of alternative understandings of people's rights and entitlements and threatening withdrawal of recognition of the College's status as an institution of higher education, did it admit its first two students of colour in 1926. The order was implemented by establishing a parallel class in the College for students of colour (Brookes, 1966, 44).

These begrudging decisions to allow a handful of people of colour into the mainstream institutions meant that by 1948, when the National Party (NP) came into power, there were only 950 black students (African, Indian and coloured) compared to almost 20,000 white students. The majority of these black students were at the Universities of Cape Town, Natal and Rhodes (Malherbe, 1977, 731). White Afrikaans universities refused to admit students of colour. The only institution to which black people would have had access at that point was UNISA.

A third phase of higher education development occurred in 1959. The NP government, responsible for introducing Bantu Education, the policy through which education was provided on strict ethnic grounds, passed the Extension of University Education Act. This Act was responsible for the creation of a generation of new universities – all of them founded on racial and ethnic grounds, in line with the separate development principle: the University Colleges of the North for Sotho/Venda and Tsonga-speaking students, Zululand for Zulu speakers, Western Cape (UWC) for coloureds and Durban-Westville (UDW) for Indians (Badat, 1999, 61). The University College of Fort Hare, which up to then had admitted Africans, coloureds and Indians, was restricted to people deemed to be Xhosa. The Rand Afrikaans University was established, specifically for Afrikaans-speaking white people, and the dual-medium, English and Afrikaans, University of Port Elizabeth, for white people. The total number of students of colour in the system at that point was 4,207 out of a total enrolment of 39, 390 students in the system (Badat, 1999, 51).

As Badat (1999, 62) points out, black student numbers rose dramatically as a result of the establishment of the new ethnic universities. Interestingly, also, in the first few years of this phase of the history of the system, black

---

[8] The institution's Council replied that it was 'not prepared to entertain the proposal' (Brooks, 1964, 43). It was tested again in 1921, when it received a second application from another 'Indian' applicant. Some members of the Council appealing to the idea of an 'open university' supported the application. It was, however, turned down.

students moved out of the historically white universities. At the beginning of this phase of development, in 1960, there were 640 students in the new ethnic institutions. Almost ten years later, in 1969, there were 3,774 (Maharajh et al., 2011, 193). The number of white students in 1968, not including UNISA, was 49,604 (ibid).

The Post-Apartheid University

What, against this history, did the new South African government inherit when it came into power in 1994? Significantly, first of all, the system was deeply racialised. Race, qualified always by complex class forces, was the primary social reality within each of the universities. Written into the narratives of every single institution during the apartheid era were the racial classifications of the period. These were challenged during the struggles against apartheid that took place between the 1970s and the 1990s. But the institutions and their students suffered. The racialised character of the institutions developed during their thirty-year histories, from the late 1950s to the 1980s, remained, for the most part, relatively intact. The University of Transkei continued, as it still does today, as Walter Sisulu University, to defend a 'Xhosa' identity; the University of Venda existed in a deep symbiosis with 'Venda' homeland politics; the University of Zululand had the unmistakeable grip of 'Zuluness' over it; and the Potchefstroom University for Christian Higher Education, North-West University today, stolidly held on to its conservative Afrikaans identity.

At the same time, and this is the second point about the apartheid legacy, from about the middle of the 1980s, as a result of internal pressure – the 1976 Soweto Uprising and the struggles in the schools, townships and places of work – and the external trade boycott against South Africa, some of the most egregious features of the apartheid system were being dismantled. This began with the abolition of what was called 'petty apartheid' – the Group Areas Act and the prohibitions on 'inter-racial' contact – and culminated in the unbanning of prohibited organisations such as the African National Congress and the Pan African Congress of Azania in 1989. The public schooling system had 'opened' up. Black children, through what was called the 'Model C approach' which gave white schools the option of opening up their admissions to children of colour, were rapidly entering privileged schools (see Carrim & Soudien, 1999). In tandem with this, historically white universities began to relax their restrictions on black people, most notably in granting them, against the law, residence places. At UCT, moves to integrate the residences were initiated in 1981 and the institution itself, from having less than 10 per cent black enrolment, was by 1993 a third black (Saunders, 2016, 10). As a result, the university system, still significantly racial in its architecture, was in dynamic flux in 1994. A large and complex system consisting of thirty-six institutions, including a new category of technically orientated higher education entities called 'technikons', it was already a landscape in reformulation.

Notwithstanding the changes taking place in the South African political situation, the primary driver of inequality in the social system at the end of apartheid continued to be racial discrimination. The first and most important step taken by the government to address this was the publication of the *Education White Paper 3* (WP3) in 1997. This WP committed the new government to the following:

- Promot(ing) equity of access and fair chances of success to all, . . . while eradicating all forms of unfair discrimination and advancing redress for past inequities.
- Meet(ing), through well-planned and co-ordinated teaching, learning and research programmes, national development needs . . . [for] a growing economy operating in a global environment.
- Support(ing) a democratic ethos and culture of human rights . . .

The second critical move was the reorganisation of the 'size and shape' of the higher education system. This arose as a result of the National Plan for Higher Education which reaffirmed the commitments of WP3 and the restructuring of the entire system (see CHE, 2000). While some of the motivation for the reorganisation was increasing efficiency, its central purpose was to lay down the architecture for a transformed post-apartheid higher education system. The proposals were contained in a Government Gazette entitled *Transformation and Restructuring: A New Institutional Landscape for Higher Education* (Maharajh et al., 2011, 202). The existing thirty-six institutions were scaled down to twenty-three through processes of mergers and consolidations.

To support this critical restructuring of the system, a National Student Financial Aid Scheme (NSFAS) was established in 1999 through the National Student Financial Aid Scheme (NSFAS) Act of 1999 (Republic of South Africa, 1999, 2). The purpose of NSFAS was specifically to establish a fund to 'redress past discrimination and ensure representativity and equal access' (RSA, 1999, 5). Between 1991 and 2011, the scheme supported 991,759 students and made available R25.1 billion in grants and R2.3 million in loans to higher education (NSFAS, 2012). The focus of this support was previously excluded, largely African students.

These developments provided the setting for the momentous changes in enrolments that took place in the system after 1993. In 1993, African enrolments in the system stood at 191,000 students (CHE, 2004, 66). By 2016, twenty-two years later, enrolments in this group had grown to 701,482 (CHE, 2018, 3).

Over the period, enrolments in the whole system went from 799,490 in 2008 to 975,837 in 2016 (figures compiled from CHE, 2008, 2015 and 2018). This growth was due to substantial increases among black students in general, particularly among the African group. Between 2008 and 2013, African enrolments increased from 515,058 to 689,503. The percentage change between 1993 (191,000) and 2016 (701,482) was 267.3 per cent. There was growth too in white enrolments until 2008 when numbers grew to 178,140. Thereafter, interestingly, numbers declined to 152,489 by 2016. Partly accounting for the decline in white student numbers was an increase in the number of students with the classification 'unknown'. These stood at 6,383 in 2011 and rose to 11,589 in 2015 (CHE, 2018, 3).

Table 5.1 provides a picture of what the changes looked like for the period 2000 to 2016.

Table 5.1 *Headcount enrolment and growth by race (2000–2016)*

Actual enrolment	African	Coloured	Indian	White
2000	317 998	30 106	39 558	163 004
2001	353 327	32 900	43 436	173 397
2002	370 072	37 906	47 567	178 871
2003	403 325	42 390	51 611	184 964
2004	453 621	46 091	54 326	188 714
2005	446 945	46 302	54 611	185 847
2006	451 107	48 538	54 859	184 667
2007	476 680	49 001	52 579	180 435
2008	515 058	51 47	52 401	178 140
2009	547 686	55 101	53 562	179 232
2010	595 963	58 219	54 537	178 346
2011	640 442	59 312	54 698	177 365
2012	663 123	58 692	52 296	172 654
2013	689 503	61 034	53 787	171 927
2014	679 800	60 716	53 611	166 172
2015	696 320	62 186	53 378	161 739
2016	701 482	61 963	50 450	152 489

Compiled from CHE, 2008 and 2015, 2018

Most critical about these statistics is, of course, the growth in the numbers of African students. Between 2000 and 2016, they increased by 120.5 per cent. In terms of participation rates for the eligible population cohorts (ages 20–24), the figure for Africans grew from 10 per cent in 2001 to 12 per cent in the years 2005 and 2006 and had reached 14 per cent in 2011 (see McGregor, 2014, para 9 and Scott, Yeld & Henry, 2007). In 2013, the rate for the whole African population, not focusing on the 20–24 age group, increased to 16.3 per cent (own calculation). For people classified coloured, it grew from 8.5 per cent to 13 per cent and Indians from 42 per cent to 51 per cent in the period 2006 to 2011. The white participation rate remained stable at 59 per cent over the period. Female participation across all the groups increased from 15 per cent to 18 per cent, while the male rate went up from 13 per cent to 14 per cent.

Importantly, most of the major institutions had become majority black by the turn of the twentieth century. By 2008, 51 per cent of the 17,896 students at UCT were deemed to be black. By 2013, this had risen to 58 per cent of the 20,078 South African students registered at the university. The proportion of white students fell to 42 per cent in 2013 (GroundUp, 2015, 1). In 2017, out of a total headcount of 28,703 students, 30 per cent were African, 16.1 per cent coloured and 7.9 per cent Indian (UCT Annual Report 2017, 39). The numbers of African students at the University of the Witwatersrand in 2017 were even greater. Out of its enrolment of 38,161 students, 81.7 per cent were black (University of the Witwatersrand, 2017, 65). Africanisation, in racial terms, had been achieved.

Engaging with South Africa's Achievement

Denyse Webstock (2016, 6), part of a Council on Higher Education(CHE) panel reflecting on the achievements of the post-apartheid government in higher education, offers a critical assessment of the significance of the changes that had taken place in the system. Referring directly to the enrolment shifts she says: 'This must count as one of the most obvious achievements in the post-apartheid era, particularly as most higher education institutions now have a majority of black students in their student complements.'

Webstock is cautious, however, in reading too much into the next phase of higher education development. Two features of the shift raised questions for her. The first was the continuing disparity in participation rates of African and white students. As African enrolments tipped over into mass status in 2013, white participation rates were over Trow's 50 per cent cut-off for universal participation. They stood at 55 per cent. The second, which is relevant for the discussion that is developed below, is that success rates, also described as 'through-put rates' in South Africa, remained highly unequal for black and white students.

A Ministerial Committee appointed to look into student financial aid in 2009 found that 'only 19 per cent (125 210) (NSFAS-supported students and largely black) had graduated, while 48 per cent (316 320) had dropped out or otherwise not completed their studies)' (DHET, 2010, xiii). Scott (2010), examining the cohort of students which had entered the system in 2000, pointed out that only 30 per cent graduated after five years and 56 per cent left the system without graduating. In relation to a target of 80 per cent set by the Department of Education, between 1996 and 2006, the success rate of African students increased from 62 per cent to 65 per cent, while that of white students remained stable at around 77 per cent. The difference between the African and white success rate was also evident in a cohort analysis of first-time entering undergraduates in 2000, indicating that the average graduation rate for white students was double that of African students. By 2004, 65 per cent of African students had dropped out and 24 per cent graduated, while 41 per cent of white students dropped out and 48 per cent graduated. Of the 69,636 African students who entered the system in 2000, 40,713 had dropped out by the end of 2003. At the end of 2000, the first year of registration, 21,096 did not return. Only 13,394 were able to graduate within that time period. The rest remained within the system without having completed their studies (all these findings are based on Scott, 2010).

The substance of Webstock's analysis is that the system had changed in critical ways. It had become more 'unified' and 'cohesive' (Webstock, 2016, 6). This 'cohesiveness', however, she argues, 'masks continuing levels of inequality for students and differences in quality of education . . .' (ibid). The 'continuing levels of inequality', for her, were manifest, as described above, in the racially skewed success rates of African and white students.

Cooper's (n.d.) thesis, in contrast to that of Webstock, is that a 'partial' revolution in African enrolments had taken place at the historically white universities in the first five years after 1994. Where the historically white Afrikaans universities began with very small African enrolments at the beginning of the 1990s, by 1998 this enrolment had grown to 23 per cent at the University of Pretoria, and over 50 per cent at the Rand Afrikaans University and the University of Port Elizabeth (Cooper, n.d., 3), a development that is consistent with Webstock's thesis. However,

Cooper then goes on to argue that more significant changes occurred after 1998 which were responsible for producing a re-stratification.

What was this re-stratification? Essentially, it was that after the major spurt of Africanisation had taken place in the 1990s, the system was beginning to reflect much stronger class-like features. According to Cooper, these class features produced enrolment patterns in the institutions that were, after 1998, distinctly more difficult to classify as neat race-defined outcomes. He found that, while African enrolments remained large and growing in absolute terms, they were dropping proportionately at research-intensive institutions, such as the University of the Western Cape (UWC), UCT, UP and SU (Cooper, n.d., 6). At the middle-level research institutions, enrolments of African students increased, while at the less research-intensive institutions African enrolments were already at over the 95 per cent level. Cooper argued:

> Although this has not been researched in detail, I hypothesize that social class is fundamental as one major factor here: African students from working/lower middle class households have been finding it financially difficult to afford a university education, while proportionately, particularly coloured middle class students have been taking up places again at UWC.

The point he was making was essentially that the 'revolution' had stalled. What had stalled it, however, were not 'race' effects but significantly now the socio-economic status of aspirant students. Poor students could not afford the costs of going to the elite universities and were entering where they could afford to.

The Growth of the African Middle Class

Cooper's thesis is informative and suggestive of how access patterns are shifting in the higher education system. As he says, however, more research is required. In particular, what is needed is a better understanding of the relationship between privilege and disadvantage in the broader society and the playing out of these dynamics in the university. Significant social changes have taken place in South Africa since the advent of democracy in 1994. These changes have not only changed the structure of inequality in the country; they are also highly significant for a discussion of inequality in the university.

The major change that has taken place in South Africa's social structure after 1994 is the growth of its African middle class. While there is disagreement among economists, sociologists and demographers about the definition of the middle class (see Southall, 2016, 43) and, as a result of these definitional differences, disagreement about the scale of the changes that have taken place, there is agreement that the African middle class has experienced significant growth as a result of the transition to democracy. While precise figures are not available, most analysts would agree that the size of this middle class was very small at the beginning of the transition. Researchers at Stellenbosch University estimate it at 350,000 in 1993 (Staff Writer, 2013). Contemporary estimates vary and, based on different analytical approaches, calculate the growth between 1993 and 2012 to be anything between 4 and 14 million (see Southall, 2016; Zizzamia, Schotte, Leibbrandt & Ranchod, 2016), with a buying power of over R400 billion as compared to the R3.8 billion buying power of middle-class adult whites (see Radebe, 2013). There are two distinctive points to take away from this analysis.

First, what emerges – of relevance to the question of black middle-class growth –is that a significant process of recomposition of the country's class structure occurred after and even as a result of the coming of democracy. This is evident in data compiled by the Southern African Labour and Development Research Unit at UCT. A recent paper published by the author and colleagues (Hino et al., 2018) shows the significant changes that occurred in household income. People had more disposable income. Hino et al. (2018, 20) argued that in households:

> [t]he distribution of income shifted slightly to the right from 1993 to 2008, mainly in the middle and in the tails of the distribution and shifted further to the right in 2015 at all levels of the income distribution, except at the very top. These results suggest that, from 1993 to 2015, there has been a rise in real incomes at all levels.

Figure 5.1 confirms that, as shifts have taken place in the South African society, they have brought with them new inequalities. Most noteworthy, inequality levels, in terms of the Gini coefficient, increased from 0.667 in 1993 to 0.698 in 2008 and fell slightly to 0.678 in 2015.

The National Income Dynamics Study data show that, in 1993, the household income distributions among the racial groups, what can be described as inter-racial differences, were quite far apart from each other, with some overlaps between the distribution of the African group and that of the coloured, but none between the African group and the white group. In 2008, the distances became less wide and the overlaps increased, mostly because the distribution of the African group shifted decidedly to the right,

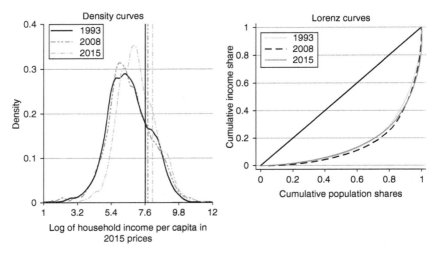

Figure 5.1 Distribution of real income per capita and Lorenz curves (1993–2015)
Source: Own calculations from weighted PSLSD 1993 and NIDS, 2008 & 2015.

signifying a decline in inter-racial inequality driven by improvement in household income in lower income brackets. At the same time, however, income inequality within racial groups increased. Measured by Gini coefficients, there have been large increases in intra-group income inequality from 1993 to 2008 for all race groups. Class distinctions, vertical inequalities, within groups grew significantly.

Much has been learnt. The work of Zizzamia et al. (2016) and his colleagues brings home several deeply important insights. Among these are the following:

1. That there is disagreement about the scale of the growth of the middle class;
2. That the African share of the middle class has expanded sharply; and
3. That, despite this expansion, Africans remain underrepresented in the middle class and have yet to consolidate their class position.

A second important takeaway from Zizzamia and his colleagues' analysis (2016), building on point 3 above, relates to the question of empowerment. How should African middle class access to higher education be approached? The approach they take is essentially a capability approach. They address the issue of access through a focus on the structural determinants that apply in a given context. A central element in the analysis is Sen's notion of capabilities 'as substantive freedoms (one) enjoys to lead the kind of life he or she has reason to value' (Zizzamia et al., 2016, 7). In terms of the outcomes of their analysis, Zizzamia and his colleagues come to important insights about ways in which the new middle class in South Africa might be approached. One of the most critical is that the vulnerability definition in its most up-to-date form is still not sufficiently sensitive to the complex social environment which it seeks to make sense of. The point they make is that 'while economic welfare is a fundamental determinant of the quality of people's lives . . . it is not a comprehensive measure of well-being' (Zizzamia et al., 2016, 20). Thus, though there is evidence of a move to middle-class status, groups within this middle class remain vulnerable. They do not yet have the protections – inherited wealth, property, insurance, other forms of capital – enjoyed by established middle-class communities, and this continues to impact on higher education through-put rates.

Conclusion

Policymakers and social analysts have worked with this new socio-economic data about the social character of South Africa in very preliminary ways. This is evident in various national studies, the studies of student demographic profiles – household income, family levels of education, schools attended – undertaken in preparation for UCT's admission policy and in the research undertaken by national enquiries around student financial aid.

Studies of the decisions of parents in relation to school integration soon after the new government formally abolished apartheid began to indicate the direction that middle-class black parents were taking. It was clear that they were beginning to invest heavily in education. Sixty-five per cent of this class were sending their children to either newly open former white public schools or private (non-state) schools. Vally and Dalamba (1999) found, for example, that by 1999, a quarter of all the children in Gauteng's former white schools were black. Hofmeyr and McCay (2010, 51–52) explained that '(n)early two decades later . . . (t)he majority of learners at independent (non-state) schools are now black . . . While the majority of the new black elite are sending their children to high-fee independent schools, the majority of learners are drawn from black middle and working-class families in the informal sector.'

These trends in the K-12 system were repeated in higher education. The UCT data showed that simple correlations between race and poverty were giving way to more complex determinants for disadvantage. A proposal for changing the admissions policy (UCT, 2014) argued that while there would have been, historically, a close correlation between race and disadvantage:

> Over the last few years, our research shows that the circumstances of black applicants have changed in various ways. Increasing numbers of our black applicants are coming out of excellent schools with very good NSC results, often from wealthy families. They can get into UCT in the general open competitive pool. They do not have to be in a different basket competing only with others of the same race. While there remain differences in cultural capital which may affect performance, these can be compensated for through weighting the marks using direct measures of parental disadvantage. We can achieve substantial diversity without needing to select students on the basis of race.

Strikingly, the UCT (2014) document explained that 'about a half of black students at UCT are now middle class. No longer can we assume that all black students are economically disadvantaged. We aspire to greater socio-economic diversity – in the interests of fairness, and equal opportunities.'

This conclusion, arrived at by UCT, was presented earlier by the Ministerial Review Committee into Financial Aid (Department of Higher Education and Training, 2010, 37) in justifying its recommendation that the racial basis for determining disadvantage should be replaced by socio-economic status:

> ... the socio-economic status of black students varies considerably across institutions. It is likely that many black students at the HAIs (Historically Advantaged Institutions) do not in fact qualify for NSFAS loans because they are not in need of financial aid. For instance, African students at UCT, are on average more affluent ... than African students at UFH. This can be seen in the respective proportions of students with negative EFCs (expected family contribution).

The Review Committee estimated that, of the 799,490 students registered in the system in 2008, 153,795 were eligible for financial aid, that is they fell below the eligibility threshold of a household income of R122,000 per annum (DoHET, 2010, 94). This could be read to suggest that approximately 20 per cent of the students enrolled in that year were deemed to be poor.

The black middle class has grown, but it is still weak. It is weak materially and in terms of the cultural capital that makes it possible for established middle-class groups to prosper in the university. It is this latter issue which was central and remains consequential in students' unhappiness with the established normative order of the contemporary university in South Africa. The material challenges experienced by this new middle class – often referred to as the 'missing middle' – are emerging in popular reports questioning the official assessment of students in need as only 20 per cent.

According to Mkansi (2014), large proportions of the almost 1 million students in the system, 843,566 in 2013, were entering on a constrained basis through either a loan or a bursary. He suggested that, in 2014, over two-thirds of the students at a rural university, such as the University of Limpopo, were beneficiaries of national student financial aid funding. A student, writing in response to Mkansi's (2014) article, said:

> My name is T, a student at the university of Limpopo doing my first year in B.Admin (local government), coming from a family of 7 with only my father working but failing to send me and my other siblings to varsity. I applied for NSFAS . . . (it) is meant to assist students like me who come from the vast rural areas of Limpopo but that did not happen as my application was not successful as the scheme doesn't have enough funds and that means me and many like me were supposed to go back and stay at home which led my father to visiting the local loan sharks so I could also at least attain my qualification looking at the current status of NSFAS and its covering of 50% of students in the country which means that many of our brothers and sisters . . . are either owing loan sharks . . . or they are seated at home . . . I'm afraid that's where me and others like me are going.

But actual socio-economic data about students' income levels, their family and household circumstances are not collected. What data we do have are inferential. It is available in the critical contribution brought to the discussion by Zizzamia et al. (2016). The essence of that insight is that the black middle class remains vulnerable. Available in the mix of data that are available is evidence of the ways in which large numbers of students are struggling in the system. But the two sets of data, that of the general population and the shifts that have taken place within it, and that for higher education, have not been correlated properly. This leaves arguments such as those advanced by Cooper incomplete. What can be said is that preliminary analyses of the present suggest that South Africa is going through a transition phase from elite education to mass education, manifesting tensions in the society which are quite different from those that characterised the early days of the system.

As Koen, Cele and Libhaber (2006, 404) noted, in 2004, at least 100,000 first-time entry students did not re-register 'because institutions exclude them on financial or academic grounds'. Current and dominant analyses of the difficulties experienced by students attribute these difficulties to race. These are most evident in the demands for free education for all made by the #FeesMustFall movement that brought South African universities to a standstill for significant periods of time between 2015 and 2017 (see Disemelo, 2015 and Msila, 2016).

That race continues to be material in shaping the life-chances of every South African young person is indisputable. What is beginning to make itself clear, however, is that very distinct class-like factors are coming into play in South African higher education. According to the Heher Commission (Commission of Inquiry into Higher Education and Training, 2017, 529) tasked with looking into the feasibility of free higher education after the student protests, 'the report accepts as its premise that free higher education (without an obligation to repay) should be available to those who cannot afford it' (ibid, 527). Recognising the vulnerability of the large majority of the country's massified student body, the report went on to state:

> Much the larger proportion of the student population today and in the foreseeable future, is and will be, through family circumstances, wholly or substantially unable to pay its way to an undergraduate or technical education. Many of those are and will be unable to support themselves and their 'dependent' (extended families) while studying, even if they can scrape together the tuition costs. In order to provide meaningful access, whether to university or College, higher education must be provided free ... (Commission of Inquiry into Higher Education and Training, 2017, 529).

This is indicative of a very important reality, that South Africa's efforts at transforming higher education remain unfinished and that, unlike previous efforts, the new frontier for transformation will need to be premised primarily, if not exclusively, on reducing the effect of socio-economic class as a determining factor for access to higher education.

REFERENCES

Adhikari, M. (2012). *A Biography of Harold Cressy, 1889–1916*. Cape Town: Juta Press.

Badat, S. (1999). *Black Student Politics, Higher Education and Apartheid: From SASO to SANSCO, 1968–1999*. Pretoria: HSRC Publishers.

Beinart, W. (1994). *Twentieth-Century South Africa*. Cape Town: Oxford University Press.

Boucher, M. (1975). Graaff-Reinet and Higher Education: A Decade of Decline, 1875–1885. *Kleio*, 7(2), 1–16.

Breckinridge, K. (2014). *The Biometric State*. Cambridge: Polity Press.

Brookes, E. (1966). *A History of the University of Natal*. Pietermaritzburg: University of Natal Press.

Buckland, R., & Neville, T. (2004). *A Story of Rhodes: Rhodes University 1904 to 2004*. Braamfontein: McMillan Publishers.

Cape of Good Hope (1854). Report on Public Education, Presented to the House of Assembly by Order of His Honour the Lieutenant-Governor, 1854. (CCP1/2/ 1/1.)

Cape of Good Hope (1860). Report of Public Education for the Year 1859, Cape Town, 1860. (CCP. 1/2/1/8 G.15.1.)

Cape of Good Hope (1891). First Report and Proceedings, with Appendices of a Commission Appointed to Inquire into and Report upon certain matters Connected with the Educational System of the Colony. Presented to Both Houses of Parliament by Command of His Excellency the Governor, 1891, Cape Town. G-9–91. (CCP 1/2/1/80.)

Cape of Good Hope. (1909). Report of the Council of the University of the Cape of Good Hope for the Year Ended 31st December, 1909. http://uir.unisa.ac.za /bitstream/handle/10500/6346/UCGHR1909.pdf?sequences=1.   Retrieved 6 June 2015.

Carrim, N., & Soudien, C. (1999). Critical Anti-racism in South Africa: Rethinking Multicultural and Antiracist Education. In S. May (ed.), *Critical Multiculturalism: Rethinking Multicultural and Antiracist Education* (pp. 153–171). London: Falmer Press.

Cooper, D., & Subotzky, G. (1999). *The Skewed Revolution: Trends in South African Higher Education, 1988–1998*. Bellville: The University of the Western Cape Education Policy Unit.

Commission of Inquiry into Higher Education and Training (2017). Report of the Commission of Inquiry into Higher Education and Training. www .justice.gov.za/commissions/FeesHET/index.html. Retrieved 6 October 2018.

Cooper, D. (n.d.). Social Justice and South African University Student Enrolment Data by 'Race', 1988–1998–2008: From 'Skewed Revolution to "Stalled Revolution"'. And Could Research-Based Policy Interventions Have Made a Difference to These Developments? Unpublished paper. www.lancaster.ac.uk /fass/events/necu7/papers/cooper.pdf. Retrieved 12 October 2018.

Council on Higher Education (2000). *Towards a New Higher Education Landscape: Meeting the Equity, Quality and Social Development Imperatives of South Africa in the 21st Century*. Pretoria: CHE.

Council on Higher Education (2004). *South African Higher Education in the First Decade of Democracy*. Pretoria: CHE.

Council on Higher Education (2008). *Vital Statistics*. Pretoria: CHE.

Council on Higher Education (2009). *Higher Education Monitor: The State of Higher Education in South Africa*. Pretoria: CHE.

Council on Higher Education (2015). *Vital Statistics*. Pretoria: CHE.

Council on Higher Education (2018). *Vital Statistics*. Pretoria: CHE.

Department of Education (1997). *White Paper 3: A Programme for the Transformation of Higher Education*. General Notice 1196 of 1997. Pretoria: Government Printer.

Department of Education (2001). *National Plan for Higher Education in South Africa*. Pretoria: Department of Education.

Department of Higher Education and Training (2010). *Report of the Ministerial Committee on the Review of the National Student Financial Aid Scheme*. Pretoria: DHET.

Department of Higher Education and Training (2011). *Green Paper for Post-School Education and Training*. Pretoria: Department of Higher Education and Training.

Disemelo, K. (2015). South African Student Protests Are about Much More than Just #FeesMustFall. *The Conversation*, October 27, 2015. http://theconversation.com /south-african-student-protests-are-about-much-more-than-just-feesmustfall-49. Retrieved 28 October 2015.

Dubow, S. (2006). *A Commonwealth of Knowledge: Science, Sensibility and White South Africa, 1820–2000*. Oxford: Oxford University Press.

GroundUp Staff. (2015). UCT and Transformation Part Two: The Students. *GroundUp*. www.groundup.org.za/article/uct-and-transformation-part-two-students_2845/. Retrieved 19 October 2018.

Hendricks, F., & Vale, P. (2005). The Critical Tradition at Rhodes University: Retrospect and Prospect. *African Sociological Review*, *9*(1), 1–13.

Hino, H., Leibbrandt, M., Machema, R., Shifa, M., & Soudien, C. (2018). Identity, Inequality and Social Contestation in the Post-Apartheid South Africa. www .opensaldru.uct.ac.za/handle/11090/946. Retrieved 29 September 2018.

Hofmeyr, J., & McCay, L. (2010). Private Education for the Poor: More, Different, Better. *The Journal of the Helen Suzman Foundation*, 56, 50–56.

Kasibe, W. (2015). Maxwele Being Denied His Rights. *The Cape Times*, Tuesday June 23, 2015, p. 13.

Kidd, A. (1910). *Higher Education in the Cape Colony, 1874–1910*. Grahamstown: Groott & Sherry Printers.

Kies, B. (1939). The Policy of Educational Segregation and Some of Its Effects upon the Coloured People of the Cape. Unpublished B Ed Thesis, University of Cape Town.

Koen, C., Cele, M., & Libhaber, A. (2006). Student Activism and Student Exclusions in South Africa. *International Journal of Educational Development*, *26*(4), 404–414.

Lulat, Y. (2005). *A History of African Higher Education from Antiquity to the Present: A Critical Synthesis*. Westport, Conn: Praeger.

MacGregor, K. (2010). South Africa: Universities and Gender and the MDGs. *University World News*, 2 May 2010. www.universityworldnews.com/post.php?story=20100502074043241. Retrieved 6 January 2019.

MacGregor, K. (2014). Higher Education in the 20th Year of Democracy. *University World News*, 27 April 2014, 317. www.universityworldnews.com. Retrieved 6 May 2015.

Macupe, B. (2013). Student Congress to March in Pursuit of Free Higher Education. *Sunday Independent*, July 21, 2013, p. 8.

Maharajh, R., Motala, E., & Scerri, M. (2011). South Africa: Reforming Higher Education and Transforming the National System of Innovation. In B. Goransson & C. Brundenius (eds.), *Universities in Transition: The Changing Role and Challenges for Academic Institutions* (pp. 193–218). Ottawa: International Development Research Centre.

Malherbe, E. (1977). *Education in South Africa, Vol. 2: 1923–1975*. Johannesburg: Juta.

Ministry of Education (2006). *Ministerial Statement on Higher Education Funding*. Pretoria: Ministry of Education.

Mkansi, L. (2014). South Africa's Funding of Higher Education. The Case of the University of Limpopo. *Projourno*, 14 August 2014. http://projourno.org/2014/08/south-africas-funding-of-higher-education. Retrieved 23 August 2016.

Msila, V. (2016). #FeesMustFall is Just the Start of Change. *Mail & Guardian Online*, 21 January 2016. https://mg.co.za/article/2016–01-20-fees-are-just-the-start-of-change/ Retrieved 22 October 2018.

National Commission on Higher Education (1996). *Report: A Framework for Transformation*. Pretoria: Government Printer.

National Student Financial Aid Scheme (2012). *Annual Report, 2012*. www .nsfas.org.za/docs/annual-reports/2012/Annual Report2012.pdf. Retrieved 20 October 2018.

Phillips, H. (1993). *The University of Cape Town 1918–1948: The Formative Years*. Cape Town: UCT in Association with Juta Press.

Radebe, K. (2013). Young, Middle Class and Black. *Moneyweb*, 8 May 2013. www.moneyweb.co.za/archive/young/middle-class-and-black.   Retrieved 8 January 2019.

Republic of South Africa. (1997). *The South African National Higher Education Act*. Pretoria: Government Printer.

Republic of South Africa (1999). *National Student Financial Aid Scheme Act, No. 56 of 1999*. Government Gazette, 413(20652).

Saunders, S. (2016). The Challenges of Politics and Collegial Relations. In Council on Higher Education (ed.), *Reflections of South African University Leaders*,

1981–2014 (pp. 1–16). Cape Town: African Minds and Council on Higher Education.

Scott, I., Yeld, N., & Hendry, J. (2007). *A Case for Improving Teaching and Learning in South Africa*. Higher Education Monitor No. 6. Pretoria: Council on Higher Education.

Scott, I. (2010). Who is 'Getting Through' in South Africa? Graduate Output and the Reconstruction of the Formal Curriculum. In D. Featherman, M. Hall, & M. Krislov (eds), *The Next 25 Years: Affirmative Action in Higher Education in the United States and South Africa* (pp. 229–243). Ann Arbor, MI: University of Michigan Press.

Soudien, C. (2010). Grasping the Nettle? South African Higher education and Its Transformative Imperatives. *South African Journal of Higher Education*, 24(6), 881–896.

Southall, R. (2016). *The New Black Middle Class in South Africa*. Auckland Park: Jacana Media.

Staff Writer (2013). South African Black Middle Class Pegged at 3 Million. *BusinessTech*, 24 October 2013. https://businesstech.co.za/news/general/48210/sa-black-middle-class-pegged-at-3-million/. Retrieved 19 December 2019.

Trow, M. (2007). Reflections on the Transition from Elite to Mass to Universal Access: Forms and Phases of Higher Education in Modern Societies since WWII. In J. Forest & P. Altbach (eds.), *International Handbook of Higher Education* (Vol. 18, pp. 243–280). Springer: Dordrecht.

University of Cape Town (2014). *'Breaking New Ground': Proposal for Modifying UCT's Undergraduate Admissions Policy*. (v. 23 April 2014). Unpublished UCT document.

University of Cape Town (2017). *University of Cape Town Annual Report 2017*. Cape Town: University of Cape Town.

University of the Witwatersrand (2017). *2017 Annual Report of the University of the Witwatersrand, Johannesburg*. Johannesburg: University of the Witwatersrand.

Vally, S. & Dalamba, Y. (1999). Racism, 'Racial Integration' and Desegregation in South African Public Secondary Schools. A Report on a Study by the South African Human Rights Commission (SAHRC). Johannesburg: SAHRC.

Webstock, D. (2016). Overview. In Council on Higher Education (eds.), *South African Higher Education Reviewed: Two Decades of Democracy*. Pretoria: CHE.

Zizzamia, R., Schotte, S., Leibbrandt, M., & Ranchhod, V. (2016). 'Vulnerability and the Middle Class in South Africa,' SALDRU Working Papers 188, Southern Africa Labour and Development Research Unit, University of Cape Town.

CHAPTER 6

Inequities in US Higher Education Access and Success
Obstacles and Opportunities for Marginal Populations

Richard Kazis

If the ladder of educational opportunity rises high at the doors of some youth and scarcely rises at the doors of others, while at the same time formal education is made a prerequisite to occupational and social advance, then education may become the means, not of eliminating race and class distinctions, but of deepening and solidifying them.
(President Harry S. Truman Foreword to Report of the Commission on Higher Education, 1947)

Across developed countries, patterns of higher education access and success have become increasingly important causes and consequences of inequality in income, wealth and social outcomes (Borgonovi & Marconi, in this volume). Every country has its own distinct disparities and inequities, reflecting complicated interactions among past patterns of individual preparation for and access to higher education, characteristics of the nation's higher education institutions, and developments in governmental policy and institutional practice.

In the United States, deep, persistent disparities in higher education outcomes exist by race/ethnicity and income. Given a legacy of exclusion from mainstream public Colleges and universities through state and federal policies, and concentration in under-resourced, low-quality elementary and secondary schools, African Americans and Native Americans significantly underperform White and Asian peers in educational attainment and achievement. Higher education outcomes for immigrants are mixed. Immigration status is not a significant barrier to higher education for newcomers from Europe, East Asia and most of South Asia. However, migrants from Mexico and other Latin American countries have great difficulty securing a College education in the United States (as do immigrants from some Southeast Asian countries, such as Laos and Cambodia)

(Baum & Flores, 2011).[1] Students from low-income households have much lower College attainment rates than do those from more affluent households – even when they demonstrate comparable levels of academic preparation (Holzer & Dunlop, 2013). The disparity in College attainment among students with similar high school academic preparation is greater by income level than by race or ethnicity (Backes, Holzer, & Velez, 2015).

Elsewhere in this volume, scholars highlight challenges facing members of two US groups: indigenous native populations; and immigrants with undocumented migration status. This chapter places those analyses in a broad framework for understanding US higher education trends and the pervasive disparities of opportunity that both reflect marginal status and contribute to further marginalisation. The chapter presents an overview of the nature and extent of inequities in College attainment, with particular attention to race/ethnicity and income. It then turns to evidence-based recommendations for narrowing these gaps, some of which can be implemented by committed institutional leaders, but others of which will require significant policy innovation – and political battles.

Key findings include:

- Disparities in College enrolment by race and ethnicity have been shrinking for several decades; at the same time, more nuanced obstacles to equitable access have emerged. Access to opportunity is affected not just by whether one attends College, but also by the institution and programme one attends.
- College success, not access alone, is the gateway to economic advancement. As the labour market value of a College credential has risen, a middle class standard of living is increasingly dependent upon completing a post-secondary degree or certificate. Completion rates vary significantly by race and ethnicity and by family income.
- Stratification of higher education opportunity by race and ethnicity and by income has been on the rise, exacerbating disparities in higher education outcomes. Elite, selective Colleges are becoming less diverse; African American and Latino students are increasingly concentrated in non-selective two- and four-year institutions.

---

[1] The top three countries of origin for US immigrants in 2017 were Mexico, China and India. By far the largest group, legal and unauthorised, has come from Mexico (Pew Research Center, 2019). Fifty-four per cent of all first- and second-generation immigrant children in 2017 were of Hispanic origin (Child Trends, 2018). Because Mexican and other Latino immigrant populations are so large and tend to have difficulty in higher education, this chapter focuses on obstacles and opportunities facing this population, not immigrants as a group. (Overall, US immigrants are better educated than at any time in the past.)

- For students from marginalised populations who complete a credential, economic and social success may still be slow compared to White and Asian peers, because of the debt load they take on in College and the comparatively weak social capital they develop while enrolled.
- Because academic preparation is so important in determining a student's post-secondary options, reducing systemic inequities in higher education will require significant improvements in elementary and secondary education for young people from marginalised populations. There is growing evidence, though, that gaps in higher education attainment can be narrowed by thoughtful, proactive innovations in governmental policy and institutional practice.

Patterns of Enrolment in US Higher Education

For low-income and other marginalised groups in the United States, higher education is an increasingly critical gateway to social mobility and economic opportunity. Rising employer demand for College-level academic, technical and social skills has boosted the economic payoff to earning a College credential. The gap between the earnings of high school and College graduates doubled between 1980 and 2000 and has stabilised at a high level since (Autor, 2014). Median lifetime earnings for individuals with baccalaureate degrees are about twice that of individuals with no more than a high school diploma (Schanzenbach, Bauer, & Breitwieser, 2017).

The labour market's reward for College-going has been pronounced since the 2008 recession. During the recession, individuals with post-secondary degrees experienced lower unemployment and steadier employment than those without (Eberly & Martin, 2012). During the recovery, as many as 95 per cent of new jobs created went to workers with a College credential (Carnevale, Jayasundera, & Gulish, 2016).

The American public has responded rationally to the rising value of a College education since World War II. In 1940, US Colleges and universities enrolled only 1.5 million students. By 1970, enrolment had jumped to just under 8 million; today, close to 17 million students attend undergraduate institutions.

Four-year public universities, two-year community Colleges, and for-profit certificate and degree-granting schools all grew rapidly at different points in the post-war era to serve the increasing number of Americans demanding access to post-secondary learning.[2] Enrolment in two-year degree-granting community Colleges, for example, grew fifteen-fold between 1950 and 1970, from 168,000 to 2.1 million, and continued to expand, reaching about 6 million students in the fall of 2017 (Thelin, 2011; U.S. Department of Education, 2019). For-profit College enrolment grew 600 per cent to around 2 million students between 1990 and 2010, targeting a population that included many who would not otherwise have enrolled in College (Beaver, 2017).[3]

As enrolments expanded, lower income and marginalised demographic groups started to narrow access gaps that had long characterised US higher education. The percentage of recent high school graduates from the lowest family income quartile who enrolled in College within a year rose steadily from 36 per cent in 1984, peaking in 2008 at 56 per cent (U.S. Department of Education, 2015). During these years, low-income students narrowed the enrolment rate gap between themselves and their middle- and upper-income peers (U.S. Department of Education, 2016).

The racial and ethnic mix of College students also became more diverse. Between 1976 and 2015, Hispanic students, as a percentage of all US residents enrolled in degree-granting post-secondary institutions, rose from 4 per cent to 17 per cent; for Blacks, the increase was from 10 per cent to 14 per cent and for Asian/Pacific Islander students from 2 per cent to 7 per cent. During the same period, White students as a percentage of all students in higher education fell from 84 per cent to 58 per cent (U.S. Department of Education, 2018).

Patterns of Completion

However, College enrolment alone is less and less a determinant of economic advancement and success. For today's high school graduates, College-going is virtually universal: roughly 90 per cent of graduates will

---

[2] A distinctive aspect of US undergraduate education is the multiplicity of institutional types that enrol students, with different origins, serving different populations, offering different programmes, and operating under different resource and cost structures. These include: public community Colleges, which grant two-year associate degrees and occupational certificates that typically require a year or less; four-year open access public Colleges and universities that grant baccalaureate degrees; selective and highly selective four-year Colleges, most of which are private, non-profit institutions (serving a surprisingly small percentage of students); and two- and four-year for-profit Colleges. For a fuller description, see Thelin, 2011.

[3] For-profit enrolments have declined after their 2012–2013 peak, as a result of a strengthening economy and growing concern about their poor performance, which spurred greater regulation of for-profit Colleges and several waves of closures and consolidations during the Obama administration.

enrol in College at some point in their lives (Commission on the Future of Undergraduate Education, 2017). The economic value of a College education is associated with completing a programme and earning a credential.[4] Here, the US story is a disturbing one of persistent disparities in attainment along socioeconomic and racial/ethnic lines. Too many students of colour (particularly Hispanic and Black students) and/or from low-income households fail to finish the programme they start. Many who do not earn a credential leave College having incurred significant debt without gaining any labour market advantage.

Disparities in the post-secondary outcomes of US demographic groups result in large part from the interaction of two dynamics: (1) patterns of access to different segments of US higher education; and (2) completion patterns within each segment. Both institutional and personal factors contribute to systematic inequities in opportunity and success (Bound, Lovenheim, & Turner, 2010; Holzer & Baum, 2017).

Recent research highlights two kinds of institution-related disparities that penalise marginalised groups. Some researchers have analysed the relationship between student outcome disparities and growing inequities in the resources and status of different types of higher education institutions (Taylor & Cantwell, 2019; The Century Foundation Working Group, 2019). A second strand of research finds that, within each type of institution, some schools pursue strategies that more effectively narrow persistence and completion gaps. (Chetty et al., 2017; The Education Trust, 2016). Each points towards promising solutions, summarised later in this chapter.

According to federal data, in 2016–2017 there were 4,360 undergraduate degree-granting institutions in the United States: about 35 per cent were two-year degree-granting community Colleges and 65 per cent were four-year institutions. The government also tracks the number of Colleges and universities by 'control' (i.e., whether they are public or private, non-profit or for-profit). There were 1,682 private non-profit Colleges and universities, 1,623 public institutions and 1,055 private for-profit institutions in 2016–2017. Public institutions accounted for 78 per cent of undergraduate

---

[4] In the aggregate, there is an established hierarchy of post-secondary credentials in terms of labour market value: the lifetime earnings premium for a graduate degree exceeds that of a four-year baccalaureate, which has a bigger payoff than an associate degree, which in turn is more valuable than a one-year or shorter-term certificate. However, the return to post-secondary credentials is not so simple. Some certificates valued by employers (e.g., in IT or allied health) provide an average return greater than many associate and even baccalaureate degrees. Twenty-eight per cent of associate degree holders earn more than the average baccalaureate graduate (Carnevale & Cheah, 2018). Programme of study matters, as does whether a graduate finds work in their chosen field.

enrolments and private non-profit institutions for 17 per cent; private for-profit institutions enrolled only 5 per cent of undergraduates (Cahalan et al., 2019).[5]

Low-income, Black and Latino students are much more likely than White and Asian students to enrol in non-selective two- and four-year institutions, where both costs and admission requirements are lower. They are much more likely than their wealthier peers to attend schools that confer certificates and associate degrees rather than baccalaureate degrees.

A smaller proportion of Hispanic and Black high school graduates enrol in a four-year College than White and Asian high school graduates; their proportion in selective and highly selective four-year institutions is even smaller. Instead, more than half of Hispanic College-goers enrol in two-year community Colleges. Black and Hispanic students are also more likely than their White and Asian peers to enrol in for-profit institutions, in part because they require minimal prerequisites and aggressive marketing to those populations (U.S. Department of Education, Office of Planning, Evaluation and Policy Development, 2016).

A study of ninth graders who graduated high school in 2013 found that students from the highest socioeconomic quintile were eight times as likely as students in the lowest quintile to attend a College categorised as most selective or highly selective (Cahalan et al., 2019). A 2011–2012 study of first-year undergraduates who had recently graduated high school found that about 50 per cent of students from the lowest family income quartile enrolled in community Colleges and another 14 per cent in the for-profit schools, compared to only 40 per cent of students from the highest income quartile enrolling in either a community College or for-profit school (Holzer & Baum, 2017).

Variations in enrolment patterns are attributable in part to individual factors. Foremost among them is academic preparation; others include family financial constraints that push students towards less costly options and schools that accommodate part-time enrolment, as well as lack of access to accurate information about College and programme choices, cost, and labour market return (Holzer & Baum, 2017).

---

[5] Two small anomalous subsets of post-secondary institutions are worth noting: in 2017, there were 102 Historically Black Colleges and Universities (HBCUs), all founded before 1964 when public higher education was essentially segregated, and 32 accredited Tribal Colleges and Universities (TCUs), funded primarily by the federal government. About 14 per cent of baccalaureates earned by African American students are earned at HBCUs; 9 per cent of native College students are enrolled in TCUs. (U.S. Department of Education, 2019).

The overall effect has been to sort College-goers in ways that present serious obstacles to economic opportunity for those trying to advance out of poverty. Low-income, Black and Hispanic, native, and older students, as well as first-generation College-goers – marginalised students – are concentrated in institutions that have lower completion rates and lower rates of economic mobility for graduates.[6] For example, the graduation rate for Hispanic students was 34 per cent at for-profit institutions in 2013–2014, compared to 52 per cent and 62 per cent at public and private non-profit institutions, respectively (U.S. Department of Education, 2016). The fact that half of Hispanic College-goers start at a community College, where the average completion rate is under 40 per cent, all but guarantees that, without changes in the patterns of enrolment or dramatic improvement in the outcomes of community Colleges, attainment rates for Hispanic students will lag those of White and Asian peers and inequities will deepen. The damage is multi-generational, as educational disparities dampen earning potential, reducing the capacity to invest in the next generation's education.

Recent research by economist Raj Chetty and his colleagues (2017) focuses on disparities in College students' economic mobility. Data on students' earnings in their early thirties and their parents' incomes were analysed for over 30 million College students from 1999 to 2013 and then summarised by institutions attended. This research, which reports on the fraction of students from the bottom quintile in family income who reach the top quintile, reinforces the view that institutional performance can either exacerbate or reduce disadvantages related to socioeconomic background. At any given College, students from high- and low-income families have similar earning outcomes over time. But two factors shape a College's ability to promote mobility: its success in helping low-income students advance to higher earnings; and the extent to which it enrols low-income students. Colleges that accelerate mobility but admit few low-income students are likely to widen rather than reduce economic inequities.

The researchers identified a group of institutions – mostly public two- and four-year Colleges and universities that serve as engines of upward mobility compared to peers nationally. At the same time, they found a disturbing trend. Access of low-income families to elite, selective

---

[6] Although students who successfully transfer from community Colleges to four-year programmes succeed at rates comparable to students who start at a four-year institution, the process of transfer is generally complex and inefficient. Many more students want to transfer than actually do so; and the transfer process itself too often acts as another barrier to earning a desired degree.

institutions increased very little between 2000 and 2011, even as these schools accelerated tuition reductions and other outreach strategies targeting high achieving low-income high schoolers. During that same period, access to more open access institutions with the highest mobility rates fell sharply, signalling a narrowing of pathways to success at those institutions.

Trend towards Increasing Disparities of Opportunity

The finding that mobility trends may be heading in the wrong direction is consistent with other recent studies of College opportunity in the United States, some of which focus on race and others on income. An analysis of enrolment trends in selective versus open access institutions by the Georgetown University Center on Education and the Workforce documents growing polarisation among the most and least selective schools – and an increase in racial stratification.[7] Among the nation's 486 most well-funded, selective four-year Colleges and universities, Whites are more concentrated today than in 1995; at the same time, concentration of African American and Latino students has increased across the more than 3,200 least well-funded two- and four-year institutions. Since 1995, 82 per cent of the increase in White enrolments has gone to the 468 most selective Colleges, while 72 per cent of new Hispanic enrolment and 68 per cent of new African American enrolment has been in open access two- and four-year schools (Carnevale & Strohl, 2013).

A new analysis of four-year institutions documents how the higher education landscape has been changing in ways that favour expansion of selective institutions and contraction of the most financially vulnerable open access Colleges and universities. Taylor and Cantwell (2019) argue that, since 1980, competition for resources and status has pushed more institutions to become selective, a trend accelerated by significant reductions in direct governmental funding of public Colleges and universities. Some institutions have improved their competitive position, but more have not. In the authors' terminology, high status and well-resourced elite and super elite institutions have held fairly stable in enrolments; the biggest change has been an increase in the number of vulnerable institutions that 'spend very little per student and rely on tuition for about

---

[7] Affirmative action admissions along racial lines is controversial and has been restricted by high-profile legal and legislative action, making it a less effective tool for increasing African American access to quality four-year schools, particularly flagship public research universities (Allen et al., 2018). Affirmative action designed to increase diversity based on income is becoming an alternative to explicitly race-based approaches.

80 percent of spending'. As the fortunes of higher education institutions have become more unequal, poorer students find their options more concentrated among lower-status institutions that have difficulty providing a quality education with available resources.

The Growing Challenge of Rising Cost, Debt and Default

In recent years, the United States public and policymakers have become concerned about the rising tide of student debt. College tuition has been climbing, state support for public higher education has been slashed, and need-based aid and scholarships have not been keeping pace – all in an era of stagnant or declining real wages. In this environment, the number of Americans securing loans to pay for College has increased rapidly (Federal Reserve Bank of New York, 2019). The media and public tend to emphasise aggregate trends: the total amount of student debt, now above $1.5 trillion, and the dramatic increase in the number of students who have taken on debt. For our purposes, of greatest interest is the extent to which the growth in student debt adds to the opportunity barriers facing low-income and particular racial and ethnic groups after leaving higher education.

Taking on student debt is generally a wise investment, assuming that the borrower earns a credential that has value in the labour market and that he or she has sufficient income and resources to pay off the loan. If that is not the case, though, the cost can far outweigh the benefit: even a small loan amount that goes into default can become a serious obstacle to further education, access to credit, and securing a home or a job.

There is growing evidence that student debt and loan default patterns are having a disparate effect on College-goers and graduates from different institutions and demographic groups. Black borrowers appear to be most disadvantaged. They are more likely to take on debt, more likely to borrow than other students pursuing the same degree, and more likely to drop out without earning a degree than White borrowers (Goldrick-Rab, Kelchen, & Houle, 2014; Huelsman, 2015). When they graduate, Black College students owe $7,400 more on average than their White counterparts ($23,400 versus $16,000). Within four years after graduation, the Black-White debt gap more than triples, reaching $25,000, due in part to higher graduate school borrowing by Blacks but also to the greater difficulty many Blacks have paying off undergraduate loans. The experience of Black and White borrowers diverges by four years after graduation: nearly half of all

Black graduates owe more on their federal undergraduate loans than they did at graduation versus only 17 per cent of White graduates (Scott-Clayton & Li, 2016).

Students at community Colleges are particularly at risk, not because they carry large debt, which they do compared to four-year students, but because they are more likely to drop out without earning a credential. Moreover, the certificates and degrees they earn often have limited labour market value, making it harder for them to repay their loans from earnings (Holzer & Baum, 2017). The reliance of students at for-profit Colleges on loans and the higher levels of debt they take on to pay for-profit tuition charges – coupled with the poor outcomes of many for-profit schools – leaves these students particularly at risk of default.

Over one million student borrowers default annually on their loans. Default rates are highest among those who started College with disproportionate barriers to success – insufficient financial resources, imperfect information on College costs and benefits, and inadequate knowledge of what it takes to navigate and persist in higher education. Compared to borrowers who do not default, defaulted borrowers are more likely to have low incomes (65 per cent of defaulters versus 36 per cent of other borrowers) and to be Black (33 per cent versus 14 per cent). They are more likely to have left school without completing their programme (49 per cent versus 23 per cent) and to have attended a for-profit institution rather than a public or non-profit school (45 per cent versus 17 per cent) (The Institute for College Access and Success, 2019). They are generally not students with above average loan balances, but rather students who have left College with no credential and/or after enrolling in only a few courses.

Researchers have recently gained access to new government data sources that allow for tracking of debt and default patterns of two student cohorts for up to twenty years. One researcher working with these data found them so troubling that she titled a paper *The Looming Student Loan Crisis Is Worse than We Thought* (Scott-Clayton, 2018). Her analysis suggests that nearly 40 per cent of students who entered College in 2004 may default on their student loans by 2023.

Institutional and individual patterns of enrolment and completion interact in ways that generate additional barriers to opportunity for groups least equipped to avoid default. The default problem is worst for students who attended a private for-profit College: 43 per cent of the 2003 cohort who started in a for-profit defaulted within twelve years, a jump of 20 percentage points over the 23 per cent rate of the 1995 cohort. And for no group are the long-term trends more troubling than for Black borrowers. Twelve years after entering College, the median Black borrower owed more than they originally borrowed, unlike the typical Latino and White students, who made progress reducing their total debt. Nearly half of African Americans who borrowed for their undergraduate education defaulted on a federal student loan. Among Blacks who completed a baccalaureate degree, fully a quarter defaulted, compared to only 9 per cent of all borrowers who completed a baccalaureate. After twelve years, three-quarters of African American borrowers who dropped out of a for-profit school had defaulted on their federal student loan (Miller, 2017).[8]

What Can Be Done to Reduce Disparities in Higher Education Opportunity?

Recent decades have seen an explosion of research and proposals about how individual institutions, and state and federal policymakers can reduce the obstacles that individuals from marginalised populations face as they make decisions about College, navigate their chosen programmes, and advance into employment or further education.[9] Some proposed solutions require significant resources, others less so. Some can be undertaken by determined and creative institutional leaders; others will make little headway without significant shifts in public opinion and policymaker readiness to invest resources in initiatives that target low-income and marginalised populations. The current 'free College' debate on expanding tuition-free public education to include the first two years of post-secondary education is a sign that the conversation has shifted, though it remains to be seen which strategies, if any, for addressing College attainment inequities will get traction in the current political environment.

No single response will be adequate: the higher education challenges facing low-income students and students of colour are complicated and intertwined. However, evidence from practice and policy point to directions for innovation and reform that, in concert, can help reduce barriers to opportunity. These include:

---

[8] Data on Hispanic students are both spottier and more complicated to use. On average, though, Hispanic completion, debt and default outcomes tend to fall between those of Whites and African Americans (see Miller, 2017).

[9] An important strand of research and practice not addressed here argues for more effective Career and Technical Education during and after high school as a way to help students from low-income families advance in today's economy (See Holzer & Baum, 2017; Stevens, 2019).

- Improving the quality of elementary and secondary education for students in low-performing schools and districts;
- Making better data available to individuals, families and others on the performance of different post-secondary institutions and specific programmes of study – disaggregated by race, ethnicity and income;
- Using disaggregated student outcome data to strengthen institutional accountability for results;
- Encouraging and incentivising evidence-based practices that have demonstrated an ability to improve outcomes for students from marginalised populations;
- Reducing the cost of College for those with limited family resources; and
- Increasing funding for the segments of public higher education that serve a disproportionate number of low-income students and Black and Hispanic students, particularly two-year degree-granting community Colleges.

Improving K-12 educational quality: Academic preparation for College begins long before the final year of high school. There is an extensive literature on the ways in which inequities in the quality and capacity of urban and rural schools penalise low-income and other potential College-goers, interacting with family background characteristics to make College-readiness less attainable (Orfield, 2009; Goldrick-Rab, 2010). While solutions to this challenge are beyond the scope of this review, reduction of disparities in elementary and secondary academic preparation will be an important part of any post-secondary success strategy. School and neighbourhood factors, including the stresses of poverty and isolation by race and/or income, will need to be addressed (Hanushek & Rivkin, 2009; U.S. Department of Education, 2016).

Making better data readily available for family and student College decisions: Inadequate data and support for good decision-making about College applications, programmes of study, and financial considerations play a role in making it more difficult for low-income students and students from marginalised groups to enrol and succeed in College. Low-income students and first-generation students with minimal support from family and friends who have previously succeeded in College face a bewildering set of decisions. If these students have attended under-resourced high schools, they are unlikely to have had much personalised advice from their academic counsellors. They may rely on the advice and experience of students from their high school, which may steer them away from applying to more rigorous Colleges (Hoxby & Avery, 2013). They may find the whole process so complicated and foreign that they make impulsive application decisions based on poor information.

More readily available and usable information about specific Colleges – presenting comparable data on completion rates, average time to degree, graduate earnings, annual and total cost of attendance – has been advocated by many as a way to reduce suboptimal decisions by students from underprepared and underinformed families (Page & Scott-Clayton, 2015). This may be particularly important for low-income students with high academic potential and record, since there is evidence that attending a higher quality institution can greatly increase the likelihood of completing College and earning a high-value credential. This is true for the decision to attend a four-year institution rather than a community College, since students who start at community College are less likely to transfer and complete a baccalaureate than those who start at a four-year institution. It is also important for low-income students and others who, with better information, could apply for and secure admission to a selective private College or state university flagship, increasing their odds of completion and success (Holzer & Baum, 2017).

Of course, for students with limited 'College knowledge', better information alone is typically insufficient: programmatic interventions that structure the College application process and simplify students' decisions are needed. Around the country, various models have emerged, some of which provide comprehensive support to groups of at-risk students and others that address specific obstacles such as completion of financial aid forms or preparation for College admissions tests (Page & Scott-Clayton, 2015). Even with better information and support, though, financial constraints can still pose a serious obstacle to College enrolment and optimal decisions about where to go to school.

Strengthening accountability for results and for reducing equity gaps: As the cost of College continues to rise, so does public concern about the return on investment for higher education. In this context, the availability of student outcome data, organised by institution and disaggregated by income level, race and ethnicity (as well as gender and age), is seen by many as an important lever for improving institutional accountability for results and equity. The popularity of the *U.S. News* College rankings demonstrates the power of public dissemination of comparative data; but the overemphasis on admissions selectivity in its rankings has had unfortunate effects on application and enrolment patterns. During the Obama administration, the federal government proposed a national ranking system that would define quality in terms of cost and outcomes and emphasise selectivity less. Although that proposal was abandoned, the Department of Education created a College scorecard that makes significant comparative cost and quality information publicly available.

States and the federal government have turned to the use of carrots and sticks – incentives and guardrails – to try to improve institutional performance. Over half the states have revamped the way they fund public higher education to be more outcomes-based, creating new formulas designed to reward institutions that do a better job of meeting state higher education priorities, including more completions, graduates in certain fields, and reduction of attainment disparities across demographic groups (Kelchen, 2018). There is little evidence, however, that these new funding models have had a significant effect on institutional decisions. Moreover, the new models run the risk of unintended heightening of income or racial/ethnic disparities (Gándara & Rutherford, 2018).

During the Obama years, the federal government took regulatory action to try to protect students from unscrupulous and poorly performing institutions – primarily in the for-profit sector. Occupational programmes covered by what was called the Gainful Employment rule were required to meet minimum thresholds with respect to their graduates' debt-to-income ratios, so that fewer students would take on debt to enrol in a programme that would not improve their earnings. Schools or programmes that failed to meet minimum requirements would run the risk of losing access to all federal financial aid for a period, which would result in losing students and perhaps having to close. The political battle over this rule was partisan and brutal. The Trump Administration's Department of Education chose not to enforce the rule and has since rescinded it (The Institute for College Access and Success, 2019).

Encouraging and incentivising investment in evidence-based institutional practices: A body of rigorous research has emerged identifying institutional practices that can improve student outcomes in College and reduce persistent attainment gaps. One important finding is the effectiveness of enhanced academic, financial and other supports for low-income students. A rigorous evaluation of the City University of New York's Accelerated Study in Associate Programs (ASAP) – which combines regular mandatory advising and student services, financial support and incentives for persistence, full-time enrolment, and early completion of remedial requirements – found that ASAP nearly doubled three-year graduation rates for low-income community College students with remedial needs (Scrivener et al., 2015). Other comprehensive initiatives that share these components show similar results of improved persistence and acceleration towards graduation (Bertrand et al., 2019).

A serious obstacle facing underprepared students when they enter College, particularly in open access institutions, is difficulty with College-level reading, writing and math skills. The approach Colleges have long used to remediate these skills – characterised by long sequences of stand-alone non-credit courses – has been shown by several decades of research to be a significant cause of College non-completion. In the early 2000s, over 60 per cent of incoming community College students and 40 per cent of four-year students were assigned to at least one remedial or developmental course (Chen, 2016). Careful research on the trajectory of these students revealed minimal gains in skills and post-secondary success and a serious dropout problem for students forced into remediation (Jaggers & Stacey, 2014). In response, institutions and states have tested a range of alternative approaches that appear to be improving outcomes, including: shorter course sequences, more accurate course placement, and curriculum redesign that embeds remediation into first College courses in English and math (Schak et al., 2017; Edgecomb & Bickerstaff, 2018).

One promising model for supporting students in simplifying their College and course selection – called Guided Pathways – is becoming popular in community Colleges and four-year open access institutions (Bailey, Jaggers, & Jenkins, 2015). Guided Pathways initiatives redesign institutional priorities to provide students with more structure and support in choosing an appropriate programme of study, taking the right courses, and progressing steadily and efficiently to credential completion. Other research suggests that engaging employers in helping to design programmes to prepare students for middle skill jobs in high demand fields – an approach called Career Pathways – can be an effective route to advancement for older workers with weak academic skills (Schwartz, Strawn, & Sarna, 2018). Guided Pathways and Career Pathways share a similar commitment to changing institutional practice in ways that invest in more structure and ongoing support, reduce the bewildering number of choices students have to make, and organise the entire institution in service of accelerated progress towards completion. This approach appears to be particularly helpful for low-income and other students with multiple risk factors increasing their odds of not graduating.

Reducing the cost of College for those with limited resources: As most state governments have reduced funding for higher education, students have seen tuition rise. Increased cost has a direct impact on College access and success for low-income students. According to one summary of the evidence, each additional $1000 in cost to students reduces enrolment by 3 to 5 percentage points and negatively impacts completion (TICAS, 2019).

Federal policymakers have addressed the high cost of College by introducing a variety of Income-Driven Repayment (IDR) plans designed to align student loan repayment and earning power. This is particularly helpful for graduates with high debt and low income. Strengthening and simplifying income-based repayment as a way to reduce the risk of default and lower overall cost to students was a priority of the Obama administration. President Trump favours maintaining IDR with some changes, but he has not yet acted on this agenda.

One response to the high cost of College that has achieved some traction is to make the first two years of College tuition-free for low-income students or students from a particular geographic area. College Promise programmes were birthed by philanthropic innovation in cities like Kalamazoo, Michigan and Long Beach, California. There are now over 200 College Promise programmes nationally. In general, they cover tuition and fees for community College degrees and occupational certificate programmes for eligible students (Miller-Adams, 2019).

The College Promise movement has evolved into a national 'free College' movement. Beginning with Tennessee in 2014, a growing number of states are implementing policy initiatives that enable students to attend community College (or the first two years of College) without having to pay tuition or fees. The models vary in their particulars: they may specify minimum grade requirements or include requirements that recipients stay in-state for several years after graduation. Most are structured as 'last dollar' scholarships, meaning that the state covers any remaining costs after students have taken advantage of all other available federal and state grants and scholarships. The evidence on these programmes is limited, since they are new; but research on Tennessee's Promise initiative finds evidence of increased College enrolment among lower-income high schoolers (Carruthers, 2019).

In the 2016 presidential election, free College became a rallying cry of the left wing of the Democratic Party, championed by Senator Bernie Sanders. Candidate Hillary Clinton countered with a proposal for 'debt-free' College. In the 2020 campaign, free College has entered the mainstream of Democratic higher education policy proposals. Candidate Elizabeth Warren pushed the debate ever further with a proposal to cancel federal student debt for the more than 44 million borrowers with student debt (McKay & Kingsbury, 2019).

Increasing the investment in institutions that serve lower-income students and students of colour: In the past year, several groups of scholars and policy experts have publicised what they see as significant underfunding of community Colleges, which contributes to unnecessarily poor student outcomes (Goolsbee, Hubbard, & Ganz, 2019; Century Foundation Working Group, 2019). They advocate for a recalibration of public investment between sectors of higher education, noting that for every dollar spent on education per student at a four-year public baccalaureate institution, only 75 cents is spent per community College student. Funding for student supports like advising, counselling and mental health resources is estimated to be 40 per cent higher on average in four-year public institutions than community Colleges, even though community College students tend to have greater academic, financial and social needs. Across public research universities, that advantage rises. Those institutions spend 60 per cent more on 'education and related spending' than do community Colleges.

Four-year open access schools also operate at a disadvantage. Selective public Colleges and universities in many states spend nearly three times as much per student as their open access counterparts – and the spending gap between selective and open access institutions has widened over time (Carnevale et al., 2018).

Resources matter, particularly at the community College level. In one study, a 10 per cent increase in community College per pupil spending in one year resulted in increased awards of certificates and degrees in the next two years of about 14.5 per cent (due perhaps to increased course offerings, shorter waiting lists, better guidance and smaller class size) (Deming & Walters, 2017).

Policy experts organised by the Aspen Institute argue for a significant new commitment to increasing the skills and productivity of the US workforce through public investment in community Colleges (Goolsbee, Hubbard, & Ganz, 2019). They estimate that raising completion rates of community College students ages 18 to 24 to the level of students in four-year institutions would result in 3.6 million young people earning College degrees by 2030, at a cost just shy of $12 billion a year. (The authors advocate another $10 billion annually to increase the share of workers age 25 to 64 with a credential, so that their workforce skills are better aligned with employer demand.) A group convened by The Century Foundation (2019) recommends that states immediately begin to increase their investment in community Colleges and that a federal-state partnership be established to support sufficient new investment across the country. Recognising that major shifts in public opinion and policymaker commitment will be needed to achieve funding adequacy, the group recommends a new body of research to establish, for the first time, what it costs to provide a quality community College education. They note: 'Much better research could greatly improve [policy] decisions, substantially boost the life chances of community College students, and jumpstart social mobility in America.'

Conclusion

Low-income students and several marginalised racial and ethnic groups in the United States (African Americans, Latinos and Native Americans, first and foremost) face serious barriers to higher education access and completion and to post-College economic success. If anything, the trend is moving towards greater polarisation and disparities of education outcomes. However, a growing body of research and practice, and an increase in public and policymaker focus on the high costs and uneven outcomes of undergraduate education, opens up possibilities for action to improve post-secondary performance and address persistent attainment disparities. As the United States tries to maintain economic vitality in the knowledge-based twenty-first century, new alliances may be able to advance a forward-looking institutional practice and public policy agenda designed to mitigate and reverse current trends.

REFERENCES

Allen, W., McLewis, C., Jones, C., & Harris, D. (2018, October). From Bakke to Fisher: African American Students in U.S. Higher Education over Forty Years. *RSF*, 4(6), 41–72. muse.jhu.edu/article/704127.

Autor, D. H. (2014). Skills, Education and the Rise of Earnings Inequality among the 'Other 99 Percent.' *Science, 344*(6186), 843–851.

Baker, R., Klasik, D., & Reardon, S. (2018). Race and Stratification in College Enrollment Over Time. *AERA Open, 4*(1), 1–28. journals.sagepub.com/doi/full/ 10.1177/2332858417751896.

Backes, B., Holzer, H. J., & Velez, E. D. (2015). *Is It Worth It? Postsecondary Education and Labor Market Outcomes for the Disadvantaged.* Washington: Center for the Analysis of Longitudinal Data in Education Research. www .caldercenter.org/sites/default/files/WP117.pdf.

Bailey, T. R., Jaggers, S. S., & Jenkins, D. (2015). *Redesigning America's Community Colleges: A Clearer Path to Student Success.* Cambridge: Harvard University Press.

Baum, S., & Flores, S. M. (2011). Higher Education and Children in Immigrant Families. *Future Child, 21*(1), 171–193.

Beaver, W. (2017). 'The Rise and Fall of For-Profit Higher Education'. *AAUP News.* January–February. www.aaup.org/article/rise-and-fall-profit-higher-education#.XQiDg9NKhoI.

Bertrand, M., Halberg, K., Hofmeister, K., Morgan, B., & Shirey, E. (2019). *Increasing Academic Progress among Low-Income Community College Students: Early Evidence from a Randomized Controlled Trial.* Chicago: University of Chicago Poverty Lab.

Bound, J., Lovenheim, M. F., & Turner, S. (2010). Why Have College Completion Rates Declined? An Analysis of Changing Student Preparation and Collegiate Resources. *American Economic Journal, 2*(3), 129–157. www .nber.org/papers/w15566.pdf.

Cahalan, M., Perna, L. W., Yamashita, M., Wright-Kim, J., & Jiang, N. (2019). *2019 Indicators of Higher Education Equity in the United States.* Washington: The Pell Institute for the Study of Opportunity in Higher Education.

Carnevale, A. P., & Strohl, J. (2013). *Separate And Unequal: How Higher Education Reinforces the Intergenerational Reproduction of White Racial Privilege.* Washington: Georgetown University Center on Education and the Workforce.

Carnevale, A. P., Jayasundera, T., & Gulish, A. (2016). *America's Divided Recovery: College Haves and Have-Nots.* Washington: Georgetown University Center on Education and the Workforce.

Carnevale, A. P., & Cheah, B. (2018). *Five Rules of the College and Career Game.* Washington: Georgetown University Center on Education and the Workforce.

Carnevale, A. P., Van Der Wurf, M., Quinn, M. C., Strohl, J., & Repnikov, D. (2018). *Our Separate and Unequal Public Colleges.* Washington: Georgetown University Center on Education and the Workforce.

Carruthers, C. (2019). *Five Things to Know about the Tennessee Promise Scholarship.* Washington: Brookings Institution. www.brookings.edu/blog/brown-center-chalk board/2019/05/06/five-things-to-know-about-the-tennessee-promise-scholarship.

Chen, X. (2016). *Remedial Coursetaking at U.S. Public 2- and 4-Year Institutions.* Washington: National Center for Education Statistics.

The Century Foundation Working Group on Community College Financial Resources (2019). *Recommendations for Providing Community Colleges with the Resources They Need.* New York: The Century Fund.

Chetty, R., Friedman, J., Saez, E., Turner, N., & Yagan, D. (2017). *Mobility Report Cards: The Role of Colleges in Intergenerational Mobility.* Working Paper No. 23618. Cambridge: National Bureau of Economic Research. opportunityin sights.org/paper/mobilityreportcards.

Child Trends (2018). *Immigrant Children.* Washington: Child Trends. www .childtrends.org/?indicators=immigrant-children.

Commission on the Future of Undergraduate Education (2017). *The Future of Undergraduate Education.* Cambridge: American Academy of Arts and Sciences.

Deming, D. J., & Walters, C. R. (2017). *The Impact of Price Caps and Spending Cuts on U.S. Postsecondary Attainment.* Working Paper 23736. Cambridge: National Bureau of Economic Research. www.nber.org/papers/w23736.

Eberly, J., & Martin, C. (2012). The Economic Case for Higher Education. *Treasury Notes.* December 13. www.treasury.gov/connect/blog/Pages/econom ics-of-higher-education.aspx.

Edgecomb, N., & Bickerstaff, S. (2018). Addressing Academic Underpreparedness in Service of College Completion. *Texas Education Review, 6*(1), 75–83.

The Education Trust (2016). *Using Data to Improve Student Outcomes: Learning from Leading Colleges.* Washington: The Education Trust.

Federal Reserve Bank of New York (2019, February). *Quarterly Report on Household Debt and Credit.* New York: Federal Reserve Bank of New York.

Gándara, D., & Rutherford, A. (2018). Mitigating Unintended Impacts? The Effects of Premiums for Underserved Populations in Performance-Funding Policies for Higher Education. *Research in Higher Education, 59*(6), 681–703.

Goldrick-Rab, S. (2010). Challenges and Opportunities for Improving Community College Student Success. *Review of Educational Research, 80*(3), 437–469.

Goldrick-Rab, S., Kelchen, R., & Houle, J. (2014). *The Color of Student Debt: Implications of Federal Loan Program Reforms for Black Students and Historically Black Colleges and Universities.* Madison: Hope Lab.

Goolsbee, A., Hubbard, G., & Ganz, A. (2019). *A Policy Agenda to Develop Human Capital for the Modern Economy.* Washington: Aspen Institute Economic Strategy Group.

Hanushek, E. A., & Rivkin, S. G. (2009). Harming the Best: How Schools Affect the Black-White Achievement-Gap. *Journal of Policy Analysis and Management*, *28*(3), 366–393.

Holzer, H. J., & Baum, S. (2017). *Making College Work: Pathways to Success for Disadvantaged Students*. Washington: Brookings Institution Press.

Holzer, H. J. & Dunlop, E. (2013). *Just the Facts Ma'am: Postsecondary Education and Labor Market Outcomes in the U.S.* IZA Discussion Paper 7319. Bonn: Institute for the Study of Labor. ssrn.com/abstract=2250297.

Hoxby, C., & Avery, C. (2013). The Missing 'One-Offs': The Hidden Supply of High-Achieving Low-Income Students. *Brookings Papers on Economic Activity*, *46*(1), 1–65.

Huelsman, M. (2015). *The Debt Divide: The Racial and Class Bias behind the 'New Normal' of Student Borrowing*. New York: Demos.

Huelsman, M. (2018). *Debt to Society: The Case for Bold, Equitable Student Loan Cancellation and Reform*. New York: Demos.

Jaggers, S. S., & Stacey, G. W. (2014). *What We Know about Developmental Education Outcomes*. New York: Community College Research Center, Teachers College, Columbia University.

Kelchen, R. (2018). *Higher Education Accountability*. Baltimore: Johns Hopkins University.

McKay, K. L., & Kingsbury, D. (2019). *Student Loan Cancellation: Assessing Strategies to Boost Financial Security and Economic Growth*. Washington: The Aspen Institute.

Miller, B. (2017). *New Federal Data Show a Student Loan Crisis for African American Borrowers*. Washington: Center For American Progress. www.americanprogress.org/issues/education-postsecondary/news/2017/10/16/440 711/new-federal-data-show-student-loan-crisis-african-american-borrowers.

Miller-Adams, M. (2019). *What Can States Learn from Local College Promise Programs?* Washington: College Promise. www.Collegepromise.org/cp-resources/policy-brief-what-can-states-learn-from-local-College-promise-programs.

Orfield, G. (2009). *Reviving the Goal of an Integrated Society: A 21st Century Challenge*. Los Angeles: The Civil Rights Project. civilrightsproject.ucla.edu/research/k-12-education/integration-and-diversity/reviving-the-goal-of-an-integrated-society-a-21st-century-challenge/orfield- reviving-the-goal-mlk-2009.pdf.

Page, L. C., & Scott-Clayton, J. (2015). *Improving College Access in the United States: Barriers and Policy Responses*. NBER Working Paper 21781. Cambridge: National Bureau of Economic Research. www.nber.org/papers/w21781.

Pew Research Center (2019, June). *Key Findings about U.S. Immigrants*. www.pewresearch.org/fact-tank/2019/06/17/key-findings-about-u-s-immigrants.

Schak, O., Metzger, I., Bass, J., McCann, C., & English, J. (2017). *Developmental Education: Challenges and Strategies for Reform*. Washington: U.S. Department of Education. www2.ed.gov/about/offices/list/opepd/educa tion-strategies.pdf.

Schanzenbach, D. W., Bauer, L., & Breitwieser, D. (2017). *Eight Economic Facts on Higher Education*. April 26. Washington: Brookings Institution. www .brookings.edu/research/eight-economic-facts-on-higher-education.

Schwartz, D., Strawn, J., & Sarna, M. (2018). *Career Pathways Research and Evaluation Synthesis*. Washington: Abt Associates.

Scott-Clayton, J., & Li, J. (2016). *Black-White Disparity in Student Loan Debt More than Triples after Graduation*. Evidence Speaks Reports 2(3). Washington: Brookings Institution.

Scott-Clayton, J. (2018). *The Looming Student Loan Crisis Is Worse than We Thought*. Washington: The Brookings Institution. www.brookings.edu/resear ch/the-looming-student-loan-default-crisis-is-worse-than-we-thought.

Scrivener, S., Weiss, M., Ratledge, A., Rudd, T., Sommo, C. S., & Fresques, H. (2015). *Doubling Graduation Rates: Three-Year Effects of CUNY's Accelerated Study in Associate Programs (ASAP) for Developmental Education Students*. New York: MDRC.

Stevens, A. H. (2019). *What Works in Career and Technical Education? A Review of Evidence and Suggested Policy Directions*. Washington: Aspen Institute. www .aspeninstitute.org/longform/expanding-economic-opportunity-for-more-ameri cans/what-works-in-career-and-technical-education-cte-a-review-of-evidence-and-suggested-policy-directions.

Taylor, B. J., & Cantwell, B. (2019). *Unequal Higher Education: Wealth, Status and Student Opportunity*. New Brunswick: Rutgers University Press.

The Institute for College Access and Success (2019). *Casualties of College Debt: What Data Show and Experts Say about Who Defaults and Why*. Washington: TICAS.

The Institute for College Access and Success (2019). *Inequitable Funding, Inequitable Results: Racial Disparities at Public Colleges*. Washington: TICAS.

The Institute for College Access and Success (2019). *What to Know about the Gainful Employment Rule*. Washington: TICAS.

Thelin, J. R. (2011). *A History of American Higher Education: Second Edition*. Baltimore: Johns Hopkins University Press.

U.S. Department of Education. Office of Planning, Evaluation and Policy Development (2016). *Advancing Diversity and Inclusion in Higher Education*. www2.ed.gov/rschstat/research/pubs/advancing-diversity-inclusion.pdf.

U.S. Department of Education. National Center for Educational Statistics (2015). *Digest of Educational Statistics 2014*. nces.ed.gov/programs/digest/2014menu_tables .asp.

U.S. Department of Education. National Center for Educational Statistics (2016). *Digest of Educational Statistics 2015*. nces.ed.gov/programs/digest/2015menu_tables .asp.

U.S. Department of Education. National Center for Education Statistics (2018). *Digest of Education Statistics 2016*. nces.ed.gov/programs/digest/d16/ ch_3.asp.

U.S. Department of Education. National Center for Education Statistics (2019). *Enrollment and Employees in Postsecondary Institutions, Fall 2017*. nces .ed.gov/pubsearch/pubsinfo.asp?pubid=2019021rev.

U.S. Department of Education. National Center for Education Statistics (2019). *Fast Facts: Historically Black Colleges and Universities*. nces.ed.gov/fastfacts/dis play.asp?id=667.

U.S. Department of Education (2019). *Tribal Colleges and Universities*. sites.ed.gov/ whiaiane/tribes-tcus/tribal-Colleges-and-universities.

CHAPTER 7

Exploring Place
Indigenous Students in US Higher Education

John L. Garland, Charlotte E. Davidson
and Melvin E. Monette-Barajas

In this chapter, we seek to explore the emerging concept of finding *place* in higher education for Indigenous students. The meaning of *place* for displaced and marginalised American Indians in the United States and their relationship with higher education moves beyond physical settings by being inclusive of language, sovereignty, self-determination, identity and data inclusion. Throughout the chapter we interchangeably use the terms *Indigenous, Native American, American Indian* and *Native* to refer to US Indigenous peoples. The chapter begins with an analysis of what *place* means to us, and possibly to Native College students. Likewise, we discuss how *place* interacts in non-Native higher education contexts. Our goal here is not to provide a literature review of various issues facing Native students in US higher education, but to explore new thoughts and applications for what it may mean to be an Indigenous person finding their *place* in US higher education. Although we provide numerous references on important new research to ground our work in this chapter, our primary intent is to extend the literature into a deeper discussion on the topic of *place*. Consistent with the theme of this text, we hope that marginalised and displaced peoples around the globe may find our discussion on *place* useful for reframing their higher education experiences.

> Where are you from? What tribe are you? What is your clan? Where is your umbilical cord buried? Although questions like these may be used to establish kinship relations and are common among many Indigenous peoples who strive to embody relational practices, these questions are rarely asked within higher education settings. Said another way, higher education has not sought to be a relative to us and, in effect, our research or scholarship (Davidson, forthcoming).

Thus, how do we find *place* in higher education? For many Native peoples in US higher education, the prior questions describe an often-painful awareness that is a result of materially contending with the systematic erosion of our umbilical connections to *place*. From our observations as Indigenous higher education leaders,[1] this process of disconnection is linked to how *Non-Native Colleges and Universities* (NNCUs) – a term used to centre the experiences of Native peoples at historically and predominantly White institutions of higher education (Shotton, Lowe, & Waterman, 2013) – have principally operated as an unapologetic colonising structure replicating US society at large. It is a structure that side-lines deeper understanding associated with how *place* uniquely affects the participation of Native students in higher education. In saying this, we are arguing that a sense of belonging – an indicator of student success often highlighted in student development literature (Strayhorn, 2019) – can be improved when a sense of *place* is made central to discussions about educational attainment; for *place* figures strongly in how we, as Native peoples, have long understood, navigated and documented our experiences (Deloria & Wildcat, 2001; Tuck & McKenzie, 2015). Correspondingly, it is impossible to speak about the dis*place*ment and marginalisation of Native Americans in society, and Native American students in US higher education, without a critical discussion of how *place* figures into how they experience these phenomena.

Likewise, as will be discussed later in this chapter, finding *place* for Indigenous students within higher education research takes on new importance in the context of historical marginalisation and dis*place*ment. The ongoing invisibility of Native Americans in higher education and in higher education research, especially in quantitative data, results in a contemporary higher education system that is generationally uninformed and/or misinformed with respect to Indigenous students. This type of systemic ignorance undermines higher education practices, policies and inclusion that seek to develop a sense-of-belonging for Native Americans.

Two concepts critical to understanding Indigenous involvement in higher education are *sovereignty* and *self-determination* which are discussed in detail later in this chapter. However, it is important to be clear now about what makes the presence of Native American students in US higher education *sovereign* and their participation *self-determined*. This is to say that 'Native students live on land that was colonised by the very institutions from which they seek an education. Treaties and other policy agreements, laws, and Native American sovereignty are part of our students' experiences. No other population comes to College with these

---

[1] We describe our backgrounds as Indigenous higher education leaders in the following section.

characteristics' (Springer, Davidson, & Waterman, 2013, 112). And, as we will discuss, the saliency of *place* and dis*place*ment, and their relationships with sovereignty and self-determination, are crucial elements for building a humanising practice of higher education.

The Authors and Higher Education

As authors, we believe it is important to be transparent to the reader when writing about higher education, especially on a topic so closely tied to our own experiences and identities. And, as participants in, and of, higher education we came to understand that an author's position within their work is rarely made explicit. As such, their work takes a settler-colonial authoritarian approach to *what* is knowledge and *who* is allowed to create knowledge and understanding. We believe that by positioning a few details of our higher education journey as Native scholars the reader may enjoy another dimension in their analysis and understanding of this chapter. In particular, we want the reader to know that as Indigenous people we may share several common intersections such as obtaining graduate degrees, attending Non-Native Colleges and Universities, and holding administrative roles. But, these experiences are also unique to each of us and while we cannot speak for other Native scholars, we do believe our analysis of higher education in the context of this chapter generally speaks to issues across individual experiences, tribal affiliations and educational backgrounds.

Charlotte E. Davidson

One of the many ways we acknowledge ourselves as Diné is as Ni'hookáá Diyiin Dine'é (Holy Earth Surface People). We are the children of Nahasdzáán (Mother Earth) and Yádiłhił Shitaa' (Father Sky) and are, therefore, stewards of ecological living systems and environmental communities, broadly, and Dinétah, specifically. Dinétah is a Diné term that means 'among the people', and refers to our ancestral homeland which is delineated by four sacred mountains and geographically encompasses northeastern Arizona, northwestern New Mexico, southwestern Colorado and southeastern Utah. Maintaining a consistent and conscious relationship with this location is achieved in social and material ways such as, but not limited to: beginning the introduction of oneself by identifying the four clan groups one is born into; wearing precious stones, such as turquoise, for purposes of well-being and protection; styling hair in the form of a Tsiyeeł (Diné hair bun); and praying to Diyin Dine'é (Holy

People) using plants sacred to Diné. This is all to say that Diné concepts – too many to additionally mention here – and the capacity to enact this grounding knowledge in the world, can and does occur outside of Dinétah. To this point, these practices served as the foundation for my undergraduate persistence at a tribal university in the Midwest region of the United States, as well as my subsequent matriculation to and graduation from a Non-Native College/University (NNCU) in Illinois.

John L. Garland

We are called the Chata People (Choctaw) and are connected to the Mississippian culture sharing a Muskogean language with the Chickasaw, Creek and other tribes. The Choctaw creation story says we emerged from earthen (Yakni) mounds in a land area known as Nanih Waiya which remains a sacred location in current day Mississippi. I am a descendent of Hushi Yukpa (Happy Bird), sister to Chief Pushmataha, and her spouse Major James Garland (a British [Irish] Soldier), and later from their son John Garland from what was known as the Six Towns District of the Choctaw (parts of present-day Mississippi and Alabama). Fortunately, many details about my family history from pre- and post-removal to southeastern Indian Territory (present day Choctaw Nation, Oklahoma) were generally documented in contrast to many tribal family histories that may have been lost during relocation. I was raised a few miles from where the Garland Choctaws ended their removal from ancestral lands to Indian Territory in the 1830s – now commonly referred to as the Choctaw Trail of Tears. My higher education journey began at a two-year Native American Serving Non-Tribal Institution affiliated with the Choctaw Nation of Oklahoma (Eastern Oklahoma State College), bachelor's and master's degrees (the first in my family) from another Native American Serving Non-Tribal Institution but affiliated with the Cherokee Nation (Northeastern State University), and finally a doctoral degree from a Non-Native College/University (University of Maryland – College Park). Collectively, these experiences led to my journey of finding *place* in higher education resulting in a career focused on Native student success.

Melvin E. Monette-Barajas

The Metis are people descended from joint Indigenous and white parents. It is both my maternal and paternal family history where my Anishinaabe (Chippewa) and Cree great-great-great grandmothers married French or

Scottish fur trappers. Metis are more commonly known as a Canadian Indigenous group; however, the Turtle Mountain Band of Chippewa Indians are descendants of these people and my homelands are located a few miles below the Canadian border in the Turtle Mountains of North Dakota. This lineage is the norm at home and it created its own culture and language – Michif, which is an identity and a language unique to my homelands. The community strives to preserve the Anishinaabe language, teaches French in the high school, and uses English as the primary language for communication which together form the Michif language. I grew up on this reservation and the Spirit Lake Nation, calling the Turtle Mountains home; the landscape of my mind. I have attended the Turtle Mountain Community College and Cankdeska Cikana Community College, both tribal Colleges, and the University of North Dakota.

Brief Historical Review of Indigenous Peoples' Place in North America with Definitions

> Through the process and structuring of settler colonialism, land is remade into property, and human relationships to land are redefined/reduced to the relationship of owner to his property. When land is recast as property, *place* becomes exchangeable, saleable, and stealable. The most important aim of recasting land as property is to make it ahistorical in order to hack away the narratives that invoke prior claims and thus affirm the myth of terra nullius 'nobody's land'
>
> (Tuck & McKenzie, 2015, 64).

One of the deep historical consequences of settler colonialism is the dominant pedagogical discourse that *place* lacks the qualities of a living educator, learning context, and loving relative; a discourse that functions to estrange us from how *place* informs our material relationships with the world. Nevertheless, Native peoples have generally resisted and refused Eurocentric sensibilities that relegate *place* to property even while participating in an often-necessary monetary relationship to land. Hence, our capacity to structure relationships to specific locations has not been entirely eliminated and, thus, it endures.

To attempt an encompassing discussion of *place* is a difficult task given the innumerable ways Indigenous peoples, both individually and communally, envision, cultivate, construct, experience, and define *place*. Likewise, applying an Indigenous pan-ethnic identity for all Native peoples in the United States as a means to solve historical injustices oversimplifies the issues at hand; yet we must begin somewhere. What we posit in these pages is a partial – unfinished – interpretation of *place* as we (re) explore *place* in the context of higher education. For Native American College students, questions such as 'Where are you from? What tribe are you? What is your clan? Where is your umbilical cord buried?' (Davidson, forthcoming) provides for opportunities of *place*ment thereby giving Native peoples primacy in that their answers are often situated in ancient stories of emergence, ancestral attributes of being-ness and principles for living; the totality of which constitutes, what Deloria and Wildcat (2001) term, *personality*. Finding a sense of *place* tends to define and validate one's social connections with others in a world that generally values higher education. Although social connections through higher education have become an important element for perceived worldly success, these connections come at a *place*-cost when Indigenous students remain literally and figuratively invisible throughout most higher education settings. In other words, how can *place* ever be complete without Indigenous peoples?

Deloria and Wildcat recognised very clearly in their book, *Power and Place: Indian Education in America*, that *personality* does not exist apart from place, for together they give epistemological direction to thought and action. To illustrate, we offer respective and very brief glimpses into this lived experience by sharing how *place* is always implicated in the production of knowledge (e.g., the writing of this book chapter) and, because this is so, we always begin such processes from who and where we originate. At this point, it is important to stress that while all Native students are living extensions of *place*, one should not assume that all Native students enter into academic environments with place-based sensibilities. These variations may occur due to historical elements of assimilation and trauma from relocation policies, family dynamics, educational opportunities, and other contributing factors. This is to say that nurturing the continuity of indigenous personality should be a shared goal of Non-Native Colleges and Universities.

An often evolving, and sometimes contradictory, aspect of nomenclature is that some terms may not adequately or accurately define people or groups. This is certainly the case for Indigenous peoples within the borders of the United States of America. As mentioned earlier and in other recent publications (Waterman, Lowe, & Shotton, 2018), the terms *Indigenous, Native American, American Indian, Indian*, and simply *Native* are used interchangeably. However, there may be unique distinctions and experiences when it comes to understanding certain Indigenous peoples in North America where these terms are applied. Some of what is discussed in this chapter applies to *Alaska Natives* and

Native Hawaiians as it does to Native Americans in the contiguous forty-eight states, but knowledge and research with the experiences of Alaska Native and Native Hawaiian College students is only now beginning to emerge, thereby illuminating the unique experiences of each. Keeping this in mind while reading this chapter will help to inform and necessarily complicate one's overall understanding of the Indigenous College student experience.

Place as Language and Sovereignty

Individual and shared experiences as tribal members whose families were historically subjected to displacement and oppression bring into focus that tribal connections to *place* are deeply relational; meaning that connection to *place* remains immutable regardless of circumstances. Further, these connections are comprised of a complicated set of human responsibilities linked to spirituality, happiness, restoration, and familial harmony. In experiencing the simultaneous combination of these states, Indigenous peoples may be unwilling to acquiesce readily to the colonising culture of higher education – a culture that can be uncompromisingly committed to sustaining itself as a hegemonic intellectual space. As Deloria and Wildcat (2001) note: 'An introduction into most American institutions of higher education should predictably result in disorientation to any person who understands their personhood as emergent from a specific environment or *place*' (p. 114). What may not be easily discernible is that Deloria and Wildcat's critical observation cannot be understood separate from foundational perspectives about language and sovereignty.

Language

In reflecting on the significance of language for Native peoples, it is essential to note that '. . . oral traditions persist and are resurging as socializing narratives for moral instruction, healing, community building, and communicative practices' (Nicholas & McCarthy, 2015, 40). In this sense, language is as beautifully distinct as Indigenous peoples themselves, given that a fundamental characteristic of language is its precise connection to knowledges that are local. When we think of individual European countries and their various languages, we often associate cultural uniqueness to those languages and their locations – or *place*. Likewise, Native tribes in the United States have unique languages connecting their knowledge with location and *place*.

Sovereignty

To open a way for understanding Indigenous conceptions of sovereignty, we look to June McCue (2007), who offers a powerful and deeply spiritual articulation of this term. It is essential to mention that while McCue is Ned'u'ten from Lake Babine in northern British Columbia, what she shares with us – as our northern relation – is a place-focused characterisation of sovereignty; one that may contradict classic Eurocentric framings:

> I can connect sovereignty and self-determination within the distinct context of my people by making an analogy to the trees on my Clan or house territory. The roots, trunk, and bark of the trees represent sovereignty to me. The special sap, food, medicines, and seedlings that come from our trees are symbiotic with the life force or energy of my people and the land, united in a consciousness and connected through the web of life. To me, this is like self-determination or the exercise of sovereignty. The specific species of the trees represents the sovereignty and self-determination inherently and uniquely intertwined within the culture of my people. We have traditional methods to keep our trees strong, healthy, productive, and secure. Like trees, we have continued to stand despite clear-cut logging and other unsustainable natural resource practices by state and industry, insect infestations, and diseases brought about through contact and climate change. We have also survived the fact that states have tried to attempt to change the way we use, regulate, and connect to our territories. Despite colonisation, our sovereignty, self-determination, and cultures live (p. 24).

Education Self-Determination and US Higher Education

Sovereignty and self-determination have become foundational elements to the process of Indigenous independence and *place* within the United States. Utilising past treaties, legal agreements and existing laws, tribes have collectively reasserted sovereignty and self-determination in many areas of tribal governance, including education.

Education Self-Determination

Indigenous communities across present day North America practised successful methods of education, language development, communication and nation-to-nation relationships regionally and across continents prior to Western colonisation – a notion that often gets lost or distorted in so-called American History. Similar to many Indigenous communities around the world where colonial education systems were imposed, the education system of the United States has earned an oppressive, violent and untrustworthy reputation. Guided by racism, broken treaties and policies of colonial assimilation, education policy for Indigenous populations over time have resulted in differential effects for American Indian tribes including the loss of many tribal cultures and languages, structural barriers to individual Indigenous identity, and legal challenges to tribes' abilities to self-govern, just to name a few. Of course, these outcomes were expectations of a US colonial government that invoked manifest destiny and had the goal of blocking Indigenous challenges to Western constructions of civilisation. Similarly, fundamental notions of Christianity have been at play throughout the formation of US education policy whose manipulative belief systems were often used as justification for many of the worst governmental human rights abuses perpetrated on Indigenous communities including forced child-family separations and forced assimilative education.

Colonial education policies towards Indigenous populations in the United States largely continued in various assimilative forms through to the *Indian Education Act of 1972* and the *Indian Self-Determination and Education Act of 1975*. These Acts, precipitated by a 1969 Senate Subcommittee on Indian Education report titled, *Indian Education: A National Tragedy – A National Challenge*, imperfectly set in motion processes by which remaining Indigenous Peoples and Tribes could begin reclaiming their education sovereignty. Aspects of Tribal sovereignty have been strengthening from the early 1800s through to the present day as Indigenous tribes reassert their places in society, especially with regard to education.

Tribal sovereignty has been built on a patchwork of legal challenges that Indigenous peoples, tribes and their allies have brought through the US legal system based on treaty violations, maltreatment, illegal land seizures, and various other legal and human rights claims. Over time, there have been many setbacks and several important legal successes (Grande, 2004). These successes have had the effect of creating opportunities for remaining tribes and their governments to begin recovering from colonial rule. However, one of the primary desired outcomes of early colonial government policy was to make invisible Indigenous peoples and their history. It was this effort at making Indigenous peoples invisible within the overall US population that persists as one of today's primary challenges for Indigenous higher education. Likewise, when tribal governments adopted early federal policies of so-called blood quantum requirements for proof of tribal membership (proving how much 'Indian blood' one has), these processes were often fraught with limited documentation of familial histories and other hurdles required to prove such connections.[2]

Many Indigenous peoples in the United States belie assuming visual constructs of race in the United States whereby citizens have been racially socialised to categorise people by phenotype (skin colour) and/or physical characteristics. As such, racist questions such as 'how much Indian are you?' persist in US education culture as a means for racialising one another and displacing marginalised racial populations. These experiences add to the overall racist experiences and psychosocial invisibility of present-day Indigenous College students who frequently come from mixed-race and mixed-tribal families but who may be culturally connected to their tribe(s). In other words, when one is assumed by others to be White/European-American because of their skin colour or physical characteristics, a Native student who is exploring their racial identity may consciously choose to pass as White in predominantly White environments that may be hostile to an Indigenous identity. Otherwise, should the student be in a supportive environment, they may find paths for safely exploring their Indigenous identity. Such psychosocial experiences during pivotal developmental periods may result in limiting or ignoring aspects of one's racial identity development. Relatedly, US blood quantum policy for federal recognition remains a barrier for many Indigenous communities and such blood quantum policies are applied to US Indigenous peoples in ways not applied to any other group or population in the United States today.

As a result of this collective history, Indigenous students are invisible on most non-Native College/university campuses. This invisibility is both structural and visual. As mentioned earlier, one of the more insidious results of racism in the United States is a hyper focus on skin colour as an indication of one's socially constructed race. In addition to possible visual ambiguity around racial identity, Indigenous identity also challenges racial categorisation since it is also directly tied to tribal citizenship (defined below).

One of the key aspects of tribal sovereignty is that tribes have regained limited nation-to-nation status as domestic dependent nations within the US federal government. This means that each federally recognised tribe's government has opportunities for a government-to-government relationship with the US federal government. As a result, tribes now retain the authority to determine who are (and are not) their citizens. Currently,

---

[2] For more information about blood quantum please visit: https://www.npr.org/sections/codeswitch/2018/02/09/583987261/so-what-exactly-is-blood-quantum.

there are over 500 federally recognised Indigenous tribes with which Native College students may affiliate. Typically, Indigenous peoples identify with a single tribe, but some may have mixed Indigenous heritage and therefore affiliate with more than one tribe. Federal recognition of Indigenous populations and tribes has been and remains a difficult and politically perilous process for Indigenous populations. Not having federal or state recognised tribal status severely limits a tribe's ability to be a sovereign entity within the United States thereby limiting access to important education resources. Federal and state limitations on tribal recognition contribute to issues of Indigenous invisibility as many higher education programs and scholarships follow federal requirements of proving citizenship, or affiliation, with a federally recognised tribe. A few tribes may have state recognition and may not be federally recognised, resulting in confusing barriers for many Indigenous students seeking funding and access to higher education today. In other words, if a tribe is not recognised by the federal government, its members may have access to even fewer Native higher education opportunities than those of federally recognised tribes.

Higher Education

The aforementioned historical issues continue to have real-world consequences for Indigenous people and their success in US higher education. As with all populations, Indigenous peoples have always been engaged in education, both pre- and post-colonial, through oral and written traditions. Indeed, today many tribes have reconstituted their education initiatives through modern education departments within tribal government structures. Although most focus on pre-College education, several tribes, such as the Navajo, Choctaw, and Ho-Chunk Nations have developed effective higher education departments and programs.

One of the major elements of contemporary Indigenous higher education initiatives was the creation of Tribal College and Universities (TCUs). Beginning with the *Tribally Controlled Colleges and Universities Assistance Act of 1978* and subsequent related acts, today there are more than thirty Tribal Colleges and Universities enrolling about 8 per cent of Indigenous College-going students (Sanders & Makomenaw, 2018).[3] The remaining majority of Indigenous College students are enrolled at Non-Native Colleges and Universities. NNCUs can include other minority-serving

---

[3] To learn more about Tribal Colleges & Universities please visit the American Indian Higher Education Consortium's website: aihec.org.

institutions (e.g. Hispanic Serving Institutions, Historically Black Colleges & Universities) and predominantly/historically White institutions – where the majority of Indigenous students are enrolled. A relatively new higher education initiative among Non-Native Colleges/Universities is the Native American Serving Non-Tribal Institution (NASNTI) designation where 10 per cent or more of their student enrolment identifies as Indigenous, as defined by the United States Department of Education – making these institutions eligible for various grants and support. NASNTI designated universities are currently working in collaboration with one another to connect their campuses with research to enhance the overall success of their Indigenous students using evidence-based approaches. Currently, there are more than twenty Colleges and universities designated as NASNTIs in the United States (WICHE, 2018).

Across the United States, Indigenous students comprise about 1 per cent of the total College-going population with the Indigenous population nearing 2 per cent of the overall US population (Waterman, Lowe, & Shotton, 2018). Although this statistic contributes to structural visibility barriers, meaning Indigenous peoples may be difficult to notice within the larger US populations, there are deeper issues at play. In order to understand the current status of Indigenous College students one should contextualise present-day higher education data availability. In quantitative research, discussed more fully later in this chapter, American Indian data are frequently missing in research studies exploring College student racial experiences due to what is known as the American Indian research asterisk (Garland, 2007).

Strides for greater inclusion of Indigenous student quantitative data across higher education settings are largely the result of the efforts by Indigenous identifying higher education researchers. To date most data inclusion has come in the form of *place*-based, or tribe-specific, qualitative research. Yet, due to the overwhelming lack of quantitative research data on Indigenous College students in comparison with other student populations, evidence-based research from large quantitative data sets remains sparse thereby allowing myths and stereotypes about the Indigenous student experiences to pervade higher education settings. These stereotypes include the notion that Indigenous peoples do not generally seek a College education or that we are unsuited for so-called modern higher education (Waterman, Lowe, & Shotton, 2018). Even more invisible within higher education data are Indigenous faculty and staff. A deeper discussion of the ethical issues surrounding Indigenous data invisibility, and possible remedies, is presented later in this chapter; however, this single issue of quantitative data invisibility remains a substantial barrier to the deeper understanding of Indigenous College students, their experiences, and their overall *place* in higher education.

In spite of these issues, an Indigenous sense of *place* is proving to be a powerful force in US higher education. Indigenous access to and success in higher education is slowly improving due to Indigenous activism as perspectives are slowly shifting to a success lens rather than a deficit lens on Indigenous College students (Shotton, Lowe, & Waterman, 2013; Waterman, Lowe, & Shotton, 2018). Historically, issues of low pre-College graduation rates and low College-going and graduation rates of Indigenous students were framed in research as problems of Indigenous students and their communities rather than issues of institutional access, climate and invisibility.

In spite of many existing and historical barriers, the last twenty years has seen concerted efforts to guide more Indigenous students towards post-secondary opportunities, including those at the graduate and professional levels, thereby shifting the landscape towards more positive and visible outcomes in the fields of education, arts, science, technology, engineering and medicine. One example is the growing American Indian Science and Engineering Society (AISES) which, in addition to supporting a growing community of Native scientists and engineers, works closely with higher education and the corporate sector providing College scholarships and direct support to Indigenous students seeking careers in Science, Technology, Engineering and Math (STEM) fields. Likewise, Indigenous communities have developed non-Indigenous education allies throughout federal, state, campus and community groups such as the College Board (home to the PSAT & SAT College preparation assessments) and Achieving the Dream (an organisation focused on supporting two-year institutions). These types of partnerships ensure that Native voices are present as initiatives are developed and research is conducted.

Likewise, as more Indigenous students have entered graduate-level education in recent decades, more Indigenous faculty and researchers are being represented in the fields of Higher Education and Student Affairs, often as visible leaders on their campuses identifying and addressing barriers to inclusive campus environments. The presence of Indigenous scholars in fields where few or none may have existed has had transformative effects across academic disciplines such as education and medicine – many of today's Indigenous graduate students, including authors of this chapter, are among the first Indigenous students to graduate from academic disciplines at their Colleges and universities.

The expanding inclusion of Indigenous perspectives and practices is shifting outdated Western notions of what is considered knowledge, research, and success towards more inclusive pedagogical outcomes for everyone especially, for those in higher education as illuminated by recent publications written by Indigenous scholars Shotton, Lowe and Waterman (2013).

Unfortunately, one of the challenges of having so few Indigenous people within large bureaucratic structures like higher education is the burdening of Indigenous students, faculty and staff with continually educating the campus community *about* Indigenous students, communities, and tribes. This is a direct contributor to a phenomenon known as racial battle fatigue (Smith, Yosso, & Solorzano, 2006) and may negatively affect Indigenous faculty, student, and staff campus experiences and threaten progress in finding *place*. Beyond simply increasing the number of Indigenous students, faculty, and staff, which has its challenges given population statistics, campuses have few immediate solutions for addressing this type of fatigue. Equally challenging is determining what solutions may be most effective for supporting Native College students, faculty, and staff who may be experiencing racial battle fatigue given an overall lack of research available to inform higher education practice.

This issue also highlights an inherent challenge around diversifying College campuses although Indigenous people share a common settler-colonial history, there is immense within-group diversity among Indigenous peoples. A citizen from one tribe is likely not an expert on another as many tribes are as distinct as European nations. Each tribe may have its own language, history governmental structure and varying degrees of higher education support. Likewise, tribes may share regional similarities and experiences, but regional differences across landscapes and bordering countries have made some tribes culturally distinct over the millennia. Alternatively, an interesting outcome of Indigenous diversity during colonisation in the United States is that tribes have turned their shared negative and oppressive settler-colonial experiences into a unifying inter-tribal catalyst for positive collective action and education advocacy. Among the best examples of this collective effort is the National Indian Education Association (NIEA) which includes all Native tribes by advocating on their behalf with US federal agencies to improve, expand and enhance funding, supportive legislation and federal policies for Indigenous-centric approaches to educational outcomes.

Asserting Indigenous *Place* through Data Inclusion and Research in Higher Education

As noted earlier, an important element of finding *place* in US higher education includes being represented in relevant higher education data and research. Until recently, Native students and faculty were generally not represented among quantitative research data meant to inform the higher education community through evidence-based publications. During the last two decades in particular, Indigenous scholars have been persisting through graduate programs in the fields of higher education administration and College student affairs administration and then into administrative and faculty ranks. This increased presence of Indigenous peoples within the academy has helped to guide new awareness and research around their higher education experiences resulting in progress for asserting an Indigenous *place* through data inclusion.

Indigenous researchers are reshaping higher education in ways unimaginable just a few decades ago, particularly in the professional practice areas of student affairs and higher education administration (Minthorn & Shotton, 2018). The field of student affairs administration in particular has become an increasingly effective vehicle for activism and inclusion for both Native professionals and research on Indigenous College student experiences. From national associations for Indigenous student affairs and higher education professionals to campus co-curricular opportunities for Native students, awareness and inclusion of Indigenous peoples and their data are incrementally improving yet remain far from equitable.

Although Native data inclusion among quantitative research on College students remains generally elusive, *qualitative* research studies and data have been more inclusive of Native students due to their person-centred nature. In particular, research is developing around the experiences of Indigenous students on the topics of improving campus climate, increasing quality campus involvement, sustaining Indigenous identity while achieving academic success and expanding access to academic offerings (Shotton, Lowe, & Waterman, 2013; Waterman, Lowe, & Shotton, 2018). However, similar studies using *quantitative* research findings across racial groups rarely include Indigenous student data due to their low statistical power in comparison with other racial group data – a phenomenon known as the *American Indian Research Asterisk* (Garland, 2007).

Although by its nature, qualitative research may be contextually limited to campus, tribal, and Native-specific communities and may not hold transferable elements across tribes or campuses, these person-centred studies have indeed provided key insights into many Indigenous College student experiences and topics where scant research previously existed. As data inclusion efforts improve for Indigenous College student research, one area that remains relatively unexamined is research on within-group differences. For example, research data on Native College students with disabilities is virtually non-existent among research on Native students or among research on College students with disabilities (Garland, 2018).

Finding our *place* in higher education is all but impossible if we tend to be invisible within data sets. Data invisibility is not just a Native American issue but likely affects any numerically small or marginalised population who finds their data missing or underrepresented in research. Quantitative researchers often say they simply cannot add statistical power to groups with few data in comparison to larger group data. Indigenous scholars have countered these concerns with calls for special reporting mechanisms within quantitative research protocols beyond simply placing an asterisk next to Indigenous data indicating the sample or population size was too small for inclusion and analysis. Proposed solutions include adding a separate section for quantitative reporting formats discussing what may be gleaned from any group data with low statistical power and for researchers to discuss the extent to which they sought data inclusivity, especially where small racial/ethnic populations and historically marginalised groups are concerned. The simple act of acknowledging whose data are missing or could not be analysed is only a first step to quantitative research transformation and inclusion. Full inclusion occurs when all quantitative group data, regardless of statistical power, finds a place for analysis and discussion within the quantitative researcher's framework.

Another prevailing ethical issue connected to Native data invisibility concerns titles for research reports and articles. This becomes an ethical concern when a given study's title says that it examines data by 'race' thereby implying it covers all races yet does not include Indigenous data within the study itself or acknowledge that it is missing. One only needs to review recent peer-reviewed journal articles that focus on research across racial groups in higher education to find examples of this phenomenon. This widely accepted practice adds to the overall invisibility of Indigenous people, raising serious ethical concerns among researcher training.

Ethical Considerations for *Place* in Research

Several aspects of Indigenous-centric approaches to research with Indigenous people have been adapted and incorporated into an ethical research framework for higher education and may provide useful applications for other marginalised and displaced populations. Unfortunately, generally accepted higher education Institutional Research Board (IRB) protocols do not necessarily require cultural competence, or deep understanding of research subjects by the researcher who engages Indigenous research participants. Due to Indigenous communities' past experience with the US education system as a tool for forced assimilation and acculturation that resulted in cultural harm (Takaki, 1993), research with Indigenous peoples should be guided by trustworthy research practices. This necessitates reversing the body of American educational research comprising methodologies and methods that are damage-centred or designed through deficit lenses that portray Indigenous peoples and communities as defeated and broken (Tuck, 2009).

American Indian researchers have proposed an array of standards and recommendations for conducting research with American Indians (Caldwell et al., 2005; Mihesuah, 2005; Mihesuah & Wilson, 2004; Tuiwai-Smith, 2006). In his study of American Indian College student involvement, Garland (2010) outlined several of these standards and recommendations, integrating them into a set of guidelines for research with Indigenous College students, which is discussed in detail below. The guidelines include: a decolonising frame of understanding; participatory involvement of Indigenous peoples; researcher cultural competence; and beneficent outcomes for American Indian students.

A *decolonising frame of understanding* is rooted in identifying and naming Western colonial imperialism related to Indigenous peoples. This is especially important within institutions of higher education where understanding differing notions of intellectual and cultural property rights are often negotiated (Tuiwai-Smith, 2006). In recent decades, many American Indian tribes have regained their sovereignty and are now ensuring that research is conducted *for* tribal members as opposed to simply *on* their people.

As late as the nineteenth century, research practices were inextricably linked to the Royal Society (London) and Paris Academy, which viewed scientific and social understanding as best researched on 'more primitive' cultures (Tuiwai-Smith, 2006). These cultures often included Indigenous peoples who were intellectually constructed as expendable subjects of society because they were considered 'savages' or 'primitive' humans thereby relieving researchers of any moral or ethical responsibility to the subjects themselves, as they furthered their desired research outcomes. Of course, US colonial actions were also influenced by this thinking as evidenced by the United States' troubled past with cultural hierarchies and social strata, including most egregiously the history of African slavery, in which human beings were ranked from most to least civilised. Although today these frameworks are mostly rejected within institutions of higher education, paternalism has frequently emerged as a philosophical approach among well-meaning but misguided researchers. Paternalism in research implies the researcher knows what is best for the participant in the pursuit of a research study and could result in unethical treatment of participants. Harding et al. (2011) explore this and other details of researcher-tribal engagement expanding on the ethical considerations mentioned here.

Participatory approaches to research, widely encouraged today when working with American Indians and their communities, fully emerged in the late twentieth century as one response to a paternalistic philosophical approach. Participatory research means that researchers and participants work together to define the research project and its purpose, and determine appropriate methods of data collection, and outcomes. Caldwell et al. (2005) describe this approach as an 'ongoing process of interaction between the researcher and research participants that allows the examination of Native strengths and emphasizes the use of Native knowledge' in solving issues (p. 8). Participatory research involving American Indians is important because it is viewed as the process of involving participants in ways that are empowering, emancipatory and ultimately beneficial to the quality of life (Macaulay, 1998). Understanding American Indian culture is crucial to full participatory research and building trust between researcher and participant.

Cultural competence in higher education research and practice is a broadly accepted expectation (Pope, Reynolds, & Mueller, 2019). However, with broad cultural differences across Indigenous tribes in the United States, cultural competence can be difficult to ensure, even as it remains a necessary element for all researchers including those identifying as Indigenous. Currently, there is no formal mechanism to ensure a researcher's cultural competence in relation to study participants. Cultural competence is defined as a skill set that enables one to effectively engage persons from culturally and racially diverse populations respectfully and ethically (D'Andrea, Daniels, & Noonan, 2003). Others expand this definition to include gender, social class, sexual orientation, and most importantly understanding how one's own worldview is used as a lens for seeing others (Constantine & Ladany, 2001; Sue & Sue, 1999). As mentioned earlier, IRB processes serve an important research review function, but study approval does not necessarily imply cultural competence on behalf of the researcher when studies include participants from other cultures and ethnicities. American Indian scholars have called for increased cultural competence when conducting research with American Indians and collecting data on American Indians (Caldwell et al., 2005; Mihesuah, 2005; Mihesuah & Wilson, 2004; Tuhiwai-Smith, 2006). Researchers should include American Indians in all research activities where American Indians are involved. When Indigenous involvement is not possible, the researcher should consult with a culturally competent advisory group including appropriate tribes to ensure the research process is in the best interest of the American Indian participants.

A final essential element to inclusive Indigenous research demands that research *benefit the Indigenous participants*. It is suggested that a research project be conducted only if American Indian participants will benefit from the research process as well as its findings (Caldwell et al., 2005). This includes how the research study is framed and designed. For example, higher education literature on College student retention has been shifting from deficit perspectives of Indigenous student success to perspectives on institutional barriers and contributions to Indigenous student success (Padilla et al., 1997). Past student deficit perspectives have aided many Colleges and universities in avoiding their responsibilities for addressing institutional barriers to student success. In other words, while certain student (research participant) characteristics may contribute (or not) to collegiate success, institutions are increasingly examining how their institutional policies, campus climate, and student and faculty diversity contribute to student success and barriers. Likewise, campuses are beginning to expand their responsibility for how certain student variables such as first-generation status, experiences of students of colour including Indigenous students, and issues with access to higher education are affecting institutional outcomes (Waterman, Lowe, & Shotton, 2018).

These and other ethical considerations for the higher education research community may be helpful for improving inclusive data collection, research and evidence-based practice. Although not a panacea, the simple awareness of what researchers have come to take for granted when conducting research studies on College campuses may itself be an act of settler-colonial resistance and Indigenous inclusion.

Full representation and participation of marginalised and displaced populations within higher education settings cannot effectively happen unless they can be positively counted, noticed and acknowledged. In other words, finding *place* in higher education research is of paramount importance. Representation within research data may at first appear to be something that could be addressed at later points in the overall work of inclusion for displaced and marginalised people, but we believe it should be primary. Without data visibility and inclusion, it is almost impossible to affect positive change for our communities in our increasingly data-driven world.

Our Hope

Discussing the power of globalisation on the future of Indigenous identity, Renn (2012) writes that, 'American Indian identity can be understood in the context of Indigenous peoples around the world, a perspective that does not negate the very real and often tragic consequences of U.S. [colonisation], but which enhances that perspective by joining the [successes] of Indigenous peoples on several continents.' (p. 25).

Our hope is that this chapter expands discussion around a sense of *place* for Indigenous peoples as we work collectively to enhance access and success for Indigenous students in higher education. Indigenous peoples continue to explore *place* in the face of displacement, violence and invisibility within US culture; but as discussed in this chapter, *place* is also an immutable aspect of being Indigenous, so it is not easily extinguished. Although much work remains, finding and asserting Indigenous places in higher education for Native students, faculty, and staff is taking root and new momentum brings cautious optimism for future positive outcomes.

REFERENCES

Caldwell, J. Y., Davis, J. D., Du Bois, B., Echo-Hawk, H., Erickson, J. S., Goins, R. T., Hill, C., Hillabrant, W., Johnson, S. R., Kendall, E., Keemer, K., Manson, S. M., Marshall, C. A., Running Wolf, P., Santiago, R. L., Schacht, R., & Stone, J. B. (2005). Culturally Competent Research with American Indians and Alaska Natives: Findings and Recommendations of the First Symposium of the Work Group on American Indian Research and Program Evaluation Methodology. *American Indian and Alaska Native Mental Health Research: The Journal of the National Centre, 12*(1), 1–21.

Constantine, M. G., & Ladany, N. (2001). New Visions for Defining and Assessing Multicultural Counseling Competence. In J. G. Ponterotto, J. M. Casas, L. A. Suzuki, & C. M. Alexander (Eds.), *Handbook of Multicultural Counseling* (2nd ed., pp. 482–498). Thousand Oaks, CA: Sage.

D' Andrea, M., Daniels, J., & Noonan, M. J. (2003). New Developments in the Assessment of Multicultural Competence. In D. B. Pope-Davis, H. L. K. Coleman, W. M. Liu, & R. L. Toporek (Eds.), *Handbook of*

Multicultural Competencies in Counseling and Psychology (pp. 287–311). Thousand Oaks, CA: Sage.

Davidson, C. E. (forthcoming). A Hidden Cartography: Navigating the Non-Matrilineal Terrain of Academe. In R. Minthorn, C. Nelson, & H. Shotton (Eds.), *Indigenous Motherhood in the Academy*. New York, NY: Routledge.

Deloria, Jr., V. (2004). Marginal and Submarginal. In D. A. Mihesuah, & A. C. Wilson (Eds.), *Indigenizing the Academy* (pp. 16–30). Lincoln: University of Nebraska Press.

Deloria, V., & Wildcat, D. R. (2001). *Power and Place: Indian Education in America*. Boulder, CO: Fulcrum Resources.

Garland, J. L. (2018). American Indian Students and Ability Status: Considerations for Improving the College Experience. In S. J. Waterman, S. C. Lowe, & H. J. Shotton (Eds.), *Beyond Access: Indigenizing Program for Native American Student Success* (pp. 139–150). Sterling, VA: Stylus.

Garland, J. L. (2010). *Removing the College involvement 'research asterisk': Identifying and rethinking predictors of American Indian College student involvement*. Dissertations & Theses: Full Text. (Publication No. AAT 3426253).

Garland, J. L. (2007). Review of the Book Serving Native American Students: New Directions for Student Services. *Journal of College Student Development*, *48*, 612–614.

Grande, S. (2004). *Red Pedagogy: Native American Social and Political Thought*. Lanham, MD: Rowman and Littlefield Publishers.

Harding, A., Harper, B., Stone, D., O'Neill, C., Berger, P., Harris, S., & Donatuto, J. (2011). Conducting Research with Tribal Communities: Sovereignty, Ethics, and Data-Sharing Issues. *Environmental Health Perspectives*, *120*(1), 6–10. DOI:10.1289/ehp.1103904

Macaulay, A. C. (1994). Ethics of Research in Native Communities. *Canadian Family Physician*, *40*, 1888–1890.

McCue, J. (2007). New Modalities of Sovereignty: An Indigenous Perspective. *Intercultural Human Rights Law Review*, *2*, 19–29.

Mihesuah, D. A. (2005). *So You Want to Write about American Indians: A Guide for Writers, Students, and Scholars*. Lincoln: University of Nebraska Press.

Mihesuah, D. A., & Wilson, A. C. (2004). *Indigenizing the Academy: Transforming Scholarship and Empowering Communities*. Lincoln: University of Nebraska Press.

Minthorn, R. S., & Shotton, H. J. (2018). *Reclaiming Indigenous Research in Higher Education*. New Brunswick, NJ: Rutgers University Press.

Nicholas, S. E., & McCarthy, T. L. (2015). The Continuum of Literacy in Native American Classrooms. In J. Reyhner (Ed.), *Teaching Indigenous Students:*

Honoring, Place, Community, and Culture (pp. 36–50). Norman, OK: University of Oklahoma Press.

Padilla, R. V., Treveno, J., Gonzalez, K., & Trevino, J. (1997). Developing Local Models of Minority Student Success in College. *Journal of College Student Development, 38*, 125–135.

Pope, R. L., Reynolds, A. L., & Mueller, J. A. (2019). *Multicultural Competence in Student Affairs*. San Francisco, CA: Jossey-Bass.

Renn, K. A. (2012). Creating and Re-creating race: The Emergence of Racial Identity as a Critical Element in Psychological, Sociological, and Ecological Perspectives on Human Development. In C. L. Wijeyesinghe & B. W. Jackson, III (Eds.), *New Perspectives on Racial Identity Development: A Theoretical and Practical Anthology* (2nd ed.) (pp. 11–32). New York: New York University Press.

Sanders, D., & Makomenaw, M. A. V. (2018). Getting Started Locally: How Tribal College and Universities Are Opening Dors to the Undergraduate Experience. In S. J. Waterman, S. C. Lowe, & H. J. Shotton (Eds.), *Beyond Access: Indigenizing Program for Native American Student Success* (pp. 51–64). Sterling, VA: Stylus.

Shotton, H. J., Lowe, S. C., & Waterman, S. J. (Eds.) (2013). *Beyond the Asterisk: Understanding Native Students in Higher Education*. Sterling, VA: Stylus.

Smith, W. A., Yosso, T. J., & Solorzáno, D. G. (2006). Challenging Racial Battle Fatigue on Historically White Campuses: A Critical Race Examination of Race-Related Stress. In C. A. Stanley (Ed.), *Faculty of Colour: Teaching in Predominantly White Colleges and Universities* (pp. 299–327). Bolton, MA: Anker.

Springer, M., Davidson, C. E., & Waterman, S. J. (2013). Academic and Student Affairs Partnerships: Native American Student Affairs Units. In H. J. Shotton, S. C. Lowe, & S. J. Waterman (Eds.), *Beyond the Asterisk: Understanding Native Students in Higher Education* (pp. 109–124). Sterling, VA: Stylus.

Strayhorn, T. (2019). *College Students' Sense of Belonging: A Key to Education Success for All Students*. New York, NY: Routledge.

Sue, D. W., & Sue, D. (1999). *Counseling the Culturally Different: Theory and Practice* (3rd ed.). New York, NY: Wiley.

Takaki, R. (1993). *A Different Mirror-A History of Multicultural America*. Toronto, Canada: Little, Brown, and Company.

The United Nations General Assembly (2007). *Declaration on the Rights of Indigenous Peoples*. Retrieved from www.un.org/esa/socdev/unpfii/documents/DRIPS_en.pdf

Tuck, E. (2009). Suspending damage: A letter to communities. *Harvard Educational Review, 79*(3), 409–427. https://doi.org/10.17763/haer.79.3.n0016675661t3n15

Tuck, E., & McKenzie, M. (2015). *Place in Research: Theory, Methodology, and Methods*. New York, NY: Routledge.

Tuhiwai-Smith, L. (2006). *Decolonising Methodologies: Research and Indigenous Peoples*. London, England: Zed Books.

Waterman, S. J., Lowe, S. C., & Shotton, H. J. (Eds.) (2018). *Beyond the Access: Indigenizing Programs for Native American Student Success*. Sterling, VA: Stylus.

WICHE: *Native American-serving nontribal College summit July 26–27 sparks progress toward budding alliance* (July, 2018). www.wiche.edu/media-release/native-american-serving-nontribal-july-2018-College-summit

Wilson, A. C. (2004). Reclaiming Our Humanity: Decolonisation and the Recovery of Indigenous Knowledge. In D. A. Mihesuah, & A. C. Wilson (Eds.), *Indigenizing the Academy: Transforming Scholarship and Empowering Communities* (pp. 69–87). Lincoln: University of Nebraska Press.

PART II

Deconstructing Marginalisation
Political and Legal Solutions to Marginalisation and Their Limitations

CHAPTER 8

Providing Access to Higher Education for Refugees in Europe

An Opportunity to Rethink the University and Its Role in the Public Sphere

Prem Kumar Rajaram

Following the arrival of over a million displaced people to Europe in 2015, the European Union (EU) and individual member states attempted to increase opportunities for migrants and refugees to access university. Several strategies formed part of this overall policy. The EU promoted mechanisms to assess and recognise migrants' and refugees' qualifications; states and individual universities set up scholarship programmes and language courses. While these measures aimed to address some of the difficulties that refugees faced in accessing higher education, they typically do not deal with the underlying political and social issues influencing how refugees are perceived and governed in Europe. That is to say, these new – and often innovative – measures stem from and reiterate the European integration infrastructure that sees refugees as cultural others.

The starting point of this paper is attempts to increase access to university for refugees are framed by the existing European integration infrastructure. This promotes a way of integrating refugees premised on their cultural and political otherness. In order to demonstrate this, I look at the contours of a 'myth of Europe'. This myth is an idea of the superior value of ways of thinking and living that are understood to be 'European', and of the social and political organisation that enables these. This myth is deployed to denigrate other ways of thinking, living and organising, and resonates with Edward Said's account of orientalism and its capacity to imagine 'Europe' as a coherent entity always in a relation of superiority across any particular relationship with 'others'. There are many aspects to this othering, but it is particularly important to note that the imagined superiority of Europe is amenable to casting 'others' as problems to be solved by the application of European norms or ideas, thus ameliorating the disruption that others can cause and furthering the imagined coherence of 'Europe' (Said, 1978).

The problematisation of others as deviant presumes also that such problems can be fixed or contained. Michel Foucault's concept of 'governmentality' is useful here (Foucault, 2007). It refers to how things – people, resources – are acted upon (by the state or government authority and by themselves) so that their conduct is amenable to the ethos and interests of state or government power, or in other words, so that they may be governed. This results in reduced complexity, often characterised by subjects learning how to understand themselves in some ways but not others. Good subjects are those that filter out aspects of their ways of thinking and living that may be disruptive to the interests of good government (Foucault, 2003).

I will argue that refugees are subject to 'governmentalisation' and that this is a key aspect of the European integration infrastructure. By this I mean that the complexity of 'refugeeness' is reduced to a series of intervenable problems centred around the question of how they may be integrated into existing systems of work and education as well as societal organisation at large. Insofar as access to education is concerned, refugees are 'governmentalised' as students, producing then an intervenable problem or situation, centred around the following question: how might refugees' qualifications and existing education be made understandable to European higher education systems and how may gaps in knowledge that impede access be addressed?

This problematisation manages potentially disruptive social forces. Governmental framing facilitates perceiving displaced individuals in terms of the potential problems they pose to government. Foucault notes that this means that the historical depth and character of people and groups become reduced to questions of systemic organisation and rule. While it may be the case that all people are subjected to governmental processes, the important point is that those who also experience forms of cultural othering are subject to a specific type of intervention centred on the idea of how to manage them as problems to the community – of the state or of Europe. Yildiz and De Genova have argued that the cultural 'othering' of Roma in Europe is similar to that experienced by migrants and refugees (Yildiz & De Genova, 2018). Both groups are denigrated in orientalist terms as representing disorder and deviance.

Against this framing of refugees as a particular type of problem, I argue that they should be understood as a group whose social and economic marginalisation is similar to the marginalisation of other communities in Europe. This is sometimes along the lines of class, and other times along the lines of religion or ethnicity (Yildiz & De Genova, 2017). Focusing on the common marginalisation (Rajaram, 2015) of refugees and others offers an opportunity to rethink how higher education access for refugees may be framed. Rather than a governmental means to ensure that refugees 'fit', the issue may be resituated to something like this: how would the entry into university of marginalised groups (including people problematised as 'refugees' requiring integration) who are aware of the historical conditionality of their marginalisation help us rethink the relationship of universities to education and the role of the university in the public sphere?

Henry Giroux has argued the 'fundamentally political nature' of university teaching has been downplayed in western states over time (Giroux, 2003, 6). The university, he argues, can become at times an adjunct to the market, providing education that is in service to existing employment opportunities thus reproducing inequalities. The reproduction of social and economic inequalities serves the interests of the elite and enables their control over state infrastructure while also then continuing the relative marginalisation and inequality of different groups defined in racial/ethnic or class terms. Giroux argues that it is important to consider the role that pedagogy and curricula have in furthering or impeding social change. Thinking about refugees as a marginalised group, and not an externalised appellant to the state as the governmental narrative would have it, might allow us to think the fuller import of critical pedagogic and inclusive practices at universities and how these may foster broader social inclusion.

The paper proceeds as follows. I begin with a brief account of what I call the 'myth of Europe' – i.e. a certain idea about the inherent value of Europeanness that normalises the idea that refugees are distinct European problems meriting solutions that protect Europe and European administrative and governing systems from potential disruption. I then go on to sketch key features of refugee integration processes in Europe before exploring two projects designed to incorporate displaced people into higher education: the European Qualifications Passport (EQP) and the Central European University's Open Learning Initiative (OLIve) programme. The EQP is an ambitious attempt to codify the education qualifications that refugees hold. It aims to create a standardised template that would allow refugees qualifications to be recognised by any national education authority or university. The EQP draws on the 1997 Convention on the Recognition of Qualifications concerning Higher Education in the European Region (generally known as the Lisbon Recognition Convention) and provides a standardised means of assessing the equivalency of qualifications to European ones. OLIve runs programmes to assist refugees to enter into higher education using funding received from the EU.[1] Both these projects are innovative, and both seek to question in different ways the hierarchies of higher education but both also encounter key limitations in doing so. I will end by arguing for policies based on thinking with Paolo Freire (1970/2005) about how universities reproduce inequalities.

Myths of Europe

In trying to understand and evaluate strategies to ensure refugee access to higher education, it is important to resituate the issue to think about how the problematisation of refugees as people requiring forms of integration relate to ideas of Europe and 'Europeanness' and how ideas of national community are boundaried. The main idea to be explored here is the framing of refugees as cultural others, enabling the particular forms of governmental responses that they are subject to.

In 2015, around one million people tried to enter the EU by crossing the Mediterranean or by land across Turkey. Narratives of crisis abounded, particularly in consideration of the deaths at the Mediterranean border (Bojadzijevic & Mezzadra, 2015). The crisis was soon enough exploited by a number of populist politicians across Europe – perils faced by people on the move were made secondary by the perceived threat to Europe's borders, community or culture (Rajaram, 2015). The Mediterranean has been subject to exclusionary bordering practices by the EU since the 1990s, with the intent of restricting the mobility of migrants from the global south. If crossings have become dangerous, it is not because of the undisciplined mobilities of migrants but rather because of the EU's bordering practices. At the same time as these bordering and immobilising practices, the Schengen space of free mobility was being created. The Schengen agreement is central to the Europeanisation of migration policies, the

---

[1] I am the current Head and one of the co-founders of the Open Learning Initiative. The two comparisons are unequal as I have no direct experience of the EQP.

crafting of a space of mobility for citizens required a common approach to border management and to asylum and refugee policy (Hess, 2010).

Scholars of European integration have argued that the Europeanisation process of Schengen and other agreements, such as the Treaty of Amsterdam may also be understood as a culturalisation process, outlining a particular idea of Europeanness (Delanty, 2008). The myth of a common space of EU citizenship – heightened by symbols harking to those used by nation states, including a flag, a hymn and a motto – fosters Europeanness. The Europeanisation process points to the emergence and production of cultural boundaries of Europeanness. Others were racialised and categorised as culturally distinct. This included EU citizens (an example of this is the exclusion and expulsion of Roma EU citizens in Italy and France). Haynes (Cantat, 2016b; Haynes, 1999) argues that Europe is organised and reproduced through cultural exclusions. In this context, European integration policies reflect the sometimes contradictory need to ensure the entry of individuals into European labour markets, while also insisting that refugees are able to adequately demonstrate their cultural adaptation.

Not having a historically or culturally merited place in Europe, refugee and asylum seekers may be framed as a problem whose solution invokes norms and practices that both strengthen the myth of Europe and enable their 'integration' into job markets and cultures. A similar framing is undertaken to address and manage the mobility of European Roma (Yilgiz & De Genova, 2017). A mode of power that enables the restriction of the field of actions of others – in this case people called refugees – is deployed (Wolf, 1990). This is governmentality: an over-determining constriction of the meaning of subjects such that they become understandable and meaningful only within the categories given by authority. The instrumental categorisation of 'refugees' strengthens the myths of Europe by concealing the political struggles inherent in migrant mobility, and simplifying complex and interconnected histories and politics through categorisations like 'refugee'.

Against this ahistoricising categorisation, we may note that Europe's internal others are connected to migrants, both commonly marginalised because of European cultural and capitalist practices that entrench particular class privileges and conceal them in a myth of Europe. The basis of the Freirean education policy that I will propose in the last section of this chapter asks what education 'integration' may look like if we begin from the perspective that political and cultural systems – including education – reflect and foster the hierarchies and inequalities that lead to these forms of common marginalisation.

The European Union's Integration Infrastructure

Until the late 1990s, there was a marked difference in approaches to migrant integration in different European states. A rights-based approach dominated in a minority of states (Sweden and the Netherlands for example) where policies were designed on the basis of fostering multi-culturalism. In the United Kingdom, the focus was similarly on diversity and equality of opportunity, realised chiefly through the welfare regime. France focused on acculturation and Germany tended to ignore the presence of non-German migrants. These differences point to different ways in which citizenship, nationhood and the state were interrelated, with those states with looser connections between nationality and citizenship being more amenable to a rights-based and diversity-focused approach to migrant tests (Penninx & Garces-Mascarenas, 2016).

The arrival of high number of non-European and eastern European migrants, including asylum seekers, western Europe in the 1990s and 2000s led to a seachange. Integration came to mean cultural adaptation, refugees and asylum seekers were differentiated from migrants on work permits: they had to be naturalised and had an obligation to prove their understanding and acceptance of what were taken to be national or European cultural norms. Amidst a flurry of attempts to define European values – tolerance, liberalism, and secularism – migrants were subject to pre-integration tests. The wider impact was the stigmatisation of migrants as culturally foreign to an imagined European way of life (Fekete, 2001; Guild et al., 2009). Otherness came to characterise migrants in general, particularly those who could be racialised. In some states, 'migrant' came to be a pejorative or stigmatising label attached to racial, ethnic or religious minorities, regardless of their 'migrantness'. In other states, like Hungary, the othering of migrants has resemblances to the cultural othering of native-born Roma. Cultural othering discourses and politics refined with regards to Roma came to be applied to racialised migrants, before being re-implemented on Roma communities (Cantat & Rajaram, 2018).

As I have noted, the EU integration infrastructure is not unitary. It does at least three things: it makes expert knowledge to disseminate to integration practitioners; cultivates symbolic meanings about migration, integration and Europe; and funds integration practices at national and sub-national scales (Geddes & Scholten, 2015). This integration infrastructure may be viewed as an assemblage, in the sense that Clarke (2015) understands the term. Clarke argues that the term assemblage may be used to talk about an object of analysis – in this case what I've called the EU integration infrastructure – that is not 'coherent, unitary or integrated but may be performed or enacted as though it were' (Clarke, 2015, 97). To refer to the EU integration infrastructure as an assemblage, is to point to the processes that come into play and the ideologies on which they depend when integration knowledge and practice is cultivated. These are not reducible to a single coherent logic though they may be deployed in ways that perform the coherence of that logic – in this case, the myth of Europe. To understand the EU integration infrastructure as assemblage is to point to the myths and ideas of Europe and to show that this myth takes place in the assemblage of the integration infrastructure.

Studying the EU integration infrastructure is thus to explore one assemblage where the ideology of Europeanism plays out. The point of the study then is not to study integration knowledge, practices or policy as specific forms of government, but to focus on how integration knowledge and practice operationalises the ideology of the myth of Europe.

European Refugee Qualifications Recognition Framework

The existing framework for recognising qualifications of refugees in Europe comes from non-mandatory clauses in the Lisbon Recognition Convention of 1997. The convention states that all signatory countries, which include all EU member states, should draw up mechanisms to recognise the qualifications of people with refugee status, including those with missing documentation. Aside from these generalities, Europe has seen moves to establish a European-wide recognitions framework, the most visible being the European Qualifications Passport, a project led by NOKUT (the Norwegian Agency for Quality Assurance in Education), whose head of foreign education outlined the reasons for the EQP 'basisically no country had made efforts to meet [the] obligations given that convention which was signed 20 years ago'. The EQP aims to upscale Norwegian practices on recognising and valourising the qualification of refugees and other migrants by creating a standardised means of assessing refugee qualifications that would be recognised by higher education authorities. The EQP began as a pilot project in Greece where of 92 individuals assessed, 73 received a qualifications passport. The project will expand between 2018 and 2020 to five different areas. From 2016–2018, a NOKUT-led project received funding from the European Commission's Erasmus+ funding programme to extend the methodology of the EQP to other countries – Armenia, Germany, France and Canada are joining the second phase of the project. In addition to the specific EQP project, the European Network of Information Centres in the European Region (ENIC) and the National Academic Recognition Information Centres (NARIC) in the EU recommends its national agencies, and universities, to adopt a flexible and dialogic method for assessing refugee qualifications, particularly in cases when documentation is missing (ENIC-NARIC, n.d.). ENIC-NARIC leaves provisions for academic assessment of knowledge as well, allowing for non-administrative assessment of qualifications where there are gaps in documentation.

These initiatives are ways of framing existing data – refugees' qualifications – so that they may become meaningful to Europe and, specifically, to European higher education. Recognition of the qualifications outlined by EQP or by ENIC-NARIC is voluntary. The documentation listing qualifications may be hampered in utility where there is a lack of political will but there has been significant interest as well as innovative methods for figuring out how to deal with qualifications recognition where there are none. In a number of European countries, however, there is a distinct lack of political will to implement aspects of the Lisbon Convention of 1997. The Hungarian qualification recognition system is daunting, involving nostrification and bureaucracy in a difficult language. The UNHCR notes that in the Czech Republic and Bulgaria, like in Hungary, degrees are only recognised after a very arduous process which discourages many refugees who lack the time, language skills and social capital to engage in this, or they are under-recognised (i.e. considered the equivalent of a high school diploma) (UNHCR, 2013). All of these countries are signatories of the 1997 Lisbon Convention.

Over-emphasis on documentation of education – through qualifications or other written evidence – can lead to the actual levels of learning and knowledge of refugees being disregarded even in the most liberal education systems. Evidence of this is not widely documented, but the OLIve project – which I will discuss below and which I direct – has encountered refugee students (from Palestine and Syria) whose learning and knowledge levels are not recognised by Norwegian and Swedish education systems because of lack of documentation. Two Palestinian applicants to OLIve's university preparatory programme who have completed most of their

Bachelor's degree lacked documentation of key high school exams and were asked to return to high school rather than given opportunity to complete their BA degrees. This was despite the fact that both students were fellows at a university in Sweden. A refugee in Norway from Syria was told she had to go back to high school as her high school certificate was not recognised, despite the fact that she was attending university in Syria at the time of her flight. These examples point to a need for systems that can put the academic assessment of the learning and knowledge-levels at the forefront. As I will describe later, OLIve has written a policy in place at CEU that enables students in such situations (i.e. those who have entered university but not completed for reasons of flight) to be assessed by academics who are able to measure, through exams or oral interviews, the level of learning of such students, and then to prescribe short-term courses (in OLIve it is about 10 months) to address gaps in disciplinary knowledge (CEU, 2017). Successful completion of this individually tailored programme makes them eligible to apply for Master's programmes (but only in CEU and only in the discipline in which they have been assessed and had a study programme designed to fill gaps).

The EQP does not directly address situations where refugees have informal learning or have entered into but not completed university studies. The focus is on recognising existing qualifications, which means effectively providing a basis for understanding how refugees and their qualifications relate to the status quo. Gaps in qualifications may be identified and an appropriate place in the education hierarchy may be found. The focus is on the presentation of key data to allow refugees to be recognisable and potentially valuable in relation to the cognitive and valuation frames of European higher education. As I will argue, a more dialogic academic assessment of existing learning and gaps in disciplinary knowledge may be a viable alternative to systems of recognition that focus on qualifications only.

Critical pedagogy studies notes that education systems may be seen as a mode of subjectification – a means of bringing people into a regime of power. The EQP and ENIC-NARIC are not to be criticised for this – their work has the potential to do more than most in providing people with the opportunities that recognition within a system can bring. Power gives agency and opportunity as much as it may also contribute to the maintenance of hierarchies.

The EQP and ENIC-NARIC projects (and OLIve as I will show later) should be understood in a wider legal, political and social framework. Insofar as refugees and their integration goes, the focus remains on how to bring groups into an existing system – of qualifications leading to study and then to work. This involves governmentality – here processes of knowledge gathering so that people are first known as refugees, and subject to specific techniques of control and pastoral care to guide their integration into host societies. Being so framed through administrative and legal means, a certain set of problems appear and others do not. The problem with integration is how the set of national and European administrative regulations that govern work and education may apply to others who have a different type of training and different qualifications. The problems are: how to approximate qualifications to the European norms, how to identify gaps and how to close these gaps.

The broader problem though is that states and other authorities see and define people in a specific way in relation to their histories, politics and techniques of government. Thus refugees are seen as refugees, legally administered people with the key problem being how to get them integrated. Things change if we see refugees also as a marginalised group, whose marginalisation in cultural, societal and economic terms bear resemblances to the marginalisation of other groups, such as Roma as I have indicated above. The end of the article focuses on what it means to think of education for marginalised groups and what happens to conceptions of knowledge and learning when we resituate the argument moving away from the governmental and integration-focused problematisation of refugees.

CEU Open Learning Initiative

The Central European University's Open Learning Initiative (OLIve) is a project devised and led by staff and faculty at the university in Budapest in cooperation with local migrant rights organisations. Since early 2016, OLIve has run projects to prepare students for university by developing academic language, academic knowledge and related academic skills. OLIve has received funding from the European Commission's Erasmus+ and Horizon2020 (Science4Refugees) grants.

OLIve is a project established from the grassroots – in this case individuals working in universities and in migrant rights organisations. Intended to fill a gap in the social provisioning for people with refugee status in Hungary, OLIve's projects focus on refining rather than transforming the educational space for students in the normalised social field of higher education, meaning that OLIve tends to identify and close gaps that prevent marginalised individuals from entering university rather than seeking to transform curricula. Students are prepared to enter into existing degree programmes in higher education in Europe. OLIve reproduces disciplines but has had reasonable success in getting students into universities, with some 65 per cent of eligible applicants doing so.

Like the EQP, OLIve seeks to make students valuable before European university systems – meaning eligible to enrol in university programmes – and also like EQP there are a number of external factors that limit OLIve's projects. The limited mobility allowed people with refugee status means that students are often only eligible for higher education support and scholarships in their countries of residence. This limits the opportunities for OLIve graduates, specifically those who may wish to continue their education at CEU (though the university has thus far offered full scholarships to OLIve graduates who get accepted on merit to their MA programmes, but this is not an institutionalised arrangement). Most of OLIve's students have refugee status in Hungary, a country with no support for prospective university students with refugee status, and no official government-sponsored language-learning classes, much less assistance in navigating the difficulties of applying to university. OLIve has also recently run afoul of the Hungarian government's punitive actions against groups that support the integration of refugees and asylum seekers, leading to a suspension by the university of the programme in August 2018 under the threat that a 25 per cent tax on the university's budget would be imposed (HHC, 2018).

In the autumn of 2018, CEU suspended OLIve. The staff were placed on paid furlough for two months as the university sought to ensure that authorities could identify that the programme was not running (CEU, 2018). The suspension sparked a social media debate, with a number of online users feeling that the university had pre-empted the authorities by suspending the programme before actually having any indication that OLIve's programmes would subject it to taxation. OLIve's suspension occurred in the middle of a long drawn-out process where CEU was subject to legal attacks by the Hungarian government (culminating in a decision to move the university in stages to Vienna). OLIve has been indirectly mentioned by Hungarian authorities or government-backed media during these legal attacks but it is debatable if the law was specifically intended to address OLIve. As the head of the programme, I spoke regularly with migration and refugee lawyers (whose business was to know the law inside out) and they doubted if CEU was actually liable under the terms of the law. But this is because the law is vaguely written, perhaps on purpose. My conversation with lawyers consistently pointed out that the law was written vaguely in order to create a climate of fear, thus impeding migration and refugee activism and support.

Six refugee students who had been accepted to the OLIve university preparatory programme had to be told in August that the programme would not run as scheduled in September, a huge blow to already vulnerable individuals who had to make significant preparations to attend university and were counting on scholarships. In 2019, the university decided that OLIve's education programmes could not be run within the university. To remedy these, the university (at the time of writing on 31 January 2019) is establishing a non-profit limited-liability company within which OLIve WP will run. The OLIve team meanwhile, working under conditions of insecurity and great emotional and other burdens following a long period of suspension, is planning to move the core of its programmes to Vienna with teaching planned to begin in September 2019. Moving two EU grants and an entire non-degree programme to a new university (CEU Vienna) still undergoing accreditation involves a series of bureaucratic acrobatics and has a significant impact on the unit's budget.[2]

OLIve is a grassroots initiative in the sense that it is not university led. The initiative was started by a group of staff, faculty and students and was only institutionalised in the university at a later date. While core staff – who are mainly volunteers – remain CEU faculty and staff, teachers include faculty and students from other Hungarian universities. OLIve is enabled by the European integration infrastructure which has as one of its core principles the political empowerment of citizens. Such empowerment may enable the transformation of the EU integration infrastructure perhaps stepping out of the governmentality framework outlined above. OLIve has established a policy intended to assist the recognition of qualifications of people with refugee status, building on ENIC-NARIC recommendations with the important qualification that the policy only applies to the CEU. The policy allows for people with incomplete degrees to enter into Master's education upon successful completion of an academic preparatory programme designed in consultation with the university degree programme to address gaps in disciplinary knowledge (CEU, 2017). This is different from other similar policies in that it does not seek to restart education but to build on existing learning without

---

[2] The OLIve unit indeed could not move to CEU Vienna due to bureaucratic hurdles. Instead, an arrangement was put in place so that the OLIve programs formerly run at CEU would run at Bard College Berlin for the duration of the Erasmus+ grant

students having to show a terminal qualification. A student who has completed all except one or two terms of work towards a degree need not restart that degree from the beginning. The gaps in learning are addressed in OLIve's preparatory programme, where specific subjects required for entry to Master's programme are focused on. Because this is an internal CEU policy, students are eligible only for entry to CEU Master's. The policy was reviewed and permitted by CEU's American accreditors and is a significant step towards assessing refugee learning academically and moving away from bureaucratic assessment of qualifications gained and their relative value before European qualifications. While still restricted to people with refugee status, and still only in place at CEU, OLIve hopes to disseminate this policy amongst its network as an example of an innovative means of addressing the qualification gaps that refugees may have, and that at least implicitly questions the governmental framing of the integration process.

Within the remit of what I have suggested is a governmental framework that seeks to bring people into a specific field of power as argued earlier, there is the possibility of contest. The ENIC-NARIC, EQP, OLIve projects further the possibility of people with refugee status entering university, and do open up a space for politicised action by and on behalf of people with refugee status. All three projects are confined by the overarching governmental focus and its techniques of control and consequent placement of refugees along a spectrum of proximity to a European norm. However, it is important when studying governmental power not to confuse the capacity of power to 'structure the possible field of actions for others' (Foucault, 1984, 428; Wolf, 1990) with the restriction of the agent's capacity to use the structure in creative, transformative or subversive ways. There have been moments evident in each of the projects examined here, where individuals have used the opportunities afforded by a large and potentially self-contradictory ideology of Europe to foster change. These different projects are however fragmented and not necessarily unifiable – their ethos is different, some projects may be supportive of the integration infrastructure while others may take note of the hierarchies and problematic normalisations that occur.

The projects looked at here have enabled people with refugee status to access university in a more straightforward way. They are constrained by European national infrastructure and politics which may restrict refugee students' right to mobility and recognition of qualifications because of a lack of political will to do so. At the same time, significant interventions have been made and these are worth preserving and strengthening. The EQP is developing an innovative qualifications recognition process that is being extended to wider geographies. Backed by the Council of Europe, the EQP project does have far-reaching potential and could be a widely accepted way of assessing how refugee qualifications compare to European ones. This may lead to the establishment of other programmes, like OLIve's preparatory programmes that can be used to fill knowledge gaps identified by the EQP.

Indeed, a key aim of OLIve's next project (also funded by Erasmus+ from 2019 through to 2020) is to develop a network of universities that can work together in creating mechanisms to assist refugees enter into university. OLIve also seeks to take this further, through its policy (CEU, 2017) ultimately allowing refugees who have had to flee before completing a Bachelor's degree to apply to Master's programmes following successful completion of a rigorous academic programme designed to address gaps in disciplinary knowledge. One aim of OLIve's next project is then to advocate for similar policies to be in place in other universities and other national education authorities. A significant issue is that this type of programme, focusing on individually tailored courses and small group study, is teacher-intensive and the cost per student is high. OLIve has been able to convince EU bodies to fund its programmes from 2016 through to 2020, but in order for the system to be sustained or to be widely disseminated in other universities, government investment will be required.

The governmentalisation of refugees as students creates a space of formal equality, where refugees like other university colleagues are seen as students first and foremost. This has a number of advantages, including the fact that refugees may not be singled out for whatever reason. However, people with refugee status do not enter equally into a space of higher education because on the one hand they experience a certain amount of dislocating shock at being in a system that tends to be structured mainly with a certain idea of a middle-class student in mind (or, depending on where they are from, someone of a specific race or other social background). The under-representation of socially marginalised groups can lead to classrooms, pedagogic practices and learning expectations to appear particularly alien. The lack of peer support can be a significant issue for students of such backgrounds (Quarry, 2018). OLIve's experience has shown also that for whatever reason the classroom and its dynamics can bring to the fore experiences of trauma that many refugees have experienced.

OLIve is developing a focus on pedagogic practices that can be better attuned to the needs of refugees and other under-represented groups in higher education. Other groups have focused energy on developing inclusive university administrative practice. The InHere Project of the

European University Association works with a consortium of universities in Spain, Italy and France and with the UNHCR to develop a short handbook for university staff members who work with or encounter refugee students (InHere, n.d.).

It can also be argued that universities, like other cultural institutions, are integral to the normalisation of systems of domination and exploitation, furthering specific accounts of knowledge and its limits, the relation of universities to a public sphere, and the capitalist system of production that underpins these. This normalisation of how universities operate and of the knowledge they foster, obscures the nature of domination and the inequalities that are fostered. In order to address this, and to think about the possibilities that may come from resituating refugee access to higher education as a problem of marginalised groups, I turn to the work of Paolo Freire (1970/2005).

Towards a Freirean Education

Paolo Freire's (1970/2005) work as an educator centres on an account of power as a way of normalising inequalities. Education can, Freire argues, prepare students for entry into a stratified economic market, thus reproducing inequalities. More fundamentally, the interests that such markets serve, and the possibility of other economic and social arrangements, become difficult to imagine, at least not without concerted work on decolonising curricula and pedagogies.

Freire argues that marginalised individuals can become conscientised (*conscientização*): understanding how he or she has been put in a position of inequality by a system that serves certain interests and is reproduced by the education system (Freire, 1970/2005, 67). Freirean pedagogy centres on assisting individuals to undertake studies of their life situation, understanding how their social and economic positions have been determined by power structures that aim to restrict and direct their economic, political and social participation. To become conscientised is to become aware of structures of power and 'their capacity to transform [this] by becoming aware of their condition as unfinished human beings' (Safta-Zecheriah, 2018, 314).

Insofar as the situation of people with refugee status is concerned, it is important to recognise that the integration infrastructural system of normalisation problematises people in a simplified category in relation to a norm. This means focusing on the problems that refugees pose to education, and seeking their remedy through knowledge-gathering processes designed to understand gaps in knowledge. Against this, we may think about the opportunities for expanding knowledge and curricula brought by thinking about what it means to bring marginalised groups into higher education. Giroux (2003) argues that the university has a specific relation to social change – it can stymie or further in progressive ways the social inclusion of marginalised groups and the critique of systems of economic and political organisation.

The migrant integration infrastructure essentially views universities as processing centres where people with refugee status may enter and successfully come out as people with the tools to further their integration into society. The conscientisation process that Freire speaks of can be aided from within the university when marginalised groups are not simply processed, but trigger reflection on the university and its relation to power. By including marginalised groups through innovative ways – perhaps such as those practised at OLIve or proposed by the EQP – the university can develop knowledge and curricula that reflect back on society its imbalances, inequalities and power structures, and how these have become resolved. Responding to the needs of marginalised groups, through innovative preparatory programmes or inclusive pedagogic and administrative practices, might lead to the university reflecting on how notions of knowledge, learning and education have fostered marginalisation.

Practically, what this looks like is a reflection on how curricula have been structured to further certain interests, or how entire universities have been structured to further the requirements of the market. In many European states, universities have become managerialised spaces geared towards the market and cost-benefit analyses of education. States have both furthered this process and taken advantage of the tendency of universities to neoliberalise – prioritising funding streams for courses and research deemed useful to the market.

A modality of policymaking that seeks to address the broader questions of access to university should then, I suggest, include the university and the re-development of its capacity to be a space of self-reflection. This is where questions of the purposes of education, the relation to society and the boundaries of knowledge (and the university itself) are re-animated as unfinished (and unfinishable). The entry of marginalised groups into university should provide fresh impetus for thinking about the foundations of the university and its ethos; the university should militate against being a processing centre for 'refugees' or any other students. This reflection on the university may involve 'decolonising curricula', meaning generally the serious study of knowledge systems that have been subjugated by dominant Euro-American ways of thinking (Foucault, 2003), so that a richer and broader account of the historical emergence of systems of power emerges.

Conclusion

The aim of this chapter was to consider the social and political contexts in which practices to increase opportunities for people with refugee status to enter higher education in Europe take place. I have noted that these practices may be connected to the EU's integration infrastructure, and to its 'governmentalisation' of refugees as students, meaning that solutions to foster university access for refugees are quite narrowly framed. I have argued that it may be useful to resituate the discussion by thinking about refugees as a marginalised group, alongside other groups in Europe, like the Roma. The entry into higher education of groups marginalised by the systems that universities often prop up offers opportunities to rethink curricula and its relation to the market, as well as the university's role in the public sphere. But whether this is done depends on the activity of the university, faculty and social organisations outside the university.

I reviewed practices of grassroots or non-state-led projects to increase refugees' opportunity to access university. While all projects (ENIC-NARIC, EQP and OLIve) have innovative aspects, they remain somewhat fragmented and rely ultimately on the widespread acceptance of their innovations by states and national education authorities. However, there is a potential there. OLIve is working to develop a wide network of universities and social organisations to advocate for innovative means of fostering refugee inclusion and success in higher education. The EQP's qualifications recognition framework has already gained much traction and is rolling out in diverse countries. Much depends on the availability of funding and (in OLIve's case) the capacity to evade animosity by national governments concerned about migrant and refugee integration. Other projects explore innovative administrative and pedagogic practices to foster the inclusion of refugees. The European University Association through its InHere project[3] has done much to foster innovative solutions and networking among refugees.

I conclude by suggesting that a pedagogic approach inspired by Paolo Freire can lead to an awareness of the power relations invested in university

---

[3] www.inhereproject.eu/

systems. Becoming aware of how universities sustain these power relations, and thus assist in the marginalisation of people with refugee status, can lead to a reflection on the ways in which curricula may serve the interests of power. Policies to foster refugee entry into higher education would thus benefit from beginning with the idea that refugees are groups subject to processes of social and economic marginalisation similar to those experienced by other groups. What happens when we think of refugee access to higher education not as integration into a pre-defined European norm and system, but as the disruptive entry of groups that fosters their marginalisation? There is much potential here for developing inclusive curricula and for rethinking the university's role in the public sphere and its capacity to foster social change.

REFERENCES

Bojadžijev, M., & Mezzadra, S. (2015). 'Refugee crisis' or Crisis of European Migration Policies? *FocaalBlog.* 12 November. www.focaalblog.com/2015/11/12 /manuela-bojadzijev-and-sandro-mezzadra-refugee-crisis-or-crisis-of-european -migration-policies. Accessed 23 October 2018.

Brigg, M. (2002). Post-development, Foucault and the Colonisation Metaphor. *Third World Quarterly, 23*(3), 421–436.

Cantat, C. (2016a). Rethinking Mobilities: Solidarity and Migrant Struggles Beyond Narratives of Crisis. *Intersections: East European Journal of Society and Politics, 2*(4), 11–32.

Cantat, C. (2016b). The Ideology of Europeanism and Europe's Migrant Other. *International Socialism* 152. http://isj.org.uk/the-ideology-of-europeanism-and-europes-migrant-other/. Accessed 23 October 2018.

Cantat, C., & Rajaram, P. K. (2018). The Politics of Refugee Crisis in Hungary: Border and Ordering the Nation and its Others. In M. Ruiz, C. Menjevar, & I. Ness (Eds.), *The Oxford Handbook of Refugee Crises* (pp. 181–196). Oxford: Oxford University Press.

Central European University (CEU) (2017). Policy on Recognition of Qualifications Held by Refugees and Asylum-seekers with a Legal Right to Live and Study in Hungary. CEU Senate Policy Document. Published online at https://documents.ceu.edu/documents/p-1705. Accessed 31 January 2019.

Central European University (CEU) (2018). CEU Suspends Education Programs for Registered Refugees and Asylum Seekers. Published online at: www.ceu.edu /article/2018–08-28/ceu-suspends-education-programs-registered-refugees-and -asylum-seekers. Accessed 31 January 2019.

Clarke, J. (2015). The Managerialised University: Translating and Assembling the Right to Manage. In J. Clarke, D. Bainton, N. Lendvai, & P. Stubbs (Eds.), *Making Policy Move: Towards a Politics of Translation and Assemblage*. Bristol and Chicago: Policy Press.

"Convention on the Recognition of Qualifications concerning Higher Education in the European Region." ETS No. 165.

Delanty, G. (2008). Fear of Others: Social Exclusion and the European Crisis of Solidarity. *Social Policy and Administration*, 42(6), 676–690.

ENIC-NARIC (n.d.). *European Area of Recognition Manual*. Published online at http://ear.enic-naric.net/emanual/index.aspx. Accessed 31 January 2019.

Fekete, L. (2001). The Emergence of Xeno-Racism. *Race and Class*, 43(2), 23–40.

Foucault, M. (1984). The Subject and Power. In B. Wallis (Ed.), *Art after Modernism: Rethinking Representation* (pp. 417–435). Boston/New York: David R. Godine/New Museum of Contemporary Art.

Foucault, M. (2003). *"Society Must be Defended": Lectures at the College de France 1975–76*. David Macey, translator. New York: Picador.

Foucault, M. (2007). *Security, Territory, Population: Lectures at the College de France, 1977–78*. Graham Burcell, translator. London: Palgrave Macmillan.

Freire, P. (1970/2005). *Pedagogy of the Oppressed*. Myra Bergman Ramos, translator. New York and London: Continuum Press.

Geddes, A., & Scholten, P. (2015). Policy Analysis and Europeanization: An Analysis of EU Migrant Integration Policymaking. *Journal of Comparative Policy Analysis: Research and Practice*, 17(1), 41–59.

Giroux, H. (2003). Public Pedagogy and the Politics of Resistance: Notes on a Critical Theory of Educational Struggle. *Educational Philosophy and Theory*, 35 (1), 5–16.

Gramsci, A. (1971). *Selections from the Prison Notebooks of Antonio Gramsci*. Translated and edited by Quintin Hoare and Geoffrey Newell Smith. New York: International Publishers.

Guild, E., Groenendijk, K., & Carrera, S. (2009). *Illiberal Liberal States: Immigration, Citizenship and Integration in the EU*. London and New York: Routledge.

Haynes, M. (1999). Setting the Limits to Europe as an 'Imagined Community'. In G. Dale & M. Cole (Eds), *The European Union and Migrant Labour* (pp. 17–41). London: Bloomsbury Academic.

Hess, S. (2010). 'We are Facilitating States!' An Ethnographic Analysis of the ICMPD. In M. Geiger & A. Pecoud (Eds.), *The Politics of International Migration Management* (pp. 96–118). Basingstoke: Palgrave Macmillan.

Hungarian Helsinki Committee (HHC) (2018). Criminalisation and Taxation. Summary of legal amendments adopted in the summer of 2018 to intimidate human rights defenders in Hungary. Published online at www.helsinki.hu/ en/ criminalisation-and-taxation/. Accessed 31 January 2019.

InHere (n.d.). *Guidelines for University Staff Members in Welcoming Refugees in Higher Education*. Published online at www.inhereproject.eu/wp-content/upl oads/2018/09/inHERE_Guidelines_EN.pdf. Accessed 31 January 2019.

Li, T. M. (2007). Practices of Assemblage and Community Forest Management. *Economy and Society, 36*(2), 263–293.

Mezzadra, S., & Neilsen, B. (2013). *Border as Method, or the Multiplication of Labour*. Durham, NC: Duke University Press.

Penninx, R. & Garces-Mascarenas, B. (2016). Analysis and Conclusions. In B. Garces-Mascarenas & R. Penninx (Eds.), *Integration Processes and Policies in Europe: Contexts, Levels and Actors* (pp. 189–202). IMISCOE Series. Springer Publishing. Open Access. www.springer.com/gp/book/9783319216737. Accessed 23 October 2018.

Quarry, J. (2018). Coming Out as Working Class. *Chronicle of Higher Education*. 25 October. Published online at www.chronicle.com/article/Coming-Out-as-Working-Class/244917. Accessed 31 January 2019.

Rajaram, P. K. (2015). Beyond crisis: Rethinking the population movements at Europe's border. *FocaalBlog*. 19 October. www.focaalblog.com/2015/10/19/prem-kumar-rajaram-beyond-crisis. Accessed 23 October 2018.

Rajaram, P. K. (2018). Refugees as Surplus Population: Race, Migration and Capitalist Value Regimes. *New Political Economy, 23*(5), 627–639.

Said, E. (1978). *Orientalism*. London: Verso.

Safta-Zecheriah, L. (2018). *Away towards the Asylum: Abandonment, Confinement and Subsistence in Psychiatric (De-)institutionalization in Romania*. PhD Dissertation submitted to Central European University. www.etd.ceu.edu/201 8/safta-zecheria_leyla.pdf. Accessed 23 October 2018.

United Nations High Commissioner for Refugees (UNHCR) (2013). *Refugee Integration and the Use of Indicators: Evidence from Central Europe*. Published online at: www.refworld.org/docid/532164584.html. Accessed 31 January 2019.

Wolf, E. (1990). Facing Power – Old Insights, New Questions. *American Anthropologist, 92*(3), 586–596.

Yilgiz, C., & De Genova, N. (2018). Un/Free Mobility: Roma Migrants in the European Union. *Social Identities, 24*(4), 425–441.

CHAPTER 9

The German Case
An Analysis of Refugee Student Supports in Higher Education

Lisa Unangst

Now nine years on from the beginning of the Syrian conflict and the first asylee arrivals in Europe, the refugee influx from the Middle East and North Africa continues to compel higher education institutions (HEIs) and stakeholders across the continent to action. Efforts have been made at the regional level to address issues of refugee student access to higher education, notably the creation of a European Qualifications Passport that recognises prior learning (Directorate of Communications, 2018), though no single initiative is comprehensive in scope. At the national and local levels, many interventions in this area have been attempted as documented by the European Commission's effort in 2016 to highlight innovative practices by HEIs (European Commission, 2016). Relevant programmes have spanned pro bono legal services for refugees offered by law students and their supervisors, therapeutic counselling and medical services, and plentiful language learning programmes, among other efforts (European Commission, 2016).

Germany has frequently been cited as a case study in the contemporary dialogue around refugee higher education (Detourbe, 2017; Korntheuer, Gag, Anderson, & Schroeder, 2018). This is partially due to its acceptance of the largest number of refugees on the continent (European Commission, EACEA, & Eurydice, 2019), though indeed the recognition rate (or acceptance rate of asylum seekers) has declined precipitously since 2016 and new arrivals have slowed in light of the EU–Turkey agreement of that same year[1] (Angenendt, Bither, & Ziebarth, 2017). It is also directly related to the federal investment of 100 million Euro specifically funding

---

[1] In brief, the agreement has meant that the German higher education system is not challenged by continuous new arrivals in the same way that HEIs in other refugee receiving contexts have been.

university programmes supporting refugee student access to higher education, which is unique in comparative context worldwide (Sobieraj, 2015).

Much of the emerging literature that focuses on refugee education in Germany has dealt with access to HEIs, profiling 'pathway' or 'bridging' programmes that prepare students for higher education and are familiar in other national settings. Further, much of the scarce literature is comprised of small-scale interviews with pathway programme students as well as the faculty and staff associated with those same initiatives (Grüttner, Schröder, Berg, & Otto, 2018). This chapter seeks to take a somewhat different approach, employing quantitative textual analysis to parse the web pages of sixteen German universities – one per federal state – that represent the 'home page' for refugee services at the given HEI (Rockwell & Sinclair, 2016). In quantifying the language used and supports offered across HEIs, the distinct policy contexts and diffusion of information available to prospective university entrants become clear. In short, the results of quantitative textual analysis reflect the disjointed nature of refugee student information and services at this sub-set of German research universities. Cohesive services for prospective students across institutions continue to be lacking years after the peak of the refugee crisis.

A particular focus of this research is on the question of whether and how women are reflected in the institutional initiatives represented on refugee 'home pages'. As observed by Wetzstein (among others), the role of gender is under-researched in academic work on migration studies in the German-speaking context (Wetzstein, 2019). I do not discuss here how 'women' are constructed by university web pages (though institutional gender constructions are a vital concern) but rather attend to essentialism, probing whether refugees are essentialised as male.

In the pages that follow, a brief description of the German higher education system is offered, followed by a summary of the contemporary refugee influx specific to the German case. I then move to provide background about university supports specifically serving women refugees, which lays the groundwork for the presentation of findings. I conclude with discussion and limitations of the present study.

Key Characteristics of the Contemporary German Higher Education System

German higher education represents a primarily public system akin to most European contexts. Roughly 400 HEIs are officially recognised as degree-granting institutions, of which 121 are research universities,

70 per cent of these being public (Finger, 2016; German Rectors' Conference, 2019). These institutions are subject to state-based policy frameworks that vary widely, and thus the higher education system is characterised by decentralisation. Accordingly, four distinct models of university governance have been identified across the sixteen federal states, including the leadership model, leadership-board model, leadership-board-academic model and the academic model that variously privilege faculty, boards of directors or elected university leaders (Hüther & Krücken, 2018, 120). Notably, in 2013 women comprised 29 per cent of all female chancellors and 15 per cent of all female presidents or rectors (Hüther & Krücken, 2018, 238).

Historically a relatively 'flat' higher education system in the sense that HEIs were of comparable quality and tended not to be stratified by prestige, German research universities are now being intentionally differentiated under the auspices of the 'Excellence Initiative' (Bloch, Kreckel, Mitterle, & Stock, 2014; Hüther & Krücken, 2018; Wolter, 2017). This process is similar to the selective investment and heightened competition seen in Russia (the 5–100 project) and China (projects 985 and 211) to achieve so-called World Class Universities as measured by *Times Higher Education*, QS and Jiao Tong ranking systems (Fang, 2012; Hazelkorn & Ryan, 2013; Wolter, 2017; Yudkevich, 2017).[2] Over four billion Euro has been invested by the German Excellence Initiative to date in supporting the research development of HEIs (Deutsche Forschungsgemeinschaft, 2013), which are expected to become more competitive in terms of admissions, faculty recruitment and public–private collaboration. Parallel processes of increasing institutional differentiation in higher education indicate a corresponding rise in access and equity issues that marginalise students at the peripheries, including migrants; these trends have been observed in many settings worldwide (Ayalon & Yogev, 2006; Boliver, 2011; Kariya, 2011). As 1 per cent of refugees have access to higher education, they are certainly included in this marginalised category (UNHCR, 2017).

Regional differences in the German context have an important role to play in refugee higher education as an uneven distribution of migrant and

---

[2] As discussed by researchers worldwide, the advent of university ranking systems has led to a clear emphasis among HEIs and national education systems on scholarly output and research production in order to advance in the rankings and attract higher quality student applicants, faculty applicants, and additional research funding. These rankings do not effectively measure teaching quality or inclusion measures, and thus efforts to achieve higher rankings are often seen as coming at the cost of improved student experience or attainment.

refugee students across the national landscape is apparent. This relates in part to the borders of the former East and West Germany and the relative prosperity of the latter. In fact, in rural areas of the East only 1.9 per cent of residents are non-nationals (Vanselow, Weinkopf, & Kalina, 2008); residents of the former East outside of Berlin have also been shown to display less acceptance of diversity (Arant, Dragolov, Gernig, & Boehnke, 2019). As most students in the country attend university within their state of residence (Spiess & Wrohlich, 2010), universities in the former East welcome distinct student bodies, and thus variation in terms of programmatic supports in these two regions is to be expected.

For all international students, whether arriving due to forced displacement or voluntary immigration, and whether from Canada or Eritrea, the language threshold for entry into German-language degree programmes is high and is set at what is defined as the C1 level. One level below 'native' fluency, C1 level proficiency requires substantial study for a new language learner before it can be achieved (Council of Europe, 2017). This C1 threshold has been identified as a key barrier for refugee students seeking to enter university by many authors across national contexts (Sontag & Harder, 2018; Subasi, Proyer, & Atanasoska, 2018; Unangst & Streitwieser, 2018).

The Refugee Influx in Germany

Refugees in contemporary Germany represent a diverse group, though rather coarse generalisations are frequently made of this heterogeneous population that elide national origin, gender, sexual orientation and other markers of intersectional identity and lived experience. In terms of age, refugees in Germany are quite young and therefore of concern to the higher education sector: slightly over 80 per cent of all non-EU asylum applicants in Germany in 2017 were between ages 0 and 34 (European Commission et al., 2019). Certainly, there is understood to be a clear responsibility to further the education of young refugees in order to support the future rebuilding of current conflict states and also to support integration into German society and the labour market. While it is possible for so-called non-traditional students to access university later in life, the number enrolling is marginal. 'In 2013 only 12,130 non-traditional students were enrolled' in the German setting (Brändle & Häuberer, 2014, 94).

The top three sending countries in 2016 were (in order) Syria, Afghanistan and Iraq (Fourier, Kracht, Latsch, Heublein, & Schneider, 2017). In academic year 2016–2017, 70 per cent of all refugee applicants to HEIs applied to research universities and 30 per cent to universities of applied sciences or specialty institutions, displaying a clear preference for more research-intensive institutions; the reason for this preference is not clear and merits further study (Fourier et al., 2017). Among both women and men aged 18–30 applying for asylum in Germany during the first six months of 2017, a broad range of educational backgrounds were reported: 17.5 per cent of women and 14.7 per cent of men noted some university education, while 15.5 per cent of women and 9.6 per cent of men reported having had no formal education (Schmidt & Kinscher, 2018).

Importantly, the Pew Research Center notes that women and girls represent fewer than 30 per cent of all refugees in Europe as a whole (Connor, 2016). Within the German university sector, it has been estimated that refugee women represent 17 per cent of university applicants. The German Academic Exchange Service (Deutscher Akademischer Austauschdienst (DAAD)) itself, the entity managing higher education programmes funded by the 100 million Euro of federal investment, has stated that clear intervention is needed to encourage increased access and participation (Fourier et al., 2017). One research university staff member interviewed by the author in summer 2017 reported that their university was making an effort to consider measures such as combining childcare with programmatic offerings in order to increase participation in this area (Unangst & Streitwieser, 2018). To my knowledge, no scholarly publication to date has parsed the myriad intersectional identities of these refugee women to borrow a turn of phrase, the 'socially and economically constructed differences – as well as similarities among them – remain hidden' (Korac, 2004, 253).

Background: Women Refugees in German Higher Education

In order to frame this inquiry of sixteen university web pages, I provide here contextual background regarding existing women-centric supports for refugee students to frame the subsequent quantitative analysis. Vitally, the overall impression is that attention is not being paid to the specific experiences of refugee women among most German HEIs. This approach must be problematised. Indeed, scholars and practitioners worldwide have cited the importance of visible programmatic supports at universities that demonstrate commitment to diversity and marginalised student groups (McRae-Yates, 2007; Morrice, 2013; Santos, Cabrera, & Fosnacht, 2010).

Academic Engagement with Intersectionality

An interesting suite of initiatives centring the experience of refugee women is demonstrated by the offerings of academic units at Universität Marburg. The Department of Gender Studies has offered various programmes on migration, notably a daylong seminar given on 3 June 2016 titled 'Hi(s)story-Herstory' with a focus on asylum and permission to remain from a gender perspective (Zentrum für Gender Studies und feministische Zukunftsforschung, 2016). Session topics included 'Feminist introduction to asylum and permission to remain' and the description of events included the assertion that German asylum processes privilege well-educated, working-age cis-gender men, as contrasted with a vision of women as 'dependents' or victims of culturally specific discrimination and violence. This programmatic menu of critical academic engagement with asylum processes invites refugee women to engage with Germany-specific structural oppressors in relation to their own migrant journeys. Simply put, it invites them to consider to what extent their own intersectional identities have influenced their experience of migration and resettlement.

Gleichstellungsbüro Connection

In some cases, programming specifically aimed at women refugees is operated through a university *Gleichstellungsbüro*, or 'equal opportunity office'. These offices were established in the 1980s, became widespread in the 1990s and are now present at all public universities. The aim of the *Gleichstellungsbüro* was originally to support women in the academy, be they students, staff or faculty (Blome, Erfmeier, Guelcher, & Smykalla, 2013). By no means have these offices taken a standardised form with respect to staffing levels, programming or other features. However, they are grounded in the same legal framework: the constitutionally protected equal rights of men and women; federal legislation requiring tertiary institutions to uphold these rights; and various state-specific laws. Substantial federal and state level support for *Gleichstellungsbüro* operation continues (Leicht-Scholten, 2008; Zippel, Ferree, & Zimmermann, 2016).

Europa-Universität Viadrina Frankfurt (Oder) provides a good example of this type of programmatic support for women. The university initiative styled 'Female Refugees @Viadrina' series seeks, broadly, to highlight university services to women, thereby increasing participation (Europa-Universität Viadrina Frankfurt an der Oder, 2018a). Importantly, childcare is provided by university affiliates during initiative offerings. These have included a campus tour for women of a refugee background, a German language course for women and a women's café. The latter includes conversation and networking with the aid of translators, as well as music and movies on occasion. These are opportunities for informal social exchange. Indeed, this specific mode of programming is common to several universities surveyed here. The German lessons focus on 'everyday language', providing an alternative to classes at the university that focus on the acquisition of academic language in pursuit of C1 level language proficiency. Additionally, offerings provided by other community partners are highlighted through the *Gleichstellungsbüro*. These include a domestic violence support phone line and local chapters of service organisations, including Caritas. A separate handbook produced by the *Gleichstellungsbüro* and aimed at women is titled *Studienbegleiter*in* – a small guide on studies and gender (Europa-Universität Viadrina Frankfurt an der Oder, 2018b). This covers topics including the gender pay gap; trans-respect, etiquette and support; as well as a substantial list of additional resources and research possibilities. Not only do *Gleichstellungsbüro* programmes offer targeted support to women refugees but there is clear emphasis on issues around agency, inclusion of women not enrolled at the university and resources for self-advocacy.

Language Diversity

Language fluencies are a critical component of identity and hold particular importance for refugee populations (Hwang & Wood, 2009; Joyce, Earnest, De Mori, & Silvagni, 2010; Kanno & Varghese, 2010; McAdams, 2001; Morrice, 2013; Ortloff & Frey, 2007; Teney, Hanquinet, & Bürkin, 2016). While not all migrants or refugees face challenges in their journey related to language (and related marginalisation), for many this is a persistent theme and particularly relevant to educational access and attainment (De Angelo, Schuster, & Stebleton, 2016; Goastellec, 2018; Muñoz & Maldonado, 2012; Oberoi, 2016; UNHCR, 2015). Specifically, language fluencies may facilitate or prevent university access based on the legal, accreditation and other frameworks at play in any given state, national or regional setting. In the German case (as noted), C1 level German proficiency is required to access most German language programmes, though programmes in English, French, Spanish and a handful of other language courses are also available (German Rectors' Conference, 2019). However, it has been recognised that many arriving refugees have only emerging German language proficiency.

If a given university is able to provide information about pathway programmes, degree programme entry and ancillary consultation among other services in a refugee student's first language, an enormous barrier to entry is lifted (Joyce et al., 2010). As an intermediate measure, making this information available in a second or third language (including a regional language such as Russian or Arabic) is helpful. Somewhat surprisingly, only a handful of universities currently make information for prospective refugee students available in languages other than English or German. This is surprising in the sense that translation of relatively static informational material need not be burdensome, particularly given the resources available at any HEI in terms of linguistic diversity. The University Of Applied Sciences Wismar represents an excellent example of clear, accessible information for speakers of at least five languages: Arabic, German, Persian, Russian and Turkish. The refugee information web page clearly links to each of these areas (Wismar, 2019). While language diversity on university websites does not only need to meet the needs of women refugees, it may be more important for this marginalised group. As is evident in other countries, women and men may differ in terms of their expectations for College programming, which may indicate a different approach to gathering information on a course of study (Crea & McFarland, 2015; Rana, Qin, Bates, Luster, & Saltarelli, 2011). Further, gendered educational pathways in sending countries may indicate distinct language fluencies among male and female refugees in any given host nation (Doyle & O'Toole, 2013; El Jack, 2010; Stevenson & Baker, 2018).

Methods

Quantitative Textual Analysis

This examination of German websites outlining refugee services uses the open-source, online textual analysis platform Voyant (Rockwell & Sinclair, 2016). While Voyant was launched in 2003 it has rarely been used in educational research, being more frequently applied in the humanities under the heading 'digital scholarship'. However, one recent contribution to the education literature used text mining to categorise university mission statements in trans-national context, assessing trends by world region (Cortés-Sánchez, 2018).

The developers of Voyant are Canadian researchers who describe Voyant as a 'web-accessible, web-based set of tools', which 'combines the capabilities of personal-computer-based pre-indexing tools, such as

TACT, with more accessible Web-based tools that can find text and create indexes in real time' (Rockwell & Sinclair, 2016, 11). In short, Voyant is a website that allows any user to either upload documents or to enter website URLs and conducts an indexing and correlation of the words contained in those documents or on those web pages. It then visualises these data in a number of ways: through word clouds (of the corpus of documents and individual documents), distribution graphs and indices of word frequency and phrase frequency (for instance, how often 'international recruitment' is used in a given document). It also offers the correlation and significance level (p-value) of sets of two words within those documents or web pages using Pearson's correlation.

Rockwell and Sinclair view Voyant as a component of a larger project they refer to as 'Agile Hermeneutics' (AH), which is defined as a pragmatic collaborative practice (pp. 7–8). Agile Hermeneutics encourages interdependence of research community members and experimentation, which is also reflective of digital scholarship as a whole. Here, improvements to software and analytic tools are largely open-source and with attribution readily given. However, it is clear that Voyant does not interpret meaning, portending 'the disappearance of the author' and, by extension, context and intentionality, in Voyant analysis (Rockwell & Sinclair, 2016, 20). It is therefore incumbent upon the researcher employing textual analysis to provide context and to situate findings appropriately.

Stratified Random Sampling

In an effort to reflect the range of state-based higher education policy frameworks as well as geographic specificities, this chapter employs stratified random sampling, where the sample consists of one research university per state (Patton, 2002). I acknowledge that analysis of sixteen institutions total is by no means representative of all institutions in operation; this instead represents an exploratory study. However, I seek to capture a range of discourses and initiatives at a sub-set of randomly selected HEIs in order to inform future research.

In defining the terms of the sample, I utilise the German Rectors' Conference database for HEIs, which offers an authoritative list of all public research universities and *fachhochschulen* (German Rectors' Conference, 2019). Each institution has been correlated with its state, as well as the official population of the institution's town or city as provided by the German Federal Statistical Office (Statistisches Bundesamt, 2018). Finally, using a list for research universities I assigned a random number to each institution. Having grouped institutions by rural/suburban/urban setting (I define rural as a municipality with fewer than 50,000 residents, suburban between 50,001 and 99,999 residents, and urban 100,000 or above, inferring from work by the Federal Employment Office) I selected institutions by assigning those closest to zero and moving towards one in each category (Bundesagentur für Arbeit, 2018; Fritsch & Jena, 2013).

Therefore, of public German research universities I select in the following order (German Rectors' Conference, 2019):

• Sixteen research universities, each representing a different federal state

Of these sixteen institutions representing the decentralised, state-based public higher education landscape (Bundesagentur für Arbeit, 2018; Fritsch & Jena, 2013):

• One institution is located in a rural area of fewer than 50,000 residents
• Two institutions are located in suburban areas of between 50,000 and 100,000 residents
• Fourteen institutions are located in urban areas of greater than 100,000 residents (77 per cent of research universities fall into this category)

Finally, I note that of the websites identified as the main 'landing page' for refugee student services (which is indeed a subjective assessment) ten are in English and six are exclusively in German. These sites are reflected in Table 9.1. Humboldt-Universität (HU) Berlin has two distinct sites that could be considered a home page, but I have chosen the more general, university-wide page rather than the page nested under 'study' options. Additionally, the website for Universität Bremen's refugee services is not hosted by the HEI but is redirected from the university website to an external page that collates refugee initiatives at all three HEIs in Bremen, including the research university.

Findings

The results of the quantitative textual analysis of the selected sixteen university websites for prospective refugee students display wide variation in length, format and content; divergent institutional approaches to prospective student information and refugee student programming are evident. The most frequent words in the corpus of HEI websites are university (205 occurrences), refugees (187), international (130), students (121) and research (109) (Sinclair & Rockwell, 2019a). The most concise content is

Table 9.1 *Universities selected for analysis by stratified random sampling*

HEI	State	Main website
Albert-Ludwigs-Universität Freiburg im Breisgau	Baden-Württemberg	www.uni-freiburg.de/universitaet-en/portrait/refugees-welcome
Universität Passau	Bayern	www.uni-passau.de/index.php?id=20890
Humboldt-Universität zu Berlin	Berlin	www.international.hu-berlin.de/en/refugees
Universität Potsdam	Brandenburg	www.uni-potsdam.de/de/international/incoming/refugees-welcome.html
Universität Bremen	Bremen	www.inhereproject.eu/universities/university-of-bremen-de
Universität Hamburg	Hamburg	www.uni-hamburg.de/uhhhilft.html
Technische Universität Darmstadt	Hessen	www.tu-darmstadt.de/studieren/studieninteressierte/internationale_studieninteressierte/angebote_fuer_gefluechtete/index.de.jsp#/veranstaltungen
Universität Rostock	Mecklenburg-Vorpommern	www.uni-rostock.de/en/international-affairs/incoming/refugees/
Technische Universität Clausthal	Niedersachsen	www.izc.tu-clausthal.de/refugees/
Universität Paderborn	Nordrhein-Westfalen	www.uni-paderborn.de/en/studium/internationale-studierende/refugees-welcome/
Technische Universität Kaiserslautern	Rheinland-Pfalz	www.uni-kl.de/en/international/refugees/
Universität des Saarlandes	Saarland	www.uni-saarland.de/studieren/refugee-students/start.html
Technische Universität Chemnitz	Sachsen	www.tu-chemnitz.de/international/iuz/projekte/refugeeswelcome/index.php.en
Otto-von-Guericke-Universität Magdeburg	Sachsen-Anhalt	www.ovgu.de/refugees.html
Christian-Albrechts-Universität zu Kiel	Schleswig-Holstein	www.international.uni-kiel.de/en/application-admission/application-admission/refugees
Bauhaus-Universität Weimar	Thüringen	www.uni-weimar.de/en/university/structure/university-management-team/board-of-governance/the-bauhaus-universitaet-weimars-support-for-refugees/

offered by Universität Saarland, with two full sentences of information presented on the home page for refugee students.

As noted, a focus of this research is to closely examine the presence or absence of programmes serving women refugees in the German university setting. Therefore, I begin by discussing the results most pertinent to that topic before moving to a more general discussion of other key findings.

Women, and Women as Mothers

Women are rarely mentioned in the corpus of sixteen refugee student 'home pages' examined here. Among all texts examined, there are eight occurrences of either Frau* (6) or women* (2) – the asterisk here operates as it does in a standard database search and reflects a query for all terms beginning with Frau (Sinclair & Rockwell, 2019b). These mentions are unevenly distributed across the relevant texts as demonstrated in Figure 9.1, where grey designates an occurrence of a word beginning with Frau and black an occurrence of women.

The HEI that references women (*Frauen*) the most is Technische Universität (TU) Darmstadt, which profiles a brown bag lunch series seeking to address what the world of work looks like for women in Germany. The programme seeks to provide a 'safe space' (*geschützten Rahmen*) for both refugee women and women with a migration background. Institutional representatives attending and presenting in

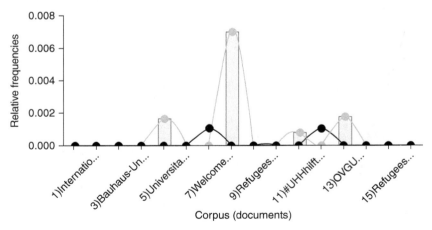

Figure 9.1 Occurrences of women* and Frau* in the corpus of web pages
(Sinclair & Rockwell, 2019d)

rotation have included faculty members and a representative of the university's 'equal opportunity office'. Given TU Darmstadt's focus on STEM (Science, Technology, Engineering and Math) fields (aligned with the German acronym MINT used on the web page in question, which refers to a focus on mathematics, computer science, natural sciences and technology), participants in the brown bag lunch series have repeatedly referenced the prejudice and preconceptions that they have encountered as women in science. This is particularly interesting and important given both the role of the equal opportunity office in support of women with migrant or refugee backgrounds and the intentional connection of these two groups. I will return to this topic in the pages that follow. Further, the multifaceted identities of participants as women, as refugee/migrant and as scientists are made clear. What does the specific discrimination look like for these individuals, and what can HEIs (and researchers) do to address it?

Additionally, the website of Universität Hamburg highlights a student-run workshop series for refugee women. The full page describing that initiative indicates that organisers welcome both women of refugee and migration background, that topics for the ongoing seminar may be determined by course participants around the general subject of women's studies and that the seminar is geared towards women who are interested in degree programme enrolment but have not yet met the requirements to do so (though they may be enrolled in pathway programmes) (Alle Frauen* Referat Uni Hamburg, 2017). Further, the programme is described as being financially supported by the university itself, and among the organising principles of the sponsoring student group are that gender is constructed and that the categories of 'man' and 'woman' are nevertheless real and impactful (Alle Frauen* Referat Uni Hamburg, 2019).

Given the scant attention to women-specific programming initiatives among the universities surveyed, it is perhaps not surprising that there are also few mentions of 'child*' (6) or 'kind*' (3) (the German word for child) (Sinclair & Rockwell, 2019a). Again, these occurrences are unevenly distributed across the web pages. Examples of the mentions of child include the referral of prospective and enrolled refugee students to the student union for childcare services (University of Freiburg, 2019), which reflects the relatively few 'wrap around' services made available in the tuition-free German context.

Multilingual Content

Referring to the previously identified issue of linguistic diversity, none of the sixteen pages surveyed here were fully available in a language other than German or English. As noted, some HEIs in the German setting do make full materials available in other languages. Given that Syrian students comprised 75 per cent of all prospective degree-seeking students enrolled in pathway programmes in 2017 (Fourier et al., 2017), it is particularly surprising that Arabic is not consistently mentioned or used. Figure 9.2 demonstrates its distribution across the web pages surveyed. In total, there were thirteen mentions of Arabi* (Arabic 11, Arabian 1, Arabische 1), many of them in relation to advising or consultation services being available in Arabic (Sinclair & Rockwell, 2019a).

Migration

Similarly, there are divergent mentions of migration: there are nine occurrences of migration*, of which three are *migrationshintergrund* (migration background), and six migration. This is significant for at least two reasons. First, as observed on the web pages of Universität Hamburg and TU Darmstadt, linking students of migration and refugee background (who may share linguistic or religious background) can be a useful tool in facilitating mutually supportive cohorts. Such student support networks have been discussed cross-nationally as

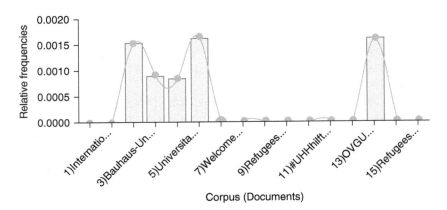

Figure 9.2 Occurrences of Arabi* in the corpus document review
(Sinclair & Rockwell, 2019c)

having the potential to engender a sense of belonging and cultural capital at the primary, secondary and tertiary education levels, though much more work in this area needs to be done (Lenette, Baker, & Hirsch, 2019; University of Tasmania Communications & Media, 2017). Still, this represents a promising area: as Elliot and Yusuf write, 'connections with members of similar ethnic groups ... [may] assist in integration through increasing health and well-being' (2014, 102).

Second, the conception of migration as a permanent part of society and therefore German higher education is remarkable. There has been much discussion in recent years (particularly since the new citizenship law of 2000) of Germany as a new immigrant-receiving context, albeit one that in some ways fails to recognise or capitalise upon this reality (Wegmann, 2014). This belies the fact that based on 2012 census figures, 30 per cent of all families in Germany now have a migration background (Henkel, Steidle, Braukmann, & Sommer, 2016). Further, the national German student union has reported that 23 per cent of university students self-identify as having a migrant background (Deutsches Studentenwerk, 2018). In this context, it is therefore both remarkable and heartening to see the following statement beginning the content of Bauhaus-Universität Weimar's refugee student page: 'Migration is not a temporary phenomenon. Our society will continue to have to deal with the manifestations, causes and consequences of migration in the future. We pledge our solidarity to those who are currently seeking refuge in Thuringia' (Universität Weimar, 2019).

Fundraising for Refugee Programmes

Finally, I note a unique innovation highlighted on the refugee home page of Universität Freiburg indicated by five occurrences of 'alumni': a Freiburg alumni fundraising campaign held specifically to support refugee student services at the institution. Based upon the decision of the alumni association's board of directors, the distribution of total funds collected (8,759 Euro) was made to two student-run initiatives in this area; a donation of 1,500 was allocated to the existing pathway programme for refugees funded by DAAD (using federal money); and an allocation was made to the programme '"Wissen+Welcome," which offers refugees a platform for communication and gives [refugees] an introduction to German society and culture through lectures on daily life in Germany held by volunteers' (University of Freiburg, 2019).

I highlight this activity for two reasons: first, the engagement of university alumni in the refugee support programmes of a university indicates both an awareness of and sensitivity to success of the constituents served. Particularly in light of recent commentary around the electoral disappointments of Angela Merkel (widely seen to have driven the so-called Welcome Culture for refugees), this is a new, positive sign of community support for refugee education in Germany. Second, the donation to the DAAD-funded pathway programme supporting access to degree courses at Uni Freiburg is notable given the implicit acknowledgement that despite 100 million Euro having been allocated to such initiatives, the funding remains insufficient. We see here a demonstration of the profound need for funding in the area of refugee student support, even in comparatively well-resourced education systems. In practice, limited funding in the German case has meant a decreased capacity of pathway and bridging programmes, routinely turning away applicants who are then likely to be excluded from future higher education opportunities (Unangst & Streitwieser, 2018).

Limitations

Several limitations to this study necessitate mention. The primary limitation is the sample size, guided by the author's experimentation with a new analytical tool producing large amounts of data. As previously noted, this sample was limited to publicly available, website-based text and cannot be seen as an exhaustive inventory of HEI programmatic offerings. Nor can the results discussed here be seen as applicable to the German higher education sector as a whole. One clear takeaway from this work is the vast diversity of language used to discuss a plethora of initiatives aimed at prospective and enrolled university students in Germany; each HEI is unique in its approach to the pressing issue of supports for refugees. Additionally, the subjective selection of refugee 'home pages' is acknowledged as a limitation, though in many cases it was abundantly clear that only one page per institution could possibly be identified as such.

Future research might use different search criteria to locate texts of interest, perhaps including student union publications for each HEI selected. Further, researchers might consider institutional case studies, drawing on memos, presidential or other senior leadership communiques, and other internal and external material to dissect a single language around refugee student support.

Discussion

How does quantitative textual analysis support a closer understanding and analysis of refugee student supports at German universities? In brief, it begins to fill a gap in the literature. German universities, increasingly supported by third-party and performance-based funding, have not been reporting in any cohesive way on their overall approaches to refugee students whether prospective or enrolled, though specific DAAD-funded pathway or bridging programmes (sometimes associated with universities) are being evaluated for the purposes of funding agencies (DAAD, 2018; Hüther & Krücken, 2018). The research presented here looks to provide relevant data on informational material for refugees who are prospective university students, whether enrolled in DAAD pathway or bridging programmes or not. To whom is it accessible, and to whom does it communicate inclusion? These questions necessitate more extensive empirical study, but this exploratory study uses a sub-set of HEIs to draw inferences and make clear textual correlations based on currently available information. This work echoes scholarship on institutional web-sites and admissions material in transnational context, though using a new method to conduct analysis (Mungo, 2017; Osei-Kofi & Torres, 2015; Thomas, Hill, O' Mahony, & Yorke, 2017).

While women refugees are under-represented in German university pathway and degree programmes alike, specific mechanisms supporting this population are sparse among the sixteen universities surveyed, which reveals relative inattention to this minoritised sub-group. It is evident that German universities operate within constrained resource environments and further within a structure of comparatively limited student services (in transnational perspective) (van der Wende, 2001). Nonetheless, given the substantial investment by federal, state and institutional actors in developing and iterating support programmes for refugees, the lack of specific focus on women calls for attention.

In this mode, I consider here not only *whether* programmes at the universities surveyed are aimed at women but whether they offer varia-tion: whether women who are mothers, women with a background in mathematics or science, or identify as a minoritised racial or ethnic group member, see themselves reflected in those programme offerings. Or are these refugee women facing invisibility at university (Harris, Spark, & Watts, 2015)? Of course, even at the most well-resourced, student services-oriented HEIs, it would be impossible to craft a targeted programme for each individual student. This is in no way the operational goal of this chapter or any university. Rather, the aim ought to be offering a menu of programmes, events and initiatives that represent a spectrum of identity, affinity and experience, allowing space within offerings for the individual to co-construct support networks and supportive resources, as well as to relate to individuals with a common interest (Clifford & Montgomery, 2017; Le Ha, 2018; Luciano, 2012; Ripamonti, Galuppo, Bruno, Ivaldi, & Scaratti, 2018).

Conclusion

The German tertiary sector has utilised the generous investment of public and private actors alike to produce a range of institution-specific supports for refugee students attending brick-and-mortar universities. This work has been both remarkable in comparative context and highly dynamic, leading to the present state of robust activity but relatively little analysis to date. I refer here not only to analysis in the scholarly sphere but also to the incorporation of feedback from refugee students themselves, largely absent from the debate over what works and what doesn't at German HEIs. This chapter foregrounds refugee women, calling attention to the relative lack of programming specifically serving this minoritised group among sixteen research universities. As El Jack has observed of the US context, 'A gender sensitive, holistic approach to the resettlement of refugees which incorporates all levels of education, particularly higher education, would allow for the full integration and the enhancement of the well-being of newly settled refugees' (El Jack, 2010, 24).

As an exploratory work, this chapter by no means seeks to be representative or generalisable. However, it aims to both describe how an intersectional frame and quantitative textual analysis might be applied to analysis of German higher education offerings for refugees. Further, it seeks to underscore the nuanced programmes already in place in the sector, which reflect some of the layers of lived experience refugee women bring to university with them. Additionally, I indicate several areas primed for further inquiry and draw initial conclusions about the current state of play in the public tertiary ecosystem.

Giles and Hyndman have written of refugees in receiving countries that 'as groups struggle to shape the meanings of spaces and create places, they reconstitute and transform social relations' (Giles & Hyndman, 2004, 6–7). Indeed, refugee students approaching higher education in Germany struggle to navigate opaque application pathways, substantial language requirements, financial stressors and, of course, the after-effects of trauma that they may have encountered in their migration journeys. They also actively reshape the brick-and-mortar universities that they attend in the German landscape: universities are challenged to consider migration – now and in the future – in terms of enrolment, student services and mission, as well as migration as an umbrella term that hides the spectrum of intersectional identity and lived experience refugee students represent. Given current enrolment patterns, these are urgent considerations for women refugees seeking to access university. Emerging good practices are in evidence in the German landscape as discussed here: can these HEIs and these institutional leaders serve as multipliers of impact and inclusion in that same sector?

REFERENCES

Alle Frauen* Referat Uni Hamburg. (2017). Kurse für Frauen* an der Universität Hamburg. 2 June 2019, https://allefrauenreferatunihamburg.wordpress.com /2017/09/27/kurse-fuer-frauen-an-der-universitaet-hamburg/

Alle Frauen* Referat Uni Hamburg. (2019). Über Uns. 2 June 2019, https://allef rauenreferatunihamburg.wordpress.com/eine-seite/

Angenendt, S., Azahaf, N., Bither, J., Koch, A., Schweiger, R., & Ziebarth, A. (2017). *More Coherence! External Dimensions of a Comprehensive Migration and Refugee Policy – Insights from Germany.* www.gmfus.org/publications/more-coherence-external-dimensions-comprehensive-migration-and-refugee-policy-%E2%80%94

Arant, R., Dragolov, G., Gernig, B., & Boehnke, K. (2019). *Zusammenhalt in Vielfalt: das Vielfaltsbarometer 2019 der Robert Bosch Stiftung.* Stuttgart: Robert Bosch Stiftung.

Ayalon, H., & Yogev, A. (2006). Stratification and diversity in the expanded system of higher education in Israel*. *Higher Education Policy, 19*, 187–203. https://doi .org/10.1057/palgrave.hep.8300119

Bloch, R., Kreckel, R., Mitterle, A., & Stock, M. (2014). Stratifikationen im Bereich der Hochschulbildung in Deutschland. *Zeitschrift Fur Erziehungswissenschaft, 17*(3), 243–261. https://doi.org/10.1007/s11618-014-0531-4

Blome, E., Erfmeier, A., Guelcher, N., & Smykalla, S. (2013). *Handbuch zur Gleichstellungspolitik an Hochschulen.* Wiesbaden: Springer VS.

Boliver, V. (2011). Expansion, Differentiation, and the Persistence of Social Class Inequalities in British Higher Education. *Higher Education, 61*(3), 229–242. https:// doi.org/10.1007/s10734-010-9374-y

Brändle, T., & Häuberer, J. (2014). Social Capital of Non-traditional Students at a German University. Do Traditional and Non-traditional Students Access

Different Social Resources? *International Journal of Higher Education, 4*(1), 92–105. https://doi.org/10.5430/ijhe.v4n1p92

Bundesagentur für Arbeit. (2018, April 16). Kleine, aber feine Studienheimat, p. 1. www.abi.de/studium/studienpraxis_campus/hochschularten/stadtflucht-studieren-auf-dem-015525.htm

Clifford, V., & Montgomery, C. (2017). Designing an Internationationalised Curriculum for Higher Education: Embracing the Local and the Global Citizen. *Higher Education Research and Development, 36*(6), 1138–1151. https://doi.org/10.1080/07294360.2017.1296413

Connor, P. (2016). *Number of Refugees to Europe Surges to Record 1.3 Million in 2015*. Washington, DC: Pew Research Center.

Cortés-Sánchez, J. D. (2018). Mission Statements of Universities Worldwide – Text Mining and Visualization. *Intangible Capital, 14*(4), 584–603. https://doi.org/10.3926/ic.1258

Council of Europe. (2017). Common European Framework of Reference for Languages (CEFR): Global scale – Table 1 (CEFR 3.3) : Common Reference Levels. 20 August 2017, www.coe.int/en/web/common-european-framework-reference-languages/table-1-cefr-3.3-common-reference-levels-global-scale

Crea, T. M., & McFarland, M. (2015). Higher Education for Refugees: Lessons from a 4-year Pilot Project. *International Review of Education, 61*(2), 229–239. https://doi.org/10.1007/s11159-015–9484-y

De Angelo, L., Schuster, M. T., & Stebleton, M. J. (2016). California DREAMers: Activism, identity, and empowerment among undocumented College students. *Journal of Diversity in Higher Education, 9*(3), 216–230. https://doi.org/10.1037/dhe0000023

Detourbe, M.-A. (2017). *Inclusion through Access to Higher Education: exploring the dynamics between access to higher education, immigration and languages.* Rotterdam: Sense Publishers.

Deutsche Forschungsgemeinschaft (2013). *Excellence Initiative at a Glance: The Programme by the German Federal and State Governments to Promote Top-Level Research at Universities.* Bonn: Deutsche Forschungsgemeinschaft. https://doi.org/10.1093/bja/aes558

Deutscher Akademischer Austauschdienst. (DAAD). (2018). *Annotated Charts on Germany's Higher Education and Research System.* Bonn. https://doi.org/10.3278/6004695w

Deutsches Studentenwerk. (2018). Studieren mit Migrationshintergrund. Retrieved April 27, 2018, from https://www.studentenwerke.de/de/node/1028

Directorate of Communications, C. of E. (2018). European Qualifications Passport for Refugees: integration through education and employment. Retrieved March 27, 2018, from https://search.coe.int/directorate_of_communications/Pages/result_details.aspx?ObjectId=0900001680796fc1

Doyle, L., & O'Toole, G. (2013). *A lot to learn: refugees, asylum seekers and post-16 learning*. London. Retrieved from www.refugeecouncil.org.uk/assets/0002/595 6/A_lot_to_learn-Jan_13.pdf

El Jack, A. (2010). "Education is my mother and father": The "invisible" women of Sudan. *Refuge, 27*(2), 19–29.

Elliott, S., & Yusuf, I. (2014). "Yes, we can; but together": Social capital and refugee resettlement. *Kōtuitui: New Zealand Journal of Social Sciences Online, 9* (2), 101–110. DOI:10.1080/1177083X.2014.951662

Europa-Universität Viadrina Frankfurt an der Oder. (2018a). Female Refugees. Retrieved August 15, 2018, from https://www.europa-uni.de/de/struktur/gre mien/beauftragte/gleichstellung/Studium/femalerefugees/index.html

Europa-Universität Viadrina Frankfurt an der Oder. (2018b). Studienbegleiter*in. Retrieved August 15, 2018, from https://www.europa-uni.de/de/struktur/gre mien/beauftragte/gleichstellung/Studium/Studienbegleiter_in/index.html

European Commission. (2016). *Inspiring practices – January 2016: Higher Education helping newly arrived refugees Inspiring practices – January 2016: Higher Education helping newly arrived refugees.*

European Commission, EACEA, & Eurydice. (2019). *Integrating Asylum Seekers and Refugees into Higher Education in Europe: National Policies and Measures, Eurydice Report*. Luxembourg: Publications Office of the European Union.

Fang, W. (2012). The Development of Transnational Higher Education in China: A Comparative Study of Research Universities and Teaching Universities. *Journal of Studies in International Education, 16*(1), 5–23. https://doi.org/10 .1177/1028315311410607

Finger, C. (2016). Institutional constraints and the translation of College aspira-tions into intentions – Evidence from a factorial survey. *Research in Social Stratification and Mobility, 46*, 112–128. https://doi.org/10.1016/j .rssm.2016.08.001

Fourier, K., Kracht, J., Latsch, K., Heublein, U., & Schneider, C. (2017). *Integration von* Flüchtlingen an deutschen Hochschulen: Erkenntnisse aus den Hochschulprogrammen für Flüchtlinge. Bonn. www.daad.de/medien/der-daad/studie_hochschulzugang_fluechtlinge.pdf

Fritsch, M., & Jena, F. (2013). *Die regionale Rolle von Hochschulen in kleinen Städten*. Jena.

German Rectors' Conference. (2019). Higher Education Compass. Retrieved May 7, 2019, from www.hochschulkompass.de/en/higher-education-institutions.html

Giles, W., & Hyndman, J. (2004). Introduction: Gender and Conflict in a Global Context. In Wenona Giles & Jennifer Hyndman (Eds.), *Sites of Violence: Gender and Conflict Zones* (pp. 3–23). Berkeley: University of California Press.

Goastellec, G. (2018). Refugees' Access to Higher Education. In J. C. Shin & P. Teixeira (Eds.), *Encyclopedia of International Higher Education Systems and Institutions* (pp. 1–7). Hamburg: Springer. https://doi.org/10.1007/978–94-017–9553-1_421–1

Grüttner, M., Schröder, S., Berg, J., & Otto, C. (2018). Refugees on Their Way to German Higher Education: A Capabilities and Engagements Perspective on Aspirations, Challenges and Support Refugees on Their Way to German Higher Education: A Capabilities and Engagements Perspective on Aspirations, Challenges. *Global Education Review*, 5(4), 115–135.

Harris, A., Spark, C., & Watts, M. N. C. (2015). Gains and Losses: African Australian Women and Higher Education. *Journal of Sociology*, 51(2), 370–384. https://doi.org/10.1177/1440783314536792

Hazelkorn, E., & Ryan, M. (2013). The Impact of University Rankings on Higher Education Policy in Europe. In P. Zgaga, U. Teichler, & J. Brennan (Eds.), *The Globalisation Challenge for European Higher Education* (pp. 79–99). Frankfurt am Main: Peter Lang GmbH.

Henkel, M., Steidle, H., Braukmann, J., & Sommer, I. (2016). *Familien mit Migrationshintergrund: Analysen zur Lebenssituation, Erwerbsbeteiligung und Vereinbarkeit von Familie und Beruf. Lebenssituation, Erwerbsbeteiligung und Vereinbarkeit von Familie und Beruf. Berlin*. Berlin: Bundesministerium für Familie, Senioren, Frauen und Jugend. http://scholar.google.de/scholar?q=Familien+mit+Migrationshintergrund.++Sommer&btnG=&hl=de&as_sdt=0,5#6

Hüther, O., & Krücken, G. (2018). *Higher Education in Germany – Recent Developments in an International Perspective*. Cham: Springer. https://doi.org/10.1007/978–3-319–61479-3

Hwang, W. C., & Wood, J. J. (2009). Acculturative Family Distancing: Links with Self-Reported Symptomatology among Asian Americans and Latinos. *Child Psychiatry and Human Development*, 40(1), 123–138. https://doi.org/10.1007/s10578-008–0115-8

Joyce, A., Earnest, J., De Mori, G., & Silvagni, G. (2010). The Experiences of Students from Refugee Backgrounds at Universities in Australia: Reflections on the Social, Emotional and Practical Challenges. *Journal of Refugee Studies*, 23(1), 82–97. https://doi.org/10.1093/jrs/feq001

Kanno, Y., & Varghese, M. M. (2010). Immigrant and Refugee ESL Students' Challenges to Accessing Four-year College Education: From Language Policy to Educational Policy. *Journal of Language, Identity, and Education*, 9(2000), 310–328. https://doi.org/10.1080/15348458.2010.517693

Kariya, T. (2011). Japanese Solutions to the Equity and Efficiency Dilemma? Secondary Schools, Inequity and the Arrival of 'universal' Higher Education. *Oxford Review of Education*, 37(2), 241–266. https://doi.org/10.1080/03054985.2011.559388

Korac, M. (2004). War, Flight, and Exile: Gendered Violence among Refugee Women from Post-Yugoslav States. In W. Giles & J. Hyndman (Eds.), *Sites of Violence: Gender and Conflict zones* (pp. 249–272). Berkeley: University of California Press.

Korntheuer, A., Gag, M., Anderson, P., & Schroeder, J. (2018). Education of Refugee-background Youth in Germany: Systematic Barriers to Equitable Participation in the Vocational Education System. In S. Shapiro, R. Farrelly, & M. J. Curry (Eds.), *Educating Refugee-Background Students: Critical Issues and Dynamic Contexts* (pp. 191–207). Bristol: Multilingual Matters.

Le Ha, P. (2018). Higher Education, English, and the Idea of 'the West': Globalizing and Encountering a Global South Regional University. *Discourse: Studies in the Cultural Politics of Education, 39*(5), 782–797. https://doi.org/10.1080/01596306.2018.1448704

Leicht-Scholten, C. (2008). Excellenz braucht Vielfalt – oder: wie Gender und Diversity in den Mainstream der Hochschulentwicklung kommt. *Journal Netzwerk Frauenforschung NRW* (23), 33–40.

Lenette, C., Baker, S., & Hirsch, A. (2019). Systemic Policy Barriers to Meaningful Participation of Students from Refugee and Asylum Seeking Backgrounds in Australian Higher Education: Neoliberal Settlement and Language Policies and (deliberate?) Challenges for Meaningful Participation. In J. L. McBrien (Ed.), *Educational Policies and Practices of English-Speaking Refugee Resettlement Countries*. Leiden: Brill. https://doi.org/10.1163/9789004401891_004

Luciano, D. (2012). *The Impact of Acculturation Strategy and Social Supports on Acculturative Stress and Academic Performance among Hispanic/Latino/a College Students*. New York: New York University.

McAdams, D. (2001). The Psychology of Life Stories. *Review of General Psychology, 5*(2), 100–122. https://doi.org/10.1037//1089-2680.5.2.100

McRae-Yates, V. (2007). *Institutionalizing Diversity: Transforming Higher Education*. Cincinnati, Ohio: Union Institute & University.

Morrice, L. (2013). Refugees in Higher Education: Boundaries of Belonging and Recognition, Stigma and Exclusion. *International Journal of Lifelong Education, 32*(5), 652–668. https://doi.org/10.1080/02601370.2012.761288

Mungo, M. (2017). Deconstructing Racism on University Websites. In J. Daniels, K. Gregory, & T. M. Cottom (Eds.), *Digital Sociologies* (pp. 233–250). Bristol: Policy Press.

Muñoz, S. M., & Maldonado, M. M. (2012). Counterstories of College Persistence by Undocumented Mexicana Students: Navigating Race, Class, Gender, and Legal Status. *International Journal of Qualitative Studies in Education, 25*(3), 293–315. https://doi.org/10.1080/09518398.2010.529850

Oberoi, A. K. (2016). *Mentoring for First-Generation Immigrant and Refugee Youth National Mentoring Resource Center Population Review.* www.nationalmentorin gresourcecenter.org

Ortloff, Debora Hinderliter & Frey, Christopher J. (2007). Blood Relatives: Language, Immigration and Education of Ethnic Returnees in Germany and Japan. *Comparative Education Review, 51*(4), 447–470. https://doi.org/10.1086/520865

Osei-Kofi, N., & Torres, L. E. (2015). College Admissions Viewbooks and the Grammar of Gender, Race, and STEM. *Cultural Studies of Science Education, 10* (2), 527–544. https://doi.org/10.1007/s11422-014-9656-2

Patton, M. Q. (2002). *Qualitative Evaluation Methods.* Thousand Oaks: Sage Publications.

Rana, M., Qin, D. B., Bates, L., Luster, T., & Saltarelli, A. (2011). Factors Related to Educational Resilience among Sudanese Unaccompanied Minors. *Teachers College Record, 113*(9), 2080–2114. Retrieved from https://search.ebscohost.com /login.aspx?direct=true&db=eric&AN=EJ951087&site=ehost-live%5Cnhttp:// www.tcrecord.org/Content.asp?ContentId=16187

Ripamonti, S., Galuppo, L., Bruno, A., Ivaldi, S., & Scaratti, G. (2018). Reconstructing the Internship Program as a Critical Reflexive Practice: The Role of Tutorship. *Teaching in Higher Education, 23*(6), 751–768. https://doi .org/10.1080/13562517.2017.1421627

Rockwell, G., & Sinclair, S. (2016). *Hermeneutica: Computer-assisted Interpretation in the Humanities.* Cambridge: The MIT Press.

Santos, J. L., Cabrera, N. L., & Fosnacht, K. J. (2010). Is 'race-neutral' Really Race-neutral?: Disparate Impact towards Underrepresented Minorities in Post-209 UC System Admissions. *Journal of Higher Education, 81*(6), 605–631. https://doi.org /10.1353/jhe.2010.0009

Schmidt, M. A., & Kinscher, B. (2018). *Geflüchtete Frauen an Hochschulen.* Berlin: Hochschule für Technik und Wirtschaft Berlin.

Sinclair, S., & Rockwell, G. (2019a). Terms. 5 June 2019, http://voyant-tools.org

Sinclair, S., & Rockwell, G. (2019b). Terms. Retrieved September 14, 2019, from http://voyant-tools.org

Sinclair, S., & Rockwell, G. (2019c). Trends. Retrieved June 5, 2019, from http:// voyant-tools.org

Sinclair, S., & Rockwell, G. (2019d). Trends. Retrieved September 14, 2019, from http://voyant-tools.org

Sobieraj, A. (2015). Facilitating access to education for refugees (Vol. 49). Bonn. Retrieved from www.daad.de/presse/pressemitteilungen/en/39606-facilitating-access-to-education-for-refugees/?c=97

Sontag, K., & Harder, T. (2018). *What are the Barriers for Asylum Seekers and Refugees Who Want to Enroll at a Swiss University?* Neuchâtel: Swiss National Center of Competence in Research (NCCR).

Spiess, C. K., & Wrohlich, K. (2010). Does Distance Determine Who Attends a University in Germany? *Economics of Education Review, 29*(3), 470–479. https://doi.org/10.1016/j.econedurev.2009.10.009

Statistisches Bundesamt. (2018). Städte (Alle Gemeinden mit Stadtrecht) nach Fläche, Bevölkerung und Bevölkerungsdichte am 31.12.2016. Retrieved October 12, 2018, from www.destatis.de/DE/ZahlenFakten/Lae nderRegionen/Regionales/Gemeindeverzeichnis/Administrativ/Aktuell/05S taedte.html

Stevenson, J., & Baker, S. (2018). Introduction. In *Refugees in Higher Education: Debate, Discourse and Practice* (pp. 1–24). Bingley: Emerald Group Publishing. https://doi.org/10.1360/zd-2013-43-6-1064

Subasi, S., Proyer, M., & Atanasoska, T. (2018). Re-accessing Higher Education: Regulations and Challenges for Refugees in Austria and Turkey. In K. Arar, K. Haj-yehia, D. B. Ross, & Y. Kondakci (Eds.), *Higher Education Challenges for Migrant and Refugee Students in a Global World* (pp. 297–310). New York: Peter Lang.

Teney, C., Hanquinet, L., & Bürkin, K. (2016). Feeling European: An Exploration of Ethnic Disparities among Immigrants. *Journal of Ethnic and Migration Studies, 42*(13), 2182–2204. https://doi.org/10.1080/1369183X .2016.1166941

Thomas, L., Hill, M., O'Mahony, J., & Yorke, M. (2017). *Supporting Student Success: Strategies for Institutional Change.* London. Retrieved from www .heacademy.ac.uk/knowledge-hub/supporting-student-success-strategies-institutional-change

Unangst, L., & Streitwieser, B. (2018). Inclusive Practices in Response to the German Refugee Influx: Support Structures and Rationales Described by University Administrators. In A. Curaj, L. Deca, & R. Pricopie (Eds.), *European Higher Education Area: The Impact of Past and Future Policies* (pp. 277–292). Cham: Springer.

UNHCR. (2015). *Ethiopia Refugee Strategy 2015–2018.* Geneva.

Universität Weimar. (2019). The Bauhaus-Universität Weimar's support for refugees. 1 June 2019, www.uni-weimar.de/en/university/structure/university-management-team/board-of-governance/the-bauhaus-universitaet-weimars-support-for-refugees/

University of Freiburg. (2019). Services and Initiatives for Refugees. Retrieved May 29, 2019, from www.uni-freiburg.de/universitaet-en/portrait/refugees-welcome

University of Tasmania Communications & Media. (2017, September 15). Program empowers those most disadvantaged to shine, p. 1. www.media.utas .edu.au/general-news/all-news/program-empowers-those-most-disadvantaged-to-shine van der Wende, M. (2001). Internationalisation Policies: About New Trends and Contrasting Paradigms. *Higher Education Policy, 14*(3), 249–259.

Vanselow, A., Weinkopf, C., & Kalina, T. (2008). *Poverty and Social Exclusion in Rural Areas.* Brussels.

Wegmann, K. M. (2014). Shaping a New Society: Immigration, Integration, and Schooling in Germany. *International Social Work, 57*(2), 131–142. https://doi.org /10.1177/0020872812446980

Wetzstein, I. (2019). The Gender Dimension of the Refugee Debate: Progressiveness and Backwardness Discourses in Austrian Press Coverage. In G. Dell'Orto & I. Wetzstein (Eds.), *Refugee News, Refugee Politics: Journalism, Public Opinion and Policymaking in Europe* (pp. 56–67). New York: Routledge.

Wismar, Hochschule. (2019). Als Flüchtling unsere Angebote nutzen. 2 November 2018, www.hs-wismar.de/international/beratung/refugees/

Wolter, A. (2017). The Expansion and Structural Change of Postsecondary Education in Germany. In P. G. Altbach, L. Reisberg, & H. de Wit (Eds.), *Responding to Massification: Differentiation in Postsecondary Education Worldwide* (pp. 115–126). Rotterdam: Sense Publishers.

Yudkevich, M. (2017). Diversity and Uniformity in the Structure of Russian Postsecondary Education. In P. G. Altbach, L. Reisberg, & H. de Wit (Eds.), *Responding to Massification: Differentiation in Postsecondary Education Worldwide.* Leiden: Sense Publishers.

Zentrum für Gender Studies und feministische Zukunftsforschung. (2016). Mobiler Studientag feministische Rechtswissenschaft: Hi(s)story – Herstory? Asyl- und Aufenthaltsrecht aus der Gender-Perspektive. Retrieved August 14, 2018, from www.uni-marburg.de/de/genderzukunft/veranstaltungen/studien tag/archiv/studientag9

Zippel, K., Ferree, M. M., & Zimmermann, K. (2016). Gender equality in German universities: vernacularising the battle for the best brains. *Gender and Education, 28*(7), 867–885. https://doi.org/10.1080/09540253.2015.1123229

CHAPTER 10

Colombian Distress Migrants in Ecuador
Limits to Higher Education

Elizabeth Donger

Introduction

Ecuador has a remarkably progressive legal framework for the social inclusion of migrants, an important contrast to current global trends of growing exclusion of non-citizen populations. However, despite constitutional guarantees of free higher education and legal commitments to equality in access, enormous gaps remain between policy and practice for the country's most vulnerable migrants. In 2015, Ecuador's national gross enrolment rate for higher education was 45.6 per cent (UNESCO-UIS, 2018). Two years later, the United Nations High Commissioner for Refugees (UNHCR) found that only 1.0 per cent of Colombian migrants with protection needs aged 18–29 years old were attending higher education in Ecuador. This is significantly lower than rates seen among the nation's lowest income quintile and among indigenous and Afro-Ecuadorean minority groups.

This chapter outlines Ecuador's vision of equal opportunity for higher education and explores why it falls short for displaced Colombians, who have historically made up the vast majority of Ecuador's refugee population. It uses the term 'distress migrant' to describe the population analysed because the Ecuadorean government, for reasons further elaborated below, does not formally recognise all Colombians with protection needs as being refugees. This more inclusive category includes registered refugees and asylum seekers, as well as migrants 'who face protection risks similar to those of refugees' but either have chosen to obtain some other form of legal status or are without any status at all (UNHCR, 2018c, 61).

The following sections map out the migration context in Ecuador and then describe the country's higher education system. National legal and policy frameworks regulating access are designed to treat officially recognised refugees and citizens entirely equally. Public education at the primary (ages 6–11), secondary (ages 12–17) and tertiary levels (ages 18–22) is all tuition-free. The government also includes refugees as one of several 'historically discriminated' groups, for whom 15 per cent of seats at private universities are reserved, tuition-free and awarded based entirely on performance on a standardised university entrance exam.

The chapter goes on to argue that Ecuador's official commitment to non-discrimination means little in a context where opportunity is distributed unevenly. An unknown but significant proportion of Colombian distress migrants remains undocumented or has pending asylum claims. These people are barred from applying to higher education. In practice, issues associated with identity documentation still act to exclude even those refugees who are formally registered with the government. There are other additional barriers to entry, including displacement-related trauma, lack of social support and information networks, discrimination and poverty. State employees' inflexible everyday interpretations of legal frameworks further limit access to higher education.

The wide gap between existing progressive frameworks for migrant inclusion and the reality of Colombians' access to higher education illustrates that impartial legal approaches are insufficient for equitable access. The chapter concludes by outlining several necessary reforms to remedy these inequalities.

This analysis draws primarily on research carried out in 2016 by the author for the FXB Center for Health and Human Rights at Harvard University (Donger, Fuller, Bhabha, & Leaning, 2017). The research evaluated the health and well-being of refugee youth ages 15–19 years living in the capital, Quito, and in Lago Agrio, the biggest city of a province that abuts 60 per cent of the Colombian border. It also evaluated the strength of the protection system in those cities. One central finding of that project was that young distress migrants craved, and yet lacked, opportunities to develop their potential and contribute to Ecuadorean society. The study involved fifteen qualitative interviews with service providers from UNHCR, government and civil society and with refugee youth. Quantitative surveys were also conducted with 299 adolescent refugees between 15 and 19 years old, reached using respondent-driven sampling.[1] These tools yielded wide-ranging data on young refugees' experiences and needs in the public and private realms.

---

[1] Respondent Driven Sampling (RDS) is an adapted chain-referral method used in epidemiologic research on hidden or hard-to-reach populations. It is intended to generate unbiased population estimates via post-stratified weights, a method for adjusting sampling weights that accounts for non-random recruitment through social networks (Heckathorn, 1997).

The chapter also integrates unpublished demographic data, provided by UNHCR Ecuador that was gathered in 2014 and 2017 for the Office's Integral Solutions Initiative. In each year, data were collected in urban areas of 9 of the country's 24 provinces using snowball sampling, reaching more than 9,000 distress migrants identified as having protection needs (including refugees, asylum seekers, undocumented migrants and other visa holders). Ninety-nine per cent of respondents were Colombian. Finally, the author carried out six additional in-depth interviews with academics and activists who work or have worked in Ecuador on refugee issues.

Distress Migrants in Ecuador

Ecuador has been a destination for refugees since the time it welcomed Jews during and after the Second World War. Its refugee population only swelled, however, as a consequence of the Colombian civil conflict, involving government, paramilitary groups, crime syndicates and left-wing guerrillas. Most Colombian distress migrants arrived after 2000 when Plan Colombia, a US military assistance package, escalated the fighting in rural areas near Ecuador (Korovkin, 2008). Today, Ecuador hosts Latin America's largest refugee population.

In 2017, after collaborating with the government to improve its database, UNHCR reported there were 145,333 'persons of concern' living in Ecuador, calling these the first 'reliable statistics . . . since 2013' (UNHCR, 2018b). This figure amounts to 0.89 per cent of the country's total population of 16.3 million (UNHCR, 2017c) and includes 47,416 recognised refugees and 11,917 asylum seekers; 45,000 'people in refugee-like situations', who are people the Office considers to be refugees but are not applying for asylum; and 41,000 'others of concern', who are people who require protection and assistance but do not 'fall under the categories of forcibly displaced or stateless' (UNHCR, 2018c, 55).

Individuals seeking refugee status in Ecuador must apply within ninety days of arrival in the country through a two-step process with appeal rights, conducted exclusively by the Refugee Office of the Ministry of Home Affairs. Status must be renewed every two years, and after three years, refugees can apply for permanent residence and Ecuadorian citizenship. This is an expensive and lengthy legal process, meaning that very few refugees are in reality able to naturalise (Donger et al., 2017, 22).

The rate of acceptance for asylum applications was 9.4 per cent in 2012, the most recent year for which data are available, down from nearly

25 per cent in 2009 (Jokisch, 2014). Ecuador's refugee determination system is highly centralised and complex and suffers from a huge backlog of pending claims, almost 15,000 in 2014. One UNHCR representative explained that the application process should only take three months but that in reality more than half the applicants wait over a year and some up to six years (Donger et al., 2017, 20).

In order to bypass this slow bureaucracy, many distress migrants choose not to apply for asylum and take advantage of other available options for legal status. Colombians in Ecuador can apply for a two-year temporary work visa, with minimal requirements, as members of the Latin American regional bloc Mercado Comun del Cono Sur (Southern Cone Common Market) or "MERCOSUR". Those with family ties to Ecuadorian citizens, such as a spouse or child born in the country, can obtain a family visa. Finally, an unknown but sizeable number of distress migrants live in the country undocumented or stay on after their asylum claims have been rejected.

Up until 2015, Colombians were consistently estimated to comprise more than 95 per cent of the registered refugee and asylum-seeking population (UNHCR, 2015). At the end of 2017, however, UNHCR estimated that Colombians made up only 70 per cent of Ecuador's recognised refugees and asylum seekers (UNHCR, 2018b). There is a growing population of migrants seeking protection in Ecuador from locations as far afield as Afghanistan, Iraq and Syria. Yet the stark change in the composition of Ecuador's distress migrant population is principally the result of the increasingly acute political, humanitarian, economic and human rights crisis in Venezuela. In the first seven months of 2018 alone, over half a million Venezuelans crossed Ecuador's borders. Though the majority continue onwards to other countries further south, up to 20 per cent remain in Ecuador (UNHCR, 2018d).

In December 2016, the Colombian government ratified a peace deal with the country's largest rebel group, the Revolutionary Armed Forces of Colombia (FARC). Despite this, other armed groups and organised criminal gangs continue to operate in Colombia, and its citizens continue to seek asylum in Ecuador. UNHCR has projected that in 2018 up to 6,500 additional Colombian asylum seekers would arrive (UNHCR, 2017b). As of early 2019, Ecuador's government had made no official statement regarding future asylum status for this population.

Ecuador takes a markedly progressive approach to migrants' rights. In 2007, Ecuador elected a left-wing government led by Rafael Correa, who declared 'a campaign to dismantle that 20th-century invention of passports and visas' (Freier, 2013, 1). Putting social and economic rights at the centre of the state model, a new Constitution was enacted in 2008 that recognised the principle of universal citizenship and human mobility as a human right (section three, article 40).

Ecuador ratified the 1951 Refugee Convention and its 1967 Protocol in 1955 and 1969, respectively, and its domestic legal and policy framework largely incorporates the international commitments inherent in these instruments. The government passed a new Human Mobility Law in 2017, which brought legal realities in line with the language of the new constitution. The law guarantees free movement for people under the State's protection; non-criminalisation of those with irregular migration status; equality under the law and non-discrimination; and the best interests of children and adolescents.

The government does not provide specialised programmes for refugees in Ecuador but integrates them into existing social services. This perspective is summed up by Laura Romero, of the Refugee Office of the Ministry of Home Affairs, when explaining the policies of the government towards refugee children: 'Any program, any project that is aimed at the refugee population also has to accommodate the native population because the refugees in Ecuador are not isolated in one specific place ... the refugee has to be just one more child' (Donger et al., 2017, 6).

Ecuador places no constraints on any migrants' freedom of movement. Registered refugees have the right to work, and, in 2014, this was also extended to asylum applicants. The Ministry of Social and Economic Inclusion provides cash transfers to qualifying low-income families in Ecuador through the Human Development Bond (BDH), and referrals for legal services for victims of rights violations. Migrants have a right to primary and secondary public education free of charge. They also are entitled to basic public healthcare provided without discrimination to citizens and foreigners alike, a guarantee that research suggests is largely honoured in practice (Donger et al., 2017, 34).

UNHCR has operated in Ecuador since 2000 and aims to play an essential role in filling the gaps in this system for refugees, providing specialised programmes for particularly vulnerable refugees through partner organisations at the local level. However, UNHCR, as in other countries, suffers from chronic underfunding: in 2017, its target budget for Ecuador was $22 million but expenditure was $11 million (UNHCR, 2018a).

Higher Education in Ecuador

Overview of the System

René Ramírez Gallegos, the secretary for higher education from 2011 to 2017 and architect of Ecuador's new law regulating higher education, writes that the country's higher education system is designed to 'build a more egalitarian and just society' (Herdoíza-Estévez, 2015, 9). The 2008 Constitution eliminated fees at public universities and guaranteed 'equality of opportunities with respect to access, permanence, passing and graduation' in both private and public institutions (Article 356). Since 2008, there have been significant reforms that have reduced the number of postsecondary institutions, attempted to increase their quality and make more equitable the admissions process.

The government raised its budget for universities from $335 million in 2008 to $2.08 billion in 2016 (2.2 per cent of GDP) to pay for fees that were previously only covered for General Basic Education (for children aged 5–15) (Secretaria Nacional de Educación Superior, Ciencia, Tecnologia y Innovacion [SENESCYT], 2017). Ecuador now invests significantly more on tertiary education than on primary or secondary. In 2015, it spent $6,004 per student in tertiary education, compared to only $576 at the secondary level and $1,025.94 at the primary level (UNESCO-UIS, 2018). One consequence of this has been to exacerbate existing inequalities between the public and private systems at the secondary level (Post, 2011).

SENESCYT is the regulatory entity for higher education, designated by the Consejo de Educación Superior (Higher Education Council). As of 2018, there are sixty universities and polytechnic schools in Ecuador. Over half are public, one-third are private and one-seventh co-financed in part by the government and in part by the private sector. One-tenth of Ecuador's students also seek higher education in Ecuador through the country's 279 Technical and Technological Training Institutes (Institutos Superiores Técnicos y Tecnológicos, ISTs), which do not offer terminal degrees (Sistema Nacional de Información de Educación Superior del Ecuador [SNIESE], 2018).

In an effort to improve the quality of higher education, the government shut down more than 14 underperforming universities, 40 polytechnics and 125 ISTs between 2008 and 2016, the majority private and in rural areas (Ramirez Gallegos, 2016). Lack of regulation and supply outside of cities had led to a 'cottage industry ... of small, privately operated universities' (Neuman, 2012). There are a very limited number of higher education opportunities in rural areas, and in particular in the provinces along the Colombian border: Sucumbíos, Carchi, Imbabura and Esmeraldas house only 1 university, 4 polytechnic schools and 17 ISTs. This is where many distress migrants, who are often displaced from rural areas, settle. While there are no reliable estimates, in 2011 UNHCR estimated that 40 per cent live in rural areas of Ecuador (UNHCR, 2011).

Access to higher education requires a secondary school diploma or 'Baccalaureate'. Secondary education, like primary education, is free for all residents in Ecuador, though completion is not legally compulsory. Since 2010, with the passing of the Higher Education Organic Law (LOES), admission to public higher education in Ecuador has also been contingent upon passing a standardised entrance exam, Examen Nacional de Educación Superior (ENES). SENESCYT states that this was intended to make the process more meritocratic and 'democratise access to higher education' (2015, 29). The ENES test was replaced in 2017 by the *Ser Bachiller*, which is similar in structure. Private universities set their own admissions criteria for admission.

After receiving their *Ser Bachiller* grade, students select their top five universities and programmes of interest through SENESCYT. Institutions elect candidates entirely based on test results, filling individual programmes by starting with applicants with the highest score. In practice, students who do not receive top marks are often placed into subjects or institutions that do not interest them or are located in cities far from their current residence. There are no publicly available data on gender, class, ethnic or racial differences in score results. What is known is that over two hundred thousand people sat the entrance exam test in 2017, competing for 77,475 available places (private and public) (El Telégrafo, 2017).

Affirmative Action Programmes

Article 11.2 of Ecuador's 2008 Constitution, supported by the subsequent 2009 Presidential Decree, calls for 'affirmative action measures' in higher education 'that promote equality in favour of those who find themselves in a situation of inequality'. LOES also calls for equal opportunity in admissions. Nevertheless, in a review of Ecuador's affirmative action policies, Catherine Walsh found that, 'despite these commitments, . . . there is still no consolidated project of affirmative action per se' (2015, 27).

The only official measure implemented is a quota policy, whereby 15 per cent of places at both public and private institutions are reserved for students defined as belonging to one of a number of historically marginalised groups, as described below, and who score highest on the entrance exam (SENESCYT, 2018). Those selected for a place at a private or co-financed university do not pay tuition and can apply for further scholarships, if available, to cover living costs.

This effort is insufficient, however, because the *Ser Bachiller* test does not account for the underlying inequality in the social and educational backgrounds of examinees: their ability to pay for tutoring, the quality of their prior educational experience, and examples set for them by university-educated parents. The old ENES entrance exam had built in affirmative action that was not carried forward to the *Ser Bachiller*, whereby students would receive additional points if they belonged to a historically disadvantaged group.

'Historically marginalised group' is also defined very widely by the Ecuadorian state. This category includes indigenous people, Afro-Ecuadorians, Montubios, people with a disability, those who belong to the lowest socio-economic quintiles, those who live in a border area, those affected by the earthquake of 2016 or those with refugee status. The details of the algorithm that SENESCYT uses to select scholarship recipients from this large group – for example, what proportion of seats are awarded to each subgroup each year – are not publicly available. None of the migration and education specialists interviewed for this chapter had insight on this point.

Recognised refugees who do not obtain one of these government-reserved private university seats can seek financial assistance for further studies through a limited number of other means. Since 2002, the private Universidad de San Francisco Quito (USFQ) has implemented an Ethnic Diversity programme to provide scholarships to indigenous and Afro-Ecuadorean youth. This programme expanded in 2015 to include refugees, and since that year nine refugees have started their studies. USFQ also operates a summer school with the non-profit FUDELA to help refugee youth develop skills and enter the job market. The founder and director of the Ethnic Diversity Programme explained that 'as far as I know we are the only private university [in Ecuador] that has an affirmative action program that is specifically for refugees' (Personal communication, 17 September 2018).

In 2018, the non-profit FUDELA covered tuition, but not living and associated, costs for five refugees in Quito and three in Santo Domingo. UNHCR runs a global DAFI scholarship programme, locally administered in conjunction with the non-profit HIAS, which covers costs for high-achieving refugee youth to attend private institutions. However, although

Ecuador is the only country in the Americas where UNHCR offers these scholarships, it awarded only 13 scholarships to refugee students from Colombia in 2016, down from the annual average of 28.1 per year to Colombians since the programme started in 2005 (UNHCR, 2017a, 27).

Trends in Enrolment

Available evidence suggests that rates of enrolment at the secondary school level in Ecuador are slightly lower for distress migrants than for the poorest quintile of the local population. This gap widens at the university level, where enrolment is far lower for distress migrants than it is for the poorest Ecuadoreans, as well as for minority groups like indigenous or Afro-Ecuadoreans.

With regard to secondary school education, Ecuador's national net enrolment rate in 2017 was 88.3 per cent (UNESCO-UIS, 2018). The most recent publicly available figures disaggregated by income are from Ecuador's National Statistics Institute (INEC) in 2014, when 68.4 per cent of residents from the lowest national quintile ages 12–17 were enrolled in secondary school (Instituto Nacional de Estadísticas y Censos, 2014). The Harvard FXB study found that secondary school enrolment rates for distress migrant youth in Quito were lower than this: 65.6 per cent among those with legal status and 47.1 per cent among those without status (Donger et al., 2017, 32).

Records on access to post-secondary education have been kept inconsistently over the past decades by various coordinating bodies, with limited cooperation, so there is no official admissions data over time (Post, 2011, 3). What evidence does exist, suggests that efforts to both increase and democratise education access in Ecuador have shown some success. Overall gross enrolment in tertiary education has gone up nationally from 38.7 per cent in 2008 to 45.6 per cent in 2015 (UNESCO-UIS, 2018).[2] Ecuador now has the highest proportion in Latin America of low-income students enrolled in university (Walsh, 2015, 30). In 2014, gross university enrolment was 5.0 per cent among those in the lowest national consumption quintile (compared to 82.4 per cent for the highest quintile) (INEC, 2014), 9.9 per for indigenous Ecuadoreans and 17.4 per cent for Afro/black/ mulatto groups.

---

[2] UNESCO-UIS defines tertiary gross enrolment as 'the number of students enrolled, regardless of age, expressed as a percentage of the official corresponding school-age population . . . the 5-year age group starting from the official secondary school graduation age'.

Equally, there is no official data on gross enrolment of distress migrants in higher education in Ecuador. What evidence does exist, however, clearly demonstrates that rates in this group are far below those seen in the aforementioned low-income and minority groups. UNHCR's 2017 study found that, of respondents between 18 and 29 years old, only 1.0 per cent were currently in university studies. Others in this age bracket were finishing their primary and secondary schooling, 2.1 per cent and 6.0 per cent respectively. This is likely an upper estimate because the UNHCR study did not capture distress migrants in rural areas, who can reasonably be assumed to have less access to tertiary education.

Barriers to Access

Why is it that Ecuador's constitutional guarantee of 'equality of opportunities' in the higher education system is not realised for distress migrants? Research suggests these migrants do not lack ambition: in the Harvard FXB study, 83.4 per cent of youth in Quito and 74.5 per cent in Lago Agrio stated that they intended to complete higher education. When asked about their priorities for assistance in a series of consultations hosted by UNHCR and the Women's Refugee Commission, adolescent refugee youth in Ecuador 'particularly focused on higher education' (2016, 8).

This section discusses several key factors that disproportionally affect distress migrants on the road to higher education: poverty; legal status and documentation; trauma, social isolation and lack of information; and discrimination and inflexible bureaucracies. Beginning well before the moment of university application, these factors profoundly shape distress migrants' mental and physical health, hopes and aspirations, and family support structures. As a result, these young people are less likely to do well in the entrance exam for public university, which is the most important step in the process. They must excel even against those educated at top-tier private schools, with stable home lives and full stomachs. If they do not, then they may be placed in a subject that does not interest them, at an institution far away from their homes (an impossibility for many given family responsibilities) and are ineligible for additional financial assistance.

Poverty

The first significant barrier that Colombian distress migrants face is financial. Many of the displaced come from the poorest sections of Colombian society, and the journey itself strips many of their assets. While recognised refugees and asylum seekers have an unrestricted right to work in Ecuador, in practice they experience 'various detailed legal and socioeconomic obstacles and gaps in implementation that prevent their access to employment' (Zetter & Ruaudel, 2016, 15). Colombians compete for work in the context of high overall unemployment, with xenophobia among some employers, and weak enforcement of labour protections (van Teijlingen, 2011, 2). As a result, most work low-wage and exploitative jobs in the informal market. Among working youth ages 15–19 living in Quito, only a small fraction (4.2 per cent) had a formally registered job (Donger et al., 2017, 36).

The 2017 UNHCR study found that these Colombian families spent the vast majority of their household income on basic subsistence needs: on average of 84.4 per cent on rent, food, clothing, transport and medicine. Young, capable and able-bodied people in these homes carry significant responsibilities: financial, emotional and otherwise. In Quito, adolescent girls ages 15–19 in the Harvard FXB study spent more than 20 hours every week on household chores and family care, while boys spent 12.8 hours (Donger et al., 2017, 32).

The economic deprivation that these distress migrants confront is starkly illustrated by the research showing this demographic suffers pervasive food scarcity. 'I worry a lot about my family', explained one 16-year-old Colombian, 'we are going through a very difficult time. I see how my mother and father don't have enough to give us food day to day' (Donger et al., 2017). The World Food Programme has estimated that about 64 per cent of recent arrivals from Colombia have poor or borderline food consumption, requiring assistance to meet their basic food needs (2017).

The university entrance exam results have been shown to be strongly impacted by family income and socio-economic background (Barahona, 2016). Even if they excel at this test and then obtain a place at a free public university, or gain a scholarship to a private institution, students bear the opportunity costs of time away from wage-earning jobs. They also still need to meet their own and their family's ongoing living expenses, making further study unrealistic for most.

In theory, recognised refugees in Ecuador have access to credit that might temporarily alleviate these burdens and allow a period of study. But in practice very few financial institutions open their doors to this population. Moscoso and Burneo found that only 26.3 per cent of recognised refugees and asylum seekers in Quito, and 20.6 per cent of undocumented respondents, had access to a savings or current bank account. Rates were much higher, 64.5 per cent, among those who had other legal status (2014, 59). A bank account is necessary even to be considered for the university quota policy. The authors concluded that, in terms of getting credit, 'being a refugee is practically the same as being ineligible' (Moscoso & Burneo, 2014, 59).

Why does it not help that university is tuition-free? Research suggests that the greatest beneficiaries of 'free' university education in Ecuador are not the poorest. In 2010, the Ecuadorean government commissioned the quantitative research scientist David Post to evaluate inequality in the higher education system from 1950 onwards, using indirect survey sources and national census information. Post found that suspending student fees for public universities in 2008 led the following year to 'an increased gap in the probability and rates of public university access between the more-advantaged and the less advantaged populations of Ecuador' (2011, 11). Children whose parents do not speak indigenous languages, those who are mestizo or white, those with upper-income fathers and those with highly educated mothers, all benefited most. The non-progressive effects of this policy have since been corroborated by other research (Ponce & Loayza, 2012).

Many of the Colombians that do gain access to university in Ecuador are middle class. According to Carmen Martinez Novo, a former professor at the private university FLASCO in Quito, and a researcher on racial discrimination in the Ecuadorian educational system, these students are not motivated by protection or survival concerns but are seeking out comparatively cheaper studies: 'FLASCO is open to giving grants to foreigners. They weren't refugees as far as I know, but it was a way for them to migrate. They were prepared, successful and active, partly because the Colombian education system is better than that in Ecuador' (Personal communication, 29 August 2018).

Legal Status and Documentation

Although Ecuador's system technically offers several options for regularisation of legal status, many Colombian distress migrants remain in legal limbo and are thus precluded outright from tertiary education. Those without legal residency in the country and those with pending status (as with asylum seekers) can enrol in secondary school, but official education policy does not allow them to formally graduate. Testimony from undocumented refugee youth in the Harvard FXB study suggests that, in practice, some without status abandon their studies midway, 'Yes I had problems, I was in school, but the [school] took me out because I didn't have documents, for this reason now I am not studying' (Donger et al., 2017, 29).

Data from UNHCR indicate that these distress migrants with uncertain legal status make up more than half of all distress migrants. The Office's 2014 study found that 35.2 per cent were undocumented, 5.2 per cent had rejected asylum claims and 18.0 per cent had pending applications.

As previously noted, many distress migrants remain without secure status because the asylum application process is so inefficient and because chances of a favourable determination are slim. Others never apply for legal status because of fear or distrust of the authorities, or because they do not have information on alternatives to the asylum system. Many Colombians in Ecuador also do not self-identify as 'refugees' (Rodriguez Gomez, 2016). As discussed in more detail below, this is in part due to pervasive bias that refugees in Ecuador experience in school, public spaces, work places and access to housing.

Many distress migrants do not apply for asylum because registered refugees in Ecuador have for some years been systematically excluded from a broad range of public services due to an issue with the refugee visa that they are issued upon receiving official status. The number printed on the visa is not compatible with Ecuador's Civil Registry, which issues national identification cards (*cédula*). A national identification card is necessary in Ecuador in order to open a bank account, get a loan, register for social security and get legal paid employment, or enrol in school. There are often bureaucratic routes around this requirement; however, in practice, refugees can only do so with the proactive support and time of service providers. For example, a national ID number is necessary to register a child for secondary school through the government's central database, *Módulo de Gestión de Atención Ciudadana* (MOGAC). A social worker at the education non-profit refugee education trust (RET) registered over eighty young refugees as her 'children', as these young people did not know anyone else with a national ID who could do this for them (Donger et al., 2017, 29).

Following sustained advocacy by civil society and by UNHCR, the 2017 Human Mobility Law addressed this significant barrier to rights. All recognised refugees (but not asylum seekers) must now be automatically issued a national identification card by the Civil Registry. The country's 47,416 formerly registered refugees can apply to receive one, by making an appointment with the Ministry for External Relations and travelling to an office in the cities of Quito, Guayaquil or Cuenca. This retroactive process is happening slowly: UNHCR reported that between November 2017 and May 2018, roughly 2.3 per cent (1,100) of all registered refugees received these cards (UNHCR, 2018b).

One last issue of documentation affects all young people displaced to Ecuador from Colombia, whether they have official refugee status or not. Secondary schools and universities require written documentation of past educational attainment for enrolment. For many distress migrants these documents are simply inaccessible, as they took little when they fled their country. These applicants are required instead to sit a placement exam. However, a staff member at the educational non-profit RET in Lago Agrio explained that distress migrants frequently fail the placement exam (Donger et al., 2017, 29). The materials to prepare, books of 200 pages each, are rarely available and much of the content is specific to Ecuador's history and culture. As a result, many are allocated after the placement exam to grades below their age and attainment level. Colombians in this situation are seen as 'lagging behind', suffer from lack of motivation, social stigma, and sometimes often drop out entirely.

'We Stay Inside': Trauma, Social Isolation and Lack of Information

Many Colombians arrive across the border with trauma as a result of their displacement, trauma that is then compounded in Ecuador by experiences of social isolation, discrimination and boredom in both public and private spheres. These factors limit their ability to excel at the university entrance exam, navigate the application bureaucracy and succeed in their studies.

Factions of the Colombian civil conflict continue to pose significant risk to some refugees living in Ecuador. 'We are very close to Colombia and they let anybody cross', explained one adolescent in Quito, 'so it's frightening that they might be looking to catch you' (Donger et al., 2017, 38). In a clear example of how this can affect schooling, one of the five refugee students attending the University of San Francisco, Quito, in 2015 started missing classes. According to the Director of the Ethnic Diversity Programme, the student explained that he feared for his life: someone had tried to kidnap his sister. The university and UNHCR were unsure whether this was true, but only a few months later the student vanished from Quito and did not return, explaining that his whole family had decided to flee Ecuador (Personal communication, 17 September 2018).

Profound levels of distrust among Colombians in Ecuador and fear of discovery mean that the diaspora is not generally a well-networked resource for information. Urban refugees can acquire information on their rights, available services and relevant administrative procedures from civil society groups in Ecuador. However, this assistance is often limited to a specific problem or issue, and many do not reach out to non-profits at all, which are significantly under-funded.

Another result of these weak peer-support networks is that Colombians often self-isolate, spending significant time at home. 'Much of the time we don't go out on the street', explained one 16-year-old woman in Lago Agrio, 'we stay inside because of fear. Because of the fear, we discuss our problems only with a few family members' (Donger et al., 2017, 37). Colombians in cities live geographically dispersed in marginal areas, often the only areas where they can find cheap accommodation and land-lords willing to rent to them. Discrimination in the housing market was an important theme emerging in the Harvard FXB study. A large proportion of these youth ages 15–19 also reported that they do not feel safe in public: 66.3 per cent in Quito and 30 per cent in Lago Agrio.

Mental health is a part of the primary healthcare system in Ecuador, and individuals are guaranteed unimpeded access to healthcare services at no direct cost, regardless of their status. Non-profit partners of UNHCR also offer psychosocial care specifically to displaced popula-tions. Nevertheless, there remain clear unmet needs regarding the mental health of distress migrants: 29.6 per cent of those aged 15–19 living in Quito and 57.1 per cent of those in Lago Agrio exhibited results indicating depression on the Mood and Feelings Scale. Only 3.4 per cent of youth in Lago Agrio and 7.9 per cent in Quito exhibited high levels of hope for their own future according to the Children's Hope Score (Donger et al., 2017, 35). These psychosocial challenges become more acute for older adolescents.

'They Judge without Knowing': Discrimination and Inflexible Bureaucracy

'Once I heard on the local radio an announcer calling Colombian women whores and accusing the Colombian men of being guerrillas', stated a 19-year-old refugee from Quito, 'what we want is respect'. Colombians in Ecuador are widely associated with criminality and sex work, and racism against Afro-Colombian refugees is pervasive. Adolescents stated that Ecuadoreans identify them easily by their accent and lexicon: 'Here, they think Colombians are all bad, we steal, we come to kill, we are very bad in practically every aspect ... they judge without knowing' (Donger et al., 2017, 38).

Outside the school system, this affects their ability to find stable housing, develop social connections, gain decent work and participate in public
spaces. More than one-third of adolescent refugees in Quito reported they
had experienced physical and verbal abuse in public, compared to
15 per cent in Lago Agrio, where refugees reported that discrimination
was not as acute because of proximity to the Colombian border.

Within education spaces, discrimination inhibits students' ability to
learn and even continue their studies. 'Xenophobia is so strong here',
explained one refugee girl in Quito, 'in school, parents do not want their
children to hang out with Colombians'. Other research has also found
evidence that Colombian youth experience negative comments in school
regarding their nationality, race, accent or lexicon; unjustified reductions
in their grades or additional punishments; and threats of low grades
(Sánchez, 2012).

An alarming number in the Harvard FXB study reported that they did
not feel safe in their secondary schools: 52.8 per cent of youth in Quito
and 24.7 per cent in Lago Agrio. Staff of the non-profit RET often see
'cases of reported physical and psychological abuse towards the students
by the teachers or by the other students ... parents often decide to
remove the kid from the school'. One student reported having moved to
five different schools to avoid severe bullying and physical abuse by peers
and teachers.

There have been several initiatives by civil society and UNHCR to
address the problem of discrimination in school. The campaign
Respiramos Inclusión ('We Breathe Inclusion') was started in 2016 to train
adults in the primary school system on forms of discrimination against
refugees and other minorities in education spaces and methods to foster
inclusion (Bermeo & Rodríguez Gómez, 2015). Workshops were carried
out in sixty schools in Guayaquil in 2016 and in twenty-five schools in
Sucumbíos and Quito in 2018. The non-profit RET also runs
a programme, *Lo Que Nos Une* (That which unites us), supporting the
formation and development of youth-led groups in Ecuador cities with
large refugee populations. These groups design campaigns and cultural
events to celebrate Colombian identity and promote integration.

In addition to explicit bias, distress migrants contend with more indirect
discrimination. For example, public officials often lack empathy for the
exceptional circumstances that distress migrants face. 'High turnover rates
in all the relevant ministries and school districts', explained an RET staff
member, '[mean that] the people involved do not have knowledge or
understanding of the issues that affect refugee youth when applying to

school. So, they do not act with flexibility when there are difficult circumstances for these youth.' The aforementioned example of refugee youth who are given insufficient time to retrieve their records of educational attainment attests to this inflexibility.

In another illustrative case also handled by RET, the three daughters of an indigenous woman from El Nariño in Colombia were each placed in different government secondary schools by district officials. There is no formal appeals process for these decisions. Officials said that this happened because the girls all had different last names, indicating they could not all be sisters. The mother explained that in her culture, children take the last name of the leaders of the indigenous community they are born in, and because of their displacement they had lived in several communities. The school officials refused to believe her or make an exception (Donger et al., 2017, 29).

Conclusions: The Way Forward

UNHCR states that refugees in Ecuador 'have access to education under the same conditions as national students, as well as the right to work' (UNHCR, 2017a). Legally speaking, this is true for registered refugees, who have access to tuition-free education in public institutions, provided they graduate secondary school and excel at the university entrance exam, the same as other citizens. This self-consciously progressive framework is a notable exception to current global trends of legalised exclusion of non-citizens. However, equality before the law means little in a context where opportunities are unequally experienced. Colombian distress migrants gain access to higher education at rates that are dramatically lower than those of other Ecuadorean minority groups.

The Ecuadorean model for higher education cannot be considered fully impartial to immigration status. Even within a context where irregular migration is decriminalised and there are various routes to legal status, identity documentation still functions as an enormous barrier to higher education for distress migrants. Though the law does not technically prohibit it, those who are undocumented or are in the process of their asylum applications cannot apply. Those with refugee visas also face significant barriers to entry unless they have been able to secure a national identity document that would facilitate their access to fair loans, work and streamlined school enrolment. Finally, migrants who opt for other forms of legal status are ineligible for any affirmative action designed to assist refugees.

The neutrality with which Ecuadorean law treats refugees does not alleviate these burdens and in fact provides gatekeepers to tertiary education with the justification to dismiss them and treat the refugee, as put by the Refugee Office, as 'just one more youth'. Public servants do not actively accommodate the additional hurdles refugee youth face to success, which arise from their status and documentation, trauma before or during displacement, experiences of discrimination, inflexible bureaucracies, weak social networks, low access to information and poverty.

Several of these barriers are also shared by other 'historically marginalised groups' in Ecuador, who are also poor and struggling with the trade-off between pursuing further education and working to meet subsistence needs. They also attend low-quality secondary schools that prepare them poorly for the entrance exam, and many indigenous and Afro-Ecuadorian students experience social stigma in the classroom.

However, as this chapter argues, there are additional challenges that refugees and migrants face that arise particularly from their experiences of displacement, lack of citizenship or perceived 'foreignness', and unfamiliarity with local people, customs or bureaucratic procedures. Importantly, the solutions to these problems are not zero-sum and where possible should be designed to benefit other marginalised groups. Allowing asylum applicants to graduate from secondary school or accelerating the rates at which registered refugees receive national identity cards does not disadvantage Ecuadoreans. Programmes like *Respiramos Inclusion* that train teachers on the methods for fostering inclusive education spaces benefit all students.

Extending loan programmes to distress migrants seeking higher education, underwritten by government guarantees, is another important step. This has been suggested elsewhere as a remedy to the regressive nature of a solely government sponsorship of universities (see Johnstone & Marcucci, 2010). Public officials who mediate access to secondary schools should receive training on the particular needs of distress migrants and be given explicit leeway to accommodate them.

Finally, informal skills development programmes for those distress migrants who cannot overcome these significant barriers are also necessary, given that under current conditions, the majority will not have an opportunity to continue their studies. Youth in the Harvard FXB study expressed the need for more skill non-formal education and night-classes, desires echoed by those in the UNHCR/WRC consultations. The programme run by USFQ and FUDELA is a useful precedent.

Helping Colombian distress migrants to develop their potential through higher education is manifestly important not only for these individuals but also for Ecuadorean society more broadly. Educated Colombians help foster social inclusion and dismantle social stigmas currently attached to this nationality around criminality. They contribute unique perspectives and skills to the job market. Educated refugees are also able to eventually return home, support a peace process and rebuild their societies: an immediately necessary task in Colombia, and one hopefully not too far off for Venezuela. The huge numbers of Venezuelans arriving in Ecuador will experience many of the same barriers to higher education as their Colombian peers, adding additional urgency to reforms.

This chapter examines the barriers that Colombian distress migrants in Ecuador encounter in accessing higher education, privileged spaces for opportunity and personal development. This analysis represents a distilled version of many of the broader social, political and economic factors that prevent these distress migrants from realising their full potential in other aspects of their lives. Ecuador's framework is in many ways inspiring and has much to teach wealthier nations that justify exclusion on the basis of limited resources. Its limitations have equally valuable lessons for those seeking to understand and enact progressive models for migrant access to and success in higher education.

REFERENCES

Barahona, K. A. G. (2016). El efecto de los factores sociodemográficos sobre los resultados educativos medidos al final del bachillerato en Ecuador en el año 2014 [The effect of sociodemographic factors on educational outcomes measured at the end of the baccalaureate in Ecuador in 2014]. Quito: Pontifica Universidad Católica del Ecuador.

Bermeo, M. J., & Rodríguez Gómez, D. (2015). Respiramos inclusión en los espacios educativos: Propuesta metodológica para educadores [We breathe inclusion in educational spaces: A methodological proposal for educators]. Quito: Ombudsman of Ecuador and UNHCR.

Donger, E., Fuller, A., Bhabha, J., & Leaning, J. (2017). *Protecting Refugee Youth in Ecuador: An Evaluation of Health and Wellbeing.* Boston: FXB Center for Health and Human Rights at Harvard University.

El Telégrafo. (2017, July 28). Las universidades del país ofertan 77.475 cupos para quienes ingresan por primera vez [The country's universities offer 77,475 seats for new applicants]. Retrieved 19 September 2018, from www .eltelegrafo.com.ec/noticias/sociedad/4/las-universidades-del-pais-ofertan-77–475-cupos-para-quienes-ingresan-por-primera-vez

Freier, L. F. (2013). Open doors (for almost all): visa policies and ethnic selectivity in Ecuador (Working Paper No. 188). Center for Comparative Immigration Studies, London School of Economics (LSE).

Heckathorn, D. (1997). Respondent-driven Sampling: A New Approach to the Study of Hidden Populations. *Social Problems, 44*(2), 174. https://doi.org/10 .1525/sp.1997.44.2.03x0221 m

Herdoíza-Estévez, M. (2015). Construyendo Igualdad en la Educación Superior: fundamentación y lineamientos para transversalizar los ejes de igualdad y ambiente [Building Equality in Higher Education: foundation and guidelines to mainstream the axes of equality and environment]. Quito: SENESCYT / UNESCO.

Instituto Nacional de Estadísticas y Censos (INEC). (2006). Encuesta de con-diciones de vida [Survey of Living Conditions]. INEC.

Johnstone, D. B., & Marcucci, P. N. (2010). *Financing Higher Education Worldwide: Who Pays? Who Should Pay?* Baltimore: Johns Hopkins University Press.

Jokisch, B. D. (2014). Ecuador: From Mass Emigration to Return Migration? Migration Policy Institute. www.migrationpolicy.org/article/ecuador-mass-emigration-return-migration

Korovkin, T. (2008). The Colombian War and 'Invisible' Refugees in Ecuador. *Peace Review: A Journal of Social Justice, 20*, 321–329.

Moscoso, R., & Burneo, N. (2014). Más allá de las fronteras: La población colombiana en su proceso de integración urbana en la ciudad de Quito [Beyond the borders: urban integration of Colombians in the city of Quito] (p. 113). Quito: UNHCR.

Neuman, W. (2012, March 18). In Ecuador, 'Garage Universities' Are Bracing for Reform. *The New York Times*. www.nytimes.com/2012/03/19/world/americas/in-ecuador-garage-universities-are-bracing-for-reform.html

Ortega, C., & Ospina, O. (2012). 'No se puede ser refugiado toda la vida ... 'Refugiados urbanos: el caso de la población colombiana en Quito y Guayaquil ['You can not be a refugee all your life ... ' Urban refugees: the case of the Colombian population in Quito and Guayaquil]. Quito: FLASCO.

Ponce, J., & Loayza, Y. (2012). Elimination of User-fees in Tertiary Education: A Distributive Analysis for Ecuador. *International Journal of Higher Education, 1* (1), https://doi.org/10.5430/ijhe.v1n1p138

Post, D. (2011). Constitutional Reform and the Opportunity for Higher Education Access in Ecuador Since 1950. *Education Policy Analysis Archives, 19*(20), 20.

Ramirez Gallagos, R. (2016). Universidad urgente para una Democracia Emancipada [Urgent university for an emancipated society]. Quito: SENESCYT-IESALC. http://reneramirez.ec/universidad-urgente-para-una-democracia-emancipada/

Rodriguez Gomez, D. (2016). The refugee label: Mapping the trajectories of Colombian youth and their families through educational bureaucracies in Ecuador. ProQuest Dissertations Publishing.

Sánchez, C. (2012). Exclusiones y resistencias niños inmigrantes en escuelas Quito [exclusion and *resistance* among immigrant children in Quito's schools]. Quito: FLASCO.

SENESCYT (2015). Informe de Rendición de Cuentas [Accountability Report]. Quito: Senescyt. www.senescyt.gob.ec/rendicion2015/assets/informe-de-rendici%C3%B3 n-de-cuentas-2015.pdf

SENESCYT (2017). Coordinación Zonal del Austro y el Sur del País: Rendición de cuentas [Zonal Coordination of the Austro and the South of the Country: Accountability]. www.senescyt.gob.ec/rendicion2016/assets/ informe-de-rendici%C3%B3 n-de-cuentas.pdf

SENESCYT (2018). Proceso de Admisión 2018 ¿Qué es Política de Cuotas? [Admissions process 2018. What is the quota policy?]. Retrieved 1 October 2018, from http://admision.senescyt.gob.ec/soluciones/que-es-politica-de-cuotas/

Sistema Nacional de Información de Educación Superior del Ecuador (SNIESE) (2018). Instituciones de educación superior acreditadas [Accredited higher education institutions], 1 October 2018, https://infoeducacionsuperior.gob.ec/ #/ies-acreditadas

UNESCO-UIS (2018). Ecuador. Retrieved 27 September 2018, from http://uis .unesco.org/country/EC

UNHCR (2011). Submission by the United Nations High Commissioner for Refugees for the Office of the High Commissioner for Human Rights' Compilation Report – Universal Periodic Review. UNHCR. www .refworld.org/pdfid/4f0e9d832.pdf

UNHCR (2015). Factsheet: Ecuador. Retrieved from www.acnur.org/fileadmin/ Documentos/RefugiadosAmericas/Ecuador/2015/ACNUR_Ecuador_2015_ General_EN_June_v3.pdf

UNHCR (2017a). DAFI Annual Report 2016. Geneva: UNHCR.

UNHCR (2017b). Ecuador 2018 Planning summary. Quito: UNHCR. htt p://reporting.unhcr.org/sites/default/files/pdfsummaries/GA2018-Ecuador-eng.pdf

UNHCR (2017c). Factsheet: Ecuador. Quito: UNHCR. http://reporting .unhcr.org/sites/default/files/UNHCR%20Ecuador%20Factsheet%20-%20 February%202017.pdf

UNHCR (2018a). Ecuador. Retrieved 30 September 2018, from http://reporting .unhcr.org/node/2543?y=2018#year

UNHCR (2018b). Ecuador 2017 Year-End Report [UNHCR]. 18 September 2018, http://reporting.unhcr.org/node/2543?y=2017#year

UNHCR (2018c). Global Trends: Forced Displacement in 2017. Geneva: UNHCR. www.unhcr.org/5b27be547.pdf

UNHCR (2018d, August 10). UNHCR ramps up response as Ecuador declares emergency. www.unhcr.org/news/briefing/2018/8/5b6d4f554/unhcr-ramps-response-ecuador-declares-emergency.html

UNHCR, & Women's Refugee Commission (2016). National Refugee Youth Consultation: Ecuador Summary Report. Presented at the Global Refugee Youth Consultations.

van Teijlingen, K. (2011). 'To have work is to have life': Refugees' experience with the right to work in Ecuador. Asylum Access Ecuador.

Walsh, C. E. (2015). Affirmative action(ing)s and postneoliberal movement in South America and Ecuador. *Cultural Dynamics*, *27*(1), 19–41. https://doi.org/10.1177/0921374014564655

World Food Program (2017). Ecuador Country Strategic Plan (2017–2021) (No. WFP/EB.1/2017/7/2/Rev.2) (p. 25). Rome.

Zetter, R., & Ruaudel, H. (2016). Refugees' Right to Work and Access to Labor Markets – An Assessment – Country Case Studies (Part 2). KNOMAD.

CHAPTER 11

Transcending Socio-cultural Barriers
Access to Tertiary Education of Muslim Minority Youth in Greece

Nelly Askouni and Thalia Dragonas

For us the university is something very big, very big indeed. You are aware that your life changes . . . your way of life . . . the way people see you . . . the way you are valued . . . you are treated very differently. Even if you have no job, people know you are a university graduate and talk to you differently, treat you differently. And this was enough for me.

These are the words of L, a young woman member of the Muslim minority in Thrace and a university graduate of economics. While Muslims, as Greek citizens, have, in theory, had the right to participate in the selection process for admission to tertiary education institutions, in practice they were up until twenty years ago de facto excluded from this educational opportunity owing to a complex set of factors, including socio-economic marginalisation, poor command of the Greek language and low educational attainment. This discrimination is but one in a nexus of multiple inequities the Muslim minority has been suffering. In 1996, an important affirmative action measure was taken as regards admission policy aiming at compensating for the years-long exclusion. The twenty years that have elapsed since the enactment of the affirmative action have witnessed important readjustment and reduction of inequalities in the fields of education and social participation. Yet this change has not followed a linear process. There is no unequivocal and unreserved acceptance of this affirmative action by the social majority; there are supporters and critics within the minority itself, and not everyone who takes advantage of this measure benefits equally.

This chapter is based on the testimonies of forty-four minority youths about their educational trajectories and their experiences as students who made use of the affirmative action measure just mentioned. The stories told and the forms of life they display reveal, as Bruner (2001) would say, a certain set of presuppositions about themselves, their relation to others, their view of the world and their place in it. The youths' accounts are not treated only as a struggle over the meaning of experience itself. They also bring to the fore the transformations that have taken place over the past twenty years, including the impressive increase in enrolment and graduation from secondary and higher education institutions. These changes in educational statistics constitute the background against which youths' stories acquire meaning. Above all, however, the youths' narratives are socio-culturally situated. Thus, the reader is provided with the social, cultural, historical and political contexts of the local world the stories are about.

The Minority in Space and Time

The Muslim historical minority, situated in the North-East region of Greece, is the result of the International Lausanne Treaty signed in 1923 following the 1912–1922 Greco-Turkish war. The Treaty stipulated, among others, the exchange of populations between Greece and Turkey and the non-exchange of 130,000 Muslims who remained in Western Thrace as well as the same number of Orthodox Greeks who stayed in Istanbul and also acquired a minority status. The fate of both these minorities has been linked to the mutually antagonistic nationalisms and the strained relations between their respective kin states (Alexandris 1992). The ninety-five years that have elapsed since the Lausanne Treaty are heavily marked by disputes and grievances on both sides. Both minorities were exposed to severely restrictive and discriminatory measures in their host country. The once flourishing Greek minority in Istanbul has currently faded to a dwindling community of a couple of thousands as a result of maltreatment and large-scale deportations in the 1950s. The Greek state, for its part, viewed the Muslim minority in Thrace as an instrument of Turkish nationalism and consequently as a threat to the Greek national interests. It endorsed policies aimed at the reduction of the minority's size (depriving its members of citizenship once they left the country), loosening its connection with Turkey, isolating it socially and turning its members into silent and obedient citizens.

Owing to the millet system[1] in force at the time the Lausanne Treaty was signed, the Muslim minority is described in the Treaty text in religious

---

[1] In the Ottoman Empire non-Muslim subjects were organised in officially sanctioned religious communities called 'millets'. They were bound to their millets by their religious affiliations rather than their ethnic origins.

rather than ethnic terms, lumping together diverse ethnic groups, such as Turks, Pomaks and Roma, that only had their faith in common. In the complex interplay of national, ethnic, religious, linguistic and cultural minority identities constituting the Muslim community in Thrace, differential categorical affiliations have played an important role both in majority–minority relations as well as in the internal politics within the minority community. The largest and highest status ethnic identity is the Turkish one, and this group has maintained a permanent grievance about the Greek State's unwillingness to acknowledge its ethnic Turkish identity (Tsitselikis 2012). The Muslim minority is estimated to be between 100,000 and 120,000, though no reliable official statistics on its exact size or ethnic composition are available.

Oppressive, rights-violating policies directed at the Muslim minority included strict limits on the official use of the word 'Turkish' for self-identification; expropriation of large parts of minority-owned land; prevention of purchase or sale of land and other forms of property; no right to set up businesses; no credit or loans by the Greek banks to minority members; restrictions on the freedom of expression, information and movement; prohibition on the restoration of old mosques or the building of new ones; obstacles to obtaining a driver's licence; and a prohibition on access to jobs in the civil service and government sector (Anagnostou 1999; Yagcioglu 2004).

As a result of these measures, the minority was both cut off from the socio-economic changes taking place in Greek society and excluded from the fruits of development, thus denied any meaningful opportunity to participate in or benefit from the society's modernisation. It thus remains a largely agrarian and economically deprived community, secluded in the main in all-Muslim areas, poorly educated, deeply traditional, patriarchal and religious (Askouni 2006; Dragonas 2004).

Civil society in Thrace has long been divided between privileged and underprivileged groups: the majority, dominant group exercising power and the minority, subordinate one remaining socially, economically and educationally disadvantaged (Akgönül 1999; Meinardus 2002). These social divisions have nurtured authoritarian attitudes and protections with respect to majority privileges, while at the same time reinforcing the minority's introversion. Rigid boundaries were set up by the majority to exclude the minority, and these were mirrored by a defensive minority in order to protect itself.[2]

---

[2]   As regards the management of the minority's cultural diversity by the Greek state on the basis of the, in ideal terms, liberal versus communitarian divide, the accommodation of the minority's cultural

The underlying goal of the Greek polity towards the Muslim minority is paradoxical. On the one hand, the measures described above have explicitly or implicitly aimed at marginalising and excluding the minority from social membership within the broader community. At the same time, however, there has been a tacit, unpublicised but pervasive effort to assimilate the minority and to prevent their integration as a discrete minority (Askouni 2006; Dragonas & Frangoudaki 2014). In tandem with these contradictory government strategies, the minority community, for its part, has continued to demand protection of its cultural and language rights, the right to self-identify as Turkish, and to preserve separate schooling and governance structures.

The Educational Framework

The socio-historical parameters just described permeate the educational system. The Lausanne Treaty affords minorities the right to establish and run schools where instruction includes the minority language and its religion. These schools, known as 'minority schools', only cater to minority children; though they are bilingual, they offer two parallel, mono-lingual curricula. While they operate as ghetto structures, perpetuating massive educational under-achievement, they continue to be cherished by the minority as bulwarks against assimilation and protectors of their ethnic identity. Seventy per cent of minority children in Thrace between the ages of 6 and 12 attend minority primary schools (Askouni 2006, 2011).

The design and delivery of minority education reflect the Muslim minority's troubled history. For a long time, the government had little investment in the education of minority children, viewing the community as easier to control and manipulate if illiterate rather than educationally empowered (Aarbakke 2000; Mavrommatis 2008). As a result, up until the year 2000, the dropout rate during the nine years of compulsory schooling was 65 per cent for minority children compared to a national average of 7 per cent. Girls in particular tended to be taken out of school at the end of primary education. Though small numbers of minority children

rights clearly does not fall under the Rawlsian liberal model (Rawls 1993). Taylor's communitarian approach (Taylor 1994) is not the case either despite the fact that the International Lausanne Treaty accorded the minority free practice of religion and the right to establish, manage and control schools using its own language and teaching the Qur'an. These liberties, equally provided to the Greek minority in Istanbul, were not intended to perpetuate both minorities' separate status but rather to integrate them within their host countries in order to secure international stability (Aarbakke 2000).

completed upper secondary education, even they could not sit for university entrance exams because of their poor command of Greek (Askouni 2006). Thus, while the minority was not formally denied a Greek higher education, in practice it was virtually impossible for them to access one. According to Aarbakke (2000), up until 1996, only two students had managed to study at a Greek higher education institution. The small number of university graduates, at the time, had conducted their studies abroad, almost exclusively in Turkey.

The sole post-secondary outlet in Greece for minority students was a two-year Teacher Training Academy, established in 1968, during the junta years. It was an authoritarian institution, born not out of concern for quality education but rather to ensure ideological and political control of teachers responsible for the Turkish curriculum of minority schools. This Academy was, for years, the only opportunity minority youths had for educational social mobility.

Limited access to quality education has resulted in social and psychological deprivation for the Muslim minority. Upward social mobility has been blocked, as well as the development of autonomy and effective social agency (Akgönül 1999). In response to this situation, the minority has for the past thirty years made improvement of the educational system and a consequent increase in educational and social opportunities one of its highest-ranking priorities. And the issue has been a central political challenge throughout this time.

New Circumstances, New Possibilities

The early 1990s marked a change in the Greek polity's attitude towards the minority. This was the result both of pressures exerted by international organisations for the protection of minority rights and of the impact of intensifying Europeanisation processes on Greece, as a whole, and Thrace, in particular. These international and domestic developments set in motion a number of social policies aimed at fairer treatment of the minority, including respect for human rights, political equality and substantial legal equality as well as the implementation of educational measures designed to prevent social exclusion (Anagnostou 2005; Dragonas 2014). The affirmative action measures in education, introduced in Thrace in the 1990s, were designed to offer educational opportunities to long-discriminated against Muslim minority youths.

The new measure regarding access to Greek tertiary education was established in 1996.[3] It allowed admission of a special 0.5 per cent minority quota to Greek universities nation-wide. Under the new law, minorities participate in the same national exams but, since extra quota places are reserved for them, they do not compete with their majority counterparts or reduce the latter's opportunities. Despite this non-competitive approach, the measure proved controversial, especially in the beginning. Within the majority community some considered it a violation of the principle of equal treatment, particularly unwelcome since access to tertiary education is of great social and symbolic importance in education-driven Greek society. For others it signalled a prospective reversal of the power structure between the two social groups. Reactions within the minority were not unequivocal either. There was widespread suspicion that the measure aimed at the assimilation of the minority-deterring youths from studying in Turkey. This initial opposition however did not discourage young people from making use of the measure. The reactions of both majority and minority communities to the educational affirmative action policy deserve systematic research because of their impact on the programme's practical efficacy.

Another important measure was a long-term educational intervention, launched in 1997, aimed at the improvement of primary and secondary education and at social inclusion of minority children. This ongoing project includes the teaching of Greek as a second language, development of multiple educational materials, remedial classes in various subjects, teacher training and extensive work within the community (Dragonas & Frangoudaki 2014; Dragonas et al. 2019).

Changing Trajectories

The affirmative measures just described propelled impressive changes, reflected in the relevant statistics. The dropout rate from nine-year compulsory education decreased from 65 per cent in the year 2000 to 28 per cent in 2010 while access to secondary education surged by 69 per cent in lower secondary and by 216 per cent in upper secondary education. Attendance changed dramatically for girls who up until the 1990s had dropped out at a very high rate upon completion of the six-year

---

[3] As regards access to tertiary education in Greece there are a fixed number of entrants admissible to tertiary education institutions (numerus clausus) and admission is the result of national exams. Candidates list the schools they aspire to, in order of preference, and on the basis of their exam results get admitted in only one school.

primary school. It increased by 147 per cent and 143 per cent in lower secondary and upper secondary respectively, approaching the national mean (Askouni and Stamelos 2013). In what follows, we demonstrate how this improved school attendance directly affected access to tertiary education.

This chapter draws from a study conducted in the academic year 2012–2013 assessing the impact of the affirmative action taken in 1997. The study made use of university records and of stories drawn from interviews with minority youths.[4]

In order to map students' trajectories and the changes brought about, data were collected on 1,706 minority students from six universities (including the University of Thrace) and four technical educational institutes across the country.[5] For every single minority student, enrolled since 1996, information was gathered on demographic data, year of enrolment, year of graduation, level of achievement, transfer or not to another university, and dropout.

The most striking development in minority youths' trajectories is the increase in access to tertiary education. In 1996, 68 students were admitted to Greek universities while in 2016 this number reached 519, equally split between male and female. This signifies a 663 per cent increase. When the measure was introduced not all minority slots were filled because the number of eligible secondary school graduates was limited. The increase in tertiary education enrolment is directly related to the increased minority student participation in secondary education. But it is reciprocal: the prospect of university education has created a much bigger demand for secondary education.

While the increase in the number of university entrants is an impressive development, individual trajectories vary. Only 37 per cent of the admitted minority students managed to graduate within the mean graduation period of six years.[6] Among the others, 25 per cent only passed a few courses, while 18 per cent seem to have been inactive. Twenty per cent had discontinued their studies. Yet this figure may be deceptive since some students do not dropout but transfer elsewhere, often to a university closer to Thrace or to

---

[4] Interviews were held by Nelli Askouni.
[5] Three universities in Athens (the National and Kapodistrian University of Athens, Panteion and the Technical University), the Aristotle University of Thessaloniki, University of Patras, the Democritus University of Thrace and the Technological Educational Institutes of Athens, Piraeus, Thessaloniki and Kavala.
[6] Undergraduate degrees are four years. The percentage of graduates refers to students who were enrolled during 1996–2008 and would have completed their studies in the academic year 2012–2013 when the study took place.

a higher education institution in Turkey. In sum, minority students' educational trajectory is rather skewed with only a little more than one out of three able to graduate on time.

Minority students face apparent difficulties. In most cases, they have problems with the Greek language, and even if they have mastered the everyday vernacular, their academic linguistic competence is limited. Moreover, their academic proficiency is lower than that of their non-minority peers, a reflection of the less competitive entrance process. Limited linguistic and academic credentials are not, however, the only reason for the minority students' low graduation rate. Research on racial and ethnic differences in academic outcomes (Bowen and Bok 1998; Jenks and Phillips 1998) has shown that minority students' graduation likelihood is a function of the compounding effect of 'overlapping disadvantages', as Alon (2007:1478) would say. These are related to social discrimination and poor quality compulsory education, factors that are compounded by gender and social class differences. (For related points, see chapters by Borgonovi and Marconi, and Crul and Lelie in this volume.) Social determination does not affect everybody in the same way.

One of the most interesting findings of the research discussed here is that the closer the higher education institution is to Thrace, the higher the rate of graduation. Whereas 61 per cent of minority students at the University of Thrace graduated, only 14.5 per cent of students at the University of Patras did.[7] Whereas 41.3 per cent of students at the Technical Educational Institute of Kavala graduated,[8] only 22.2 per cent from the comparable institute in Athens did. Minority students have more visibility at the University of Thrace, and their needs are more closely attended to by university personnel than is the case at the other universities. A clear preference for the University of Thrace is indicated by the number of transfers from other institutions. Students report that transfers are driven by economic considerations. Studies far from Thrace are costly for minority families who, as a rule, find the expenses hard to defray. But other reasons also motivate students' preferences for staying closer to home.

The difficulties encountered by minority students should not detract from the overall benefits of the affirmative action measure, which have been impressive. However, it may be high time for policymakers to think of additional adjustments to ensure that all students have as much of a chance to benefit from the measure as possible. Precedents from other countries show that the mere establishment of special favourable measures

---

[7] Patras is a city in the South.   [8] Kavala is a city bordering Thrace.

is not a sufficient condition for good academic results. They need to be supplemented by additional economic and educational interventions, including language training, academic and peer support, and increased quality education at the primary and secondary levels. The twenty-two-year educational intervention mentioned above (Dragonas and Frangoudaki 2014) has played this supportive role. By improving achievement and enhancing students' positive relationship with school it lays the foundation for future academic success at the tertiary level. It has also offered, on a small scale, the possibility of ongoing support for students who need it at the university level.[9]

Youths Sharing their Stories

The quantitative information presented only describes one aspect of the minority students' trajectories and the significance they have for the students themselves. The figures say nothing about how the huge leap of accessing tertiary education is experienced by the students, their families and their communities. In modern societies, higher education is universally considered a critical driver of socio-economic advancement. The questions raised are as follows: what does this mean for its users? What does it mean for them to penetrate a system from which they have been excluded? How do their interests and desires grow in a terrain that, until recently, was both alien and inaccessible? We tried to explore these questions through our interviews with students.

Forty-four youths between the ages of 24 and 38 took part in the study: twenty were male and twenty-four female. They were clustered in three groups: sixteen were still students; eighteen were graduates; and ten had either never attended or they had dropped out. All interviews, with the exception of a group discussion, were on a one-to-one basis and were conducted in Thrace, Athens and Patras. The group discussion took place in the premises of the 'Western Thrace Minority Scientists Association', an organisation representing the minority's official political

---

[9] In order to help students meet learning standards supportive classes were offered at the University of Patras catered to needs in Greek language and scientific terminology. Moreover, recommendations were also made towards the Ministry of Education for individual tutoring of minority students in all Greek universities. Additionally, visits were set up, upon the demand of the Department of Biology at the University of Athens, in order to assist faculty organise tutorials for minority students. Yet such supportive actions cannot be successful if they have an ad hoc character. They must obey to some organised educational services and the allocation of resources designed to accelerate minority students' learning progress.

line. In this discussion, while youths did raise many personal experiences, the political references prevailed.

Drawing from the potential of narrative inquiry our aim was to use the youths' stories, shared during the interviews, as an expressive embodiment of their experience as students, as a mode of communication with someone who is not a member of the minority community and as a way for understanding their world. While talking, students, explorers of their own paths, constructed their selves and their lives in the process.

Each individual is a locus where a plurality of (often contradictory) factors interacts. Our interest, however, goes beyond the individual youths. It is the modes of youths' operation composing a 'culture', as de Certeau (1988) would say, that interest us. We are seeking to comprehend their actions as the minority/dominated element in Thracian society, a community that is nevertheless neither passive nor lacking in agency.

We aimed to analyse youths' experiences as students in a dynamic process determined by lived identities and inequalities. This mechanism, however, simultaneously leads to a possible transformation of the minority sociocultural structures (Archer & Leathwood 2003). The way minority youths experience novel educational opportunities, deal with difficulties and construct their social trajectories is a function of their ethnic, class and gender identities and of the material and symbolic resources they have access to. While the affirmative action measure is, doubtless, a privilege they benefit from, it also highlights the difference between themselves and their counterparts, members of the majority. In any case identities are neither uniform nor static. They are in a continuous process of construction and deconstruction depending on the temporality and the respective definitions of social divisions (Rattansi 1994). While one can discern common motifs in students' stories, there are important differences in the way they perceive their position in the university world, differences that ultimately define their particular choices and consequently their own course of action.

We have taken up two themes that highlight these differences between youths. One refers to the way positive discrimination is discursively represented and the other has to do with the way students position themselves in terms of how close or how far from home they choose to study.

Affirmative Action: Ambivalence and Contradictions

Affirmative action dates back to 1961 when the United States first instituted programmes designed to promote non-discrimination in various fields.

Preferential admission to tertiary education was one of these interventions. The affirmative action introduced in Greece was not the result of a social movement from below as was the case in the United States with the Civil Rights Movement. It was introduced from above as a way to enhance social inclusion with the tacit aspiration of assimilation.

The concept of affirmative action has been widely debated and contested (Holzer & Neumark 2006; Martiniello & Rea 2004). Arguments in favour are equity and social justice, compensation for lost opportunities, redress of social imbalance by raising aspirations of the disadvantaged and benefit to students of all backgrounds. Meritocracy, so the argument goes, ostensibly undermined by this social redress legitimises oppressive societal structures that determine personal choices and opportunities (Moses 2001). Thus, there is no equity without social justice (Dubet 2004; Duru-Bellat 2009). Counterarguments claim that two-tiered universities undermine the aspiration of fairness within an educational system. That is, ethnic minorities are patronised and stigmatised and underlying problems in education, such as insufficient funding and preventing underprivileged children from fulfilling their potential, are covered up and not addressed (Glaser 1975; Sowell 2004; Steele 1990; Thernstrom & Thernstrom 1999).

Some patterns emerge from the repeated claims made in the student interviews, patterns that echo the relevant literature and the desire to break away from the constraints of minority life. For them, tertiary education signifies a better future; a flight from isolation; a change in social status; and a prospect of enhanced employment opportunities. At the same time, the students acknowledge that affirmative action provides a redress for social injustice, bringing within reach previously inaccessible tertiary education on an equal footing with the rest of their counterparts, members of the majority. They are well aware that it permits their appropriation of a space that was, up until recently, in effect forbidden and that the new opportunity implies a major change in their lives.

> It is positive that they allowed students access to tertiary education . . . Our constitutional rights are protected . . . a human right . . . fifteen or twenty years ago this was a dream – literally an impossible dream. (Male, student at Law School, University of Thrace)

The representation of a constricted system one cannot escape from is very unsettling for the youths. They thus mobilise every argument that justifies the need for the measure highlighting the educational, political and social injustices they have been subjected to. Many see it as 'necessary aid' to minority youths, as compensation for the difficulties in Greek language use.

> I explain to them [his non-minority fellow students] that Greek is not our mother tongue, we speak another language and many children need the quota in order to enter some School. They do not have private coaching and they cannot perform in the national exams. I believe that [the affirmative action] must continue because otherwise many children would be left out, myself included. (Female, student at English Language and Literature Department, University of Athens)

Others claim that it is the poor quality of primary and secondary education that explains the linguistic and academic deficit and maintain that this is the product of a conscious political project on the part of the Greek polity. They reply to the argument that affirmative action is preferential treatment, by invoking their community's long-standing marginalisation and exclusion.

> [Affirmative action] is necessary owing to the very difficult conditions in primary and, even more so, secondary education. As long as we have such teachers (graduates from the Teacher Training Academy)[10] who, without knowing how to read Turkish became teachers of our children, it is understandable why our children cannot receive the education they are entitled to. (Male, graduate of Polytechnic School, University of Thrace)

> Most people, some are friends of mine, claim it is an unjust measure. It certainly is ... yet was there no injustice towards these people? (Male, graduate of School of Education, University of Thrace)

Besides the political arguments, minority youths highlight the social obstacles they are confronted with and the great inequalities they experience, as a social group, in relation to their counterparts, members of the majority.

> We do not fight with the same weapons. One has a gun and the other has an arc. (Male, student at Economics Department, University of Thrace)

Discrimination is not to be found only between minority and majority groups. It exists within the minority itself. Thus, young people highlight the economic and socio-cultural inequalities within their own community. City-dwellers are more privileged living under more favourable conditions

---

[10] The speaker refers to two-year Teacher Training Academy, the authoritarian institution established by the Greek junta in 1968.

while the 'others' who live in the mountainous villages are cut off from civilisation and cultural opportunities.

> All minority children do not live under the same conditions ... those who live in the village do not come in touch with the [Greek] language ... if there was no measure these children would not have been able to access the university ... in descending from the village they will mingle with students and they will become socialized ... they will see that there exists a world other than their village ... if they stayed back I do not know what kind of education they would have had. (Male, graduate of School of Education, University of Thrace)

At the same time youths try to negotiate the widespread counter-arguments expressed by members of the majority. They seem to recognise the 'unfairness' inflicted upon their fellow students. It is a strategy to save face and cope with the feeling of being patronised.

> On the one hand, I say to myself that it may be unfair for the other kids who sit for the exams. I have thought 'maybe it shouldn't have been this way' ... on the other, I think that they have been speaking Greek since they were very young while we haven't. (Female, graduate of School of Economics, University of Thessaloniki)

> I understand them ... they feel the injustice because [the exams] are very difficult ... but they do not know the real inequalities that exist here. (Female, student at School of Education, University of Thessaloniki)

Yet acknowledgement that positive discrimination is a much-needed measure brings up youths' own limitations, thus feeding an insecure and ambivalent self-concept. Doubt and ambivalence surface as a result. Defence mechanisms come into play. In trying to negotiate their self-doubts their arguments revolve around the needs of 'others' rather than their own.

> For me there was no problem ... but for some others it can be very difficult. (Male, graduate of Law School, University of Thessaloniki)

> I would enter university without making use of the affirmative action. I needed no additional coaching ... It is, however, a very good measure. It helps students that have had limited opportunities to study at the university. (Male, graduate of Polytechnic School, University of Thrace)

A young man describes the positive discrimination measure, in a very self-debasing fashion, as 'a special personal favour', 'a small gift' bestowed upon him by the polity. Another one, internalising inferiority, brings up feelings of shame: 'I know quite a few that do not admit it to their fellow students ... they may be feeling ashamed.' And yet another throws an aggressive comment: 'Some admit to themselves that they are second-class citizens and benefit by having it easy.'

The image of the recipient is painful and clearly comes across as a stigma. Despite the many arguments legitimising affirmative action, in the youths' consciousness it is still represented as illegitimate. An ambivalent discourse emerges. By refusing the value of the measure for their own benefit and projecting its value onto 'others' and by dissociating themselves with the use of the third-person plural, youths discursively construct a 'false' self, competent and unaffected by ethnic, class and educational constrains. At the same time, however, there is shame and a feeling of inferiority.

Internalised inferiority does not only evoke shame. It also elicits guilt. Since the affirmative action is there to correct a social imbalance, failure and dropout are criticised by the students who most often take it upon themselves for not having invested as much, while once more, they project it onto the 'others': '... some kids drop out because they do not try enough'; 'they do not try because their access to the university is a given'; 'those who try make it'.

Projection is at work once more when they find comfort in the idea that minority students do not constitute the only category that benefits from special entrance exams – Greeks abroad have the same privilege.

Ambivalence runs through all the stories provided by the minority youths. They refer to affirmative action as a very positive measure for addressing social injustice but at the same time they feel belittled. They implicate political and social parameters for their educational deficit, yet guiltily they attribute low achievement to not trying hard enough. The latter obfuscates the structural educational, social and cultural obstacles minority youths encounter.

Lastly, many youths criticise the measure as a deceptive process whereby they get admitted easily and then they are confronted with great difficulties. They underline the disproportionately low rate of graduates.

> You may get admitted with very low grades but when you actually get there you realise it is a different world ... If you had pressured yourself ... to study you wouldn't have encountered such great difficulties. I saw it in myself. The second time [she sat the entrance exams] that I had studied harder I could see the great difference. (Female, student in the Pharmacy Department, University of Patras).

Several youths support a more rigorous selection process and a reformulation of the current measure by suggesting alternative regulations to the current measure, even if they do not clearly know what could take its place: '[The measure] could change a bit . . . they could, maybe, raise the threshold'; 'it could be more strict'; 'it is necessary but not so very much . . . not everyone should have access . . . they could raise the prerequisites'; 'a prep year in the university would help students who enter the university with insufficient background knowledge'.

Youths realise that affirmative action is a transitional measure intended to offer an opportunity that would redress injustice, and once this is restored it will not apply any longer. They tend to agree, however, that affirmative action alone cannot cope with the as-yet unrealised long-term commitment to creating an educational setting geared to upward mobility for all. The students at the Western Thrace Minority Scientists Association, using systematically political arguments, were more sceptical than the rest. They claimed that accessing the university may be easy but the number of graduates is disproportionately low. They worry about the extent to which inequalities are inherent in minority status and whether they can be rectified. In sum, minority youths make use of affirmative action; they believe they deserve this positive discrimination but do not seem comfortable about it. They feel patronised; their fear of being 'second class' citizens is reconfirmed; and they know that the real cause of the problem has not been rectified.

How Close or How Far from Home

Under the Greek system of tertiary education, many students leave home to attend university in a different part of the country. This geographic mobility brings with it social and symbolic transitions for many minority youths. It represents a huge social leap that demands the transcendence of multiple social and cultural barriers related to discrimination, geographical seclusion and past isolation. For most of these students this transition is a novel experience. Geographical mobility associated with university education has not until recently been part of the minority's habitus. Studies on minority and working-class students underline this complicated transition. They highlight the strains experienced and the ambivalence towards the milieu of origin, and they identify the inclusion strategies used (Reay 2001; Reay, Crozier & Clayton 2009; Pasquali 2014). The Muslim minority's traditional, patriarchal and religious customs bring an additional dimension to the unfamiliarity of the university experience for many Muslim students (Trubeta 2001; Tsitselikis 2007).

The most frequently repeated observation in students' narratives is their ambivalence about leaving home and distancing themselves from their familiar environment. One's in-group and shared culture are a source of great comfort and support. Yet moving away is not only a source of apprehension. It is also an aspirational dream. In students' narratives there are three distinct themes. The first is a claim for autonomy. However, only a small number unreservedly voice their desire to break away from the closed environment of their community and from their parents' control.

> I felt very happy because I wanted to leave ... I wanted to lead a different life, to be farther away, to meet people, to study. (Male, student, History Department, University of Crete)

> I went crazy. A big city ... I was on my own, I didn't have to worry that my parents were there ... I was independent. (Female, graduate of School of Education, University of Thessaloniki)

For most youths, however, emancipation from restrictions of the familiar collides with fears of the unknown. The proximity of the place of study to Thrace represents a safe resolution of these conflicting forces. The University of Thessaloniki being only a few hours away from Thrace ranks very high in students' preferences.

> Athens scared me ... I thought it was very chaotic and I wanted a city closer to my home-town ... I wanted though to leave home ... I wanted to live on my own ... to get to know the world ... it certainly frightened me, but I liked it at the same time. It was the unknown that I was to explore. (Male, graduate of Law School, University of Thessaloniki)

A third group (all students at the University of Thrace), mainly women, seek the security of the familiar and confess that their emotional dependence on their family inhibits them from distancing themselves from home.

> I chose Komotini [a Thracian city] for its proximity. I was going back and forth ... I did not want to break away from my hometown [half an hour away from Komotini]. I was feeling bad, i.e. I was not feeling ready to move away from Xanthi. One reason was financial but it was also emotional ... I would have felt lonely ... I was afraid to go far away. (Female, graduate of History Department, University of Thrace).

The most common strategy for remaining close to home is to transfer to the local university in Thrace. This way, on the one hand, the strong identification with the community is retained, but, on the other, the symbolic opening up to the wider Greek society is enabled but restricted.

> I transferred from the University of Patras . . . A small town is better . . . You get to know more people . . . I have not regretted it at all . . . You go out for a walk and you always meet someone . . . every weekend I went home. (Male, graduate of School of Education, University of Thrace).

As shown earlier, students graduate at a higher rate from the University of Thrace than from more distant institutions. Being close to one's place of residence is also less expensive. The reduced cost is coupled with the real and symbolic security associated with one's familiar environment. For the members of the minority moving away to study involves increased difficulties compared to the rest of the Greek students who leave home to pursue their studies. Confined to Thrace and with limited experience of travelling, many youths feel alienated when they find themselves in other parts of Greece. In Thrace they do not have to explain who they are; minority identity is a given and their language, religion and culture are known to everyone. The uncanny environment of a strange city, language difficulties and the common disadvantage in their academic training weigh heavily on minority students. Non-minority students may consider them strange and they feel they have to account for their difference. By contrast, at home one's own group is a source of support that may contribute to higher academic achievement.

Separating oneself from home is a function of both social class and gender. The cost of studies away from home prevents geographic mobility which in turn hampers social mobility. For poorer students, university enrolment is only conceivable if it is close to home. If this is not the case most abandon the prospect of pursuing their studies. Sometimes when families cannot afford to send all their children to university, they just choose to support one of them.

> I was very happy I was admitted up to the moment my father told me that I cannot go since my sister is already a student . . . if it wasn't for my sister I would have definitely gone. (Female, admitted but never attended)

In the case of girls, especially those from the mountainous area where the traditional structures are very strong, there is an intricate interplay of economic and gender constraints. Families particularly resist letting girls study if this means leaving home and moving away from family control. We have however witnessed changes in the twenty years since we have been working with the minority.

It was my mother mostly who was afraid and was telling me 'I do not know whether you will go' and I said 'please let me, I want to go', and she said 'ok, you will go ... of course ... you got admitted'. They were afraid in the beginning; it is natural, you come from the village to a huge city, they resented it, they were used to my being there all the time. In the beginning whenever I was leaving, she cried incessantly and up to now she still has not accepted it. (Female, student at Biology Department, University of Athens)

We are indeed a closed society. In the past they would not let girls study, let alone let you live somewhere far. Now that they have opened up ... they let girls move. In the past my parents used to say: 'be close', thus I have not experienced what it is to be away from parents. I may have liked it ... I now say if only I had left ... (Female, graduate of History Department, University of Thrace)

Regardless of whether minority youths study close to or far from home, their student life is a decisive phase that redefines their relationship with their own community. Most students describe themselves as socially active, mixing with their counterparts and not sticking to their minority peers. These extrovert practices co-exist with strong in-group ties. Very often close friends are also members of the minority. Moreover, minority students usually reside in student dorms that tend to favour ethnically in-group relations nurturing thus introversion. The words of a young woman reflect this ambivalent relationship: 'With one leg you are rooted in tradition, in your home town, and with the other you see the change and you want to touch it.'

The choice about how close or far from home to move is posed again once students graduate and have to face the future. Youths describe the transition back to Thrace as a difficult one. It is only a small number of youths that describe their familiar environment as a reassuring one. For most youths returning home and living with the family once again represents a comedown. One female student attributes her decision to stay on for graduate studies to her inability to face return. She portrays herself as 'a stranger in her own home'. Another wishes she could remain in Athens with none of the minority–majority conflict. While she describes this fantasy she divulges her dream of becoming a nursery school teacher in her village. Students' stories reveal their trepidation about being alien in a world either too vast or too small to be their own. In reality almost all return because of the limitations in their choices. Homecoming, however, does not represent defeat for all. Many youths negotiate multiple identities and contribute to the formation of new social models.

If you asked me a year ago I would certainly say that I would not go back. Yet because I have a job here that allows me to be myself, I made the decision to return although I knew that it would be difficult . . . after all it is not so difficult because it is me who is not the same. I am stronger, more independent, more assertive and I have all this strength I have gained from this experience, from the fact that it is me that has managed to pull through. And I cannot say I have grudges, they respect me and in comparison to the girls who grew up and stayed in the village, they give me more leeway to be different. (Female, graduate of Social Anthropology Department, Panteion University of Athens).

University studies are described as a decisive factor leading to personal changes, empowerment and growing autonomy. At the same time the returning youths are enlisted in family social mobility strategies. Accessing tertiary education is the most important vehicle for the realisation of the youths' dreams for a better future, a process that presupposes distancing themselves from the social world of their parents.

Coming from this type of society and family, university was the ticket to change my life. This is how we grew separate from our parents. That is, because we were also involved during the summer in agricultural work, I always remember my parents saying: You will not be like us! You will have a better future; you will find a better job. So, I went to the university clearly with a view to changing my life. (Female, graduate student, School of Education, University of Athens)

Reconciling the Poles of Contradiction

The Muslim minority has been the subject of domination for many years. Broader societal and political contradictions were enacted in the complex relationship between majority and minority. It is on this politically and culturally contentious terrain that youths construct and reconstruct their selves and their relationships with others. Fine and Sirin's (2007) frame of hyphenated selves referring to youths living in conflict, striving to make meaning and negotiating the contradictory messages that swirl through them, is very pertinent in the case of the Muslim minority youths.

In contrast to the divisions and marginalisation of the past, the policy of affirmative action, introduced twenty years ago, opened up the prospect of social inclusion and decisively reinforced the transformation of minority social characteristics which were already in the process of changing. The impressive improvement in access to secondary and tertiary education reflects, and at the same time shapes, broader socio-cultural developments, the most important being the weakening of traditional communal structures. Class, culture and gender interact amidst rapid social change. Studies on gender have revealed a multitude of social practices enacted by Muslim minority women whereby 'modernity' is a synonym of progress, emancipation and improved life conditions (Zaimakis & Kaprani 2005; Zografaki & Askouni 2013).

In this chapter we examined students' capacity to make choices and to define and transform their society as they experienced a process of emancipation. Minority youths directly reflect the process of modernisation because of the benefits of the affirmative action measure which has enabled them to transcend familiar geographical and symbolical boundaries and redefine their position in the society they belong to. This process is not linear or uniform. As is the case in societies in transition, youths in Thrace vacillate between tradition and modernity. New norms and practices may be incompatible with norms and practices of the past. As Giddens (2000) has observed, when traditional ways become eroded, identity must be created and recreated more actively than before.

This laborious process entails tensions between adaptation and transformation that were expressed in students' ambivalences about the extent to which they wished to make use of affirmative measures. Students' narratives oscillated between the position of passive adaptation to the environment and active agency negotiating and transforming it. The youths expressed both a fear of distancing themselves from the familiarity of their community and also a desire to break away from tradition and family constraints and make a life of their own. These tensions reveal a dynamic contradiction between delimitation and mobility. Youths' ways of operating – multiform and fragmentary – even if concealed, conform to certain rules. Settling down away from one's culture would be a transgression of the limit, a disobedience to tradition and a 'betrayal' of one's community. Yet at the same time youths dream of a departure from the enclosure and a flight to an alternate life they encountered in their student years. They may not be completely ready, but the foundations for an autonomous life have been laid.

REFERENCES

Aarbakke, V. (2000). *The Muslim Minority of Greek Thrace*, Unpublished doctoral dissertation, Bergen: University of Bergen.
Akgönül, S. (1999). *Une Communauté, deux Etats: la Minorité Turco-musulmane de Trace Occidental*, Istanbul: ISIS.

Alexandris, A. (1992). *The Greek Minority of Istanbul and Greek-Turkish Relations, 1918–19*, Athens: Center for Asia Minor Studies.

Alon, S. (2007). Overlapping Disadvantages and the Racial/Ethnic Graduation Gap among Students Attending Selective Institutions. *Social Science Research*, *36*(4), 1475–1499.

Alon, S. & Tienda, M. (2005). Assessing the 'Mismatch' Hypothesis: Differences in College Graduation Rates by Institutional Selectivity. *Sociology of Education*, *78*(4), 294–315.

Anagnostou, D. (1999). *Oppositional and Integrative Ethnicities: Regional Political Economy, Turkish Muslim Mobilization and Identity Transformation in Southeastern Europe*, Doctoral Dissertation, Ithaca, NY: Cornell University.

Anagnostou, D. (2005). Deepening Democracy or Defending the Nation? The Europeanisation of Minority Rights and Greek Citizenship. *West European Politics*, *28*(2), 335–357.

Anderson, E. (2010). *The Imperative of Integration*, Princeton, NJ: Princeton University Press.

Archer, L. & Leathwood, C. (2003). Identities, Inequalities and Higher Education. In L. Archer, M. Hutchings, & A. Ross (Eds.), *Higher Education: Issues of Inclusion and Exclusion* (pp. 175–191). London: Routledge.

Askouni, N. (2006). *Η Εκπαίδευση της Μειονότητας στη Θράκη: από το Περιθώριο στην Προοπτική της Κοινωνικής Ένταξης* [Minority Education in Thrace: From the Margins to the Prospect of Social Inclusion], Athens: Alexandria.

Askouni, N. (2011). Μειονοτικό ή Ελληνόγλωσσο Σχολείο για τα Παιδιά της Μειονότητας στη Θράκη; Εκπαιδευτικές Επιλογές, Πολιτικά Διλήμματα, Κοινωνικές Αλλαγές [Minority or Greek Language School for the Children of the Minority in Thrace? Educational Choices, Political Dilemmas, Social Changes. In A. Androusssou & N. Askouni (Eds.), *Πολιτισμική Ετερότητα και Ανθρώπινα Δικαιώματα: προκλήσεις για την εκπαίδευση* [Cultural Otherness and Human Rights] (pp. 208–222). Athens: Metaihmio.

Askouni, N. & Stamelos, G. (2013). Η Διαρροή των Μαθητών της Μουσουλμανικής Μειονότητας της Θράκης από το Γυμνάσιο [The Dropout of Muslim Minority Students in Thrace from Lower Secondary Education]. Unpublished report, The Project on the Education of the Muslim Minority Children.

Bowen, W. G. & Bok, D. (1998). *The Shape of the River: Long-Term Consequences of Considering Race in College and University Admissions*, Princeton, NJ: Princeton University Press.

Bruner, J. (2001). Self-making and World-making. In J. Brockmeier & D. Carbaugh (Eds.), *Narrative and Identity* (pp. 25–37). Amsterdam: John Benjamins Publishing Company.

de Certeau, M. (1988). *The Practice of Everyday Life*, Transl. S. Rendall, Berkeley: University of California Press.

Dragonas, T. (2004). Negotiation of Identities: The Muslim Minority in Western Thrace. *New Perspectives on Turkey, 30*, 1–24.

Dragonas, T. (2014). The Vicissitudes of Identity in a Divided Society: The Case of the Muslim Minority in Western Thrace. In K. Featherstone (Ed.), *Europe in Modern Greek History* (pp. 135–152). London: Hurst & Co.

Dragonas, T., Dafermou, C., Zografaki, M., Assimakopoulou, I., Dimitriou, A., Katsiani, O. & Lagopoulou, V. (2019). 'Language is Freedom': A Multimodal Literacy Intervention Empowering the Muslim Minority in Greece. *The International Journal of Learning: Annual Review, 26*(1), 1–15.

Dragonas, T. & Frangoudaki, A. (2006). Educating the Muslim Minority in Western Thrace. *Islam and Christian-Muslim Relations, 17*(1), 21–41.

Dragonas, T. & Frangoudaki, A. (2014). 'Like a Bridge over Troubled Water': Reforming the Education of Muslim Minority Children in Greece. In V. Lytra (Ed.), *When Greeks and Turks Meet* (pp. 289–311). Surrey: Ashgate.

Dubet, F. (2004). *L'école des Chances. Qu'est-ce qu'une école juste?*. Paris: Seuil.

Duru-Bellat, M. (2009). *Le Mérite contre la justice*. Paris: Presses de Sciences Po.

Fine, M. & Sirin. S. (2007). Theorizing Hyphenated Selves: Researching Youth Development in and across Contentious Political Contexts. *Social and Personality Psychology Compass, 1*(1), 16–38.

Giddens, A. (2000). *Runaway World: How Globalization is Reshaping our Lives*. New York: Routledge.

Glazer, N. (1975). *Affirmative Discrimination: Ethnic Inequality and Public Policy*. New York: Basic Books.

Holzer, H. J. & Neumark, D. (2006). Affirmative Action: What Do We Know? *Journal of Policy Analysis and Management, 25*(2), 463–490.

Jencks, C. & Phillips, M., eds. (1998). *The Black-White Test Score Gap*. Washington, DC: Brookings Institution Press.

Martiniello, M. & Rea, A., eds. (2004). *Affirmative Action. Des discours, des politiques et des pratiques en débat*. Louvain-La-Neuve: Academia-Bruylant.

Meinardus, R. (2002). Muslims: Turks, Pomaks and Gypsies. In R. Clogg (Ed.), *Minorities in Greece: Aspects of a Plural Society* (pp. 81–93). London: Hurst & Company.

Mavrommatis, G. (2008). Εθνικισμός και ιστορία εκπαιδευτικής πολιτικής: η εκπαίδευση των Θρακιωτών μουσουλμάνων μειονοτικών 1945–1975 [Nationalism and the history of educational policy: The education of Thracian Muslim minority 1945–1975], Unpublished doctoral dissertation, Athens: Panteion University.

Moses, M. S. (2001). Affirmative Action and the Creation of More Favorable Contexts of Choice. *American Educational Research Journal, 38*(1), 3–36.

Pasquali, P. (2014). *Passer les Frontières Sociales. Comment les « filières d'élite » entrouvrent leurs portes*, Paris: Fayard.

Rattansi, A. (1994). 'Western' Racisms, Ethnicities and Identities in a 'Postmodern' Frame. In A. Rattansi & S. Westwood (Eds.), *Racism, Modernity and Identity: On the Western Front* (pp. 15–85). Cambridge: Polity Press.

Rawls, J. (1993). *Political Liberalism*, New York: Columbia University Press.

Reay, D. (2001). Finding or Losing Yourself? Working-class Relationships to Education. *Journal of Education Policy, 16*(4), 333–346.

Reay, D., Crozier, G. & Clayton, J. (2009). 'Strangers in Paradise'? Working-class Students in Elite Universities. *Sociology, 43*(6), 1103–1121.

Sowell, T. (2004). *Affirmative Action around the World*. New Haven, CT: Yale University Press.

Steele, S. (1990). *The Content of Our Character: A New Vision of Race in America*, New York: St. Martin's Press.

Taylor, C. (1994). The Politics of Recognition. In A. Gutmann (Ed.), *Multiculturalism: Examining the Politics of Recognition* (pp. 25–73). Princeton, NJ: Princeton University Press.

Thernstrom, S. & Thernstrom, A. (1999). *America in Black and White: One Nation Indivisible*. New York: Simon & Schuster.

Trubeta, S. (2001). *Κατασκευάζοντας ταυτότητες για τους μουσουλμάνους της Θράκης. Το παράδειγμα των Πομάκων και των Τσιγγάνων* [Constructing Identities for the Muslim in Thrace: The Example of Pomaks and Gypsies], Athens: Kritiki.

Tsitselikis, K. (2007). The Pending Modernisation of Islam in Greece: From *Millet* to Minority Status. *Südosteuropa, 55*(4), 354–373.

Tsitselikis, K. (2012). *Old and New Islam in Greece. From Traditional Minorities to Immigrant Newcomers*. Leiden: Martinus Nijhoff Publishers.

Yagcioglu, D. (2004). *From Deterioration to Improvement in Western Thrace: A Political Systems Analysis of a Triadic Ethnic Conflict*, Doctoral Dissertation, Fairfax, VA: George Mason University.

Young, I. M. (1990). *Justice and the Politics of Difference*. Princeton, NJ: Princeton University Press.

Zaimakis, G. & Kaprani, K. (2005). "Μουσουλμάνες" γυναίκες και πολιτισμική αλλαγή: Ετερότητα, φύλο και θρησκεία σε έναν αγροτικό οικισμό στη Δυτική Θράκη ["Muslim" Women and Cultural Change: Otherness, Gender and Religion in an Agricultural Settlement in Western Thrace.] *Επιθεώρηση Κοινωνικών Ερευνών* [Social Research Review], *116*(A), 79–100.

Zografaki, M. & Askouni, N. (2013). Education des filles, pratiques de famille et ruptures à la tradition: le cas de la minorité musulmane en Grèce. In F. Hatchuel (Ed.), *Transmettre ? Entre Anthropologie et Psychanalyse: Regards croisés sur des pratiques familiales* (pp. 129–158). Paris: L'Harmattan.

CHAPTER 12

Combating the Exclusion and Marginalisation of Persons with Intellectual Disabilities in Higher Education in the United States

Matthew S. Smith and Michael Ashley Stein

Introduction

With considerable justification, the United States takes pride in its dis-ability-related civil rights laws and policies prohibiting discrimination. Further to these mandates, students with disabilities are largely able to access higher education and receive reasonable accommodations that enable their equal participation. This category of students includes a range of individuals with autism, as well as physical, cognitive, learning, visual, hearing, and multiple impairments (Hehir & Gamm, 1999). However, most students with intellectual disabilities (ID)[1] are barred from mainstream higher education on the premise that they lack adequate qualifications, and are thereby shunted towards segregated settings (Task Force on Higher Education, 2014). This situation predominates despite the promise of equality and inclusion contained in civil rights and education ideals, and even though the rationales supporting increased access to higher education generally resound with equal force for students with ID (Sannicandro, Parish, Fournier, Mitra, & Paiewonsky, 2018).

Correspondingly, emerging postsecondary education opportunities for students with ID have confirmed common knowledge. Postsecondary education is a gateway to fuller participation in society for historically marginalised groups (McMahon, 2009) and correlates with vastly improved employment and income opportunities (Baum & Ma, 2007; Bureau of Labor Statistics, 2010; Mischel, Bernstein, & Allegretto, 2007). Thus, even segregated education schemes – euphemistically called 'inclusive' postsecondary education (IPSE) or 'inclusive' higher education (IHE)

---

[1] According to the American Association on Intellectual and Developmental Disabilities, intellectual disability denotes 'significant limitations both in intellectual functioning and in adaptive behavior as expressed in conceptual, social, and practical adaptive skills' (Schalock et al., 2010, 1).

programmes – nevertheless have instrumental value. Yet, ironically, many IPSE programmes also discriminate against the students they purport to include. Hence, a delicately balanced and complex picture emerges. There is urgent social need to break down barriers to mainstream higher education for students with ID, as well as to continue to support inroads into higher education made on their behalf by IPSE programmes, all the while warding against unintended marginalisation.

The first section describes American legislation and case law that is generally helpful to students with ID but has not enabled these students to enrol in mainstream higher education. The next section recounts the emergence of IPSE programmes that have provided students with ID historically excluded from mainstream higher education some positive opportunities to learn beyond high school settings. Because IPSE programmes and practices are evolving, the third section notes three types of discrimination that marginalise students with ID *within* these programmes: suspect admissions criteria, second-class status and biased disciplinary procedures. The last section presents a case study illustrating how these barriers manifest in practice.

Students' with ID Right to (Some) Education

Access to education for students with ID has improved over the last fifty years. From the 1880s through the 1970s, individuals with ID were typically deemed social misfits and 'uneducable', segregated from the rest of society and placed in large warehouse institutions (Stein, Stein, & Blanck, 2009). As a result of a social movement led by families on behalf of their children with ID (Weiner & Hume, 1987), the United States Congress and federal courts eventually granted children with ID the right to an education. Statutory recognition, enshrined in the 1975 Education for All Handicapped Children Act (EHCA),[2] came on the heels of constitutional litigation in 28 of 50 states (Hehir & Gamm, 1999).

The EHCA was rooted in *Brown* v. *Board of Education*, the landmark Supreme Court decision that separate education facilities are inherently unequal (1954). Although *Brown* applied to racial discrimination, it heralded a normative shift towards equal access to education. Courts subsequently extended *Brown*'s desegregation imperative to students with disabilities seeking access to public schools (Waterstone, 2014; *Pennsylvania Ass'n for Retarded Children* v. *Pennsylvania*, 1971). The

[2] Pub. L. No. 94–142, 20 USC §§ 1400 *et seq.* (1976).

EHCA took on even greater significance after the Supreme Court made it easier for the federal and state governments to discriminate against persons with ID than against racial or ethnic minorities or women (*City of Cleburne, Texas* v. *Cleburne Living Center*, 1986).[3] Although *Cleburne* centred on housing, this lower standard tipped the balance in favour of governmental exclusionary practices and prompted disability rights advocates to rely increasingly on statutes,[4] rather than the US Constitution, to safeguard their rights (Silvers & Stein, 2002). Consequently, the pointed constitutional protections used to desegregate schools racially are much blunter instruments for students with disabilities seeking educational inclusion.

When the EHCA was enacted, fewer than half of the 8 million American children with disabilities were receiving an 'appropriate' education: 1.75 million were excluded outright from public schools, with another 2.5 million 'sitting idly in regular classrooms awaiting the time when they were old enough to "drop out"' (House of Representatives Report No. 94–332, 1975). The EHCA ensured that these children could participate in public education (Grigal, Hart, & Lewis, 2012). In 1990 – the same year that the momentous Americans with Disabilities Act (ADA) (42 USC §§ 12101 et seq.) was passed – the EHCA was revised and amended as the Individuals with Disabilities Education Act (IDEA) (Pub. L. No. 94–142, 20 USC §§ 1400 et seq. (2006)). The IDEA continues to guarantee all students with ID and other enumerated types of disabilities a right to a 'free and appropriate public education' by requiring school authorities to develop 'individualised educational programs' (IEPs) for each eligible student, and also providing federal funds and processes to implement these IEPs.[5]

The Supreme Court was initially parsimonious when interpreting what constituted a 'free and appropriate public education'. In 1982, it ruled that schools need only provide access to a 'basic floor of opportunity' of 'some

---

[3] The *Cleburne* Court ruled that governments needed only a 'rational basis' to justify excluding persons with ID from social opportunities, a lower standard than the 'strict' or 'intermediate' scrutiny applied to other marginalised groups under the U.S. Constitution's Equal Protection Clause (ibid).

[4] Prominently, the country's first general disability rights protection law, the Rehabilitation Act of 1973, prohibited any recipients of federal funds (including public schools) from discriminating against persons with disabilities (Pub. L. No. 93–112, 29 USC § 794 (1976); Aron & Loprest, 2012).

[5] Students or their parents who believe their IEPs fall short of providing an appropriate education may initiate administrative due process hearings and appeal hearing officers' decisions to federal courts (20 USC § 1415).

educational benefit' (*Bd. of Educ. of the Hendrick Hudson Central Sch. Dist. v. Rowley*). In other words, schools were required merely to demonstrate that IEPs were 'reasonably calculated to enable the child to receive educational benefits' without having to prove that a student *actually* benefited (ibid), and not that they 'maximize academic and social development, consistent with the goal of full inclusion' (CRPD, 2006, art. 24(2)(e)). Although a minority of courts interpreted *Rowley* more expansively, low expectations for students with disabilities combined with traditional deference to school expertise significantly affected the scope of students' with ID right to education (Eckrem & McArthur, 2001).

The EHCA and IDEA proved instrumental for many students with ID to gain entry to public schools (Morningstar, Bassett, Cashman, Kochar-Bryant, & Wehmeyer, 2012). Once enrolled, *Rowley*'s minimal standard ensured that access to a quality, inclusive education remained illusory for many students. And, although the IDEA created detailed procedures by which parents could advocate for more generous IEPs, in practice these procedural protections 'have been reduced to mere empty ritual for all but the most educated and wealthy' (Kotler, 1994). Moreover, chronic federal budgetary shortfalls incentivise schools to skimp on educational programmes, especially for minority students or those without fierce parent advocates (Colker, 2013). Together, obfuscatory procedures and resource constraints engender pervasive low expectations for students with disabilities that in turn corrode educational planning (Griffin, McMillan, & Hodapp, 2010; Uditsky & Hughson, 2012).

While the Supreme Court has recently broadened the scope of an appropriate education under the IDEA,[6] it has yet to adjudicate how the IDEA applies to higher education access for students with ID. This gap increasingly warrants attention. The IDEA generally requires school districts to provide these students with education through age 21 (20 USC § 1412), but because it was enacted when few if any students with ID were

---

[6] In 2017, the Supreme Court expanded the IDEA's scope, unanimously ruling that IEPs should be 'appropriately ambitious', give 'every child . . . the chance to meet challenging objectives', and enable 'progress appropriate in light of the child's circumstances' (*Endrew F. v. Douglas Cnty. Sch. Dist. Re-1*, 2017). This ruling effectively (although not technically) has reversed *Rowley*'s minimal standard and opened the door for legal challenges to inadequately sponsored primary and secondary school programmes for students with ID. However, the scope of those challenges will broaden only insofar as courts are inclined to mitigate the traditional deference afforded school authorities in education disputes. Echoing the *Cleburne* "rational basis" standard, the *Endrew F.* Court clarified that judges should determine no more than 'whether the IEP is reasonable, not whether the court regards it as ideal' (ibid). Consequently, school and parent expectations, as reflected in IEPs, continue to play a crucial role in defining the extent of the right to primary education by students with ID (McGrew & Evans, 2004).

expected to attend postsecondary education programmes, the IDEA does not specify where education of College-age students with ID should occur. Moreover, due to ambient stereotypes, courts have not construed the IDEA to require 'age-appropriate' placements for College-age students,[7] resulting in students aged 18 and over rarely continuing their education alongside their peers in postsecondary settings (Grigal, Hart, & Migliore, 2011). On paper, the IDEA requires schools to develop for each student with ID a 'transition plan' that is 'focused on improving academic and functional achievement', including, expressly, movement from primary school to postsecondary education (20 USC § 1401(34)(A)). But in practice, many educators do no more than simply acknowledge the possibility that certain students with ID might continue on to higher education (ibid).

Consequently, instead of the IDEA, in postsecondary education settings, students with disabilities' right to education hinges on different statutes: the Rehabilitation Act and the ADA (Dept. of Educ., 2017). These disability non-discrimination statutes clearly apply to postsecondary programmes,[8] although they provide different kinds of protections. Whereas the IDEA evaluates what measures or conduct is appropriate in light of an individual student's circumstances,[9] the Rehabilitation Act and ADA investigate whether that conduct applies disparately to students with disabilities, either specifically or as a group. Thus, under the IDEA a student with ID seeking to receive free educational services on a College campus has to demonstrate both that the College programme is appropriate within the context of the student's individualised educational goals and that the secondary school setting is not. By contrast, the same student under the Rehabilitation Act or ADA would have to show that her exclusion is discriminatory – that is, based on disability and despite possible reasonable accommodations. Indeed, the Rehabilitation Act or ADA may be more adept than the IDEA at remedying certain forms of disability-based discrimination against students, such as denials of entry for service animals (*Fry* v. *Napoleon Cmty. Sch.*, 2017; 34 CFR § 104.44(b)).

---

[7] While students with ID may be free to enrol in postsecondary education programmes, courts have not yet found that they are entitled to have IDEA funds underwrite those placements. Instead, IEP teams certify students with ID seeking tertiary education as ready for graduation from their secondary school placements, thereby relieving public schools of their obligation to provide a free and appropriate education under the IDEA.

[8] The following statutory and regulatory provisions specifically implicate postsecondary education programmes: 29 USC § 794(b)(2), 34 CFR § 104.43, 42 USC § 12131(1), and 28 CFR §§ 35.104 & 130.

[9] In other words, since IEPs contain individualised educational goals that differ from student to student, schools are evaluated against expectations specific to each student.

Crucially, the Rehabilitation Act and ADA apply to students with ID in postsecondary programmes irrespective of their matriculation or degree-seeking status (Dept. of Educ., 1998; 34 CFR § 104.43).

However, unlike the IDEA's wide-ranging implications for the content of students' with ID educational offerings, the Rehabilitation Act and ADA likely do not compel higher education institutions to modify their admission criteria or graduation requirements deemed to be essential or fundamental to existing programmes. This is so even though in effect such criteria and requirements categorically bar certain groups from attending or graduating. Indeed, students with ID must be 'otherwise qualified' in order to trigger statutory protections: that is, they must meet the same basic admission requirements, with or without reasonable accommodations, as students without disabilities. Further, Rehabilitation Act regulations expressly permit exclusionary admission criteria having 'a disproportionate, adverse effect' on students with ID so long as the criteria have 'been validated as a predictor of success in the education program or activity' and alternate standards having a less disproportionate, adverse effect are not readily available (34 CFR § 104.42(b)(2)). The Supreme Court has therefore upheld interpretations of the Rehabilitation Act allowing postsecondary institutions considerable discretion in defining the parameters of programmes of study (e.g. *Southeastern Cmty. Coll.* v. *Davis*, 1979). This includes discretion to require 'reasonable' physical qualifications for graduation (*Doherty* v. *So. Coll. of Optometry*, 1988) or to dismiss students for 'unprofessional behavior' (*Halpern* v. *Wake Forest Univ. Health Scis.*, 2012).

Consequently, the IDEA and disability civil rights statutes have been only marginally effective in facilitating students with ID to continue their education in age-appropriate settings. Indeed, federal and state laws and regulations on high school graduation requirements only compound the academic and attitudinal barriers faced by students with ID seeking higher education. Strikingly, many American states have open enrolment to their community College systems, allowing anyone with a high school diploma to register. This creates pathways to undergraduate degrees for those choosing not to enrol in traditional four-year College or university programmes for financial, academic or other reasons (Hart, Mele-McCarthy, Pasternack, Zimbrich, & Parker, 2004). However, following the No Child Left Behind Act of 2001, students must pass a mandatory exit exam to be eligible for a high school graduation diploma (Katsiyannis, Zhang, Ryan, & Jones, 2007). Many students with ID, despite having successfully completed high school, are unable to pass additional state-based tests and obtain their high school diplomas and are thereby barred from enrolling in higher education (Task Force on Higher Education, 2014).

Simultaneously, piecemeal policy guidance and regulatory fixes have sown confusion among students, parents and federal and state disability services agencies alike, resulting in unnecessary denials of services and funds to which students with ID seeking higher education should be entitled (Lee, Rozell, & Will, 2018). Thus, campuses that lack adequate supports for students with ID miss crucial opportunities to supplement their offerings by using available federal dollars designated for youth with ID seeking pathways to employment (Task Force on Higher Education, 2014). Although in theory the IDEA, disability civil rights statutes, and vocational and pre-employment funding schemes might be applied creatively and robustly to cut through administrative barriers to accessing higher education, rational bases for continuing to exclude students with ID from higher education remain instantiated following *Cleburne.*

The Rise of IPSE Programmes

A century ago, approximately 300 US higher education institutions offered coursework on eugenics and were thereby complicit in grisly experiments conducted on persons with ID living in other kinds of institutions (Dolmage, 2017). By contrast, 270 postsecondary programmes for students with ID now exist nationwide (Lee, Rozell, & Will, 2018). Roughly 38 per cent serve students with ID dually enrolled in high school and College, i.e., individuals needing little more than reasonable accommodations in order to make the transition (ibid). The remainder serve students with ID who are otherwise excluded from higher education settings due to the academic criteria described above.

The slow conversion of higher education institutions from facilitating human rights abuses against persons with ID to promoting alternative sites for their inclusion was catalysed by disability rights advocates in the second half of the twentieth century. Concurrent with parental advocacy efforts on behalf of their children with ID accessing primary school education, the People First movement of self-advocates with ID precipitated the emptying of large congregate institutions in the 1980s (Carey, 2010). Among the many positive consequences of transitioning people to living within their own communities was the development of programmes on College campuses for adults with ID, some as early as the 1970s (Neubert, Moon, Grigal, & Redd, 2001). These initial schemes centred on creating occasions for socialisation and integration, or provided occupational skills training to prepare participants for employment (ibid). Increasingly, these programmes focus on how to support students in maximally inclusive College experiences designed to mirror the undergraduate experiences of mainstream students (Grigal, Hart, & Weir, 2013; Caroll, Blumberg, & Petroff, 2008).

The majority of American IPSE programmes emerged within the last decade, following passage of the Higher Education Opportunities Act of 2008 (HEOA) (20 USC §§ 1001 et seq.), which targeted a number of barriers to postsecondary education for students with ID through two innovations. First, the HEOA allocated financial aid for students with ID enrolled in federally approved comprehensive transition and postsecondary (CTP) programmes on College campuses (VanBergeijk & Cavanagh, 2012). Although CTP programme students do not attain degrees,[10] they need not have high school diplomas and take at least half of their coursework alongside students without disabilities (Grigal, Hart, & Weir, 2013). Moreover, because CTP programmes focus on preparing students with ID for 'gainful employment',[11] funds for pre-employment services administered by state vocational rehabilitation agencies can offset programme costs, so long as students' individualised employment goals[12] require a postsecondary credential (Lee, Rozell, & Will, 2018). As of September 2018, 92 US institutions of higher education have created CTPs (Dept. of Educ., 2018), up from just 10 in January 2012 (VanBergeijk & Cavanagh, 2012).

Moreover, the HEOA created a funding stream for Transition and Postsecondary Programs for Students with Intellectual Disability (TPSID). TPSID projects aim to operationalise the expressed intention of the 2004 IDEA to enable students with ID to participate in higher education (20 USC §§ 1140g). In eight years, the TPSID initiative has supported the creation or expansion of programmes at 93 Colleges and universities serving 3,350 students with ID across 31 states (Lee, Rozell, & Will, 2018). Over this same period TPSIDs have engendered demonstrable positive outcomes. Paid employment among TPSID graduates rates increased from 30 per cent in 2010 (Grigal, Hart, Smith, Domin, & Weir, 2016) to 61 per cent in 2014–2015 (Papay, Trivedi, Smith, & Grigal, 2017), more than tripling the employment rate among adults

---

[10] The relevant HEOA provisions are 20 USC §§ 1091(s) & 1140, and its regulations at 34 CFR § 668.231(a)(5).
[11] The relevant HEOA provision is 20 USC § 1140(1)(B), and its regulations at 34 CFR § 668.231(a)(3).
[12] Somewhat confusingly, adults with ID eligible for vocational rehabilitation services can have employment goals that significantly differ from their educational goals set forth in their IEPs.

with ID the same year (17 per cent) (National Core Indicators, 2017). This surge may be attributable to TPSID students' employment rate while completing their programmes being double the rate for all transition-age youth with ID (Grigal et al., 2016; Smith, Grigal, & Papay, 2018). Both CTP programmes and TPSID projects receive technical assistance from and are evaluated by Think College, the designated National Coordinating Center (NCC) based at the University of Massachusetts Boston (Grigal et al., 2016). In this way, in just a decade the HEOA has created more well-defined pathways to postsecondary education programmes for students with ID than older, disability-specific education and civil rights statutes have done.

The transformative potential of such schemes cannot be overstated. Among students with disabilities, students with ID have historically been the least likely to participate in higher education and experienced the most dismal post-school outcomes (Thoma et al., 2011), including low rates of competitive (i.e., non-segregated) employment and highest poverty rates (US Senate Committee for Health, Education, Labor and Pensions, 2011). In 2010, for example, adults with ID participated in the work force at a rate of 22.8 per cent (Butterworth et al., 2012). Migliore, Mank, Grossi, and Rogan (2007) found that 76 per cent of persons with ID who worked were employed in facility-based programmes or sheltered workshops. Only about 150,000 persons with ID work in community-based settings outside the sheltered work environment (President's Committee on Persons with Intellectual Disabilities, 2009; Ross, Marcell, Williams, & Carlson, 2013).

However, the quality of IPSE programmes varies vastly (President's Committee on Persons with Intellectual Disabilities, 2016).[13] Still, '[a]pproximately half the courses in which students are enrolled are segregated and specialized' (ibid). Moreover, IPSE programmes differ with regard to the availability of 'campus housing, peer mentoring, specialized orientation programs, family participation, cost and other program components' (ibid). Indeed, uniform standards are only just emerging through NCC-led efforts to develop model accreditation standards (Institute for Community Inclusion, 2018). Especially as educators grapple with the practical implications of the relatively

---

[13] Despite the common source of funding and common goals across IPSE programmes, they range from 'substantially separate' programmes allowing students with ID to participate only in classes with other students with disabilities, to highly individualised and integrated 'inclusive individual support' programmes affording students with ID access to mainstream courses and degree programmes either for audit or credit, while many 'mixed' or 'hybrid' programmes combine certain elements of both (Grigal & Hart, 2010).

recent and radical notion of including students with ID in higher education programmes, there are a number of ways in which these programmes can improve in order to ensure that they deliver on their aims of inclusion, as described in the following section.

Discrimination *within* IPSE Programmes

The nationwide opening of postsecondary education pathways to students with ID demonstrates progress in higher education and is leading to better employment outcomes. Nevertheless, and despite achieving significant goals, sundry IPSE programmes mistakenly discriminate against their own students in at least three areas: admissions criteria, academic credentials, and disciplinary procedures.[14] Consequently and ironically, in pursuing academic excellence and reputation, certain IPSE programmes belie in practice the very premise that students with ID have an equal claim to participate in higher education for which they purportedly stand. Even as students with ID increasingly access College campuses, they and their allies must remain vigilant to stamp out the persistent vestiges of the discriminatory attitudes that had once barred their entry.

Suspect Admission Criteria

The admission criteria of IPSEs 'vary considerably in their expectations and prerequisites of students and ... often diverge from stated policies' (McEathron, Beuhring, Maynard, & Mavis, 2013). Nonetheless, apparent trends in admission criteria used by IPSEs are cause for concern. Most IPSE programmes restrict admission to students with 'mild' or 'moderate' ID whom they describe as 'high-functioning' (University of Arkansas, n.d.; University of Cincinnati, n.d.; West Texas A&M University, n.d.). Other programmes, like UNC Greensboro's Beyond Academics, bar students who have legal guardians (UNC Greensboro, n.d.), despite the prevalence of guardianship.[15] For its part, the HEOA defines a student with ID without regard to degrees of severity that bear the hallmarks of outmoded and offensive measures (20 USC § 1140(2)(A)). Hence, the HEOA does not

---

[14] Recently, parents of a student with ID sued his federally approved CTP programme for failing to provide advertised inclusive opportunities (Johnson, 2018).

[15] Perversely secondary school special educators are deeply complicit in promoting guardianship, acting as the gatekeepers of the 'school-to-guardianship pipeline' (Jameson et al., 2015; National Council on Disability, 2018).

recognise sub-classifications of students with ID who are College ready and those who are not. Nor does it permit programmes to cream-skim students with ID who will be easier to accommodate than others (ibid). Moreover, it is difficult to understand how diagnosis-driven admission criteria would be justified as 'reasonable' even by the broad decades-old Supreme Court standard in *Cleburne*, when such stratification is inapposite to the purported aim of IPSEs to create opportunities for students with ID excluded from higher education.

Furthermore, many four-year, on-campus programmes expressly require that aspiring students with ID conform to vague behavioural standards smacking of ableism. The University of Arkansas EMPOWER programme, for instance, admits only students 'who do not demonstrate significant behavioral or emotional problems' (University of Arkansas, n.d.). Coastal Carolina University's LIFE programme requires that each admitted student '[n]either has nor exhibits a history of difficult, challenging behavior' (Coastal Carolina University, n.d.). Ohio State University's Transition Options in Postsecondary Settings (TOPS) programme requires each student to 'demonstrate the ability to maintain appropriate behavior in a variety of settings'. And ClemsonLIFE requires that students not be 'defiant toward authority' (Clemson College of Education, n.d.). Although the Rehabilitation Act may allow students with ID to be dismissed from study programmes based on their documented inability to adhere to 'professional' standards of conduct (*Halpern* v. *Wake Forest Univ. Health Scis.*, 2012), it seems certain that such broad characterisations of behaviour as problematic, challenging, inappropriate, or defiant reflect retrogressive stereotypes about persons with ID and discriminatory attitudes about presumed 'normal' on-campus conduct.

Many programmes likewise require applicants to have parents who are prepared to support them by absorbing operating costs. UCLA's Pathway programme, for example, requires that each student '[h]ave family support' (University of California Los Angeles Extension, n.d.). ClemsonLIFE mandates each student to have 'parents who will support his/her independence' (Clemson College of Education, n.d.). Millersville University's Integrated Studies programme obliges each student to '[h]ave support from family' (Millersville University, n.d.). The University of Colorado Inclusive Services programme requires a '[c]ommitment from the applicant's family/caregivers to support the goals of the student' (University of Colorado, n.d.). It borders on paradoxical that IPSEs tasked with preparing students with ID for competitive integrated employment and other facets of independent living permit admission of only those individuals with ready familial supports. Such preconditions bar students with ID who lack supportive family environments or who rely on non-family members for support needed to achieve independence, thereby excluding the persons with ID perhaps in greatest need of a stepping stone to independent living. These requirements likewise reflect socio-economic biases about successful students with ID, as well as assumptions about the extent to which IPSE programmes may prevail on unpaid family-centred supporters to supplement their offerings.

Clearly, analogous admission criteria would be deemed intolerable if applied to mainstream College aspirants. Yet within the realm of IPSE, programmes openly advertise these preconditions. That students with ID must pass through these sieves to show themselves worthy of continuing their education in age-appropriate settings suggests that some of these IPSE programmes have some distance to traverse in eradicating attitudes that contribute to the exclusion of students with ID, despite their formal role as gatekeepers to higher education.

Second-Class Status

The HEOA specifically and intentionally omitted the requirement for students with ID to attain traditional degrees or certificates. Instead, it authorised a new type of postsecondary credential for these students by defining a CTP programme to signify 'a degree, certificate, or nondegree program' (Lee, Rozell, & Will, 2018). Additionally, the HEOA mandated that TPSID programmes create and offer 'meaningful credentials' without defining further the content or scope of such a credential (20 USC § 1140g (d)(8)). Although developing a meaningful credential is a required condition of federal funds, empirical research relates that 'many' TPSID programme directors 'described uncertainty about how to meet or measure this goal' (Thoma, 2013). Accordingly, although most TPSID programmes offer 'some type of credential', these vary widely (Grigal & Smith, 2014).

To be fair, '[t]he process for developing a credential that is meaningful both within and outside of the IHE takes significant resources and time' (ibid). Nevertheless, the relative stagnancy across three years of TPSID project implementation, during which very few funded programmes have expanded their credential offerings (ibid), speaks volumes regarding entrenched attitudes of administrators regarding the proper place for students with ID in the realm of higher education. So, too, the fact that only 2 of 44 TPSID programmes surveyed offer a path for students with ID to an undergraduate degree (ibid). Consequently, students with ID in non-degree programmes cannot count their classes for credit towards a degree, no matter whether these are completed in segregated or mainstream classrooms (Shanley, Weir, & Grigal, 2014). Thus, students with ID who excel in an IPSE programme and wish to pursue an associate's degree, for example, need to start from scratch. In this way, IPSE programmes appear committed to opening their doors for historically marginalised students with ID but not yet prepared to treat them equally in all aspects of credentials and status.

Although the HEOA regulations entrust its National Coordinating Center (NCC) to define 'meaningful credential' and to measure TPSID programmes' performance (80 FR 36777), the NCC's current model accreditation standards do not expressly require qualifying programmes to build bridges to traditional degree-seeking programmes (National Coordinating Center Accreditation Workgroup, 2016). While institutional cordons may help assuage ableist concerns that traditional degrees will be diluted as a result of students' with ID access to them,[16] systematically shunting students with ID towards distinct credentials might unintentionally erect barriers for future efforts to make mainstream higher education accessible. One can thus wonder if the HEOA, in carving out a special space for students with ID on College campuses within the confines of non-degree programmes that offer a 'meaningful credential', might have inadvertently entrenched ableist notions about the aims of higher education (Dolmage, 2017; Hehir, 2000). It remains to be seen whether the HEOA's 'meaningful credential' standard results in inequitable inclusion, and if so, whether this second-tier status can be justified as a temporary handhold in the perilous climb up ivied walls. So long as educators with specialised subject-matter expertise develop these credentials, the notion that postsecondary education programmes advertise themselves as inclusive – while they preclude students from obtaining traditional degrees – only underscores the persistent gap between rhetoric and practice that many of these programmes must close.

Biased Disciplinary Procedures

Last, some IPSE programmes do not provide students with ID the same due process protections afforded matriculated students in disciplinary proceedings, even though the Constitution has long guaranteed students

---

[16] Indeed, such fears about full inclusion of lower-achieving students only belie the extent to which the prestige of postsecondary degrees depends circularly on their exclusivity.

at public institutions of higher education a right to notice and a hearing when facing disciplinary action (*Dixon* v. *Ala. State Bd. of Educ.*, 1961). Instead, these IPSE programmes imposes their own internal rules and regulations on students with ID to issue disciplinary sanctions or even dismissals. This policy could result from well-intentioned desires to minimise the visibility of students with ID who may be perceived as 'acting out'. Nevertheless, applying disciplinary procedures without recognised safeguards is discriminatory.

Existing literature on IPSE programmes make scant mention of disciplinary or grievance procedures, even though the NCC model accreditation standards envision some complaint filing mechanism being made available. The College of New Jersey (TCNJ) is unique in publishing its standards for students in its Career and Community Studies (CCS) programme. That programme reserves the right to summarily 'dismiss' a student if s/he fails to 'display appropriate dispositions' within the programme or to 'display[] an acceptable level of emotional and behavioural stability to allow for increasing independence in academic, vocational and social activities' (TCNJ, 2016). The CCS programme does not provide further guidance on these standards (ibid). By contrast, it is much more unlikely that mainstream TCNJ students will be dismissed. They may be investigated and notified in writing of charges for a number of conduct violations, including harassment, stalking, abuse, damage to property, upon which they can select an informal or formal hearing. Either way, the hearing results in a decision that the student may appeal. Available sanctions range from written warnings and housing termination to probation or suspension and ultimately to expulsion and degree revocation (ibid). Given the limited protections that non-discrimination statutes and the IDEA afford students with ID in higher education, providing these individuals with fewer safeguards than their mainstream peers runs contrary to the goals of IPSE programmes.

Case Study

Despite the aforementioned defects, academic discussion of IPSE programmes has generally and rightfully been adulatory. Effectively implemented IPSE programmes can indeed be 'transformative' for students with ID (Folk, Yamamoto, & Stodden, 2012). Nonetheless, while IPSE programmes may be transforming students with ID, it is less clear how rapidly students with ID are transforming their host institutions. Put another way, while data indicates that students with ID are more likely to have competitive integrated employment after completing their IPSE programmes, there is less information about whether students with ID are treated on campus as coequals. We hope that over time students with ID will find greater acceptance in IPSE programmes, and that these programmes will increasingly embrace divergent learning modalities as a desired element of diversity, consistent with the public commitment of many institutions of higher learning to including other traditionally excluded and marginalised groups.

For now, anecdotal evidence indicates that within manifold IPSE programmes students with ID face discriminatory attitudes that undermine opportunities to maximise their potential and create incentives against investing in the development of their own human capital. The vast majority of the ever-growing body of literature on the promise of IPSE programmes overlooks this reality. Conversely, a rights-based approach to education urges greater attention to the processes and safeguards needed to protect students' rights within IPSE settings.

The anonymised case study below, which relates the experiences of a student with ID named 'Rosa', is based on facts known personally to the authors. Used anonymously with the permission of the student and her parents, it helps illustrate how discriminatory attitudes persist within IPSE programmes, undermining such programmes' claims to 'inclusiveness' and at times subjecting students to discrimination otherwise prohibited by law.

Rosa attended public high school. Attending College was a goal included in Rosa's IEP since she began the IDEA-mandated transition planning process. She expected to attend College after high school, as her non-disabled older siblings had done. Rosa was admitted to a four-year 'hybrid' model IPSE programme on a state College campus, where students with ID participated in both self-contained and inclusive classes, but were not eligible for accumulating College credits. Following a contentious mediation process with the school district, Rosa's parents managed to secure partial funding for her IPSE programme through age 21.

Although IPSE programme classes and activities were on campus, Rosa and other students with ID faced barriers to services available to mainstream College students. For example, they were not deemed eligible for housing, despite the Rehabilitation Act (*Fialka-Feldman* v. *Oakland Univ. Bd. of Trs.*, 2009; 34 CFR § 104.45). So, Rosa's parents networked with parents of other students in the IPSE programme to lease a house off-campus. In addition, although the IPSE programme provided stipends to mainstream students to serve as 'house mentors' in off-campus residences, it required that parents of students with ID offer them free boarding and lodging. Nor were Rosa and her peers eligible to receive student health services from the campus infirmary, even though students in Rosa's programme paid the same healthcare fees in addition to their tuition that mainstream College students did.

The IPSE programme also imposed ambiguous behavioural requirements on students with ID. House mentors, ostensibly there to support programme students' transition to College life, were deputised to monitor students' behaviour, on and off campus, and to report any behaviour that triggered health and safety concerns. For instance, Rosa's house mentor filed an incident report when Rosa crossed a street on her way to campus just after the crosswalk signal had turned from 'walk' to a flashing cautionary hand. IPSE programme administrators summoned Rosa's parents to campus and informed them that based on this and other reports the programme had been surreptitiously collecting, Rosa would be 'asked' to leave the programme if she again put the health and safety of both herself and other IPSE students at risk. When Rosa's parents requested to view other incident reports made about Rosa, the administrators asserted that those records were not subject to release, notwithstanding federal laws guaranteeing students access to their educational records.

Indeed, Rosa's behaviour was under heightened scrutiny not only from programme administrators but also from other members of the College community. In Rosa's second year, a College official unaffiliated with the IPSE programme observed her in the student centre lying face down on a couch and moaning with her hands placed underneath her stomach. When s/he approached Rosa, Rosa refused to respond to the official and did not move her hands. The official reported Rosa to the College for masturbating in a public space. The incident was relayed to IPSE administrators, who again summoned Rosa's parents to campus, again without first discussing the incident with Rosa. Unaware of the report, Rosa explained matter-of-factly that she had been experiencing painful menstrual cramps that day, was lying down and holding her pelvic area, and did not respond to the official because it would have been inappropriate to discuss private matters with a stranger. Rosa's parents asked that the official's report be expunged from College records or that a written record of Rosa's explanation be included alongside the official's report. These requests were denied; the IPSE administrators insisted that it would be better not to make a fuss and simply move on.

Throughout Rosa's time in the programme, administrators actively attempted to deal with perceived behavioural issues internally and informally. They asserted broad authority to suspend or expel IPSE programme students, independently of the College's disciplinary processes for mainstream students, believing that shielding students with ID from these procedures to be in their best interests. This belief materialised when a College student observed Rosa crying outside the campus library after having fallen and twisted her knee. The student summoned campus police, who without first asking her whether she wanted to go to student health services, offered to call an ambulance for her. (Rosa later explained that she had assented because she had understood the officer's suggestion as a directive, given the officer's position of authority.) Rosa was sent to a local hospital in an ambulance unaccompanied and police informed the programme administrators, who then notified Rosa's parents. While leaving the hospital with Rosa, whose emergency room visit required nothing more than an elastic bandage and crutches, a programme administrator instructed Rosa's parents not to allow Rosa to return to campus for the semester's final week while the programme assessed whether Rosa would be 'asked to return' the next semester. Only after Rosa's parents pressed programme administrators at an in-person meeting after classes ended did the programme concede to having in effect summarily suspending Rosa. They apologised to Rosa, who failed to understand why she had been sent home.

Ultimately, Rosa completed the programme. Although she received a non-degree certificate of completion and was not permitted to receive College credit for coursework she completed in inclusive classrooms, she participated in the College's graduation exercises alongside degree-seeking students. It is unlikely that she can use her certificate to pursue further studies, and it is unclear how prospective employers will value this certificate relative to other, better recognised credentials. Notwithstanding the discriminatory attitudes she encountered, she experienced tremendous personal growth at College and learned valuable lessons on and off campus. Indeed, she looks back at her College experience fondly overall, remembering primarily her positive interactions with fellow students, her house mentor, and other members of the College community both affiliated and unaffiliated with the programme.

Conclusion

American laws and policies have slowly but progressively recognised an equal right to education by students with ID, but significant barriers remain to making this right a lived reality, especially at the postsecondary level, and in particular regarding mainstream higher education. IPSE programmes provide socially meaningful and instrumentally valuable opportunities for these students, but are nonetheless challenging due to their segregated nature, and are problematic when they discriminate against the very students they are designed to enable. The future of postsecondary education for students with ID lies in dismantling administrative barriers to their participating in mainstream higher education, while at the same time acknowledging and supporting the progressive opportunities afforded by IPSE programmes. In both instances, great care must be taken to ward against discrimination and marginalisation.

REFERENCES

Americans with Disabilities Act of 1990, Pub. L. No. 111–2, 42 USC §§ 12101 et seq. (1994), and its implementing regulations, 28 CFR Part 35.

Aron, L. & Loprest, P. (2012). Disability and the Education System. *Future of Children*, 22(1), 97–122.

Baum, S. & Ma, J. (2007). *Education Pays: The Benefits of Higher Education for Individuals and Society*. Washington, DC: The College Board.

Bd. of Educ. of the Hendrick Hudson Central Sch. Dist. v. Rowley, 458 U.S. 176 (1982).

Brown v. Bd. of Educ. of Topeka, 347 U.S. 483 (1954).

Bureau of Labor Statistics (2010). Employment Status of the Civilian Population 25 Years and Over by Educational Attainment, Sex, Race and Hispanic or Latino Ethnicity. In *Labor Force Statistics from the Current Population Survey*. Washington, DC: Author.

Butterworth, J., Smith, F. A., Hall, A. C., Migliore, A., Winsor, J., Domin, D., & Timmons, J. C. (2012). *State Data: The National Report on Employment Services and Outcomes*. Boston, MA: University of Massachusetts Boston, Institute for Community Inclusion.

Carey, A. C. (2010). *On the Margins of Citizenship: Intellectual Disability and Civil Rights in Twentieth-Century America*. Philadelphia: Temple University Press.

Caroll, S. Z., Blumberg, R. E., & Petroff J. G. (2008). The Promise of Liberal Learning: Creating a Challenging Postsecondary Curriculum for Youth with Intellectual Disabilities. *Focus on Exceptional Children*, 40(9), 1–12.

Clemson College of Education (n.d.). *ClemsonLIFE Application and Admissions*. 3 October 2018 from ClemsonLIFE website: www.clemson.edu/education/cul ife/application-admissions/index.html

Coastal Carolina University (n.d.), *LIFE Program*. Retrieved October 3, 2018 from LIFE Program website: www.coastal.edu/biddlecenter/lifeprogram.

Colker, R. (2013). *Disabled Education: A Critical Analysis of the Individuals with Disabilities Education Act*. New York: New York University Press.

Conroy, M., Hanson, T., Butler, J. & Paiewonsky, M. (2013). Massachusetts Inclusive Concurrent Enrollment: Shifting from state funds to IDEA funds. Think College. Boston: University of Massachusetts Boston, Institute for Community Inclusion.

Dixon v. Ala. State Bd. of Educ., 294 F.2d 150 (5th Cir. 1961).

Doherty v. So. Coll. of Optometry, 862 F.2d 570 (6th Cir. 1988).

Dolmage, J. T. (2017). *Academic Ableism: Disability and Higher Education*. Ann Arbor, MI: University of Michigan Press.

Eckrem, J. O. & McArthur, E. J. (2001). Is the Rowley Standard Dead? From Access to Results, *University of California Davis Journal of Juvenile Law and Policy*, 5, 199–217.

Education for All Handicapped Children Act of 1975, Pub. L. No. 94–142, 20 USC §§ 1400 et seq. (1976), reauthorized as Individuals with Disabilities Education Act of 1990, Pub. L. No. 94–142, 20 USC §§ 1400 et seq. (2006), and its implementing regulations, 34 CFR Part 300.

Endrew F. v. Douglas Cnty. Sch. Dist. RE-1, 137 S. Ct. 988 (2017).

Fialka-Feldman v Oakland Univ. Bd. of Trs., No. 2:2008cv14922 (E.D. Mich. 2009).

Folk, E. D. R., Yamamoto, K. K., & Stodden, R. A. (2012). Implementing Inclusion and Collaborative Teaming in a Model Program of Postsecondary Education for Young Adults with Intellectual Disabilities. *Journal of Policy and Practice in Intellectual Disabilities*, 9(4), 257–269.

Griffin, M. M., McMillan, E. D., & Hodapp, R. M. (2010). Family Perspectives on Post-Secondary Education for Students with Intellectual Disabilities. *Education and Training in Autism and Developmental Disabilities*, 45(3), 339–346.

Grigal, M., Hart, D., Smith, F. A., Domin, D., & Weir, C. (2016). Think College National Coordinating Center: Annual report on the transition and postsecondary programs for students with intellectual disabilities (2014–2015). Boston: University of Massachusetts Boston, Institute for Community Inclusion.

Grigal, M. & Smith, F. (2014). Current Status of Meaningful Credentials for Students With Intellectual Disabilities Attending TPSID Model Demonstration Programs, (Think College Insight Brief 5). Boston: University of Massachusetts Boston, Institute for Community Inclusion.

Grigal, M., Hart, D. & Weir, C. (2013). Postsecondary Education for People with Intellectual Disability: Current Issues and Critical Challenges. *Inclusion*, 1(1), 50–63.

Grigal, M., Hart, D., Smith, F. A., Domin, D., & Sulewski, J. (2013). Think College National Coordinating Center: Annual report on the transition and postsecondary programs for students with intellectual disabilities. Boston: University of Massachusetts Boston, Institute for Community Inclusion.

Grigal, M., Hart, D. & Lewis, S. (2012). A prelude to progress: The evolution of postsecondary education for students with intellectual disabilities (Think College Insight Brief 12). Boston: University of Massachusetts Boston: Institute of Community Inclusion.

Grigal, M., Hart, D., & Weir, C. (2012a). A Survey of Postsecondary Education Programs for Students with Intellectual Disabilities in the United States. *Journal of Policy & Practice in Intellectual Disabilities*, 9(4), 223–233.

Grigal, M., Hart, D. & Weir, C. (2012b). Think College Standards Quality Indicators, and Benchmarks for Inclusive Higher Education (Insight Brief 10). Boston: University of Massachusetts Boston, Institute for Community Inclusion.

Grigal, M., Hart, D., & Migliore, A. (2011). Comparing the Transition Planning, Postsecondary Education, and Employment Outcomes of Students With Intellectual and Other Disabilities. *Career Development for Exceptional Individuals*, 34(1), 4–17.

Grigal, M. & Hart, D. (2010). *Think College!: Postsecondary Education Options for Students with Intellectual Disabilities*. Baltimore: Brookes Publishing Co.

U.S. House of Representatives (1975). Report No. 94–332 on H.R. 7217. A bill to amend the Education of the Handicapped Act to provide educational assistance to all handicapped children, and for other purposes; with amendment, 1975 USCCAN 1425.

Halpern v. Wake Forest Univ. Health Scis., 669 F.3d 454 (4th Cir. 2012).

Hart, D., Grigal, M., Sax, C., Martinez, D., & Will, M. (2006). Postsecondary Options for Students with Intellectual Disabilities (Research to Practice Brief 46). Boston: University of Massachusetts Boston, Institute for Community Inclusion.

Hart, D., Mele-McCarthy, J., Pasternack, P. H., Zimbrich, K., & Parker, D. R. (2004). Community College: A Pathway to Success for Youth with Learning, Cognitive, and Intellectual Disabilities in Secondary Settings. *Education and Training in Developmental Disabilities*, 39(1), 54–66.

Hehir, T. & Gamm, S. (1999). Special education: From legalism to collaboration. In J. Heubert (ed.), *Law and School Reform* (pp. 205–227). New Haven, CT: Yale University Press.

Hehir, T. (2000). *New Directions in Special Education: Eliminating Ableism in Policy and Practice*. Cambridge, MA: Harvard Education Press.

Higher Education Opportunity Act of 2008, Pub. L. No. 110–31, 20 USC §§ 1001 et seq. (2012), and its implementing regulations, 34 CFR § 68 et seq.

Jameson, M. J., Riesen, T., Polychronis, S., Trader, B., Mizner, S., Martinis, J., & Hoyle, D. (2015). Guardianship and the Potential of Supported Decision Making With Individuals with Disabilities. *Research and Practice for Persons with Severe Disabilities*, 40(1), 36–51.

Johnson, J. (10 December 2018). The Case for BUILD. *The Bethel University Clarion*. Retrieved 22 January 2019 from: https://bethelclarion.com/2018/12/10/the-case-for-build

Katsiyannis, A., Zhang, D., Ryan, J. B., & Jones, J. (2007). High-Stakes Testing and Students with Disabilities: Challenges and Promises. *Journal of Disability Policy Studies, 18*(3), 160–167.

Kotler, M. A. (1994). The Individuals with Disabilities Education Act: A Parent's Perspective and Proposal for Change. *University of Michigan Journal of Law Reform, 27*, 362–397.

Lee, S., Rozell, D., & Will, M. (2018). *Addressing the Policy Tangle: Students with Intellectual Disability and the Path to Postsecondary Education, Employment and Community Living.* Washington, DC: Inclusive Higher Education Committee.

McEathron, M. A., Beuhring, T., Maynard, A., & Mavis, A. (2013). Understanding the Diversity: A Taxonomy for Postsecondary Education Programs and Services for Students with Intellectual and Developmental Disabilities. *Journal of Postsecondary Education and Disability, 26*(4), 303–320.

McGrew, K. S. & Evans, J. (2004). Expectations for students with cognitive disabilities: Is the cup half empty or half full? Can the cup flow over? (Synthesis Report 55). Minneapolis, MN: University of Minnesota, National Center on Educational Outcomes.

McMahon, W. (2009). *Higher Learning, Greater Good: The Private and Social Benefits of Higher Education.* Baltimore: Johns Hopkins University Press.

Migliore, A. & Butterworth, J. (2008). Postsecondary education and employment outcomes for youth with intellectual disabilities (DataNote Series, Data Note XXI). Boston: Institute for Community Inclusion.

Migliore, A., Mank, D., Grossi, T., & Rogan, P. (2007). Integrated Employment or Sheltered Workshops: Preferences of Adults with Intellectual Disabilities, their Families, and Staff. *Journal of Vocational Rehabilitation, 26*(1), 5–19.

Millersville University (n.d.). *Admissions.* Retrieved 3 October 2018 from Integrated Studies website: www.millersville.edu/integratedstudies/admissions/index.php

Mischel, L., Bernstein, J., & Allegretto, S. (2007). *State of Working America, 2006/2007*, 10th edn, Washington, DC: Economic Policy Institute.

Moore, E. J. & Schelling, A. (2015). Postsecondary Inclusion for Individuals with an Intellectual Disability and its Effects on Employment. *Journal of Intellectual Disabilities, 19*(2), 130–148.

Morningstar, M. E., Bassett, D. S., Cashman, J., Kochar-Bryant, C., & Wehmeyer, M. L. (2012). Aligning Transition Services with Secondary Educational Reform: A Position Statement of the Division on Career Development and Transition. *Career Development and Transition for Exceptional Individuals, 35*(3), 132–142.

National Coordinating Center Accreditation Workgroup (2016). Report on Model Accreditation Standards for Higher Education Programs for Students with Intellectual Disability: A Path to Education, Employment, and Community Living. Boston: University of Massachusetts Boston, Institute for Community Inclusion.

National Core Indicators. (2017). *Chart generator 2014–15.* National Association of State Directors of Developmental Disabilities Services and Human Services Research Institute. Retrieved 4 October 2018 from www .nationalcoreindicators.org/charts/

Neubert, D. A., Moon, M. S., Grigal, M., & Redd, V. (2001). Post-secondary Educational Practices for Individuals with Mental Retardation and other Significant Disabilities: A Review of the Literature. *Journal of Vocational Rehabilitation, 16*(3), 155–168.

Ohio State University (n.d.). *Prospective TOPS Students.* Retrieved 3 October 2018 from Transition Options in Postsecondary Settings (TOPS) website: http://ni songer.osu.edu/adult/adult-clinics-services/tops/prospective-students

Papay, C., Trivedi, K., Smith, F., & Grigal, M. (2017). One year after exit: A first look at outcomes of students who completed TPSIDs (Think College Fast Facts 17). Boston: University of Massachusetts Boston, Institute for Community Inclusion.

Pennsylvania Ass'n for Retard. Child. v. Commonwealth of Pa., 334 F. Supp. 1257 (E. D. Pa. 1971).

Ross, J., Marcell, J., Williams, P., & Carlson, D. (2013). Postsecondary Education, Employment, and Independence: Living Outcomes of Persons with Autism and Intellectual Disability. *Journal of Postsecondary Education and Disability, 26* (4), 337–351.

Sannicandro, T., Parish, S. L., Fournier, S., Mitra, M., & Paiewonsky, M. (2018). Employment, Income, and SSI Effects of Postsecondary Education for People with Intellectual Disability. *American Journal on Intellectual and Developmental Disabilities, 123*(5), 412–425.

Schalock, R. L., Borthwick-Duffy, S. A., Bradley, V. J., Buntinx, W. H. E., Coulter, D. L., & Craig, E. M. (2010). *Intellectual Disability: Definition, Classification, and Systems of Supports,* 11th edn, Washington, DC: American Association on Intellectual and Developmental Disabilities.

Section 504 of the Rehabilitation Act of 1973, Pub. L. No. 93–112, 29 USC § 794 (1976), and its implementing regulations, 34 CFR Part 104.

Shanley, J., Weir, C., & Grigal, M. (2014). Credential Development in Inclusive Higher Education Programs Serving Students with Intellectual Disabilities (Think College Insight Brief 25). Boston: University of Massachusetts Boston, Institute for Community Inclusion.

Silvers, A. & Stein, M. A. (2002). Disability, Equal Protection, and the Supreme Court: Standing at the Crossroads of Progressive and Retrogressive Logic in Constitutional Classification. *University of Michigan Journal of Legal Reform, 35,* 81–136.

Smith, F., Grigal, M., & Papay, C. (2018). Year one employment and career development experiences of College students attending Cohort 2-TPSID model demonstration programs. Boston: University of Massachusetts Boston, Institute for Community Inclusion.

Southeastern Cmty. Coll. v. Davis, 442 U.S. 397 (1979).

Stein, M. A., Stein, J. S. & Blanck, P. (2009). Disability. In S. N. Katz et al. (eds.), *Oxford International Encyclopedia of Legal History.* New York: Oxford University Press.

Task Force on Higher Education for Students with Intellectual Disabilities and Autism Spectrum Disorder (2014). Report to the Massachusetts Legislature. Boston: Joint Committee on Higher Education.

Think College National Coordinating Center (2017). Higher education access for students with intellectual disability in the United States (Think College Snapshot). Boston: University of Massachusetts Boston, Institute for Community Inclusion.

Thoma, C. A. (2013). Postsecondary Education for Students with Intellectual Disability (ID): Complex Layers. *Journal of Postsecondary Education and Disability, 26*(4), 285–302.

Thoma, C. A., Lakin, K. C., Carlson, D., Domzal, C., Austin, K., & Boyd, K. (2011). Participation in Postsecondary Education for Students with Intellectual Disabilities: A Review of the Literature 2001–2010. *Journal of Postsecondary Education and Disability, 24*(3), 175–191.

Uditsky, B. & Hughson, E. (2012). Inclusive Postsecondary Education – An Evidence-Based Moral Imperative. *Journal of Policy and Practice in Intellectual Disabilities, 9*(4), 298–302.

UNC Greensboro (n.d.). *Admissions.* Retrieved 3 October 2018 from Beyond Academics website: https://beyondacademics.uncg.edu/admissions.

United Nations Convention on the Rights of Persons with Disabilities, New York, 12 December 2006, opened for signature on 30 March 2007, entered into force on 3 May 2008, 999 UNTS 3.

University of Arkansas (n.d.). *Admissions.* Retrieved 3 October 2018 from EMPOWER website: https://empower.uark.edu/admission.php.

University of California Los Angeles Extension (n.d.). *Admissions.* Retrieved 3 October 2018 from Pathway website: http://education.uclaextension.edu/path way/admissions

University of Cincinnati (n.d.). *Transition and Access Program (TAP).* Retrieved 3 October 2018 from TAP website: https://cech.uc.edu/education/ats/tap.html.

University of Colorado (n.d.). *Application*. Retrieved 3 October 2018 from Inclusive Services website: www.uccs.edu/inclusiveservices/application.

U.S. Department of Education, Office for Civil Rights (1998). *Auxiliary Aids and Services for Postsecondary Students with Disabilities*. Washington, DC: Author.

U.S. Department of Education, Office of Postsecondary Education (July 2, 2010). Overview Information; Coordinating Center for Transition and Postsecondary Programs for Students With Intellectual Disabilities; Notice Inviting Applications for New Awards for Fiscal Year (FY) 2010. 75 FR 38506.

U.S. Department of Education, Office for Civil Rights (2011). *Students with Disabilities Preparing for Postsecondary Education: Know Your Rights and Responsibilities*. Washington, DC: Author.

U.S. Department of Education, Office of Postsecondary Education (June 26, 2015). Applications for New Awards; Coordinating Center for Transition Programs for Students with Intellectual Disabilities into Higher Education. 80 FR 36777.

U.S. Department of Education, Office of Special Education and Rehabilitative Services (2017). *A Transition Guide to Postsecondary Education and Employment for Students and Youth with Disabilities*. Washington, DC: Author.

U.S. Department of Education, Federal Student Aid (2018). *Students with Intellectual Disabilities*. Retrieved 3 October 2018 from https://studentaid.ed.gov/sa/eligibility/intellectual-disabilities

VanBergeijk, E. O. & Cavanagh, P. K. (2012). Brief Report: New Legislation Supports Students with Intellectual Disabilities in Post-secondary Funding. *Journal of Autism and Developmental Disorders*, 42(11), 2471–2475.

Waterstone, M. (2014). Disability Constitutional Law. *Emory Law Journal*, 63(3), 527–580.

Weiner, R. & Hume, M. (1987). *And Education for All: Public Policy and Handicapped Children*, 2nd edn, New York: Aspen Publishers.

West Texas A&M University (n.d.). *Where the Learning Continues (WTLC)*. Retrieved 3 October 2018 from WTLC website: http://wtamu.edu/academics/eod-where-the-learning-continues.aspx

CHAPTER 13

'Invisible' Disabilities in South Africa's Higher Education Sector

An Analysis of the Inclusion of Persons with Psychosocial and Intellectual Disabilities

Faraaz Mahomed

Introduction

The United Nations (UN) Convention on the Rights of Persons with Disabilities (CRPD), introduced in 2007, highlights the significance of equality as a fundamental guiding principle for society's treatment of people living with disabilities. It recognises a specific right to education and acknowledges the value of education as a facilitative right, viewing it as a means to enable effective participation in society. Education is an enabler of numerous other rights, representing an opportunity that should be available to all people on an equal basis. For this reason, the Convention requires state parties to provide access to secondary and tertiary education to persons with disabilities on an equal basis as those without disabilities.

Despite these provisions, people living with disabilities face numerous challenges in attempting to navigate the higher education space. These include stigma and discrimination, lack of accommodations and lack of appropriate access to services, often compounded by racial, gender and class inequalities that are also determinants of access. Even where disability is accommodated for, as demonstrated in this chapter, these accommodations often do not extend to the realm of 'invisible' disabilities, namely psychosocial and intellectual disabilities. The term 'psychosocial disability' refers to the barriers to participation in society that arise out of an individual's mental health status, whether diagnosed with a specific mental health condition or not (Manderscheid, Ryff, Freeman, Dhingra, & Strine, 2010), while the term 'intellectual disability' refers to challenges in cognitive learning abilities and developmental delays that may result in difficulties in participating fully and equally in society (Katz & Lazcano-Ponce, 2008).

The CRPD's socially oriented paradigm illustrates the need for a significant shift in how we might view 'pathology' and what we might conceive of as solutions to disabilities. Recognising that psychosocial and intellectual disabilities are social phenomena that arise from the individual's interaction with their environment is a first step to counteracting those factors in the environment that militate against inclusion. This approach thus addresses the 'pathological' environment with which an individual interacts rather than, as has predominantly been the case with medical interventions, simply ascribing a clinical label and offering a solution that seeks to correct a deficit in the person (Shakespeare, 2006).

The social model of disability notwithstanding, prevalence statistics still tend to focus on the proportion of people who have been diagnosed with a mental health condition or an intellectual or developmental impairment, ignoring undiagnosed and 'invisible' disabilities, suggesting that these statistics may very well be significant underestimates if the broader social conception of disability is taken into account. Even by these narrower definitions, the prevalence of mental health and intellectual impairments globally is alarmingly high. In 2014, a meta-study of prevalence surveys quantifying psychosocial disabilities found that 29.2 per cent of people will be affected by such a condition in their lifetime (Steel et al., 2014). Using clinical and public health terminology, the World Health Organization (WHO) noted that depressive 'disorders' are estimated to be the fourth most common contributors to the 'global disease burden' presently and, due to increasing prevalence, are likely to be the second most commonly diagnosed health condition overall by 2020 (WHO, 2001). Intellectual disabilities are even more difficult to quantify because they exist on such a broad spectrum. A 2011 meta-study estimated global prevalence of intellectual and developmental disabilities of roughly 1 per cent, suggesting that about 70 million people are living with some form of diagnosable impairment (Maulik, Mascarenhas, Mathers, Dua, & Saxena, 2011).

In South Africa, the vast majority of research conducted into disabilities in the higher education system relates primarily to physical and sensory disabilities (Bell, 2013; Engelbrecht & De Beer, 2014; Fitchett, 2015; Losinsky, Levi, Saffey, & Jelsma, 2003; Lourens, 2015; Maotoana, 2014; Mokiwa & Phasha, 2012; Mutanga, 2018; Seyama, Morris, & Stilwell, 2014). While some stressors and barriers to participation may be similar regardless of disability type, it would be prudent to consider what specific challenges may be faced by students with psychosocial and intellectual disabilities and to ensure that accommodations provided sufficiently cater to the needs of this population. Research from the United States (US) illustrates that students with psychosocial and intellectual disabilities make up the largest proportion of higher education students with disabilities overall (Koch, Lo, Mamieseishvili, Lee, & Hill, 2018). These students are enrolling in higher education in increasing numbers, but they also withdraw from higher education at higher rates than any other group, including students with physical disabilities (Koch et al., 2018). This demonstrates that improved accommodations and substantial changes in higher education policy and practice are needed to cater to the needs of students with 'invisible' disabilities.

Adapting to higher education is notoriously challenging, for students with disabilities and those without. However, these challenges can be particularly onerous for students with existing psychosocial and intellectual disabilities. Research shows that factors such as increased distress and maladaptive coping mechanisms, including alcohol and drug abuse, can be common sequelae, resulting in progressive withdrawal among students with psychosocial and intellectual disabilities (Wolf, 2001). Anxiety relating to the demands of education has been shown to be more common among students with intellectual disabilities than those without (Trainin & Swanson, 2005), while social isolation and difficulties with relationships have also been documented as part of the higher education experience of this group (Yang, Lin, Zhu, & Liang, 2015). Importantly, students with psychosocial and intellectual disabilities also experience anxiety about their prospects for future employment and integration into society post-graduation, demonstrating the acute awareness of difference that is a prevailing feature of their lives (Yang et al., 2015). Moreover, Newman et al. (2011) suggest that accommodations for 'invisible' disabilities, such as psychosocial and intellectual disabilities, are more complex and more difficult to tailor than those for the 'visible' disabilities. This, therefore, requires a more nuanced approach to accommodation than is often applied.

In this chapter, I explore the specific complexities of South Africa's post-apartheid higher education landscape, examining the evolution of national legislation and higher education policies as they pertain to people with psychosocial and intellectual disabilities. In addition, I consider the results of four interviews with key stakeholders and look at a sample of existing institutional policies for disability inclusion, noting the significant variations in accommodations for people with psychosocial and intellectual disabilities. I also seek to highlight ways in which minimum standards for accommodations provided may be instituted in light of substantial resource differentials between institutions and the mandate for disability policies in all institutions for higher education in terms of the 2013 White Paper for Post-School Education and Training. Acknowledging the significant implementation challenges that lie ahead, I also draw attention to the need for an enabling environment for effective execution of evolving policy provisions.

Disability in Higher Education: The South African Context

Prior to democracy, access to higher education in South Africa was racially determined, with preferential funding and political support for white universities (Jansen, 2003). Howell, Chalken and Alberts (2006, 78) note that, with respect to persons with disabilities in the apartheid era higher education system, 'attitudes and institutional practices ... have perpetuated some of the deepest inequalities and most severe forms of discrimination in our country's history'. Students with disabilities were, therefore, not spared from discriminatory policies and practices in South Africa's higher education landscape. In fact, they are likely to have been particularly disadvantaged by them.

Following the renunciation of apartheid as government policy, preferential access and funding policies were dismantled and efforts to transform higher education began.[1] The Constitution of the Republic of South Africa, adopted in 1996, establishes a universal right to 'a basic education, including adult basic education' and a right to 'further education, which the state, through reasonable measures, must make progressively available and accessible'. The Higher Education Act, No. 101 of 1997 (HEA, as amended), governs all tertiary education in the country, while additional legislation, such as the Continuing Education and Training Act, No. 16 of 2006 (CETA, as amended), and the Adult Education and Training Act, No. 52 of 2000 (AETA, as amended), govern other aspects of the higher education system. The HEA does not mention disability specifically, instead mentioning the need to ensure non-discriminatory access more broadly. Meanwhile, the CETA and the AETA refer to a set of directive principles for national education policy. Importantly, these principles incorporate a provision to 'ensure that no person, as a result of physical disability, is denied the opportunity to receive [an education]'. However, the principles do not mention psychosocial or intellectual disabilities. The HEA requires the establishment of institutional forums in all universities.

---

[1] The chapter by Crain Soudien in this volume provides a useful overview of transformation efforts in South Africa's higher education system.

These are bodies made up of management, faculty and students whose aim is to foster dialogue and create environments where specific needs are identified and solutions sought.

South Africa has 26 public universities, as well as almost 400 private 'Further Education and Training' (FET) Colleges (DHET, 2014), now referred to as 'Technical and Vocational Education and Training' (TVET) Colleges. In 2015, nine 'third tier' Community Education and Training (CET) Colleges were inaugurated – one in each province of the country – whose aim is to enhance post-school education and training either for the purpose of promoting employability or for preparing students for entry into a TVET College or university (DHET, 2015). Based on census data from 2011, the proportion of people with disabilities in South Africa who enrol in higher education is less than 1 per cent (DHET, 2016). This compares to a figure of approximately 4 per cent of the general population enrolled in higher education (DHET, 2013). Regarding overall completion of higher education in the South African population, the Department of Social Development (DSD) noted in 2016 that 5.3 per cent of people with disabilities in South Africa had graduated from a higher education institution. This compares with a post-secondary completion rate in the general population of 15.5 per cent (UNESCO, 2018). Unfortunately, due to the lack of accurate and comprehensive data, conclusions cannot be drawn specifically about psychosocial and intellectual disabilities. Despite the dismantling of the apartheid financing architecture for higher education, funding dependent on research outputs and on student fees has not been proportional between institutions, with the result that formerly white universities continue to be far better resourced than their former non-white counterparts (Habib, 2016). This is significant because resource allocation substantially affects the availability of accommodations for students with disabilities, perhaps most starkly illustrated by the fact that under-representation of students with disabilities, while a challenge in all institutions of higher education, is particularly pronounced in formerly black universities (DHET, 2015).

According to the Department of Higher Education and Training (DHET, 2018), people with psychosocial disabilities are particularly under-represented in national data regarding disability and represent the most marginalised and, indeed, 'invisible' group of disabled individuals. Lack of sufficient and accurate assessment for psychosocial and intellectual disabilities is a major challenge, and this is particularly true in rural parts of the country (Christianson et al., 2000). Stigma and discrimination against people with psychosocial disabilities are a key barrier to disclosure, meaning it is often difficult to gauge prevalence or support needs, and this is true also in higher education settings. By their nature, psychosocial and intellectual disabilities are easier to conceal than the physical disabilities, and environments that discourage disclosure often result in further concealment (Allen & Carlson, 2003), suggesting that there may be a higher proportion of people with psychosocial and intellectual disabilities in higher education than has been diagnosed or disclosed, pointing to substantial unmet needs for supports and accommodations.

Students with psychosocial and intellectual disabilities are also being educated within a broader system which presents numerous co-occurring obstacles to equality. South Africa's National Development Plan Agenda 2030 contains a target of 2 per cent for employees with disabilities in the public workforce (National Planning Commission, 2011). To date, progress towards this goal has been slow, with the figure at less than 1 per cent in 2016 (Enca, 2016). Ensuring equal participation in higher education is both an unequivocal obligation in terms of the CRPD and a major avenue through which progress towards these employment goals (themselves obligations in terms of the CRPD) can be met. In the next section, I consider the policy aspects of higher education for people with psychosocial and intellectual disabilities in South Africa, examining the shifts towards more inclusive higher education spaces, while also highlighting the specific emphasis (or lack thereof) on psychosocial and intellectual disabilities in the relevant instruments.

Post-apartheid South African Higher Education Policy: Psychosocial and Intellectual Disability in the Context of Transformation

Since the end of apartheid, a handful of policy instruments have been adopted in South Africa to engage with the subject of transforming the higher education system. These have largely taken the form of White Papers (White Paper 3 and White Paper 6 specifically), which have contained only cursory reflections on disability-specific needs, particularly in relation to higher education.

In 2013, the White Paper for Post-School Education and Training was introduced and it contained a specific section on disability, a first for South African higher education policy. This policy notes the need for improved data collection to inform accurate assessments of the accommodations needed. It also recognises that a significant concern is the lack of a uniform standard for institutional frameworks to meet the needs of students with disabilities. In practice, this has meant that institutions were left to decide on an individual basis what their specific commitments would be and what resources they would devote to disability (DHET, 2013). To address some of these concerns, the White Paper proposed compulsory development of institutional policies for the inclusion of students with disabilities, while still differentiating between institutions based on their available resources, expecting more accommodations from institutions that have historically been better resourced (i.e. formerly white institutions) (DHET, 2013). Despite some progressive shifts, the White Paper did not differentiate between the accommodations needed for different types of disability, thus failing to recognise the potential specificities associated with psychosocial and intellectual disabilities in comparison with physical disabilities.

In 2018, the Strategic Policy Framework for Disability in the Post-School Education and Training System (hereafter, the Strategic Framework or the framework) was adopted (DHET, 2018) to operationalise the provisions of the 2013 White Paper. The framework mandates the establishment of dedicated Disability Rights Units (DRUs) in all institutions of higher education and includes a broader classification of disabilities (including physical, sensory, psychosocial, intellectual and developmental disabilities). According to the framework, all institutions of higher education in the country should have institutional policies regarding disability in place by March 2021 (DHET, 2018). There is, however, no requirement as to what the actual content of these policies ought to be, meaning that, while institutions might seek to apply standards or to establish DRUs, the actual mechanics of their implementation (and arguably the effectiveness thereof) are left to the individual institutions. Funding for disability accommodations has not been specifically provided for in the South African education budget, and there is no guideline or plan in place to secure such funding, despite the fact that the Strategic Framework, like the 2013 White Paper, highlights the need for 'differentiated approaches'[2] where substantial resource differentials exist (DHET, 2018). Similarly, human resource capacity is mentioned, with the aim of 'professionalising' the DRUs of all institutions by March 2021, but the framework does not offer clarity around

---

[2] The provision allowing for differentiated approaches seems to be a way of acknowledging the fact that some institutions may have better resources or may be better prepared to address the needs of students with intellectual and psychosocial disabilities. However, beyond this provision, there is no clear guidance on the constitution of differentiated approaches, nor is there any discussion in the White Paper or the Strategic Framework of what a minimum standard ought to be regardless of resource differentials.

the parameters of such professionalisation. Of particular relevance is the framework's mention of the role of disabled peoples' organisations (DPOs), which can significantly aid in providing expertise, monitoring implementation and supporting advocacy (DHET, 2018). This is significant, particularly because of the CRPD's emphasis on the participation of people with disabilities in all aspects of life, including in governance and advocacy related to higher education.

Judging by the introduction of the White Paper and the Strategic Framework, some progress has been made in developing a stronger understanding of the needs of students with disabilities in higher education. It is especially encouraging that the framework acknowledges the need to differentiate between different types of disabilities. Despite this progress, a common challenge in South Africa is the actual translation of policies into implementation. Numerous policies have not been implemented for reasons that include poor planning and lack of capacity (Engelbrecht, 2006; Frykberg, 2018; Muller, 2011). Another major concern is the lack of resources to actualise well-meaning policy objectives. Acknowledging that these may be real concerns, it may be sensible to allow for differentiated approaches as reflected by the Strategic Framework. Even so, it is worth reiterating that equal access to higher education for students with disabilities remains a fundamental right under the CRPD, and failure to uphold this right constitutes unfair discrimination. Therefore, the provision for differential approaches in no way absolves the state of its responsibility in terms of the CRPD to promote the equal participation of students with psychosocial and intellectual disabilities in higher education. For this reason, minimum standards for reasonable accommodation of students with psychosocial and intellectual disabilities can help to ensure that these obligations are met regardless of the differentiated approaches envisaged by the framework. Following on from the aforementioned, in order to establish what good practices have been adopted and how these might be incorporated into minimum standards for institutional policies, I consider the current state of efforts to include people with psychosocial disabilities in higher education in South Africa.

The Inclusion of People Living with Psychosocial and Intellectual Disabilities: An Analysis of Existing Policies and an Indication of Good Practices in South Africa

Currently, the way in which institutions of higher education in South Africa approach disability inclusion differs substantially between institutions. In order to assess the present situation, to highlight implementation challenges and to shed light on good practice, I examined existing policies and programming. My aim is to document what South Africa's institutions of higher education are doing to accommodate students with psychosocial and intellectual disabilities, what challenges and gaps exist in inclusion and what practices can be replicated as part of the standardisation process. To gather the necessary data, I used a mixed methods approach, interviewing two researchers with an interest in the topic of disability in higher education in South Africa, a representative of a DPO and an official of a university involved in the development of a disability inclusion policy. In addition, I contacted disability focal points at all universities and conducted a random sample of two TVETs in each province in order to access disability inclusion policies. I also used more rudimentary internet searches for policy documents and institutional information. Below is an exploration of the results.

Establishment of DRUs and a Clear Plan for Activities to be Conducted

The establishment of DRUs in higher education institutions in South Africa is difficult to gauge. According to a 2007 study, 21 per cent of institutions had developed formal policies by that time (Matshedisho, 2007), although this number is thought to have increased since then (Ndlovu, 2016). Unfortunately, efforts to arrive at a definitive number of institutions with formal DRU policies were not fruitful, signifying that centralisation of information and standardisation of policy implementation remain key challenges.

Moreover, the mere existence of a DRU does not necessarily signify its functionality, with some DRUs serving 'only ceremonial' functions in the words of an interviewee. Some DRUs are considered more 'functional' than others, with regular activities that include awareness-raising of the rights of students with disabilities on campus and the development of spaces for social interaction among students with disabilities. Others, however, are merely products of 'compliance' and lack the rigour required to cater to the needs of students with disabilities. Interviewees suggested that specific activities would need to be highlighted in DRU strategies over and above their establishment.

Adoption of Accommodation Policies that Explicitly Cater to the Needs
of Students with Psychosocial and Intellectual Disabilities

From a search of university websites and engagements with researchers, I was able to access disability policies for less than half of the universities. Just two TVETs mentioned disability specifically on their websites, and neither had a dedicated disability policy. I was able to obtain one draft policy on diversity and inclusion (including disability) from a CET College. Efforts to engage with the DHET to obtain further information or consider whether monitoring took place were not successful.

In total, I was able to obtain ten policies, ranging in length from a one-page 'code of conduct' document to a lengthier guideline that specifies the roles of students and staff in creating an inclusive higher education environment. Importantly, just three policies highlighted the need to differentiate between physical disabilities and psychosocial and intellectual disabilities. As one interviewee noted, this can be problematic because it makes it possible to ignore or marginalise 'invisible' disabilities. Instead, it was suggested that 'explicit reference' should be made to psychosocial and intellectual disabilities to ensure that they are not 'left behind'. Similar to the distinction between 'mere existence' and rigour mentioned above, interviewees noted the need for action-oriented approaches in institutional policies.

Specialised and Non-specialised Mental Health Services

All universities mentioned the availability of mental health support services, while 6 of the 18 TVETs mentioned that they provide these services. Accommodations that are commonly utilised to support students with psychosocial and intellectual disabilities include psychotherapy and counselling to address emotional difficulties.

The policies accessed varied considerably in terms of their provision of such services, ranging from provision of psychiatrists and psychologists to a clear recognition of the need for spaces that would foster social inclusion, allow for the development of meaningful relationships, facilitate life skills training and promote self-efficacy. Three universities mentioned the use of peer support groups to assist students in building communities of peers and in fostering social inclusion, while the TVETs did not offer such services. This model has been shown to be an effective mechanism to build community among students with disabilities and to provide necessary care without the use of specialised services (Prince, 2015). Importantly, this raises questions related to the goal of 'professionalising' support services as stated by the 2018 Strategic Framework. One interviewee suggested that an approach that focused only on specialised mental health services without recognising the value of peer-supported and peer-led initiatives would be 'misguided' and 'in tension with the CRPD'. This suggests that further refinement of the mix of services suggested by the Strategic Framework might be warranted.

The conditions under which supports are provided can also be important determinants of their efficacy in improving educational outcomes and may also determine their utilisation. For psychosocial disabilities in particular, concerns about confidentiality and the stigma associated with utilisation of supports can be major contributing factors to non-utilisation or non-adherence (Prince, 2015). Less than half of the policies mentioned the need for confidential service provision, representing something of an oversight that might hinder service utilisation.

Guidelines for Instructors and Administrators, and Engaging These Actors as Advocates for Inclusive Education

Providing guidance to instructors and administrators is an essential avenue for addressing the needs of students with psychosocial and intellectual disabilities. One interviewee, for example, noted that these stakeholders represent 'key variables for success or failure [of diversity measures]'. Measures that can be utilised by instructors and administrators might include the provision of extra time for examinations, referrals to specialised mental health services where needed, allowances for the use of assistive devices and the provision of assistance with note-taking.

Just one institution included a guideline for specific accommodations for each type of disability, giving instructors and administrators clear and feasible options for supporting students with psychosocial and intellectual disabilities. Importantly, this guideline also emphasised the human rights of students with disabilities and noted that instructors and administrators were key stakeholders in ensuring that these students were able to access their rights. Another interviewee highlighted the significance of this, saying that 'when lecturers become advocates for and supporters of the rights of students, they [the students] are likely to feel more included and more supported'.

Mentorship of Students with Psychosocial and Intellectual Disabilities
to Support Self-efficacy in Personal and Academic Pursuits

Mentorship support provided by institutions of higher education has also been shown to promote the well-being and self-efficacy of students with psychosocial and intellectual disabilities (Ames et al., 2016). One university did offer such a programme, noting its availability to all students with disabilities. This service did not pay specific attention to the needs of students with psychosocial and intellectual disabilities, instead stating that it 'catered for all aspects of difference'.

Career Counselling Specific to Students with Psychosocial
and Intellectual Disabilities

Career counselling was available in all but two of the institutions, although this was not specific to students with psychosocial and intellectual disabilities. Considering the vocational and occupational challenges that these students may face, and the specific anxieties that these students experience regarding their prospects for future employment and integration into society post-graduation (Yang et al., 2015), it is possible that further emphasis on specialised support is required.

An interviewee also highlighted that career and vocational counselling that catered to the needs of students with psychosocial and intellectual disabilities requires 'a greater deal of sensitivity because we know that the employment landscape is also different'. This refers to the fact that reasonable accommodations may be required by students with intellectual and psychosocial disabilities when they seek or undertake employment and that counsellors and students alike would need to be aware of, and sensitised to, this reality.

A Clear and Comprehensive Screening Protocol for Identifying Students
with Intellectual Disabilities that Recognises Disability
as an Evolving Concept

While all policies recognised the need for accommodations for intellectual disabilities, they provided little detail about how intellectual disabilities would be assessed, and only one recognised the need to consider disability as an evolving concept with key opportunities and challenges that needed to be continuously assessed.

Research has demonstrated that many accommodations provided to students with intellectual and developmental disabilities tend not to be based on rigorous assessments and are not tailored to the needs of the individual student, with the result that they do not actually meet the needs of the student in question (Weis, Dean, & Osborne, 2016). Further tailoring of accommodations, such as the incorporation of an emphasis on needs assessment and individualised interventions, was lacking in the policies analysed.

Awareness-raising and Stigma Reduction Activities

Stigmatisation of psychosocial and intellectual disabilities can have a detrimental impact on student retention (Young et al., 2015), meaning that the creation of an inclusive and tolerant space through awareness-raising and stigma reduction is, itself, a necessary accommodation, while also representing a cardinal requirement of the CRPD.[3] An interviewee stated that 'stigma is probably the single biggest discouraging factor for students with psychosocial and intellectual disabilities', suggesting that addressing this barrier to participation can be extremely impactful.

Policies adopted by six South African universities incorporate an emphasis on building inclusive communities through advocacy and awareness-raising initiatives. That said, it is unclear what such initiatives consist of and how their efficacy might be gauged, meaning further elaboration and standardisation may be needed. Moreover, all of the policies which incorporated an emphasis on stigma reduction emphasised disability in its entirety. Considering that psychosocial and intellectual disabilities are particularly stigmatised and marginalised due to their 'invisible' nature (Yang et al., 2015), specific programming to counter any problematic beliefs or attitudes in this sphere may also be necessary.

Mechanisms for Including Students with Psychosocial and Intellectual Disabilities in Institutional Forums and Student Representative Councils

A key feature of the CRPD's approach to disability is the fostering of participation of people with psychosocial and intellectual disabilities in

---

[3] Article 8 of the CRPD:

  1.   States Parties undertake to adopt immediate, effective and appropriate measures:
       (a)   To raise awareness throughout society, including at the family level, regarding persons with disabilities, and to foster respect for the rights and dignity of persons with disabilities;
       (b)   To combat stereotypes, prejudices and harmful practices relating to persons with disabilities, including those based on sex and age, in all areas of life;
       (c)   To promote awareness of the capabilities and contributions of persons with disabilities.

decisions governing their well-being. This means active efforts to support the participation of students with disabilities in governance structures in universities. Engagement with DPOs to aid in supporting the participation of students with particular accommodation needs may also assist in ensuring that participation occurs on an equal basis as students without disabilities.

Participation of students with disabilities in institutional forums and student councils was highlighted by about half of the institutional policies accessed. Five institutions had established formalised mechanisms for including students with disabilities in institutional forums and student representative councils. These included dedicated seats in these mechanisms, as well as specific measures for outreach to student organisations and DPOs to recruit representatives. It is important, however, to highlight that these efforts do not specifically mention psychosocial or intellectual disability, with an interviewee raising concern that this might result in a bias towards physical disability. It may therefore be necessary to consider supports that allow participation by students with psychosocial and intellectual disabilities, including assistive devices or use of visual medium aids to assist with interpreting documentation.

Gender, Race, Sexual Orientation, Culture and Language-Appropriate Accommodations

The stressors faced by students with psychosocial and intellectual disabilities can vary greatly depending on their backgrounds, so the nature and orientation of interventions, too, may require nuance. In China, for example, an emphasis on local models of mental health has been incorporated into mental health supports in a higher education setting, with demonstrable success (Yang et al., 2015). Similarly, students from varying gender and cultural backgrounds experience the higher education environment in different ways, and efforts aimed at accommodating those differences in the realm of psychosocial and intellectual disability need more attention (Young, Anderson, & Stewart, 2015).

Just one policy mentioned the significance of culture as an important factor in addressing the needs of students with (all) disabilities, while two incorporated some emphasis on gender. According to interviewees, gender, race, sexual orientation, culture and language-appropriate accommodations are of special importance given the need for an emphasis on equal participation in the educative experience, meaning that additional attention is required on measures to foster inclusivity in all accommodations provided. Measures to reach specific groups in one policy included a support group for lesbian, gay, bisexual, transgender and queer (LGBTQ) persons' mental health and training for providers of support to intellectually disabled students on specific cultural attributes such as idiomatic language and the use of appropriate visual and symbolic cues to aid learning.

Mechanisms for Redress to Address Discrimination and Exclusion Affecting Students with Psychosocial and Intellectual Disabilities and Provision of Accommodative Supports to Seek Redress When Necessary

Complaints-handling for students who are seeking redress when they experience discrimination on the basis of their disability status is available at all institutions whose policies I was able to access. However, just one institution made note of the availability of accommodative supports (e.g. assistance with filing complaints and with interpreting legal or technical documents) that would assist students to seek redress in the event that they needed it.

This is significant, because it illustrates that the mere existence of a recourse mechanism is not sufficient if the barriers to its utilisation are not addressed. An interviewee suggested that mechanisms for redress were severely under-utilised because they were difficult for students with psychosocial and intellectual disabilities to navigate. He suggested that measures to reach these students should include clear language aids, the provision of qualified support persons and accommodations for peer support for complainants where necessary.

The Way Forward: Fostering Inclusive Institutions through an Enabling Environment for Effective Implementation

In this section I build on some of the evidence of good practices identified earlier to consider how minimum standards for institutional policies can incorporate the two practices below, as well as place an emphasis on effective implementation.

Ensuring Accountability and Engaging in Continuous Monitoring and Evaluation

A key aspect of effective implementation of good practice is the development of mechanisms for promoting accountability. Accountability could be fostered through the development of a mechanism for oversight of disability inclusion in the DHET, and through the introduction of appropriately costed plans with explicit timelines for implementation.

Given the absence of policies for disability inclusion in several institutions, the need for accountability and enforcement mechanisms is evident. Similarly, accountability can also be fostered by continuous monitoring and evaluation of progress, both by institutions themselves and by DHET, considering not only enrolment but also completion, given the propensity of students with intellectual and psychosocial disabilities to withdraw from higher education at a higher rate than other students (Koch et al., 2018). It is significant that none of the policies referred to above mention student satisfaction. Research has noted considerable dissatisfaction with supports and has also highlighted how this limits efficacy and utilisation of services (Kundu, Dutta, Schiro-Geist, & Crandall, 2003). It may therefore be useful to consider an emphasis on gauging service user satisfaction as part of the standardisation process in future. This is particularly important in light of the CRPD's emphasis on user-centred supports and accommodations and the participation of service users in the development and governance of supports (DSD, 2016).

As the Strategic Framework acknowledges, the development of sound data collection and monitoring mechanisms can aid in gauging support needs and progress made towards inclusion. Disaggregation by disability could significantly aid in developing a more accurate understanding of psychosocial and intellectual disability prevalence and accommodation than currently exists. Accountability can also be enhanced through engagements with DPOs such as the South African Disability Alliance, the South African Federation for Mental Health and Autism South Africa to build monitoring and evaluation frameworks that are indicative of best practice and that can be monitored independently by these organisations.

Building Capacity for 'Professionalisation', While Acknowledging the Value of Peer Support

As noted, the lack of individualised supports can be an impediment to inclusion, and this may be affected by lack of appropriate personnel or the over-stretching of existing resources (Weis et al., 2016). Capacity development can contribute to the development of a cohort of health and social service providers who are familiar with the specific needs of students with psychosocial and intellectual disabilities.

Ultimately, while this might require tailoring to the specific circumstances of each institution, technical assistance from DHET to identify the optimal mix of services can be helpful. Given its substantial potential to improve participation and foster cohesion, peer support could be considered alongside the goal of 'professionalization' of support services (Prince, 2015). Training of instructors and administrators on the human rights of students with psychosocial and intellectual disabilities may also be incorporated into a minimum standard for institutional policies on disability inclusion.

Table 13.1 summarises key findings and recommendations, highlighting good practices identified. These can be considered minimum standards for institutional policies, as envisaged by the Strategic Framework.

Table 13.1 *Summary: Key Features of Good Practice in Supporting Students with Psychosocial and Intellectual Disabilities*

- Establishment of the disability rights unit and a clear plan for activities to be conducted
- Adoption of policies to regulate the provision of accommodations to students with disabilities, with explicit reference to accommodations for students with psychosocial and intellectual disabilities
- Specialised and non-specialised mental health services catering to disability-specific challenges, comprising an appropriate mix of clinical and social service professionals and peer support activities
- A guideline for specific accommodations for each type of disability, offering instructors and administrators clear and feasible options for supporting students with psychosocial and intellectual disabilities and engaging these actors as advocates for inclusive education
- Mentorship of students with psychosocial and intellectual disabilities to support self-efficacy in personal and academic pursuits
- Career counselling specific to students with psychosocial and intellectual disabilities
- A clear and comprehensive screening protocol for identifying students with intellectual disabilities that recognises disability as an evolving concept
- Awareness-raising and stigma reduction activities that contain substantive guidance on implementation and tangible outcomes-based activities
- Mechanisms for including students with psychosocial and intellectual disabilities in institutional forums and student representative councils
- Gender, race, sexual orientation, culture and language-appropriate accommodations
- Mechanisms for redress to address discrimination and exclusion affecting students with psychosocial and intellectual disabilities and provision of accommodative supports to seek redress when necessary
- Continuous monitoring and evaluation of disability inclusion policies and initiatives, including supporting monitoring by DPOs and mechanisms to gauge user satisfaction of supports provided
- Development of capacity to cater to a diverse population of students with psychosocial and intellectual disabilities

Conclusion

The marginalisation of students with psychosocial and intellectual disabilities by institutional policies and practices that fail to accommodate their needs is a significant impediment to the realisation of the CRPD's vision of equal access to higher education. Given the continued stigmatisation of students with psychosocial and intellectual disabilities, the lack of policy coherence and the historic discrimination that these students have faced, the finding that they are more likely to withdraw from higher education than non-disabled students or even students with physical disabilities (Koch et al., 2018) is unsurprising. This continued marginalisation highlights the importance of investing more vigorously in supports for students with psychosocial and intellectual disabilities. The fact that some institutions have been able to develop stronger policies and practices is encouraging. Nevertheless, significant divergences in policy and practice between institutions are indicative of the need to develop minimum standards for all institutional policies dedicated to disability inclusion regardless of resource differentials.

Undoing the historic marginalisation of people with psychosocial and intellectual disability in and from higher education in South Africa is likely to require broader shifts than those developed at institutions themselves. Efforts by DHET and others to engage in effective monitoring and oversight can aid in the fostering of accountability. Similarly, engagements with DPOs to develop good practices, to encourage collaboration and to monitor implementation can be useful avenues for participatory governance and the fostering of accountability as well, in keeping with the provisions of the CRPD. Initiatives to develop the capacity of a workforce that is adept at catering to the needs of students with psychosocial and intellectual disabilities while also engaging the peer support model can help to address the challenge of resource constraints. Ultimately, these measures can shift the way in which actors in the higher education space and beyond view their role, acknowledging their contribution not simply as service providers but also as stakeholders in more equal societies, wherein the aspirations of well-meaning political instruments may reach fruition.

REFERENCES

Adult Education and Training Act, 52 of 2000 (as amended)
Allen, S. & Carlson, G. (2003). To Conceal or Disclose a Disabling Condition? A Dilemma of Employment Transition. *Journal of Vocational Rehabilitation, 19* (1), 19–30.

Ames, M. E., McMorris, C. A., Alli, L. N . . . & Bebko, J. M. (2016). Overview and Evaluation of a Mentorship Program for University Students with ASD. *Focus on Autism and Other Developmental Disabilities, 31*(1), 27–36.

Bell, D. (2013). Investigating Teaching and Learning Support for Students with Hearing Impairment at a University in the Western Cape. PhD diss., Stellenbosch University. http://scholar.sun.ac.za/handle/10019.1/80004. Retrieved 30 April 2019.

Christianson, A. L., Zwane, M. E., Manga, P . . . & Kromberg, J. G. R. (2000). Epilepsy in Rural South African Children: Prevalence, Associated Disability and Management. *South African Medical Journal, 90*(3), 261–266.

Constitution of the Republic of South Africa, Act No. 108 of 1996

Continuing Education and Training Act, No. 16 of 2006 (as amended)

De Cesarei, A. (2015). Psychological Factors that Foster or Deter the Disclosure of Disability by University Students. *Psychological Reports, 116*(3), 665–673.

Department of Education (1997). *Education White Paper 3: A Programme for Transformation of Higher Education.* Pretoria: Government Printer.

Department of Education (2001). *Education White Paper 6: Special Needs Education: Building an Inclusive Education and Training System.* Pretoria: Government Printer.

Department of Higher Education and Training (2013a). *White Paper for Post-School Education and Training.* Pretoria: Government Printer.

Department of Higher Education and Training (2013b). Statistics on Post-School Education and Training in South Africa. www.dhet.gov.za/DHET %20Statistics%20Publication/Statistics%20on%20Post-School%20Educati on%20and%20training%20in%20South%20Africa%202013.pdf. Retrieved 30 April 2019.

Department of Higher Education and Training (2014). The list of Private FET Colleges. www.saqa.org.za/docs/misc/2014/Private%20FET.pdf. Retrieved 30 April 2019.

Department of Higher Education and Training (2015a). Statement by the Minister of Higher Education and Training Dr Blade Nzimande, MP: The establishment of the Community Education and Training Colleges (CETCs). www.dhet.gov.za/RegionalOffices/educational-institutions/CET %20Colleges/MINISTER%20Statement%20on%20Community%20Colle ges.pdf. Retrieved 30 April 2019.

Department of Higher Education and Training (2015b). *Annual Report 2014/2015.* Pretoria: Government Printer.

Department of Higher Education and Training. (2018). Strategic Policy Framework for Disability in the Post-School Education and Training System. www.dhet.gov.za/SiteAssets/Gazettes/Approved%20Strategic%20Disability% 20Policy%20Framework%20Layout220518.pdf. Retrieved 30 April 2019.

Department of Social Development (2016). White Paper on the Rights of People with Disabilities. www.health-e.org.za/wp-content/uploads/2016/04/White-Paper-on-the-Rights-of-Person-with-Disabilities-.pdf. Retrieved 30 April 2019.

Enca (2016). SA falls behind in efforts to employ disabled people. www.enca.com/south-africa/sa-falls-behind-efforts-employ-disabled-people. Retrieved 30 April 2019.

Engelbrecht, L. & de Beer, J. J. (2014). Access Constraints Experienced by Physically Disabled Students at a South African Higher Education Institution. *Africa Education Review, 11*(4), 544–562.

Engelbrecht, P. (2006). The Implementation of Inclusive Education in South Africa after Ten Years of Democracy. *European Journal of Psychology of Education, 21,* 253.

Engelbrecht, P., Nel, M., Smit, S., & van Deventer, M. (2016). The Idealism of Education Policies and the Realities in Schools: The Implementation of Inclusive Education in South Africa. *International Journal of Inclusive Education, 20*(5), 520–535.

Fitchett, A. (2015). Exploring Adaptive Co-Management as a Means to Improving Accessibility for People with Reduced Mobility at the University of Witwatersrand. In E. Walton & S. Moonsamy (eds.), *Making Education Inclusive* (pp. 130–146). Newcastle: Cambridge Scholars Publishing.

Frykberg, M. (2018). State of human rights in South Africa under spotlight at seminar. www.iol.co.za/news/south-africa/gauteng/state-of-human-rights-in-south-africa-under-spotlight-at-seminar-13766500. Retrieved 30 April 2019.

Habib, A. (2016). Transcending the Past and Re-imagining the Future of the South African University. *Journal of Southern African Studies, 42*(1), 35–48.

Higher Education Act, No. 101 of 1997 (as amended)

Howell, C., Chalklen, S., & Alberts, T. (2006). A History of the Disability Rights Movement in South Africa. In B. Watermeyer, L. Swartz, T. Lorenzo, M. Schneider & M. Priestley (eds.), *Disability and Social Change: A South African Agenda* (pp. 46–84). HSRC: Cape Town.

Jansen, J. (2003). Mergers in South African Higher Education: Theorising Change in Transitional Contexts. *Politikon, 30,* 27–50.

Katz, G. & Lazcano-Ponce, E. (2008). Intellectual Disability: Definition, Etiological Factors, Classification, Diagnosis, Treatment and Prognosis. *Salud Publica Mex, 50*(S2), S132–S141.

Koch, L. C., Lo, W., Mamieseishvili, K., Lee, D., & Hill, J. (2018). The Effect of Learning Disabilities, Attention Deficit Hyperactivity Disorder, and Psychiatric Disabilities on Three-year Persistence Outcomes at Four-year Higher Education Institutions. *Journal of Vocational Rehabilitation, 48*(3), 359–367.

Kundu, M., Dutta, A., Schiro-Geist, C., & Crandall, L. (2003). Disability-Related Services: Needs and Satisfaction of Postsecondary Students. *Rehabilitation Education*, *17*(1), 45–54.

Losinsky, L. O., Levi, T., Saffey, K., & Jelsma, J. (2003). An Investigation into the Physical Accessibility to Wheelchair Bound Students in an Institution of Higher Learning in South Africa. *Disability and Rehabilitation*, *25*, 305–308.

Lourens, H. (2015). The Lived Experiences of Higher Education for Students with a Visual Impairment: A Phenomenological Study at Two Universities in the Western Cape, South. PhD diss., Stellenbosch University. http://scholar.sun.ac.za/handle/10019.1/96732. Retrieved 30 April 2019.

Manderscheid, R. W., Ryff, C. D., Freeman, E. J., Dhingra, S., & Strine, T. W. (2010). Evolving Definitions of Mental Illness and Wellness. *Preventing Chronic Disease*, *7*(1), A19.

Maotoana, M. R. (2014). The challenges experienced by Students with Physical Disability at the University of Limpopo (Turfloop Campus). (Masters thesis) University of Limpopo, South Africa.

Matshedisho, K. R. (2007). The Challenge of Real Rights for Disabled Students in South Africa. *South African Journal of Higher Education*, *21*(4), 706.

Maulik, P. K., Mascarenhas, M. N., Mathers, C. D., Dua, T., & Saxena, S. (2011). Prevalence of Intellectual Disability: A Meta-analysis of Population-based Studies. *Research in Developmental Disabilities*, *32*(2), 419–436.

Mokiwa, S. A. & Phasha, T. N. (2012). Using ICT at an Open Distance Learning (ODL) Institution in South Africa: The Learning Experiences of Students with Visual Impairments. *Africa Education Review*, *9*(1), 136–151.

Muller, H. (2011). The right to water and sanitation: The South African Experience. Presentation at the Consultation with State Actors – Good Practices in Water, Sanitation and Human Rights. UN, Geneva, 20–21 January 2011. www2.ohchr.org/english/issues/water/Iexpert/docs/StateActors/SouthAfrica.pdf. Retrieved 30 April 2019.

Mutanga, O. (2018) Inclusion of Students with Disabilities in South African Higher Education, International Journal of Disability, *Development and Education*, *65*(2), 229–242.

National Planning Commission (2011). *National Development Plan*. Pretoria.

Ndlovu, S. (2016). Preparation of Students with Disabilities to Graduate into Professions in the South African Context of Higher Learning: Obstacles and Opportunities. *African Journal of Disability*, *5*(1), 1–8.

Newman, L., Wagner, M., Knokey, A., Marder, C., Nagle, K., Shaver, D. . . . & Schwarting, M. (2011). *The Post-high School Outcomes of Young Adults with Disabilities Up to Eight Years after High School: A Report from the NLTS-2.* Menlo Park, CA: SRI International.

Prince, J. P. (2015). University Student Counselling and Mental Health in the United States: Trends and Challenges. *Mental Health and Prevention, 3*(1–2), 5–10.

Rajohane-Mathshedisho, K. (2007). Access to Higher Education for Disabled Students in South Africa: A Contradictory Conjuncture of Benevolence, Rights and the Social Model of Disability. *Disability & Society, 22*(7), 685–699.

Seyama, L., Morris C. D., & Stilwell, C. (2014). Information Seeking Behaviour of Blind and Visually Impaired Students: A Case Study of the University of KwaZulu-Natal, Pietermaritzburg Campus. *Mousaion: SA Journal of Information Studies, 32*(1), 1–22.

Shakespeare, T. (2006). The Social Model of Disability. In Lennard J. Davis (ed.), *The Disability Studies Reader* (pp. 2–197) Hove: Psychology Press.

Steel, Z., Marnane, C., Iranpour, C., Chey, T., Jackson, J. W., Patel, V., & Silove, D. (2014). The Global Prevalence of Common Mental Disorders: A Systematic Review and Meta-analysis 1980–2013. *International Journal of Epidemiology, 43*(2), 476–493.

Trainin, G. & Swanson, H. L. (2005). Cognition, Metacognition, and Achievement of College Students with Learning Disabilities. *Learning Disability Quarterly, 28*, 261–272.

UN Committee on the Rights of Persons with Disabilities (2015). Initial Reports of States Parties due in 2009: South Africa-CRPD/C/ZAF/1. http://docstore .ohchr.org/SelfServices/FilesHandler.ashx?enc=6QkG1d%2fPPRiCAqhKb7yh st4eZ%2bvBhJ1Wb4RWrHF%2bzS6eeqUZjCorR9VzAmM9ZRBV%2bM9 AAcTpyvNF03juBmVkkdFoM5CWkyBvATpBHrPS9VdBhfEo%2f1u6Xl%2 b2SXMA52BG. Retrieved 30 April 2019.

UNESCO (2018). UNESCO Institute for Statistics Data. https://knoema.com/UN ESCOISD2018/unesco-institute-for-statistics-data. Retrieved 30 April 2019.

UN General Assembly (2007). Convention on the Rights of Persons with Disabilities. http://www.un.org/disabilities/documents/convention/convopt prot-e.pdf. Retrieved 30 April 2019.

Van Hees, V., Moyson, T,. & Roeyers, H. (2015). Higher Education Experiences of Students with Autism Spectrum Disorder: Challenges, Benefits and Support Needs. *Journal of Autism and Developmental Disorders, 45*(6), 1673–1688.

Weis, R., Dean, E. L., & Osborne, K. J. (2016). Accommodation decision-making for Postsecondary Students with Learning Disabilities: Individually tailored or One size fits all? *Journal of Learning Disabilities, 49*(5), 484–498.

WHO. (2001). World Health Report: Mental disorders affect one in four people. http://www.who.int/whr/2001/media_centre/press_release/en/. Retrieved 30 April 2019.

Wolf, L. E. (2001). College Students with ADHD and Other Hidden Disabilities. *Annals of the New York Academy of Science, 931*(1), 385–395.

Xaba, W. (2017). Challenging Fanon: A Black radical feminist perspective on violence and the Fees Must Fall movement. *Agenda, 31*(3–4), 96–104.

Yang, W., Lin, L., Zhu, W., & Liang, S. (2015). An introduction to mental health services in universities in China. *Mental Health and Prevention, 3*(1–2), 11–16.

Young, K., Anderson, M., & Stewart, S. (2015). Hierarchical microaggressions in higher education. *Journal of Diversity in Higher Education, 8*(1), 61–71.

PART III

Confronting Marginalisation
Narratives of Affected Students and Educators and Innovations in Higher Education Settings

CHAPTER 14

'Now I Constantly Challenge Society by Bringing My Existence Forward'

Creating Counter-Spaces/Stories with Sanctuary Students Transitioning to Higher Education in Toronto

Paloma E. Villegas and Tanya Aberman

Introduction

Walking into the classroom on the first day of class was a nerve-wracking and exhilarating experience for us. The room, hidden in the back of an unfamiliar building, had tables organised into a rectangle so everyone could see each other, with a chalkboard on one side. Students stepped in hesitantly at first. Some knew each other and sat together, others sat in silence waiting for the class to begin. We felt the weight of the task ahead of us. We were responsible for facilitating a bridging course, titled 'Critical Approaches to Migration and Uprootedness', that would allow migrant students, who had previously been unable to access higher education (HE) because of their immigration status, entry to York University (YU) in Toronto for the first time.

The students with whom we worked were mainly non-status migrants and refugee claimants. However, because migrants can experience shifts in their legal status categorisation across time, we have decided to opt for the term, sanctuary students. In conceptualising this term, we draw on literature on migrant precarity that argues against undocumented/documented and refugee/economic migrant binaries (Goldring, Berinstein, & Bernhard, 2009). Instead, the focus is on recognising the range of legal status categories outside of permanent residence or citizenship, including refugee claimants/asylum seekers, temporary migrant workers, temporary permit holders, sponsored spouses/family members and non-status/undocumented migrants.[1] These statuses are often conditional and

---

[1] Non-status is often used in Canada, and is similar to the undocumented migrant category in the United States. Non-status migrants may have expired visas or their immigration applications may have been refused, leading them to have no legal status in Canada and no protection from deportation.

dependent on third parties, such as family members, employers, immigration adjudicators or other civil servant decision makers who hold power to support, grant or revoke status (Goldring & Landolt, 2013). They can also be fluid, as migrants can transition across legal status categories, particularly as those categories multiply and become more exclusionary in current immigration management regimes. This context of precarity produces specific vulnerabilities for migrants including detention and deportability – the ever-present possibility of deportation (De Genova, 2002).

The term 'sanctuary student' specifically refers to those migrants who wish to enrol in HE but face barriers because of their legal status. In the United States, such students are mainly undocumented migrants, popularly referred to as DREAMers. Our use of sanctuary student draws on research about DREAMers as well as the term 'Sanctuary Scholar', coined by Article 26, an organisation working with universities to increase access for migrant students across the United Kingdom (Article 26, n.d.). For Article 26, 'Sanctuary Scholar' 'refers to any *forced migrant* who is undertaking, or seeks to undertake, a higher education course or programme in the UK' (Hudson & Murray, 2018, emphasis added). Sanctuary student therefore links populations facing similar educational barriers in different geographic regions; it also adapts and extends this definition to include a broader population of migrants.[2]

In Ontario, Canada, sanctuary students are required to obtain government-issued study permits (and other documentation), as well as to pay international student fees, which are roughly three times the domestic fees, without access to government loans, bursaries or private scholarships. These bureaucratic and financial barriers create insurmountable obstacles for most sanctuary students, leading them to avoid enrolling altogether. We hoped that for the first time in a Canadian HE institution, the bridging course would change, or at least attenuate, those barriers in a systemic way.

The course was part of a larger Access Programme, which minimises barriers by allowing sanctuary students to study at domestic fee rates and without study permit obligations. This Access Programme has consisted of

---

[2] We recognise that in isolating 'students' there is a danger of falling into deservingness tropes of the 'value' HE brings to migrants vis-à-vis ideas of incorporation and contribution (Anguiano & Nájera, 2015). However, our intent is to discuss a relatively invisibilised population in Canada, while recognising the relative privilege of having access to HE. Scholars have also identified the dangers with the term sanctuary and its potential to highlight 'exceptional' cases and exclude others (Houston & Morse, 2017). As we discuss below, the participants of the bridging course promoted a broader sense of inclusion, which is also our intention with the term.

two entry pathways, recognising that sanctuary students in Toronto have different access needs. The bridging course offers semester-long (three month) academic and social support, solidarity-building between students who had few previous interactions with peers in similar legal status situations, and introductions to university procedures and services. The course is housed in a Sociology department, given existing connections with faculty therein, and therefore draws on discipline-based theory and practice. Once students complete the bridging course successfully, having demonstrated their academic capabilities, they are eligible to transition into the larger Access Programme and pursue a variety of undergraduate degrees, without study permit requirements and at domestic fee rates. Sanctuary students who do not feel they need the upgrading or support of the bridging course have the option of applying directly to undergraduate programmes and still benefitting from domestic fee rates.

The Access Programme stemmed from a considerable amount of advocacy and awareness-raising by a variety of community members, as well as sanctuary students themselves. It was a collaboration between a refugee centre and YU, both in Toronto. When we walked into that classroom in 2017, it was only a pilot project with little guarantee of success. However, now in its second year, the course has been buoyed by students' relative success, as well as positive media coverage (Weins, 2018) that encouraged more sanctuary students to participate.

Nonetheless, the programme has faced challenges, as some students engaged in the bridging course and the undergraduate degree programmes struggled due to financial pressures and the stress of dealing with immigration processes and officials. Only a little over half of the sanctuary students who enrolled in the bridging course were able to complete it successfully, and of those, several are not yet ready or able, to begin their bachelor's degrees. However, YU considers the programme a success, and three additional bridging courses have since been mounted, with over thirty sanctuary students admitted to undergraduate programmes in 2018.

This chapter considers the bridging course as a point of departure for analysing the barriers experienced by sanctuary students in Canada due to their immigration status. Using the concepts of counterspaces and counterstorytelling (Yosso, 2006), which we expand on in detail below, we consider how bridging students negotiated barriers and challenged existing norms regarding borders, racism and activism. We posit that students drew on their personal and community knowledge to counter negative framings of migrants and articulate alternative narratives. This counterstorytelling not only gave students opportunities to reimagine their experiences and their place in Canadian society, but also emboldened them to imagine making demands on the state for inclusion.

We also examine the bridging course as a counterspace that challenges notions of belonging based on immigration status. The counterspace created through the course permitted students to expand their understanding of the systemic issues and power relations at play in their immigration experiences and status, as well as connect with others in similar precarious and illegalised situations. We argue that reducing barriers for sanctuary students increases counterspaces for learning where students can re-imagine their futures while pursuing their goals along with their peers.

Conceptual Framework: Precarity, Migrant Illegalisation and Critical Race Theory

Our conceptual framework brings together scholarship on migrant precarity, 'illegality' and critical race theory (CRT). Precarious immigration status describes a varied and changing landscape of immigration status categories: non-status/undocumented migrants, refugee claimants/asylum seekers, temporary migrant workers, temporary permit holders and sponsored spouses/family members (Goldring et al., 2009). Such precarity can be understood under the framework of migrant illegalisation, which involves the criminalisation, dehumanisation and exploitation of migrants who have precarious status (De Genova, 2005; Gonzales & Sigona, 2017).

Given this context, our analysis draws on CRT, and particularly the concepts of counterspaces and counterstorytelling (Yosso, 2006) to examine the effects of migrant illegalisation on sanctuary students seeking to access HE. CRT works to disrupt normative understandings of race and racialisation in order to work towards transformative change (Solórzano, Ceja, & Yosso, 2000, 63). It therefore 'challenges claims of objectivity, meritocracy, color blindness, race neutrality, and equal opportunity, asserting that these claims camouflage the self-interest, power, and privilege of dominant groups' (Yosso, Smith, Ceja, & Solórzano, 2009, 663). Initially emerging out of legal studies, CRT promotes inter/transdisciplinarity in the academy (Solórzano et al., 2000), and while centring race, CRT also defines various forms of oppressions as relational and interlocking. This approach promotes an understanding of how, for instance, framings of migrant 'illegality' and racialisation co-constitute each other. As a result, scholars who employ CRT often focus on the situated lived experiences of affected individuals, such as sanctuary students (Yosso et al., 2009).

Counterspaces and counterstorytelling are theoretical and methodological tools to describe lived experience, particularly in education scholarship. Counterspaces challenge exclusionary spaces and access to education (Muñoz, Espino, & Antrop-Gonzalez, 2014), and are sites where students can disrupt the negative perceptions imposed upon them and their communities (racism, xenophobia, anti-refugee rhetoric and migrant illegalisation), perceptions which seep into how they experience their everyday lives, including access to university (Solórzano et al., 2000). Specifically, counterspaces include:

> academic and social spaces that foster . . . learning at the university . . . such as: study groups where students' social groups develop into academic support groups; centres where students receive tutoring or assistance with academic skills; or student organisations that enable students to give back to their communities (Muñoz & Maldonado, 2012, 295).

These counterspaces, and the skills developed within them, facilitate and encourage educational outcomes for the students who are marginalised from access to HE because of their immigration status. They also operate to create solidarity among students and support the negotiation between students' experiences in school, home and within their communities.

Part of the process of creating counterspaces involves the ways students articulate and re-articulate counterstories of belonging (Chang, 2011; Muñoz, Espino, & Antrop-Gonzalez, 2014; Muñoz & Maldonado, 2012; Yosso, 2006). As Muñoz and Maldonado (2012) argue, counterstories are

> told by those who are marginalized about their own experiences, stories which are not often told, acknowledged, or valued. The term has also been used to refer to a methodological approach which aims to expose, analyse, and challenge the stories of those in power – the dominant discourse, the 'majoritarian story' in education ... storytelling is a cultural practice through which groups affirm identities and resist oppressions. (pp. 295–296)

Counterstories are important interventions because they nurture the building of community among affected individuals, promoting what Yosso (2006) defines as community cultural wealth. This perspective draws on critical education theory (Freire, 2004) and challenges the understanding that students arrive in an educational space as empty vessels. Instead, this approach highlights how students bring with them layered and complex knowledge garnered from their experiences, families and communities (Yosso, 2006). Chang (2011) argues that counterstories are therefore important to '[challenge] the commonsense, or perceived wisdom, that undocumented immigrants are uneducated, powerless, and ignorant' as per common anti-migrant representations (Chang, 2011, 510).

As re-articulations, counterstories may not address the legal barriers that sanctuary students experience, but they can lead to the reframing of hegemonic ideas that they may have internalised or that circulate in their communities. Counterstories may also lead those who narrate them to re-draw boundaries associated with im/migrant deservingness, for example, by rejecting notions of who is a 'good immigrant' and how they are expected to behave. Finally, they can be used as tools to challenge and advocate for a reworking of existing laws and policy.

Contextualising Barriers and Strategies for Access to HE for Sanctuary Students

Access policies for sanctuary students transitioning to HE vary depending on geographic location, legal status and the priorities set by individual institutions. While the issue of HE education access has gained more attention in the last few years in light of the global so-called refugee crisis, as well as the plights of the 'DREAMers' in the United States, access policies internationally remain incomplete and often ad-hoc (de Wit & Altbach, 2016). Beginning in the 2000s, some US states began to pass policies allowing undocumented migrants to register and pay in-state tuition fees at public Colleges, and more recently access financial aid, if they met specific residency requirements (Flores, 2010; Najafi, 2008). These policies were a direct result of strong and sustained advocacy work by various communities (Najafi, 2008), but they continue to be in constant flux, producing uncertainties for sanctuary students. A key example is the 2017 announcement that DACA (Deferred Action for Childhood Arrivals), would be cancelled. At the time this chapter was written, DACA has not been cancelled but the announcement produced a chilling effect across migrant communities in the United States and transnationally. However, many HE institutions continue to support undocumented students by declaring their campuses as spaces of sanctuary (Ngai, 2017).

In the United Kingdom, access to HE gained increased attention when it was identified by a group of asylum-seeking youth as their paramount priority through the Save the Children's 'Brighter Futures' project (Article 26, n.d.). The barriers these students faced stemmed from the different categorisation of migrants and associated tuition rates: refugees granted *limited* or *indefinite leave to remain* and those with *Humanitarian protection* paid domestic fees, but *asylum seekers* and refugees with *discretionary leave to remain* paid international student fees (Refugee Council, 2013). A programme titled Article 26 was developed as a result of the 'Brighter Futures' project (Article 26, n.d.). Those associated with Article 26 work with universities to facilitate access for refugees and asylum seekers but *not* undocumented migrants (Murray, Hope, & Turley, 2014). Like US access policies, Article 26 supports students through undergraduate degrees to graduate school, and partner universities offer a limited number of scholarships to cover tuition.

In Ontario, Canada, access to HE schooling has been piecemeal (Aberman & Ackerman, 2017; Kamal & Killian, 2015). Sanctuary students face barriers given their legal status and deportability, because anyone who is not a permanent resident or citizen is expected to apply for a study permit for most programmes. Most sanctuary students are also classified as international students for tuition purposes, except for convention refugees and the dependants of permanent residents and citizens.

Counterspaces and Migrant Students in HE

Despite common barriers in all three countries described above, research from the United States highlights some innovative ways that undocumented students participate in the creation of counterspaces in universities and other educational institutions (Muñoz et al., 2014; Muñoz & Maldonado, 2012; Soltis, 2015; Trivette & English, 2017; Yosso, 2006). Examples of counterspaces for sanctuary students include DREAMer/undocumented student clubs, which advocate for immigration reform and provide support for undocumented members (Villegas, 2006) and student resource centres, which offer a range of outreach, advising, and other support designed to attract and retain them (Manalo-Pedro, 2018).

Counterspaces have also included sites developed specifically to counteract the lack of access to HE, including Freedom University in Georgia and Uprooted U in Toronto, Canada. Freedom University, based on freedom schools developed during the 1960s civil rights movement, was created to counter Georgia's exclusionary policies which bar undocumented students from accessing university. The goal of the programme is to 'emphasise the importance of safe spaces to cultivate education for liberation ... [and provide] a tangible example of how to build alternatives in the face of separate and unequal access to education' (Soltis, 2015, 23). As such, Freedom University was established as a space of transformational resistance where faculty members and students rejected the exclusion of undocumented students and worked 'towards developing a more socially just community' (Muñoz, Espino, & Antrop-Gonzalez, 2014, 20).

Uprooted U was also created to challenge the exclusion of sanctuary students from HE in Canada's largest city, Toronto, a key immigrant gateway. The programme offers a grassroots HE experience to bridge the gap faced by youth graduating from high school. While Ontario's HE policies do not officially exclude sanctuary students, as Georgia's do, the study permit and international fee requirements leaves students with few possibilities for equitable access. The Uprooted U programme was developed as a collaborative effort by a refugee centre, community educators, and youth and students working on specific community-engaged projects (Aberman, Villegas, & Villegas, 2016). Faculty members at institutions across the city voluntarily offered their time to provide lectures to the sanctuary students, introducing them to new areas of study, while also recognising their knowledge and academic potential. For their part, the students developed solidarity among themselves, as they came to understand their common challenges and engage in critical interventions (counterstories about the representation of migrants in popular discourse) brought about by the counterspace created (Aberman, Villegas, & Villegas, 2016).

In what follows, we use a similar analytical approach to examine the YU bridging course, which is part of the larger Access Programme. We also discuss how sanctuary students who participated in the course articulated and re-articulated their experiences with, and perceptions of, borders, racialisation, and activism, sometimes in complex or contradictory ways.

Methods

We conceptualise our participation in the bridging course as contributing to a counterspace in, and counterstorytelling about, HE in Canada. Crawford and Arnold (2016) argue that 'there is little clarity on the motivating factors that compel educators to act on behalf of [undocumented] students, to increase their access to the full educational pipeline and to help them attain educational capital and opportunities' (p. 198). We came to the YU bridging course and larger access project because of our personal, professional and political experiences. Paloma grew up undocumented in the United States and benefited from access policies during her HE education. Given this experience, her research and political practice centres on making visible and working to improve the experiences of precarious status migrants, including sanctuary students. Tanya has been working with sanctuary students in the Greater Toronto Area for over five years and has followed their lead in advocating for increased access to education, as well as other social rights. Tanya invited Paloma to teach in Uprooted U, leading to continued collaboration when the YU Access Programme was announced. Through this process, we were influenced by the work of other scholar activists seeking to open up access to HE, including those who participate in Freedom University, whose pedagogy focuses on:

> (1) creating a safe space based on mutual care and respect for each other's human rights, whereby teachers are also students and students are also teachers, (2) teaching subjects and skills that are relevant to students' lives and deepen their understanding of their own history and identity, and (3) using students' everyday knowledge as tools to analyse their own oppression and the oppression of others. (Soltis, 2015, 23)

By discussing precarious status as an individual experience, as well as a social, systemic process, and problematising discourses of illegalisation and meritocracy, we seek to disrupt ideas of deservingness prevalent in work related to sanctuary students (Anguiano & Nájera, 2015).

Our analysis draws on data collected by Paloma in 2017, as well as Tanya's experience of participating in the design and implementation of the Access Programme. The data came from a project with eleven students who successfully completed the bridging course in 2017. Participants came from different regions including Africa, the Caribbean and Latin America. Some had university experience in their countries of origin while others completed their secondary education in Canada. Legal statuses included refugee claimants (n=5), non-status (undocumented) (n=5) and one person transitioning from non-status to permanent residence, demonstrating the malleability of legal status. The majority of participants were women (n=8). Names used are pseudonyms chosen by participants.

Data include interviews, as well as course assignments including essays, creative projects and reading reflections. To avoid students feeling coerced to participate in this project, interviews took place after they completed the course (which was taught by Paloma). Interviews focused on participants' experiences attempting to enrol in HE prior to the bridging, their perceptions and evaluations of the course, and their future plans. Assignments focused on the course topic: critical approaches to migration and uprootedness.

The Access Programme as a Counterspace

While Uprooted U, the precursor to the YU Access Programme, was a counterspace wherein students could reflect on and challenge their exclusion from HE, its impact was limited because it did not offer academic credit or lead to automatic enrolment in Bachelor degree programmes. The YU Access Programme and specifically its bridging course built on, and institutionalised, the work done through Uprooted U in several ways. First, it facilitated students' enrolment in undergraduate university programmes. Second, it was located at the university, whereas Uprooted U was housed at a refugee centre in the city. Students explained feeling proud to be taking courses *at* the university, stating that they felt like 'real' students travelling to and from campus and walking among other students. They now said that they felt included in a university space. Nonetheless, the space was not fully accessible given institutional restrictions, participants' work, familial, and other responsibilities and language barriers. A number of sanctuary students who inquired about the course were unable to take up the opportunity due to these responsibilities and barriers; others who had started the course were unable to finish successfully for similar reasons.

Third, students welcomed the fact that their peers in the bridging course shared some of their immigration status challenges. Counterspaces offer students a refuge from the discrimination and violence they face in society (Muñoz, Espino, & Antrop-Gonzalez, 2014). While no counterspace is 100 per cent safe, the YU classroom was a space where students could openly discuss their personal concerns and connect them to larger systemic processes they were learning about in the course. Specifically, students were able to disclose and examine their precarious status, which most could not do in other environments. The course curriculum, described below, was also specifically designed to be 'relevant to students' lived experiences, valuing students' culture and prior knowledge as a way to construct meaning of their own experiences' (Muñoz, Espino, & Antrop-Gonzalez, 2014, 19). Through this pedagogy, and in this place, students individually and collectively analysed the ideological and institutional forces responsible for their situations and experiences.

Counterstories

The course presented students with critical migration studies scholarship including historical and contemporary explanations for migration, theorisations of migrant precarity, borders, detention, deportation, immigrant and refugee education, and social movements. During the course, students' reading reflections and course discussions illustrated the ways they participated in an active process of counterstorytelling. They combined what they learned with their own experiences to challenge specific conceptions of migrants (which sometimes included themselves). Joey said:

> One of this week's readings is on the concept of legality/illegality in Canada and comparing it to the USA. As I read further into it, I kept thinking how most of the things being analysed within the reading were things I already have extensive knowledge of due to lived experiences.

While Joey, and other students, recognised the importance of scholars' critical interventions in issues of migrant 'illegality', they also began to see themselves and their communities as holding expert knowledge on these topics. As we had hoped, the academic articles, and collective discussions of their content, bolstered and deepened the students' counterstories about their lived realities of precarity. Given this depth of knowledge, we identify four types of counterstories discussed by students: borders and status; race and the myth of multiculturalism; precarious work and status; and migrant activism. These counterstories frequently intersect, as the students made connections between systems of power and their experiences.

Borders and Status

Borders and bordering practices were a central topic in the course, given its focus on migration and uprootedness. Students' counterstorytelling targeted the links between borders and the ways global practices of exploitation and capital accumulation intersect with racist practices through colonialism, imperialism and neoliberalism (Melamed, 2015; Robinson, 1983). For example, Maria, a non-status woman, asked in one of her reading reflections:

> Should borders exist, are they to keep people out or in? Should rich and powerful governments be able to extract minerals from so called poor countries for very little money, polluting water, soil and air, and at the same time close their borders . . . [and implement] visas so the poor people cannot go in?

Similarly, Thomas Jefferson, whose refugee application had been refused, asked 'are physical borders just a social construct created to control human populations to benefit certain people?' Both participants articulated a link between economic displacement in the Global South and border regimes that work to keep displaced migrants out of the Global North (Casas-Cortes et al., 2015).

Given their readings on border regimes, students began to question and challenge migrant illegalisation and its work to mark certain bodies as 'illegal'. Specifically, after reading Goldring et al. (2009), Magalhaes et al. (2010) and Villegas (2014), students discussed the ways migrant illegalisation operates through the production of multiple legal statuses. Laura, a refugee claimant, commented:

> I realised that I tend to make comparisons between the different precarious statuses which I guess many people do. I also tend to analyse which situation is better or worse but at the end, I conclude there is not a secure status when it comes to precariousness . . . Identifying myself as someone with precarious status, I have discovered that, despite the specific precarious status each one possesses, we all share similar fears, anxieties, instability, [lack of a] sense of belonging, and the inability to make long-term plans.

Migrant illegalisation often isolates precarious status migrants, making them feel that they are the only ones experiencing precarity and/or fear of exposure leading to deportation (Ledesma, 2015). Laura reflected on the ways she had internalised Canadian immigration system categories (undocumented/non-status, refugee claimant, and 'economic' migrant) using them to assign 'deservingness'[3] to other migrants. She then explained how, during the course, her thinking shifted when she realised that one way migrant illegalisation and deportability work is by pitting migrants against one another (e.g. people informing or policing one another). This shift led her to rearticulate her situation by claiming precarious status, a broader concept that placed her in solidarity with her peers and other migrants while rejecting the hegemonic imposition of migrant illegalisation, stating: 'we [precarious status migrants] are all considered within the term "illegality", even though this is not a quality that is inherent to a person upon crossing a border'.

Rayan described a similar realisation as he read for the course, listened to course lectures, reflected on his immigration experience and the state's role in re/producing precarious statuses. He was a refugee claimant under what is termed the legacy file: claimants who submitted their applications before 2012 when the Canadian refugee determination system was amended.

---

[3] 'Deservingness' refers to the allocation of value or worth to each category according to conceptions of 'good' vs. 'bad' immigrants (Willen, 2015).

From that point, the government prioritised adjudicating new cases under the logic of efficiency, and as a result, legacy cases were stalled, making applicants live in precarious status for several years (Immigration and Refugee Board of Canada, 2018). He said:

> I have also come to the realisation of my own status in this country . . . it's like the government has no regard for us, we are not that important. Laws and regulations are made not for the purpose of making it easier for precarious status people to become Canadian citizens or permanent residents. It is my belief that the laws put precarious status people at a greater risk. Wouldn't it be easier and safer for the government to put in place regulations and laws that protect people living with precarious status so that they can be protected from discrimination and abuse?

Rayan's comments raise important questions about Canada's legal system and identify how laws maintain the privilege of (some) citizens while excluding others.

Race and the Myth of Multiculturalism

Another example of counterstorytelling involved disrupting hegemonic understandings of Canadian nation-building. Canada is often framed as a multicultural haven. Multiculturalism is embedded in the Canadian constitution and popular discourse and internalised by those living in Canada including im/migrants and racialised peoples (Ali, 2008). Yet the discourses of inclusion and equality that are assumed inherent to multiculturalism are non-performative; they 'do not do what they say' (Ahmed, 2004). Multiculturalist policy and state discourse reify racial/ethnic/cultural differences while portraying the Canadian state as liberal and inclusionary (Bannerji, 2000; Giles 2002, 119–123).

In class, students identified the ways multiculturalist discourse worked to exclude them through the language of diversity and inclusion. Many expressed how they had internalised this discourse that refers to Canada as open and welcoming. As the semester went on however, the course material and class discussions led students to critically analyse their preconceived ideas in their writing assignments. Gabriella referred to Canada as 'coated with multiculturalism', even though: 'Canada as a nation needs immigrants to build their prosperity, security for the nation and also help improve their labor market.' Similarly, Djemba, a refugee claimant, described in a writing assignment:

> I wish that Canada and its people realize and understand the struggles of refugees, to understand that I did not choose to be in the situation which I found myself in, as well as all other refugees ... How beautiful and colourful Canada will be if all this diversity and multiculturalism was fully welcoming and people were given a second chance to make it in life.

Djemba's statement counters the framing of refugees as 'opportunistic rational-choice decision makers' (Pratt & Valverde, 2002, 146). It also questions multiculturalist representations of Canada that ignore the mistreatment of refugee claimants and other precarious status migrants.

Students also disrupted inclusive understandings of multiculturalism through their observations of the experiences of racism they had encountered. In class, they read an article about Black refugee students in Canada (Schroeter & James, 2015). Reflecting on the reading, they drew on their own experiences to link racism with migrant illegalisation (Villegas & Aberman, 2019). Djemba, described his schooling experiences including professional streaming, which pushes students towards technical rather than academic courses:

> I cannot recount the number of times career counsellors, job developers and guidance counsellors have tried to convince me to do a profession more physical than academic. Mostly because they believe as a strong Black male from Africa, the best career path for me will be construction or some physical labour as opposed to my choice of academics.

Djemba had challenged his counsellors' expectations of his probable educational trajectory through his participation in the YU bridging course. In fact, his engagement in the course emerged from a concerted effort on his part to overcome obstacles imposed by counsellors, a process that he described as stressful and unnecessarily time-consuming.

Precarious Work and Status

Like Djemba's description of being pushed into manual labour, the students' counterstorytelling frequently involved discussions of the workplace and precarious working conditions. Precarious work refers to insecure, temporary, often difficult and poorly paid work that disproportionately affects working-class, women, im/migrant and racialised peoples (Fudge, 2012; Kalleberg, 2009; Vosko & Clark, 2009). In class, students read a report on precarious work and well-being by Lewchuk et al. (2013). For Maria, the report led to a reflection on income disparities and the dehumanisation of workers like herself:

> How can we stop this dehumanisation? . . . We are the majority, we are the work force, and without us the 1% could not be as privileged as they are. I really believe in the popular chant 'The people united will never be defeated.' As much as we need jobs to survive, they need us.

Maria's words turn the association of immigrants as alienated, isolated, workers on its head. Instead, like Djemba, she points out that under current economic conditions, employers and nation-states need precarious exploitable labour. Her reference to 'the people united will never be defeated' reclaims ideas of the humanity and solidarity of migrants/precarious workers. Thomas Jefferson articulated a similar broad understanding of the relationship between work, community, and solidarity stating, 'The goal of work is to earn a living, pay the bills, provide for loved ones and give back to the community they live in.' Through their counterstorytelling, these students disrupt neoliberal framings of personal responsibility and meritocracy. As instructors, we could see in their writing and class discussions, the building blocks for social change that can ultimately lead to more concrete transformations at policy and legal levels.

Migrant Activism

Students also used counterstorytelling to discuss their engagement, or future plans to engage, in social justice projects. For instance, after reading about DREAMers in the United States, Laura stated: 'This . . . makes me think about my next step and makes me wonder, how can I contribute to causes like this here in Canada that would benefit those in precarious situations like my own family?' Laura's conception of justice/activism included not only her individual and family circumstances but also other migrants facing similar situations.

Part of students' social justice work involved making themselves, and their migration statuses/experiences visible. For instance, Joey explained:

> It wasn't until I moved to Canada that I truly began understanding the meaning of stating your immigration status for activist purposes. Actually, I didn't see myself being one of those people doing so for others. Before, I was comfortable just stating that I was there, that I was different, but that I was there. Now, I constantly challenge society by bringing my existence forward in the place of others, or at least I'd like to believe I constantly do this. Fighting for what's right, fighting to make a difference. These are battles I never thought myself being capable of doing. It makes me wonder, what my old younger self would think of me now? Am I someone she would consider brave as well?

Joey described a shift that led her to reimagine how precarious status migrants are expected to behave, from 'needy', vulnerable victims, to resourceful, active participants of social change. As we discussed with our students, visibility can be an important 'political strategy [for migrants] for responding to the pressures to hide themselves in fear or shame' (Hart, 2015, 9). Further, this approach can be interpreted by scholars and migrants as a refusal to accept hegemonic framings and to build community with those who are similarly affected (ibid, 9). However, Hart goes on to argue that 'legibility is neither universally coherent nor automatically liberatory' (ibid, 9). It can lead immigration enforcement agents to arrest, and potentially deport migrants. Rayan was cognisant of the punishment that public action can impose onto migrants. His recommendation was to call for collective solidarity:

> I am truly proud to know that there are people who are willing to stand up for what they believe in, in spite of their precarious status and not having documents ... Just imagining if all people who are undocumented and precarious would unite and stand together with the help of people who are secure; just imagining the progress we could have in this day and age. I do understand that speaking out for some is not possible due to the impact that speaking out might have on not just them, but their family as well. But I do pray that those who do have a voice will learn to use that voice to help those who can't. We all have a part to play, and the sooner we become more unafraid to speak about our insecure status, only then we will get the word out there.

Rayan's recommendations draw everyone who participates and benefits from the Canadian immigration system into a process of working for collective transformation. Cognizant of the limits to visibility and pressure for precarious status migrants to 'come out', Rayan proposes a flexible process where everyone participates according to their abilities.

Discussion and Conclusion

Participants' counterstories emerged as a result of their participation in the counterspaces created within the course where they linked their personal experiences with course texts, class discussions and their community cultural wealth (Yosso, 2006).

In doing so, the counterstories outlined above disrupt normative understandings of migrant belonging in several ways.

First, students' counterstories challenged the spaces imagined as available in Toronto and in Canada for precarious status migrants. Students' critiques of borders, racism and precarious work contributed to their re-imaginings of their equitable inclusion into employment and academic settings. The space created in the bridging course provided a place for students to create a sense of community with peers with similar experiences, and to discuss issues relevant to their lives that they might not be able to discuss in other contexts of their lives.

Second, the students' counterstories challenge a 'divide and conquer' immigration environment in Canada that is at least partly brought about by the existence of multiple different immigration categories. While sanctuary students are often pitted against each other and pushed to present themselves as more deserving than other immigrants (Anguiano & Nájera, 2015), participants began to reflect on the ways such practices prevent solidarity. In their course assignments and grassroots activism, they called on the Canadian government and other decision makers to implement changes on multiple levels; a social justice process they felt was needed for their humanity to be recognised and respected.

Third, and related to the above, students challenged hegemonic projects of Canadian nation-building and multiculturalism. To do this, they drew on their personal experiences and social locations, often linking their immigration status to their experiences of racialisation. Questioning the racism and xenophobia they have felt in Canada provided counterstories to multicultural narratives of inclusivity and welcome. They also went beyond their personal experiences to call on the Canadian government to change policies and practices that affect all im/migrants (Weins, 2018).

While critiques of the systemic issues that produce migrant 'illegality' and precarity disrupt neoliberal processes of individualisation and personal responsibility, students' material realities, in terms of their financial and immigration status situations, did not change because of the bridging course or the counterstories that emerged through it. Most participants continued to engage in precarious work after the bridging course, and did not see the potential for their situation improving until they received secure immigration status. However, within the first bridging cohort, six of the eleven students have since acquired a more secure status, either having their refugee claim or permanent resident application approved. For some of these students, their participation in HE helped their applications by showing establishment in Canada. Of those six, four are pursuing full-time studies at the university. For the other seven students, financial concerns have been the primary factor keeping them from their studies.

Finally, the broader Access Programme created a counterspace which influenced other actors and institutions to begin conversations about access to HE for sanctuary students. This process led those working to create change in isolated ways within their institutions to meet each other and share strategies and experiences, what Rayan above referred to as everyone having a 'part to play'. For instance, faculty and staff members at several Colleges and universities across Toronto (and to a lesser extent the province of Ontario) began to explore the possibility of increasing access and potentially creating similar counterspaces for sanctuary students. While provincial policy amendments could facilitate this process, these are unlikely due to the recent conservative swing in provincial politics. However, universities have mandates which allow them to set their own admission criteria, providing opportunities to advocate for counterspaces within individual institutions.

Nonetheless, more work is needed. While the bridging course and other sites within the university can be understood as counterspaces, the university remains an inaccessible and exclusionary space for many sanctuary students given the interlocking of legal status and financial situation (among other factors). Given this, access should be conceptualised as more than getting sanctuary students through the door (Villegas, 2016). Finally, from our experience liaising with university officials we learned about the importance of institutional support of the programme – in terms of funding for the bridging course, access to resources and information, as well as a knowledgeable staff who interact with sanctuary students.

More research is needed to understand the barriers that affect sanctuary students' success in HE as well as how their educational outcomes positively or negatively affect their ability to achieve secure status and work in Canada. This work would contribute to filling some of the knowledge gaps concerning precarious status migrants' inclusion in Canada and would contribute to further advocacy for and by sanctuary students.

REFERENCES

Aberman, T., & Ackerman, P. (2017). Isn't the Right to an Education a Human Right? In S. Carpenter & S. Mojab (eds.), *Youth as/in Crisis* (pp. 127–144). Rotterdam: Sense Publishers.

Aberman, T., Villegas, F., & Villegas, P. E. (eds.). (2016). *Seeds of Hope: Creating a Future in the Shadows*. Toronto: FCJ Refugee Centre.

Ahmed, S. (2004). Declarations of Whiteness: The Non-Performativity of Anti-Racism. *Borderlands, 3*(2). www.borderlands.net.au/vol3no2_2004/ahmed_declarations.htm

Ali, M. A. (2008). Second-generation Youth's Belief in the Myth of Canadian Multiculturalism. *Canadian Ethnic Studies, 40*(2), 89–107.

Anguiano, C. A., & Nájera, L. G. (2015). Paradox of Performing Exceptionalism: Complicating the Deserving/Underserving Binary of Undocumented Youth Attending Elite Institutions. *Association of Mexican American Educators Journal, 9*(2), 45–56.

Article 26. (n.d.). *Approach & Values.* article26.hkf.org.uk/about-us/what-we-dl/approach-values

Bannerji, H. (2000). *The Dark Side of the Nation: Essays on Multiculturalism, Nationalism and Gender.* Toronto: Canadian Scholars' Press.

Casas-Cortes, M., Cobarrubias, S., De Genova, N., Garelli, G., Grappi, G., Heller, C., ... Peano, I. (2015). New Keywords: Migration and Borders. *Cultural Studies, 29*(1), 55–87.

Chang, A. (2011). Undocumented to Hyperdocumented: A Jornada of Protection, Papers, and PhD Status. *Harvard Educational Review, 81*(3), 508–521.

Crawford, E. R., & Arnold, N. W. (2016). Exploring the Meaning and Paths of Advocacy for Undocumented Students' Access to Education. *Journal of Latinos and Education, 15*(3), 197–213.

Dauvergne, C. (2008). *Making People Illegal: What Globalization Means for Migration and Law.* Cambridge: Cambridge University Press.

De Genova, N. (2002). Migrant 'Illegality' and Deportability in Everyday Life. *Annual Review of Anthropology, 31*, 419–447.

De Genova, N. (2005). *Working the Boundaries: Race, Space, and 'Illegality' in Mexican Chicago.* Durham: Duke University Press.

de Wit, H., & Altbach, P. (2016). The Syrian Refugee Crisis and Higher Education. *International Higher Education, 84*, 9–10.

Flores, S. M. (2010). State Dream Acts: The Effect of In-state Resident Tuition Policies and Undocumented Latino Students. *Review of Higher Education, 33* (2), 239–283.

Freire, P. (2004). *Pedagogy of the Oppressed* (M. B. Ramos, Trans.). New York: The Continuum International Publishing Group.

Fudge, J. (2012). Precarious Migrant Status and Precarious Employment: The Paradox of International Rights for Migrant Workers. *Comparative Labor Law & Policy Journal, 34*(1), 95–131.

Giles, W. (2002). *Portuguese Women in Toronto: Gender, Immigration and Nationalism.* Toronto: University of Toronto Press.

Goldring, L., Berinstein, C., & Bernhard, J. (2009). Institutionalizing Precarious Migratory Status in Canada. *Citizenship Studies, 13*(3), 239–265.

Goldring, L., & Landolt, P. (2013). The Conditionality of Legal Rights and Status: Conceptualizing Precarious Non-citizenship. In L. Goldring, & P. Landolt (eds.), *Producing and Negotiating Non-Citizenship: Precarious Legal Status in Canada* (pp. 3–27). Toronto: University of Toronto Press.

Gonzales, R. G., & Sigona, N. (2017). Mapping the Soft Borders of Citizenship: An Introduction. In R. G. Gonzales, & N. Sigona (eds.), *Within and Beyond Citizenship: Borders, Membership and Belonging* (pp. 1–16). London: Routledge.

Hart, C. (2015). The Artivism of Julio Salgado's I Am Undocuqueer! Series. *Working Papers in Education*, *1*(2), 1–14.

Houston, S. D., & Morse, C. (2017). The Ordinary and Extraordinary: Producing Migrant Inclusion and Exclusion in US Sanctuary Movements. *Studies in Social Justice*, 11(1), 27–47.

Hudson, B., & Murray, R. (2018). *Guiding Principles on Sanctuary Scholars in UK Higher Education*. London, UK: Article 26, a project of the Helena Kennedy Foundation. http://article26.hkf.org.uk/_/uploads/Article_26_-_Guiding_Pri nciples.pdf

Immigration and Refugee Board of Canada (2018, July 4). Legacy Fact Sheet. https://irb-cisr.gc.ca/en/information-sheets/Pages/legacy-fact-sheet.aspx

Kalleberg, A. L. (2009). Precarious Work, Insecure Workers: Employment Relations in Transition. *American Sociological Review*, *74*, 1–22.

Kamal, F., & Killian, K. D. (2015). Invisible Lives and Hidden Realities of Undocumented Youth. *Refuge: Canada's Journal on Refugees*, *31*(2), 63–74.

Ledesma, A. (2015). On the Grammar of Silence: The Structure of My Undocumented Immigrant Writer's Block. *Harvard Educational Review*, *85* (3), 415–426.

Lewchuk, W., Laflèche, M., Dyson, D., Goldring, L., Meisner, A., Procyk, S., . . . Vrankulj, S. (2013). *It's More than Poverty: Employment Precarity and Household Well-being*. Toronto, ON: Poverty and Employment Precarity in Southern Ontario.

Magalhaes, L., Carrasco, C., & Gastaldo, D. (2010). Undocumented Migrants in Canada: A Scope Literature Review on Health, Access to Services, and Working Conditions. *Journal of Immigrant Minority Health*, *12*(1), 132–151.

Manalo-Pedro, M. R. (2018). The Role of a Dream Resource Center at a CSU: How Institutional Agents Advanced Equity for Undocumented Students through Interest Convergence (Unpublished doctoral dissertation), Los Angeles, CA: University of California.

Melamed, J. (2015). Racial Capitalism. *Critical Ethnic Studies*, *1*(1), 76–85.

Muñoz, S., Espino, M. M., & Antrop-Gonzalez, R. (2014). Creating Counter-spaces of Resistance and Sanctuaries of Learning and Teaching: An Analysis of Freedom University. *Teachers College Record*, *116*(7), 1–32.

Muñoz, S., & Maldonado, M. M. (2012). Counterstories of College Persistence by Undocumented Mexicana Students: Navigating Race, Class, Gender, and

Legal Status. *International Journal of Qualitative Studies in Education, 25*(3), 293–315.

Murray, R., Hope, J., & Turley, H. (2014). *Education for All: Access to Higher Education for People Who Have Sought Asylum; a Guide for Universities* www .hkf.org.uk/_/uploads/Article26-SSG-FINAL.pdf

Mutsaers, P. (2014). An Ethnographic Study of the Policing of Internal Borders of the Netherlands. *British Journal of Criminology, 54*(5), 831–848. DOI:10.1093/ bjc/azu033

Najafi, A. M. (2008). Legislation. In G. Madera, K. Wong, J. Monroe, G. Rivera-Salgado, & A. A. Mathay (eds.), *Underground Undergrads: UCLA Undocumented Immigrant Students Speak Out* (pp. 2–18). Los Angeles, CA: UCLA Center for Labor Research and Education.

Ngai, M. M. (2017). A Call for Sanctuary. *Dissent, 64*(1), 16–19.

Pratt, A., & Valverde, M. (2002). From Deserving Victims to 'Masters of Confusion': Redefining Refugees in the 1990s. *The Canadian Journal of Sociology, 27*(2), 135–161.

Refugee Council (2013). *Fees and Funding.* www.refugeecouncil.org.uk/wp-content/uploads/2019/03/Fees_and_funding.pdf

Robinson, C. J. (1983). *Black Marxism: The Making of the Black Radical Tradition.* North Carolina: University of North Carolina Press.

Schroeter, S., & James, C. (2015). 'We're Here because We're Black': The Schooling Experiences of French-speaking African-Canadian Students with Refugee Backgrounds. *Race Ethnicity and Education, 18*(1), 20–39.

Solórzano, D. G., Ceja, M., & Yosso, T. J. (2000). Critical Race Theory, Racial Microaggressions, and Campus Racial Climate: The Experiences of African American College Students. *Journal of Negro Education, 69*(1/2), 60–73.

Soltis, L. E. (2015). From Freedom Schools to Freedom University: Liberatory Education, Interracial and Intergenerational Dialogue, and the Undocumented Student Movement in the US South. *Souls, 17*(1–2), 20–53.

Trivette, M. J., & English, D. J. (2017). Finding Freedom: Facilitating Postsecondary Pathways for Undocumented Students. *Educational Policy, 31* (6), 858–894.

Villegas, F. (2006). Challenging Educational Barriers: Undocumented Immigrant Student Advocates. (Master of Arts Master's Thesis), San Jose: San Jose State University.

Villegas, F. (2016). 'Access without Fear!': Reconceptualizing 'Access' to Schooling for Undocumented Students in Toronto. *Critical Sociology, 43* (7–8), 1179–1195.

Villegas, P. E. (2014). 'I Can't Even Buy a Bed because I Don't Know if I'll Have to Leave Tomorrow': Temporal Orientations among Mexican Precarious Status Migrants in Toronto. *Citizenship Studies, 18*(3–4), 277–291.

Villegas, P. E., & Aberman, T. (2019). A Double Punishment: The Context of Postsecondary Access for Racialized Precarious Status Migrant Students in Canada. *Refuge, 35*(1), 72–82.

Vosko, L. F., & Clark, L. F. (2009). Canada: Gendered Precariousness and Social Reproduction. In L. F. Vosko, M. MacDonald, & I. Campbell (eds.), *Gender and the Contours of Precarious Employment* (pp. 26–42). New York: Routledge.

Weins, M. (2018). Grade 12, Then What? Canadian Dreamers and Their Quest for Higher Education. www.cbc.ca/news/grade-12-then-what-canadian-dreamers-and-their-quest-for-higher-education-1.4803832

Willen, S. S. (2015). Lightning Rods in the Local Moral Economy: Debating Unauthorized Migrants' Deservingness in Israel. *International Migration, 53*(3), 70–86.

Yosso, T. J. (2006). *Critical Race Counterstories along the Chicana/Chicano Educational Pipeline.* New York: Routledge.

Yosso, T. J., Smith, W., Ceja, M., & Solórzano, D. G. (2009). Critical Race Theory, Racial Microaggressions, and Campus Racial Climate for Latina/o Undergraduates. *Harvard Educational Review, 79*(4), 659–691.

CHAPTER 15

Towards an Emergent Theory of Fallism (and the Fall of the White-Liberal-University in South Africa)

A. Kayum Ahmed

Introduction

The white-liberal-university (deliberately hyphenated) occupies a paradoxical position for Black and other marginalised people. It is simultaneously empowering and dehumanising; it offers the possibility of acquiring knowledge that could serve as a liberatory tool from the violence of socioeconomic marginality (Black liberation), while at the same time, the physical and epistemic architecture of the university can create an oppressive, alienating space for Black, queer and disabled people among others (Black pain).

Fallism is an attempt to make sense of this Black liberation/Black pain paradox. The idea of Fallism first emerged at the end of 2015 as a collective noun to describe student movements at universities in South Africa that use the 'Must Fall' hashtag, including #RhodesMustFall (#RMF) and #FeesMustFall. These Fallist movements employed decolonial theories centred on Pan-Africanism, Black Consciousness and Black radical feminism to argue that the university's epistemic architecture is deeply rooted in coloniality and, that consequently, the white-liberal-university as we know it, must fall.

While these arguments were initially developed in March 2015 by #RMF student activists at the University of Cape Town (UCT) in South Africa, they were subsequently exported to the University of Oxford in the United Kingdom (UK) where students created the #RhodesMustFall Oxford movement. Oxford students were inspired by the #RMF Cape Town movement's call to decolonise the university, and employed similar language and tactics to argue for the decolonisation of Oxford.

Based on my analysis of the #RMF Cape Town and Oxford movements, I seek to establish Fallism as an emergent theoretical framework for understanding the university as the 'authorised center of knowledge production'

(Mamdani, 2016, 69). This chapter draws on a combination of ninety-eight interviews, one year of observations, and document analysis, to offer insights into the formation and evolution of the #RMF student movements at UCT and Oxford, as a contribution to advancing Fallism as a theory that exposes the university's paradoxical epistemic architecture.

The Backstory

On 9 March 2015, Chumani Maxwele, a black student at the University of Cape Town (UCT) in South Africa, took containers filled with human feces and emptied their contents onto a bronze statue of Cecil John Rhodes located on the university's campus (Jansen, 2017; Mamdani, 2016; Nyamnjoh, 2016). Maxwele's defacement of the Rhodes statue was an important catalyst in the formation of #RhodesMustFall (#RMF)[1] – a radical student movement centred on decolonising the university by confronting questions of institutional racism, access to education and reforming the Eurocentric university curriculum (Gibson, 2016; Luescher, 2016; Mbembe, 2016). While the statue glorified the white British imperialist and racist Rhodes, and was characterised in the #RMF's mission statement (2015) as 'an act of violence' as well as 'the perfect embodiment of black alienation and disempowerment', it served primarily as a symbolic focal point for the movement's broader decolonial objectives. According to the #RMF mission statement (2015), '[w]e stress that this movement is not simply about the removal of a statue, and removing the statue is only the first step towards the radical decolonization of this university'.

At the same time, the #RMF mission statement published by the Johannesburg Workshop in Theory and Criticism (2015) acknowledges that '[t]his movement was sparked by Chumani Maxwele's radical protest against the statue of Cecil John Rhodes on Monday, 9 March 2015' (JWTC, 2015, 6). Maxwele chose 9 March 2015 to collect human waste from the poor, black township of Khayelitsha on the outskirts of Cape Town, and throw it onto the Rhodes statue at UCT – located on the mountainside of the wealthy, white suburb of Rondebosch – because it coincided with the start of Infecting the City; an annual public art event that wanted 'to re-claim public space for the public' through performance art and exhibitions in open spaces across Cape Town (Infecting the City,

---

[1] The hashtag (#) that precedes the name 'RhodesMustFall' is used on social media networks such as Twitter to identify and search for messages on a particular issue.

n. d.). Recognising that he could face serious legal and disciplinary consequences for his actions, Maxwele used the annual public art event as a cover for his protest. His protest was therefore deliberately masked as a performance to avoid disciplinary action; it was a performance of a performance.

The #RMF movement comprised three pillars centred on Pan-Africanism, Black Consciousness and Black radical feminism (Personal communication with Chumani Maxwele, 31 August 2016). Maxwele specifically mentioned Frantz Fanon's (2004) work on decolonisation, Steve Biko's (1978) Black Consciousness philosophy, and Kimberlé Crenshaw's (1991) intersectionality framework as he explained the intellectual foundations of the #RMF movement. The three pillars of Pan-Africanism, Black Consciousness and Black radical feminism are collectively referred to in this chapter as #RMF's 'decolonial framework'.

In #RMF's mission statement, decolonisation was understood as the antithesis of 'transformation' – a term often associated with South Africa's transition from apartheid to democracy. But decolonisation was also referred to by #RMF as the 'very destruction' of 'a violent system of power' which defines 'our existence as black people' (JWTC 2015, 12). While #RMF sought to destroy rather than transform the power structures that defined black existence embedded in the university's architecture, the movement simultaneously recognised the advantages of being located within the university space. Masixole Mlandu, a student representative from the Pan-Africanist Student Movement of Azania (PASMA) and a prominent member of #RMF, noted that the university 'is the only space that we, as black people, have to think … they are spaces for organising and mobilising … so to me … #RhodesMustFall can be seen as the awakening to a cry that has always been there … #RhodesMustFall was … at the heart of it was a critique of how the university is structured' (Personal communication with Masixole Mlandu, 30 June 2017).

Mlandu's assertion that #RMF's formation can be characterised as a critique of the university, but that the university 'is the only space that we, as black people, have to think' leads me to argue that the university occupies a paradoxical position for Black and other marginalised people. The #RMF's mission statement invokes the idea of 'black pain' which student activists define as 'the dehumanization of black people' informed by the 'violence exacted only against black people by a system that privileges whiteness' (#RMF, 2015).

In their attempts to decolonise UCT, the #RMF movement employed disruptive tactics, such as the illegal occupation of the university's central administration building, culminating in the burning of artwork that students believed, depicted black bodies in dehumanising ways. Some students involved in these disruptive moments indicated that they were influenced by #RMF's decolonial framework centred on Pan-Africanism, Black Consciousness and Black radical feminism. In developing this decolonial framework, #RMF simultaneously delinked from Eurocentric ideas (Mignolo, 2009), rejecting human rights discourses embedded in South Africa's progressive constitution. While the rejection of human rights can be characterised as delinking, the burning of artwork appears more like erasure, suggesting that student activists engaged in actions that could be characterised as a radical extension of delinking.

While epistemic disobedience requires a process of delinking that may include replacing the offensive paintings with artwork from the margins, #RMF activist Masixole Mlandu described the burning of artwork as 'tak[ing] the struggle to another level' (Personal communication with Masixole Mlandu, 30 June 2017). This new level, which involves the erasure of knowledge, could be interpreted as an extension of delinking. At the same time, my interviews with several students involved in burning the artwork reveal that their actions were largely unplanned. Alex Hotz (Personal communication, 13 July 2017), the first appellant listed in the Supreme Court of Appeal case pertaining to the burning of paintings, stated that 'there was no plan ... ' It is therefore difficult to develop a conclusive understanding of what motivated the spontaneous actions of student activists to burn the artwork.

The students involved in the #RMF movement were referred to by various actors as 'activists' as well as 'hooligans' (Hodes, 2015), and were also compared to Boko Haram (Mbembe, cited in Laing, 2016). Sometimes, these student activists were called 'Fallists' (Bofelo, 2017; Davis, 2016; Healy-Clancy, 2016) and their movement to decolonise the university was referred to as 'Fallism' (Ngcaweni, 2016). The term 'Fallism' denoted the students' demand to remove the Rhodes statue from UCT; for the statue to fall. But Fallism appears to have several meanings. According to Sizwe Mpofu-Walsh (2016, 82), '"Fallism" is a nascent, complicated and emerging viewpoint ...', while Godsell and Chikane (2016, 59) suggest that 'the basic foundations of Fallism reside within the ambit of the decolonisation project of the African university ...'

A few weeks after the formation of #RMF at UCT, students at the University of Oxford, who were inspired by the decolonial movement in Cape Town, created their own #RMF Oxford movement also centred on the removal of a Rhodes statue located at Oriel College in Oxford's High

Street (Gebrial, 2018; Mpofu-Walsh, 2016; Newsinger, 2016). Student activists at Oxford indicated that they were inspired by the #RMF movement in Cape Town (Personal communication with Ntokozo Qwabe, 3 August 2016), and therefore started a similar movement using the Rhodes statue located at Oriel College as a symbolic reference point in their call to decolonise the university (Mpofu-Walsh, 2016). This flow of knowledge and ideas from the global South to the North – from the colonised to the coloniser – suggests that Fallism has the ability to travel and can be replicated in white-liberal spaces.

While the Rhodes statue was eventually removed from UCT precisely one month after Maxwele threw feces onto it, the statue remains standing at Oxford. This difference in the outcome of the two movements offers some indication of the varying strategies and tactics employed, and leads to questions about the ways in which the #RMF movement in Oxford was shaped by #RMF in Cape Town. Despite important differences between the two movements, this chapter finds that the formation of #RMF Oxford may contribute to what Comaroff and Comaroff (2011) refer to as a 'theory from the South'. I therefore consider whether the emergence of the #RMF movement in Cape Town and its subsequent exportation to Oxford can be assessed through the Comaroffs' (2011) theory, which contests the assumption that knowledge is developed in the North and travels southward. For the Comaroffs (2011), the South is able to prefigure historical trends and export them to the global North.

In developing an emergent theory of Fallism, I will draw on articulations of Fallism gathered through interviews with #RMF activists. At the same time, my development of Fallism is not necessarily endorsed by student activists who have multiple and sometimes conflicting understandings of Fallism. I therefore experiment with developing Fallism as a concept that originated through the #RMF movement into a decolonial theory that flows from acts of epistemic disobedience and delinking. However, I suggest that Fallism extends decolonial theories of delinking and disobedience through disruption and counter-violence on the one hand, and because of its ability to travel from South to North on the other.

Constructing a Decolonial Framework

The #RMF movement's mission statement was crafted over five days during the student occupation of the Bremner administration building which was renamed 'Azania House'. Students, workers and faculty adopted the mission statement on 25 March 2015, which starts with the following line: 'We are an independent collective of students, workers and staff who have come together to end institutionalised racism and patriarchy at UCT' (#RMF, 2015). The statement acknowledges Maxwele's 'radical protest' and how it 'brought to the surface the existing and justified rage of black students'. While the statement specifically mentions Black Consciousness and intersectionality, Pan-Africanism is introduced slightly later in official #RMF documents. During interviews with #RMF activists, they refer to Black Consciousness, Pan-Africanism and Black radical feminism (which includes intersectionality) as the three pillars of the movement.

These three pillars establish the basis for #RMF's decolonial framework which constitute an act of epistemic disobedience. The students' invocation of decolonial theorists such as Fanon and Biko, and of concepts such as intersectionality, was symptomatic of this disobedience since these scholars were not often taught at the university. Black students on the margins of the white-liberal-university space rejected UCT's privileging of European theorisations of power by developing a framework centred on Black Consciousness, Pan Africanism and Black radical feminism. #RMF's disobedience, directed towards the university, was primarily based on student experiences of dehumanisation or black pain within the university space. These experiences included a sense of alienation because of the dominance of Euro-American academic literature, taught by white professors in spaces historically designed to celebrate white power through statues and other iconography. At the same time, #RMF's formulation of a decolonial framework that demanded black liberation took place in the same physical space that their black pain was generated in.

Prominent #RMF activist Ntokozo Qwabe, who was involved in both the #RMF UCT and Oxford protests, reflected on the idea of black pain in an extensive Facebook post published on 9 November 2016. Qwabe indicated that he was completing his fourth degree, of which two were Master's degrees from Oxford. Before becoming a student at Oxford, Qwabe attended law school from the age of 16 at the University of Kwa-Zulu-Natal, but had to drop out due to financial constraints:

> ... the only company willing to hire under-aged me was Shoprite Checkers – first as a trolley boy (yes, those people that push customer trolleys from outside stores), then as a Till Packer (yes, the people who put your items in your bags at the till), and finally as a Cashier (when I had turned 17).

After working at the Shoprite Checkers grocery store chain for three years, Qwabe returned to university with just enough money to complete his studies. But he continued to face several financial and administrative obstacles, noting that:

> [W]hat shatters me the most is that the university seemed to do all it could to spit me out – when it was supposed to be a place of hopes and dreams for me. A place where I could escape the cycle of black poverty I had been born to ... as a black person, university nearly broke me to pieces – never to recover, and with no hope of repair. You know, many people will not understand why we call for free decolonised education. They will never understand why we call for our universities to be decolonised and to cease inflicting pain on black bodies.

Ntokozo Qwabe's experiences in South Africa and the United Kingdom reflect the paradoxical position of the university as 'a place where I could escape the cycle of black poverty' (Black liberation), and the university that 'inflicts pain on black bodies'. For Qwabe, 'racism at Oxford has grave psychological and mental health implications for black students' (Personal communication with Ntokozo Qwabe, 1 August 2017). The Black pain/ Black liberation thesis I advance in this chapter flows from this paradox and can be better understood through an assessment of the three pillars of the movement.

Black Consciousness

One of the major themes that run through #RMF's mission statement centres on the idea of blackness; on Black Consciousness, what it means to be 'black', and to experience 'black pain'. Leila Khan, a law student and member of the Muslim Youth Movement at UCT, noted during our interview that the very first time the idea of 'black pain' was introduced as a concept in the #RMF context, was during a meeting of Black student organisations on 13 March 2015.

In the #RMF mission statement (2015) under a subheading, 'centering black pain', it equates black pain with dehumanisation. However, the mission statement also defines 'black' as 'all people of colour'. This definition reflects Biko's (2017, 52) philosophy of Black Consciousness which argues that blacks are 'those who are by law or tradition politically, economically and socially discriminated against as a group in South African society and identifying themselves as a unit in the struggle towards the realisation of their aspirations'. According to Leila Khan:

> As far as Black Consciousness ... it was a really good way to make sense of all the critiques that we were making about white people being involved and

limiting the space. I think we had all been reading Biko by ourselves . . . and then also . . . the practical stuff that comes from his writing: so, how do you actually organise and how it's actually more effective to organise without white people. We used that as a point of departure . . . And also just this unifying idea of 'black' which is also very important because that was not pervasive. You don't find people just identifying as black like in a non-phenotypical way.

The #RMF mission statement (2015) acknowledges that blackness as a 'political identity' should not ignore 'the huge differences that exist between us'; it aims to build 'unity to bring about our collective liberation'. According to Biko (2017, 52), 'being black is a reflection of a mental attitude' rather than pigmentation, and by adopting blackness as an identity, 'you have started on a road towards emancipation . . . ' However, in several conversations with student activists, many indicated that when a coloured or Indian person self-identified as black, they were referred to as 'Biko black', whereas those who were black Africans were referred to as 'black black'. This distinction between Biko blacks and black blacks seemed to emerge later in the movement as a way of signalling the significant class differences within the broad category of black.

It is important to note that while Black Consciousness is a concept taken directly from Biko's work, 'black pain' is a new idea developed by the #RMF movement at its 13 March 2015 meeting. In the #RMF's collation of writing, poetry and statements compiled through the Johannesburg Workshop in Theory and Criticism (2015, 108), student activist Khumo Sebambo reflected on the notion of black pain which she described as a 'real affliction' invoked during the movement 'as an important aspect of identity formation'. The formation of a collective black identity using the notion of Black Consciousness and black pain became a helpful way of articulating the feelings of alienation that black students encountered at UCT. By delinking from Eurocentric knowledge systems and adopting Black Consciousness as one of the pillars of #RMF's decolonial framework, students created opportunities to 'link (instead of delinking) with knowers who are dealing with conditions of coloniality and projects of decoloniality . . . ' (Mignolo, 2011, 62). Collective identity within #RMF is therefore facilitated through acts of epistemic disobedience directed toward the university.

Black Radical Feminism

In an opinion piece written by Mbali Matandela (also known as Mbalinhle Matandela) (2015) on her involvement in the #RMF movement, she writes:

'After the movement's first meeting, myself and a small group of black radical feminists decided that we needed to stake our claim in talks about the university and its institutional racism . . . We were not going to let only men lead the movement.' #RMF's mission statement, which was released five days before Matandela's article, appears to support her narrative when it states that, 'while this movement emerged as a response to racism at UCT, we recognise that experiences of oppression on this campus are intersectional and we aim to adopt an approach that is cognisant of this going forward' (#RMF, 2015).

Crenshaw's (1991, 139) intersectional framework is a 'Black feminist criticism' of treating race and gender as mutually exclusive resulting in the erasure of black women's experiences. Intersectionality therefore considers how different elements of identity such as race, gender and sexual orientation, which are often viewed separately, are in fact connected. Her paper analyses how United States' (US) courts dealt with black women plaintiffs to reveal the 'conceptual limitations of the single-issue analysis that intersectionality challenges' (Crenshaw, 1989, 149). In addition to challenging patriarchy, intersectionality also challenges white feminism, which privileges the experience of white women. Consequently, by recognising the experiences of 'Black women as the starting point' (Crenshaw, 1989, 140), intersectionality extends beyond a simple merger of identities to recognise how black women can simultaneously belong to more than one category of identity.

The #RMF mission statement (2015) distinguishes between the emergence of the movement as a response to racism sparked by Maxwele's protest on the one hand, and its evolutionary trajectory as an intersectional movement that extends beyond race on the other. Two ideological dimensions can already be discerned at this early stage in the development of #RMF: the first is the adoption of Black Consciousness as a founding pillar of the movement which incorporates and centres the idea of black pain. The second dimension reflected in the #RMF mission statement (2015) builds on Black Consciousness and develops the idea of black pain by employing intersectionality as a way of 'tak[ing] into account that we are not only defined by our blackness, but that some of us are also defined by our gender, our sexuality, our able-bodiedness, our mental health, and our class, among other things'.

In the Johannesburg Workshop in Theory and Criticism (2015, 122) publication that compiles various #RMF statements, poetry, art and writing, Gamedze states that, 'There is power in collective pain, in collective rage, if only we might see it, recognize it, and acknowledge it within each other. Intersectionality collectivizes.' However, Gamedze also finds that, 'The intersectional agenda of Azania house is in direct response to the history of patriarchy in Black Consciousness movements. The popular imagination of Black Consciousness resides in black heterosexual maleness.' This analysis points to a tension between Black Consciousness and intersectionality, while simultaneously recognising intersectionality as a tool for building collective resistance alongside Black Consciousness philosophy.

I suggest that the decision to include intersectionality as the second pillar of the movement constitutes another layer of epistemic disobedience that is directed internally toward the #RMF movement, more so than the university. Black radical feminists within #RMF appear to delink from the patriarchy embedded in Black Consciousness while supporting the overarching philosophy of black liberation and black identity. Their act of epistemic disobedience within the movement therefore complicates Mignolo's (2009) delinking framework which centres on the margins delinking from dominant Western thought and ideology. While Black radical feminists were engaged in a process of delinking from the university's Eurocentric knowledge systems, they were also delinking from 'black heterosexual maleness' within Black Consciousness (Gamedze, 2015, 122).

Pan-Africanism

The term 'Pan-Africanism' is not mentioned in the #RMF mission statement (2015). It is however expressly mentioned in an official #RMF document entitled, the 'Bremner Occupation Statement' published on #RMF's Facebook page two days earlier on 23 March 2015. The statement follows the occupation of UCT's central administration building and indicates that 'We, the Rhodes Must Fall movement, are occupying the Bremner building with the intention to 1) disrupt the normal processes of management and 2) force management to accept our demands' (#RMF 2015).

The statement revealed that #RMF activists occupied the administration building as the start of their decolonisation of the university and began 'a programme of rigorous political education under the guidance of a group of black lecturers from UCT and other South African universities that interrogates and problematizes the neo-colonial narratives pertaining to Africa' (#RMF 2015b). As part of this programme of political education, the students wanted to discuss how to organise and mobilise, but also,

'How do we resolve the tensions between Pan-Africanism and intersectionality, moreover how does that implicate our own movement?'.

Professor Amina Mama (2017, 1), who served as the former Director of the Africa Gender Institute at UCT, argues that, 'The varied grassroots Pan-African movements of the past have been reduced into a hegemonic Pan-Africanism narrative that has become an institutionalised support for patriarchal values.' The tensions between the Pan-Africanists and the Black radical feminists occupied the #RMF activists from the very start of the movement. While Chikane (2018: Location 2245 Kindle edition) acknowledges that 'Black Radical Feminism wasn't let into the space; it brought a crowbar and forced its way through the movement's male gatekeepers', he argues that the rise of Pan-Africanism and the collapse of the #RMF movement is strongly linked to class and particularly, the movement's inability to deal with class. Based on my interviews with student activists, it is not so much class, but rather the #RMF movement's struggle to fully incorporate intersectionality into its decolonial framework that resulted in fractures in the movement.

When I asked Alex Hotz, a former member of the Students' Representative Council, about how the factionalism within the #RMF was tied to the three pillars of the movement, she indicated that the three pillars of the movement were not reflective of three distinguishable factions. Instead, student activists often identified with all three pillars. However, as Hotz points out, there were 'different schools of thought around Pan-Africanism' (Personal communication with Alex Hotz, 13 July 2017) that resulted in the 'tensions between Pan-Africanism and intersectionality' captured in the Bremner occupation statement (#RMF, 2015b).

Brian Kamanzi, who served as a member of the education subcommittee in the #RMF movement, supports Hotz's assertion when he poses the following question: 'We must begin to ask ourselves, if decolonisation and Pan-Africanism are important contributions to the present struggle, then why have we collectively not made more efforts to include the rapidly growing communities of Africans, from outside South Africa, into the debates and conceptualisation around what an inclusive education could look like?' (Kamanzi, 2016).

In an interview with Kamanzi in which he described the three pillars of the movement, he indicated that 'Pan-Africanism, I think, comes through a lot more shallow than the others' (Personal communication with Brian Kamanzi, 27 June 2017). For Masixole Mlandu, a member of PASMA and the UCT Students' Representative Council in 2017, 'the third pillar of the movement was Pan-Africanism, which is also an important one, you know. Because our issues here are not unique to South Africa or the continent; these are issues that affect the entire world' (Personal communication with Masixole Mlandu, 30 June 2017). Mlandu critiqued the notion of South African exceptionalism, arguing that 'we are all affected by imperialism' which results in a 'shared collective experience'.

While Pan-Africanism is not specifically mentioned in #RMF's mission statement, the list of twenty-eight demands at the end of the statement contain strong references to Pan-Africanist ideas. For instance, under a sub-heading entitled 'our long-term goals', the second goal demands that the university rename buildings to 'tak[e] seriously its African positionality'. Furthermore, the fifth long-term goal listed in the mission statement demands that UCT:

> Implement a curriculum which critically centres Africa and the subaltern. By this we mean treating African discourses as the point of departure – through addressing not only content, but languages and methodologies of education and learning – and only examining western traditions in so far as they are relevant to our own experience (#RMF, 2015).

This goal reflects epistemic disobedience in that it seeks to delink from Western knowledge and theory by privileging African thought and ideas. At the same time, #RMF recognises the value of Western ideas 'in so far as they are relevant to our own experience' (#RMF, 2015). Their approach is not dismissive of Western thought, but recognises its incompleteness; Western thought has value if it is complemented by or grounded in the black experience.

The Rise of Fallism

The earliest references to Fallism that I could identify can be traced back to the '#fallist' hashtag that emerged on Twitter for the first time on 9 December 2015 when it was used by #RMF student activist, Lindiwe Dhlamini, whose Twitter handle is @IAmAFallist. The #RMF Facebook page employs the term for the first time on 27 February 2016 when it refers to Black radical feminist, Wanelisa Xaba, as a 'Fallist'. The notion of Fallism therefore seems to emerge nine months *after* the formation of #RMF in March 2015. These references to Fallism appear as the #RMF movement begins to dissipate one year after its formation. Its contested origins appear in the cracks of the movement in December 2015 and become more widely used during 2016, initially by black, queer women, but later, also by black men involved in the movement.

Of the students I spoke to, there were some who identified very strongly with Fallism, others who rejected the concept altogether, and a few students who previously referred to themselves as Fallists but subsequently became disillusioned with the idea. The contested nature of what constitutes Fallism creates difficulties when attempting to define it. Alex Hotz (Personal communication, 13 July 2017) eloquently captured this difficulty when she stated: '. . . I'm beginning to wonder what the fuck Fallism is . . . I just think there are so many contradictions . . .' Just before making this statement, Hotz suggested that Fallism emerged out of the three pillars of the #RMF movement, namely, Pan-Africanism, Black Consciousness and Black radical feminism. These three pillars therefore constitute a decolonial framework that gives birth to the idea of Fallism. It is the weaving together of these pillars, which I have referred to as #RMF's decolonial framework, that creates the tapestry for the emergence of Fallism.

Defining Fallism

But what exactly is Fallism? For Booysen (2016, 4), '[t]he notion of Fallism highlights the demand for far-reaching change'. She also cites #RMF activist, Athabile Nonxuba's definition of Fallism as 'an oath of allegiance that everything to do with oppression and conquest of black people by white power must fall and be destroyed'. In the same edited volume, Sizwe Mpofu-Walsh (2016, 82), who was a leading student activist in the #RMF Oxford movement argued that '"Fallism" is a nascent, complicated and emerging viewpoint, combining aspects of decolonial thought, Black consciousness, radical feminism and pan-Africanism.' For Mpofu-Walsh (2016, 82), 'no protest movement as wide as "Must Fall" can claim coherence. The Must Fall umbrella is not, nor does it aspire to be, a body of literary thought, or a full social theory. Rather, it is a programme of political action.'

Gillian Godsell and Rekgotsofetse (Kgotsi) Chikane (2016, 58–59) reflect on what they refer to as the 'philosophy of Fallism' which is understood as the 'reinvigorated process in which the decolonisation project has been renewed in the higher education system and in society at large'. While they acknowledge that the philosophy of Fallism has varied meanings across academic institutions, they suggest that 'the basic foundations of Fallism reside within the ambit of the decolonization project of the African university ...' Godsell and Chikane (2016) draw on Ndlovo-Gatsheni's scholarship to assert that this decolonisation project is centred on radically transforming the curriculum, institutional structures and the underlying values that shape the university.

In one edited volume, Fallism is described as an 1) oath of allegiance, 2) a viewpoint, and 3) a philosophy. It is linked to the oppression of black people, considered as a programme for political action and as a continuation of the decolonisation project in African higher education. The ubiquitous nature of Fallism is similarly reflected in my conversations with students, faculty and workers. Like Godsell and Chikane (2016), student activist Wandile Kasibe (Personal communication, 28 June 2017) also characterised Fallism as a philosophy. Sandy Ndelu (Personal communication, 17 July 2017), a trans activist and member of #RMF who used to identify as a Fallist, stated that Fallism was about 'being part of a community of young people'. Black radical feminist, Wanelisa Xaba (2017, 98), refers to 'Fallism as an ideology' in her writing.

During my interview with student activist Simon Rakei (Personal communication, 12 July 2017), he indicated, 'I think Fallism is a real thing as an ideological, theoretical construct to try and understand the world.' For Rakei, Fallism is 'disruptive in nature ... it was a really powerful tactic'. He suggested that the creativity of the #RMF protests disrupted spaces that he asserted were 'abnormal' spaces. 'We are taught to be normal in an abnormal space', according to Rakei. This suggests that in addition to being interpreted as an ideological, philosophical or theoretical construct, Fallism also embodies a physical dimension; this physicality requires radical, performative action that 'abnormalises' a space through disruption.

Piven (2006, 23) describes disruption as a 'power strategy that rests on withdrawing cooperation in social relations'. This form of disruption offers the voiceless an opportunity to express their demands but does not necessarily translate into a shift in power. For the social movement to gain momentum and to sustain its collective action, McAdam et al. (1996, 3) argue that a more formal organisational structure is required that is dependent on various factors including 'disruptive tactics'. These tactics operate outside 'proper channels' and include occupying spaces and disrupting public order. Tarrow (1994) adopts a similar position finding that disruption or the threat of disruption is what makes social movements effective.

At the same time, Fallism is not only about disruption. By employing public pedagogy as a theoretical framework to analyse this idea, Fallism appears to take on the characteristics of public intellectualism and performative social activism, suggesting that student protestors are 'public pedagogues' (Burdick et al., 2014) 'who create a social space within which they engage the larger society in learning about equity, accountability, and democracy' (Sandlin et al., 2011, 358).

Patricia Bevie, the chairperson of the workers' union, NEHAWU, indicated that she joined the student discussions every evening after work:

> It was a developing process and a growing process for me like you won't believe it. I tell you, I used to sit open mouth listening to these students. They created this boldness within me ... They were the intellectuals, they never made you feel less than them. It was just, it was just amazing ... I learnt such a lot. I'm 52 years old. I have never heard any of these things in my life ... (Personal communication with Patricia Bevie, 26 July 2017).

The kind of public pedagogy that the #RMF movement adopted occurred within, but simultaneously outside, the university's designated learning spaces. In other words, while disruptive moments occur within the precinct of the university, which is a traditional learning space, it also occurs outside the classroom in administrative buildings, lobbies of departments and in the streets that run between the university buildings. The public pedagogy of the movement challenges existing designated learning spaces, thereby inverting the architecture of the university. Fallism appears to exist in the in-between spaces of the university – the cracks – where ideas developed by the margins conveyed through public pedagogy serve to widen the cracks.

Fallism and the Question of the Human/Non-Human

During my interview with #RMF activist, Masixole Mlandu, he asserted that 'in South Africa, the problem is whiteness ... anything that is not white is expelled from the category of being human ...' While most constructions of Fallism have thus far centred on its epistemological and pedagogical dimensions, Mlandu also introduced a dimension to Fallism that raises questions about what/who constitutes the human. But Mignolo and Walsh (2018, 153) argue that '[t]he question is not "what is human and humanity" but rather who defined themselves as humans ...'

The construction of the human, and who gets to define who is human, is further complicated by #RMF activists such as Wandile Kasibe (Personal communication, 28 June 2017), who stated that:

> Fallism cannot be understood outside of the framework of the land. Fallism then becomes a much bigger process whereby we claim our humanity; at the

same time that humanity cannot be delinked from land. It is a humanity that is attached, that is basically connected to the ground, to the land that was taken from black people. Even if we claim free education, it is free education that is part of the land. It is free education that is meant to produce people to think creatively about how they will use the land. So the land then becomes an integral part of the Fallist movement. It becomes the national question for us.

Kasibe connects the epistemological dimensions of Fallism that centre on disrupting the university as the dominant curator of knowledge, with a Fallist construction of humanity that confronts the human/non-human binary and that is deeply rooted in the land. The connection between land and humanness is also reflected in Fanon's (1963, 43) writing: 'For a colonized people, the most essential value, because the most concrete, is first and foremost the land: the land which will bring them bread and, above all, dignity.'

The connection between humanness and the land is further explored in Lewis Gordon's (2015) analysis of Franz Fanon's *Les Damnés de la terre* (1961), popularly known as The Wretched of the Earth. Gordon (2015) argues that the title of Fanon's work should be read as, The Damned of the Earth. During an interview, Lewis explained how he arrived at this interpretation by considering the etymology of 'human'. Gordon (2015) argues that the word 'human' derives from the Latin word 'homo', which in turn, stems from the word 'humus', meaning 'dirt' or 'clay'. Similarly, the word 'damned' is associated with being pushed back into the earth. At an existential level, Gordon argues that the human being emerges from the earth, 'a creature with feet on the ground while reaching for the skies' (cited in Aksan, 2018).

Mbembe (2015) critiques #RMF's employment of decolonisation as a conceptual framework, arguing that student activists have used it to describe 'a psychic state more than a political project in the strict sense of the term'. He asserts that '[i]f we cannot find a proper name for what we are actually facing, then rather than simply borrowing one from a different time, we should keep searching' (2015). Acknowledging Mbembe's (2015) critique, I suggest that Fallism could potentially constitute the 'proper name' that reflects what #RMF activists were attempting to achieve in challenging the white-liberal-university.

Fallism as a Theory for Decolonising the University

Achille Mbembe would most likely argue against the development of Fallism as a decolonial theory. At the launch of his book, *A Critique of*

Black Reason, which I attended in Cape Town, he responded to a question about the appropriation of the concept of coloniality in relation to the #RMF student movement as follows:

> It's too easy to pick up a little bit of intersectionality here, a little bit of black feminism there, a little bit of queer theory ... and make a potpourri of things ... it doesn't make intellectual coherence ... I am for the articulation from this part of our world of ideas, and concepts and theories that speak beyond our own boundaries, that can travel, make sense in America, in Europe, in Asia and elsewhere. We haven't been able to do that. Because to some extent we are too self-centred, we are too isolationist, we are not even linking with our own continent. We still hear people in South Africa saying 'we are going to Africa'.

Mbembe's critique of the #RMF movement's decolonial framework as a self-centred, South African potpourri of ideas that cannot travel to other parts of the world, merits further consideration. The framework is indeed a combination of Pan-Africanism, Black Consciousness and Black radical feminism; a compilation of old ideas. Furthermore, given the #RMF students' own scepticism about how these old ideas translate into the concept of Fallism, as well as the uncertainty about what Fallism actually constitutes, it may seem futile to want to develop Fallism into a decolonial framework.

However, I think that Fallism could nevertheless be constituted as an emergent decolonial theory comprised of three dimensions: first, Fallism emerges from the disruption of dominant constructions of what constitutes knowledge and how knowledge is developed (epistemic disobedience). For #RMF, this disruption included demands to replace the Eurocentric university curriculum with one that was more African centred. Second, Fallism exposes the paradoxical nature of the university as both a space for black people to think (Black liberation), and a space that simultaneously dehumanises black people (Black pain). This paradox derives from the university's position as the authorised centre of knowledge production and its engagement in epistemic coloniality. Third, Fallism facilitates the intersections between creative forms of activism and learning (public pedagogy). For #RMF, this dimension of Fallism involved reclaiming the non-academic, in-between spaces of the university and turning them into disruptive pedagogical spaces.

My attempt at developing Fallism into an emergent theory should be interpreted as advancing the #RMF's decolonial cause which is deeply connected to the body-politics of knowledge and takes the form of black pain. Consequently, Fallism, as a theory, is a lens through which the paradoxical positioning of the university as simultaneously empowering and dehumanising for black people, can be better understood. It is therefore not only a collective noun to describe the student movements, but a decolonial option that emerges from the university's margins to crack the epistemic architecture of the university's epicentre. However, Fallism moves beyond the limits of epistemic disobedience and delinking directed outward towards the university, to also disrupt the internal patriarchal frameworks that shape the ideological character of the movement itself.

In addition to its disruptive epistemic and pedagogical dimensions that challenge the coloniality of knowledge, Fallism is also concerned with the continuous construction and reconstruction of what constitutes the human (coloniality of Being). This recognition of humanness, as an ongoing process of becoming, is rooted in the idea of black pain reflected in the #RMF's mission statement. Consequently, Fallism as a decolonial theory deliberately conspires towards the fall of the coloniality of knowledge and the coloniality of Being. In the context of the #RMF movement, Mbembe (2015) asks:

> If everything 'must fall', then what exactly must stand in its place? Unless we extend our imagination and properly articulate what 'must stand' in lieu of what will have been overthrown, we might end up privileging the politics of ruins over a genuine politics of creative emancipation. To distribute property and the wealth of the nation in a different way, we will need to massively reinvest in various generic human potentialities.

Mignolo (2011) however takes a different approach from Mbembe (2015); while Mbembe (2015) is concerned about 'privileging the politics of ruins', Mignolo (2011, 11) recognises that decolonial options are 'built on the ruins of imperial knowledge'. For Mignolo and Walsh (2018, 83), '[h]ow do we, and can we, move within the cracks, open cracks, and extend the fissures?' As a decolonial theory, Fallism creates the space for alternative ideas to emerge through cracks in the wall of coloniality, eventually leading to its fall. Fallism, however, is not only about the fall of colonial knowledge; it also connects those who are engaged in developing decolonial options, thereby facilitating the creation of new structures and building coalitions within and between people and institutions.

Fallism as a Theory from the South

Fallism, as a theory, can also be distinguished from epistemic disobedience and delinking because of its ability to travel. Its formation as a theory that emanated in Cape Town and was subsequently exported to Oxford, warrants further attention. When I asked #RMF Oxford activist, Sizwe Mpofu-Walsh, whether he identified with the concept of Fallism, he responded:

> I'm not sure. It seems that when Fallism as an ideology emerged, the ideology became a little bit more rigidified and a little less welcoming of outside views and a politics of hyper-reflexivity emerged . . . at some point, the politics of reflexivity becomes so inward that you lose sight of the social circumstances that you're trying to overcome. So in that sense I am some-what reluctant to describe to myself as a Fallist. On the other hand, I'm very happy to embrace the politics of decolonial practice as practiced by #RMF and say that I'm a Fallist and say that I took a Fallist debate into Oxford. But I don't sort of go around espousing Fallist ideology.

Mpofu-Walsh's position on Fallism can be contrasted with that of #RMF Oxford activist, Ntokozo Qwabe, who stated that,

> I do identify as a Fallist. And really, being a Fallist is identifying with the ideology of Fallism, which of course has its pillars. Being a person who identified with Black Consciousness, with Pan-Africanism and Black fem-inism and who identifies with the decolonial cause, or with the decolonial struggle so to say . . . in a world that remains infested by coloniality (Personal communication with Ntokozo Qwabe, 1 August 2017).

While these views are not diametrically opposed, they offer two distinct approaches to the concept of Fallism within the #RMF Oxford movement. Mpofu-Walsh (Personal communication, 31 July 2017) is only willing to acknowledge that he 'took a Fallist debate into Oxford' whereas Qwabe strongly identifies with Fallism. Based on their responses, Fallism as a concept appears to have at least resonated with #RMF Oxford activists and was taken up in varying degrees by individual students rather than by the #RMF Oxford movement. However, student activists with no ties to South Africa did not appear to expressly adopt the idea of Fallism. For Brian Kwoba, 'identifying as a Fallist wasn't something that I saw' within the #RMF Oxford movement. Kwoba went on to state that, 'Fallism as like a more general category . . . I don't think that really developed in the UK in the way that it did in South Africa. So I would be happy and honored to call myself a Fallist . . . because I'm for the things that people identified as Fallists are for' (Personal communication with Brian Kwoba, 21 September 2017).

The lack of consistency among #RMF Oxford activists about the adop-tion of Fallism as a concept in their movement makes it difficult to conclude that Fallism was an idea exported from Cape Town to Oxford.

At best, elements of Fallism including the language of Fallism may have been taken up by individual #RMF Oxford activists, but not by the movement as a collective. However, if Fallism is understood as a theory that unveils the paradoxical nature of the university as simultaneously empowering and dehumanising for black bodies, could #RMF Oxford's aims not be considered as reflective of Fallism? For students such as Qwabe (Personal communication, 1 August 2017) who self-identified as a Fallist,

> Black pain is the foundational basis of Fallism . . . Being a Fallist does not mean going to a protest. It means identifying with the ideologies of the Fallist movement and embodying that in your work and your daily life.

Qwabe's strong affinity with Fallism may have to do with the fact that he was actively involved in both the Oxford and Cape Town movements unlike his fellow #RMF Oxford activists. This raises some difficulty when trying to delineate between the two movements. At the same time, Qwabe's active involvement in both the Cape Town and Oxford movements suggests that he has important comparative insights that other activists may not have had the opportunity to develop.

I therefore argue that the #RMF movement in Oxford exhibited some elements of Fallism suggesting that it could constitute what Comaroff and Comaroff (2012) refer to as a theory from the South. My assertion is based on the fact that both #RMF movements sought to deliberately disrupt the geographies of knowledge by contesting 'core and periphery, relocating Southward . . .' (#RMF, 7). In this way, #RMF Cape Town's engagement with, and contestation of the effects of coloniality, their decoding of these effects theoretically, and their innovative political responses which were then exported to the global North, reflects the Comaroffs' theory. Consequently, #RMF's formation at Oxford could support key elements of the Comaroffs' thesis, including the idea that the South is anticipating and driving some of the political, economic, and cultural modalities of the Euro-American future.

During my conversation with Dr. Zethu Matebeni (Personal communication, 21 July 2017) at UCT, she indicated that students involved in #RMF UCT failed to fully appreciate the international dimensions of their movement: 'I was teaching a course now at Yale on "Gender and Sexuality and Decolonising South African Universities" . . . What was interesting for me was that [the students at Yale] were looking for leadership from South Africa. And I don't think South African students realised that.' After arranging a Skype conversation with activists from the Trans Collective who formed part of the #RMF UCT movement, Dr. Matebeni found that the students in her class at Yale 'got energy and power from what was happening here . . . so they used #RhodesMustFall as a thing for them to mobilise and to say the things that they needed to say . . . all they wanted to hear about was #RhodesMustFall'.

According to Matebeni (Personal communication, 21 July 2017), many Yale students 'were really considering the idea of Fallism. A lot of them were writing their thesis on Fallism and wanted to learn more about this new way of understanding who they are'. While her students at Yale were also critical of certain elements of the #RMF movement, she recognised that #RMF activists at UCT 'gave people a language'. Reflecting on the global impact of the #RMF UCT movement, Matebeni concluded our interview stating that '[m]aybe one day they will realise that they really did change the world. And it was a powerful thing to be part of and to experience'.

Conclusion

My analysis builds on scholarship that recognises the centrality of the university as knowledge producer, but does not always fully comprehend the oppressive dimensions of the university's epistemic architecture. I argue that black students at UCT, with the support of workers and faculty, played a fundamental role in unearthing and articulating the paradoxical role of the university as a simultaneously empowering (Black liberation) and dehumanising (Black pain) space for those on the margins of the university.

Since the university's engagement in epistemic coloniality forms the basis for its paradoxical construction, the #RMF movement engaged in a process of epistemic disobedience, creating a decolonial framework centred on Black Consciousness, Black radical feminism and Pan-Africanism. This framework inspired a new grammar of Fallism, creating a paradigm shift from the dominant Eurocentric model of knowledge production, to one centred on decoloniality and disruption. Calling for the fall of the white-liberal-university using symbols such as the Rhodes statue, student activists employed disruptive tactics to create public awareness of their demands, engaging in a form of public pedagogy.

Through a combination of epistemic disobedience and public pedagogy, I argue that the #RMF movement was not only engaged in demanding the fall of the university, but also in generating the emergent theory of Fallism. The multiple understandings of Fallism and what it meant to be a Fallist speak to its nascent disposition as a concept emerging from protest and disobedience. What I try to do in this chapter is experiment with developing Fallism into an emergent decolonial theory informed by the multiple and divergent perspectives extracted from students involved in the #RMF movements at UCT and Oxford. I argue that Fallism can be constituted as a decolonial theory to challenge the paradoxical nature of the university as a space that simultaneously empowers and dehumanises marginalised bodies.

REFERENCES

Biko, S. (1978). *I Write What I Like*. Chicago: University of Chicago Press.

Biko, S. (2017). *I Write What I Like*. Cape Town: Pan Macmillan South Africa.

Bofelo, Mphutlane wa. (2017). Fallism and the dialectics of spontaneity and organization disrupting tradition to reconstruct tradition. *Joburg Post* 4 August 2017. www.joburgpost.co.za/2017/08/04/fallism-dialectics-spontaneity-organisationdisrupting-tradition-reconstruct-tradition/

Burdick, J., Sandlin, J., & O'Malley, M. (2014). *Problematizing Public Pedagogy*. Routledge: New York.

Chikane, Rekgotsofetse. (2018). *Breaking a Rainbow, Building a Nation: The Politics Behind #MustFall Movements* (Kindle Edition). Johannesburg: Picador Africa.

Comaroff, J., & Comaroff, J. (2011). *Theory from the South: Or, How Euro-America Is Evolving toward Africa*. New York: Paradigm.

Crenshaw, K. (1991). Mapping the Margins: Intersectionality, Identity Politics, and Violence against Women of Color. *Stanford Law Review, 43*(6), 1241–1299.

Davis, Rebecca. (2013). The man behind Cape Town's poo protests: But who does Andile Lili represent? *The Daily Maverick* (4 December 2013).

Fanon, Frantz. (2004). *The Wretched of the Earth*. Translated by Richard Philcox. New York: Grove.

Gebrial, Dalia. (2018). Rhodes Must Fall: Oxford and Movements for Change. In Gurminder K. Bhambra, Dalia Gebrial, & Kerem Nişancıoğlu (eds.), *Decolonising the University* (pp. 19–36). London: Pluto Press.

Gibson, Nigel C. (2016). The Specter of Fanon: The Student Movements and the Rationality of Revolt in South Africa. *Social Identities 23*(1), 1–21.

Godsell, Gillian & Chikane, Rekgotsofetse. (2016). The Roots of the Revolution. In Susan Booysen (ed.) *Fees Must Fall* (pp. 54–73). Johannesburg: Wits University Press.

Gordon, L. R. (2015). *What Fanon Said: A Philosophical Introduction to His Life and Thought*. New York: Fordham University Press.

Healy-Clancy, Meghan. (2016). The Everyday Politics of Being a Student in South Africa. *African Studies Association Annual Meeting Paper*. https://papers.ssrn.com/sol3/papers.cfm?abstract_id=2751105

Hodes, Rebecca. (2015). How Rhodes Must Fall Squandered Public Sympathy. The Daily Maverick (20 August 2015).

Infecting the City (n.d.). Home. www.africacentre.net/infecting-the-city/ 5 May 2019.

Jansen, J. (2017). *As by Fire: The End of the South African University*. Tafelberg: Cape Town.

Johannesburg Workshop in Theory and Criticism (2015). *The Johannesburg Salon, Volume 9.* www.jwtc.org.za/resources/docs/salon-volume-9/FINAL_FINAL_Vol9_Book.pdf. Retrieved 5 May 2019.

Kamanzi, Brian. (2016). ShackvilleTRC: An opportunity to turn the page. *The Daily Maverick* 8 June 2016. www.dailymaverick.co.za/opinionista/2016-06-08-shackvilletrc-anopportunity-to-turn-the-page/#.WuiYpdMvyT8

Luescher, T. M. (2016). Student Representation in a Context of Democratisation and Massification in Africa: Analytical Approaches, Theoretical Perspectives and #RhodesMustFall. In T. M. Luescher, M. Klemenčič, & J. Otieno Jowi (eds.), *Student Politics in Africa: Representation and Activism* (pp. 27–60). Cape Town: African Minds.

Mama, A. (2017). The Power of Feminist Pan-African Intellect. *Feminist Africa, 22*, 1–15.

Mamdani, M. (2016). Between the Public Intellectual and the Scholar: Decolonization and Some Post-independence Initiatives in African Higher Education. *Inter-Asia Cultural Studies, 17*(1), 68–83.

Mbembe, A. (2001). *On the Postcolony*. Berkeley: University of California Press.

Mbembe, A. (2016). Decolonizing the University: New Directions. *Arts & Humanities in Higher Education, 15*(1), 29–45.

Mbembe, A. (n.d.). *Decolonizing Knowledge and the Question of the Archive*. Africa Is a Country. https://africaisacountry.atavist.com/decolonizing-knowledge-and-the-question-of-the-archive. Retrieved 5 May 2019.

McAdam, Doug, McCarthy, John D., & Zald, Mayer N. (1996). *Comparative Perspectives on Social Movements: Political Opportunities, Mobilizing Structures, and Cultural Framings*. Cambridge: Cambridge University Press.

Mignolo, W. D. (2009). Epistemic Disobedience, Independent Thought and De-Colonial Freedom. *Theory, Culture & Society, 27*(7–8), 1–23.

Mignolo, W. D. (2011). Epistemic Disobedience and the Decolonial Option: A Manifesto. *Transmodernity, 1*(2), 44–66.

Mignolo, W. D. (2011). *The Darker Side of Western Modernity: Global Futures, Decolonial Options*. Durham: Duke University Press.

Mignolo, W. D. (2013). Geopolitics of Sensing and Knowing: On (De)coloniality, Border Thinking, and Epistemic Disobedience. *Confero, 1*(1), 129–150.

Mignolo, W. D., & Walsh, C. E. (2018). *On Decoloniality: Concepts, Analytics, Praxis*. Durham: Duke University Press.

Mpofu-Walsh, S. (2016). The Game's the Same: 'MustFall' Moves to Euro-America. In S. Booysen (ed.), *Fees Must Fall: Student Revolt, Decolonization and Governance in South Africa* (pp. 74–86). Johannesburg: Wits University Press.

Newsinger, John. (2016). Why Rhodes Must Fall. *Race & Class*, *58*(2), 70–78.

Ngcaweni, Wandile. (2016). Revisiting the ABCs of the Decolonial Paradigm of Fallism. *The Daily Vox* 30 September 2016. www.thedailyvox.co.za/wandile-ngcawenirevisiting-abcs-decolonial-paradigm-fallism/

Nyamnjoh, F. B. (2016). *#RhodesMustFall: Nibbling at Resilient Colonialism in South Africa*. Mankon: Langaa Research and Publishing.

Piven, Frances F. (2006). *Challenging Authority*. Lanham: Rowman and Littlefield Publishers.

RMF Oxford (2015). *RMF Oxford Press Release: Oxford Students Call for Cecil John Rhodes Statue to Fall*. RMF Oxford, 4 November 2015. https://rmfoxford.files.wordpress.com/2015/12/041115rmfpressrelease1.pdf. Retrieved 5 May 2019.

RMF Oxford (2018). *Rhodes Must Fall: The Struggle to Decolonise the Racist Heart of Empire*. London: Zed Books.

Sandlin, J., O'Malley, M., & Burdick, J. (2011). Mapping the Complexity of Public Pedagogy Scholarship: 1894–2010. *Review of Educational Research*, *81*(3), 338–375.

Tarrow, S. (1994). *Power in Movement*. Cambridge: Cambridge University Press.

Xaba, W. (2017). Challenging Fanon: A Black Radical Feminist Perspective on Violence and the Fees Must Fall Movement. *Agenda*, *31*(3–4), 96–104.

CHAPTER 16

Family Sacrifice, Faltering Systems
The Case of First-Generation College Students in Rajasthan

Orla Kelly, Jacqueline Bhabha and Aditi Krishna

Even though the financial condition of our family is not good, my parents have always motivated us to study well, so that we children do not have to work as labourers. My mother is very supportive of my studies. She is often pressurised by our relatives for my marriage and told that if you educate her too much you will not be able to find a match for her. She always tells me – do not bother about the comments made by the relatives and neighbors – just concentrate on your studies. – Meera, 19

Introduction

India has made significant strides in enabling access to primary education for its vast population since the legacy of widespread illiteracy left by the British. In recent decades, considerable attention has also been paid to expanding the scope of secondary educational opportunities for previously excluded communities. These phenomena, expanded primary and secondary educational engagement, have both attracted scholarly attention. As a the result a detailed picture now exists regarding the rapidly changing scope, variation, and distribution of school enrolment and its impact across India. Much less scholarly attention has been paid to tertiary education. In part, this reflects a widespread view that, with the school improvement agenda still incomplete, the focus of educational interventions and assessments should not be deflected to less urgent priorities. However, in a rapidly changing society, with social and economic advancement increasingly dependent on active participation in a knowledge and technology economy, tertiary education is a critical instrument of social inclusion and inequality reduction. Where caste, class, religious, gender, and other barriers to social mobility persist, education across the spectrum has a vital role to play in redrawing boundaries and reversing hierarchies.

Glass ceilings of privilege and power are more likely to be effectively impacted by those with than without a College degree. This stance has informed a body of work we have undertaken together with Indian partners over the past few years.

In this chapter we show how poor young Indian women's educational participation is shaped by a multiplicity of interconnected factors across various domains: girls' own preferences and choices, as well as those of their parents, siblings and extended family; the nature of schools; the composition and perspective of communities; and a range of macro-level factors related to the state in which students reside. Our chapter highlights the power and limits of familial, particularly parental, support in promoting educational outcomes for an under-represented group. We also address the high personal and familial costs of College participation, due to weak institutional and community support. Specifically, We summarize the findings of a mixed methods study, which involved more than 700 young women from economically, educationally, and socially marginalised backgrounds in the north-west Indian state of Rajasthan. Two-thirds of the participants were enrolled in tertiary education at the time of the study. We compare their experiences to a group of young women, matched in age, location and parental education level, who dropped out at the secondary school level, to highlight some of the familial dynamics and broader social processes that may have allowed the enrolled young women to advance educationally despite considerable odds. By focusing on the uncommon circumstances of this successful minority rather than the barriers to educational progression, this project employs a 'positive deviance' approach. We find several significant trends within the 'College' compared to the 'non-College' group. Specifically, in socially conservative Rajasthan, families have protected and promoted self-confidence and educational aspiration among adolescent girls, through financial and moral support, and a loosening of gendered expectations regarding marriage and household work. Together, this set of inputs has supplemented, and in many cases compensated for, weak societal and institutional support.

Our data adds to the large body of research which suggests that young women's participation in education cannot be encouraged by financial incentives alone. Normative change and in particular, attitudes within a broad familial and societal context are crucial variables that public policy must address. More specifically, our findings support the vast body of interdisciplinary work, which shows that inclusive education policy must move well beyond targeting access through enhanced infrastructure, geographic proximity, or financial aid, important though these inputs are.

Sustained and widespread educational participation of women from marginalised communities requires mechanisms to navigate and neutralise inhibitive social norms such as early marriage and burdensome household responsibilities. Further, if first-generation learners are to convert their educational training into upward social mobility, through enhanced career prospects, the absence of formalised academic and career guidance support must be addressed.

Historical and Regional Context

In the decades since independence, the government of India has made remarkable strides in increasing average per capita years of education (UNESCO, 2015). It has built a large-scale national education system, developing an infrastructure that was largely absent when the country emerged from colonial rule.

However, access to education has been uneven and mostly reflective of broader entrenched social hierarchies. The causes of disparities in long-term educational achievement in India are well researched and multifactorial and vary considerably across the vast and heterogeneous nation. However, some common trends have been identified at the macro level. Urban location strongly favours educational achievement; poverty plays a defining role in determining access; economic deprivations tend to be closely related to the legacies of gender, caste, and religious discrimination (Government of India, 2012; Siddhu, 2011). A growing proportion of Indian school children attend private institutions; those who rely on government institutions are typically from the most marginalised communities, particularly girls. Public schools are the most overburdened and underfunded, and some are experiencing a crisis in learning outcomes (ASER, 2014). Additional hurdles result from the endemic discrimination related to gender, caste, and income, also woven into the school experience in a variety of ways. Notably, researchers in the field have identified stereotyping in school materials, exposure to gender-based violence, teacher biases, and gender-biased subject streaming (Plan, 2008; Rampal, 2007; Unterhalter, 2005). In some areas, restrictive gender norms compound deeply engrained social hierarchies and increase the opportunity costs of school participation for girls. These norms include early marriage (Moore, 2009), familial insistence on limited mobility within the public domain and onerous domestic responsibilities (Kelly & Bhabha, 2014), low levels of parental, particularly maternal, education (Azam & Kingdon, 2013; Woodhead, Frost, & James, 2013) and lack of support for girls' education because of lower perceived returns from educating girls (Probe, 1999).

Despite these challenges, national data show that an increasing number of children from economically and socially disadvantaged backgrounds are accessing the education system every year. The Indian government has succeeded in raising educational attainment rates through the national policy to universalise primary education – Sarva Shiksha Abhiyan (SSA) – first codified in 2009.[1] Implementing a central policy goal, the government has achieved universal enrolment and gender parity at the primary level. At the secondary level, too, year-on-year increases in enrolment are being achieved with more planned for the future: the government aims to attain a universal enrolment by 2020 (Government of India (GOI), 2014). Similarly, tertiary level enrolment was at 24 per cent in 2013, up from 10 per cent in 2000 (World Bank).

This educational progress is the outcome of several interrelated factors. The supply of education is increasing through government and private investment. The country has experienced significant economic growth accompanied by a lowering in fertility rates over the last two decades, trends that have enabled more families to afford education for all their children (Kingdon, 2007). Over this period there has also been a sizeable increase in demand for girls' education (Khera et al., 2011; Probe Team, 1999) due to decreases in absolute poverty, greater access to educational institutions (Tiwari & Ghadially, 2009) and campaigns for girls' education led by both government and civil society (GOI, 2015).[2]

Also, state and district level programmes such as the supply of bicycles (Burde & Linden, 2013), conditional cash transfers (Kremer et al., 2009), explicit challenges to biased gender attitudes (Beaman et al., 2012) and information on access to real opportunities for return on educational investment through the availability of 'pink collar' jobs (Jensen, 2010) have been found to have a significant effect.

Rajasthan, where this research took place, is the largest state in India, with a population size similar to Thailand and a history of

---

[1] The government's flagship programme for the achievement of Universalization of Elementary Education began in 2001. Thanks to the programme, the country has achieved near universal enrolment at the lower primary level. Critical elements of the programme have been massive infrastructural development, teacher training and community mobilisation. In 2009, the programme was codified by the 86th amendment to the Constitution of India which made free and compulsory education a fundamental right for all children aged 6–14 years.

[2] Issues of education quality continue to be debated but are beyond the scope of this chapter.

Table 16.1 *Gross enrolment ratio in Rajasthan*

	Lower primary I–V (6–11 yrs)		Upper primary VI–VIII (11–14 yrs)		Secondary IX–X (14–16 yrs)		Upper secondary XI–XII (16–18 yrs)	
	Boys	Girls	Boys	Girls	Boys	Girls	Boys	Girls
2004–2005	125	116	85	55	58	28	29	14
2010–2011	110	110	91	73	72	50	50	31

Source: Educational Statistics at a Glance, Government of India Ministry of Human Resource Development Bureau of Planning, Monitoring & Statistics, New Delhi, 2012 Select Education Statistics 2004–2005, Ministry of Human Resource Development, New Delhi 2007

entrenched gender discrimination as evidenced by a range of social indicators.[3] Particularly relevant to the present research is the comparative data on literacy: in 2011, Rajasthan recorded a female literacy rate of just 52 per cent as opposed to a 79 per cent rate for males (GOI, 2011). It is noteworthy, therefore, that, despite this challenging context, the state has followed the national trend of a significant reduction in gender inequality over the last decade. In the educational context, progress in gender equity is being made at all levels, as Table 16.1 shows. Between 2004 and 2010, the gross enrolment ratio (GER) for girls at the upper primary level increased from 55 to 73 per cent. At the lower secondary level enrolment rates for girls almost doubled with an increase from 28 to 50 per cent.

As a result of these significant shifts in educational attainment at the primary and secondary levels, a stream of students, many of them first-generation learners, are entering into the tertiary education system. As Table 16.2 illustrates, in Rajasthan in 2015–2016 the GER was 22.2 and 18.5 per cent for males and females, respectively. For scheduled castes (SCs), the most recent tertiary level enrolment rate was 16.7 per cent for males and 13.4 per cent females. Similarly, among the scheduled tribe (ST) group, the rate was 16.9 versus 13.5 respectively (Government of India (GOI), 2016).

---

[3] Rajasthan has the fourth lowest child sex ratio at birth in India, with 870 girls born to 1,000 boys (GOI, 2011). High levels of under-five mortality persist among girls: while both under-five mortality and infant mortality rates in Rajasthan have declined, the rate of decline among girls is lower with 79 deaths per 1,000 live births compared with 60 deaths for males. This disparity is indicative of the continuing neglect of girls during infancy and early childhood.

Table 16.2 *Gross enrolment rate in tertiary education, by gender and social group*

Year	State	All			Scheduled caste			Scheduled tribe		
		Both	Male	Female	Both	Male	Female	Both	Male	Female
2015–16	All India	24.5	25.4	23.5	19.9	20.8	19.0	14.2	15.6	12.9
	Rajasthan	20.2	21.8	18.5	15.2	16.7	13.4	15.2	16.9	13.5
2010–11	All India	19.4	20.8	17.9	13.5	14.6	12.3	11.2	12.9	9.5
	Rajasthan	18.2	20.9	15.2	11.2	13.5	8.5	13.0	15.7	10.3

Data Source: All India Survey on Higher Education (2015–2016)

The improved equity in enrolment rates at the tertiary level is partly due to the progressive impact of a caste-based educational reservation system that retains 5 per cent of seats in central government-funded institutions for SCs, 6 per cent for STs and 25 per cent for other backward classes (OBCs). Further, one-third of seats within each caste group, including the general category, are reserved for women.

As a result of these significant shifts in educational attainment over a short period, millions of families have children entering primary, secondary and even tertiary education for the first time. Little is known about the household dynamics that have contributed to this shift, a lacuna we hope to address in this chapter.

Methodology

The data presented in this chapter are part of a multi-state project. The project was designed to explore how female College students from socially and economically marginalised, low-literacy families across India managed to progress to a tertiary level of education, successfully overcoming significant economic, social, infrastructural and cultural barriers to girls' higher education. In our study, the 'College' group is defined as young women, enrolled in their second year of an undergraduate degree at a government College, whose parents have completed at most a primary school education. By focusing on the successes of this atypical minority, rather than on the barriers to educational progression, a 'positive deviance' approach, we hoped to distil lessons that might eventually contribute to strategies for magnifying the educational success we observed (Marsh et al., 2004).

Data Collection

Participants were drawn from government Colleges in five districts in different administrative zones. In partnership with our colleagues at the Institute of Development Studies, Jaipur, we selected the districts based on their socio-economic diversity. In each district, we gathered lists of government Colleges with female enrolment from the state education department. We used proportionate random sampling based on female tertiary enrolment rates to select Colleges and their respective participant quotas. With state government support for the project, one staff member in each College coordinated with the research team to schedule data collection. The field research team were all young women from Jaipur, Rajasthan's state capital, relatively close in age to the research participants, and many of them were also first-generation learners.

At each of the selected Colleges, all-female second-year students were convened and asked to complete a short eligibility questionnaire to ascertain their parents' education level. Results from this initial screening questionnaire were tabulated, and a list of eligible students compiled – namely, students neither of whose parents had completed more than a primary school education. If more than the required quota of participants in a particular College met the study selection criteria, a lottery system was used to randomly select participants for inclusion in the full study. In total, 739 students completed the initial eligibility questionnaire across the 13 government Colleges studied; among these, 430 of those identified as eligible for participation were invited to complete the full study questionnaire, with 413 agreeing to participate.

Non-College Comparison Group. An amended version of the survey was also administered to a comparison group of young 'non-College' women, who were matched with the College group on age, home location, and parental education level. To find the comparison group participants, the research team asked the College administration and study participants for details of the participants' former secondary institutions. The research team approached these feeder secondary schools in each respective district. The schools provided lists of students who had enrolled in Standard VIII or IX at the same time as the College group but had not progressed beyond their Standard X (lower secondary school graduation) exams. Among this group, the research team randomly selected 280 households to visit; 223 young women in these households were available and interested in participating in the study. Only girls who were still living in their natal family homes were included in the study.

A subgroup of 34 members of the College group took part in a qualitative 'empowerment' workshop, hosted by the Institute of Development Studies in Jaipur. The qualitative tools used for this workshop were developed by the Krantijyoti Savitribai Phule Women's Studies Centre, University of Pune in the State of Maharashtra, under the direction of Dr Sharmila Rege, our Indian research partner in an earlier phase of this project. The qualitative narratives generated in this empowerment workshop, and from which narrative quotes in this report are drawn, supplemented the study's quantitative findings. A subset of students who participated in the quantitative research were invited to participate in an empowerment workshop. The workshop asked participants to create visual and written journeys of their lives, through the use of games, facilitated group discussions, poster making and essay, letter and diary writing. Participants also wrote narratives in response to open-ended questions.

Findings

Demographic Profile: As illustrated in Table 16.3, the College group is slightly older than the non-College group. Slightly more members of the College group are single. There are significant differences in the caste membership of the two groups. More non-College than College group members belong to general castes; conversely more College group members belong to OBC and ST/SC castes.

According to the 2011 national census, the religious profile of the population in Rajasthan is 89 per cent Hindu and 8.5 per cent Muslim.

Table 16.3 *Participant profiles*

College Group (*n* = 413)								
Average Age	Religion %		Caste %		Marital Status %		Household Income (INR) %	
18.8	Hindu	97	General	17	Single	78	<50,000	76
	Other	2	ST/SC	38	Engaged	13	51–100,000	14
							100,000+	
	Muslim	1	OBC	45	Married	9		10
Non-College Group (*n* = 223)								
17.9	Hindu	78	General	36	Single	75	<50,000	60
	Muslim	18	ST/SC	31	Engaged	9	51–100,000	27
							100,000+	
	Other	4	OBC	33	Married	16		3

Muslims are therefore under-represented within the College population (<1 per cent) and over-represented among the non-College group (18 per cent), as shown in Table 16.3. The lower representation of young Muslim women among the College population reflects a lower rate of educational attainment among Muslim girls in the state as whole. This finding is consistent with other research on the challenges faced by this religious minority (Azam & Bhatt, 2015) and corresponds to a larger state-wide trend of exclusion of Muslim girls at higher levels of education (GOI, 2013).

Parental Education: An inclusion criterion for the study was that participants' parents had completed no more than primary school education. For the College group, 71 per cent of their mothers and 23 per cent of their fathers had absolutely no formal education. An additional 16 per cent of mothers and 14 per cent of fathers had not completed the lower primary level. For these families, the daughter's enrolment in tertiary education represents a significant generational shift, a clear instance of contemporary Indian upward mobility. Even though the parental educational threshold required for all study participants was low, the non-College group's parents had even lower average levels of education than the College group's parents. This correlation confirms the well-established positive relationship between parental education level and increased child educational attainment, even at the very lowest levels of educational attainment.

Education levels were particularly low for mothers across the two groups. Rajasthan has the largest difference between male and female literacy rates in the country (GOI, 2011). It is therefore unsurprising that fathers' education levels are conspicuously higher than mothers' across both the College and non-College groups. Several of the College group's essays noted mothers' low levels of education and how the concomitant economic and social limitations were key motivating factors in maternal decisions to support their daughters' education.

> My mother had never got an opportunity to study, she was very supportive of my goals. My brother was not keen that I go to College, but my mother and sisters supported me and I got admission in College. (Nidhi, 19)

Given parental educational disadvantage, it is unsurprising that the majority of participants in both groups reported low household incomes (though we did not expect to find that more of the College than the non-College group reported family income in the lowest income category of less than 50,000 Rupees per annum). Table 16.3 records the fact that the majority of study participants in each group was living around or below the national poverty line. According to the National Planning Commission of India, an urban family surviving on less that 57,000 INR[4] per annum is living below the poverty line (GOI, 2011).

The qualitative narratives confirm that financial concerns loomed large for the College group. Even small costs associated with educational participation created significant challenges:

> The economic situation of the family was not good. When I had to be admitted to College, my father arranged for some money. Even the transport charge of Rs. 12 per trip to College was difficult to bear by [my] parents. (Jaya, 19)

This economic insecurity was often compounded by family adversity, such as death or serious illness in the family.

> Post the elementary level I had to struggle to continue my studies. Both my parents had no formal education and most people in the village used to discourage me. My father fell ill when I was in Class VIII, and since then there has been no source of regular income in the household. I was under a lot of pressure to drop out of school before completing Class X. I tried to convince my parents that I should be allowed to study further as I did not want to struggle like them for money. (Ritu, 20)

Another salient difference between groups was in parental employment. Fewer of the College group's mothers (91 per cent versus 72 per cent) worked outside the house. One might expect households with only one working parent to have lower household income, which is what our data suggest. However, in India, working mothers are most often observed in the poorest households (Neff, Sen, & Kling, 2012; Olsen & Mehta, 2006), which may suggest greater income insecurity among non-College households. Relatedly, nearly a third of College fathers were salaried employees whereas more than half of non-College fathers were employed as precarious casual labourers (p. value <.001), which may have led to more income insecurity among the non-College households. Another hypothesis is that having a mother at home may have eased the housework expectations directed at the College group, allowing them to focus on their studies. The College group on average had 0.87 fewer siblings than the non-College group, which may indicate greater availability of intra-household economic resources.

Apart from these demographic differences, other more subtle contrasts emerged between the College and non-College group. They concerned

---

[4] This is equivalent to less than $2 a day.

household norms regarding the conduct of family relationships as well as gender expectations relating to marriage and housework.

Support from the Social Network: We investigated the extent to which participants from each of the two groups felt supported by family, teachers and friends in relation to their educational goals. Respondents were asked to rate the level of support from their social network on a scale from one to five, with five being extremely supportive. The difference in reported levels of support between the two groups was striking, particularly at the family level. Paternal and sibling support were markedly higher among the College than the non-College group: 70 per cent of the former reported that their fathers had been extremely supportive of their educational goals, compared with only 16 per cent of the non-College group. Similar trends are evident among mothers and siblings. Strikingly, nearly four out of five of the non-College group reported that grandparents were extremely unsupportive of their educational goals. In the close-knit and traditional, extended family context of Rajasthan, resistance to long-term educational participation from grandparents may have played a role in stopping the girls' education. Grouping the results, we found that the College group scored far higher on a 'support for educational goals' scale with an average score of 27.64 out of a possible 35 as compared to the comparison group who scored 20.

High levels of family support for education correlated with increased pressure on limited household resources; 22 per cent of the College group reported that their parents had taken out loans to support their education during secondary school, though less than one in five reported that this created tension within the household. In comparison, none of the non-College group indicated that their parents had taken out loans to support their secondary school education. Relatedly, the College group was asked to rate on a scale of *1 to 3* about the top three factors they thought contributed to reaching tertiary education: 97 per cent rated parental support as the top factor. In the qualitative workshop, many of the College group stated that their parents placed great faith in educational attainment as a path for upward mobility:

> Even though the financial condition of our family is not good, my parents have always motivated us to study well so that the children do not have to work as laborers. My mother is very supportive of my studies. She is often pressurized by our relatives for my marriage and told that if you educate her so much you will not be able to find a match for her. She always tells me – do not bother about the comments made by the relatives and neighbors, just concentrate on your studies. (Meera, 19)

It appears from participants' responses that parents' dedication to their education often contrasted with considerable censure from the wider community. Like Meera, Usha notes that her extended family was quite concerned that her educational success might adversely affect her marriage prospects:

> My parents were always pressurised by family members to get us married. Even today, we have to hear comments like – even if girls are educated, they will not earn; if you invest in a boy he will at least earn and support the family. (Usha, 20).

Marriage: A loosening of gendered expectations, particularly in terms of marriage age, was shared across the College group. Rajasthan has long had one of the highest rates of child and early marriage in India. According to the most recent national census, 12.9 per cent of girls in Rajasthan got married between the ages of 10 and 17 years and 44 per cent between the ages of 18 and 20 (GOI, 2011). By contrast, the vast majority of both cohorts in this study were single though over the age of 19 – 78 and 75 per cent in the College and non-College groups, respectively (p-value < 0.00). Differences were apparent in the choice of a marriage partner. A larger proportion of the College group reported being able to make decisions about their choice of partner compared to their non-College counterparts. Only 24 per cent of the College group reported having no control over the choice of marriage partner compared to 81 per cent of the non-College group. Conversely, 38 per cent of the College group reported having complete or a lot of control over their marriage match as opposed to only 6 per cent of the non-College group.

Housework: Both the groups reported spending long hours on housework from a young age, as illustrated in Table 16.4. However, with the exception of lower primary level, the non-College group reported spending more time on housework than the College group throughout their schooling. For example, 42 per cent of the non-College group versus 29 per cent of the College group reported spending more than two hours a day on household chores at the upper primary level. Similar patterns were reported at the higher levels of schooling. Indeed, 11 per cent of the non-College group cited household responsibilities as the main reason they dropped out of school. And despite the high levels of reported parental support for education, the College group was not shielded from onerous chores. Even at the upper secondary level, 52 per cent of the College group reported spending more than three hours a day on housework.

Table 16.4 *Hours engaged in housework, by level of schooling*[1]

		Non-College (n = 223)	College (n = 413)	p-value[2]
Lower primary school	5 or more	0.00	10.41	<0.00
	3–4 hours	0.00	13.08	
	1–2 hours	43.05	34.14	
	None	56.95	42.37	
Upper primary school	5 or more	10.31	10.17	<0.00
	3–4 hours	31.84	18.89	
	1–2 hours	44.84	42.37	
	None	13.00	28.57	
Lower secondary school	5 or more	8.07	12.83	<0.00
	3–4 hours	49.78	31.23	
	1–2 hours	40.81	47.46	
	None	1.35	8.47	

1 Numbers represent means or proportions with standard errors in parentheses.
2 *p*-values are from significance tests, examining differences between non-Colleges and Colleges.

Some concessions may have mitigated the impact of household responsibilities on their educational progression: 70 per cent of the College group reported being relieved from chores very often around exam time.

Some qualitative narratives illustrate the complex balancing of household obligations and academic demands required of the College group:

> As I grew up I started helping my mother with household chores as I was the eldest. Even today I do most of the housework and farm work. This is a reason why sometimes it is difficult for me to concentrate on my studies and I am not able to get good grades. I get up early to study. I realise that I needed to put in more effort and time to improve my grades. I complete all the housework including cooking before going to College. (Meena, 20)

Community Censure: By contrast with the differences reported at the family level, both groups experienced similar broader structural challenges. Notably, participants in both the College and non College groups reported experiencing similar levels of harassment and community censure in the public sphere. By the time they reached lower secondary school, one in two of the non-College group and one in three of the College group reported experiencing stalking. By the lower secondary

Table 16.5 *Experience of sexual harassment in public, by level of schooling*

	Lower primary		Upper primary		Lower secondary		Upper secondary[1]
	CG (%)	NCG (%)	CG	NCG (%)	CG (%)	NCG (%)	CG (%)
Derogatory gestures	2	0 ***	14%	12	16	21	21
Verbal harassment	9	3 ***	26%	25	29	48 ***	32
Stalking	4	1***	21	41 ***	31	51 ***	35
Unwelcome touching	0	4 ***	36%	4 ***	44	10 ***	54

[1] Only for College group as non-College participants did not attend upper secondary school.
*** p<0.01, ** p<0.05, * p<0.1 n = 413 CH n = 223 NC

level, 44 per cent of the College group reported experiencing unwelcome touching, rising to 54 per cent by the time they reached the upper secondary level. Clearly, education-related journeys undertaken by participants were often fraught with the danger of sexual harassment. The support of their friends and families may have helped the College group to deal with this harassment, but for many of the non-College group, this threatening behaviour contributed to the decision to drop out of school. More than one in ten of the non-College group cited lack of safety on the journey to school as the main reason that they dropped out. The negative implications of these troubling findings are compounded by the lack of opportunities available to young women to discuss matters related to sexuality, including harassment and abuse. Only half of the participants reported receiving any sex education (51 per cent of the College and 47 per cent of the non-College group, NCG). Of those who did receive sex education, only 18 per cent of the College group (CG) and a mere 7 per cent of the non-College group received it in school.

The qualitative data shed light on the nature and extent of this harassment, as well as on the young women's frustration with the impunity afforded to abusers:

> Girls have to face violence and harassment on a daily basis. When I was in school I have faced harassment many times. Once I was returning from school and a boy from the village started following me, he held my hand and started touching me inappropriately and wanted my mobile number. I was scared and I just ran from there. The same boy then started troubling my

friend and one day took her away forcefully to an isolated spot and misbehaved with her. She also somehow pushed him away and ran. Such incidents are increasing day by day and many men/boys go unpunished. (Aarti, 21)

The study participants drew attention to the urgent need to enhance public safety for young women. Among the many suggestions articulated by participants in the course of the empowerment workshop were the provision of safe transportation facilities in both rural and urban areas, an increase in the availability of girls-only hostels, installation of CCTV cameras at bus stops and other key public places, the organisation of helplines and public discussion fora in communities, schools, local government committees and police stations. Clearly, the pervasive presence of unchecked sexual harassment continues to act as a significant deterrent to more rapid tertiary educational opportunities for India's less privileged young women who may experience more vulnerability in the public sphere.

Institutional Challenges

To understand the effect of the institutional environment on the educational trajectory of both the groups in this study, the study survey included scales to measure various school factors, including infrastructure, peer relationships, teacher absenteeism, across the different levels of schooling. We hypothesised that the College group would report a more positive experience than their non-College peers – however, this was not uniformly the case. The most striking difference was that a higher proportion of the non-College than the College group attended government schools, at every level of education. As a result, on average, the College group reported paying much higher fees than their non-College counterparts. On average, the College group reported paying fees nine times higher than the non-College at the lower secondary level. One advantage of enrolling in private schools is enhanced physical accessibility. At every level of schooling, the non-College group reported longer travel times than the College group. Otherwise, despite the fees and higher revenues of the private schools, many of the experiences of schooling across the two groups were similar in terms of teachers performing basic duties, school infrastructure, the experience of violence, and teacher absenteeism (Kelly, Krishna, & Bhabha, 2016).

There was no significant difference between the two groups in terms of take-up of household-level poverty alleviation schemes: one in five of each group reported having below poverty line cards. More than half of the participants in each group reported benefiting from government programmes administered at the primary and lower secondary level – most commonly, the provision of free meals, books and uniforms. Despite the fact that most participants came from low-income and traditionally marginalised ST, SC and OBC backgrounds, the number of students that received scholarships was remarkably low. Just 15 per cent of College participants reported receiving any governmental monetary support for their education at the upper primary level, a figure that increased to 25 per cent at the lower secondary level. Overall, fewer of the College group benefited from government subsidies than the non-College group, partly because many more of the College group attended non-government schools where restrictions on eligibility reduce accessibility of government schemes. The financial hardships of covering education costs experienced by participants' families grew more pressing as children progressed through the education system. For example, 22 per cent of the College group reported that their parents had taken out loans to support their education.

Limits of Familial Support

As we have illustrated, family support was critical to the College goer's educational progression in several ways. However, our data also illustrate the inherent limits to this support, due to parents' lack of familiarity with educational terrain. For example, one in four of the College group found the College application process difficult or very difficult. Just 15 per cent of this group received help with the process from parents. Most commonly, the College group received support from friends (47 per cent), siblings (41 per cent), and teachers (27 per cent).

The impact of familial education deficits was particularly evident in relation to technology: seven out of ten of the College group had never used the internet. This finding is consistent with a nationwide survey of rural youth according to which 76 per cent of rural females aged 14–18 had never used the internet (ASER 2018). Given these low levels of internet use it is unsurprising that none of the College group reported getting information on the College or scholarship application process online.

Parental inexperience with higher-level educational intuitions may also explain the heavy concentration of students from traditionally marginalised groups within the general Arts subject stream. Specifically, individuals in the general castes chose non-Arts tracks much more often than those in SCs or STs, as Table 16.6 illustrates.

The portion of the College group studying Arts (66 per cent overall, and 83 per cent of those from STs) is notably higher than the national average (35 per cent of those who graduated in 2016).

Table 16.6 *Choice of course, by caste group (College only)*

	SC	General	ST	SBC	OBC	Total
Arts	71.21	55.71	82.76	65.62	62.7	65.86
Science	25.76	28.57	17.24	28.12	32.43	28.33
Commerce	3.03	10	0	6.25	4.86	4.84
Law	0	5.71	0	0	0	0.97

Pearson *chi2*(15) = 35.2858 *Pr* = 0.002

An alternative explanation for the clustering of ST/SC groups in the general Arts concentration relates to participants' career choice; half of the survey respondents among the College group reported wanting to become a teacher as their career goal.[5] This career choice might reflect a lack of professional role models outside the school setting. Eligibility for government teaching posts reserved for socially marginalised groups under the national reservation policy may also have been a factor. Career considerations are likely to have been salient given that 97 per cent of participants reported plans to pursue professional occupations after graduation, in sharp contrast to their mothers, 91 per cent of whom were not working outside the household. This aspiration is also a departure from national practice where female formal workforce participation lies at just 29 per cent, one of the lowest in Asia (ILO, 2013).

Conclusion

This chapter describes differences between two groups of young Indian women matched by age, geographical location and parental education levels, where one but not the other group attended College. It highlights some of the drivers of educational success among previously excluded populations, some of the outstanding challenges, and many of the factors that require further attention and public engagement. It underscores the urgent need for more work in this field and the significant transformational potential of higher education as a tool for social mobility, gender justice, and economic empowerment.

Among the striking differences noted between the two groups compared in our study is religious affiliation: whereas only 1 per cent of the College group identified as Muslim, almost 20 per cent of the non-College group

[5] A rate twice as high as the rate found among rural women aged 14–18 in a nationally representative survey (ASER, 2018).

did. This finding is consistent with other research on the challenges facing the Muslim minority (Azam & Bhatt, 2015) and corresponds to a concerning, statewide trend of exclusion of Muslim girls at higher levels of education (GOI, 2013). Another notable finding relates to caste membership. More of the College than non-College cohort identified as coming from SC, ST or OBC backgrounds; groups which have historically been under-represented at higher educational levels (Hnatkovska, Lahiri, & Paul, 2013), but they have, since Independence, been targeted through affirmative action government education programmes. By contrast with the lack of progress made in including Muslim minorities in higher education, caste has been the focus of these targeted educational reforms. Differences in the caste composition of the College and non-College group point to some success in dismantling caste-based barriers to higher educational attainment through the reservation policy. The welcome higher representation of lower-caste groups contrasts with the religious disparities we continued to observe, disparities which have not been the focus of targeted educational reforms. Indeed contemporary developments in India with rising levels of anti-Muslim conduct may foreshadow concerning trends in the opposite direction.

Other disparities between the two groups emerge from our data. The College group had 0.87 fewer siblings than their non-College peers, a difference that may have had an impact on the amount of disposable household income available (including with loans levied) to support education. Moreover, both groups had parents with no more than a primary education, and the College group parents were somewhat more educated than the non-College group: 29 per cent of mothers and 77 per cent of fathers in the College group had some education compared to only 17 per cent of mothers and 69 per cent of fathers in the non-College group. This correlation confirms the well-established positive relationship between parental education level and increased child educational achievement, even at the very lowest levels of educational attainment (Azam & Kingdon, 2013; Dreze & Kingdon, 2001; Woodhead et al., 2013). It underscores the spillover and likely multiplier impact of education for future generations.

Among the most significant differences noted between the College and non-College group were attitudinal and behavioural disparities in family dynamics. Ninety-seven per cent of the College group cited parental support as the most instrumental factor in their educational success. This support was not just emotional. One in four of the College group parents took out loans to support their daughter's education.

We also found a dramatic willingness to challenge established but perhaps weakening, social norms regarding gender roles and marriage in particular. Marriages are viewed by many as the cornerstone of kin and caste relations (Oberoi, 1998), and arranged marriage is still the dominant tradition in India. Girls from uneducated families are the least likely to have a say in the choice of a spouse and the most likely to be married at a very young age (Banerjee, Duflo, Ghatak, & Lafortune, 2013). The College group's deferral of students' marriage to allow for study time represents a significant departure from a tightly guarded community norm, a bold act by the parents, and a norm that needs to become more diffuse if girls' access to College education is to increase. The drivers of this critical, independent parental stance are poorly understood and merit further scrutiny. Timing is not the only relevant marriage variable promoting female autonomy. Our study found that girls in the College group were consulted more in the choice of marriage partner compared to the non-College group, a reflection of the overall differences in respect of the right to express a view, in autonomy and individual agency in the two sets of households. Personal growth and a sense of personal independence were also positively impacted by the opportunity to study. Almost all participants saw their educational achievement as a path to economic independence, with 97 per cent intending to work, before and after marriage, once they had finished their studies.

Despite these changes, some traditional norms persisted, among them the skewed allocation of domestic chores to young women. The College group reported onerous housework responsibilities (somewhat reduced during exam time) which limited the time available for homework and studying, a challenge to educational progression for adolescent girls well documented in the literature (Assaad, Levison, & Zibani, 2010; Kelly & Bhabha, 2014; Levison, 1998). The transition to new social norms and gender roles is gradual, an uneven, uphill, and inconsistent process facing young women as they, together with their families, navigate uncharted territory within and beyond their homes.

Also, a large portion of both groups reports experiencing regular and invasive forms of sexual harassment. Harassment is stressful and intimidating for young women, a disincentive to navigating the public sphere in the teeth of community opposition. The lack of confidential and trusted facilities for reporting this oppressive behaviour compounds its negative impact, particularly for young women who fear that any complaints they may make to parents or other close relatives may jeopardise their permission to continue studying. As those participants in the empowerment workshop stressed, the issue of harassement must be addressed more systematically, through rigorous enforcement of recent legal reforms and discussions to stimulate broader norm change. Otherwise, this harassment will continue to hamper significant advances in female educational access and mobility, whatever the economic investment in promoting these goals.

Both groups studied experienced difficulty accessing government social supports. More than half of the participants reported benefiting from government programmes administered at the primary and lower secondary level – most commonly, the provision of free meals, books, and uniforms. However, although most participants came from low-income and traditionally marginalised ST, SC, and OBC backgrounds, the number of students that received scholarships was remarkably low. Just 15 per cent of participants from the College group reported receiving any governmental monetary support for their education at the upper primary level, increasing to 25 per cent at the lower secondary level. Overall far fewer members of the College than the non-College group reported benefiting from government education programmes, partly because many more of the College group attended non-government schools where penetration of government schemes is low due to restrictions on eligibility. The financial hardships experienced by participants' families in covering the costs of education grow more pressing as children progress through the education system. For example, 22 per cent of the College group reported that their parents had taken out loans to support their education. Relying on parents to secure loans (often high-interest) to enable their daughter to complete secondary school can put a strain on both individual students and their families. The College group that participated in the qualitative workshop commented on the fact that many students eligible for government assistance were struggling to navigate an unfamiliar and confusing administrative terrain. Some participants noted that the lack of transparency concerning the application process for grants and scholarships at the upper secondary and College levels had been particularly problematic for them. Increased clarity surrounding the process and targeted assistance in applying for scholarships at the school level would help low-income families take advantage of government and scholarship programmes that exist but are underutilised where most needed.

Although more non-College than College students benefited from educational subsidies, this financial assistance does not seem to have been decisive in terms of their educational progress: the non-College group still failed to progress beyond the lower secondary level, thus suggesting a need to refocus resources and priorities. Many of the disadvantaged young women within the sample who attended low-cost private schools were ineligible for government education programmes as a result of their private school enrolment status. This restriction will need to be considered in light of the government's growing reliance on private schools to serve low-income communities.

Our study shows the importance of familial support in generating an enabling environment for first-generation women College enrolees, to pursue higher education. It shows how parents' permission, encouragement, and financial backing are still essential supports in the process of moving from the familiar context of school and home community to the broader environment beyond, despite decades of public pronouncements about the importance of female education.

Our findings suggest that first-generation learners need institutionalised support once admission to College is secured. Perhaps partly owing to lack of guidance for the young women in this study, the majority were enrolled in general Arts degrees, rather than in more specific professional degrees. Students from the most marginalized caste backgrounds were significantly less likely to have specialised in a non-Arts subject: 83 per cent of those from the ST group was in the general Arts concentration as opposed to 56 per cent of the Other group. This choice may leave this group comparatively disadvantaged for future job prospects.

A salient question that remains is what the increased level of education will mean for these first-generation learners in a national context with low levels of female workforce participation within the formal sector. Studies in a range of contexts, including India, documents the difficulties first-generation learners can have navigating higher education itself and translating their educational experience into professional opportunity because of a lack of familial social and cultural capital (Agrawal, 2012; Jeffery & Jeffery 2004). To navigate the unfamiliar College environment effectively and to leverage its gains for future benefit, additional types of support are needed that illiterate parents do not have the capacity to provide. Students need advice on what courses to take, on what career opportunities flow from different trainings, on what pre-employment experiences are available and on how to find effective mentors. These are resources that students from privileged backgrounds, from families with prior experience of higher education, take for granted. But they are elusive for first-generation learners.

Enhancing access to tertiary education for traditionally excluded groups is an urgent priority for a country like India, with rapidly increasing technological growth and an ambitious modernisation agenda. If future growth and economic development are going to benefit sections of the population who need it most, government policies will need to strengthen the support available to constituencies such as those discussed in this chapter. Impacting parental norms (or indeed community norm change more generally) so that more elders follow the behaviour of the College group parents is not an easy or short-term target for government policy. But it can be accelerated through financial incentives to support College enrolment of young women, rigorous enforcement of prohibitions on child marriage and sexual harassment, enhancement of safety and monitoring within communities, consistent and decentralised messaging about the value of gender equality and non-discriminatory obligations. Lower hanging fruit, perhaps, for policy reform exists in the other area of support we have discussed: the need for mentorship, for clear advice on the College application process and on course enrolment, for financial aid and student loan opportunities, for internships, trainee opportunities and pre-employment work experience. Here government policies directed at expanding and supporting first-generation learners, including the young women described in this chapter, could have a catalytic effect. It would be exciting to see these possibilities realised so that a much larger cohort of young women could access the opportunities they deserve.

REFERENCES

Agrawal, T. (2012). *Returns to education in India: Some recent evidence*. www .igidr.ac.in/pdf/publication/WP-2011-017.pdf

ASER India (2014). Annual status of education report (rural) 2013. New Delhi: ASER Centre. www.asercentre.org/Keywords/p/234.html

ASER India (2018). Annual status of education report (rural) 2013. New Delhi: ASER Centre. www.asercentre.org/Keywords/p/337.html

Assaad, R., Levison, D., & Zibani, N. (2010). The Effect of Domestic Work on Girls' Schooling: Evidence from Egypt. *Feminist Economics*, *16*(1), 79–128.

Azam, M., & Kingdon, G. G. (2013). Are Girls the Fairer Sex in India? Revisiting Intra-household Allocation of Education Expenditure. *World Development, 42*, 143–164.

Azam, M., & Bhatt, V. (2015). Like Father, Like Son? Intergenerational Educational Mobility in India. *Demography, 52*(6), 1929–1959.

Banerjee, A., Duflo, E., Ghatak, M., & Lafortune, J. (2013). Marry for What? Caste and Mate Selection in Modern India. *American Economic Journal: Microeconomics, 5*(2), 33–72.

Beaman, L., Duflo, E., Pande, R., & Topalova, P. (2012). Female Leadership Raises Aspirations and Educational Attainment for Girls: A Policy Experiment in India. *Science, 335*(6068), 582–586.

Burde, D., & Linden, L. L. (2013). Bringing Education to Afghan Girls: A Randomized Controlled Trial of Village-based Schools. *American Economic Journal: Applied Economics, 5*(3), 27–40.

De, A., Khera, R., Samson, M., & Shiva Kumar, A. K. (2011). PROBE revisited: A report on elementary education in India. *OUP Catalogue.*

Government of India (GOI) Planning Commission (2012). *Twelfth Five Year Plan (2012–2017) Social Sectors.* planningcommission.nic.in/plans/planrel/12thplan/pdf/vol_3.pdf last accessed 06/04/16

Government of India (GOI) (2007). *Selected Educational Statistics 2004–2005 Ministry of Human Resource Development Bureau of Planning, Monitoring & Statistics New Delhi.* www.educationforallinindia.com/SES2004-05.pdfi

Government of India (GOI) (2012). *Statistics of School Education 2009–2010.* http://mhrd.gov.in/sites/upload_files/mhrd/files/SESSchool_201011_0.pdfi

Government of India (GOI) (2014). *Framework for Implementation of Rashtriya Madhyamik Shiksha Abhiyan.* http://rmsaindia.org/images/files/website_detail_contents/guidelines/rmsa/Framework 20for 20Implementation 20of 20RMSA.pdf

Government of India (GOI) (2015). *Steps Taken by Government for Survival, Protection and Education of Girl Child.* https://pib.gov.in/newsite/PrintRelease.aspx?relid=132980

Hnatkovska, V., Lahiri, A., & Paul, S. B. (2013). Breaking the Caste Barrier Intergenerational Mobility in India. *Journal of Human Resources, 48*(2), 435–473.

Huebler, F. (2005). Educational attainment in India, 1950–2000. http://huebler.blogspot.com/2005/10/educational-attainment-in-india-1950.html

ILO (2013). India: Why Is Women's Labour Force Participation Dropping? www.ilo.org/global/about-the-ilo/newsroom/news/WCMS_204762/lang-en/index.htm, last accessed 09/08/16

Jeffrey, C., Jeffery, R., & Jeffery, P. (2004). Degrees without Freedom: The Impact of Formal Education on Dalit Young Men in North India. *Development and Change, 35*(5), 963–986.

Jensen, R. (2010). The (perceived) Returns to Education and the Demand for Schooling. *Quarterly Journal of Economics, 125*(2), 515–547.

Kelly, O., & Bhabha, J. (2014). Beyond the Education Silo? Tackling Adolescent Secondary Education in Rural India. *British Journal of Sociology of Education, 35* (5), 731–752.

Kelly, O., Krishna, A., & Bhabha, J. (2016). Private Schooling and Gender Justice: An Empirical Snapshot from Rajasthan, India's Largest State. *International Journal of Educational Development, 46,* 175–187.

Khera, R., De, A., Samson, M., & Shiva Kumar, A. K. (2011). PROBE Revisited: A Report on Elementary Education in India. *OUP Catalogue*.

Kingdon, G. G. (2001). School Participation in Rural India. *Review of Development Economics*, *5*(1), 1–24.

Kingdon, G. G. (2007). The Progress of School Education in India. *Oxford Review of Economic Policy*, *23*(2), 168–195.

Kremer, M., Miguel, E., & Thornton, R. (2009). Incentives to Learn. *The Review of Economics and Statistics*, *91*(3), 437–456.

Levison, D. (1998). Household Work as a Deterrent to Schooling: An analysis of adolescent girls in Peru. *The Journal of Developing Areas*, *32*(3), 339–356.

Marsh, D. R., Schroeder, D. G., Dearden, K. A., Sternin, J., & Sternin, M. (2004). The Power of Positive Deviance. *BMJ*, *329*(7475), 1177–1179.

Moore, A. M. (2009). Adolescent Marriage and Childbearing in India: Current Situation and Recent Trends. www.guttmacher.org/pubs/2009/06/04/AdolescentMarriageIndia.pdf

National Sample Survey Office (2015). *Key Indicators of Social Consumption in India Education: NSS 71st Round (January-June 2014)*. Ministry of Statistics and Programme Implementation: Government of India.

Neff, D. F., Sen, K., & Kling, V. (2012). The Puzzling Decline in Rural Women's Labor Force Participation in India: A Reexamination. www.readkong.com/page/the-puzzling-decline-in-rural-women-s-labor-force-5379691

Oberoi, P. (1998). *Family Kinship and Marriage in India*. Delhi: Oxford India Paperbacks.

Olsen, W., & Mehta, S. (2006). Female Labour Participation in Rural and Urban India: Does Housewives' Work Count? *Radical Statistics*, *93*, 57.

Plan India (2008). Learn without Fear the Campaign to End Violence in Schools Challenges in India New Delhi. http://plan-international.org/apprendresanspeurLa/files-es/india-the-campaign-to-end-violence-in-schools-english

PROBE Team (1999). *Public Report on Basic Education in India*. New Delhi: Oxford University Press.

Rampal, A. (2007). Ducked or Bulldozed? Education of Deprived Urban Children in India. In W. T. Pink, & G. W. Noblit (eds.), *International Handbook of Urban Education* (pp. 285–304). New Delhi: Springer.

Siddhu, G. (2011). Who Makes It to Secondary School? Determinants of Transition to Secondary Schools in Rural India. *International Journal of Educational Development*, *31*(4), 394–401.

Tiwari, N., & Ghadially, R. (2009). Changing Gender Identity of Emerging Adults. *Journal of the Indian Academy of Applied Psychology*, *35*(2), 313–321.

UNESCO (2015). Education for All 2000–2015: India Is First in the Race to Reduce Out of School Children. www.unesco.org/new/en/newdelhi/about-this-office/si

ngle-view/news/education_for_all_2000_2015_india_is_first_in_the_race_to_re
duce_out_of_school_children/#.V8BiJZgrI2w

Unterhalter, E. (2005). Fragmented Frameworks? Researching Women, Gender,
Education and Development. In S. Aikman, & E. Unterhalter (eds.), *Beyond
Access: Transforming Policy and Practice for Gender Equality in Education* (pp.
15–35). London: Oxfam.

Woodhead, M., Frost, M., & James, Z. (2013). Does Growth in Private Schooling
Contribute to Education for All? Evidence from a Longitudinal, Two Cohort
Study in Andhra Pradesh, India. *International Journal of Educational
Development, 33*(1), 65–73.

World Bank (n.d.): Data Bank. https://data.worldbank.org/indicator/SE
.TER.ENRR?locations=IN

Zeitlin, M. (1991). Nutritional Resilience in a Hostile Environment: Positive
Deviance in Child Nutrition. *Nutrition Reviews, 49*(9), 259–268.

CHAPTER 17

DACAmented
Impossible Realities, Deferred Actions, Delegated Dreams and Stories of Resilience

Carlos Aguilar and Roberto G. Gonzales

Introduction

The journey to higher education by undocumented students has been one of legal, financial and informational barriers. Despite ensured equal access to primary and secondary education (*Plyler* v. *Doe*, 1982), federal policies addressing access to postsecondary education are non-existent – a lack of action that has motivated some states to provide additional access and others to erect further barriers. While the implementation of the Deferred Action for Childhood Arrivals (DACA) programme in 2012 has attenuated the transition to 'illegality' that many undocumented young people experienced after high school graduation, access to postsecondary education remains a challenging endeavour for most undocumented youth. The recent announcement to rescind DACA and the lack of a solution for comprehensively managing immigration further obscure the future of this constituency. Placed at the intersection of contrasting political, economic and social contexts, this chapter explores the experiences of three undocumented immigrant youths in Texas who enter adult transitions at differing levels of educational attainment. This chapter illustrates how policies, school practices and families' legal structures continue to create conflicting educational experiences of exclusion and belonging for undocumented young people living in the United States.

An estimated 10.7 million undocumented immigrants, largely from Mexico and Central America, reside in the United States (Krogstad, Passel, & Cohn, 2018). Made up mostly of long-term settlers, the status of this population is the result of decades of unauthorised migration and increasingly restrictive immigration laws and policies (Massey, Durand, & Malone, 2002). While media accounts tend to paint this population in broad brushstrokes, it is quite diverse. In fact, more than 2.1 million undocumented immigrants have lived in the United States since childhood (Batalova & McHugh, 2010). Unlike first-generation immigrants who migrate as adults and the American-born second-generation, undocumented youth and young adults have developed values, identities and aspirations rooted in their experiences growing up in the United States. But their lives are also deeply impacted by their undocumented status, a reality that becomes increasingly salient and detrimental to life-course trajectories as they reach adolescence (Gonzales, 2011).

Because of their young age on arrival, primary and secondary schools are a key socialising force in the lives of undocumented youth (Gonzales, 2010; Gonzales, Heredia, & Negrón-Gonzales, 2015). In 1982, the United States Supreme Court held in *Plyler* v. *Doe* that states could not deny children access to a K-12 education based on their immigration status (Olivas, 2011). But beginning around the age of 16, undocumented youth confront a growing set of obstacles and face more uncertain futures (Abrego, 2006; Enriquez, 2011; Gonzales, 2011). In addition, research suggests that making it through high school and to College is not an easy feat for undocumented immigrant youth as they face multiple barriers on the road to and through postsecondary education (Abrego, 2006; Enriquez, 2011; Gonzales & Ruiz, 2014).

On June 15, 2012, educational prospects changed for many of these young people with the introduction of the Deferred Action for Childhood Arrivals (DACA) programme. Introduced by the Obama Administration, this policy offers eligible undocumented young people temporary protection from deportation and access to a work authorisation permit, along with other forms of legal access to the polity such as obtaining a driver's licence, improved access to higher education, and increased spatial mobility (Abrego, 2018; Batalova, Hooker, Capps, Bachemeir, & Cox, 2013). In the programme's seven years, more than 814,000 young people have become 'DACAmented' and through this new status have begun to enjoy previously unavailable life opportunities. Nevertheless, notable limitations curbed DACA's effectiveness in diminishing certain aspects of the experience of illegality: it did not lead to a pathway to citizenship; it was by nature partial and temporary; and it did not address the legal circumstances of beneficiaries' family members (Gonzales, Ellis, Rendón-García, & Brant, 2018). On September 5, 2017, the Trump administration announced the rescission of DACA. At the time of this writing, the future of the programme is being challenged in the courts, and Congress has yet to find a long-term solution for comprehensively managing immigration.

While the future of DACA remains uncertain, the lived experiences of DACA beneficiaries provide important insight into the educational experiences of undocumented immigrant youth and young adults, and the ways in which policies and integrative practices may impact their educational and life-course trajectories. In this chapter, drawing from our own research and the burgeoning scholarship on the experiences of undocumented immigrant youth, we examine how policies, school practices and families' legal structures continue to create conflicting experiences of exclusion and belonging for undocumented young people living in the United States. To contribute to this analysis, we examine the experiences of three undocumented young adults in Texas who enter adult transitions at differing levels of educational attainment.

Undocumented Youth and the Implementation of the Deferred Action for Childhood Arrivals

Undocumented immigrant youth and young adults embody the complexity of the human experience and the adaptability that characterises it. As they grow up, undocumented immigrant youth vacillate between experiences of belonging and exclusion. Owing to their legal inclusion in K-12 schools, undocumented immigrant youth are afforded opportunities to become integrated into the country's social framework. However, their undocumented status plays an increasingly constricting role at a time when young people begin to transition to lives of greater independence and responsibility. Just as their peers begin to seek after school employment, postsecondary careers, driver's licences and prepare for College, they realise that many of these pursuits are not available to them. This process has been conceptualised as a 'transition to illegality' (Gonzales, 2011, 2016). While the educational system encourages undocumented immigrant students to dream and to aspire alongside their documented peers, they soon confront a life of blocked opportunities and limitations. In this transitional phase of their lives, some undocumented youth continue to pursue postsecondary goals and aspirations thanks to their academic resilience (Gonzales, 2008). For others, legal barriers force them into hopelessness, lowering their aspirations and academic performance (Gonzales & Chavez, 2012; Suárez-Orozco, Yoshikawa, Teranishi, & Suárez-Orozco, 2011).

Participation in K-12 schools is undoubtedly a defining and integrative experience. Yet undocumented immigrant students experience schooling within the broader context of a stratified public educational system (Gonzales et al., 2015) that structures opportunities for all of its pupils.

Schools often make decisions regarding how students are integrated into the larger curriculum, determining student access to scarce resources.[1] These decisions benefit a small portion of students while disadvantaging much larger segments. While access to school resources has an important bearing on the success of all students, curriculum tracking decisions that negatively affect the more general student body can be especially detrimental to undocumented students (Gonzales, 2010). Due to legal exclusions from financial aid and limited family finances, undocumented students' pursuit of postsecondary education is prohibitively difficult. Their parents tend to lack knowledge of the US education system, and their own undocumented status often keeps them from seeking help from teachers and counsellors. Taken together, these barriers can have a direct effect on undocumented students' ability to take advantage of critically needed services (Hagan, Rodriguez, & Castro, 2011; Menjívar & Abrego, 2012; Rodríguez & Hagan, 2004), limiting their access to guidance and advocacy needed to succeed in high school and advance to College.

Though tens of thousands of undocumented students graduate from US high schools each year, exclusions in federal and state financial aid severely limit the number of undocumented students able to enrol in postsecondary education. Even as some are able to challenge the limits of an undocumented status, most undocumented students encounter a legal ceiling and a 'constrained inclusion' (Negrón-Gonzales, 2017). For those able to transition to postsecondary institutions, limited financial resources coupled with a lack of educational support and feelings of shame, frustration and fear hinder their ability to persist in postsecondary endeavours (Gonzales, 2016; Negrón-Gonzales, 2013; Perez, Espinoza, Ramos, Coronado, & Cortes, 2009).

Tuition equity bills and the implementation of the Deferred Action for Childhood Arrivals (DACA) programme have provided a small but significant number of undocumented students with additional opportunities to achieve postsecondary success. As many studies now document, the implementation of DACA has allowed many of its beneficiaries to access paid internships and new and better paying jobs, acquire driver's licences, new forms of health care, begin to build credit through bank accounts and credit cards, as well as improve their spatial mobility (Abrego, 2018; Gonzales, Terriquez, & Ruszczyk, 2014; Guarneros, 2017; Wong, Richter, Rodriguez, & Wolgin, 2015). The opportunities and benefits

---

[1] See chapters in this volume by Borgonovi and Marconi, and by Crul and Lelie advancing similar arguments in the European context.

facilitated by DACA transcend the individual. With increased economic power, DACA recipients have been able to acquire cars, seek better living arrangements, and create jobs through entrepreneurial investments (Wong et al., 2016), leading to improved circumstances for their family members (Gonzales, Ellis, Rendón-García, & Brant, 2018).

DACA has played a pivotal role in increasing undocumented students' first-time and re-enrolment rates into postsecondary educational institutions (Gonzales, Roth, Brant, Lee, & Valdivia, 2016; Wong et al., 2015). As relative economic stability has improved for many, so have opportunities to pay for an education out of pocket and to handle other personal, occupational, and educational responsibilities. In the absence of comprehensive immigration reform at the federal level, the devolution of immigration policy to states, counties, and municipalities has created unevenness, complicating the lives of immigrants who reside in states hostile to undocumented migrants (Hsin & Ortega, 2018; Silver, 2018; Terriquez, 2015).[2] However, efforts by undocumented students, parents, academic advisors and mentors have in some cases countered these challenges, creating positive outcomes for students with respect to postsecondary institutions (Aguilar, 2017; Aguilar, Marquez, & Romo, 2018; Perez et al., 2010).

Methodology

This chapter draws data from three in-depth interviews, part of a larger exploratory research project conducted by the first author in Texas during the summer of 2018. The interviews examined the aspirations, goals and experiences of DACA beneficiaries in particularly harsh contexts: (1) the Trump administration announcement terminating DACA, and (2) the implementation of Texas Senate Bill 4 (SB4), a state measure allowing local police to engage in immigration enforcement and requiring them to cooperate with immigration agencies like Immigration and Customs Enforcement (ICE). The narratives of three DACA beneficiaries who entered adult transitions at differing levels of educational attainment 'show different perspectives on' how policies, school practices and families' legal structures influence the lived experiences of undocumented students (Creswell, 2007, 74).

All respondents were born in Mexico and were at least 18 years of age at the time of the interview. Christopher was enrolled in high school,

---

[2] States like Arizona, Oklahoma, Missouri, Indiana, Ohio, Alabama, Georgia, North Carolina, South Carolina, and New Hampshire deny in-state tuition rates for undocumented students, See https://uleadnet.org/

Miranda in community College and Haley in a four-year university.[3] Respondents were recruited by the first author and agreed to be interviewed in a location of their choosing. Although an Institutional Review Board (IRB) allowed for a signed consent form to be waived, all respondents provided verbal consent and received a document with contact information, purpose of the study, steps for protecting confidentiality and interview procedures.

All interviews were conducted in English, audio recorded and transcribed. After listening to the interviews, we used open coding techniques. We placed conceptual labels on responses that described discrete events, experiences, and feelings reported in the interviews. We then analysed each interview across all questions to identify meta-themes. All interviews were conducted by the first author, an undocumented researcher currently benefiting from DACA. Respondents were all informed about the interviewer's circumstances. This academic rendering is then shaped by our personal and professional endeavours at the intersection of unforgiving academic rigour and rebellious manifestations of individual and communal lived experiences.

The Texas Context: A Mixed-Immigration Stance

Of the estimated 10.7 million undocumented immigrants living in the United States, more than 1.7 million live in Texas.[4] Despite its history and proximity to Mexico, Texas's record on immigration is mixed. It recently led a seven-state coalition challenging both DACA and the Deferred Action for Parents of Americans and Lawful Permanent Residents (DAPA) programme, an additional Obama administration measure designed to protect undocumented parents of children with a secure immigration status. The state has also implemented Texas Senate Bill 4, an anti-immigrant bill that, among other things, requires police departments to engage in immigration enforcement. These actions break from a history of integrative policies, including the 2001 tuition equity bill (SB 1403, SB 1503)[5] that made Texas the first US state to allow undocumented students to attend public universities at in-state rates and qualify for state funded financial aid.[6] In 2013, approximately 25,000 undocumented students were benefiting from this policy, accounting for roughly 2 per cent of the

[3] All names used are pseudonyms.
[4] See Immigrants in Texas www.americanimmigrationcouncil.org/research/immigrants-in-texas
[5] SB 1528 is an amendment to the initial provisions of House Bill 1403 in 2005.
[6] See In-State Tuition for Undocumented Students: 2017 State-Level Analysis, www.naspa.org/rpi/posts/in-state-tuition-for-undocumented-students-2017-state-level-analysis

total number of students enrolled in Colleges across the state. Nearly three-fourths of undocumented students who benefited from SB 1528 that year were enrolled in community Colleges.[7]

Recent studies show that tuition equity bills reduce high school drop-outs, teen pregnancy rates and increase the likelihood of high school graduation (Bozick & Miller, 2014; Koohi, 2017; Potochnik, 2014). The implementation of tuition equity bills demonstrably increases enrolment rates at postsecondary institutions among undocumented students (Flores, 2010; Darolia & Potochnick, 2015). As of this writing, and despite having the second largest population of DACA beneficiaries – approximately 113,000 – Texas has yet to release a report on the impact of its tuition equity bill. Given its years of operation improving undocumented and DACA students' postsecondary success, however, the bill is likely to have substantially increased the number of undocumented students enrolled in Texas Colleges and universities. Questions nevertheless remain regarding the persistence of other types of barrier on undocumented students' road to and through postsecondary education in the state of Texas.

Analysis

Who They Focus on . . . It's Not Us

Seventy miles west of San Antonio, Texas, in a relatively small conservative town that sits at the heart of the Texas Hill Country,[8] Christopher dreams of attending College and eventually becoming an anaesthesiologist. Working at a local hardware store during the summer, he looks forward to graduating from high school in the upcoming academic year. While Christopher speaks confidently about attending College, he is a long way from achieving his goals. Unable to identify a support network in high school to guide him through the College application process, Christopher faces many obstacles to a postsecondary education despite benefiting from DACA and qualifying for SB 1528. As he prepares to complete the last year of high school, Christopher is hard pressed to identify any positive relationships he has formed with academic or institutional mentors at school. This lack of institutional support has compelled Christopher to consider the Scholastic Assessment Test (SAT) an obstacle to College rather than

---

[7] See "Lawmakers likely to wage in-state tuition fight again this year", www.texastribune.org/2017/01/19/lawmakers-likely-see-state-tuition-policy-fight-ag/
[8] The Texas Hill Country is a region located at the intersection of West, Central, and South Texas.

simply a necessary and achievable step towards a higher education. When we spoke to him, Christopher had no prior knowledge of his eligibility for in-state tuition and state financial aid through SB 1528. Christopher explained that he had not reached out to his counsellor because:

> I don't feel like walking up there and just tell them that I have the DACA. I mean they probably know that I am an immigrant. But at the same time, some of them probably go against [undocumented immigrants], because some of them be like 'oh what are they doing here?'

Christopher's narrative is not unique. Despite the implementation of the Texas SB 1528 almost two decades ago, schooling continues to demotivate, decelerate and derail the life-course trajectories of many undocumented students (Aguilar, 2018; Valenzuela, 1999). While an undocumented status represents a significant obstacle to further educational opportunity, so too does the absence of a clearly signalled pathway to postsecondary education in school. As of this writing, and despite having identified an ally counsellor in his school during the interview, Christopher has yet to contact or be contacted by an academic counsellor.

At a community College in Austin, Texas, Miranda is expected to graduate in the upcoming academic year with a bachelor's degree through a partnership programme with a four-year institution in Central Texas. Like Christopher, Miranda navigated high school in a rural Texas town without the guidance and support of academic mentors. Although Miranda started her postsecondary education in 2015, the high costs of this education and the lack of information about SB 1528 pushed her to transfer to a community College last year. She explained:

> In high school, the counsellors, who they focus on it's not us. I was thinking about that the other day. High school should really have some guidance. I know [another local university] just opened a centre for Dreamer ... I mean DACA recipients. That's good. I feel that they should do that for high school, too, because when you are in high school, it's a really confusing time. So yeah, when I graduated, I really didn't know what to do. So over two years, I paid everything out of pocket. I know I could have gotten help somewhere else, but I had no idea where to get it from.

Today, Miranda benefits from DACA, in-state tuition, and state financial aid. Unfortunately, at the time of the interview Miranda had not been able to identify any resources or support systems at the community College to support her mental or physical well-being.[9] Like her, many undocumented students in Texas continue to confront information barriers and knowledge gaps. Even when information is provided, undocumented students are often cautioned about restrictions on their access rather than reminded of their entitlements.

Fortunately, some undocumented students in Texas do learn to navigate the educational system despite their lack of institutional support. When asked whether she was benefiting from the Texas SB 1528, Haley, a senior at a university in Corpus Christi exclaimed.

> What? See! I didn't know about that! What is this? . . . oh my God, can you give me this information because I am trying to find financial aid for my last semester and this whole time I was told I couldn't [fill out the financial aid form], but was never told I could do this thing.

Though Haley, Miranda and Christopher's educational experiences differed, they also exhibited several commonalities: insufficient academic and institutional support, and inadequate information about the financial options available to them. It is likely that Miranda and Haley partially benefited from the Texas SB 1528 because they both graduated from a high school in Texas and had resided in the state throughout their high school years. Yet, in the context of the lived experiences encountered by undocumented students in educational institutions, whether or not Miranda and Haley actually benefited from the Texas SB 1528 is not as important. Rather, central to our interest as sociologists is what their narratives convey about the contexts they navigate and their experiences in doing so.[10]

Parental 'sacrificios': An Important Form of Capital

The lack of academic and institutional support and knowledge about existing tuition equity bills poses great challenges to undocumented students intent on securing a higher education. The complexities arising out of membership in mixed-status families (families including members with differing immigration statuses) further stratify educational experiences and trajectories. Though Haley and Christopher's parents were supportive throughout their education (Cuevas, 2018), Miranda described her family

---

[9] The community College that Miranda attends has a website where they provide DACA updates and information, a commitment statement where the College is identified as a support, a resource, and an ally, as well as contact information should undocumented students like to speak to a counselor.

[10] The concept of the irrelevance of factual veracity is drawn from Mitchell Duneier's approach during one of his talks on his seminal book 'Sidewalks', www.youtube.com/watch?v=pPs8hIePpZc&t=297s

as reticent to provide financial support. Due to her undocumented status and the potential termination of DACA, her family feared that their efforts would be in vain should DACA be rescinded. Thus, although Miranda recalls that her mother immigrated to the United States to secure a better education for her daughter, she thought of this in terms of a high school diploma. When asked whether or not a postsecondary education had been an option, Miranda elaborated:

> In my mind it was. In my parents' [minds], it really wasn't but I didn't realize this till I graduated [from high school]. I was receiving acceptance letters and stuff and I was really excited, and I was like 'mmm, where to go?' and then I started seeing that my parents started saying 'you need to calm down, we don't get a lot of help [have a lot to give]'.

Many undocumented students find themselves navigating the postsecondary system without financial support from their parents. Parental *sacrificios*, emotional, and financial support remain pivotal as undocumented students navigate educational institutions in the United States (Aguilar, 2017, 2018; Aguilar et al., 2018; Cuevas, 2018; Enriquez, 2011; Gonzales, 2016). For some undocumented students, such as Miranda, both emotional and financial support are missing because families lack familiarity with the US educational system and fear that an uncertain future and the potential termination of DACA may lead to truncated educational and professional careers, negatively impacting their children's wellbeing (Aguilar, 2017). This parental reticence is a product of current fears about anti-immigrant policies rather than any dismissal of the intrinsic value of education. Such response further complicates our understanding of undocumented students' experiences in their road to and through a postsecondary education as the educational system has historically represented a haven for undocumented children and youth.

While many undocumented students speak of parental *sacrificios* and the associated love and care (Aguilar, 2018; Cuevas, 2018), Miranda's narrative reflected her resentment regarding the invisible tax that an undocumented status levied on her and her family throughout her childhood.

> I want my family to be different. When I have kids, I want to be able to dedicate time to them. Hopefully when they are born, [I will] just take some time off and be there for them.

For Haley, on the other hand, while she hoped 'not to live [her parents'] life', she stressed the supportive role her family played throughout her education and the DACA application and renewal process.

> My mom is really good at doing the research for [immigration], so she just kind of gives me the paperwork for this and I just do it with her . . . [In terms of education], I think my mom was just trying to not give me a whole bunch of answers at the same time because I do not think she knew either. [But] my parents have always been like, you just work hard, you don't get in trouble, and you'll be good. You know, and that is all I was really told.

Haley's parents have been able to adjust their status to that of legal permanent residents. As a result, their family lives more comfortably and her parents are less reticent to interact with community institutions. Despite their lack of a formal education, Haley's parents developed a range of connections within their community, including with people within law enforcement and immigration agencies, that provided her with information and support. When Haley was asked about the role of mentors throughout her education, she stated:

> No, I really didn't tell anybody [that I was undocumented] till I went to College. That's when I told people that I was DACA. In high school, nobody helped me or nothing, [The process to applying to College] was confusing and annoying. I hate applying for stuff, and specially for [DACA], it's worst because they ask you all of these questions that you don't even know. But I mean my mom helped me, my mom definitely helped me, we know a lot of people that work in the justice system for immigration, so they were able to help us, too.

Haley often referred to her family's involvement in her education and her overall development in a positive light. Yet, she also projects resentment towards individuals she feels have 'been given everything by their parents'. Holding strong meritocratic values, Haley sees the United States as a 'spoiled place' where citizens are blessed, and immigrants, like herself, are 'unlucky' due to the hostile contexts many have to navigate. Relatively speaking, however, Haley has been well-provided for by her parents. Though she was awarded a soccer scholarship to attend College, and currently holds two jobs to support herself, the *sacrificios* and the emotional and informational support that her parents provide are also a form of valuable capital (Aguilar, 2018; Cuevas, 2008; Yosso, 2005).

Rescinded Actions but Continued Resiliency ...

The political environment that DACA beneficiaries navigate in the state of Texas is distinctive. Although they can benefit from in-state tuition rates and state financial aid, efforts to rescind DACA and the implementation of the Texas SB 4 threaten DACA recipients in many ways. As Miranda explained, her educational trajectory could be characterised as an uphill battle as well as a feat to be performed against the clock.

> Miranda: [after U.S. Attorney General Jeff Sessions' announcement to rescind DACA], I was mad about it, angry, you know. What are we doing wrong? But I have a lot of family from Monterrey (Mexico) and they live there. Some of my uncles, they went to school and they did all that, so now I am kind of just, I am just motivated to finish my school before my DACA expires. It's pretty selfish, I know but that's just my feelings now. I just need to finish before that happens, and once I have my degree, I don't know, whatever happens . . .
>
> Interviewer: Have you thought about going back to Mexico?
>
> Miranda: Like . . . I feel like I would be more appreciated over there. Sometimes I just feel exhausted, being here, working my butt off on everything and then people still don't want you here, it's kind of . . . frustrating.

While none of the respondents had concrete plans to return to Mexico if DACA was to be terminated, Miranda and Christopher had thought about the possibility and were confident of their ability to succeed in Mexico. Haley, on the other hand, spoke of plans to marry her US-citizen boyfriend. Yet, the uncertainty of her DACA status in the long term and the current political context still placed a big question mark on her educational endeavours. She expanded:

> I don't know, I don't know what would happen, if I would be able to work, if I would be able to finish school, if I didn't . . . I would be devastated, all that for nothing, I was literally this close, that would suck.

Having secured jobs after College graduation, both Miranda and Haley experienced high levels of anxiety. Miranda explained:

> My anxiety is the timing, you have this much time to get things done and after that you don't know what is going to happen. That feeling of uncertainty, you don't know what's going to happen and then fear with my family, my parents don't see themselves living [in Mexico] because they don't have any type of education so there is no way they can get a better job. For me is, well I am working on this education . . . my fear is my parents.

She continued:

> I want to graduate by next summer, and then I am actually going to be under contract with an Independent School District, so I would work [there] two years, and then probably move into a less urban area . . . My plans [have not changed], I just don't know if they can happen or not, because I don't know if after, can you still work, you know? if you don't have

your work permit, what good does your degree do? . . . [It's] like a due date for an assignment, you need to get this done before that time, or else, you don't know what is going to happen.

Christopher acknowledges his persistent fear as well as his efforts to not let these anxieties frame his whole life. As he continues to dream about higher education, Christopher reflects on what he considers necessary to improve the opportunities for undocumented students in higher education:

Just to let [undocumented students] know that they can do it. That there will be professors or counsellors in College that will help them. To see how they can help them with their life, with school, financially, just let them know that they are there, and that they don't have to worry about anything.

Despite increased anxiety, ambivalence, and uncertainty, 'the fear [that such decision caused can be] juxtaposed with its transformational power . . . [functioning] as a platform on which [DACA beneficiaries' lived experiences and narratives] are transformed' into expressions of resilience, persistence and survivance (Aguilar, 2018, 11). Essential throughout these challenging times are also the experiences and stories that emanate from the larger community of undocumented immigrants. As Christopher explained:

If they want to remove [DACA] or not, I am still going to be myself, I am still going to be living, I am still going to look for a job, if I get barred, or whatever. I am not really worried about it.

Later in the interview he added:

[other undocumented immigrants here] are just living life, they get through it, they make it, they go all out, with the DACA, without the DACA, they live life to the fullest, they still live here. They are just loving their job, some of them may even have their own business. [Even if they do not get supported by the state or their local town], they still go all out.

While identifying DACA as a turning point in their lives and acknowledging the detrimental consequences of its potential termination, the narratives by Christopher, Haley and Miranda exemplify the diverse, complex and at times contradictory experiences of this resilient constituency (Aguilar, 2018). This complexity is illuminated by their testimonies, lived experiences and adaptability for they have bloomed despite recurring historical legislative droughts.

Conclusion

The absence of a legal status complicates the educational trajectories of undocumented immigrant students. Though many persevere through the porous educational pipeline, their journey can be both physically and emotionally injurious. While policies such as DACA and, in some cases, state-level tuition equity bills, have temporarily addressed some of the problems encountered by undocumented immigrant youth, the lack of academic and institutional support, coupled with their membership in mixed-status families, and growing anti-immigrant rhetoric reinforce the urgency of securing a permanent and comprehensive legal fix.

By focusing on the state of Texas, this chapter has explored the experiences of three DACA beneficiaries who entered adult transitions at differing levels of educational attainment. The narratives of Haley, Miranda, and Christopher suggest that implementation of helpful policies such as the tuition equity policy in Texas, does not always translate into programme utilisation or even awareness. While Miranda and Haley benefited from the ability to attend College at in-state tuition rates, the fact that they were not initially aware of SB 1528 and did not feel safe reaching out to academic agents despite being DACA recipients reflects an institutional failure to advance the support needed by this constituency.

This chapter has also highlighted the important contribution of families, including both their social and economic capital, to the undocumented students' educational trajectories. The lack of a permanent solution to the legal misfortunes of mixed-status families directly influences the educational experiences of undocumented youth and young adults. Although undocumented parents continue to make *sacrificios* to improve the lives of their families, uncertainty about a legal future may push some parents to curb support for their children as a way to protect them from future disappointments. For many, on the other hand, having a legal immigration status provides for the creation and extension of networks that transmit information and support in the educational and life-course trajectories of their children. In some cases, as with Haley's parents, the networks may include individuals otherwise experienced as threatening, such as 'people that work in the justice system for immigration'. Either way, and despite a lack of institutional support and of policy awareness, some undocumented students are able to capitalise on the messages, whether negative or positive, that their parents convey to them. Finally, and as the main focus of this chapter, the imminent termination of DACA at the time of the interviews fostered feelings of fear and anxiety. While feelings like these have been previously recorded in literature on undocumented youth, the potential termination of their deferred action concretised the fears that had led Miranda's parents to withhold emotional and financial support in the first place.

All three respondents benefited from DACA at or before the age of 18. Although they had become aware of the vulnerability engendered by their undocumented status through failed or uncomfortable attempts at rites of passage such as obtaining a driver's licence, taking the SATs, or travelling out of state with their friends, their imminent immersion into a pool of illegality through DACA's potential termination amplified their fears and anxieties, and jeopardised their plans. However, at the time of the interviews quoted in this chapter, they also expressed confidence in their capabilities. While DACA has increased beneficiaries' life opportunities, the impressive educational and occupational gains that DACA facilitated are also a reflection of resilient individuals and a consequence of individual, familial and communal support. Today, it is time for elected officials to step up; they ought to secure a permanent solution that improves and validates the lived experiences of this community. Neglecting this issue presents the possibility of catastrophic consequences for individuals, families, communities, and society in general.

With this chapter, our intention is not to argue that tuition equity bills are inefficient. To the contrary, we believe they have been of tremendous benefit in helping undocumented students to access postsecondary opportunities. They are pivotal measures that can increase the number of undocumented students in postsecondary institutions. Yet, little is known, in the Texan context specifically, about the intersection of local, state, and federal political conservatism and how it shapes the experiences of undocumented students as they navigate ambivalent social and institutional environments. This chapter presents a first exploration of these complexities. In the case of the three respondents discussed here, despite financial, emotional, institutional, and political hurdles, Miranda and Haley have been able to attend and excel in postsecondary institutions. Christopher, on the other hand, and many undocumented students like him whose postsecondary trajectories are yet to take off, continue to battle the invisible informational barriers that prevent so many resilient young people from testing the boundaries of their immigration status.

REFERENCES

Abrego, L. J. (2006). 'I Can't Go to College Because I Don't Have Papers': Incorporation Patterns Of Latino Undocumented Youth. *Latino Studies; London, 4*(3), 212–231.

Abrego, L. J. (2018). Renewed Optimism and Spatial Mobility: Legal Consciousness of Latino Deferred Action for Childhood Arrivals Recipients and Their Families in Los Angeles. *Ethnicities, 18*(2), 192–207.

Aguilar, C. (2017). *Mi Casa es Tu Casa: DACAdemics Redefine Citizenship* (M.S., The University of Texas at San Antonio). Retrieved from http://search .proquest.com/docview/1949775500/abstract/228AADF41C47445FPQ/1.

Aguilar, C. (2018). Undocumented Critical Theory. *Cultural Studies ↔ Critical Metodologies*, 1–9.

Aguilar, C., Marquez, R., & Romo, H. (2018). From Dreamers to DACAdemics: A la escuela sin pasaporte. In *Seen but Not Heard: Interdisciplinary Perspectives on Child Migrants and Refugees*. Lanham, MD: Lexington Books.

Batalova, J., Hooker, S., Capps, R., Bachmeier, J., & Cox, E. (2013). *Deferred Action for Childhood Arrivals at the One-Year Mark: A Profile of Currently Eligible Youth and Applicants*. Retrieved from http://search.proquest.com/docview/182 0758318/?pq-origsite=primo.

Batalova, J., & McHugh, M. (2010). *DREAM vs. Reality: An Analysis of Potential DREAM Act Beneficiaries*. Retrieved from Migration Policy Institute website: www.immigrationresearch-info.org/system/files/DREAM-Insight-July2010 .pdf.

Bozick, R., & Miller, T. (2014). In-State College Tuition Policies for Undocumented Immigrants: Implications for High School Enrollment among Non-citizen Mexican Youth. *Population Research and Policy Review, 33* (1), 13–30.

Creswell, J. W. (2007). *Qualitative Inquiry and Research Design: Choosing among Five Approaches* (2nd ed.). Thousand Oaks, CA: Sage Publications, Inc.

Cuevas, S. (2018). *Apoyo Sacrificial, Sacrificing Support: Understanding Undocumented Latina/o Parents' Engagement in Students' Post-Secondary Planning and Success* (Ph.D., Harvard Graduate School of Education). http s://dash.harvard.edu/ handle/1/37935837.

Darolia, R., & Potochnick, S. (2015). Educational 'When', 'Where', and 'How' Implications of In-State Resident Tuition Policies for Latino Undocumented Immigrants. *The Review of Higher Education, 38*(4), 507–535.

Enriquez, L. (2011). 'Because We Feel the Pressure and We Also Feel the Support': Examining the Educational Success of Undocumented Immigrant Latina/o Students. *Harvard Educational Review, 81*(3), 476–500.

Flores, S. M. (2010). State Dream Acts: The Effect of In-State Resident Tuition Policies and Undocumented Latino Students. *The Review of Higher Education*, *33*(2), 239–283.

Gonzales, R. G. (2010). On the Wrong Side of the Tracks: Understanding the Effects of School Structure and Social Capital in the Educational Pursuits of Undocumented Immigrant Students. *Peabody Journal of Education*, *85*(4), 469–485.

Gonzales, R. G. (2011). Learning to Be Illegal: Undocumented Youth and Shifting Legal Contexts in the Transition to Adulthood. *American Sociological Review; Washington*, *76*(4), 602–619.

Gonzales, R. G. (2016). *Lives in Limbo: Undocumented and Coming of Age in America*. Oakland, CA: University of California Press.

Gonzales, R. G., & Chavez, L. R. (2012). 'Awakening to a Nightmare': Abjectivity and Illegality in the Lives of Undocumented 1.5-Generation Latino Immigrants in the United States. *Current Anthropology*, *53*(3), 255–281.

Gonzales, R. G., Ellis, B., Rendón-García, S. A., & Brant, K. (2018). (Un)authorized Transitions: Illegality, DACA, and the Life Course. *Research in Human Development*, *15*(3–4), 345–359.

Gonzales, R. G., Heredia, L. L., & Negrón-Gonzales, G. (2015). Untangling Plyler's Legacy: Undocumented Students, Schools, and Citizenship. *Harvard Educational Review*, *85*(3), 318–341.

Gonzales, R. G., Murillo, M. A., Lacomba, C., Brant, K., Franco, M. C., Lee, J., & Vasudevan, D. S. (n.d.). Taking Giant Leaps Forward. Retrieved October 6, 2018, from Center for American Progress website: www.americanprogress.org/issues/immigration/reports/2017/06/22/434822/taking-giant-leaps-forward/.

Gonzales, R. G., Roth, B., Brant, K., Lee, J., & Valdivia, C. (2016). *DACA at Year Three: Challenges and Opportunities in Accessing Higher Education and Employment*. Special Report, American Immigration Council, pp. 30.

Gonzales, R. G., & Ruiz, A. G. (2014). Dreaming Beyond the Fields: Undocumented Youth, Rural Realities and a Constellation of Disadvantage. *Latino Studies*, *12*(2), 194–216.

Gonzales, R. G., Terriquez, V., & Ruszczyk, S. P. (2014). Becoming DACAmented: Assessing the Short-Term Benefits of Deferred Action for Childhood Arrivals (DACA). *American Behavioral Scientist*, *58*(14), 1852–1872.

Guarneros, N. (2017). *Freedom of Movement: A Qualitative Study Exploring the Physical Mobility and the Undocumented Spatial Consciousness of DACA Beneficiaries in Higher Education* (Ph.D., The Claremont Graduate University). http://search.proquest.com/docview/1955178374/abstract/C54503DE39804785PQ/1.

Hagan, J. M., Rodriguez, N., & Castro, B. (2011). Social Effects of Mass Deportations by the United States Government, 2000–10. *Ethnic and Racial Studies, 34*(8), 1374–1391.

Hsin, A., & Ortega, F. (2017). The Effects of Deferred Action for Childhood Arrivals on the Educational Outcomes of Undocumented Students. *Demography, 55*(4), 1487–1506.

Koohi, S. (2017). College Prospects and Risky Behavior among Mexican Immigrant Youth: The Effects of In-State Tuition Policies on Schooling and Childbearing. *Economics of Education Review, 58*, 162–174.

Krogstad, J. M., Passel, J. S., & Cohn, D. (2018). 5 facts about illegal immigration in the U.S. Retrieved February 23, 2019, from Pew Research Center website: www.pewresearch.org/fact-tank/2018/11/28/5-facts-about-illegal-immigration-in-the-u-s/.

Massey, D. S., Durand, J., & Malone, N. J. (2002). *Beyond Smoke and Mirrors: Mexican Immigration in an Era of Economic Integration*. Russell Sage Foundation.

Menjívar, C., & Abrego, L. (2012). Legal Violence: Immigration Law and the Lives of Central American Immigrants. *American Journal of Sociology, 117*(5), 1380–1421.

Negrón-Gonzales, G. (2013). Navigating 'illegality': Undocumented Youth & Oppositional Consciousness. *Children and Youth Services Review, 35*(8), 1284–1290.

Negrón-Gonzales, G. (2017). Constrained Inclusion: Access and Persistence among Undocumented Community College Students in California's Central Valley. *Journal of Hispanic Higher Education, 16*(2), 105–122.

Olivas, M. A. (2011). The Political Efficacy of Plyler v. Doe: The Danger and the Discourse. *UC Davis Law Review, 45*(1), 1–26.

Perez, W., Espinoza, R., Ramos, K., Coronado, H., & Cortes, R. (2010). Civic Engagement Patterns of Undocumented Mexican Students. *Journal of Hispanic Higher Education, 9*(3), 245–265.

Perez, W., Espinoza, R., Ramos, K., Coronado, H. M., & Cortes, R. (2009). Academic Resilience Among Undocumented Latino Students. *Hispanic Journal of Behavioral Sciences, 31*(2), 149–181.

Potochnick, S. (2014). How States can Reduce the Dropout Rate for Undocumented Immigrant Youth: The Effects of In-state Resident Tuition Policies. *Social Science Research, 45*, 18–32.

Rodríguez, N., & Hagan, J. M. (2004). Fractured Families and Communities: Effects of Immigration Reform in Texas, Mexico, and El Salvador. *Latino Studies, 2*(3), 328–351.

Silver, A. M. (2018). *Shifting Boundaries: Immigrant Youth Negotiating National, State, and Small-Town Politics*. Stanford, CA: Stanford University Press.

Suárez-Orozco, C., Yoshikawa, H., Teranishi, R. T., & Suárez-Orozco, M. (2011). Growing Up in the Shadows: The Developmental Implications of Unauthorized Status. *Harvard Educational Review, 81*(3), 438–472.

Terriquez, V. (2015). Dreams Delayed: Barriers to Degree Completion among Undocumented Community College Students. *Journal of Ethnic and Migration Studies, 41*(8), 1302–1323.

Valenzuela, A. (1999). *Subtractive Schooling: U.S.-Mexican Youth and the Politics of Caring.* Albany: State University of New York Press.

Wong, T. K., Richter, K. K., Rodriguez, I., & Wolgin, P. E. (2015). Results from a Nationwide Survey of DACA Recipients Illustrate the Program's Impact. Retrieved October 6, 2018, from Center for American Progress website: www .americanprogress.org/issues/immigration/news/2015/07/09/117054/results-from-a-nationwide-survey-of-daca-recipients-illustrate-the-programs-impact/.

Wong, T. K., Rosas, G. M., Reyna, A., Rodriguez, I., O'Shea, P., Jawetz, T., & Wolgin, P. E. (2016). New Study of DACA Beneficiaries Shows Positive Economic and Educational Outcomes. Retrieved October 6, 2018, from Center for American Progress website: www.americanprogress.org/issues/immi gration/news/2016/10/18/146290/new-study-of-daca-beneficiaries-shows-posi tive-economic-and-educational-outcomes/.

Yosso, T. J. (2005). Whose Culture Has Capital? A Critical Race Theory Discussion of Community Cultural Wealth. *Race Ethnicity and Education, 8* (1), 69–91.

CHAPTER 18

Building Ethical Relationships through the Borderless Higher Education for Refugees Project in Dadaab, Kenya

Wangui Kimari and Wenona Giles

Introduction

The Borderless Higher Education for Refugees (BHER) project, located in the refugee camps and town of Dadaab in northeastern Kenya, engages with university students and faculty in a context of continually shifting tensions. Our efforts in the BHER project to build ethical and equitable student–professor relationships, in one of the largest and most insecure refugee camps in the world, continuously collide with inequities that result in what is defined by Mezirow (1995, 50) as ongoing 'disorienting dilemmas' (Giles & Dippo, 2019). These are 'reconcilable and irreconcilable dilemmas that may always be unsettling' (Mezirow, 1995, 50). Since ethical relationships are not always characterised by equity, despite one's best intentions, they require sustained efforts, and it is moments of equity failure, spoken to within this chapter, that can elucidate gaps in the work directed towards building equitable dynamics. We build on these 'disorienting dilemmas' to develop the term 'equity failure'. With this term we reference key moments that reveal gaps in the foundations and planning of futures – moments that indicate the lack of fulfilment and temporary failures. While these gulfs emerge in unanticipated ways and may be initially challenging, as we demonstrate in this chapter, they may ultimately be productive since they compel those involved towards better understandings of contextual inequities not considered previously. These new understandings provoked by the moments of 'rupture' (i.e. when it is evident that ongoing equity efforts have not been adequate enough) can then be directed towards (re)making and fortifying equity goals and practices in North–South partnerships[1] and beyond.

[1] We acknowledge the shortcomings of the language 'global North' and 'global South', but opt for it over 'Third World', a term associated with a Cold War context. It was recently estimated that at least 86 per cent of refugees live in the global South (Hyndman & Giles, 2017, 25).

Undoubtedly, lessons learned by university partners in the BHER project have engendered a productive reshaping of institutional and pedagogical praxis. The continuous reencounters between different worldviews, positionalities and personalities and, as well, the logistical and cultural challenges inherent in enabling access to higher education in a context rife with disparities have revealed challenges underlying the project's founding assumptions. Here we examine two core BHER project spaces that are interrelated and characterised by many inequalities: BHER partnership institutional fora and pedagogical initiatives in BHER classrooms. Related, we ask what impact students have had on this project, especially in moments of equity failure, and the extent to which the limited success of BHER has depended on their forthrightness, openness to expand our understandings of them and their communities, and their determination to find a future beyond precarity. Our analysis is influenced by theoretical reflections on positionality and equity, which challenge us to examine our roles as educators and administrators in each of the two spaces we address in this chapter.

Critical reflections on teaching in precarious contexts have interrogated the power hierarchies and coloniality intrinsic to what has been historically established as 'knowledge' of a particular context or, in the case of BHER, a particular group of faculty or students (Choi, 2006, 437). Similar discussions have been taken up in debates on institutionalised pedagogy (Freire, 2000 [1970]; hooks, 1994). We hope that the knowledge we share here about this complex and challenging project speaks to power, privilege and also unexpected opportunities for learning that have occurred across the BHER partnership and the classrooms of its university partners.

We begin by detailing the history of the BHER project and the various elements that characterise BHER in its present iteration. This is followed by a discussion of two project spaces[2] where issues related to the tuition-free aspects of the BHER initiative and classroom discussions about the construction of identity and forced migration are raised. In the first space, the engagement is between students and administrators. In this case, we seek to make evident the challenges faced at the level of North–South interuniversity interactions necessary for project operations and the ways in which pedagogy and funding are intertwined. In the second space, students engage with their professor, and here moments of equity failure are highlighted in

---

[2] We rely on several sources of data for this chapter, including monthly and annual partnership meeting minutes of the BHER project that were compiled over five years (2013–2018); interviews in the spring and summer of 2018 with students, as well as those faculty and staff involved in administering the BHER project partnership for their university; and co-author Kimari's personal experience as a BHER project teaching assistant and course instructor between 2014 and 2018, when she taught for York University.

order to show how they encourage more ethical considerations for future pedagogical practices. We conclude by reiterating the importance of learning from equity failure to engender more ethical relationships within North–South partnerships that may unintentionally replicate power and knowledge disparities that are not always immediately visible.

The Locations of the BHER Project

Located in northeastern Kenya, not far from the border with Somalia, the Dadaab camps have been described as one of the largest sites of extended asylum[3] in the world and are currently home to some 235,269 registered refugees and asylum seekers (as of the end of January 2018) who have fled civil war, famine and other disasters since 1991 (UNHCR, 2018a).[4] Residents currently live in the main camps of Hagadera, Dagahaley and Ifo (see Figure 18.1). Of these, 200,886, or 85 per cent, are nationals of Somalia (UNHCR, 2018b). The camps are characterised by 'spatial sequestration, a lack of citizenship, and limited access to education or livelihood' (Giles and Orgocka, 2018, 416). Few refugee youth in Dadaab complete high school, and fewer yet manage to access university through scholarships provided by institutions outside of Dadaab. This is a gendered outcome that is much more extreme for women, who are many times less likely than men to enter and complete high school in the camps (ibid).

BHER is a development project comprised of a partnership between two Kenyan and two Canadian universities that, with the support of the office of the United Nations High Commissioner for Refugees and Windle International Kenya, offer accredited university courses to refugees in the Dadaab camps and to some Kenyans who live in Dadaab town.[5] It was formed in response to research on long-term refugee situations[6] and a 2010

---

[3] Otherwise known as a 'protracted refugee situation' in policy discourse, the office of the United Nations High Commissioner for Refugees (UNHCR) defines this as a situation in which 25,000 or more refugees originating from the same country have sought asylum in another country (or countries) for at least five consecutive years. This definition does not refer to individuals but to a specific national group of people.

[4] For a review of the history of the Dadaab refugee camps, see (Hyndman & Giles, 2017, 49–59).

[5] Our description of the BHER project in this section is derived from various project documents, as well as Giles and Dippo (2019), and Giles (2018).

[6] BHER is built upon research that began in 2005 on the long-term displacement of refugees (Hyndman and Giles, 2017) and that revealed a dearth of attention to higher education in extended exile. Further exploration of this issue in international workshops on access to higher education for refugees, a feasibility study and two videos (Dippo, Orgocka, & Giles, 2013; Murphy 2012, 2016) revealed the possibilities as well as challenges related to such an international project (see also www .bher.org/).

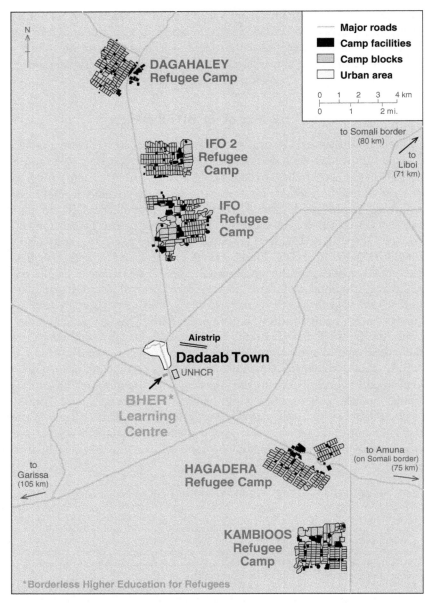

Figure 18.1 The BHER Learning Centre in the town of Dadaab and the Dadaab refugee camps in Kenya
Source: Courtesy of Joseph Mensah and Carolyn King, York University

request from Dadaab town and camp residents to have higher education in situ. This request was transmitted by the NGO Windle International Kenya, which promotes educational opportunities for marginalised communities in Kenya. The appeal was motivated by the recognition among local communities in Dadaab of the limited number of scholarships to study elsewhere in Kenya and beyond. In addition, as the BHER Partnership developed, it became more evident to us that offering university diplomas and degrees in the region, rather than expecting students to leave for Nairobi and other cities, towns and countries, could significantly enhance the local knowledge base in the region and help to avoid what has been dubbed by theorists as 'brain drain'.[7]

Both on-site and online university credit courses are offered through the BHER project, enabling mainly uncertified teachers, but also others who have graduated with a high school degree and are working in various sectors, from refugee and Kenyan communities in Dadaab, to earn a certificate, diploma and/or degree in a variety of fields, including Public Health Promotion, Education (Science), Education (Arts) and Geography. Refugee and local students in Dadaab, as well as students located at partner universities, can benefit directly through online exchange opportunities and by being able to participate in what BHER partner universities call *facilitated online learning*. This refers to a pedagogical model that includes on-site (in a Learning Centre in Dadaab town) and online courses (from the four university partners) in which students benefit from a variety of robust remedial and mentorship supports from professors, teaching assistants and project administrators and technicians.

The BHER project began with a complex preparation period in 2011 that included fundraising, a feasibility study and the development of the global North–South partnership. The choice of institutional partners was prompted by a decision to have academic anchors inside and outside the country where the Dadaab refugee camps are located, as well as to ensure that an adequate number of courses and programmes would be available for the students. While in principle each university agreed to recognise the

---

[7] There is some debate about the benefits or losses to the country of origin of human capital flight or brain drain, but context, class and gender relations matter. In the case of those Dadaab refugees in northeastern Kenya who reached out to us, who may at some future time consider returning to rebuild their war-torn and environmentally challenged country (some BHER students who have graduated with diplomas or degrees have already begun to return to homelands), or migrate to employment opportunities in the region, they did not see that it was in their personal and community interest to claim one of the few scholarship opportunities offered by those funders who required the displacement of students to a global North or other country.

others' course credits and to adhere to a tuition-free model of course delivery, these were among the most challenging aspects of the project, and ones that we turn to later in this chapter.

In 2011, discussions began with prospective students from the Dadaab camps and town, Kenyan professors and the Kenyan Ministry of Education about the types of programmes to be offered. Based on the ratio of refugees living in the camps to local Kenyan citizens, it was decided that about 75 per cent of the students would be refugees from the Dadaab camps (mostly Somalis) and 25 per cent would be Kenyan citizens from Dadaab town and the surrounding region (including many ethnic Somalis). Consultations with the Dadaab town community, the two local Members of Parliament and one of the Kenyan partner universities led to the offer of land for the construction of the BHER Learning Centre in Dadaab. By August 2014, this site housed two computer labs and several seminar rooms (see location in Figure 18.1). The BHER refugee students, like all refugees in Kenya, are not legally permitted to live or travel outside the refugee camp but received permission to visit the Learning Centre in the town of Dadaab. The first cohort of 200 students began their studies in the summer of 2014; a second cohort of 200 students began in 2015. The project has been funded primarily by the Canadian government and more recently by the Open Society Foundations.[8]

BHER's North–South Partnership

The literature on partnerships is sizeable and significant (e.g. Baud, 2002; Chernikova, 2011; Hynie, McGrath, Young, & Banerjee, 2014; Jazeel & McFarlane, 2007; Ogden & Porter, 2000; McGrath & Young, 2019). Drawing on these and other authors, one of the most relevant claims about partnerships for our chapter builds on Chernikova's analysis that 'a successful partnership can support and meet different goals for the

[8] Global Affairs Canada (GAC) [formerly the Canadian International Development Agency (CIDA)], the aid and development arm of Canada, took an international lead in supporting the implementation of the BHER project in 2013–2019. Open Society Foundations (OSF) began to support the BHER project in 2017, and continues to do so as we write this chapter. We thank both GAC and OSF for their financial support, and their strong encouragement over the long-term. MasterCard Foundation funded the initial Feasibility Study (Dippo, Orgocka, & Giles, 2013) and the first of two videos (Murphy, 2012). The Social Sciences and Humanities Research Council of Canada funded early research and the development of a partnership between two Kenyan and two Canadian universities, Windle International Kenya and the UNHCR. York University and the University of British Columbia have provided generous financial and in-kind support to the BHER project from its earliest days. The UNHCR has also been supportive, especially with the funding of student transport and lunch.

partners but that success is contingent on the partnership valuing this diversity of goals' (Chernikova, 2011; Hynie et al., 2014, 6). However, as Hynie et al. also point out, respect for diversity 'is challenged by the context in which community-university partnerships occur (2014, 6; Chernikova, 2011, 75; Rip, 2001 & Box, 2001 in Baud, 2002, 155). We consider how ethical relationships in partnerships that are intentionally non-hierarchical and attentive to how the power of class, race, geography and gender belonging may impact operational and everyday processes. In exploring equity failures within such operations, we document how the BHER partnership and classrooms are spaces of continually shifting situational tensions where participants (students, faculty and administrators) come up against unexpectedly fraught and challenging contextual dynamics. This has led some of us, associated in different ways with the BHER project, to examine strategies for developing more ethical relationships within this project. We suggest that one way of entering into an analysis of the meaning of inequity in global North–South relationships is through thinking with, learning from and being open to equity failures, a discussion that we take up here.

Both Kimari and Giles, women and privileged scholars, though different in age, academic seniority and racial backgrounds, grappled with many questions about their positionality while engaged with the BHER project. We both 'stick out' in this project. Kimari, an anthropologist from Nairobi, found that working at 'home' in Kenya did not insulate her from unfamiliar complicated encounters, partly because of her relative material privilege. Furthermore, the historical southern–northern Kenya divide, which has been consistently and violently re-entrenched via national and international social and political events, had an impact, at times unexpected, on her experience as an instructor.[9] She was concerned and constantly alert to the ways this background would shape how and what her students thought of her. Theorising similar dynamics, Tsuda (1998) and Jacobs-Huey (2002) argue that being from the same 'place' as one's 'informants' is not a guarantee of insider status. This is because class, gender and other situational privileges are always defining not only of one's initial encounters but of subsequent interactions as well. Giles, a Canadian anthropologist, Co-Lead of the BHER project and Chair of the Kenyan-Canadian BHER Partnership Committee, was positioned uneasily

[9] Both before and after independence, northeastern Kenya has been consistently marginalised by consecutive governments in political and economic ways. The ongoing local war against terrorism, which has undue bearing on the lives of Somali refugees read as Al-Shabaab sympathisers, has exacerbated the violence and historical marginalisation enacted by the state in this region.

between the major global North funders of the BHER project to whom she was responsible and recipients of that funding (e.g. university partner institutions, BHER staff, course directors and students), in both Canada and Kenya, to whom she was also answerable. Related to this positioning, she has said elsewhere (with Dippo) that an education project, such as BHER, funded by global North agencies and hosted at a Canadian university, necessarily struggles to understand itself in relation to the historical legacy of colonialism (Giles & Dippo, 2019).

Thus, our positions in relation to those with whom we worked in this project, despite our best intentions, were primed to lead to uncomfortable but inevitable equity disparities in both our institutional and pedagogical activities. The ethnographic episodes that we describe below elucidate these events and the lessons they enabled. As a consequence, these reflections have also strengthened our view that equity failures should not only cause 'disorienting dilemmas'. Rather, they should stimulate ongoing attempts to build truly ethical relationships. We argue that this is the case in the BHER project.

Inequality in a Global North–South Partnership

The partnerships involved in the development of the BHER project range from transnational institutional and organisational relationships, such as the BHER Canadian–Kenyan universities and NGO partnership, to partnerships at the most interpersonal level, between teachers and students. The first example on inequity discussed below pertains to a BHER-defined tuition-free approach, which was among the most challenging aspects of the BHER North–South partnership.

One of the key areas of institutional negotiation among the BHER partners was the creation of a tuition-free model for the delivery of university programmes. The leadership of the BHER project at the host Canadian university promoted this approach within the BHER consortium. Their rationale was not simply that students in Dadaab are unable to pay tuition but, rather, that a tuition-free model is not based on an individual student's success (i.e. in winning scholarships). Instead, such a model would encourage a collective student identity: support students to work together so that as many of the group as possible would succeed. This goal is captured by a Swahili phrase oft raised by BHER students with us: *pamoja tutashinda* (together we will win). Whereas scholarship programmes focus on the so-called best and brightest, a tuition-free model promotes a more equitable focus on the group, encouraging individuals in the group to support one another, in order to ensure that all or most successfully complete their academic programme. We were fairly certain from the outset that the success of the BHER students, who were all living in or near the impoverished and isolated Dadaab campus and engaged in many distance or online and compressed university courses, would depend on their development of strong student support groups. Time has proven this to be true. Of the four universities engaged in the BHER project, students in three of these institutions that most wholly and readily adopted a tuition-free and non-competitive approach to teaching and learning have had the highest retention and graduation rates.

The absence of tuition fees or scholarships meant that the BHER team at the Canadian host university had to look to other funding models to convince their university administration to host the project. A cost-recovery budget model was adopted, built on estimates of the elements that tuition pays for (including the cost of course directors' and teaching assistants' teaching time, internet access, registration and graduation administrative costs). Our model was further developed through discussions and negotiations among partners and funders. Of course, the four universities involved in the negotiations did not come to the table as equally resourced parties. What works in a global North university may not be possible in its counterpart in the South. This disparity notwithstanding, prior to the beginning of the project, and after many meetings and discussions, all the BHER partners formally agreed to both tuition-free and cost-recovery approaches and signed a partnership agreement to this effect.

However, as the project progressed, it became apparent that at least one of the Kenyan universities was barely able to sustain the consequences of a cost-recovery model for the delivery of tuition-free programmes. The financial requirements of the funders for detailed budgets, forecasts and specific forms of evidence of financial expenditures, as well as different hiring practices in Canada and Kenya, and the lack of familiarity or experience of the Kenyan university with all of these Canadian accounting requirements not only seriously challenged partnership relations but percolated down to students' access to their courses, as highlighted by the interview excerpts below. By contrast, after many internal consultations within their universities, both of the Canadian universities were able to accept that BHER students would not pay tuition. One Canadian university rationalised this approach from a humanitarian or 'charity' perspective and simply absorbed any tuition costs that went above and beyond the funds they received. As mentioned above, at the other Canadian university where the grant was hosted, tuition-free and cost-recovery approaches were readily adopted.

Recent reflections of a student and several project administrators lay bare the 'tyranny', in the words of one interviewee, of the inequalities in global North–South relations and, especially, in trying to work together across different university cultures to deliver courses. The comments below focus on the challenges that the project partners and students confronted, as a result of an interruption in the transfer of funds from the Canadian host university due to the delayed financial reporting by a Kenyan university. The point we are making here is not that one approach or model may be worse or better than another, but that in the context of a global North–South project, any partnership may be fraught with inequity, which will often be revealed in unanticipated ways. What's more, the impact of these challenges is, perhaps inevitably, experienced most acutely by the Southern partners, a reflection of the broader global inequity within which any such North–South project is situated.

In this case, students registered in one of the Kenyan universities were left without access to their course materials because the Kenyan university would not register students and upload the course materials that were required by the students to begin their course. Due to their different financial reporting infrastructure and their push back against the BHER project's cost-recovery model, it was a struggle for this Kenyan university to provide timely and accurate forecasts and documentation related to cost clearance.[10] One result of the delay in receiving funding was that the university would not register students in its courses until additional funds were received, but the Canadian host university could not transfer new funds until most of the documentation for the previous tranche of funds was received. The frustration that this situation created for the students is further elaborated below and demonstrates the close correlation between the financial and pedagogical aspects of the project. The politics in Kenya at this time towards refugees may also have contributed to the lack of flexibility on the part of the university towards the registration of mostly Dadaab refugee students. A sense of mistrust of refugees and fear that the Dadaab camps harbour terrorists[11] meant that, unlike the other Kenyan and Canadian partners, this large and renowned university was not willing

---

[10] Once a tranche of funds, based on a financial forecast (developed by each partner), is advanced to a partner in the BHER project, 80 per cent of that funding must be cleared by the accounting offices at the lead Canadian university before the next tranche of funds (based on a forecast) can be forwarded.

[11] There is no evidence that any refugees have been involved in recent violent attacks in Kenya.

to treat refugees differently (i.e. with more flexibility) than its regular Kenyan students.

In the spring of 2018 we interviewed Amani, an ambitious 28-year-old single-parent Kenyan student, who lives in Dadaab town and is taking BHER courses to qualify as a primary school teacher. The reason she gave for coming to Dadaab six years ago was 'because of finding bread' (i.e. the need to create a livelihood for herself and her family). Despite the hardships she experienced in this area of northeastern Kenya, Amani affirmed that 'it is a place that I have come to achieve my goals and ambition'. While in Dadaab she has had various jobs, including as a cleaner in hospital operating rooms, as a distributor of food for the World Food Programme and as a security guard. Amani told us about her frustration with the lengthy delays in receiving electronic course materials on her tablet and the burdens that placed upon her and her fellow students:

> Sometimes you register for the semester; we are there waiting for the notes, no notes you see. Let's say, September, we are there waiting for the notes and registration is already done. We are waiting for the notes; no one is communicating. Then all of a sudden, we are being told the exam is on the 20th of December. Can you imagine you are being told to prepare for the exam from what you have learned from September thru November, but you still don't have the notes even though registration was done early enough.

However, she has no illusions about who is to blame:

> What is the problem? If at all, the problem is for those people who are giving us this education, we are requesting them [the Canadians] to pay the [Kenyan] university early, because I heard that maybe when they give the school fees early enough, they [the Kenyan University] will release the notes.

From the perspective of one of the senior administrators at this Kenyan university, the delivery of student course materials has been onerous because of institutional politics, donor-reporting requirements, as well as the technological challenges of making material available online. A senior Kenyan BHER project administrator, responsible for ensuring the production of university financial reports for the Canadian funder, stated:

> We have had many challenges. Well, having understood the refugee world and trying to understand our models of education and what we want to do. Now getting that [the requirements of the funder] to be understood by the stakeholders [senior administrators] in the [Kenyan] university has been a painstaking experience.

As mentioned above, these difficulties become enmeshed in a Kenyan geopolitical context that is hostile to refugees. The ascendancy of narratives that frame refugees as perpetrators of terrorist violence, or as fraudulent refugee claimants, for example, has made it extremely difficult for Kenyan administrators of BHER-related programmes to sustain the project at their institutions, especially amidst taunts by university colleagues that they were supporting potential terrorists. On this, the same administrator said:

> And then you can be called names by people who think you are a burden. And you are called names on one side, and then on the other side you are told that the [financial aspect of the] partnership is also struggling. And then students are complaining; they say that this is not what they were told it would be.

Furthermore, the administrator confirms the close relationship between pedagogy and finances and specifically the difficulty of working with a cost-recovery model:

> Because of all of these itemised budgets – it is something the university has never done before, and so it is one other reason why I have been called names. So, I would suggest that students simply pay fees like any other student, and whatever else we are doing differently for any other student, like a class in Dadaab that is not being done elsewhere, then this can be supervised by the donor. This is important.

Despite the issues raised above, the administrator shared:

> But I am very happy to see the students who have graduated with the diploma, and we are looking forward to seeing those who will graduate with a degree. The fact that we have survived through the storm is something we should celebrate.

A university administrator from another Kenyan university also referred to the stringent requirements for the release of funds to partner institutions upheld by both the Canadian funder and host university, and the serious difficulties this causes to the Kenyan institutions. What's more, they added:

> Also, when the money comes it goes to a central place [in the respective university], and so it is hard to get it from there, and this can bring about delays. So maybe, if you want something to go on for the program you need to use your own money for this initially. We also need more understanding from Canada about what we go through here; the university cultures are different, and we operate differently.

Echoing these sentiments, a Canadian administrator of the BHER project describes the inequity present in this initiative that, despite all efforts to the contrary, structures the project in a financially unequal way, leading to very problematic issues in course delivery for the Kenyan universities. They refer to a

> North-South divide that is hegemonic: it is structured to reinforce the tyranny that the person who has the money is the person who has the final say. And to try and overcome that and maintain respect and good relationships has been a very big challenge.

Inherent in the North–South power relation described above, which we refer to in this chapter as having led to an equity failure, are cultural/political differences between universities involved in the BHER project, as well as the geopolitics of the Kenyan state. On the one hand, the Canadian university partner that received project funds had to distribute them according to the requirements of the funder and their own accounting requirements. The Canadian accountability requirements were standard accounting practices and monthly partnership meetings, as well as numerous individual institutional meetings in Canada and Kenya were arranged to explain the financial requirements of the donor and host university so as to ensure transparency and equity. On the other hand, despite these supports, the financial aspects of the project, including an emphasis on a tuition-free model, created a situation that the Kenyan partner universities found extremely difficult to adapt to their own priorities and financial structures. The geopolitics of this North–South funding relationship meant they had little or no say in changing these requirements.

Regardless of this very real barrier to the development of an equitable relationship, partners in the BHER project have so far, and against great odds, persisted in the BHER partnership. The tensions in this space of inequity reverberate in the space of the classroom, as described in the following examples.

Equity Failure in a Classroom

Since 2016, the co-author of this chapter, Wangui Kimari, has been teaching an introduction to anthropology course, *Making Sense of a Changing World*, to Dadaab students enrolled in BHER-supported education programmes. In Toronto, the course was oriented around getting students to understand global trends (often shaped by Northern political economies) by drawing from an anthropological toolbox. Similarly, when it came to teaching in

Dadaab, Kimari wanted students to use the course to develop visions of other worlds, see the connections across histories and geographies, while using established anthropological concepts to articulate these associations. Since offered both online and on-site, the course was designed to be cognisant of the infrastructural issues that could sometimes affect course delivery in Dadaab: in particular, electricity and internet outages. To these ends, on both a content and infrastructural front, she reworked the course for 'fit' to Dadaab, keeping 'the unique challenges of refugee camps in mind' (BHER, 2019). Her solutions were, for example, the incorporation of previously unplanned tools such as WhatsApp as course delivery support (to make announcements, speak with students, share assignment information) and the development of a synthesis of topics and course material that she felt students would be interested in and relate to. Kimari also carefully considered strategies to approach topics, such as sexuality, which, she felt, might not 'hit the ground' in the ways desired.

Despite all the intentional work directed towards this course, Kimari learned that no class, or effort, directed towards establishing equity is ever infallible and that the gaps in this practice could become evident when least expected. Though discussions about gender, marriage and even birth across the world (the discussion of in vitro fertilisation and whether the test tube could also be considered a parent of the conceived child was certainly memorable) were illuminating, two episodes highlighted key learning moments about equity and underscored (1) the significance of students' voices in contextualising the BHER project in the Dadaab camps and (2) the learning opportunities afforded by equity failures for future projects.

In a class examining identity construction, subject formation and habitus among 'youth', one of the readings focused on how young people in various places, including Dakar, used their clothing to speak about their own lives – to write their own biographies. The young voices contained in the assigned text, describing the performance of aspiration through dress, resonated with Kimari and had, a year earlier, also resonated with the classroom in Toronto where she had used this material.

In Dadaab, however, the reaction was quite different. Most of the young women in this cohort wore, more or less, the same shade of *chador*, *abaya* and/or *hijab*, conservative but not ostentatious or elaborate. The young men, like their counterparts throughout Africa, exhibited more variation in their chosen clothing. Kimari felt that an outsider like herself could not completely understand these students as performing similar material generational aspirations, as the Dakar youth or her Toronto students, because of religious, social and economic restrictions, and this is not something they admitted to in the classroom discussion. One student however, in seeking to 'make sense' of this mode of seemingly foreign identity formation that was being debated, said bluntly: 'but Madam, that does not happen here in Dadaab, we do not perform anything through our clothing because we just wear whatever clothes we are given by the agencies'.

Though the instructor had been conscious of how class impacts one's access to material goods and how these can be used to construct identity, she had not foregrounded the very real material limits that mould the lives of many of our Dadaab students, including the frequent dependence on NGOs for many items, including clothing. It was at the moment of this student's revelation that the depth of this inequity in access to clothing was made more explicit, and not their inability to write their own biographies through what they wore. Certainly, in this instance it became clear that generalisations about the modes through which youth perform their identity could not have the same purchase in this context, and in failing to 'hit the ground' as these discussions normally did, they engendered a moment of equity failure.

Some months later in the same course, Kimari was again stopped in her tracks by her students.

No longer obliged to promote a territorially bound 'culture' as was the norm in the early days of the discipline, it has become commonplace for anthropology course in Canada to attend to the many aspects of human life, including migration. Kimari's class, *Making Sense of a Changing World*, was not to be left behind in this regard. To these ends she dedicated at least two classes to thinking about chain migration, displacement, push-and-pull factors and borders, and how these phenomena worked to reshape local practices and territories. From the outset she was very conscious of her position as a 'migrant' to Canada (as a recently graduated foreign student) who *chose* and was not *forced* to leave her home. Above all, and particularly in Dadaab, she recognised that she was the citizen of a country (Kenya) intent on ensuring that BHER students, despite the majority's birth in Kenya, remain non-citizens. So even while she and her Dadaab students were technically from the same country, at different moments she could be, as Choi (2006) discusses, 'simultaneously an insider, outsider, both and neither', while her students could not have the same diversity in identity: here they were almost always outsiders.[12] As a result,

---

[12] Kenyan citizens living in the northeastern region of the country are also outsiders in the sense that they are very likely to be impoverished and/or ethnic Somalis, who face ongoing and serious historical discrimination.

migration was a topic that she taught with much trepidation, even when the course content was intended to be critical.

The class on migration was, therefore, structured as an engagement with the readings through the lens of the students' own experiences. Certainly, they made it clear that their direct experience of key course concepts such as cultural relativism and displacement qualified them to lead the discussion: the stories they shared about living together in a 'city of thorns',[13] within refugee communities fraught by deep and painful tensions relating to ethnocentrism and migration, were extremely relevant and guided our conversations.

Despite her best intentions, Kimari's equity failure moment in this class became apparent in her inability to know how to proceed in face of the unexpected revelation by one student that his brother had left Dadaab in search of a better life in Europe and while in Libya, as this is the route that he took, had been kidnapped and continued to be held for ransom by an ISIS-affiliated faction. Due to both the gravity and unexpectedness of this revelation, Kimari was not sure what to do. Though she felt certain that there *may* have been a right way to respond, at this instant she was unsure, frustrated by this uncertainty, and remained silent.

This moment, without a doubt, exposed gaps in Kimari's knowledge about some of the experiences students were facing, even against the very real attempts to have their lives shape both the pedagogic and administrative operations of the BHER project. In reflecting on this instance, Kimari continues to ask herself: how can we use moments like this to build towards ethical relationships more attuned to local dynamics and effects?

In both of these situations, in the discussion about youth, clothing and identity construction in Dadaab and the inability of the instructor to act after a painful student revelation, the best intentions of the teacher and the university are rendered irrelevant. Despite the foregrounding of equity in both institutional and curricula activities, as well as Kimari's own seeming familiarity with the context, these two situations, among many, showed blind spots – gaps in the understandings of local realities that impeded an expansion of the ethical attention that contributes to more equitable relationships.

That many people around the world are unable to choose clothes they can use to 'perform their identity' and that the gravities of forced migration include a limitless continuum of very violent force were not elements that the instructor had, admittedly, comprehensively and emotionally factored

---

[13] This is how Rawlence describes the Dadaab camps in his recent book (2016).

in. At the same time, the empathy and humanity accorded to Kimari by the students, as they bluntly but patiently reoriented her to the particular realities of the place (beyond what she thought she knew and her most critical intentions), certainly established the importance of equity failure as a learning opportunity. At their most powerful, and this is our suggestion, these moments are catalysts for better ethical relationships within North–South partnerships – both in and outside of the classroom, and need to be coupled with consistent reflections on the positionalities of both institutions and personnel, so as to be more, much more, than 'disorienting dilemmas'.

Conclusion

In this chapter, we have examined our efforts at building ethical relationships through learning from equity failure in the BHER project in Dadaab, Kenya. To these ends we have reflected on two spaces within the BHER North–South partnership: within institutional interactions and in the classroom. The challenges with partnership sustenance and course delivery, as well as unexpected learning moments during classroom activities, have been brought together to show the different ways in which inequity and the gaps in knowledge it indicates become evident and can impact collaborations.

The histories and the snapshots we have provided indicate the very real and ongoing challenges attendant to establishing a transcontinental partnership that foregrounds equity and that takes place in contexts that are highly uneven and precarious. This precarity refers to situations of not only severely unequal citizenship opportunities but also to those that do not have the required provision of services needed to run project activities, such as a consistent electricity and internet connection. To reflect on these moments, we have also taken seriously our positionalities and those of our institutions and recognised how historical trajectories of colonialism, class, gender and even geographical location in Kenya, for instance, contribute to equity failures. Notwithstanding these recognitions, and the compelling insights afforded by such moments, we understand that building good and strong relationships requires sustained efforts. We suggest that any global North–South educational initiative should build on the kinds of failures that occur in the life of a project by taking them seriously and dialogically working to redress the gaps they indicate.

Against these hard lessons, we are also conscious of the very real efforts of the students – their hard work, dreams and determinations – that are primarily responsible for the success of this project. The students taking courses at one of the four BHER-related universities continue to direct their sights on their goals: graduation and, finally and hopefully, access to better lives, jobs or indeed further education and graduate degrees. However, the students' articulations of their ambitions, frustration, anger, intellectual excitement and step-by-step progress towards graduation may well be among the most important reasons for the continuation of the BHER project. We have seen their complaints about project hardships dissipate over the last four years, to the point that, while there is still concern about many aspects of course delivery among some of the students, most now have longer sights on the end goal – of their graduation and beyond. In this regard, Khadija, a 25-year-old Kenyan who is doing a BA degree in education, shared:

> We never believed that we would reach this path. The BHER team [staff in Dadaab and instructors] are our role models. Through their support, I have been encouraged to complete this. So, whenever I think about dropping [out] I see that there are people who have guided me [to this point].

Olal speaks of the education he is receiving:

> This program is shaping people. It has changed my life. I've learnt so much from education [the Kenyan and Canadian courses he has taken] and I now see that it's the most crucial tool in life because it can take you out of poverty. This learning is helping us form a community. It has taught us so much. The other thing is people knowing that we're learning. The community is realising that we can help them and we are now given responsibilities [by the Dadaab refugee community, NGOs, national and international agencies].

The resilience of southern institutions, and particular administrators, in sustaining North–South collaborations, is also recognised as important for building from equity failures. For them, the differences in their resourcing and institutional approaches, when compared to their Canadian partners, brought about frictions that were ultimately worked through in order to prioritise and support the students. At the same time, establishing a more inclusive North–South relationship continues to be work in progress.

REFERENCES

Baud, I. (2002). North-South Partnerships in Development Research: An Institutional Approach. *International Journal of Technology Management and Sustainable Development, 1*(3), 153–170.

Borderless Higher Education for Refugees (BHER) (2019). *About BHER.* Retrieved 2 February 2019, from https://www.bher.org/about%20bher/

Chernikova, E. (2011). *Shoulder to Shoulder or Face to Face? Canada's University-Civil Society Collaborations on Research and Knowledge for International Development.* Ottawa: International Development Research Centre.

Choi, J. A. (2006). Doing Poststructural Ethnography in the Life History of Dropouts in South Korea: Methodological Ruminations on Subjectivity, Positionality and Reflexivity. *International Journal of Qualitative Studies in Education, 19*(4), 435–453.

Dippo, D., Orgocka, A., & Giles, W. (2013). *Feasibility Study Report: Reaching Higher: The Provision of Higher Education for Long Term Refugees in the Dadaab Camps, Kenya.* 14 April 2014, http://refugeeresearch.net/ms/bher/workshops/feasibility-study-report/

Freire, P. (2000 [1970]). *Pedagogy of the Oppressed.* New York: Continuum.

Giles, W. (2018). The Borderless Higher Education for Refugees Project: Enabling Refugee and Local Kenyan Students in Dadaab to Transition to University Education. *Journal on Education in Emergencies, 4*(1), 164–184.

Giles, W., & Dippo, D. (2019). Transitions from Knowledge Networked to Knowledge Engaged: Ethical Tensions and Dilemmas from the Global to the Local. In S. McGrath, & J. Young (eds.), *Ethical Networking for Research and Practice: Reflections on the Refugee Research Network.* Calgary: University of Calgary Press.

Giles, W., & Orgocka, A. (2018). Adolescents in Protracted Refugee Situations: The Case of Dadaab. In J. Bhabha, D. Senovilla Hernandez, & J. Kanics (eds.), *Research Handbook on Migration and Childhood.* Cheltenham: Edward Elgar Publishing.

hooks,b. (1994). *Teaching to Transgress.* New York: Routledge.

Hyndman, J., & Giles, W. (2017). *Refugees in Extended Exile: Living on the Edge.* Abingdon-on-Thames: Routledge.

Hynie, M., McGrath, S., Young, J. E., & Banerjee, P. (2014). Negotiations of Engaged Scholarship and Equity through a Global Network of Refugee Scholars. *Scholarly and Research Communications, 5*(3), 1–18.

Jacobs-Huey, L. (2002). The Natives are Gazing and Talking Back: Reviewing the Problematics of Positionality, Voice and Accountability among 'Native' Anthropologists. *American Anthropologist, 104*(3), 791–804.

Jazeel, T., & McFarlane, C. (2007). Responsible Learning: Cultures of Knowledge Production and the North–South Divide. *Antipode, 39*(5), 781–789.

McGrath, S., & Young, J. (eds.). (2019). *Ethical Networking for Research and Practice: Reflections on the Refugee Research Network.* Calgary, Canada: University of Calgary Press.

Mezirow, J. (1995). Transformation Theory of Adult Learning. In M. R. Welton (ed.), *Defense of the Lifeworld*. New York: SUNY.

Murphy, P. (2012). Hunger for Education on the Edge of the Planet. Toronto. http://www.bher.org/bher-videos/ (video)

Murphy, P. (2016). Borderless Higher Education: Bringing Higher Education to Refugees in Dadaab. http://www.bher.org/bher-videos/ (video)

Ogden, J. A., & Porter, J. D. (2000). The Politics of Partnership in Tropical Public Health: Researching Tuberculosis Control in India. *Social Policy & Administration, 34* (4), 377–391.

Rawlence, B. (2016). *City of Thorns: Nine Lives in the World's Largest Refugee Camp*. New York: Picador.

Sultana, F. (2007). Reflexivity, Positionality and Participatory Ethics: Negotiating Fieldwork Dilemmas in International Research. *ACME: An International E-Journal for Critical Geographies, 6*(3), 374–385.

Tsuda, T. (1998). Ethnicity and the Anthropologist: Negotiating Identities in the Field. *Anthropological Quarterly, 71*(3), 107–124.

UNHCR. (2018a). *Dadaab Refugee Complex*. 1 February 2019, www.unhcr.org/ke/dadaab-refugee-complex

UNHCR. (2018b). *Refugees and Asylum Seekers in Kenya by Country of Origin and Location*. Retrieved 1 February 2019, from Statistical Summary as of 31 December 2018: Refugees and Asylum Seekers in Kenya: www.unhcr.org/ke/wp-content/uploads/sites/2/2019/01/Kenya-Statistics-Package-December-2018.pdf

CHAPTER 19

The 'Jungle' Is Here; The Jungle Is Outside
University Teaching in the Calais Refugee Camp

Corinne Squire and Tahir Zaman

Introduction

Less than 1 per cent of refugees and asylum seekers worldwide enter higher education (HE) (UNHCR, 2016). This chapter explores the borders of HE in Europe, in relation to the ongoing arrival of displaced people, predominantly from Africa and West Asia. These new arrivals are mostly male, young and single, from varying economic and educational backgrounds. Almost all are fleeing violent conflict or situations of protracted displacement in countries of origin or first refuge. While many were or planned to become students, in almost all cases, access to HE has been lost or cut off.

This chapter addresses the possibilities raised by relocating the 'university' to the informal Calais 'Jungle' refugee camp, where the authors and colleagues from Social Sciences and Humanities at the University of East London (UEL) taught an accredited 'Life Stories' short course in 2015–2016 and worked on a number of other education-related initiatives.[1] We draw on our observations of HE by and for refugees and asylum seekers as practised in these programmes. We focus on these programmes because they provide striking instances of refugees themselves generating new conditions for learning and teaching (Hall, Lounasmaa, & Squire, 2018). The chapter analyses HE in refugee spaces not only as a humanitarian response and an assertion of a human right but also as a partial construction of a largely refugee-initiated, political formation characterised by reciprocity. Within this context, the area outside the camp, more than the camp itself, appears as a 'jungle' – a dangerous space that denies humanity. By contrast, the 'Jungle' sustains safety and a generous and humane outlook, including through epistemically open,

---

[1] We describe these programmes collectively as 'Educating without borders'. See: https://educatingwithoutborders.wordpress.com/university-for-all-2/ – on Life Stories in Calais, Manchester, London, and (by online learning) in Lebanon and Jordan.

dialogic forms of what Mbembe (2016) has called 'pluriversal' university education.

We begin by describing the context in which the 'Life Stories' course at the Calais camp operated. We then consider what a 'need' for and a 'right' to education mean in situations of heightened humanitarian need and for illegalised humans. The heart of the chapter is an exploration of how HE practised by and with refugees in contemporary Europe may generate forms of 'university' that depart from the dominant, commercially driven model: pursuing a citizenry of learning, centring on students and linking HE to other kinds of intellectual work. We argue that such initiatives can move beyond humanitarian and rights frameworks to more reciprocal frames of coalition, commons and association. All these frames have different possibilities and limits. We suggest that educational citizenships grounded in such reciprocities, rather than in fundamentally asymmetric humanitarian and rights exchanges, are more mobile and wide-ranging and that, within those reciprocal frameworks, associational education practices in particular, and as discussed below, demonstrate the value of heterogeneous, adaptable relationships.

Life Stories

The informal gathering established in the post-industrial scrublands on the periphery of the Northern French port of Calais was named the 'Jungle' by French media, but then also by the site's residents. For residents, this term emphasised the camp's abject conditions – not even fit, many said, for animals. From the early 2000s, the 'Jungle' hosted thousands of residents, until in October 2016 it was demolished. A wall paid for by the UK was built around the Calais port, and the majority of the then roughly 8000 residents was registered and distributed to Centres d'Acceuil et Orientation (CAOs) across France. About 700 refugees are still thought to be living around Calais and trying to reach the United Kingdom, sleeping in patches of scrub and woodland, with occasional, heavily policed access to volunteer-provided tents, blankets, food, water, and medical care (RRDP, 2018). The 'Jungle' was several kilometres from Calais's centre, making it hard for refugees to use town services; some Calaisians were also hostile and aggressive towards them. The camp was two hours by foot, across numerous razor wire fences and a heavy, violent police presence, from the port and station, setting up exhausting and dangerous nightly expeditions for those attempting to reach the United Kingdom – an effort known as 'trying'. At the site, vegetation thinly covered potentially toxic landfill, including broken-up asbestos. The camp lacked shelter and sanitation, creating a dire public health situation. The French state's neglect was justified by its policy of not formally recognising the camp – part of a wider border enforcement regime that seeks to create a hostile environment for illegalised migrants and asylum seekers (Castro, 2015; Dhesi, Isakjee, & Davies, 2018).

The 'Jungle' was a dangerous and depressing place for residents, many of whom, concerned only with leaving, hardly engaged with camp structures, including 'Life Stories'. Nonetheless, the city had given the land to refugees to live on, and many stayed for months, so some residents also viewed the camp as a home-like community. Large numbers of residents worked, often alongside volunteers who came from France, the United Kingdom and other countries, to provide for residents' needs and to build spaces of residence, nutrition, faith, art, sport and education (Hall et al., 2018).

When we started teaching in the 'Jungle', in September 2015, there was already some English and French teaching at L'Ecole des Arts et Metiers, L'Ecole Laique du Chemin des Dunes and the Jungle Books Library, all of which were established and built by residents with help from visiting volunteers. Between then and October 2016, when the camp was demolished, we travelled to the camp roughly every two weeks to teach 'Life Stories', deliver photography workshops and help students with their coursework. Over 90 per cent of camp residents were male, and most students were men. While women's childcare responsibilities left them little time for study or writing, we conducted a day's art workshop with some of the 200 'vulnerable' women in the government-run Jules Ferry Centre. A book project, *Voices from the 'Jungle'* (Africa et al., 2017), affording students' work a broader audience, and including the work of a woman author, was also developed.

The churn of new student faces was hard to keep pace with, as residents regularly made successful attempts to cross the heavily fortified and policed border between mainland Europe and the United Kingdom. Nevertheless, some residents stayed in the camp long enough to finish a course. Others contacted us afterwards by phone or social media, to continue studying and working on assignments or for education advice. Those with less economic and social capital, who did not have phones or phone credit, were less likely to stay in touch, though some called or messaged months later. One Afghan man in his thirties, whose educational aspirations had been curtailed by poverty, submitted by Facebook Messenger, over several months, a 10,000-word assignment which made a substantial contribution to the *Voices* book. Injured while 'trying', he stayed in France, continuing the French lessons he had started in the 'Jungle' and re-qualifying as a heavy goods vehicle driver, able to support his family though not yet to begin university. A Sudanese man in his twenties with an English Literature background completed the Calais course, and then, when he reached the United Kingdom, the UEL Open Learning Initiative (OLIve) course, a bridging programme for refugees into HE. He received a UEL foundation-year fee waiver and is now taking a Political Sciences degree. An Iraqi teenager who attended many 'Life Stories' classes, now awaiting UK asylum, still regularly seeks advice on qualifying for HE.

The character of the 'Life Stories' course was simple but flexible and participatory. Students had often had, and might want again, more conventional courses. In this context of resource constraint and disempowerment, though, pedagogical adaptability, student-centredness and attention to the knowledge students brought with them were central to the course process. The course aimed to provide space for the reading, discussion, telling and writing of life stories, of the students, those close to them or others; to introduce camp residents to European HE systems; and to encourage them to continue education, circumstances permitting. It involved three three-hour teaching sessions, seminar-style, based on readings, questions and discussion, with follow-up assignment sessions and one-to-one face-to-face and online (if feasible) tutoring. Students set the curriculum, including the writings of Nelson Mandela, Malala Yousafzai, Warsan Shire, JJ Bola, Chinua Achebe, Malcolm X, Martin Luther King, WEB DuBois, Plato and Mahmoud Darwish. Assignments involved a mix of writing and visual work, mostly photography and personal stories. Over 100 students attended the course, which ran three times, with 55 completing; another 100 participated in advice workshops. A further 100 people from refugee and asylum-seeker backgrounds have formed subsequent cohorts of the course in Manchester and London and, most recently, via online teaching, in Jordan and Lebanon. In Calais, many students engaged in extended writing projects, including the co-authored *Voices from the Jungle* (Africa et al., 2017). Some produced films and participated in photography exhibitions. Others have sought more advice on HE, or have passed into HE or preparation for it, for instance via UEL's OLIve courses.

'Life Stories' has been taught with wide support from UEL-based students, colleagues and administrative staff, as well as colleagues outside the university. As it has proved helpful in reaching those who are among the least eligible to access HE in Europe and the Middle East, it may now be expanded to reach others in that situation within the United Kingdom, such as young people leaving foster care and children's care homes.

While 'Life Stories' initially received UEL 'civic engagement' funding for travel, and 'impact' funding for visual projects and workshops, it is now sustainable from UEL's teaching budget, which supports fee waivers and travel contributions, and through staff's regular 'civic engagement' volunteering, with some additional civic engagement and impact funding. This structure has enabled instructors to team-teach the course in Calais, Manchester, and London; to pay undergraduate teaching assistants, many from refugee and asylum-seeker backgrounds themselves; and to deliver professional creative art and writing workshops. The course's resource 'investments' are justified to and by UEL, as with all courses, via a 'business case'. In this justification, the 'Life Stories' course contributes to UEL's civic engagement 'mission', as well as to UEL staff and student helpers' teaching and learning skills, UEL 'access' figures for refugees and, through 'Life Stories' students themselves, to the broader learning and teaching environment of the university.

Our 'Life Stories' teaching was not linked to research; no ethical approval has been sought, no research interviews or observations conducted. Valuable and rigorous research on resident conditions needs was done in the 'Jungle' by, for instance, MSF and the Refugee Rights Data Project (RRDP) (Bouhenia et al., 2017; RRDP, 2016). 'Educating without borders' may in future conduct some research with ex-students to map educational and life trajectories. This chapter, however, is based not on empirical research but on theoretical analysis, drawing on data from and about the camp, the *Voices from the 'Jungle'* book and other publicly available accounts, personal reflections on our teaching and media reports.[2]

In what follows, we consider, first, the possibilities and limits of humanitarian and rights theories of refugee HE provision – theories which are the basis of most policy arguments for such provision – and, second, the possibilities and constraints of what we call 'reciprocity' theories of refugee HE. In our view, reciprocity theories better describe many of the innovative patterns of education provision we saw developing in the camp – patterns of coalitional, commoning and associational provision.

---

[2] For the 'Jungle', see: www.calaidipedia.co.uk/

Humanitarian and Rights Accounts of Refugee Higher Education

We move now to what are perhaps the most common and powerful theoretical accounts of refugee HE, those based on humanitarianism and human rights arguments and their limitations.

Within humanitarian discourses of human welfare, education is viewed as an essential component. Indeed, when requesting resources for the 'Life Stories' course, we tactically deployed humanitarian arguments about the humanitarian necessity of education. However, such humanitarianism not only cloaks refugee agency and self-sufficiency but also obfuscates education's substantial market benefits. Refugees' and migrants' labour, crucial to European economies and to refugees' own sense of themselves and their effectiveness, is enhanced by their education. Indeed, humanitarian justifications of refugee student fee-waivers are frequently accompanied by assertions of the likely future value of educating such students, while refugees' own accounts (as in Africa et al., 2017) repeatedly reject positioning themselves as charity recipients to situate themselves as producers of value.

Arguments about educational humanitarianism are further qualified by the arguments' limited purchase, especially in relation to HE, since humanitarianism's primary legal application is to relieve suffering from war and other conflicts. While there has been a move towards the expansion of humanitarianism beyond emergency relief, towards development agendas – the so-called humanitarian-development nexus – much of this work is carried out with limited success, in a framework of containment. In such cases, the humanitarian–development nexus is deployed in the interests of powerful states in the global North to curtail the onward mobility of displaced people stranded in countries of first refuge in the global South (Duffield, 2008). Less understood is the significance of educational spaces for those who refuse to be contained, who make their way to countries further afield, searching for security and improved life chances.

Going beyond ideas of humanitarian succour to arguments about justice, appeals for support for the 'Life Stories' course also tactically mobilised human rights claims, drawing on Article 26 of the UN's Universal Declaration on Human Right which affirms that 'higher education shall be equally available to all on the basis of merit'. More broadly, the UK organisation called Article 26 invokes this right to campaign for fee-waived and scholarship HE provisions for refugees and asylum seekers across the United Kingdom.[3]

---

[3] For Article 26, see: http://article26.hkf.org.uk/

Rights discourse was common among 'Jungle' residents. However, their rights expectations within Europe, most fundamentally to be treated fairly and without discrimination, as human beings rather than rights-suspended 'refugees' to whom no services were due, were undermined by the camp. The 'Jungle' was a place that, as Muhammad (all 'Voices' author names are pseudonyms, unless otherwise indicated) wrote, 'belonged to the European Middle Ages'. In the end, Muhammad decided not to go to the United Kingdom, 'a country whose government talks all the time about human rights and helping refugees but closes their borders against them' (Africa et al., 2017, 113, 202). In response to this rights abrogation, some, for instance Zimako Jones, founder of the Ecole Laique du Chemin des Dunes,[4] instead constructed the camp as the true repository of 'European' values of freedom and democracy: a new republic and city of the future, taking forward French Enlightenment ideals betrayed elsewhere (Loud Minority, 2016). For Jones, the 'jungle' of irrationality lay outside the camp. This assertion of rationalism and rights was successful in gaining media and public support for the Ecole. Though eventually demolished like the rest of the camp, the school was the last building standing, used to house unaccompanied minors who remained, pawns in custody disputes between France and the United Kingdom, after all other residents were evicted and buildings razed.

Discourses and practices of 'human rights' appear well before and outside of contemporary (Sikkink, 2017) Western instantiations. However, current Western human rights arguments often 'Eurocentrise' those rights, leaving out large fields of human interaction. Consequently, rights arguments may work better as tactics within broader struggles for justice, rather than as social justice frameworks in themselves. Moreover, even within Western rights frameworks, 'rights' are contested; they compete with each other (Mouffe, 2014). And despite human rights' allegedly universal character, they are also differentiated by *whose* rights they may be. Western countries tend to award rights mostly to national citizens, of whom concomitant responsibilities can be demanded, and less to 'othered' subjects within their borders (Dembour & Kelley, 2011). For example, Jones'

---

[4] The Ecole Laique du Chemin des Dunes was set up by a camp resident, Zimako Mel Jones, in collaboration with the French organisation working against educational exclusion, Solidarité Laique. It first hosted English and French classes. At its second, larger site, it developed a children's classroom and teaching schedule; a playground; a meeting room and movie theatre; small accommodation rooms for volunteers; and a nurse-staffed clinic. It also hosted Université Lille III staff who recruited 80 camp residents for a year-long bridging course into French HE, which began after the camp had closed.

reassertion of the French Enlightenment, welcomed by left publications like *Liberation*, was viewed by the French political right as an usurpation of 'rights' discourse by someone with, as yet, no citizenly 'right' to it. In UK universities, asylum seekers who have no irregularities in their forced migration history are often favoured for fee waivers and scholarships, and thus given education rights, over asylum seekers who face more obstacles to citizenship.

The rights approach to university education in the Calais camp was complex and problematised by specific circumstances. Camp residents were often already well educated, up to high school level or above, making university their most relevant educational choice. Others held HE as a more distant goal. However, while university education was useful for and popular with residents, NGOs working in the camp could argue for rights to and resources for language education much more effectively, given European governments' preoccupations with refugees' rapid progress towards employment and social 'inclusion'. Even then, rights to food, fuel, sanitation, shelter, health and citizenship were often higher priorities for both refugees and the volunteer initiatives supporting them (than any kind of education). 'Life Stories' courses were patchworked between residents' mornings of sleep to recover from nights spent 'trying' or freezing, and NGO meal distributions; and had to work alongside food, shelter, legal, medical and therapeutic services. Rights' claims, then, were a starting point, but not a full or sustained argument, for HE in the camp.

In what follows, we move on from humanitarian and rights-based approaches, which seem to us insufficient to understand educational spaces' significance for camp residents, to refugee education. The following section explores the idea of a politics of reciprocity to describe what happened in the camp around education, particularly HE, and what may happen in other similar spaces. This shift to a reciprocity framework is at the same time a shift away from the fundamental asymmetries of humanitarianism and rights arguments wherein the former continues to lock the figure of the refugee into the role of grateful beneficiary and the latter recognises the citizen as the rightful bearer and carrier of rights.

Reciprocities

It has long been understood that the modern humanitarian enterprise is anchored in a relation of asymmetry to displacement-affected people, reduced to the passivity of beneficiary or end-user (Harrell-Bond, 2002). Awards of rights, too, are usually in the end adjudicated asymmetrically by powerful national and international actors, however strong the rights claims made by the displaced. Moreover, to be recipients of humanitarian or rights largesse, displaced people are expected to respond in highly specific and predetermined ways: to show gratitude and conform to norms set out by humanitarian actors and agencies (Moulin & Nyers, 2007), or to acknowledge and meet others' rights definitions and the responsibilities attached to them. Such asymmetrical relations underpinning the unreciprocated humanitarian 'gift' or rights award make the recipient 'inferior' (Maus, 2009 [1950], 83). Where displaced people behave otherwise they are seen as 'pulling the wool over the eyes' of institutional actors (Kibreab, 2004) or are disavowed by the very agencies purporting to protect them (Moulin & Nyers, 2007). Without the possibility of meaningful reciprocation, displaced people may seek to evade the Medusa-like gaze of humanitarian and rights enterprises that petrify them into passive recipients or mechanical responders. Spaces such as the 'Jungle', lying outside of the formal humanitarian and rights systems, allow residents to reconfigure relations of exchange between themselves and non-resident volunteers and workers engaged in practices of informal humanitarianism and rights (Zaman, 2019). By a 'politics of reciprocity', we are thus referring to processes occurring in camp spaces, through which residents were able to respond reciprocally – actively and on their own terms – to the arrival of informal humanitarians and migrant rights activists.

In this chapter, 'reciprocity' indicates interactions on the basis of acknowledged humanness, not gifting and receiving, or exchanging some goods for others. As in theories of altruism, we are describing positive reciprocity, treating it as related to social responsibility.[5] In relation to HE, such reciprocity works at a tangent to humanitarian or rights-based provision and is characterised by residents' own activities.

The effects of this reciprocity in the 'Jungle' were wide-ranging. Residents' active educational engagements put distinctions between 'teachers' and 'students' in question; there was learning and teaching in each group. Accounts from teachers who were not residents emphasised what *they* had learned. In *Voices from the 'Jungle'*, authors often noted the educative effects of dialogue with people of different backgrounds from all over the world. Such dialogue, in the camp's small, makeshift schools, helped develop wider practices like the residents' council, an 'organic

---

[5] In social psychology, the reciprocity norm is viewed narrowly as involving expectations of mutual exchange, and is contrasted to the norm of social responsibility which involves expectations that people will depend on each other for help (Berkowitz, 1968). Here we define reciprocity differently, as a broader foundation for social responsibility, similar to 'recognition' in the work of Honneth (1995).

democracy' in which residents from all national and religious groups, though skewed towards older, English-speaking, male residents, worked with non-resident volunteers on, for instance, developing new schools as new groups of residents arrived with different skills and needs. Residents also cultivated and initiated a range of collaborative activities – teaching, but also arts and sports programmes, advocacy and activism – with non-resident volunteers. This reciprocity linked academic HE to other forms of education – photo, theatre and radio workshops, language learning – and to less obviously 'educational' practices like art, social protest and legal debate. One camp resident described the library, for instance, as a multifaceted place where he attended 'Life Stories' and other classes, met legal advisors and friends, but also relaxed:

> . . . my mind is too busy. All people here, all, have the stress . . . Today I was at Jungle Books library for more than eight hours. Sometimes I sleep there. Sometimes I learn some English. I go there every day. (Africa et al., 2017, 149)

In what follows, we will not therefore distinguish HE from related activities, as discourses and practices of reciprocity occurred across educational and other practices in the camp.

Of course, reciprocities were limited and imperfect. Our use of this concept is not meant to indicate that reciprocity is ever fully symmetrical, non-hierarchical or conflict-free. We are suggesting, rather, that educational and other initiatives in the 'Jungle' operated as heuristic and pragmatic practices of reciprocities, forms of relationality that in this case, as in others, prefigured cooperative action (Hall et al., 2018; Romano & Balliet, 2017).

How could these fields of reciprocity develop in the 'Jungle', and perhaps similar contexts? We propose that such developments were possible because the camp was both a space of abjectification and something very different: a city. The 'Jungle' met the criteria for what Isin and Rygiel (2007) describe as 'abject space'. Yet the patrolling police were not omnipresent, and 'Jungle' borders were much like borders everywhere – porous. In the daytime, residents often made their way to the city centre, despite the distance and the hostility of some local people and the police, to access resources and even take 'tourist' snaps of themselves to send home. The 'Jungle' and the town existed in the same city space. Moreover, the camp space itself became at times a site of politics, as well as abjectification, despite attempts by the state to 'render refugee life invisible and inaudible' by creating a hostile environment outside of the camp and corralling those who would attempt the journey across the channel into a wasteland on the periphery of Calais. The duality of such a space, as Isin and Rygiel argue, contributes to the suspension of the logic of the nation-state, making acts of resistance possible (2007, 184–185). The 'Jungle' space was not and could not be fully abjectified. Residents explicitly and deliberately made the space, themselves; they were not corralled into invisibility and silence. The camp, while having an abjectified look and sound in popular media – sad faces, violence, fires, mud, shouts and cries in 'unknown languages' – produced its own resistant images and soundtrack through residents' political arguments, their generation of photographs, paintings, music, radio, writing, film and poetry, and the flows of hospitality, such as food and other goods, art, legal advice and education, that moved around, into and out of camp space.

How did reciprocity become 'politics' in the camp? The political vector for reciprocal action and resistance from within abjection was, we suggest, a form of reciprocity-founded *citizenship* – not quite of the kind Jones described. By 'citizenship', we mean assemblages of effective public engagements. They do not need to be seen in relation to nation states and colonialism, contexts which forced migration renders problematic (Smith & Rogers, 2016). Rather, the citizenly engagements we are interested in are mobile resistances in and to coloniality and post-coloniality. In this case, they are part of the 'expansive project' of democracy and of 'pluriversities': universities reciprocally permeable to knowledge interchange (Mbembe, 2016), embedded in power relations, but moving away, through various routes, from marketised exchanges.

These types of reciprocal, citizenly engagements in the 'Jungle' came about, we propose, because conditions in that site were similar to other sets of circumstances that engender resistance within cities. While there was expectation and hope on the part of residents that the precarity of their situation would be short-lived, such a transitory, unplanned space could still operate as a '(site) of urban stabilization' (Agier, 2011, 45). Indeed, reading the 'Jungle' as part of the urban landscape, rather than a site of exception, invites us to consider how many city or citizenship spaces can be understood as '(machines) for learning' (McFarlane, 2011). In this case, being located partly in abjectified space – not swallowed up by abjection, but in a situation characterised by the near-invisibility of the state as welfare provider – engendered a 'makeshift' urbanism manifested in the construction of tea-houses, restaurants, places of worship, language schools and improvised universities, all sustained by, and themselves supporting, the emergent reciprocal citizenship and public engagement we have described.

The place of the university among the camp's reciprocal, citizenly engagements was a significant one. Many residents had been at university or had been planning to attend. In the conflicts which had driven people from their countries, university students, drawn into discussion and activism, were particularly likely to have clashed with military, political or religious forces. For others, just the desire for university education was powerful. Shaheen, from Afghanistan, for example, wrote:

> I opened my eyes in a poor family. It was very difficult to get education, but my father was dreaming for me that I would get an education. I was the first child. So, my father struggled so much for me to get an education ... I did medicine for two years only. Because of my economic problems, I then left my education. (Africa et al., 2017, 30–31)

The wish for HE was never the first reason given for migration in the Jungle. Rather, residents' situations were well captured by the first lines of Warsan Shire's poem *Home*, 'no one leaves home unless/home is the mouth of a shark', which resonated with many in the 'Life Stories' classes. Nevertheless, residents often defined themselves as actual or potential students. The camp was replete with reciprocal intellectual interactions – in conversation classes or around braziers burning plastic as people attempted to keep warm, often truncated, with rapidly shifting personnel. One 'Life Stories' student noted the similarities of course discussions to long university evenings spent putting the world to rights over coffee – without, of course, the coffee, or any of the other resources he'd taken for granted at the time.

A key feature of the camp's reciprocity-founded, makeshift citizenship, and the provisional universities that were part of it, was willingness to 'make do' with the scarce resources at hand. Improvised yet coordinated systems emerged to counter poor sanitation, insufficient power supplies, inadequate shelter – and lack of education. 'Urban learning in the context of improvisation', McFarlane (2011, 368) tells us, 'involves acting within assemblages of multiple relations – reciprocal relations stretched between family and friends, negotiating the "modern" and "traditional", and delimiting the possibilities of resistance – which are coordinated in order to manage a field of uncertainties'. In the 'Jungle', the stretching and re-imagining of reciprocal relations – and resources – among residents, and between residents and non-residents, was central to the longevity of the camp in the face of the French state's constraints and violence. It also allowed for a persistence of improvised education, including HE.

We now analyse a number of different manifestations of reciprocally founded HE operating in the 'Jungle'. These are of course overlapping, heuristic categories, but they help us understand the opportunities and limits of varying reciprocity practices. We start by describing reciprocity strategies of *coalition*, which involved explicit reciprocal co-operations that developed more or less unified aims and practices, albeit temporarily.

Educational Coalitions

Coalitions were the most obvious form of reciprocity operating within 'Jungle' educational practices, since they overtly brought into dialogue many different stakeholders – residents who were heterogeneous in terms of nationality, class, ethnicity, sexuality, gender and how far they identified as refugees, teachers, other volunteers, NGOs and state agencies. Across these heterogeneities, a coalitional citizenship often arose, comprising alliances between residents, and between residents and volunteers, geared to planning, delivering and promoting educational services. Such coalitions drew on diverse histories of progressive coalitional politics (Agustin & Jorgensen, 2016). They looked beyond humanitarian provision of education as part of human welfare, or as a right, to education as transformation. Participants in these coalitions valued HE as they did other educational fields, and so supported the delivery of the 'Life Stories' course within a predominantly arts and crafts school, and alongside French and English classes.

Frequently, the coalitions involved groups of residents of different nationalities, religions and generations, who articulated the need for schools, planned and built them, while non-resident volunteers found financial and physical resources and did the teaching. Residents also managed classrooms and administered classes, and linked education to legal, health and social welfare provision by making referrals from schools to other services. Higher-level English students taught introductory classes. The School Bus scheme and Crisis Classroom trained residents as 'English as a Second Language' teachers and continue this work.[6] In two 'Life Stories' Plato seminars, students translated extensively and with commentary into Farsi, becoming the main teachers for half the class. In a 'Life

---

[6] For the School Bus Project, see: www.facebook.com/TheSchoolBusProject/
For Crisis Classroom, see: www.facebook.com/CrisisClassroom/

Stories' course taught later for the Greater Manchester Refugee Support Network, students translated and discussed concepts from Mandela's *Long Walk to Freedom* into Arabic and Kurdish.

In Calais, educational involvement often led to new language and occupational skills. Several camp residents began attending Jungle Books Library classes with little English and ended up as 'librarians'. At the same time, most residents supporting or providing education through such coalitional services distanced themselves from professionalised or financialised models of knowledge like those currently dominating Western universities. Residents expressed resistance to profiting from education, vocationally or economically, when, as sometimes happened, French or UK volunteers helping with the schools offered references or payments for hours worked as administrators or teachers. As Shikeb, who had learned English in the camp and was now teaching English to beginners himself, explained,

> I have practised [English] for four months. I have a dictionary in my phone; I try to learn with this. In the school, I sometimes help the teachers arranging books, and sometimes I read ... I have worked in one of the schools, but I never wanted money for that. I think knowledge should be pure and beautiful, never for money. (Africa et al., 2017, 175)

Residents also played a large role within educational coalitions in determining curricula and pedagogies. Eurocentrism and decoloniality were familiar ideas for many 'Life Stories' students, who pointed out our lack of knowledge of, for example, Arabic literary traditions and Islamic histories of reading Plato. The attention they drew to this epistemic violence, the marginalisation and trivialisation of non-Western ways of knowing, being and acting, served as a reminder that alongside learning on both sides, there was a specific need for non-resident teachers to 'unlearn' their perspective on the worlds inhabited by 'Jungle' residents (Danius, Jonsson, & Spivak, 1993). Processes of unlearning generated through interactions between teachers and students open the door for new relationships and knowledges that can become 'constituents of alternative social visions and practices', as well as 'enabling new political identities and initiatives' (Gibson-Graham, 2002, 108).

Activism was also refugee-led within the coalitional educational citizenship of the camp. While some external volunteers offered advice about activist engagements, the practices we are describing bore little relation to such advice, arising rather from residents' own coalitional activities, for instance, communalising the ownership of educational resources like classrooms and books, promoting inclusive teaching, and linking education to other fields of practice. Such coalitions stand in contrast to more paternalistic volunteer-led approaches, for example, those that seek to 'teach' European understandings of solidarity and activism to migrants and refugees occupying buildings in Athens as squats (Zaman, 2019).

Coalitional forms of educational reciprocity were thus not simply balanced alliances in the 'Jungle'. They were often refugee-led. As the Syrian thinker Yassin al-Haj Saleh suggests, 'refugees' offer a much greater challenge to Europe, politically, than terrorism. There is, he proposes, a strong potential for a refugee-associated 'alter politics' (Hage, 2015) that could make up another Europe, operating in addition to the anti-state politics of contradictions and gaps that must also be conducted. For Saleh, this possibility is not about a conversation between political forms; the 'alter-politics' of refugees' 'Europe' reaches out and over existing political formations. Such politics therefore lead us in new directions (Saleh cited in Heintz, 2018), and initiatives such as the 'Life Stories' courses and other coalitional educational activities in the 'Jungle' provide examples. They contribute actively to the production and transformation of discourses and processes. In so doing, they create 'new subject positions and imaginative possibilities that can animate political projects and desires' (Gibson-Graham, 2002, 105).

As with many coalitions, however, educational coalitions in the 'Jungle' proved problematic to maintain. Specific educational goals held coalitions together for a while, but limited their scope. Coalitions were undermined by high resident mobility, variable volunteer investment, and large imbalances of economic, social and symbolic capitals. Yet some coalitions have continued with much the same group of now-ex residents and volunteers, and similar activities – for example, the Hopetowns project in North London, the Crisis Classroom/Refugee School Bus project, and 'Life Stories' itself. UEL's OLIve project, too, while part of a 2017-start four-country EU Erasmus programme to "bridge" refugees into HE, brought together again, in London, many of those involved in the Calais 'Life Stories' courses, both as teachers and students; some of the latter are now OLIve or 'Life Stories' tutors themselves. The project also took on and developed the student-centred orientation and the breadth of the 'Life Stories' courses.

It is important to recognise that reciprocity was and is key to these educational coalitions. Structural reciprocities, as well as personal exchanges between residents, and between residents and volunteers, founded and sustained projects like the Jungle Books Library, Ecole

Laique du Chemin des Dunes and the Darfuri School. We could characterise these structures and exchanges as 'working' partnerships and
friendships that extended beyond 'balanced' alliances that blurred the
lines of conventional relationships on the basis of, for instance, ethnicity
or kinship. These relationships were particularly frequent and intense in
the field of education which, perhaps more than many other areas of
potential collaboration, crosses language, national, religious and class
differences. There was a recognition that such 'working' relationships,
more than taken-for-granted organisation, kin or friend relations, required
active, ongoing effort.

This 'working' on reciprocity was less obvious in the second kind of
'communing' strategy which characterised the camp's educational citizenship, where reciprocity was more embedded, but also more implicit.

Educational 'Commoning'

An alternative, 'communing' form of educational reciprocity appeared
regularly within the 'Jungle'. Commoning as a gerund, Linebaugh reminds
us, denotes action or doing, anchored in 'human deeds'. It is a 'customary
activity; rather than a natural resource' (Linebaugh, 2008, 45, 79). It
demands that we move beyond territorialised understandings of the self
that produce and reproduce ownership of, and exclusion from, shared
resources; the resource divides that occupy coalitional citizens have less
significance here. Instead, commoning calls for an acknowledgment of
inter-subjectivities and reciprocal exchanges located in persons, rather than
property (Anderson et al., 2012). Movement is built into commoning,
rather than needing to be negotiated. In relation to forced migration,
commoning is often articulated in terms of religious conventions of
sanctuary; anti-colonial articulations of democracy are also relevant
(Mbeki, 1999; Shoukri, 2011).

This mobile, 'communing' reciprocity, even more than coalitional
reciprocity, brackets off concepts of the legal status of citizen, UN
Convention refugee, or undocumented migrant, as well as language and
ethnic divisions, and instead generates a citizenship of socio-cultural relations. It is in indeed in such a 'commoned', socio-culturally reciprocal
world that the various 'categories' of people on the move exist. They
inhabit and construct, along with resident or visiting others, a 'world of
knowledge, of information, of tricks for survival, of mutual care, of social
relations, of services exchange, of solidarity and [a] sociability that can be
shared' (Hardt & Negri, 2011, 190). In the 'Jungle', resources of water, food

and building materials reached into the camp via volunteer contributions; yet hospitality was also generated internally by residents offering what they had of shelter, tea, meals and friendship to each other and to volunteers. As Africa, a long-term resident, put it:

> You (volunteer) can try this. Go anywhere in the 'Jungle', say, 'Hi', and you will hear, 'Hi, please come on in'. You will find people saying, 'Hi, hi my brother', and inviting you in. It is because of this, that I find (the "Jungle") wonderful. (Africa et al., 2017, 157)

Along the lines Isin and Rygiel (2007) describe, a negotiated and learned grammar of sociability – a practical ethic – produced what Africa called 'a wonderful place' where he not only had neighbours but had 'made six thousand persons [*sic*.] my brothers'. This, he said, meant he was 'a rich man', adding, 'because of that I sleep in safety'. This practical ethic was founded in a reciprocated respect for one another where 'respect with a little smile [. . .] can solve everything here in the Jungle – everything' (Africa et al., 2017). Here, we find articulated a contemporary *mu'ākhā* (brotherhood – a term, the gendering of which, accurately reflected the numbers of men in the camp)[7] among residents, contrasted with life outside the 'Jungle' in French cities where interaction was often hostile. As Mani wrote,

> I like the 'Jungle' nights. I am feeling that the 'Jungle' in the night belongs just to us. Belongs to us refugees. In the nights, especially at midnight. You can't see any volunteers, police, or journalists. I am feeling more safe, more comfortable at these times. (Africa et al., 2017, 171)

This 'communing' reciprocity within the camp supported a 'communing' politics, distinct from the coalitional model. Residents articulated it through the residents' council, which was a form of camp collectivity as well as a coalition, in religious settings, and in joint cultural and educational endeavours. This framework allowed joint resident action across different political and religious views, national and cultural backgrounds, and resource levels. The camp council, for instance, helped resolve conflicts between national resident groups, negotiated with local actors in the Calais region, and campaigned for specific classes and schools.

More generally, this 'communing' reciprocity was exemplified by how refugees themselves planned, built and taught in the schools, often with

---

[7] This term refers to the contract set forth by the Prophet Muhammad between the early Meccan exiles and the host community of Madina to promote mutual care, protection and assistance, providing Muslims with a model of how to respond to displacement (Zaman, 2016).

little early input from external volunteers. This is clear in the case of l'Ecole Laique du Chemin des Dunes, but similar stories could be told about the Jungle Books Library, the Ecole des Arts et Metiers, and the Darfuri and Oromo schools. Residents also adjudicated curricula and delivery collectively. Before running 'Life Stories' in the Ecole Laique and the Darfuri School, we presented the project to resident school administrators and existing students, who discussed and decided together if and how it should run.

This 'communing' reciprocity and its consequent educational citizenship works against the grain of the contemporary marketised university, not resisting so much as bracketing it off. Because 'communing' values customary activities, and recognises existing resources, it does not need to oppose the conventional university. Instead, the alternative, 'communing' university simply arises in everyday contexts, and persists or fades away, depending on what other sociocultural factors are in play. For example, the relatively quickly decided-upon 'Life Stories' classes we held with small groups of camp residents outside the schools, often around a fire, accompanied by tea or breakfast, might end because of a hastily called community meeting or for lunch; or might continue across weekly visits, distributions of photocopies and books, and students' own reading and discussion. Commoning strategies can come into play anywhere, at any time, weaving education into the changing patterns of everyday lives. Such 'communing' reciprocity was so locally embedded and contingent, though, that despite its ubiquity, it could be overridden, at least temporarily, by anything 'uncommoning' – by the mobility of residents and volunteers, the dramatic resource disparities between them, or more locally, by police demolitions of some camp areas, or volunteer organisations changing where and to whom they distributed resources.

Additionally, as with educational coalitions, educational 'communing' can be undone by differences in economic, social and cultural capital. Residents were better able to keep in touch with teachers, and other students, if they had English or French skills, and to learn online, if they had smartphones; and to continue learning when the camp was destroyed, if they had strong relations with NGOs, and phone credit. As between the Greek squats in Athens (Zaman, 2019) there were pronounced geographical resource differences within the camp, too. Living close to a "school" in the Jungle – that is, to a wooden shelter hosting volunteer language teaching in French or English, and perhaps some other classes – was something usually related to nationality since camp neighbourhoods were broadly nationally organised; it allowed easier access to educational resources for 'communing'.

We turn now to a third form of educational citizenship that developed in the camp, which, working alongside the other forms, built reciprocities across spaces and life practices, without explicit coalition-building or implicit commoning.

Educational 'Associationalism'

The 'makeshiftness' and 'throwntogetherness' (Massey, 2005) of the 'Jungle' meant that reciprocities did not only emerge from building links with like-minded people, or working with fundamental similarities, as in coalitional or 'communing' initiatives. Significant reciprocal practices also developed associationally, at functional locations like schools, tea-houses and places of worship, where people gathered. For instance, the Refugee Youth Service, located close to the theatre, therapy centre and library, often made use of the spaces of these nearby institutions for its activities, because young people themselves often explored these places. The Unofficial Women's and Children's Centre, relocated after the March 2016 partial demolitions to a family caravan area, built reciprocal exchanges of service request and provision between nearby residents and volunteers. These associational, 'neighbourhood' citizenships within the larger camp 'city' worked alongside coalitional and commoning politics. They lacked the bonding capitals and resource-fulness of commoning; but the bridging of social capital across ethnic groups and with volunteers was more persistent, albeit weaker, than those generated by commoning and coalitional initiatives. For the churning of volunteer initiatives at the Jungle, the regular arrival and departure of residents, and resource differentials within and between the groups, made the more explicit alliances within coalitions and the more universalised assumptions of commoning difficult to maintain; associational links were less demanding and more adaptable. Such horizontally spreading practices generated non-material forms of capital such as skills learned and relationships that have been maintained beyond the dismantling of the camp; sustaining change, rebuilding after forced relocations, for instance. In the United Kingdom, part of HopeTowns' language teaching practice has involved re-establishing prior links, starting from where former residents now are. A number of other advice and service groups which began in the camp also operate, post-'Jungle', in France and the United Kingdom. This continuity and adaptability challenges conventions of what a 'camp' is.

In the camp, associational educational citizenship generated flows of people and knowledges, which established learning as both outcome and process. The library, for example, founded and run by a wide variety of residents and volunteers, supporting reading, study and discussion, was physically and socially linked to the next-door Eritrean church, one of the first-established public spaces in the camp; at night, each protected the other. The library added buildings and functions: a larger classroom, a children's space, which later housed Iranian hunger strikers, a smaller room for meetings for instance on 'safeguarding', a radio station, wooden librarians' huts. Buildings' functions and learning processes changed often. Popular English classes led to the large space's use for conversation classes; the library hosted information-gathering by the organisation Safe Passage. 'Life Stories', too, operated at times with this associational form of reciprocity, its classes connecting students to legal and health advice but also to photography workshops, language classes, and – the most popular sessions we offered – workshops about HE possibilities across Europe.

This associational (Hirst, 2013) educational citizenship can be creatively independent of other political forces. Even when those forces curtail associational reciprocities, such reciprocities may move, and appear elsewhere.

Conclusions

At the end of his contribution to 'Voices from the 'Jungle' (Africa et al., 2017), a young Eritrean man then in the United Kingdom, about to start university, wrote a 'thank you' to God, his parents, and 'those who helped me to pass the difficulties and who are still helping me, my lovely friends' (Africa et al., 2017, 258). This dedication encompassed Eritrean friends in the United Kingdom and elsewhere; other refugee friends from the journey, including Calais; and a shifting group of non-resident camp volunteers, including those from the 'Life Stories' courses, with whom he had occasional but consistent interactions in Calais and the United Kingdom – interactions which helped him move through many small steps towards university.

Within refugee educational citizenship, the outside of the camp, more than the camp itself, can appear as a jungle, denying humanity, rights and reciprocities. Paradoxically, it is the 'Jungle' space and similar 'makeshift' living and educational spaces that contest marketised HE and counterpose their own subaltern "universities". Education carried on in other refugee spaces, the opening up of universities across Europe to refugee education initiatives, and the cascade effect of such work on programmes for others with very low HE access, all provide examples. There remain criticisms of university-oriented initiatives for refugees and asylum-seekers: they may skew towards individuals whose legal status conforms to the notion of a 'good refugee'; they may cherry-pick refugees and asylum-seekers whose capitals – strong European language skills, prior attainment within educational institutions valued within Europe – approximate those of a European 'good student'; the reciprocal educational citizenship practised within refugee spaces may be difficult to sustain against contemporary university pressures.

Initiatives that are able to strategically adopt a variety of framings may be the most effective in working through the gaps and contradictions of the traditional university without institutional, conceptual or political co-option. Following from the cities of sanctuary model, for instance, the 'universities of sanctuary' movementsup[8] is an initiative that seeks to promote Article 26, arguing that since universities are powerful institutions 'anchored' in their towns and cities, Article 26 can leverage resources for the benefit of local populations (Zaman, 2018). 'Universities of sanctuary' recognises that those with unresolved immigration statuses as well as recognised refugees need the resources of universities. Aside from bursaries and fee waivers, it campaigns for access to facilities like libraries, sports halls and student union events for all forced migrants. The movement relates perhaps most strongly to the commoning form of educational citizenship described above. Yet it is strategic enough to develop coalitions, and porous enough to be associational too. It is, indeed, purposefully heterogeneous in strategies and forms.

Such examples suggest that to characterise the projects we have discussed as working within the gaps of university discourse and practice, or else as unsustainably 'othered' by the university assemblage, is too dualistic. 'Universities of sanctuary' work within universities, but also reach back out; the 'Life Stories' courses do something similar; HopeTowns and OLIve work outside, but bridge into HE institutions. If we look at such reciprocally framed, 'alter-university' initiatives, we can see that education – including university education, a practice characterised from its beginning by a reciprocal and open citizenry of learning and teaching – can be a space where alter-politics can, for refugees and those working in solidarity with them, have powerful effects.

---

[8] See: https://universities.cityofsanctuary.org/

REFERENCES

Africa, Ali Haghooi, Ali Bajdar, Babak Inaloo, Eritrea, Habibi et al. (2017). *Voices from the 'Jungle'*. London: Pluto.

Agier, A. (2011). *Managing the Undesirables*. London: Polity.

Agustin, O., & Jorgensen, M. (eds.) (2016). *Solidarity without Borders*. London: Pluto.

Anderson, B., Sharma, N., & Wright, C. (2012). 'We Are All Foreigners': No Borders as a Practical Political Project. In P. Nyers, & K. Rygiel (eds.), *Citizenship, Migrant Activism and the Politics of Movement*. London: Routledge.

Berkowitz, L. (1968). Responsibility, Reciprocity and Social Distance in Helping. *Journal of Experimental Social Psychology*, 4(1), 46–63.

Bouhenia, M., Ben Farhat, J., Caldiron, M., Abdallah, S., Visentin, D., Neuman, M., Berthelot, M., Porten, K., & Cohuet, S. (2017). Quantitative Survey on Health and Violence Endured by Refugees during Their Journey and in Calais, France. *International Health*, 9(6), 335–342.

Castro, A. (2015). From the 'Bio' to the 'Necro': The Human at the Border. *Resisting Biopolitics: Philosophical, Political, and Performative Strategies* 71, 237.

Danius, S., Jonsson, S., & Spivak, G. (1993). An Interview with Gayatri Chakravorty Spivak. *Boundary 2*, 20(2), 24–50.

Dembour, M., & Kelly, T. (eds.) (2011). *Are Human Rights for Migrants?* London: Routledge.

Dhesi, S., Isakjee, A., & Davies, T. (2018). Public Health in the Calais Refugee Camp: Environment, Health and Exclusion. *Critical Public Health*, 28(2), 140–152.

Duffield, M. (2008). Global Civil War: The Non-Insured, International Containment and Post-interventionary Society. *Journal of Refugee Studies*, 21 (2), 145–165.

Gibson-Graham, J. (2002). Beyond Global vs Local: Economic Politics Outside the Binary Frame. In A. Herod, & M. Wright (eds.), *Geographies of Power: Placing Scale*. Oxford: Blackwell, 25–60.

Hage, G. (2015). *Alter-Politics Critical Anthropology, Political Passion and the Radical Imagination*. Melbourne: Melbourne University Press.

Hall, T., Lounasmaa, A., & Squire, C. (2018). From Margin to Centre? Practising New Forms of European Politics and Citizenship in the Calais 'Jungle'. In T. Birey, C. Cantat, E. Maczynska, & E. Sevinin (eds.), *Challenging the Political*. Budapest: CEU Press.

Hardt, M., & Negri, A. (2011). *Commonwealth*. New York: Belknapp.

Harrell-Bond, B. (2002). Can Humanitarian Work with Refugees be Humane? *Human Rights Quarterly*, 24(1), 51–85.

Heintz, A. (2018). Dissidents of the left: In conversation with Yassin al-Haj Saleh. www.aljumhuriya.net/en/content/dissidents-left-conversation-yassin-al-haj-saleh. Accessed 13 November 2018.

Hirst, P. (2013). *Associative Democracy*. Oxford: Wiley.

Honneth, A. (1995). *The Struggle for Recognition*. London: Polity.

Isin, E., & Rygiel, K. (2007). Abject Spaces: Frontiers, Zones, Camps. In E. Dauphinee, & C. Masters (eds.), *The Logics of Biopower and the War on Terror*. New York: Palgrave Macmillan.

Kibreab, G. (2004). Pulling the Wool over the Eyes of the Strangers: Refugee Deceit and Trickery in Institutionalized Settings. *Journal of Refugee Studies, 17*(1), 1–26.

Linebaugh, P. (2008). *The Magna Carta manifesto*. Berkeley, CA: University of California Press.

Loud Minority (2016). Who opens a school . . . http://loudminority.co.uk/?port folio=who-opens-a-school. Accessed 13 November 2018.

Mauss, M. (2009 [1950]). *The Gift*. London and New York: Routledge.

Mbeki, T. (1999). *African Renaissance: The New Struggle*. Tafelberg: Mafube.

McFarlane, C. (2011). The City as a Machine for Learning. *Transactions of the Institute of British Geographers, 36*, 360–376.

Massey, D. (2005). *For Space*. London: Sage.

Mbembe, A. (2016) Decolonising the University: New Directions. *Arts and Humanities in Higher Education, 15*(1), 29–45.

Mouffe, C. (2014). Democracy, Human Rights and Cosmopolitanism. In C. Douzinas, & C. Gearty (eds.), *The Meanings of Rights*. Cambridge: Cambridge University Press.

Moulin, C., & Nyers, P. (2007). '"We Live in a Country of UNHCR"- Refugee Protests and Global Political Society'. *International Political Sociology*, (2007) 1, 356–372.

RRDP (2016). Still waiting: Filling the information gaps around the Calais camp. London: RRDp. http://refugeerights.org.uk/wp-content/uploads/2018/08/RR E_StillWaiting.pdf. Accessed 14 June 2019.

RRDP (2018). Twelve months on. London: Refugee Rights Data Project. ht tp://refugeerights.org.uk/wp-content/uploads/2018/08/RRE_TwelveMonths On.pdf. Accessed 13 November 2018.

Romano, A., & Balliet, D. (2017). Reciprocity outperforms conformity to promote cooperation. *Psychological Science*, 095679761771482 DOI:10.1177/ 0956797617714828

Shoukri, A. (2011). *Refugee Status in Islam*. London: I.B. Tauris.

Sikkink, K. (2017). *Evidence for Hope*. Princeton, NJ: Princeton University Press.

Smith, B., & Rogers, R. (2016). Towards a theory of decolonising citizenship. Citizenship Education Research Journal 5, 1. ejournals.ok.ubc.ca/index.php/C ERJ/article/download/11/248 Accessed 13 November 2018.

UNHCR (2016). Missing out: Refugee education in crisis. Geneva: UNHCR. www.unhcr.org/57d9d01d0. Accessed 13 November 2018.

Zaman, T. (2016). *Islamic Traditions of Refuge in the Crises of Iraq and Syria.* London: Palgrave.

Zaman, T. (2018). The 'humanitarian anchor': a social economy approach to assistance in protracted displacement situations. HPG Working Paper May 2018. London Overseas Development Institute (ODI).

Zaman, T. (2019). 'What's So Radical about Refugee Squats? An Exploration of Urban Community Based Responses to Mass Displacement in Athens'. In T. Birey, C. Cantat, E. Maczynska, & E. Sevinin (eds.), *Challenging the Political Across Borders.* Budapest: CEU Press.

CHAPTER 20

Culture, Gender and Technology
Mediating Teacher Training Using Text Messaging in Refugee Camps

*Dacia Douhaibi, Negin Dahya, Olivier Arvisais
and Sarah Dryden-Peterson*

Introduction

> ... in [Gender Responsive Pedagogy] we are trained on how to handle girls. It is trying to rectify past mistakes [social inequities] that happen to them. For example, a boy and a girl, both of them they start learning but a boy ends up in the University, but the girl cannot go up to University. She drops out from class eight, or form two in secondary school, like that. Now what is the problem?
>
> (Kalid, Group Interview 1, Kakuma, 19 April 2016)

By the time students in Dadaab or Kakuma refugee camps reach secondary school, gender imbalances are clear. Students who are men outnumber women students, and women typically sit together at the back of the classroom (field notes, April 2016). As class proceeds, men overwhelmingly raise their hands to respond to questions posed by the teacher, and they are more likely to be chosen to respond, even when both men and women have raised their hands (Taylor, 2015). Women tend to miss more classes than their male counterparts, and their grades are, on average, lower (Arvisais, 2016).

As highlighted by Kalid, a teacher in the Kakuma refugee camp, our research also finds that the barriers to education that women students face in this context are exacerbated by the reality that few teachers have received gender-sensitive training. Many refugee teachers are concerned about the educational outcomes of girls. This local concern paired with international interest in gender-equity has led many refugee teachers in Kenya to seek out ways to improve their teaching and learning practices to better support girls and young women. This occurs through formal gender-based training opportunities and also through peer-to-peer knowledge sharing and development (see Dahya & Dryden-Peterson, 2017; Dahya, Dryden-Peterson, Douhaibi, & Arvisais, 2019; Dryden-Peterson, Dahya, & Adelman, 2017).

Post-secondary training programmes have been created in response to community-driven interests to support teachers and their gender-equity work in Dadaab and Kakuma. These include training programmes offered by Kenyan nationals as well as higher education programmes delivered by international institutions and instructors. Two examples are the Kenyan Equity in Education Project (KEEP) project and the Borderless Higher Education for Refugees (BHER) project. The majority of the courses and trainings offered through these programmes have been provided in traditional face-to-face classroom contexts. In the case of BHER, however, several instructors from partner universities offered courses that assumed a blended structure, where students in Dadaab participated in courses offered partially or completely online, connected with instructors and students in Canada. KEEP programmes were primarily delivered face-to-face over short or intermittent training workshops, although ongoing communication and support were sometimes facilitated by Kenyan national instructors using mobile phones; students also used mobiles to build and nurture professional development locally through peer-to-peer networks (Dahya et al., 2019).

In this chapter, we explore the use of text and instant messaging among refugee teachers who have enrolled in or completed one or both of these programmes in Dadaab or Kakuma as well as across refugee teachers and course instructors.[1] In particular, we consider how the use of mobile phones and social networks support more gender-sensitive and equitable teaching and learning environments both in and outside of the classroom. We draw on research conducted in 2016 to explore two questions: how are refugee teachers in teacher training programmes using text and instant messaging to support their learning? How can mobile and text messaging technology be constructed and used to support culturally relevant, gender equitable, community-grounded teacher training among refugee teachers in refugee camps? Our data include surveys and group interviews with refugee teachers, as well as semi-structured interviews with instructors of teacher training programmes with origins in Kenyan and Canadian iNGOs and universities.

---

[1] The term 'student-teacher' is used to refer to teachers in the Dadaab and Kakuma refugee camps that participated in teacher training courses offered through the KEEP or BHER projects. The term 'instructor' refers to instructors who taught refugee teachers in either project.

Our findings identify that the use of technology, and in particular mobile platforms like SMS and WhatsApp chat groups, has become a common complement to these teacher training programmes. We have documented this practice as being part of both formal and informal training, as pedagogical tools used by instructors to support the delivery of courses, and by student-teachers during and following their training to extend class discussions and share best practices once applying those tools in their classrooms (Dahya et al., 2019). In our exploration of these practices, we draw on theories of post-colonialism and transnationalism to consider the power dynamics interwoven throughout these engagements. Specifically, we describe how group chats and SMS have extended gender-equity training beyond the temporal and physical space of the classroom, as teachers-in-training continued to discuss and remind one another about pedagogical tools and learning strategies during and after their training. We also share how mobile phones and social networks have been used to increase the reach of these ideas to the surrounding communities, including parents and community leaders, to support education for girls and women.

The peer-to-peer engagement and professional development at the community level illuminate the ways in which mobile technology and group chat applications like WhatsApp can amplify existing strengths and opportunities within refugee communities. We consider the importance of culturally relevant curriculum in these settings and explore tensions among educational projects devised outside the camps compared to emergent learning and professional development among refugee teachers in camps.

Mobile Technology and Refugee Education: A Review of the Literature

In 2016, UNHCR reported that as well as being essential for keeping in touch with loved ones and facilitating livelihood opportunities, mobile phone and internet access are as critical to refugee safety and security as food, shelter and water (UNHCR, 2016). In 2017, the GSMA Mobile for Development Foundation similarly reported that many refugees arriving in Europe from Syria, Iraq, Afghanistan and other locations had smartphones if little else and saw them as a critically important tool for organising their journey and staying in touch with friends and family. Consequently, because communication through mobile platforms is a commonplace and familiar way of seeking information and being connected to social networks, it is a potentially valuable educational resource and tool.

While a rich body of work has been produced on refugee education broadly (Burde et al., 2016; Dryden-Peterson, 2010, 2016; Preston, 1991; Waters & Leblanc, 2005; Winthrop & Kirk, 2008) and refugees and communication technologies (Charmarkeh, 2013; Danielson, 2013), the merging of these areas to investigate the relationship between refugee education and mobile technology is a recent addition to the fields of education and refugee studies (see Dahya, 2016). The impact of technology on gendered learning outcomes in refugee education is a particular area within these literatures that remains largely unexplored (see Anderson, 2013; Dahya & Dryden-Peterson, 2017). Initial work in this area points to the ways in which mobile technology offers opportunities to mitigate otherwise persistent challenges in these contexts, such as inconsistent and failing internet, low computer literacy and mobility challenges that result in face-to-face or central technology programming being difficult to pursue (Dahya, 2016). Additionally, Dahya and Dryden-Peterson (2017) and Boškić et al. (2018) have recently identified how, in Dadaab, mobile phones and their text messaging and chat-based applications are being used to engender knowledge sharing and community building to pursue and succeed in education.

Despite these possible benefits, higher education institutions in developing countries, particularly public ones, often suffer from poor network infrastructure and limited internet access (Sobaih et al., 2016; Mian, 2014); thus, they typically lack the technology and technological literacy that would invite communication and connection with students working remotely from locations like refugee camps. The use of mobile phones, a device most people own or have access to in developing countries (Poushter, Bishop, & Chwe, 2018), and which can rely on a cellular network in addition to the internet, presents an opportunity to circumvent some current technological limitations. Mobile learning (or *m-learning*) is often considered more convenient than traditional e-learning because it allows people who could not have access to an education otherwise to gain access to resources to learn independently. For this reason, mobile phones show great promise to increase access to higher education in developing countries (Kaliisa & Picard, 2017).

The use of mobile phones in education has been praised for its flexibility and the easy access to resources it offers (Baran, 2014; Lamptey & Boateng, 2017). According to Pouezevara and Khan (2007), who conducted a training programme for teachers in Bangladesh, mobile phones allowed teachers to attend training without having to leave their families or their workplace. Interview and focus group data in this case suggested that teachers strongly preferred mobile supported training that allowed them to remain in their homes and classrooms. Empirical research investigating this domain of education and technology in refugee camps specifically remains under explored, though several reports document the presence, persistence and perceived value of mobiles across stakeholders, educators, technologists and beneficiaries working in refugee settings (see Dahya, 2016; Pimmer, 2018).

Post-coloniality and Transnationalism: Conceptualising Power and Culture in Mobile Technology Use in Refugee Education

In this landscape, international education programmes and related transnational networks evoke important questions about the dynamics of power and culture embedded in teacher education and using mobile technology. Post-colonial theory addresses ongoing differences between countries as well as between individuals where shared histories of colonisation define social, economic, political and cultural relations or power (Ahmed, 2000; Loomba, 2005; Said, 1979). From a post-colonial perspective, individuals from dominant and coloniser groups represent socio-cultural norms while once colonised groups are positioned as non-white, non-colonial 'Others'. In the case of refugees in Kenya from neighbouring African countries, the role of coloniality and post-coloniality is multidirectional. Alongside Somalia's independence in the 1960s, Kenya went through its own movement to achieve independence from the British around the same time. Somalia's history of colonialisation by Italy and Great Britain also continued to inform the fight for power and conflict resulting in an exodus of refugees from the country into Kenya starting in the 1990s and ongoing. This past and contemporary post-colonial situation promotes consideration of the significance of relationships among refugees and nationals in Eastern Africa and among refugees and white and/or Western educators. We pay particular attention to how mobile technology and the availability of vast and transnational social networks impact these socio-cultural relations. From a transnational perspective, we explore how, in education, transnational connections can be forged with instructors and students from other countries through online learning, and in the use of mobile phones, SMS and instant messaging communication (see Toukan, Gaztambide-Fernández, & Anwaruddin, 2017; Roudometof, 2005). What kinds of power structures circulate across these communication networks? How do those involved in these networks perpetuate and disrupt them? We explore these questions throughout our study findings and discussion.

Context: Dadaab and Kakuma, Kenya

Kenya is home to the one of the oldest and largest refugee communities in the world; hosting nearly 500,000 refugees in two refugee camp complexes in Dadaab and Kakuma, northwest and northeast Kenya respectively (UNHCR, 2018). Many teachers in primary and secondary schools are refugees who have had little, if any, formal post-secondary teacher training. Typically, they have successfully completed secondary school and move directly into positions as teachers in primary and secondary schools across the camps (Flemming, 2017; Morris & Voon, 2014).

Access to education for refugees in Dadaab and Kakuma is lower than the national average in Kenya – a result of lack of infrastructure, societal pressures, instability and domestic burdens. These barriers disproportionately affect women and girls who often do not progress beyond the class 6 (grade 6) level, a result of poverty and socio-cultural conceptions of education for girls and gender roles, including early marriage and family duty (Abdi, 2016; Jackline, 2012; Wright & Plasterer, 2010). A lack of sanitary facilities and sanitary wear further frustrates women's and girls' participation in school. For those young women and girls who do attend, our interview participants suggest that the belief that women students will not perform well because they are girls is pervasive. Teachers tend to overwhelmingly be men as a product of the disproportionate number of men who complete secondary school (Kinoti & Philpott, 2017). This male-dominated educational orientation further contributes to the small number of women students who complete secondary school, as they lack female role models and often do not receive equitable attention and support in the classroom in relation to their male counterparts.

It is within this context that teacher training programmes such as KEEP and BHER entered to support gender-inclusive teaching and learning. KEEP, run by Windle International Kenya and the World University Services of Canada (WUSC), provides support to female secondary school students and generates broad community support for girls' education through teacher training programmes and community outreach and engagement programmes, involving men and women refugee teachers and community members in Dadaab and

Kakuma.[2] KEEP directly tackles gender discrimination and gender-based barriers in schools and the broader community through training in gender responsive pedagogy (GRP) and employing community mobilisers who work with parents and community leaders to support girls' education. BHER, a consortium of Canadian and Kenyan universities, UNHCR and Windle International Kenya, launched in Dadaab in 2013 with the aim of making post-secondary educational programmes available to refugees where they live.[3] BHER works with four partner universities (the University of British Columbia, York University, Kenyatta University and Moi University) to support the delivery of university courses that lead to a Certificate, and Diplomas, to teach at the secondary or primary level and degrees in Education, Public Health and Geography, while encouraging the emulation of gender-equitable learning environments through the pedagogy employed by course instructors.

Computer and mobile technology, in the form of course websites, course Moodle sites, Skype tutorials and email and mobile communication platforms are intimately woven into the delivery of these teacher training programmes, particularly for BHER, which combined face-to-face classroom instruction with remote online course delivery. Such possibilities for advanced education, whereby instructors from universities across the world are connected with teaching students in refugee camps in Kenya, have only been made possible by advances in internet connectivity and mobile phone technology.

Methodology

Our methodological stance throughout this project has been as feminist researchers. We paid close attention to the particular experiences of women and girls in this educational context, and to the evident, perceived and potential effects of the research findings on the lived realities of girls and women. As argued by Huilman and Winters (2011), feminist approaches to education research can offer useful interpretations of social interactions and, potentially, provide possibilities for changes in education. Key considerations in this work included what role boys and men played in the

---

[2] Windle International Kenya supports the education of refugees and other conflict affected communities in East Africa through the provision of educational programs and teacher training opportunities. Please see http://windleinternational.org/. See https://wusc.ca/initiatives/keep/ for details on the KEEP project.

[3] See www.bher.org/ for details on the BHER project.

movement for greater gender equity in teaching and learning in these camps, and if or how access to mobiles and the nature of their use among women teachers influenced these same efforts. A gendered approach to research is critical in this case, where gender operates as a key organising characteristic in society and where gender-based expectations are influenced by norms and practices often juxtaposed in postcolonial settings where multiple cultural standards are at play.

In 2016, two members of our researcher team in Dadaab and Kakuma met with refugee teachers who were enrolled or had completed courses offered by KEEP and/or BHER. We used a concurrent research design (Creswell, 2014) whereby we conducted a survey and qualitative interviews during a single phase of data collection.

Our surveys about teachers' access to and use of mobile phones, SMS and instant messaging chat groups captured specific information about what kind of mobile phones, chat programmes and curricular content teachers used. The goal of our survey was to understand the diversity of participant perspectives, accounts and evaluations of their use of text and instant messaging to support teacher training in the refugee camps (see Jansen, 2010). We distributed surveys to teachers in both Kakuma and Dadaab in April 2016. In total, we collected 203 survey responses (119 surveys in Dadaab by teachers participating in the BHER programme, 35 surveys in Dadaab by teachers in KEEP and 49 surveys by teachers in KEEP located in Kakuma). In Dadaab, we collected contact details from survey respondents willing to participate in follow-up interviews via WhatsApp or Skype. We sought this possibility of virtual interviews since it was not possible to conduct interviews with teachers in Dadaab due to tight restrictions on time and mobility for both refugees and ourselves in the camps at that time. Our efforts to secure follow-up interviews remotely with teachers in early 2017 were unsuccessful.

We conducted semi-structured interviews with course instructors via Skype or in person in Nairobi. We were also able to interview refugee teachers enrolled in KEEP training in Kakuma, a somewhat less restrictive space of study than Dadaab, to understand their experiences and perspectives on using text and instant messaging as part of their teacher training programmes. Groups of teachers met with one researcher in Kakuma for interviews. Five group interviews took place with a total of eighteen refugee men and three refugee women who were teachers. The twenty-one teachers interviewed were all from Kakuma, and several were working as 'community mobilisers' to promote education and the importance of girls going to school.

This mixed methodological approach brought together group interviews, individual interviews with instructors, surveys and observation of everyday activities. It can be understood as a form of 'periscoping', whereby researchers employ various lenses, through a variety of methodological approaches, to produce coherent understandings of processes, subjects and spaces not easily encountered (Hiemstra, 2017). There are natural limitations to this approach, which, while illuminating details that researchers may otherwise not be able to gather at all, still leaves aspects of the context and research participants' experiences out of range.

Findings

Our research produced a number of key insights on the benefits, challenges and limitations of text and instant messaging chat groups in support of education in refugee camps' contexts. First, we present general findings that provide insights into the roles of formal and informal mobile messaging in teacher training programmes in Dadaab and Kakuma. Second, we demonstrate how group chats and peer-to-peer SMS communication serve to extend gender equity in both the classroom and the broader community. Third, we present findings related to challenges in transnational communication and the ways that formal and informal mobile messaging tools are used to support refugee teacher networks and refugee teacher and instructor networks that extend between the camps and Canadian cities.

The Role of Mobile Messaging in Teacher Training

It was central to our research to understand the capacity of mobile technology – specifically text and instant messaging – to support formal instruction: whether or not the majority of student-teachers had mobile phones and whether they had reliable access to mobile networks. Our survey findings indicate that the vast majority of refugee teachers (199 of 203 survey respondents) did have access to a mobile phone, including all 40 women respondents. The vast majority of survey respondents also indicated that mobile phones were the most used tool in their teacher training programmes, superseding tablets, computers or other devices.[4] Of note, WhatsApp, Facebook Messenger and SMS were used most frequently of all applications.

---

[4] Sixty per cent of respondents used mobile phones, while 17 per cent reported using a tablet at school and only 12 per cent reported using a computer at school.

While many student-teachers did interact with instructors through SMS and/or WhatsApp, discussions were primarily between students who were peers in teacher training programmes during and following teacher training, rather than between instructors and students. Thus, communication is happening vertically across programme instructors and refugee teachers and horizontally between refugee teachers in camps; the latter happening to a greater degree with clear and robust examples from refugee teachers about how these peer-to-peer networks and chat groups support teacher practice and professional development.

Reliable access to mobile networks was a challenge in both Dadaab and Kakuma. Barriers to connectivity – specifically the cost of data and airtime, sufficient access to electricity and unstable internet and mobile network connections – were widely cited. Some were not connected to chat groups and left out of these conversations, though some refugee teachers described information disseminated through these mobile tools also being shared by word of mouth to those who were offline. Our research also shows variation in the quality of the phone that refugee teachers had and in their levels of technical literacy.

Despite these challenges to mobile connectivity, instructors working with refugee teachers in Kakuma and Dadaab described how mobile phones were used to mitigate challenges in connectivity, as mobile-based network access proved more reliable than computer connectivity. For example, as noted by one instructor who worked in Dadaab with the BHER programme:

> I think people have learned to use their phones in very interesting and flexible ways because that's the only way that most of them have the access to the internet or to easy communication with not only one another but with instructors . . . So definitely, I saw how when students were struggling to get online in the computer lab, they would pull their phones out instead. (Instructor Interview 1, Dadaab, 26 April 2016)

In addition to documenting this baseline responsive application of mobile phones, our research findings illuminate two outcomes in the use of text messaging, and particularly group instant messaging, to support teacher training in Kenyan refugee camps. First, SMS and WhatsApp were demonstrated to have significant capacity to support the implementation of pedagogical tools learned through teacher training, such as gender-responsive pedagogy taught by KEEP instructors, in the classroom and community. Importantly, findings from interviews highlight the ways that instant messaging group chats facilitated community engagement outside the classroom walls and through peer networks to support gender equity in education, intersecting horizontal and vertical axes of communication taking what is learned from the 'top down' and expanding that learning 'across' the community. In addition, the strategies learned in training were revisited and concretised through SMS and group chats where teachers were able to reiterate what they had learned and share successful applications from their experiences in their classrooms.

This first outcome points to community-generated opportunities for refugee teachers to engage in peer-to-peer professional development that incorporated learning from international teacher training programmes but did not necessarily depend on that formal and traditional educational structure to grow their practice. Second, mobile communications highlighted cross-cultural learning, especially for international instructors, as well as challenges and embedded power dynamics across transnational social relations for refugee teachers, instructors and sometimes Canadian teachers in training also communicating with refugee teachers in the camps. These dynamics were complex, laden with tensions of insider/outsider cultural dynamics and simultaneous growing and learning about cultural difference and about teaching and learning across these networks. We explore each of these two main findings below.

Group Chats and Peer-to-Peer SMS Communication: Refugee Teachers Extending Gender Equity in the Classroom and the Community

While we have survey data from refugee teachers enrolled in KEEP in both Dadaab and Kakuma, and that data show comparable patterns of use across the two locations, a more detailed picture of how chat groups are used at the peer-to-peer level is evident through our interview data collected in Kakuma. Group interviews in Kakuma clarified key relationships between teacher training and the use of text and instant messaging on mobile phones. Mobile communication through SMS and WhatsApp conversations had a significant capacity to support the implementation of gender-equity teaching strategies in schools and classrooms, and there is an intersection between teaching/learning environments and the community that is facilitated over instant messaging. The strategies learned in KEEP teacher training were revisited and concretised through SMS and group chats where teachers were able to reiterate what they had learned, adopted it in culturally situated and relevant ways and share successful applications from their experiences of implementing GRP in their classrooms.

For example, one student-teacher explained that he participates in a group chat with friends and colleagues working with the KEEP programme and who discuss various issues that surface related to their daily teaching practices. 'Like if we have a problem in school, we can discuss it and a find a solution before we take it forward to our line supervisor or the community mobiliser' (Participant 1, Group Interview 1, April 2016). He continues with an example explaining that two girls had a fight one evening and the teachers were informed and able to discuss the issue the same evening over WhatsApp to then resolve the problem in the classroom the next morning. Although the teacher did not articulate the specific approach used to solve this problem, the group chat with KEEP-trained teachers was the place where informed and engaged conversation took place towards a peaceful resolution of the problem in support of the girls rather than with a penal approach.

In this way, we found that group chats and peer-to-peer SMS communication extended gender-equity training beyond the temporal and physical space of the classroom, as teachers-in-training continued to discuss and remind one another about pedagogical tools and strategies learning in their programmes during, and after their training. As one teacher explained:

> In the follow up [of the gender responsive pedagogy training] I was involved in developing or coming up with ten WhatsApp groups and the WhatsApp groups were supposed to help teachers talk about the challenges that they are receiving – these were region based and also subject based, so teachers were talking about the varied [issues] that we're seeing in their classroom – for example shyness in girls was emerging as a big issue . . . So, teachers in those WhatsApp groups were able to present the challenges they were receiving, and other teachers were giving what they have done to overcome if somebody has ever had the same type of challenge. (Instructor Interview 1, Kakuma, May 20, 2016)

Gender-based approaches to teaching introduced in teacher training were then put in practice, discussed and further refined through collaborative groups and individual messaging. The impact of GRP training extended geographically and temporally through the iterative process of discussing implementation strategies and addressing challenges and questions within collegial chat groups and across the camp communities.

Mobile phones and social networks are also being used to engage the broader community, and particularly male community members, parents and community leaders, to support girls' education. Within the subregional communities of the camps, teachers and community mobilisers were working directly with parents to engage them in critical conversations pertaining to the importance of girls' education. The form and function of these community networks are analysed in depth in our upcoming article (Dayha, Dryden-Peterson, Douhaibi & Arvisais, in review). WhatsApp groups were used, for example, for a community advocacy outreach project engaging men and boys around violence against women, including early marriage. Teachers and community mobilisers would knock on doors and talk to men and boys in the community outside of school about the importance of girls' education. They would invite these fathers, husbands and brothers to join chat groups to discuss the gender equity in education priming the discussion for face-to-face workshops and community meetings. In doing so, teachers and community mobilisers 'spread the word' and the values underpinning their gender-responsive pedagogy training to the community at large, using both online and offline tools.

The Challenges of Transnational Communication and the Application of Formal and Informal Mobile Messaging Tools as Mediating Mechanisms

Group chats and peer-to-peer SMS communication were important tools for supporting formal instruction across geographic boundaries both within and between camps, and between students in different parts of the world. Mobile spaces facilitated problem-solving and engagement in meaningful dialogue and information sharing. Data from Dadaab specifically provide an indication of the prevalence of mobile phone use in support of instruction, challenges incorporating mobile technology in instruction and dilemmas about how to structure pedagogies that use text and instant messaging originating from outside refugee camps. While some of the international instructors taught their teacher training courses in both Dadaab and Kakuma, all of them taught in Dadaab and this is also where the majority of our survey data was collected. Data from Dadaab illuminate some of the complexities related to the development and deployment of both gender equitable and culturally relevant curriculum in these settings, and in particular through mobile platforms.

In Dadaab, there was a marked degree of variation in the formal use of SMS and WhatsApp communication platforms between instructors and refugee teachers in the BHER programme. Not all instructors believed that learning outcomes were supported by the use of computer or mobile-based platforms. A Kenyan instructor stated, for example: 'I think there is an overestimation of the role technology has played because it is mostly onsite relationships that make things work . . . I intentionally did not ask students to do anything online' (Instructor interview 5, Dadaab, 4 June 2016). Two Canadian instructors shared the perspective that incorporating more technology in an already complex teaching context would prove distracting and might complicate the learning process. Conversely, three of the eight instructors from BHER partner universities interviewed indicated that they intentionally used WhatsApp, as a platform already familiar to student-teachers, to communicate with students about assignments, answer questions, share course information and documents, accept assignments and facilitate discussion between students outside of the classroom. For these instructors, mobile communication tools provided a more reliable method than other platforms, including the Learning Management System *Moodle* and email, to send and receive information to and from students. This included instructions and assignments and enabled students to maintain access to course activities beyond the confines of the face-to-face instruction that happened periodically at the centrally located Learning Centre. This was particularly true to support the delivery of online courses delivered by instructors offsite, located in Canada. One Canadian instructor explained:

> I was also able to set up a WhatsApp group to talk to students who are struggling particularly on assignments. They often corresponded with me in the evenings that way . . . And then I connected groups of people together that were working on similar topics so that they could have discussions that I could interject in from time to time if I saw that they were getting off track. That worked quite well. (Instructor Interview 1, Dadaab, 26 April 2016)

Notably, this use of mobile chat platforms served as a mechanism to ensure that students could continue course work despite challenges noted in connectivity in the camps that limited broader use of computers and mobile communication platforms. According to another Canadian instructor:

> I think that we were led to believe, we did expect and we were told that electricity was unreliable and internet connectivity would be intermittent but I think we weren't prepared about how big of a challenge electricity was going to be that it was in the first year that we were operating the students were more offline than they were online. (Instructor Interview 4, Dadaab, 27 June 2016)

In these cases, while gender-sensitive and responsive pedagogical approaches were encouraged in the courses delivered in Dadaab, student-teachers who are women did not always utilise formal course group chats or participate in them with the same frequency as their male colleagues. An important consideration, accordingly, is whether women students are aided or constrained by the supplemental use of mobile communication tools by international instructors.

Even when some instructors opted not to use mobile communication strategies to support their formal instruction, support staff with the BHER programme did, either in addition to or in the absence of, what instructors were doing. A support staff working in Dadaab noted:

> I actually send in two batches. So, I will tell them there is this, maybe it's a discussion forum, you are not communicating to your lecturer, they are requesting you to communicate. So, I broadcast to all of them . . . I realized most of them they don't go to their emails and they would say I didn't see this. So, the effective method from my analysis is SMS because they will get it. Emails they will have to get to the computer again which is connected to the internet. An SMS it is there. (Support staff interview, 14 April 2016)

The vast majority of teachers do have access to mobile phones regularly; however, their involvement in education-related chat groups varied; some teachers used them regularly throughout the duration of their courses or training programmes, while others participated sparingly or were unclear about which chat groups existed and how to participate in them. One instructor said:

> When I started the WhatsApp group, the [refugee] teachers were very enthusiastic but it proved a bit hard because largely in Dadaab the network coverage is low and so with low coverage in network some [student] teachers were not able to get information in time thereby they became fatigued and some of them dropped out. (Instructor interview 7, 20 May 2016)

The above interview excerpts highlight several key considerations for the use of transnational mobile networks to support refugee education. First, peer-to-peer networks created organically across student-teachers and community members may fare differently than those created by instructors of internationally managed programmes, carrying distinct iterations of power in the relationship between refugee teachers and the instructors of teacher training programmes. Sharing of information in practice across community members complicates and perhaps challenges notions of cultural and educational imperialism that assume unidirectional, top-down distributions of knowledge in transnational learning settings. We observe that through instant messaging, information received through formal instruction is re-envisioned in lived, changing practices and dialogues among refugee teachers in the camps. Second, a question emerges about the value and purpose of the refugee teacher groups where instructors are involved; we question if or how the dynamics of chat groups were mis/aligned with both the instructor and participant expectations or needs, and note how the ethno-racial and geopolitical differences literally across the world (including time differences and language/literacy constraints) impacted the dynamics of engagement in these chat groups. We consider the example of Dadaab as compared to Kakuma, where refugee teachers tended to establish and manage their own peer-based chat groups to address specific pedagogical concerns as they emerged rather than responding to formal curriculum. Instructors delivering courses to students in Dadaab, in comparison, attempted to use WhatsApp group chats to support more instrumental dimensions of instruction and management from a distance, with some challenges to understanding each other and working through differing temporal engagements online.

It was clear, in speaking with international instructors from Canadian universities, prior expectations about what Dadaab would be like and how to appropriately structure courses in order to ensure cultural and context relevance were not in line with what instructors encountered, particularly at the onset of the programmes. Refugee teachers familiar with teaching in the local context and international instructors may, thus, have found their approaches to teaching and learning quite at odds with realities in these particular sites, particularly during the earliest courses delivered.

There were notable challenges constructing course content that would be meaningful, relevant and implementable in classrooms in this particular setting. Simply transferring teaching approaches used in Canadian schools would not work in Dadaab and Kakuma; the ideas of social life and gender roles that international instructors take for granted were not what they found in their classrooms in Dadaab (Field notes, April 2016). An indication of this, one instructor remarked:

> I think I was surprised you know when we were putting this program together we had imaginary refugee students who were prepared, you know, to walk a hundred miles in order to access post-secondary education and when we arrived there again I admit to being surprised. In retrospect I don't know why I was surprised, but there was the full range of student and student commitment than you would find anywhere else. (Instructor interview 8, 27 June 2016)

Another instructor explained:

> The first thing I was thinking about when I started conceiving the course is how can I really help these people because I have never been to a refugee

camp before. I know the context is very different, is very complex you know. And so here we have got to help them as developing teachers, they are teaching the Kenyan curriculum, most of them are Somali, although not all, and Somalia itself has a wide range of ethnic groups, which you know is something on the ground there which I don't even know about it, so I start seeing it. (Instructor interview 3, 6 June 2016)

A third instructor adds:

My biggest challenges as an educator were not the educating part itself but were stuff around that like how to organise class to fit in a rather short and non-predictable time period. How to divide the groups of people by gender so that they would accept and be attentive to and learn some materials that was worrisome for them like culture reasons and so forth. (Instructor interview 2, Dadaab, 10 June 2016)

Some instructors made efforts to bring refugee teachers enrolled in university courses in Canada together with Canadian students enrolled in the same course. Cultural differences combined with accessibility challenges, outlined above, made efforts to create and sustain cross-cultural and transnational learning networks hard to achieve. For example, one Canadian instructor noted that long posts shared on Moodle from Canadian students seemed difficult for the Dadaab students to respond to in similar length, related perhaps to the amount of time they had at a computer and the time it might take them to type such a post in a non-native language or on a mobile device. The topics of interactions also influenced participation. The instructor explained:

You know there were kind of equal threads that had equal participation students in Toronto and students in Dadaab. And then there were other things that you know Dadaab students talked among themselves and Toronto students didn't know really how to participate. Particularly subjects around [Female Genital Mutilation] FGM and gender-based violence. Students in Toronto really were kind of taken aback by some of what was appearing in the forum and didn't really know how to engage in a productive or constructive kind of ways. (Instructor interview 8, 27 June 2016)

In this context, internationally situated instructors have no control over the learning environment and little clarity on precisely how the content being taught is taken up by students or translated at the peer-to-peer level. Further, power dynamics related to insider/outsider positions and historical post-colonial social structures related to whose knowledge is valued is somewhat inevitable in a formal classroom context. A productive insight of this work is introducing the ways that both sharing knowledge and information using text and instant messaging serves to connect local insider and outsider knowledge, changing the role and position of the geographically removed 'outsider' related to how the curriculum and pedagogy are both taught and adopted to suit the realities of community members in the camps. While post-colonial power structures might be alive and well, they are also transformed as communities are more and more regularly connected using mobile technology. Despite certain challenges faced by instructors to manage formal course curriculum using group chats, we found there is meaningful learning beyond and outside of the scope of formal curricula – and that learning can be distributed in multiple directions across instructors and refugee teachers, and refugee teachers and community members. This horizontally oriented peer-to-peer teaching and learning ecosystem offers a conceptual shift from rigidly teacher- and curriculum-focused training programmes that often assume that teachers, including refugee teachers, are simply a conduit to transmit already-existing knowledge to their students.

Conclusion

The nature of SMS messaging and WhatsApp group chat across the camp communities demonstrates possibilities for ways that networked communication and mobile telephones can change the landscape of education in refugee camps, particularly vis-à-vis gender equity and girls' engagement initiatives. Moreover, the impact of the training teachers have received, and the substantiating conversations that took place over SMS and WhatsApp following their training, will not only touch students in schools across Dadaab and Kakuma but also students in schools in countries of origin as some refugee teachers return home.

Despite these opportunities, connectivity is not reliable nor equitable, and mobile/technical competency is not ubiquitous. Further, there is an important question about situating power in and across these groups with regard to who starts groups and how they are maintained. In our findings, the success of peer-to-peer networks and groups emergent from among student-participants asks us as outsiders to the community to reconsider not only the role of text and instant messaging but our role in supporting teachers and teacher training in refugee camps using this tool.

From these findings we are encouraged to consider whether, and how, effort could be made to take account of the experience of locally situated teachers in developing context-relevant approaches to teaching and learning that might respond to their daily and emergent needs and practices. Although time constraints make it difficult to co-produce course curricula with refugee teachers familiar with their teaching and learning environment, this may be an important aspect for the ultimate success and relevance of teacher training programmes, particularly when instructors are so unfamiliar with the terrain. On the other hand, as our research demonstrates, student-teachers and community members often take up content delivered in courses and training programmes, re-envisioning that information through their lived and changing experiences of teaching in the camps. In this way, refugee teachers take what they will from the remote learning that occurs and the virtual participation available to them and refine it for their own purposes, in their own context, complicating and perhaps challenging notions of cultural and educational imperialism or post-colonial power structures.

Finally, further research must contribute to identifying how and where technology is being used and how contents are being reconceptualised to support learning among young adults, considering learning in day-to-day life experiences across communities, schools, and homes. New veins of study should also consider differences in the use of technology to support learning for men and women, identify how girls/women report on their own learning experiences with technology and analyse the perspectives of men and women with regard to gender differences in the use of technology for learning.

REFERENCES

Abdi, F. (2016). Behind Barbed Wire Fences: Higher Education and Twenty-First Century Teaching in Dadaab, Kenya. *Bildihaan, 16*, 21–35.

Ahmed, S. (2000). *Strange Encounters: Embodied Others in Post-Coloniality.* London: Routledge.

Anderson, J. (2013). Policy Report on UNHCR's Community Technology Access Program: Best Practices and Lessons Learned. *Refuge, 29*(1), 21–30.

Arvisais, O. (2016). AEP Research Project: Dadaab Refugee Camp, No. 00154799. Geneva, Switzerland: The UN Refugee Agency.

Baran, E. (2014). A Review of Research on Mobile Learning in Teacher Education. *Journal of Educational Technology & Society, 17*(4), 17–32.

Burde, D., Kapit, A., Wahl, R. L., Guven, O., & Skarpeteig, M. I. (2016). Education in Emergencies. *Review of Educational Research, 87*(3), 619–658.

Charmarkeh, H. (2013). Social Media Usage, Tahriib (Migration), and Settlement among Somali Refugees in France. *Refuge, 29*(1), 43–52.

Creswell, J. W. (2014). *Research Design: Qualitative, Quantitative, and Mixed Methods Approaches*, 4th edn. Thousand Oaks: SAGE Publications.

Danielson, N. (2013). Channels of Protection: Communication, Technology, and Asylum in Cairo, Egypt, *Refuge, 29*(1), 31–42.

Dahya, N. (2016). *Education in Conflict and Crisis: How Can Technology Make a Difference? A Landscape Review*. Germany: GIZ, USAID, WVI.

Dahya, N., & Dryden-Peterson, S. (2017). Tracing Pathways to Higher Education for Refugees: The Role of Virtual Support Networks and Mobile Phones for Women in Refugee Camps. *Comparative Education, 53* (2), 284–301. Published online 1 December 2016. http://dx.doi.org/10.1080/03050068.2016.1259877

Dahya, N., Dryden-Peterson, S., Douhaibi, D., & Arvisais, O. (2019). Social Support Networks, Instant Messaging, and Gender Equity in Refugee Education. *Information, Communication and Society Special Issue on Transnational Materialities, 6*, 774–790.

Dryden-Peterson, S. (2010). The Politics of Higher Education for Refugees in a Global Movement for Primary Education. *Refuge, 27*(2), 10–18.

Dryden-Peterson, S. (2016). Refugee Education: The Crossroads of Globalization. *Educational Researcher, 45*(9), 473–482.

Dryden-Peterson, S., Dahya, N., & Adelman, E. (2017). Pathways to Educational Success among Refugees: Connecting Locally and Globally-Situated Resources. *American Educational Research Journal.* http://journals.sagepub.com/doi/abs/10.3102/0002831217714321

Flemming, J. (2017). *Case Study Report: Norwegian Refugee Council, Dadaab, Kenya*. Education in Crisis and Conflict Network: University of Massachusetts. Accessed 1 September 2018. https://scholarworks.umass.edu/cgi/viewcontent.cgi?article=1000&context=cie_eccn

GMSA (2017). *The Importance of Mobile for Refugees: A Landscape of New Services and Approaches*. Accessed 5 September 2018. www.gsma.com/mobilefordevelopment/programme/disaster-response/the-importance-of-mobile-for-refugees-a-landscape-of-new-services-and-approaches

Hannah, J. (1999). Refugee Students at College and University: Improving Access and Support. *International Review of Education, 45*(2), 153–166.

Hiemstra, N. (2017). Periscoping as a Feminist Methodological Approach for Researching the Seemingly Hidden. *The Professional Geographer, 69*(2), 329–336.

Jackline, M. K. (2012). Factors Influencing Performance of Girls in Primary Schools in Dadaab Refugee Camp in North Eastern Kenya, Master's Thesis: University of Nairobi. Accessed 25 August 2018. http://erepository.uonbi.ac.ke/bitstream/handle/11295/7367/Murithi_Performance%20of%20girls%20in%20oprimary%20schools.pdf?sequence=1

Kaliisa, R., & Picard, M. (2017). A Systematic Review on Mobile Learning in Higher Education: The African Perspective. *Turkish Online Journal of Educational Technology-TOJET, 16*(1), 1–18.

Kinoti, T., & Philpott, L. (2017). *Remedial Education Program: An Innovation to Improve Girls' Academic Performance in Refugee Contexts.* Promising Practices in Refugee Education: World University Service of Canada. Accessed 10 September 2018. http://assets.wusc.ca/wuscwebsite/reportsandfinancials/rep ortsandpublications/PPIRE_WUSC_Remedial_Education_Program.pdf

Lamptey, H. K., & Boateng, R. (2017). Mobile Learning in Developing Countries: A Synthesis of the Past to Define the Future. *World Academy of Science, Engineering and Technology, International Journal of Social, Behavioral, Educational, Economic, Business and Industrial Engineering, 11*(2), 414–421.

Loomba, A. (2005). *Colonialism/Postcolonialism: The New Critical Idiom*, 2nd edn. New York: Routledge.

Mian, B. S. A. (2014). Les usages des TIC pour la formation continue des enseignants en Côte d'Ivoire : cas de l'université de vacances de l'ENS d'Abidjan. *Ernwaca Outreach Journal* 1, 25–28.

Morris, H., & Voon, F. (2014). *Which Side Are You On? Discussion Paper on UNHCR's Policy and Practice of Incentive Payments to Refugees.* UNHCR. Accessed 29 August 2018. www.unhcr.org/5491577c9.pdf

Pimmer, C., Zelezny-Green, R., & Gröhbiel, U. (2018). *A Lifeline to Learning: Leveraging Technology to Support Education for Refugees.* In F. Miao, M. Pagano, & M. West (eds.), UNESCO-Report. http://unesdoc.unesco.org/images/002 6/002612/261278e.pdf

Pimmer, C., Linxen, S., & Gröhbiel, U. (2012). Facebook as a Learning Tool? A Case Study on the Appropriation of Social Network Sites from Mobile Phones in Developing Countries. *British Journal of Educational Technology, 43* (5), 726–738. DOI:10.1111/j.1467-8535.2012.01351x

Pouezevara, S. L., & Khan, R. (2007). *Learning Communities Enabled by Mobile Technology: A Case Study of School-Based, In-Service Secondary Teacher Training in Rural Bangladesh* (Project Number TA No. 6278-REG). Manila: Asian Development Bank.

Poushter, J., Bishop, C., & Chwe, H. (2018). Smartphone Ownership on the Rise in Emerging Economies, Pew Research Centre. Accessed 15 September 2018. www.pewglobal.org/2018/06/19/2-smartphone-ownership-on-the-rise-in-emerging-economies/

Preston, R. (1991). The Provision of Education to Refugees in Places of Temporary Asylum: Some Implications for Development. *Comparative Education, 27*(1), 61–81.

Ropers-Huilman, R., & Winters, K. T. (2011). Feminist Research in Higher Education. *The Journal of Higher Education 82*(6), 667–690.

Roudometof, V. (2005). Transnationalism and Cosmopolitanism: Errors of Globalism. In R. P. Appelbaum, & W. I. Robinson (eds.), *Critical Globalization Studies* (pp. 65–74). New York: Routledge.

Said, E. (1979). *Orientalism*. New York: Random House.

Sobaih, A. E. E., Moustafa, M. A., Ghandforoush, P., & Khan, M. (2016). To Use or Not to Use? Social Media in Higher Education in Developing Countries. *Computers in Human Behavior, 58*, 296–305. DOI:10.1016/j.chb.2016.01.002

Taylor, J. (2015). *UNHCR Mission to Dadaab: Accelerated Education (AE) (Field Mission)*. Geneva: UNHCR.

Toukan, E. V., Gaztambide-Fernández, R., & Anwaruddin, S. M. (2017). Shifting Borders and Sinking Ships: What (and Who) Is Transnationalism 'Good' For? *Curriculum Inquiry, 47*(1), 1–13. DOI:10.1080/03626784.2017.1281049

UNHCR (2016). *Mobile Connectivity a Lifeline for Refugees, a Report Finds.* Accessed 10 August 2018. www.unhcr.org/afr/news/latest/2016/9/57d7d4478/mobile-connectivity-lifeline-refugees-report-finds.html

UNHCR (2018). *Figures at a Glance, UNHCR Kenya*. Accessed 10 August 2018. www.unhcr.org/ke/figures-at-a-glance

Waters, T., & Leblanc, K. (2005). Refugees and Education: Mass Public Schooling without a Nation-State. *Comparative Education Review, 49*(2), 129–147.

Winthrop, R., & Kirk, J. (2008). Learning for a Bright Future: Schooling, Armed Conflict, and Children's Well-Being. *Comparative Education Review, 52*(4), 639–661.

Wright, L. A., & Plasterer, R. (2010). Beyond Basic Education: Exploring Opportunities for Higher Learning in Kenyan Refugee Camps. *Refuge, 27*(2), 42–56.

Xu, Y., & Maitland, C. (2016, June). Communication Behaviors when Displaced: A Case Study of Za'atari Syrian Refugee Camp. *Proceedings of the Eighth International Conference on Information and Communication Technologies and Development* (pp. 58–62). ACM.

Index

473